Debates on the Measurement of Global Poverty

D1483841

The Initiative For Policy Dialogue Series

Initiative for Policy Dialogue (IPD) brings together the top voices in development to address some of the most pressing and controversial debates in economic policy today. The IPD book series approaches topics such as capital market liberalization, macroeconomics, environmental economics, and trade policy from a balanced perspective, presenting alternatives, and analyzing their consequences on the basis of the best available research. Written in a language accessible to policymakers and civil society, this series will rekindle the debate on economic policy and facilitate a more democratic discussion of development around the world.

Debates on the Measurement of Global Poverty

Edited by
Sudhir Anand, Paul Segal, and Joseph E. Stiglitz

OXFORD
UNIVERSITY PRESS

1-25-13

OXFORD
UNIVERSITY PRESS

Debates on the measurement

Great Clarendon Street, Oxford OX2 6DP

Oxford University Press is a department of the University of Oxford.
It furthers the University's objective of excellence in research, scholarship,
and education by publishing worldwide in

Oxford New York

Auckland Cape Town Dar es Salaam Hong Kong Karachi
Kuala Lumpur Madrid Melbourne Mexico City Nairobi
New Delhi Shanghai Taipei Toronto

With offices in

Argentina Austria Brazil Chile Czech Republic France Greece
Guatemala Hungary Italy Japan Poland Portugal Singapore
South Korea Switzerland Thailand Turkey Ukraine Vietnam

Oxford is a registered trade mark of Oxford University Press
in the UK and in certain other countries

Published in the United States
by Oxford University Press Inc., New York

© Oxford University Press 2010

The moral rights of the authors have been asserted
Database right Oxford University Press (maker)

First published 2010

British Library Cataloguing in Publication Data
Data available

Library of Congress Cataloging in Publication Data
Data available

Typeset by SPI Publisher Services, Pondicherry, India
Printed in Great Britain
on acid-free paper by
Clays Ltd., St Ives Plc

ISBN 978-0-19-955803-2 (Hbk)
ISBN 978-0-19-955804-9 (Pbk)

1 3 5 7 9 10 8 6 4 2

Contents

Contents

List of Figures

List of Figures

List of Tables

List of Tables

List of Abbreviations

ACC	Ahluwalia, Carter, and Chenery
AHFC	Actual Household Final Consumption
BLS	Bureau of Labor Statistics
BMI	Body Mass Index
CASEN	National Characterization Socio-economic Survey (Chile)
CBN	Cost of Basic Needs
CDF	Cumulative Density Function
CE	Consumer Expenditure
CEPAL	Comisión Económica para América Latina el Caribe
CES	Consumer Expenditure Survey
CEX	Consumption Expenditures *or* Consumption Expenditure Survey
CHIP	China Household Income Project
CIS	Commonwealth of Independent States
CPD	Country Product Dummy
CPI	Consumer Price Index
CPIP	CPI for the Poor
CPS	Current Population Survey
DA	Domestic Absorption
DHS	Demographic and Health Survey
ECLA	Economic Commission for Latin America
ECLAC	Economic Commission for Latin America and the Caribbean
EECA	Eastern Europe and Central Asia
EFS	Expenditure and Food Survey
ELI	Entry Level Item
EKS	Eltetö-Köves-Szulc
ESCAP	Economic and Social Commission for Asia and the Pacific
EU	European Union
EUS	Employment–Unemployment Survey
FES	Family Expenditure Survey

FGT	Foster-Greer-Thorbecke
FISIM	Financial Services Indirectly Imputed
FSU	Former Soviet Union
HCR	Headcount Ratio
HDI	Human Development Index
HES	Household Expenditure Survey
HFCE	Household Final Consumption Expenditure
HS	Household Survey
ICP	International Comparison Program
ICT	Information and Communication Technology
IDB	Inter-American Development Bank
IMR	Infant Mortality Rate
IPL	International Poverty Line
GDP	Gross Domestic Product
GK	Geary-Khamis
GNP	Gross National Product
IMF	International Monetary Fund
LAC	Latin America and the Caribbean
LCU	Local Currency Unit
LSMS	Living Standards Measurement Study
MDG	Millennium Development Goal
MENA	Middle East and North Africa
MIDEPLAN	Ministerie de Planificación y Cooperación
MPCE	Monthly Per capita Consumer Expenditure
MRP	Mixed Reference Period
NA	National Accounts
NAS	National Accounts Statistics
NBS	National Bureau of Statistics (China)
NGO	Non-Governmental Organization
NIPA	National Income and Product Accounts
NPISH	Non-Profit Institutions Serving Households
NSS	National Sample Survey
NSSO	National Sample Survey Organisation
OECD	Organisation for Economic Co-operation and Development
PCTE	Per Capita Total Expenditure
PCE	Per Capita Expenditure
PGI	Poverty Gap Index

PL	Poverty Line
PPP	Purchasing Power Parity
PPPP	PPP for the Poor
PWT	Penn World Tables
SDE	Shape of the Distribution Elasticity
SI	Sen Index
SME	Small and Medium Enterprise
SNA	System of National Accounts
S/NA	Survey to National Accounts means
SNAk	Survey to National Accounts ratio (at constant 1987 level)
SOE	State-Owned Enterprise
SPG	Squared Poverty Gap
SSA	Sub-Saharan Africa
SWB	Survey World Bank
UN	United Nations
UNCTAD	United Nations Conference on Trade and Development
UNDP	United Nations Development Programme
UNICEF	United Nation Children's Fund
UNRISD	United Nations Research Institute for Social Development
UNU-WIDER	United Nations University—World Institute for Development Economics Research
URP	Uniform Reference Period
WDR	World Development Report
WHO	World Health Organization
WIID	World Income Inequality Database
WTO	World Trade Organization

Contributors

Sudhir Anand is Professor of Economics at the University of Oxford and Official Fellow of St Catherine's College, Oxford.

Bettina H. Aten is an Economist in the Bureau of Economic Analysis in Washington, DC.

Albert Berry is Professor Emeritus of Economics at the University of Toronto.

Surjit S. Bhalla is Chairman of Oxus Investments, a New Delhi-based economic research, asset management, and emerging-markets advisory firm.

Shaohua Chen is a Senior Statistician in the World Bank's Research Department.

Angus Deaton is the Dwight D. Eisenhower Professor of International Affairs and Professor of Economics and International Affairs at the Woodrow Wilson School of Public and International Affairs and the Economics Department at Princeton University.

Sakiko Fukuda-Parr is Professor of International Affairs at The New School for Social Research.

Qin Gao is Assistant Professor at Fordham University in New York City.

Ivo Havinga is a staff member of the United Nations Statistics Division, Department of Economic and Social Affairs.

Alan Heston is Professor Emeritus at the University of Pennsylvania.

Robert Johnston is retired from the United Nations Statistics Division. He continues to work as consultant to United Nations programs on development of statistics and indicators in developing countries.

Gisèle Kamanou is a staff member of the United Nations Statistics Division, Department of Economic and Social Affairs.

Thomas Pogge is Leitner Professor of Philosophy and International Affairs at Yale University, Professorial Fellow at the ANU Centre for Applied Philosophy and Public Ethics and Research Director at the University of Oslo Centre for the Study of Mind in Nature.

Martin Ravallion is Director of the World Bank's Research Department.

Sanjay G. Reddy is Associate Professor of Economics at The New School for Social Research.

Carl Riskin is Distinguished Professor of Economics at Queens College of the City University of New York and Senior Research Scholar at the Weatherhead East Asian Institute, Columbia University.

David E. Sahn is a Professor of Economics at Cornell University.

Paul Segal is a Research Fellow at the Oxford Institute for Energy Studies and New College, University of Oxford.

T. N. Srinivasan is the Samuel C. Park, Jr. Professor of Economics at Yale University and Visiting Professor, Stanford Center for International Development, Stanford University.

David Stewart is Chief of the Policy Advocacy Unit, Policy, Advocacy and Knowledge Management Section, Policy and Practice, UNICEF.

Joseph E. Stiglitz is Co-President of the Initiative for Policy Dialogue and University Professor at Columbia University.

K. Sundaram is a member of the Centre for Development Economics at the Delhi School of Economics.

Suresh D. Tendulkar is a member of the Centre for Development Economics at the Delhi School of Economics.

Vu Quang Viet is a retired staff member of United Nations Statistics Division, Department of Economic and Social Affairs.

Stephen D. Younger is Associate Director of the Cornell University Food and Nutrition Policy Program and Scholar in Residence at Ithaca College.

Acknowledgments

This book originated in a workshop on global poverty organized by Sudhir Anand and Joseph Stiglitz in 2003, under the auspices of the Initiative for Policy Dialogue (IPD) at Columbia University. The meeting was motivated by the first Millennium Development Goal of the United Nations—the halving of world poverty by the year 2015. Our purpose was to examine the many important measurement issues—methodological and empirical—raised in the definition, estimation, and tracking of global poverty.

The papers presented at the original workshop have undergone very substantial revision, and several new papers have been added to represent the different sides of the debate and to take account of recent developments. We are extremely grateful to the authors for their willingness to revise and restructure their papers, taking note of the editors' and referees' comments.

We wish to acknowledge the assistance of Shari Spiegel, Shana Hofstetter, Sarah Green, Farah Siddique and other IPD staff members who helped to organize the original workshop or to coordinate the production of this book. We would also like to thank Sarah Caro and Jenni Crosskey for seeing the book through Oxford University Press.

We are grateful to the Swedish International Development Cooperation Agency (SIDA), the Ford Foundation, and the John D. and Catherine T. MacArthur Foundation for funding the original workshop on global poverty, out of which this book was conceived. In addition, Sudhir Anand wishes to acknowledge research support from the Rockefeller Foundation (to the Global Equity Initiative at Harvard University), and from the DKR/CAR Fund. Finally, we acknowledge the Rockefeller Brothers Fund for their support of IPD's work.

1

Introduction

Sudhir Anand, Paul Segal, and Joseph E. Stiglitz

Global poverty is higher on the public agenda than ever before. While it has always been a central concern of development economists and professionals, it has never before been studied so intensively, and has never been as prominent in the public consciousness as it has become over the last few years. This new focus is due in part to the commitment of the international community to the United Nations Millennium Development Goals (MDGs)—the first of which is to halve, between 1990 and 2015, the proportion of people living in extreme poverty. It is due also to substantial progress in the collection and analysis of data. While we can now say much more about global poverty than in the past, considerable controversy has developed about how to analyze and interpret the data, and what they tell us about the magnitude and rate of change of global poverty.

In many ways, the controversy should not come as a surprise. If the world's attention were not focused on poverty, we would have little need to measure it. Differences among economists and statisticians in the estimates would be of little significance. But with a global commitment to halve poverty, how we measure it makes a great deal of difference. If in one system of metrics we have already achieved our goal, the MDGs will not be able to serve as the rallying cry for more assistance (whether of aid or trade). At least some of the moral weight behind the demands by civil society is that the persistence of poverty at this level is unconscionable in a world of such wealth.

The issue of measurement is thus of more than just academic interest. What we measure affects what we do. The focus on poverty has directed scarce resources towards poverty reduction. Many of those who believe that we have made great strides in reducing poverty—that we have already achieved the MDG of halving poverty since 1990—believe that these scarce resources should be devoted to maximizing growth. Other critics of poverty measurement worry that focusing excessive attention on numbers in poverty encourages governments to direct resources towards those just below the poverty line as this is the easiest way to reduce the number of poor. But this is not the best way to improve the well-being of the poor.

All of the poverty lines used to measure global poverty represent living standards that are hard to fathom by those in advanced industrial countries. What would it be like to live on $1 a day, or $2 a day—on an annual income of $365 to $730? For most of us, it is beyond conception. The poverty standards in the US are closer to $15 a day, and a visit to the slums of Detroit or New York provides a picture of what life is like for those with incomes at this low level. Having applied for a graduate fellowship very late in his third year in college, and without a degree, Stiglitz was fortunate enough to receive a small fellowship from MIT which left him with just $1 a day for food (in 1963 prices— equivalent to $7 in today's prices). Even with careful planning, it was not sustainable: Stiglitz lost weight rapidly during the year (which he was happily able to regain subsequently). For Stiglitz it was an experiment—one which he knew would end in twelve months. But for those in the developing world, it is not an experiment, and for many no end to starvation level diets is in sight. There can be a vicious circle with poor diets leading to low productivity, and low productivity leading to low wages (see, for example, Stiglitz, 1976).

Every once in a while, the neglected field of national income statistics finds itself at the center of controversy. For example, the measurement of inflation in Argentina has been disputed in recent years: has the government cooked the books so that true inflation is higher than measured inflation? Is it trying to allay the longstanding concerns of that society about inflation, not by lowering inflation, but by lowering the measurement of inflation? Ten years ago, when Stiglitz served as Chair of the Council of Economic Advisers in the US, another such controversy flared up. Were we overestimating inflation, thereby giving social security recipients (whose payments go up with inflation) far too much year after year, and undermining the financial viability of the entire social security system? A report by a former Chair of the Council of Economic Advisers (Boskin Commission, 1996) found that inflation was overestimated by 1.3 percentage points per year from 1978 to 1996.

In some cases, there is a strong rationale for measuring things one way or another. In others, it is simply a matter of convention—though if we are to make comparisons across countries or over time, the comparisons must be done in a consistent way. With prices and products changing all the time and differing across and within countries, making consistent comparisons is harder than it might seem, and some of the controversies relate to these differences. With brie and croissants relatively more expensive in the US, and McDonalds hamburgers relatively more expensive in France, a Frenchman might find his cost of living in the US far higher than in France; but at the same time, an American might find maintaining his life style in Paris more difficult than in the US. Economists have, over the years, developed standard, if imperfect, techniques for dealing with these problems.

Even if there were not these price and product differences, there is another question. How do we define poverty? Some of the original poverty measures were devised as basic measures of survivability. Below those levels, it was hard to sustain life—to meet nutritional needs and provide the basic necessities of shelter, energy for cooking and heating, and clothing. Of course, these basic necessities could differ in different parts of the world—illustrating that a global standard (e.g., $1 or $2 a day) must be viewed simply as an approximation, a point of reference. It should be noted, though, that measured poverty corresponding to different poverty lines can show contrary trends depending on changes in the income distribution. Moreover, updating the poverty line over time in a world of changing products and prices leads to further challenges.

Beyond national income statistics, there are also serious issues regarding the household surveys that are used to measure living standards within countries. Most data on the distribution of income come from asking people their income and consumption levels. It is often difficult for individuals to recall this information perfectly. We know that something is wrong because the total amount reported, when extrapolated to the whole economy, does not add up to the national accounts estimate of total income of the economy. Is this due to conceptual differences between surveys and national accounts, or to under-reporting in surveys? If the latter, is the underreporting uniform, or are the rich underreporting more than the poor? The answer to these questions, as we shall see, makes a great deal of difference to one's view about what is happening to global poverty.

This volume brings together some of the leading researchers in the field, from both academia and international organizations, in order to provide a thorough examination of the challenges and uncertainties involved in measuring global poverty. The chapters in Part I of the book discuss questions on the measurement of poverty at a global level, including conceptual issues such as what we really mean by poverty—and whether we can apply the concept at the global level—to the more empirical questions of whether to use national accounts data or household survey data, and the difficulties posed by the use of purchasing power parity (PPP) exchange rates. Part II then presents studies on specific regions and countries of the world in order to provide an overview of the challenges faced.

Estimates of global poverty

The standard estimates, most commonly cited by academics and the media, are due to Shaohua Chen and Martin Ravallion (2001, 2004, 2007, 2008) at the World Bank. Using the World Bank's "PPP$1-a-day" poverty line,[1] Chen and Ravallion's (2008) estimates are that 1,377 million people were living in extreme poverty in 2005, compared with 1,813 million in 1990 (see Table 1.1).[2] Poverty is going down, but slowly. At this pace, assuming a

Introduction

Table 1.1. Estimates of global poverty, 1980–2005 (millions)

Year	1980	1990	2000	2005
Chen and Ravallion (2008) PPP$1.25, 2005 prices	1,896[a]	1,813	1,696[b]	1,377
Chen and Ravallion (2007) PPP$1.08, 1993 prices	1,470[a]	1,248	1,109[b]	969[d]
Bhalla (this volume, Ch. 4) "SNAk" PPP$1.08, 1993 prices	1,489[a]	1,216	770[c]	456
Bhalla (2002) adjusted HFCE PPP$1.50, 1993 prices	1,479	1,056	647	
Bhalla (2002) survey means PPP$1.30, 1993 prices	1,581	1,208	899	
Sala-i-Martín (2006) PPP$1.36, 1996 prices	498	363	322	

[a] 1981 estimate;
[b] 1999 estimate;
[c] 2001 estimate;
[d] 2004 estimate.

linear trend in global poverty reduction would yield a total of 1,086 million poor in 2015. But performance varies widely across regions. China has had enormous success in reducing poverty. In Africa, however, the prospects of meeting the MDGs are bleak, with poverty going up from 299 million in 1990 to 391 million in 2005.

The World Bank's canonical estimates have been challenged by researchers from both the left and the right. Some believe that the World Bank numbers underestimate the level of poverty and overestimate its reduction (see, in particular, Reddy and Pogge, Ch. 3 in this volume); while others (Surjit Bhalla, Ch. 4 in this volume, and Sala-i-Martín, 2006) believe that the World Bank numbers overestimate the level of poverty and underestimate its reduction. Table 1.1 and Figure 1.1 present estimates of global poverty by Chen and Ravallion (2007, 2008), by Bhalla (2002, and this volume), and by Sala-i-Martín (2006). As can be seen, their estimates vary substantially. Chen and Ravallion's 2007 estimates are much lower than their 2008 estimates, but their rates of poverty decline are not very different. Bhalla in his chapter, ostensibly using the same World Bank poverty line, estimates the number in extreme poverty to decline dramatically from 1,216 million in 1990 to only 456 million in 2005. Sala-i-Martín (2006) estimates global poverty at just 363 million in 1990 and 322 million in 2000—a slower rate of decline, but from a much lower level. In the context of trying to achieve the first MDG, our views on both the extent of global poverty and its rate of decline have great policy relevance. Is a concerted international effort required? Or is it true, as Sala-i-Martín claims, that "[t]he world might just be in better shape than many of our leaders believe!"[3]

4

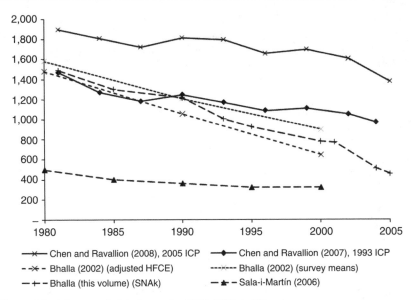

Figure 1.1 Estimates of global poverty, 1980–2005 (millions)

The measurement of global poverty

The large divergence in estimates of global poverty arises from the use of different methodologies and datasets, which we now describe in greater detail. First, the authors use different poverty lines. Second, they use different PPP exchange rates to convert incomes in local currencies into a common international currency.[4] Third, they take different approaches to estimating within-country distributions of income. Fourth, they calculate mean incomes within countries differently.

The definition of poverty

The first question in the measurement of global poverty is: what do we mean by poverty? Put another way, we have to define a poverty threshold. The income poverty lines used by Bhalla, Sala-i-Martín, and the World Bank (i.e. Chen and Ravallion) are all derived, in some sense, from the original World Bank PPP$1-a-day poverty line at 1985 prices (World Bank, 1990). This poverty line was informally chosen as being representative of the subsistence poverty lines of the poorest countries, translated into 1985 PPP$. Yet, while all authors base their poverty line on the same concept, they adopt different numbers. Chen and Ravallion (2007) use PPP$1.08 at 1993 prices.

5

Bhalla (2002) states that the "equivalent to $1 a day at 1985 prices is $1.30 a day at 1993 prices and not $1.08 a day" (p. 67). He thus uses a line of $1.30 at 1993 prices with survey data, while his "most preferred" method (p. 140) is to use national accounts data and adjust the poverty line to $1.50.[5] In his chapter in this volume (Ch. 4), Bhalla uses the Chen and Ravallion (2007) line of $1.08 at 1993 prices. Sala-i-Martín (2006) states that the poverty line of $1 a day at 1985 prices is equivalent to PPP$1.36 per day, or PPP$495 per year, at 1996 prices. In their most recent update based on a new global price survey (discussed below), Chen and Ravallion (2008) adopt a line of PPP$1.25 at 2005 prices. How can these differences be explained?

The disagreement arises over how to update a 1985-based PPP$ value. Within a single country, one would usually update a poverty line using a price index based on measured inflation. Thus if prices are estimated to have risen by 10 per cent after the poverty line was established, then the poverty line today should be 10 per cent higher. If we are expressing everything in US dollars, then all we need to do is to look at US inflation over the period 1985 to 1993. But updating a poverty line that is denominated in PPP$ is not so simple. Calculating a set of PPP exchange rates involves the prices of *all* countries (discussed below), so changes in a country's PPP exchange rate will depend on price changes in all countries. Bangladesh's 1985 poverty line at 1985 PPP$ scaled up by US inflation over 1985–93 would not be expected to be equal to Bangladesh's 1993 poverty line at 1993 PPP$.[6]

This is part of the more general "index number problem" that there is no simple, or uniquely best, way to convert overall price levels across space or time when relative prices are changing—and relative prices do change, across both space and time. PPPs are multilateral price indexes, and they have no analytical relationship with the price indexes used within countries to measure inflation. In fact, Deaton (2001, p. 127) observes that "the PPP international dollar has strengthened relative to the currencies of the poor countries whose poverty lines are incorporated into the international line."

This is indeed what Chen and Ravallion (2001) find. They calculate afresh a global poverty line for 1993 using a similar method to that for the original 1985 poverty line, deriving it as the median of the lowest ten poverty lines in their data set[7] converted into PPP$—this time using 1993 PPPs. This re-doing of the original method results in a poverty line of PPP$1.08 per day of consumption at 1993 PPP dollars, referred to as "$1 a day" for convenience. This represents a much lower rate of inflation than experienced in the US over 1985–93. As Chen and Ravallion (2001, p. 288) point out, "the fact that $1.08 in 1993 has a US purchasing power less than $1 in 1985 does not mean that the real value of the poverty line has fallen. Indeed, if we had simply adjusted the $1 per day line for inflation in the US between 1985 and 1993 we would have obtained a poverty line which is well above the median of the ten lowest poverty lines at 1993 PPP."

Sala-i-Martín (2006) appears to be unaware of this point, however, going so far as to claim that "this mysterious change in the poverty threshold has never been explained by the World Bank" (p. 370). Instead, he bases his calculation of a poverty line on US inflation, stating that the 1985 poverty line corresponds to $495 a year in 1996 prices (pp. 370, 372). Bhalla (2002) maintains that "international inflation . . . is what is needed to convert incomes (or consumption) from one base to another" (p. 65). Unfortunately, this ignores Deaton's point regarding the depreciation of the currencies of poor countries relative to international PPP$. For these reasons the poverty lines used by Bhalla (2002) and Sala-i-Martín (2006) are higher in real terms than those used by the World Bank.[8]

All three of these methods of constructing a global poverty line use a money metric threshold of poverty, converting estimates of household consumption, measured in national currency units, into PPP$. Reddy and Pogge in this volume challenge the money metric approach to global poverty measurement. Their primary objection to the PPP$1-a-day poverty line is that it does not correspond to any "achievement concept" or set of capabilities that are common across countries. That is, there is no reason to think that PPP$1 a day in one country will enable the same set of achievements—e.g. in terms of nutrition or shelter—as PPP$1 a day in another country. While domestic poverty lines are often set according to some achievement concept, this interpretation is lost when a global poverty line is constructed using standard PPP exchange rates. Reddy and Pogge argue that an explicit achievement-based threshold should be used to define a global poverty line. This would require costing the minimal standard set of capabilities in each country to yield a money-metric poverty line denominated in local currency. Thus the global capability-based poverty threshold would be represented in income space by the set of these national poverty lines, one for each country.[9]

T. N. Srinivasan (Ch. 5) is equally critical of the World Bank's definition of a global poverty line. He argues that poverty should be seen as a multidimensional concept, but that if it is to be considered in monetary terms it should be defined at the national level only—as the cost of a bundle of basic goods and services specific to each country. He is more pessimistic than Reddy and Pogge regarding the possibility of defining a global poverty line for international comparison and aggregation of poverty across countries. In his view, measures of global poverty will in practice never be satisfactory and are at best just advocacy tools for focusing public attention.

Robert Johnston's chapter contributes a historical discussion on the measurement of poverty, tracing it back over more than a century. He argues that the concept of extreme poverty as "distress and degradation" developed by early researchers remains appropriate for the measurement of global poverty today.

David E. Sahn and Stephen D. Younger's chapter on Africa in this volume follows the achievements-based approach of the human development literature by focusing on non-monetary measures of poverty. As indicators of well-being they use anthropometric measures (height-for-age and body mass index) and years of schooling. The authors make the point that these non-income indicators have a number of practical advantages over monetary indicators, including their being easier to measure reliably,[10] and their being defined at the individual rather than the household level. To these one could add Reddy and Pogge's point that they do not suffer from the difficulties of the PPP$1-a-day line, and are thus more comparable across countries. On the other hand, they are measures of a longer-term conception of well-being than those based on current real income or consumption, because they depend on nutrition and health, or schooling, over a number of years. Thus they are unlikely to respond to short-run changes in policy or economic environment. Sahn and Younger's data on Africa indicate a mixed picture: no clear trend in health indicators, but a widespread (though not ubiquitous) decline in education poverty.

Sakiko Fukuda-Parr and David Stewart in their chapter similarly provide a multidimensional picture of poverty and development, presenting a broad overview of recent trends in human poverty and human development. Using such wide-ranging indicators as life expectancy and rates of hunger and schooling, in addition to income, they illustrate the point that a full picture requires the use of numerous measures of well-being.

While the above authors use non-monetary measures of deprivation, Riskin and Gao in their chapter on China consider several income poverty lines that are based on the cost of achieving minimum levels of calorie intake. They find that the direction of change of urban poverty between 1988 and 1995 depends on the poverty line used, but there appears to have been a clear decline from 1995 to 2002. The social safety nets put in place by the government do not seem to be behind this reduction, but the government's strategy to make growth more equitable, including its targeted investment programs, may have played a role. Riskin and Gao also analyze a range of factors associated with urban poverty and find, for instance, that while employment in a state-owned enterprise reduced the probability of being poor in 1988, it increased the probability in 1995 and had no impact in 2002. While being unemployed contributes substantially to the probability of being poor, most heads of poor urban households are in fact employed.

Purchasing power parity exchange rates

Assuming one adopts the money-metric approach to poverty measurement, household consumption in national currencies has to be converted into a common currency for international comparison. The use of PPP exchange rates is intended to take account of the fact that, for instance, a dollar's worth of rupees, bought on the currency markets, will buy more of most goods and services in India than the same dollar would buy in the US. But $1 converted into rupees at the PPP exchange rate should buy approximately the same quantity of goods and services in India as $1 does in the US. Incomes in developing countries can be three or four times higher when measured at PPP exchange rates than when measured at market exchange rates.

PPP exchange rates are calculated using price surveys across countries conducted by the International Comparison Program (ICP). But these surveys are not done every year, so the country's real growth rate (measured using its own market basket of goods to adjust for inflation) is used to estimate PPP income in other years. However, real PPP income estimates calculated in this way can turn out to be very different from estimates based on a new price survey (for instance, see World Bank, 2008b).[11] Thus estimates of real income using PPPs based on different benchmark years will not be comparable.

ICP price surveys were benchmarked in 1985, 1993–96 (referred to as the 1993 ICP), and 2005. Apart from the latest World Bank estimates (Chen and Ravallion, 2008) which are based on the 2005 ICP, all estimates of global poverty in Table 1.1 use PPPs based on the 1993 ICP. Other researchers have not yet used the 2005 ICP data to generate estimates of global poverty. One advantage of the new ICP round is that a much more comprehensive price survey has been undertaken for China—its PPP exchange rate had previously been estimated on the basis of limited data from a few cities. It is also the first time since 1985 that an ICP price survey has been conducted for India. For both countries, the estimates of GDP using the new PPP exchange rates are substantially lower than previous estimates (World Bank, 2008b). Chen and Ravallion's chapter in this volume discusses the implications of the new price data for China and presents new poverty estimates. China is found to have more poverty than previously thought, but its record in poverty reduction remains just as impressive. This is not, of course, surprising: the new PPP data indicate that income levels in China are lower than implied by previous PPP estimates, but estimates of growth rates are unchanged.

The most widely used set of PPP data are from the Penn World Tables (PWT), and Bettina Aten and Alan Heston in their chapter discuss the use of PWT data in the measurement of global poverty. The PWT PPP estimates are based on the Geary-Khamis (GK) method, in which a vector of "average international prices" is constructed to value the output of each country. Both Bhalla and Sala-i-Martín make use of PWT in their estimations of global poverty.[12] On the other hand, the World Bank, for both its GDP and global poverty estimates, uses the Elteto-Köves-Szulc (EKS) method. This method does not involve constructing a vector of international prices but is based on bilateral (Fisher) price indices computed using each country's output vector as weights; the PPP exchange rate for a given country is then defined as the geometric average of its bilateral price indices with respect to all other countries.[13]

The use by the GK method of a vector of "average international prices" leads to a potential problem. As Aten and Heston (Ch. 6) explain, the "international price" of a good is a weighted average of its price in each country in international dollars, where the weights are the country's share in world output. This implies that prices in larger economies get a larger weight, so the resulting relative international prices are closer to relative prices in larger economies, which tend to have higher incomes per capita. When incomes are measured at these international prices, substitution bias (the Gershenkron effect)—the fact that people buy more of the goods that are relatively cheap in their own country—implies that the incomes of poor countries are likely to be overestimated relative to the incomes of rich countries. Since the global poverty line is the median of the lowest ten poverty lines at EKS PPP$ (Chen and Ravallion, 2001), calculating global poverty relative to this line through use of incomes converted at GK PPP will lead to an underestimate.[14] Using the same basic methodology as Sala-i-Martín, a study by Ackland et al. (2004) finds that estimates based on incomes at EKS PPP imply a global poverty incidence nearly 60 per cent higher than those based on incomes at GK PPP (from PWT). In published global poverty estimates, Sala-i-Martín (2006) is alone in making exclusive use of PWT GDP data (based on GK PPPs),[15] and this is likely to be part of the explanation for his much lower estimates of global poverty compared with the World Bank's EKS-based estimates.

Aten and Heston (Ch. 6) discuss the possibility of "poverty PPPs," or PPP exchange rates designed specifically to convert the incomes of the poor. They observe that existing consumption PPPs, based on prices only of consumption goods and services, are an improvement on GDP PPPs, which include investment goods and government expenditures. But, as they point out, the consumption basket of the poor will typically be different from the average consumption basket, with food expenditure comprising a larger fraction of the budget of the poor than of the average consumer. The poor may also face different prices from the average consumer. In principle, one could restrict PPP calculations to goods consumed by the poor, and also use prices faced by the poor, but such data are typically not available.[16] These questions regarding the appropriate expenditure weights and prices in the construction of poverty PPPs apply to both the GK and EKS methods.

The fact that standard PPPs are not designed for converting the incomes of the poor is also highlighted by Reddy and Pogge (Ch. 3). They observe that use of these PPPs implies that estimates of global poverty depend on some prices that are irrelevant to the poor. They comment that "whether a household in India lives in absolute poverty by the $1 PPP per day standard cannot reasonably depend on information about Japanese real estate prices, but under the current methodology of poverty assessment it may."[17] The use of poverty PPPs would mitigate this problem.

The distribution of income within countries

For measuring global poverty we need an estimate of the distribution of income within each country. Household income or consumption surveys in countries are the main source for this information. World Bank researchers have access to the primary unit record data in such surveys, which enables them to compute a country's income or consumption distribution directly (for convenience, henceforth referred to simply as "income distribution").[18] Other authors who did not have access to unit record data of household surveys have used secondary published information on within-country inequality.

Bhalla (2002) thus uses a two-step method to estimate global poverty. First, he takes estimates of relative inequality within countries from secondary datasets (Deininger and Squire, 1996, and UNU-WIDER's World Income Inequality Database[19]), which provide quintile shares for most countries and decile shares for some. For each country Bhalla scales these income shares to an exogenous estimate of average income or consumption.[20] His favored method (2002) is to scale to a constant fraction of the national accounts category of per capita Household Final Consumption Expenditure (HFCE),[21] but he also provides estimates where income shares are scaled to the mean income as measured in surveys. In his chapter in this volume (Ch. 4), Bhalla presents three sets of estimates. Two estimates are based on survey means from different sources (World Bank and non-World Bank website data respectively). The third method, which he favors, uses the survey mean in 1987 and projects this mean backwards and forwards using the growth rate of consumption from the national accounts, thus keeping constant the ratio of the mean of the distribution to HFCE at its 1987 value; he refers to this method as "SNAk" (estimates reported in Table 1.1 and Figure 1.1). Sala-i-Martín also follows a two-step method, taking quintile share data from Deininger and Squire (1996 updated dataset) and scaling them to per capita GDP. The quintile numbers are then converted to smoothed within-country distributions using a technique called kernel density estimation.[22]

Perhaps the most important methodological difference between alternative estimates of global poverty is the choice of mean for within-country distributions: the survey mean itself, (adjusted) per capita HFCE, or per capita GDP. This choice would seem to account for much of the difference in estimates of levels of and changes in global poverty.

Both Bhalla and Sala-i-Martín scale within-country distributions to national accounts categories, viz. adjusted per capita HFCE and per capita GDP, respectively. One reason given by Sala-i-Martín for scaling to per capita GDP is that he wishes to measure income and not consumption poverty. This, however, would require the use of a national accounts category of aggregate personal or household income. But following the 1993 System of National Accounts, most countries do not include such a category in their published national accounts.

11

GDP is therefore the only national accounts measure of income available across a wide range of countries. However, its use in the measurement of poverty is problematic. GDP includes retained earnings of corporations, the part of government revenue (taxes) that is not distributed back to households as cash transfers, and GDP does not net out depreciation. For illustration we can take the example of the US, which is one of the few countries that does report measures of household income (referred to as personal income) in its National Income and Product Accounts (NIPA). In 2006, US GDP was $13,246.6 billion, personal income $10,891.2 billion, and disposable personal income $9,529.1 billion (NIPA Tables 1.1.5 and 2.1). Disposable personal income was therefore only 72 per cent of GDP. Hence scaling to GDP per capita can substantially overestimate personal incomes and underestimate income poverty.

The Millennium Development Goals monitor consumption poverty,[23] which is what the World Bank estimates. Ravallion (2004) argues that the difference between consumption and income poverty (and Sala-i-Martín's use of GDP to measure income) may account for the difference between Sala-i-Martín's and the World Bank's 1993 PPP$-based estimates (reported in Chen and Ravallion, 2007).

The category of HFCE does not include those components of GDP mentioned above that are not part of aggregate household or personal income. Moreover, HFCE is reported for all countries in the IMF's *International Financial Statistics*. Hence we find Bhalla's (2002) (adjusted) HFCE-based global poverty estimates are higher than Sala-i-Martín's estimates and closer to the World Bank's (see Figure 1.1 and Table 1.1). However, Bhalla's estimates (SNAk) in this volume based on the growth rate of HFCE decline more rapidly than his or the World Bank's (1993 PPP$) survey mean-based estimates, and by 2001 they have fallen to approximately half of the World Bank's estimates.

The divergence between survey mean-based and HFCE-based estimates of global poverty is due to a growing divergence between survey means and per capita HFCE. Deaton, Ch. 7 in this volume, finds that, for his sample of non-Organisation for Economic Co-operation and Development (OECD) countries during 1990–2000, "the growth rate of survey consumption is approximately half of the growth rate of national accounts consumption." In India, for example, the ratio of survey to NA (national accounts) consumption declined over time from 0.68 in 1983 to 0.56 in 1999/2000. There has been heated debate about the source of this divergence in the context of poverty measurement in India (e.g. Ravallion, 2000; Bhalla, 2002; Deaton and Kozel, 2005).

Although both surveys and the national accounts measure "household consumption", household expenditure in surveys differs from HFCE in the national accounts in both concept and method of estimation. This issue is discussed in detail by Ivo Havinga, Gisèle Kamanou, and Viet Vu in their chapter (Ch. 9). In terms of concept, HFCE includes imputed values of financial intermediation services and consumption by "non-profit organizations serving households."[24] HFCE also includes imputed rents from owner-occupied housing, which are often not estimated in household surveys. It should be noted that neither survey expenditure nor HFCE includes imputed values of government-provided healthcare, education, or other services.[25]

The two categories also differ greatly in their method of estimation.[26] To calculate HFCE, the national accounts typically starts with an estimate of national production of a commodity such as rice from crop-cutting data, aerial or farm surveys, etc. As such surveys are conducted infrequently, gross production figures may have to be estimated without up-to-date information. Moreover, the methods used to arrive at these figures are not applied uniformly and can be unreliable. From an estimate of national production thus generated, government consumption and firms' consumption are subtracted, and the residual is attributed to households. Data on government consumption may be adequate, but firms' consumption is typically poorly estimated. It is often based on outdated firm surveys, and extrapolations or assumed changes over time. In India, the divergence between survey and national accounts consumption is partly due to the underestimation by NA of firms' consumption of intermediate goods. This has led to double-counting where, for instance, the edible oil consumed in restaurant meals was attributed to HFCE under both the "edible oil" category and the "restaurant meals" category.[27]

NA estimates of HFCE are thus indirect and subject to three sources of error: the initial estimate of aggregate production, the estimate of government consumption, and the estimate of firms' consumption. There is no reason to suppose that the data and methods used to estimate these, which include surveys of various types, are more reliable than household surveys. Moreover, their sources and methods are generally less well-documented (in terms of the surveys employed, how and when they were conducted, etc.) than household surveys. Finally, because it is calculated as a residual, the errors in the estimate of HFCE will tend to get compounded. By contrast, household surveys measure personal consumption and income directly.

Household income and consumption measured through surveys will, however, also be subject to errors. One reason is that there may be underreporting of incomes. If all incomes were underreported by the same fraction, then uniform scaling to an accurate estimate of mean income would correct the problem. However, the underreporting is not uniform across the distribution. As Ravallion (Ch. 2, this volume) discusses, the rich tend to underreport proportionately more than the poor.

Differential underreporting by the rich and poor can help to explain the growing divergence between mean income or consumption measured in surveys and in the national accounts. As the income share of the rich rises, which has occurred for instance in both India and China (and in other countries where inequality has risen), greater underreporting by the rich compared with the poor will imply growing underestimation of average household income and consumption as measured in surveys.

Underreporting by the rich will not by itself imply any bias in the measurement of poverty when individual income or consumption levels are obtained directly from surveys. In this case, individuals above the poverty line are of limited interest, and scaling to national accounts categories can lead to underestimation of the incidence of poverty. In his chapter, Ravallion (p. 33, this volume) provides a simple illustration of this point as follows:

> The true but unobserved distribution of income is (say) 1, 2, 3 (person 1 has an income of 1, person 2 has income 2, person 3 has 3). The poverty line is slightly above 1, so the true poverty rate is 1/3. We do a survey, and the three people respond that their incomes are 1, 1.5 and 2. Income of person 2 is underestimated by one-quarter, while it is underestimated by one-third for person 3. The survey gives the right poverty rate. However, the survey underestimates the true mean; the survey mean is 1.5. Now let's assume (for the sake of argument) that the national accounts do give the right mean of 2. If we assume that the survey under-estimation is distribution-neutral then we multiply all three incomes by 4/3. The 'corrected' incomes are 1.3, 2 and 2.7—implying that there is no poverty. We get the mean right, but the poverty measure is way off the mark.

Moreover, if a rise in within-country inequality leads to a growing underestimation of the mean, then the extent of underestimation of poverty due to scaling to the NA mean may be increasing over time—which will imply an overestimation of poverty reduction.

A further problem with household surveys is that the respondents may not be representative of the population. The very rich are reluctant to respond for tax and other reasons. Korinek et al. (2006) find that in the US the rich tend to respond less than the poor. In developing countries, on the other hand, the very poor and marginalized—particularly the homeless who have no fixed address, or those living in remote rural areas—may be excluded from the sample frame and are thus also likely to be under-represented.

The implication of under-representation of both the rich and the poor in surveys is different from that of underreporting. In this context even data taken directly from the survey may underestimate poverty. Extending Ravallion's example, suppose that the true distribution is 1, 1, 2, 3, 3, and hence the true poverty rate is 2/5. Now suppose that half of the poorest are missed from the sample frame and half of the richest fail to respond, so the survey reports only the three incomes 1, 2, 3. The survey mean remains correct at 2, but the survey underestimates poverty at 1/3 when the true incidence is 2/5.

Even though surveys are prone to measurement error, there is little reason to think that scaling the mean to some NA category, while using within-country relative distributions from surveys, will reduce the error in measuring poverty. On the other hand, it is doubtful that the decline in survey means relative to NA means could be attributed entirely to underreporting by the rich. Bhalla's method of using the survey mean in 1987, and projecting this mean forwards and backwards with the growth rate of NA consumption, provides a useful alternative for comparison with the purely survey-based estimates of the World Bank. As seen above, his estimates indicate a more rapid rate of poverty reduction after 1987 than the World Bank's, owing to the growing divergence between survey and NA means.

Clearly there is scope to improve data collection in household surveys. Albert Berry (Ch. 11 in this volume) on the measurement of poverty in Latin America, describes the difficulties in measuring several components of household income including production for own consumption at the lower end of the distribution, and capital income at the upper end of the distribution. Data collection is improving over time, but he believes that confidence intervals around estimates of the Gini coefficient should be of the order of 4 or 5 percentage points. These limitations in the data, he argues, make it hard to determine the impact of the policy reforms in Latin America on poverty. K. Sundaram and Suresh Tendulkar, Ch. 14 in this volume, discuss further problems in the collection of household survey data in India, including reference periods that have changed, and their implications for estimates of poverty. On the basis of a close analysis of the survey data they conclude that, despite numerous sources of non-comparability between the surveys over time, the finding of declining poverty in India in the 1990s is robust.

Data coverage and comparability

As we have seen, all estimates of global poverty rely on household surveys to provide income or consumption distributions within countries. But while the availability of survey data has improved substantially in recent years, the coverage of countries remains a problem. In particular, the coverage of countries in sub-Saharan Africa is a major concern.

Chen and Ravallion's (2008) estimates of global poverty for the World Bank are based on 675 surveys across 116 countries. Ninety per cent of the population of the developing world is represented by a survey within two years of 2005 (Chen and Ravallion, 2008, pp. 13–16). But this includes only 71 per cent of the population of sub-Saharan Africa. Moreover, coverage for this region is very low in the 1980s, and Chen and Ravallion (2008, p. 16) report that "our estimates for the early 1980s rely heavily on projections based on distributions around 1990." Sahn and Younger, Ch.15 in this volume, argue that the World Bank's reported figures for consumption poverty are somewhat implausible for a number of African countries, and reflect the difficulties of collecting expenditure data. Chen and Ravallion (2008, p. 16) also note that their survey data for China in the early 1980s "are probably less reliable than later years." The lack of good quality data will contribute to uncertainty in estimates of global poverty.[28]

In addition to coverage, there is also the question of data comparability.[29] In some country surveys, incomes are gross of tax and in others net of tax; for some they refer to cash incomes and for others certain items of income in kind are included. The rental value of owner-occupied housing is imputed in some surveys but not in others. In studies that use secondary data for within-country distributions, different distributions may have different population units—individuals or households (sometimes families)—and these units may be ranked in a variety of ways, such as individuals ranked by income received, individuals ranked by household income per capita (or per equivalent adult), households ranked by household income per capita (or per equivalent adult), or households ranked by total household income. The population unit and ranking concept used to construct the distribution can make a huge difference to measured inequality and poverty. For example, Anand (1983) found that the income share of the lowest 40 per cent varied from 9.6 per cent to 17.7 per cent for differently defined distributions of income from the *same* Malaysian household survey. Chen and Ravallion, on the other hand, use unit record data from household surveys in each country to construct comparable distributions—of individuals ranked by per capita household income (or consumption).

The data comparability issue has been discussed at length by Atkinson and Brandolini (2001) in their review of secondary datasets used in studies of income inequality. On the basis of a detailed analysis of distribution data for OECD countries, they find that problems of comparability, including those described above, are present even in the "high quality" subset of the Deininger and Squire (1996) compilation, used by both Bhalla (2002, and this volume) and Sala-i-Martín (2006). Atkinson and Brandolini (2001, pp. 777–8) conclude that "users could be seriously misled if they simply download the Deininger and Squire 'accept' series [i.e. the 'high quality' subset]." Recent World Bank distributional data, described in Chen and Ravallion (2004, 2008), are subject to fewer problems of non-comparability than Deininger and Squire (1996)—but some problems remain, such as the unavoidable mixing of income and consumption distributions.

The coverage of PPP data based on the 1993 ICP has also been a significant concern. In the World Bank's previous global poverty estimates (Chen and Ravallion, 2007), the PPPs for 69 of the 100 countries were based on data collected in the 1993 ICP, while most of the remainder were based on interpolations from cross-country regressions. China and India were important exceptions: India's PPP was extrapolated from its 1985 estimate, while China's was "based on a credible independent (non-ICP) study of price levels in ten cities of China" (Chen and Ravallion, 2004, p. 9). As we saw earlier, the 2005 ICP has much wider coverage than the 1993 ICP and includes data for both China and India. The improved coverage has made a substantial difference to estimates of global poverty, which is due in part to the finding that both China and India are approximately 40 per cent poorer than indicated in previous estimates.

Conclusion

The international community's commitment to halve global poverty by 2015 has been enshrined in the first Millennium Development Goal. How global poverty is measured is a critical element in assessing progress towards this goal. The chapters in this volume address a range of problems in the estimation of global poverty, from a variety of viewpoints. Given their political salience, it is not surprising that controversy surrounds both "official" and independent estimates, and that a lively debate has ensued.

In this introduction, we have discussed different views concerning the possibility of defining and using a meaningful global poverty line. We have examined different PPP exchange rates that have been used to map a global poverty line across countries, and the complications that arise in the periodic re-estimation of PPPs on the basis of different ICPs. One of the most significant differences between the studies is whether they use survey or national accounts means for within-country distributions in the estimation of global poverty. It will be clear from our discussion of the issues that we have reservations about some of the approaches adopted. We have nonetheless tried to include the full range of viewpoints to allow the reader to form his or her own judgment about their relative merits. The debate on the measurement of global poverty will surely continue, and with this volume we hope to illuminate this important topic.

Notes

1. As we discuss below, the original "PPP$1-a-day" poverty line has been updated to PPP $1.25 at 2005 prices.
2. Chen and Ravallion (2008, Table 8).
3. Sala-i-Martín (2006, p. 392).
4. PPP exchange rates convert, say, pounds into dollars, not at the official exchange rate but at a rate reflecting the differences in purchasing power. The official exchange rate may be US$1.50 to UK£1, even if one can buy about the same market basket of goods with a pound in the UK as with a dollar in the US. In this case, the PPP exchange rate would be 1 to 1, not 1.5 to 1. (Not surprisingly, different patterns of consumption will give rise to different PPP exchange rates.)
5. Bhalla (2002) states that "the errors inherent in [National Accounts] means are corrected by increasing the poverty line by approximately 15 percent, from $1.30 per capita per day to $1.50 per capita per day" (p. 121). We discuss the use of National Accounts means below.

6. More generally, GDP at PPP\$ calculated in year $t+n$ is not equal to GDP at PPP\$ calculated in year t multiplied by intervening domestic growth and deflated by intervening US inflation.

7. The ten countries are: Bangladesh, China, India, Indonesia, Nepal, Pakistan, Tanzania, Thailand, Tunisia, and Zambia (Chen and Ravallion, 2001, p. 285).

8. While Bhalla (2002) and Sala-i-Martín (2006) both use a higher real poverty line than Chen and Ravallion (2007), Sala-i-Martín's estimates of poverty are lower in all years and Bhalla's (2002) are lower from about 1990. This is due to other methodological differences, such as their use of National Accounts data for scaling household incomes, which we discuss later.

9. One could then use the relative cost of this capability set in different countries to infer the implied "PPP" exchange rates. There is no reason to think that such exchange rates would be similar to extant PPP exchange rates.

10. Although it is possible to measure years of schooling reliably, a year of schooling in one country may differ from that in another in quality or in total hours spent at school.

11. Given a benchmark year t, GDP in PPP\$ in year $t+n$ is calculated by scaling GDP in PPP\$ in year t up or down by the country's real growth rate (nominal growth minus a price deflator). In the case of Penn World Tables there is a further stage of reconciliation after this updating (Aten and Heston, Ch. 6). As mentioned in note 6 above, GDP in PPP\$ in year $t+n$ calculated in this manner can be very different from that obtained by use of a new ICP conducted in the year $t+n$.

12. In the case of Bhalla (2002), PWT is only one of several cited sources—see note 15 below.

13. See Anand and Segal (2008, pp. 70–3) for formulas and discussion of the GK and EKS methods.

14. Of course, if the global poverty line itself were re-estimated as the median of the lowest ten poverty lines in GK PPP\$, then the overestimation of incomes in poor countries would also lead to a higher poverty line in GK PPP\$, and such a bias would not be present.

15. Bhalla (2002) mixes PPP sources, which is problematic for a different reason. On p. 140 he reports using the World Bank's *World Development Indicators* as his source for PPPs, but on p. 207 he reports using PPPs additionally from the Penn World Tables, the IMF's *International Financial Statistics*, and Maddison (2001), benchmarked in various years. The PPPs in these sources are inconsistent because some are based on EKS and others on GK, and they are benchmarked to different years (Anand and Segal, 2008, pp. 81–2).

16. It would also require knowing "the poor" in advance, implying a certain circularity. However, this is not a major practical problem.

17. By itself, of course, this does not tell us whether global poverty is under- or overestimated.

18. All estimates of global poverty are based on datasets that include both income and consumption surveys. The World Bank, wherever possible, chooses consumption surveys over income surveys. Mixing income and consumption surveys raises questions of comparability, which are discussed in Anand and Segal (2008, pp. 73–4).

19. The United Nations University World Institute for Development Economics Research (UNU-WIDER) World Income Inequality Database (WIID) is available at <http://www.wider.unu.edu/research/Database/en_GB/database/> (accessed June 13, 2009).
20. Bhalla (2002) also smoothes within-country distributions by fitting a three-parameter Lorenz curve to the quintile shares through regression. After this regression he performs a "filtering" procedure (pp. 133–4), but it is unclear precisely what this procedure involves (Anand and Segal, 2008, p. 81).
21. Bhalla (2002, p. 128) scales to 0.867 times HFCE.
22. The smoothing technique used by Sala-i-Martín (2006) is problematic (see Anand and Segal, 2008, pp. 78–9). First, the theory of kernel density estimation assumes that the income observations are independent identically distributed draws from the underlying income distribution, which is not the case for quintile means. Second, his use of a constant bandwidth across all countries' datasets is incorrect because the appropriate bandwidth for a distribution depends on its spread. Minoiu and Reddy (2008) find that the use of alternative bandwidths makes a large difference to poverty estimates. Finally, non-parametric kernel density estimation is intended for large datasets, whereas each of Sala-i-Martín's country distributions is constructed from just five data points (the quintile means).
23. This is, however, somewhat ambiguous. The "Official List of MDG Indicators" on the Millennium Development Goals Indicators website (<http://mdgs.un.org/unsd/mdg/>, accessed June 13, 2009) states the reduction of *income* poverty as the goal, whereas under "Data Availability" the data used to monitor this goal are described as measuring consumption poverty.
24. The latter includes expenditure by organizations such as political parties and religious associations.
25. Aten and Heston (Ch. 6) state that the latest PWT, version 6.1, includes expenditures on health and education by government and non-profit institutions in "Household Actual Final Consumption" for OECD countries, but not for other countries.
26. Much of this paragraph closely follows Deaton (2003, pp. 367–8).
27. See Kulshreshtha and Kar (2005).
28. The coverage and quality of data in Bhalla (2002) are questionable. According to his Table A.1 (p. 209) there are 317 surveys for the period 1950–80, and 604 for the period 1980–2000, implying a total of 921. But he also reports using "more than 1,000 household surveys" (p. 38). Moreover, Ravallion (2002, p. 8) observes that only "[a]bout half of Bhalla's 600 distributions over 1980–2000 would pass the quality standards applied to the [World] Bank's calculations."
29. This paragraph draws on Anand and Segal (2008, p. 74).

Bibliography

Ackland, R., Dowrick, S., and Freyens, B. (2004) 'Measuring Global Poverty: Why PPP Methods Matter'. Paper presented at the 2004 Conference of the International Association for Research in Income and Wealth, Cork, Ireland (August).

Ahmad, S. (2003) 'Purchasing Power Parity for International Comparison of Poverty: Sources and Methods'. Mimeo, Development Data Group, World Bank, Washington, DC. <http://www.worldbank.org/data/ICP> accessed on January 15, 2007.

Anand, S. (1983) Inequality and Poverty in Malaysia: Measurement and Decomposition. Oxford and New York: Oxford University Press.

—— and Segal, P. (2008) 'What Do We Know about Global Income Inequality?' Journal of Economic Literature, 46(1), pp. 57–94.

Atkinson, A. B. and Brandolini, A. (2001) 'Promise and Pitfalls in the Use of "Secondary" Datasets: Income Inequality in OECD Countries'. Journal of Economic Literature, 39(3), pp. 771–99.

Bhalla, S. S. (2002) Imagine There's No Country: Poverty, Inequality and Growth in the Era of Globalization. Washington, DC: Institute for International Economics.

Boskin Commission (1996) 'Toward a More Accurate Measure of the Cost of Living'. Final report to the Senate Committee from the Advisory Commission to study the consumer price index, December 4. <http://www.ssa.gov/history/reports/boskinrpt.html> accessed on March 6, 2009.

Chen, S. and Ravallion, M. (2001) 'How Did the World's Poorest Fare in the 1990s?' Review of Income and Wealth, 47, pp. 283–300.

—— —— (2004) 'How Have the World's Poorest Fared since the Early 1980s?' World Bank Research Observer, 19(2), pp. 141–69.

—— —— (2007) 'Absolute Poverty Measures for the Developing World, 1981–2004'. World Bank Policy Research Working Paper 4211, Washington, DC.

—— —— (2008) 'The Developing World is Poorer than We Thought, But No Less Successful in the Fight against Poverty'. World Bank Policy Research Working Paper 4703, Washington, DC.

Deaton, A. S. (2001) 'Counting the World's Poor: Problems and Possible Solutions'. World Bank Research Observer, 16(2), pp. 125–47.

—— (2003) 'How to Monitor Poverty for the Millennium Development Goals'. Journal of Human Development, 4(3), pp. 353–78.

—— and Kozel, V. (eds.) (2005) The Great Indian Poverty Debate. New Delhi: Macmillan.

Deininger, K. and Squire, L. (1996) 'A New Data Set Measuring Income Inequality'. World Bank Economic Review, 10(3), pp. 565–91. Updated dataset available at <http://econ.worldbank.org>.

Korinek, A., Mistiaen, J. A., and Ravallion, M. (2006) 'Survey Nonresponse and the Distribution of Income'. Journal of Economic Inequality, 4(1), pp. 33–55.

Kulshreshtha, A. C. and Kar, A. (2005) 'Estimates of Food Consumption Expenditure from Household Surveys and National Accounts'. In A. S. Deaton and V. Kozel (eds.) The Great Indian Poverty Debate, New Delhi: Macmillan, pp. 102–18.

Milanovic, B. (2005) Worlds Apart: Measuring International and Global Inequality. Princeton, NJ: Princeton University Press.

Minoiu, C. and Reddy, S. G. (2008) 'Kernel Density Estimation Based on Grouped Data: The Case of Poverty Assessment'. IMF Working Paper WP/08/183, International Monetary Fund, Washington, DC.

Ravallion, M. (2000) 'Should Poverty Measures be Anchored to the National Accounts?' Economic and Political Weekly, August 26 and September 2.

—— (2002) 'Have We Already Met the Millennium Development Goal for Poverty?' *Economic and Political Weekly*, November 16.

—— (2004) 'Pessimistic on Poverty?' *The Economist*, April 10.

—— and Chen, S. (1997) 'What Can New Survey Data Tell Us About Recent Changes in Distribution and Poverty?' *World Bank Economic Review*, 11(2), pp. 357–82.

Sala-i-Martín, X. (2006) 'The World Distribution of Income: Falling Poverty and... Convergence, Period'. *Quarterly Journal of Economics*, 121(2), pp. 351–97.

Stiglitz, J. E. (1976) 'The Efficiency Wage Hypothesis, Surplus Labor and the Distribution of Income in L.D.C.s'. *Oxford Economic Papers*, 28(2), pp. 185–207.

United Nations (2000) *We the Peoples: The Role of the United Nations in the 21st Century*. Secretary-General's MDG Report, New York.

World Bank (1990) *World Development Report 1990: Poverty*. New York: Oxford University Press.

—— (2008a) *Global Purchasing Power Parities and Real Expenditures: 2005 International Comparison Program*. Washington, DC.

—— (2008b) 'Comparison of New 2005 PPPs with Previous Estimates'. Revised Appendix G to World Bank (2008a), Washington, DC.

Part I
Measuring Global Poverty

2

The Debate on Globalization, Poverty, and Inequality: Why Measurement Matters[1]

Martin Ravallion[2]

Introduction

What has been happening to the living standards of poor people in the world lies at the heart of the globalization debate. Indeed, as Amartya Sen has argued, the real concern of the "anti-globalization" protestors is surely not globalization per se, for these protests are among the most globalized events in the modern world; rather, their concerns seem to stem in large part from the continuing deprivations and rising disparities in levels of living that they see in the current period of globalization (Sen, 2002).

Are their concerns justified? There is no denying the *perceptions* held by the critics of globalization that poverty and inequality are rising. For example, the website of the International Forum on Globalization confidently claims that "globalization policies have contributed to increased poverty, increased inequality between and within nations."[3] Whether this is a valid generalization, or even a valid characterization for any specific group of countries, is another matter.

Both sides in the debate have sought support from "hard" data on what is happening to poverty and inequality in the world. A "numbers debate" has developed, underlying the more high-profile protests and debates on globalization. By some accounts, the proportion of people living in extreme poverty in the developing world has fallen sharply in the 1990s (Bhalla, 2002; Sala-i-Martín, 2002). Other assessments suggest much more modest gains, including those regularly published by the World Bank (the latest published update is Chen and Ravallion, 2008). Yet others claim that globalization has led to greater poverty (International Forum on Globalization, 2001).

There have been similar disagreements about what has been happening to inequality. By some accounts, income inequality has been rising in the world (see for example, International Forum on Globalization, 2001, and Galbraith, 2002, commenting on Dollar and Kraay, 2002a), while by others (including Bhalla, 2002, and Sala-i-Martín, 2002) it has been falling, though not continuously.

Who should we believe? To answer that question, we need to probe more deeply into the sources of the differences between the conflicting assessments. This calls for closer scrutiny of the concepts being used, which are not always in agreement between the two sides of the debate. It also requires closer inspection of the data sources and methods of analysis, even when there is agreement on the concept one is trying to measure. Only then can one form a judgment as to what the available data can really tell us about progress against poverty and inequality in the new era of globalization. This chapter offers a non-technical commentary on the conceptual and methodological differences underlying the "numbers debate" on globalization.

Ambiguous concepts make deceptive statistics

Before trying to quantify anything, one must first be clear about the concept to be measured. Specialists are (typically) precise about these things, but that is not so true in the popular debate on globalization.

Most observers have a reasonably clear idea about the difference between "poverty" and "inequality." As these terms are normally defined, poverty is about *absolute levels of living*—how many people cannot attain certain predetermined consumption needs. Inequality is about the *disparities in levels of living*—for example, how much more is held by rich people than poor people. Measures of poverty and inequality are typically based on household consumption expenditure or income normalized for differences in household size and the cost of living. Aggregate measures of poverty at country or global levels tend to get the most attention, though finer breakdowns (such as by geographic area or ethnic group) are often brought into the picture. Some commentators are less careful about an equally important distinction lingering under the surface of the globalization debate—between the ideas of "relative poverty" and "absolute poverty." The latter typically means that the poverty line has fixed purchasing power. Relative poverty typically means that the poverty line has higher purchasing power in richer countries or areas within countries. How much higher is a matter of debate; this depends on how important relative deprivation is to a person's assessment of his or her well-being, and that is not something we know much about (Ravallion, 2009). Economists have traditionally assumed that people only care about their own consumption, but there is now a body of evidence suggesting that people do hold "social preferences," and that relative deprivation is an important determinant of welfare and behavior.[4] There is wide agreement that a person's own income is far too narrow a basis for judging economic well-being. To the extent that this depends on relative income, measures of poverty in terms of welfare will need to use poverty lines that vary with the mean income of some relevant reference group. Putting that into practice in a convincing way is another matter.

The measurement choice does matter. Roughly speaking, the more "relative" a poverty measure, the less impact economic growth will have on its value. Those who say globalization is good for the world's poor tend to be undisguised "absolutists." By contrast, many critics of globalization appear to think of poverty in more relative terms. At one extreme, if the poverty line is proportional to mean income then it behaves a lot like a measure of inequality. Fixing the poverty line relative to mean income has actually been popular in poverty measurement in Western Europe. This method can show rising poverty even when the levels of living of the poor have in fact risen. That is surely an extreme position that would seem hard to defend. While we can agree that relative deprivation matters, it appears to be very unlikely that individual welfare depends *only* on one's relative position, and not at all on absolute levels of living, as determined by incomes. Instead, Ravallion and Chen (2009) propose a class of "weakly relative" poverty measures, whereby the poverty line rises with mean consumption, but with an elasticity less than unity.

A further distinction is between the ideas of "relative inequality" and "absolute inequality." In applied work, economists typically mean "relative inequality" when they talk about the effects of greater trade openness on inequality. Relative inequality depends on the *ratios* of individual incomes to the overall mean. (The precise nature of that dependence—the weight given to income disparities at different levels, for example—has been the subject of a large literature.)[5] So if all incomes grow at the same rate then relative inequality is unchanged. A common finding in the academic literature is that greater trade openness has roughly the same effect on the growth rate of income at different levels of income (see, for example, Dollar and Kraay, 2002a, b). Then openness can be said to be "distribution-neutral" in that (relative) inequality is unchanged on average.

But that is not the only defensible concept of inequality. "Absolute inequality" depends on the *absolute differences* in levels of living, rather than relative differences, as captured by the ratios to the mean. Consider an economy with just two household incomes: $1,000 and $10,000. If both incomes double in size then relative inequality will remain the same; the richer household is still ten times richer. But the absolute difference in their incomes has doubled, from $9,000 to $18,000. Relative inequality is unchanged but absolute inequality has risen sharply.

Perceptions on the ground that "inequality is rising" appear often to be referring to this concept of inequality. Indeed, in experiments used to identify which concept of inequality is held by people, it was found that 40 per cent of participants thought about inequality in absolute terms (Amiel and Cowell, 1999).[6] It is not that one concept is "right" and one "wrong." They simply reflect different value judgments about what constitutes higher "inequality."

These value judgments carry considerable weight for the position one takes in the globalization debate. Finding that the share of income going to the poor does not change on average with growth does not mean that "growth raises the incomes (of the poor) by about as much as it raises the incomes of everybody else" as claimed by an article in the *Economist* (May 27, 2000), referring to Dollar and Kraay (2000a). Given existing inequality, the income gains to the rich from distribution-neutral growth will of course be greater than the gains to the poor. In the above example of two households, the income gain from economic growth is ten times greater for the high income person; to say that this means the poor share fully in the gains from growth is clearly a stretch. And the example is not far fetched. For example, for the richest decile in India, the income gain from aggregate growth will be about four times higher than the gain to the poorest quintile; it will be fifteen to twenty times higher in Brazil or South Africa.

The common empirical finding in the literature is that changes in (relative) inequality have virtually zero correlation with rates of economic growth naturally carries little weight for those who are concerned instead about absolute inequality. The latter does tend to rise with growth, and fall with contraction. Across 117 spells between successive household surveys for forty-seven developing countries (the same data set used in Ravallion, 2001) I find a strong positive correlation—a correlation coefficient of 0.64—between annualized changes in the absolute Gini index (in which absolute differences in incomes are not scaled by the mean) and annualized rates of growth in mean household income or consumption, as estimated from the same surveys. Yet there is virtually zero correlation (a coefficient of –0.06) with relative inequality, as measured by the ordinary Gini index in which absolute differences are scaled by the mean.

A further source of confusion underlying the conflicting claims that have been made about what has happened to "inequality" in the world in the current period of globalization stems from lack of clarity about whether one is talking about inequality between countries or between people (wherever they live). Some of the claims about rising "inequality" have been based on the fact that, looking back over the past forty years or so, initially poorer countries have tended to experience lower subsequent growth rates (see, for example, Pritchett, 1997). But of course countries vary enormously in population size. If one takes account of this, then the picture of rising inequality changes dramatically. Total inequality between people in the world can be thought of as having two components: the amount of inequality *between* countries and the amount *within* countries. Since one naturally weights by population when calculating overall inequality, the between-country component is also population weighted. Given the population weighting, the between-country component has tended to fall, even though poorer countries have not tended to have higher growth rates (see, for example, Schultz, 1998, and Bhalla, 2002). The two largest countries naturally figure prominently in this finding. China and (more recently) India have enjoyed high growth rates and this has been a major contributing factor to lowering overall inequality in the world.

Nor can it be denied that there is evidence of rising inequality within many countries, including China and India. Rising inequality is not, however, correlated with growth rates; indeed, among growing economies, inequality tends to fall about as often as it rises (Ravallion and Chen, 1997; Ravallion, 2001).

Combining the between- and within-country pictures, there is no convincing sign of a significant trend increase in overall inequality between people over the past twenty years or so; nor is there convincing evidence of a trend decline in inequality.

The devil is in the details

Conceptual ambiguities are not the only reason for the conflicting claims in the globalization debate. There are also differences in how the available data have been interpreted and differences in the underlying assumptions made in measurement.

Let us now focus on absolute poverty. All the estimates I have seen suggest a trend decline in the incidence of poverty and the total number of poor since about 1980.[7] Progress has not been even over time. There is evidence of an increase in the number of poor in the late 1980s and early 1990s (Chen and Ravallion, 2000).[8] However, this sub-period is not typical, and it is not too surprising that progress against poverty was stalled then, given simultaneous macroeconomic difficulties in the two largest countries, China and India, on top of the weak growth in Africa. If one focuses instead on the period since about 1990, all sources I know of suggest a sustained decrease in the number of poor by any absolute standard. This is also evident if one looks at estimates going back to 1980 and before (Bourguignon and Morrisson, 2002; Sala-i-Martín, 2002; World Bank, 2002; Chen and Ravallion, 2004, 2008).[9]

While there appears to be broad agreement that absolute poverty is tending to fall, there are some large discrepancies among the available estimates of the rate of progress being made against absolute poverty. I will focus on two estimates. In the first, Bhalla (2002) presents estimates of the incidence of absolute poverty in the developing world that imply that the United Nations' Millennium Development Goal (MDG) of halving the 1990 "$1-a-day" poverty rate by 2015 was in fact already reached in 2000.

Contrast this with the World Bank estimates for the 1990s, which suggest that the MDG for poverty will be reached on time if the rate of progress since 1990 is maintained (World Bank, 2000). This is based on the numbers reported in World Bank (2000), comparing 1990 and 1998. This implies a drop in the $1-a-day poverty incidence of about 0.6 percentage points per year, which would be sufficient to halve the 1990s poverty rate by 2015.[10] On updating this estimate using the latest available data, we find a mean annual rate of decline over the 1990s of 0.7 points per year, which (if maintained) would mean that the MDG for poverty would be achieved slightly ahead of time.[11]

These two sources differ in other respects. For example, Bhalla's estimates indicate that the incidence of poverty in South Asia is well below average for the developing world as a whole, while the World Bank finds above average poverty for that region. However, here I will focus on the difference in the aggregate numbers—similar reasons underlie the differences in regional composition.

How could two estimates of roughly the same thing be so different? Have we really achieved the MDG for poverty, fifteen years ahead of time, as Bhalla claims? To answer this question we need to look inside the black box of poverty measurement.

To measure poverty one first needs a poverty line. Different people naturally have different ideas of what "poverty" means. This is true between countries as well as within a given country. Richer countries tend to have higher poverty lines when converted to a common currency at exchange rates that attempt to assure purchasing power parity (PPP). Among poor countries, there is very little income gradient in the poverty lines—absolute consumption needs tend to dominate in a poor country. But as incomes rise, societies naturally tend to alter their views as to what minimum standard of living is deemed acceptable. So poverty lines rise with mean consumption.

Recognizing this feature of how poverty lines vary, how should we measure poverty in the world as a whole? There are two approaches that have been taken. The relative poverty approach uses poverty lines that increase with mean income of the country. For example, Ravallion and Chen (2009) present results for a relative poverty line which rises with mean income above a critical level, as determined by the aforementioned empirical relationship between actual poverty lines and mean consumption across countries. This is arguably a better approach than setting a poverty line that is proportional to mean income, which tends to give either absurdly low poverty lines in poor countries, or absurdly high ones in rich countries.

However, all such relative poverty lines do not treat people with the same level of consumption the same way, and so the resulting measures would clearly lose meaning as measures of absolute income poverty. Since 1990, the World Bank has chosen instead to measure global poverty by the standards of what poverty means in poor countries, which gave the "$1-a-day" line (Ravallion et al., 1991; World Bank, 1990, 2000). This poverty line is then converted to local currency using the latest PPP exchange rates for consumption and local consumer price indices are then used to convert the international poverty line in local currency to the prices prevailing at the time of the survey.

It is fully acknowledged that this is a conservative definition; while one could hardly argue that the people in the world who are poor by the standards typical of the poorest countries are not in fact poor, there are many more poor people in the world who are poor by the standards of middle-income countries. Some observers have argued that the World Bank has systematically underestimated the extent of poverty using its $1-a-day line and argue that a higher line should be used;[12] still others have argued for a lower line. However, there is no escaping the fact that there is a degree of arbitrariness about any poverty line. Provided one is consistent across countries, one can test whether the regional comparisons and assessments of progress over time are robust to such differences.

Having set a poverty line, one counts how many people live below it. Over the past twenty-five years there has been considerable expansion in the coverage and frequency of the household surveys that allow one to calculate the proportion of the population living in households with consumption expenditures and/or incomes per person below the poverty line. Such surveys are currently the most widely used source of data for measuring poverty in the world.

It is important to recognize that these surveys come with numerous problems. In the international comparisons of the "$1-a-day" poverty rates done by the World Bank, only surveys that meet certain quality criteria—arguably quite minimal criteria—are included. The surveys must be nationally representative, include a sufficiently comprehensive consumption or income aggregate (including consumption or income from own production) and it must be possible to construct a correctly weighted distribution of consumption or income per person.

The World Bank's researchers found that the latter requirement was often not met by pre-existing data sources, so they have insisted on being able to get back to the original "raw" household-level data sets rather than rely on summarized tabulations from secondary sources to assure that the calculations are done consistently. By building up the global poverty numbers from the primary data—either the raw micro data or special purpose tabulations designed to meet uniform quality criteria—past errors or inconsistencies in estimating distributional statistics can be dealt with. The latest published update used almost 700 surveys since about 1980 for measuring global poverty, representing 115 countries (Chen and Ravallion, 2008). At the time of writing, the database included 400 surveys representing 100 countries.

Nonetheless, there are still numerous comparability problems across these various surveys. For example, some use income while some use consumption to measure well-being. There are also comparability problems among surveys in the questionnaires used—such as differences in recall periods for consumption—that can greatly influence the results obtained. Some observers in the globalization debate have chosen to largely ignore these differences. Yet others find casual anecdotal observations more persuasive. For example, Secor (2003) quotes an academic contributor to the globalization debate as rejecting existing quantitative data showing lower inequality in Indonesia than Australia; the support given by the academic for his claim that the existing data are wrong is that "You can check that out by going to the capital city and driving in from the airport. You can see it ain't so." Thankfully, most observers would not find a drive into the capital city from the airport more persuasive than a well-designed nationally representative sample survey of households (as is done in both Australia and Indonesia).

But even if the surveys are entirely accurate, it must be acknowledged that the measure of poverty obtained can still miss important aspects of individual welfare. Using household consumption ignores inequalities within households. Nor does it reflect people's concerns about uninsured risk to their incomes and health as well as their feelings about relative deprivation, as already discussed. A conventional poverty measure can hardly be considered a sufficient statistic for judging the quality of people's lives.

Even putting these concerns to one side, there are numerous differences in the methods used to measure the incidence of poverty in the world.[13] How one deals with the diversity in the underlying survey data is an important factor. Some researchers have indiscriminately mixed distributions that vary in important ways. For example, some are distributions of household income (not per capita) and the poorest x per cent in some surveys refers to households while others follow the methods used by the World Bank's researchers in which they refer to people. These differences can matter greatly to the measures one obtains of poverty and inequality. The fact that household (rather than per capita) distributions were more common in the 1960s and 1970s than the 1980s and 1990s also biases comparisons over time, given that household distributions tend to show higher inequality (given that, when measuring inequality between individuals, inequality within households is invariably ignored for lack of data). Signs of falling inequality may simply reflect this fact, rather than a real change in distribution.

However, these differences may well be less important than others. While many researchers prefer to use the consumption expenditures or incomes reported in surveys, some have preferred to anchor their poverty measures to the consumption or GDP means obtained from a country's national accounts. This is the method used by Bhalla (2002), Sala-i-Martín (2002) and UNCTAD (2002). This method ignores the absolute levels of consumption or income found in all these surveys. By exploiting the mathematical properties of poverty measures, the published quintile shares from surveys are combined with the published national accounts aggregates to come up with estimates of the incidence of poverty. This method tends to show a higher rate of poverty reduction over the past twenty years than the survey-based method.

The researchers who measure poverty using the national accounts admit that they are doing so partly as a matter of convenience; it is just a whole lot easier to do it this way than by going back to all those messy micro household-level data sets. But they also argue that it is better to obtain mean household consumption or income from the national accounts rather than the surveys that were designed for that purpose. To support this, they argue that surveys tend to underestimate mean household consumption and income (especially income).[14] They point to the discrepancies between survey aggregates and national accounts aggregates. To some extent, these discrepancies reflect differences in the coverage and definitions of the two data sources. The differences also stem from measurement errors in both sources.

However, for the purpose of estimating the extent of poverty it is actually immaterial which gives the better estimate of average household consumption or income. The key question is which data source gives the better estimate of the poverty measure—that is after all the object of the exercise. Even if one agreed that the national accounts are right, there is no reason for assuming that the errors in the surveys leave inequality unaffected. For various reasons (including fear of taxation or legal action), the rich tend to underreport their incomes, and this is thought to be a much more serious problem (in both its absolute level and proportionately) than for the poor. It has not been established, and is quite unlikely from what we know, that the discrepancy between these two data sources is entirely due to underestimation of consumption or income levels in the surveys but that they still get inequality right. More plausibly, underestimation of mean income from a survey tends to come hand-in-hand with an underestimation of the extent of inequality.

To see why anchoring poverty measures to the national accounts can go so wrong, consider the following simple example. The true but unobserved distribution of income is (say) 1, 2, 3 (person 1 has an income of 1, person 2 has income 2, person 3 has 3). The poverty line is slightly above 1, so the true poverty rate is 1/3. We do a survey, and the three people respond that their incomes are 1, 1.5, and 2. Income of person 2 is underestimated by one quarter, while it is underestimated by one-third for person 3. The survey gives the right poverty rate. However, the survey underestimates the true mean; the survey mean is 1.5. Now let's assume (for the sake of argument) that the national accounts do give the right mean of 2. If we assume that the survey underestimation is distribution-neutral then we multiply all three incomes by 4/3. The "corrected" incomes are 1.3, 2, and 2.7—implying that there is no poverty. We get the mean right, but the poverty measure is way off the mark.

This is just an example. However, it may not be far fetched. One study found that the mean income of the ten highest income households in each of eighteen surveys for countries in Latin America was generally no more than the average salary of the manager of a medium to large sized firm (Szekely and Hilgert, 2000). Clearly there is massive underreporting by the rich.

Careful data work has also been revealing about the sources of the discrepancies between surveys and national accounts, and has thrown considerable doubt on methods of measuring poverty that assume that the national accounts get the mean right while the surveys get inequality right. For India it has been found that for categories of consumption accounting for over 75 per cent of the consumption of the poor, the divergence between the national accounts and the national household surveys is small (Sundaram and Tendulkar, 2001). Simply multiplying all incomes or consumptions by a single number so that the survey gives the same mean as the national accounts results in a serious overstatement of the consumption expenditure of the poor and hence produces a spurious reduction in the headcount index.

Recent research has studied how poverty and inequality measures from survey data can best be corrected for the tendency of richer households to not want to participate in such surveys. Results for the US suggest that without such corrections, surveys tend to appreciably underestimate both the mean and the extent of income inequality, but that these two effects are roughly offsetting for measures of poverty (Korinek, Mistiaen, and Ravallion, 2006). Very little correction is needed for the incomes of the poorest few deciles, but the correction factors are as high as 30–50 per cent for the richest decile. Again this makes clear just how wrong one can be in assuming that the income underestimation in surveys is distribution-neutral.

The key point is that simply correcting the survey mean need not get you a better measure of poverty, even if you believe that the national accounts give you the correct mean for measuring poverty, which is far from obvious. If you do not believe the overall survey mean, how can you believe the distribution of income obtained from the same survey?

Dubious claims about the welfare impacts of globalization

People on both sides of this debate have been quick to draw conclusions about the impacts of "globalization" from their favorite poverty numbers. The title of a book by the International Forum of Globalization asks: "Does globalization help the poor?" and the book answers with a confident "no." The back cover of Bhalla (2002) asks: "Who has gained from globalization?" and answers with equal confidence: the poor. Yet readers of neither book will come away any wiser about the answer to these questions than when they started. In fact, neither book contains the sort of analysis that would be needed to credibly allow attribution of the claimed changes in poverty and inequality to "globalization." We are not given any evidence that would allow one to identify the role played by greater openness to external trade (as one aspect of globalization) in the distributional changes observed, versus other factors such as rising agricultural productivity, demographic factors, changes in the distribution and returns to education, and internal policy reforms.

More careful analytic work has attempted to identify the causal effects of (for example) greater trade openness on aggregate inequality, with controls for at least some of the other factors that are likely to matter. A number of attempts to throw empirical light on the welfare effects of trade liberalization have been made using aggregate cross-country data sets, whereby levels of measured inequality or changes over time in measured inequality and/or poverty are combined with data on trade openness and other control variables.[15] An example can be found in the careful econometric analysis using cross-country panel data sets in Dollar and Kraay (2002a), who discovered no sign that greater openness to external trade is either good or bad for (relative) inequality, and hence that the poor tend to benefit (absolutely).

However, there are also reasons to be cautious in drawing implications from these studies. There are concerns about data and methods and it is unclear how much power cross-country data sets have for detecting any underlying effects of greater openness or other covariates. The attribution of inequality impacts to trade policy reforms per se is particularly problematic.

One way in which the correlations (including lack of correlation) found in these studies can be deceptive is that starting conditions vary a lot between reforming countries. Simply averaging across this diversity in initial conditions can readily hide systematic effects of relevance to policy. For example, countries differ in their initial level of economic development. It is often argued that greater openness to external trade will have very different effects on inequality depending on the level of economic development—increasing inequality in rich countries and decreasing it in poor ones.[16] However, the opposite outcome is possible when economic reforms, including greater openness to external trade, increase demand for relatively skilled labor, which tends to be more inequitably distributed in poor countries than rich ones. There is some evidence of a *negative* interaction effect between openness to trade and initial GDP per capita in regressions for inequality across countries (Barro, 2000; Ravallion, 2001).

These problems can be dealt with using more sophisticated methods to analyze the compilations of country aggregates, such as by allowing for nonlinearities through interaction effects between trade openness and initial conditions. However, the problems go deeper. Aggregate inequality or poverty may not change with trade reform even though there are both gainers and losers at all levels of living. In cases in which the survey data have tracked the same families over time, it is quite common to find considerable churning under the surface.[17] Some people have escaped poverty while others have fallen into poverty, even though the overall poverty rate has moved rather little. Numerous sources of such diverse impacts can be found in developing country settings. For example, geographic disparities in access to human and physical infrastructure between and within developing countries can impede prospects for participating in the growth generated by reform, and these disparities tend to be correlated with incomes.[18]

Consider the case of China, which has recently undertaken a major trade reform, namely its accession to the WTO in 2001. One cannot possibly understand how this reform will affect the population simply by looking at its impact on (say) the aggregate poverty rate or overall inequality. The economic geography of poverty and how this interacts with the geographic diversity in the welfare impacts of policy reforms is crucial to understanding its impact. In the aggregate, the results of Chen and Ravallion (2004) indicate a small positive impact on mean household income, with slightly lower poverty in the short term as a result of the reform.[19] However, there is still a sizable, and at least partly explicable, variance in impacts across household characteristics. Rural families tend to lose; urban households tend to gain. There are larger impacts in some parts of the country than others; for example, one finds non-negligible welfare losses among agricultural households in the North-East—a region in which rural households are more dependent on feed grain production (for which falling relative prices are expected from WTO accession) than elsewhere in China.

Past analyses in the literature that simply averaged over these differences would miss a great deal of what matters to the debate on policy. Reforms may well entail sizable redistribution between the poor and the rich, but in opposite directions in different countries or different regions within countries. One should not be surprised to find that there is no correlation between growth and changes in inequality, or that there is no overall impact of policy reform on inequality. Yet there are real welfare impacts under the surface of this average impact calculation. Claims made about the distributional impacts of trade reform using cross-country comparisons are of questionable relevance for policy in any specific country.

Lessons for how to achieve pro-poor growth

What is "pro-poor growth"? By one definition it is a situation in which incomes of the poor grow at a higher rate than the non-poor.[20] The problem with this definition is that distributional changes can be "pro-poor" with no absolute gain to the poor or even falling living standards for poor people. Equally well, "pro-rich" distributional shifts may have come with large absolute gains to the poor. Instead, Ravallion and Chen (2003) define pro-poor growth as growth that reduces poverty by some agreed measure.

Among those who know the survey-based evidence, there is unlikely to be much disagreement with the claim that economic growth is typically (though by no means invariably) pro-poor, in the specific sense that absolute poverty (measured against a poverty line with fixed real value) tends to fall with growth. Many observers have gone from this observation to conclude that policies that are known to be good for growth are good for poverty reduction.[21] This does not follow. Growth-promoting policies often have distributional implications that cannot be ignored if one is interested in the impacts on poverty.

The case of India is instructive. Poverty incidence in India has been falling at a trend rate of about 1 percentage point per year since about 1970, and the country appears now to have returned to this trend decline since the macroeconomic difficulties of the early 1990s (Datt and Ravallion, 2002). However, performance has been uneven between states. Some states have been doing far better than others, both in the longer term, and in the wake of economic reforms over the past ten years.

But the growth rate needed to achieve this trend decline has been rising over time. The responsiveness of national poverty incidence to both non-agricultural output per capita and agricultural yields have been declining over time, especially so for non-agricultural output (Datt and Ravallion, 2002; Ravallion and Datt, 2002).

Here the geographic composition of India's growth has played an important role: widening regional disparities and limited growth in lagging areas has made the overall growth process less pro-poor over time. By and large, economic growth in India has not occurred in the states where it would have the most impact on poverty nationally. These differences in the impact of growth on poverty relate in turn to differences in access to infrastructure and social services (health care and education) that make it harder for poor people to take up the opportunities afforded by aggregate economic growth (Ravallion and Datt, 2002).

Such heterogeneity in the impact of growth on poverty holds important clues as to what else needs to be done by governments to promote poverty reduction, on top of promoting economic growth. According to some observers "such actions are not needed . . . Growth is sufficient. Period." (Bhalla, 2002). The basis of this claim is the evidence that poverty reduction has generally come with economic growth.

But that misses the point. Those who are saying that growth is not enough are *not* typically saying that growth does not reduce absolute income poverty, which (as an empirical generalization) is hard to deny. They are saying that combining growth-promoting economic reforms with the right policies to help assure that the poor can participate fully in the opportunities unleashed by growth will achieve more rapid poverty reduction than would be possible otherwise. Redressing the antecedent inequalities of opportunity within developing countries as they open up to external trade is crucial to realizing the poverty-reducing *potential* of globalization. That is the real challenge facing policy-makers striving for pro-poor growth.

Notes

1. These are the views of the author, and should not be attributed to the World Bank or any affiliated organization. This is a revised and updated version of a paper of the same title that appeared in *International Affairs*, July 2003.
2. Development Research Group, World Bank.
3. <http://www.ifg.org/store.htm>
4. See, for example, the discussion in Fehr and Fischbacher (2002) and references therein. On the implications for poverty measurement, see Ravallion (1998).
5. See Cowell (2000).
6. Participants in these experiments were students in the UK and Israel.
7. Bhalla (2002), Bourguignon and Morrison (2002), Chen and Ravallion (2000, 2001, 2008), Sala-I-Martin (2002), World Bank (2000, 2002).
8. This is apparently why Fischer (2003, p. 8) claims that "For some time it was the accepted view is that the proportion of people living in poverty in the world has been declining but their absolute number has been increasing" (a view which he then takes issue with); Fischer refers to the "World Bank" as the source.
9. World Bank (2002) claims that 200 million people escaped absolute poverty in the world as a whole over 1980–2000. This estimate has been questioned by Wade (2002) and others on the grounds that it is obtained by combining different sources (namely the estimates of Bourguignon and Morrison, 2002) up to 1992 and those of Chen and Ravallion (2000) after that. Shaohua Chen and I have subsequently re-estimated our series back to the early 1980s to check the claim made in World Bank (2002). Data coverage and quality deteriorate as one goes back further in time. While recognizing this limitation, our estimates suggest that if anything the 200 million figure is probably an underestimate.
10. Reddy and Pogge (2002, and Ch. 3 in this volume) and Wade (2002, though apparently drawing solely on Reddy and Pogge) argue that the World Bank's estimates (as reported in World Bank, 2002, and Chen and Ravallion, 2002) underestimate the level of poverty and overstate its rate of decline; however, they do not present alternative estimates to support this claim. Elsewhere, I have addressed in detail the methodological concerns raised by Reddy and Pogge (Ravallion, 2002a).
11. This calculation was made by Shaohua Chen using the same methods documented in Chen and Ravallion (2000, 2001) but updating the data set used there to include surveys not available at that time. The estimates for India in the 1990s used an adjustment method proposed by Deaton (2001) to deal with a serious comparability problem between the 1999/2000 survey design and previous surveys.
12. Examples include Wade (2002) and Reddy and Pogge (2002).
13. For a detailed discussion of the differences between the methods used by Bhalla (2002), for example, and the World Bank, see Ravallion (2002b).
14. For evidence on this point for developing and transition economies, see Ravallion (2003).
15. Examples include Bourguignon and Morrison (1990), Edwards (1997), Li et al. (1998), Lundberg and Squire (1999), Barro (2000), Dollar and Kraay (2002).
16. Wood (1994) makes a qualified argument along these lines.
17. Baulch and Hoddinott (2000) compile evidence for a number of countries.

18. In the context of China's lagging poor areas, see Jalan and Ravallion (2002).
19. The study used a general equilibrium model to estimate the effects of the trade reform on prices and wages and a large household survey to estimate the household level welfare impacts; for further details, see Chen and Ravallion (2002).
20. See, for example, Kakwani and Pernia (2002), who define pro-poor growth as a situation in which the actual change in poverty over time is greater than the change that would be expected if inequality (strictly the Lorenz curve) did not change.
21. For example Fischer (2003, p. 3) argues that " ... the surest route to sustained poverty reduction is economic growth. Growth requires good economic policies." Fischer then goes on to discuss policies that are thought to be good for growth.

References

Amiel, Y. and Cowell, F. (1999) *Thinking about Inequality: Personal Judgment and Income Distributions*. Cambridge: Cambridge University Press.

Barro, R. (2000) 'Inequality and Growth in a Panel of Countries'. *Journal of Economic Growth*, 5, pp. 5–32.

Baulch, B. and Hoddinott, J. (2000) 'Economic Mobility and Poverty Dynamics in Developing Countries'. *Journal of Development Studies*, 36(6), pp. 1–24.

Bourguignon, F. and Morisson, C. (1990) 'Income Distribution, Development and Foreign Trade'. *European Economic Review*, 34, pp. 1113–32.

—— —— (2002) 'The Size Distribution of Income Among World Citizens, 1820–1990'. *American Economic Review*, 92(4), pp. 727–44.

Bhalla, S. (2002) *Imagine There's No Country: Poverty, Inequality and Growth in the Era of Globalization*. Washington, DC: Institute for International Economics.

Chen, S. and Ravallion, M. (2000) 'How Did the World's Poorest Fare in the 1990s?' World Bank Policy Research Working Paper 2409.

—— —— (2001) 'How Did the World's Poorest Fare in the 1990s?' *Review of Income and Wealth*, 47, pp. 283–300.

—— —— (2004) 'Welfare Impacts of China's Accession to the World Trade Organization'. *World Bank Economic Review*, 18(1), pp. 29–58.

—— —— (2008) 'The Developing World is Poorer than We Thought, But no Less Successful in the Fight against Poverty'. Policy Research Working Paper 4703, Washington DC: World Bank.

Cowell, F. A. (2000) 'Measurement of Inequality'. In A. B. Atkinson and F. Bourguignon (eds.) *Handbook of Income Distribution*, Amsterdam: North-Holland.

Datt, G. and Ravallion, M. (2002) 'Has India's Post-Reform Economic Growth Left the Poor Behind?' *Journal of Economic Perspectives*, 16(3), pp. 89–108.

Deaton, A. (2001) 'Adjusted Indian Poverty Estimates for 1999–2000'. Mimeo, Research Program in Development Studies, Princeton University, NJ.

Dollar, D. and Kraay, A. (2002a) 'Growth *is* Good for the Poor'. *Journal of Economic Growth*, 7(3), pp. 195–225.

—— —— (2000b) 'Spreading the Wealth'. *Foreign Affairs*, 81(1), pp. 120–33.

Edwards, S. (1997) 'Trade Policy, Growth and Income Distribution'. *American Economic Review: Papers and Proceedings*, 87(2).

Fehr, E. and Fischbacher, U. (2002) 'Why Social Preferences Matter: The Impact of Non-Selfish Motives on Competition, Cooperation and Incentives'. *Economic Journal*, 112, pp. C1–33.

Fischer, S. (2003) 'Globalization and its Challenges—Ely Lecture to the American Economics Association'. *American Economic Review*, 93(2), pp. 1–30.

Galbraith, J. K. (2002) 'Is Inequality Decreasing?' *Foreign Affairs*, 81(4), p. 178.

International Forum on Globalization (2001) *Does Globalization Help the Poor? A Special Report*. San Francisco, CA: International Forum on Globalization.

Jalan, J. and Ravallion, M. (2002) 'Geographic Poverty Traps? A Micro Model of Consumption Growth in Rural China'. *Journal of Applied Econometrics*, 17(4), pp. 329–46.

Kakwani, N. and Pernia, E. M. (2003) 'What is Pro-Poor Growth?' *Asian Development Review*, 18(1), pp. 1–16.

Korinek, A., Mistiaen, J., and Ravallion, M. (2006) 'Survey Nonresponse and the Distribution of Income'. *Journal of Economic Inequality*, 4(2), pp. 33–55.

Li, H., Squire, L., and Zou, H-F. (1998) 'Explaining International and Intertemporal Variations in Income Inequality'. *Economic Journal*, 108, pp. 26–43.

Lundberg, M. and Squire, L. (1999) 'Growth and Inequality: Extracting the Lessons for Policy-Makers'. Mimeo, World Bank.

Pritchett, L. (1997) 'Divergence, Big Time'. *Journal of Economic Perspectives*, 11(3), pp. 3–17.

Ravallion, M. (1994) *Poverty Comparisons*. Chur, Switzerland: Harwood Academic Press.

—— (1997) 'Can High Inequality Developing Countries Escape Absolute Poverty?' *Economics Letters*, 56, pp. 51–7.

—— (1998) *Poverty Lines in Theory and Practice*. World Bank Livings Standards Working Paper 133, Washington, DC.

—— (2000) 'Should Poverty Measures be Anchored to the National Accounts?' *Economic and Political Weekly*, 34 (August 26).

—— (2001) 'Growth, Inequality and Poverty: Looking Beyond Averages'. *World Development*, 29(11), pp. 1803–15.

—— (2002a) 'How *Not* to Count the Poor: A Reply to Reddy and Pogge'. Mimeo, World Bank Development Research Group.

—— (2002b) 'Have We Already Met the Millennium Development Goal for Poverty?' *Economic and Political Weekly*, November 16.

—— (2003) 'Measuring Aggregate Economic Welfare in in Developing Countries: How Well do National Accounts and Surveys Agree?' *Review of Economics and Statistics*, 85, pp. 645–52.

—— (2009) 'On the Welfarist Rationale for Relative Poverty Lines'. In K. Basu and R. Kanbur (eds.), *Arguments for a Better World: Essays in Honor of Amartya Sen*. Volume I: *Ethics, Welfare and Measurement*, Oxford: Oxford University Press.

—— and Chen, S. (1997) 'What Can New Survey Data Tell Us about Recent Changes in Distribution and Poverty?' *World Bank Economic Review*, 11(2), pp. 357–82.

—— —— (2003) 'Measuring Pro-Poor Growth'. *Economics Letters*, 78, pp. 93–9.

—— —— (2009) 'Weakly Relative Poverty'. Policy Research Working Paper 4844, Washington DC: World Bank.

—— and Datt, G. (2002) 'Why Has Economic Growth Been More Pro-Poor in Some States of India than Others?' *Journal of Development Economics*, 68, pp. 381–400.

—— —— and van de Walle, D. (1991) 'Quantifying Absolute Poverty in the Developing World'. *Review of Income and Wealth*, 37, pp. 345–61.

Reddy, S. G. and Pogge, T. W. (2002) 'How *Not* to Count the Poor', Mimeo, Barnard College, New York.

Sala-i-Martín, X. (2002) 'The World Distribution of Income (Estimated from Individual Country Distributions)'. Mimeo, Columbia University.

Schultz, T. P. (1998) 'Inequality in the Distribution of Personal Income in the World: How it is Changing and Why'. *Journal of Population Economics*, 11(3), pp. 307–44.

Secor, L. (2003). 'Mind the Gap: The Debate Over Global Inequality Heats Up'. *Boston Globe*, January 5.

Sen, A. (2001) 'Globalization, Inequality and Global Protest,' *Development*, 45(2), pp. 11–16.

Sundaram, K., and Tendulkar, S. D. (2001) 'NAS-NSS Estimates of Private Consumption for Poverty Estimation: A Disaggregated Comparison for 1993–94'. *Economic and Political Weekly*, January 13.

Székely, M. and Hilgert, M. (2000) 'What's Behind the Inequality We Measure? An Investigation Using Latin American Data'. Mimeo, Office of the Chief Economist, Inter-American Development Bank, Washington, DC.

UNCTAD. (2002) *The Least Developed Countries Report*. Geneva: United Nations.

Wade, R. (2002) 'Are Global Poverty and Inequality Getting Worse?' *Prospect Magazine*, March.

Wood, A. (1994). *North-South Trade, Employment and Inequality. Changing Fortunes in a Skill-Driven World*. Oxford: Clarendon Press.

World Bank (1990) *World Development Report: Poverty*. New York: Oxford University Press.

—— (2000/1) *World Development Report: Attacking Poverty*. New York: Oxford University Press.

—— (2002) *Globalization, Growth and Poverty*. Washington, DC.

—— (2003), *Global Economic Prospects*. Washington, DC.

3

How *Not* to Count the Poor*

Sanjay G. Reddy[1] and Thomas Pogge[2]

Introduction

How many poor people are there in the world? This simple question is surprisingly difficult to answer at present.

Building on earlier exercises going back to the late 1970s,[3] the World Bank (henceforth Bank) has, in the 1990 and 2000/1 World Development Reports (WDRs), as well as periodically thereafter, presented comprehensive estimates of the extent of poverty in the world and in particular regions and countries in different years. These estimates have been widely accepted and employed in a range of analyses and assessments. They have been used to describe the world, to determine resource allocation priorities, and to judge which policies and programs reduce poverty the most. Recently, they have played a central role in monitoring the first Millennium Development Goal, which calls for the halving of global poverty as defined by the Bank's estimates.

Among the questions that the Bank's global income poverty estimates have been used to answer is whether the world is "on the right track" in terms of poverty reduction strategy. The Bank's recent estimates have led many to conclude that the world is indeed on the right track. Former Bank President, James D. Wolfensohn, for example, stated in 2001:

> Over the past few years, [these] better policies have contributed to more rapid growth in developing countries' per capita incomes than at any point since the mid-1970s. And faster growth has meant poverty reduction: the proportion of people worldwide living in absolute poverty has dropped steadily in recent decades, from 29 per cent in 1990 to a record low of 23 per cent in 1998. After increasing steadily over the past two centuries, since 1980 the total number of people living in poverty worldwide has fallen by an estimated 200 million—even as the world's population grew by 1.6 billion.[4]

Barely two years earlier, the Bank had painted a strikingly different picture: "the absolute number of those living on $1 per day or less continues to increase. The worldwide total rose from 1.2 billion in 1987 to 1.5 billion today."[5]

Global poverty estimates also influence assessments of the seriousness of the problem of world poverty, the scale of resources that should be devoted to reducing it, and the regions to which these resources should be directed. WDR 2000/1 argued, for example, that the largest number of the world's poor were in Africa rather than in South Asia, as earlier believed. The questions of how many poor people there are in the world, how poor they are, where they live, and how these facts are changing over time are clearly very important ones. The Bank's answers to these questions have been highly influential in part because, until quite recently, there were no other estimates.[6] Alternative estimates that have been produced recently adopt in central respects the same methodology as the Bank.

It is argued in this chapter that the Bank's estimates of the level, distribution, and trend of global poverty are marred by three serious problems. The first is that the Bank uses an arbitrary international poverty line that is not adequately anchored in any specification of the real requirements of human beings. The second problem is that it employs a concept of purchasing power "equivalence" that is neither well defined nor appropriate for poverty assessment. These difficulties are inherent in the Bank's "money-metric" approach and cannot be credibly overcome without dispensing with this approach altogether. The third problem is that the Bank extrapolates incorrectly from limited data and thereby creates an appearance of precision that masks the high probable error of its estimates. It is difficult to judge the nature and extent of the errors in global poverty estimates that arise from these three flaws. It will be argued, however, that there is some reason to believe that the Bank's approach may have led it to understate the extent of global income poverty and to infer without adequate justification that global income poverty has steeply declined in the recent period. We refer in what follows to the Bank's methodology of poverty assessment as it was applied to produce the estimates of poverty published in the 1990 and 2000/1 WDRs and in accompanying papers by Shaohua Chen and Martin Ravallion (as well as subsequent updates on the Bank's Povcalnet website[7]). However, the criticisms we present of this method apply also to the approach (as described, for instance, in Ravallion, Chen, and Sangraula, 2008) that the Bank is using to generate its most recent revised estimates of poverty.

It is possible to describe a practicable methodology for assessing global income poverty that would be more reliable. The current income poverty estimates should no longer be employed, and new ones corresponding to a defensible methodology should be generated.

A meaningless poverty line

A procedure frequently used in national poverty assessment exercises is to define a poverty line in terms of the cost of achieving certain ends. These ends are most often elementary requirements (such as the ability to be adequately nourished). The commodities that are deemed necessary for an individual to achieve a set of elementary requirements can be allowed to vary across groups of persons (defined for instance by age, gender, and other relevant criteria) if that is thought appropriate. Procedures of this kind have the advantage that, once established, they offer a consistent basis for determining the level of the poverty line in different years and locations. They also result in a poverty line that has a meaningful and relevant interpretation in terms of access to resources that are sufficient for achieving basic human requirements. For this reason, many countries have used such procedures in their domestic poverty estimates.

In contrast to this human requirements centered approach, the Bank has adopted what can be referred to as a "money-metric" methodology that does not directly refer to such requirements but rather to a relatively arbitrary international poverty line (IPL) defined in abstract money units and to local currency amounts that it deems to be "equivalent." In 1990, the Bank constructed an IPL from a set of domestic poverty lines (some from governmental, others from non-governmental sources) for thirty-three countries during the mid-1980s. These domestic poverty lines were scaled upward or downward according to changes in the national consumer price index (CPI) to determine their "equivalent" in 1985 national currency units. These 1985 national currency amounts were then converted into a common unit of "real purchasing power" equivalence using the 1985 purchasing power parity (PPP) conversion factors for consumption (expressed in local currency units per "international dollar," on which see below) calculated by Summers and Heston (1988). An IPL of $31 per month was chosen. The reason provided is that the domestic poverty lines of eight of the poorer countries in the sample, converted into dollars in this way, were very close to this IPL, which was thus deemed to reflect a poverty line that was "most typical" for poor countries.[8] This "$1 (PPP 1985) a day" (actually $1.02 PPP 1985) poverty line was applied in WDR 1990. In the Bank's later poverty measurement work (starting with Chen et al. 1994), this IPL was revised downward, without explanation, to $30.42 per month or $1 per day PPP 1985 (Chen and Ravallion, 2001, pp. 285 n. 7).

This IPL was then converted into the national currency units of different countries using the Penn World Tables (Summers and Heston 1988) PPP conversion factors for 1985. The resulting national poverty lines were then adjusted in proportion to changes in the national CPI (as reported in the IMF's *International Financial Statistics*) and applied to estimates of per capita household consumption from household survey data to derive the number of poor persons in a particular country and year.

For the 2000 poverty estimation exercise and more recent ones, the Bank established a new IPL. For the same list of thirty-three countries it had used earlier, it identified the ten countries whose domestic poverty lines—converted into 1993 national currency units and then, via 1993 general-consumption PPPs, into 1993 international dollars—were the lowest. The Bank then chose the median of these (so converted) domestic poverty lines—$32.74 per month or $1.08 per day 1993—as its new IPL. No justification has been offered for this change in approach. One reason may be that when 1993 PPPs are used to convert the list of thirty-three poverty lines into international dollars a cluster of poverty lines that may be deemed "most typical" no longer appears.

Is the new IPL "higher" or "lower" than the old one? This question is impossible to answer, as PPP dollars from different years are not comparable (as will be discussed below). The Bank claims that "This [new $1.08 per day PPP 1993] line has a similar purchasing power to the $1-a-day line in 1985 PPP prices, in terms of the command over domestic goods" (WDR 2000/1, p. 17). However, as PPP units in different years are non-comparable, this statement has no meaning. Chen and Ravallion (2001) offer as justification for their claim the observation that the global poverty headcount is approximately the same for the most recent common year (1993) in which both methodologies were applied. In offering this fact as a justification for the ostensible "equivalence" of the new IPL with the old they make a serious error in reasoning. It is obvious that, when employing *any* method of poverty assessment, one can define an IPL that is just high enough to yield whatever rate of poverty incidence one wishes to match (because it had resulted from a method previously used). There will necessarily be some level of the IPL defined in terms of the new method at which the aggregate number of poor people will be equal to the number previously estimated by the old method. Such coinciding results are easily achievable between any pair of methods and therefore do not show two methods to have any particular consistency with each other, nor do they provide any reason to believe that either method is appropriate for assessing the purchasing power of the poor.

An alternative approach to judging the Bank's claim that the new IPL maintains "a similar purchasing power . . . in terms of the command over domestic goods" involves using each country's CPI to transform its 1985 national poverty line (equivalent to $1 per day PPP 1985) into 1993 national currency units and then comparing the result with this country's 1993 national poverty line (deemed equivalent to $1.08 per day PPP 1993). We present the result of this exercise in Table 3.1, which shows 1985 national poverty lines updated to 1993 through a country's CPI to be as much as 30 per cent lower (for Nigeria) and as much as 157 per cent higher (for Mauritania) than the 1993 poverty line for the same country. Since national CPIs are used to convert each country's national poverty line from the base-year amount into equivalent amounts for other years, the Bank's change in IPL has raised Nigeria's national poverty lines uniformly for all years, and dramatically lowered Mauritania's national poverty lines uniformly for all years. Changes of this kind can potentially affect estimates of the trend as well as the level of poverty in each country.

Such large revisions in national poverty lines, up and down, cannot be reconciled with the claim of Chen and Ravallion (2001) that the new IPL maintains the "same" real level of purchasing power as the old. These adjustments

Table 3.1a. 1985 World Bank Poverty Line, updated by CPI versus 1993 WB Poverty Line at PPP (in national currency units)

Country	CPI Updated Old Poverty Line (1*PPP85*CPI)	New Poverty Line (1.08*PPP93)	Ratio: Updated Old PL/New PL	Country	CPI Updated Old Poverty Line (1*PPP85*CPI)	New Poverty Line (1.08*PPP93)	Ratio: Updated Old PL/New PL
Algeria	15.08	11.94	1.26	Kuwait	0.31	0.25	1.24
Australia	2.13	1.43	1.49	Lesotho	1.67	1.20	1.39
Austria	18.22	14.84	1.23	Luxembourg	48.13	39.71	1.21
Bahrain	0.29	0.28	1.01	Madagascar	665.13	567.64	1.17
Bangladesh	10.90	13.59	0.80	Malawi	2.75	1.63	1.69
Barbados	2.03	1.19	1.70	Malaysia	1.56	1.69	0.92
Belgium	48.76	39.40	1.24	Malta	0.25	0.26	0.98
Botswana	1.54	1.49	1.04	Mauritania	93.28	36.24	2.57
Burkina Faso	160.95	110.66	1.45	Mauritius	12.98	7.41	1.75
Burundi	120.05	60.27	1.99	Morocco	5.31	3.30	1.61
Cameroon	341.47	152.42	2.24	Mozambique	631.85	864.85	0.73
Canada	1.56	1.37	1.14	Nepal	10.10	9.89	1.02
CAR	198.10	116.14	1.71	Netherlands	2.77	2.20	1.26
Chad	156.82	94.94	1.65	New Zealand	2.45	1.61	1.52
Chile	257.70	222.71	1.16	Niger	175.61	107.70	1.63
China	1.59	1.52	1.05	Nigeria	8.68	12.33	0.70
Colombia	317.76	214.39	1.48	Norway	11.25	9.84	1.14
Congo	376.58	219.11	1.72	Pakistan	8.12	8.85	0.92
Costa Rica	84.02	57.85	1.45	Panama	0.74	0.48	1.55
Denmark	11.66	9.88	1.18	Paraguay	1018.92	801.80	1.27
Dominican Rep.	7.37	4.47	1.65	Philippines	13.94	6.68	2.09

Country				Country			
Ecuador	1107.22	890.63	1.24	Portugal	182.30	124.98	1.46
Egypt	2.38	1.25	1.91	Rwanda	106.04	58.69	1.81
El Salvador	9.52	4.78	1.99	Saudi Arabia	4.80	2.52	1.90
Ethiopia	1.14	1.39	0.82	Senegal	210.63	136.64	1.54
Fiji	0.95	0.90	1.06	Sierra Leone	281.97	250.47	1.13
Finland	8.52	6.93	1.23	Singapore	1.53	1.71	0.90
France	8.36	7.05	1.18	South Africa	2.13	1.79	1.19
Gabon	470.04	326.38	1.44	Spain	151.55	125.72	1.21
Gambia	6.24	2.62	2.38	Sri Lanka	12.47	13.75	0.91
Germany	2.83	2.17	1.30	Sudan	77.28	50.89	1.52
Ghana	292.17	191.51	1.53	Swaziland	1.66	1.29	1.28
Greece	257.75	194.31	1.33	Sweden	14.35	10.80	1.33
Guatemala	2.92	1.98	1.48	Switzerland	3.25	2.36	1.38
Haiti	5.60	2.60	2.15	Syria	9.95	11.48	0.87
Honduras	3.63	2.08	1.74	Tanzania	99.47	126.44	0.79
India	8.23	7.51	1.10	Thailand	10.96	14.40	0.76
Indonesia	651.49	680.38	0.96	Togo	189.00	95.93	1.97
Iran	257.73	275.01	0.94	Trini.-Tobago	3.66	3.50	1.05
Ireland	0.91	0.71	1.27	Tunisia	0.55	0.37	1.48
Italy	1983.72	1600.92	1.24	Turkey	8190.38	6351.30	1.29
Jamaica	14.39	12.64	1.14	UK	0.86	0.68	1.28
Japan	277.70	200.49	1.39	United States	1.34	1.08	1.24
Jordan	0.34	0.32	1.05	Venezuela	60.17	40.70	1.48
Kenya	23.70	12.60	1.88	Zambia	326.81	239.14	1.37
Korea, Rep.	736.56	743.48	0.99	Zimbabwe	3.24	2.45	1.32

Table 3.1b. Summary of data in Table 3.1a

Summary	
Number of Countries	92
Number of Countries With Ratio > 1	77
Number of Countries With Ratio < 1	15
Geometric Mean Ratio of Old PL to New PL (unweighted)	1.31
Percentage of Sample Population for Whom Ratio > 1 (1985 Population)	81.62%
Geometric Mean Ratio of Old PL to New PL (weighted by 1985 population)	1.12

Notes: For method, see text. Following the World Bank, we draw the PPP conversion factors for 1985 from Table 3 of Summers and Heston (1988). China's PPP for 1985 is drawn from the online Penn World Tables 5.7 as it is not available in Summers and Heston (1988). PPP conversion factors for 1993 are from the table "The World Bank 1993 Consumption PPP in 1993 Price," available from <http://siteresources.worldbank.org/INTPOVCALNET/Resources/PPP1993.xls> (accessed on July 4, 2009). We draw the country-specific CPI data from the 1998 WDI ("Consumer price index (1987 = 100)," series code: FP.CPI.TOTL). Data for a small number of countries were dropped due to wildly improbable differences between the 1993 poverty lines calculated according to the two methods. We confirmed through examination of Economist Intelligence Unit country reports that in each of these cases a hyperinflation or change of currency was experienced.

entail huge revisions in estimates of the poverty headcount for any given year, substantially increasing poverty estimates for some countries and dramatically lowering poverty estimates for others. In 1999, applying its method with the old ($1 per day PPP 1985) IPL, the Bank reported very similar poverty rates for Nigeria and Mauritania of 31.1 per cent and 31.4 per cent respectively. In 2000, applying its method with the new ($1.08 per day PPP 1993) IPL, the Bank reported poverty rates for Nigeria and Mauritania of 70.2 per cent and 3.8 per cent respectively. Depending on which PPP base year is used, Nigeria's poverty rate is either slightly lower or eighteen times higher than Mauritania's.

Chen and Ravallion (2001, p. 291) concede that the Bank's IPL revision has produced a substantial shift in the geographical distribution of poverty. This shift is illustrated in Table 3.2, which focuses on the three years (1987, 1990, 1993) for which the Bank has successively evaluated the same income and consumption data relative to two different IPLs. Table 3.2 shows that the IPL revision has greatly increased the reported incidence of poverty in Sub-Saharan Africa (raising the poverty headcount ratio reported for 1993, for instance, from 39.1 per cent to 49.7 per cent) and has greatly reduced the reported incidence of poverty in Latin America (lowering the poverty headcount ratio reported for 1993 from 23.5 per cent to 15.3 per cent). The Bank's revision of its IPL appears to have produced substantial changes in its poverty estimates, suggesting that the Bank's underlying methodology is unreliable.

The Bank's method is unreliable because its results are excessively dependent on the chosen PPP base year, which is entirely arbitrary. In order to see why, it is helpful to examine how the Bank compares the consumption expenditure of a person in one country and year with that of another person from another country and year. This comparison is made by the Bank in two steps. First, national CPIs are used to deflate or inflate the two national currency amounts into "equivalent" amounts of a common base year. Second, PPPs for this base year are then used to

Table 3.2. Changes in estimates of the prevalence and regional distribution of poverty due to methodological revision

	Headcount ratio for 1985 PPP PL (% of population living below $1.00 a day at 1985 PPP)			Headcount ratio for 1993 PPP PL (% of population living below $1.08 a day at 1993 PPP)			Percent change in headcount ratio from 1985 to 1993 PPP PLs		
	1987	1990	1993	1987	1990	1993	1987	1990	1993
East Asia	29.70	28.50	26.00	26.60	27.58	25.24	–10.44	–3.23	–2.92
Eastern Europe & Central Asia	0.60	–	3.60	0.24	1.56	3.95	–60.00	–	9.72
Latin America & Caribbean	22.0	23.00	23.50	15.33	16.80	15.31	–30.32	–26.96	–34.85
Middle East & North Africa	4.70	4.30	4.10	4.30	2.39	1.93	–8.51	–44.42	–52.93
South Asia	45.40	43.00	43.10	44.94	44.01	42.39	–1.01	2.35	–1.65
Sub-Saharan Africa	38.50	39.30	39.10	46.61	47.67	49.68	21.06	21.30	27.06
Total	30.70	–	29.40	28.31	28.95	28.15	–7.79	–	–4.25

Notes: The estimates relative to the $1 per day PPP 1985 IPL of the prevalence and distribution of global poverty in the years 1987, 1990, and 1993 are from Table 5 of Ravallion and Chen (1997; cf. WDR 1999/2000, p. 25). The corresponding estimates relative to the $1.08 per day PPP 1993 IPL are from Table 2 of Ravallion and Chen (2000; cf. WDR 2000/1, p. 23). The variations between these sets of estimates are also discussed in Chen and Ravallion (2001, pp. 290–3).

compare the resulting national currency amounts. The problem with this method is that the PPPs of different base years and the CPIs of different countries each weight prices of underlying commodities differently, as they reflect distinct global and national consumption patterns. As a result, international comparisons are highly dependent on the arbitrary choice of base year for the PPPs used to undertake the spatial component of these comparisons.

Poorly defined and inappropriate measures of purchasing power "equivalence"

At the heart of the money-metric approach to inter-country poverty comparison and aggregation is the translation of the IPL from the abstract money units (international dollars) in which it is defined into the local currencies actually used by persons in different countries. For this purpose, measures of purchasing power equivalence or *purchasing power parities* (PPPs) are used. These are defined in terms of a number of units of a country's currency that are deemed equivalent to a unit of the currency of a base country. PPPs for a given base year are typically interpreted as describing the number of units of a country's currency necessary to purchase the "same amount" of commodities as can be purchased for one unit of the base country's currency at the base country's prices.[9]

How can appropriate PPPs, suitable for deriving the amount of local currency that is "equivalent" in purchasing power to the IPL, be determined?[10] This question is difficult because price ratios between any two countries vary from commodity to commodity. The PPP importantly depends on the weights assigned, explicitly or implicitly, to the various commodities. Allowing such weights to be determined by actual consumption patterns does not avoid arbitrariness: consumption patterns vary from country to country due to diverse tastes, price vectors, and income distributions. And the fact that only a small fraction of a country's consumption expenditure is for medicines, for example, does not show that the price of medicines is of little importance for gauging the standard of living of its inhabitants.

Ultimately, the concept of an "equivalent" amount of currency is only substantively meaningful in relation to an *achievement* concept. One currency amount at a point in time and space can be deemed "equivalent" to another currency amount at another point in time and space if both quantities are just sufficient to achieve a common end.[11] Since amounts that are equivalent in relation to one end may not be equivalent in relation to another, the end must be carefully specified and justified so that it generates cost comparisons that are appropriate for the purpose at hand. Very different cost comparisons (and PPPs) may apply to comparisons of the cost to governments of achieving a given level of military capability, the costs to corporate executives of achieving an accustomed standard of living, or the costs to persons of avoiding extreme poverty.

One obvious way of specifying the end in relation to which a set of PPPs is defined is to fix a reference bundle of commodities. The least cost of purchasing this reference bundle in different countries in national currency units at the prevailing local prices establishes a set of PPPs.[12] A generalization of this approach specifies the end as some final achievement (for example, the attainment of a specified degree of subjective preference satisfaction—utility—or the possession of a specified set of human requirements however conceived) which is dependent on the ability to obtain commodities. In this case, the least cost (in national currency units at the prevailing local prices) of bringing about this final achievement in different countries establishes a set of PPPs. In order to conduct such an exercise, it is necessary to specify a transformation function which specifies the manner in which command over commodities is transformed into final achievements. This transformation function can be held to be common across countries or be informed by subjective preferences and relevant contextual features (such as environmental or cultural conditions). Since persons can vary in their ability to transform commodities into final attainments, more fine-grained index numbers (specific to persons within countries as well as to individual countries) can also in principle be constructed. It is unavoidable, however, to specify an invariant level of achievement (in some achievement space) to which the PPPs refer, if they are to be deemed to characterize "equivalent" levels of purchasing power.

It is obvious that there cannot be one set of PPPs that is appropriate for all purposes. Rogoff (1996) is one of many to note: "Ultimately, there is no 'right' PPP measure; the appropriate variation of PPP depends on the application." More fundamentally, the appropriate PPP is determined by the underlying achievement concept in relation to which equivalence is specified. If PPPs are to be meaningful and relevant to their purpose, distinct achievement concepts must be specified to ground cost of living adjustments for corporate executives, comparison of poverty lines across countries, and conversion factors used to determine the relative size of military expenditures. It is an empirical question whether the PPPs associated with distinct achievement concepts are sufficiently different in magnitude to make it necessary to adopt different PPPs for each purpose.

In practice, two methods of calculating PPPs have been most widely used. The World Bank currently uses the EKS (Elteto-Koves-Szulc) method in its calculations of poverty headcounts, while the Penn World Tables and earlier World Bank publications use the GK (Geary-Khamis) method (see for example Kurabayashi and Sakuma, 1990; and Ward, 1985). Both methods suffer from three problems.

The first problem with existing PPPs is that they do not in fact refer to any specified achievement concept. In practice, the dominant motivation for producing PPPs to date has been to undertake broad comparisons of the quantity of real national income and its components and of relative prices. These "broad gauge" PPPs have been used to compare living standards or to permit comparative assessments of poverty and income distribution despite the possibility that they may be inappropriate for these purposes. Considerations of whether PPP calculation methods permit consistent inter-country orderings (obeying such properties as base country invariance and "fixity" of rank orderings[13]) have been of greater interest than considerations of whether they permit a meaningful and appropriate basis for comparison of individuals' living standards and of the cost of achieving specific ends such as the avoidance of deprivation.

The second problem is that the measure of average prices constructed in existing PPPs is quite inappropriate for poverty assessment. This is because existing methods for calculating PPPs involve aggregating information on the quantities of a wide variety of commodities demanded in different countries and the (explicit or implicit) prices at which these commodities are exchanged. As such, PPPs from existing methods reflect quantities and prices that have no relevance to absolute poverty assessment. PPPs from existing methods are influenced by *irrelevant* information in the following ways, among others:

(i) Commodity Irrelevance: They are influenced by information about the prices and quantities of commodities consumed disproportionately by the non-poor, both within the same country and in other countries. In principle, the price of *some* such commodities could be relevant to determining the cost of avoiding absolute poverty. In particular, this will be true of commodities that are essential to maintaining an adequate level of well-being and unaffordable for many poor people. However, most commodities consumed disproportionately by the non-poor do not have this feature.

(ii) Country Irrelevance: PPPs that are meant to reflect how much currency in one country is required to purchase the "same" amount of goods and services as can be bought with one unit of the currency of a base country are influenced by information about prices and quantities of commodities consumed in *third* countries. There are reasons why this sensitivity to third country information could sometimes be appropriate in the multilateral comparison of aggregate levels of real national income (see Reddy and Plener, 2006). However, this sensitivity is quite inappropriate in the case of absolute poverty assessment. Sensitivity to third country information will imply that a poverty line in a country (calculated by converting an IPL expressed in a base country's currency using a PPP conversion factor) will fluctuate simply because of changes in prices in a third country, even though nothing has changed either in the country in which poverty is being measured or in the base country. Whether a household in India lives in absolute poverty by the $1 PPP per day standard cannot reasonably depend on information about Japanese real estate prices, but under the current methodology of poverty assessment it may. How serious the impact of such "country irrelevance" is in practice is difficult to judge.

Both country and commodity irrelevance are instances of the violation of a principle of independence of irrelevant alternatives: *poverty estimates for a country should not change simply because other countries' consumption patterns or price levels have changed, nor because the consumption pattern or price level of goods that are not needed to avoid poverty have changed.* A method of measurement that fails to satisfy this requirement is flawed.

The problem of dependence on irrelevant alternatives can be avoided by starting from an appropriate achievement concept and constructing PPPs which accurately reflect the relative costs of attaining this achievement in different countries.

The third problem with existing PPPs is that PPPs of different base years are not comparable. They are designed to provide spatial rather than spatio-temporal comparisons. The changing structure of the global and national economies over time gives rise to substantial changes in PPPs. Because of the lack of a clear and invariant achievement concept to which the PPPs refer, it is difficult to adjudicate among inter-country comparisons that invoke PPPs from different base years. Moreover, such adjudication is necessary since estimated trends in poverty levels can differ according to the base year used. Table 3.1 shows that poverty lines in individual countries are greatly influenced by the base year. Since different countries' poverty lines are influenced differently, this problem cannot be remedied by adjusting the levels of the IPLs associated with different PPP base years. For example, raising the level of the Bank's new IPL to $1.343 per day PPP 1993 would achieve a perfect fit with the old IPL ($1 per day PPP 1985) for the US, would improve the fit with the old IPL for Mauritania, and would worsen the fit for Nigeria.[14] Nor can the problem be avoided by using the PPPs of one base year in perpetuity, because the choice of this base year would still be arbitrary. It would still be true that very different results would have been obtained if a different PPP base year had been chosen instead.

National poverty headcounts and hence also the geographical distribution of poverty are greatly influenced by the choice of base year. As our tables, and indeed the Bank's own tables (comparing Table 4 of WDR 1999/2000 with Table 4 of WDR 2000/1), show these variations are intolerably large. This is a problem that is inherent to the money-metric approach and the use of existing PPPs (see Pogge and Reddy, 2006, for a full exposition and some dramatic examples). It is unknown at this point to what extent these variations can be reduced by combining the money-metric approach with more appropriate PPPs that better reflect the basic requirements and/or empirical consumption patterns of those deemed very poor.

A dilemma therefore arises when attempting to use existing PPPs to estimate the value of any aggregate (including the extent of severe poverty) over time. One option is to commit to some PPP base year once and for all, and then to use the resulting PPPs for the comparison and conversion of household consumption data generated in all subsequent years. This option has the advantage that it provides a stable basis of comparison. However, this option has an important drawback: the global consumption pattern will shift and is likely over time to diverge from the original pattern that once prevailed in the chosen PPP base year. It becomes increasingly difficult to justify the application of the previously fixed PPPs to the assessment of poverty in the most recent years; the PPPs used do not refer to the relative costs of purchasing goods and services in the most recent years.

The second option is the one the Bank has chosen. Here the previously chosen PPP base year is periodically replaced by a later one, thus avoiding the use of PPPs that reflect an outdated consumption pattern. However, this second option also has its drawbacks: each time a PPP base year is abandoned, all the previous estimates of the extent and trend of poverty calculated via these PPPs must be discarded too. This may undermine public understanding of and confidence in the exercise. The deeper drawback of the second option mirrors that of the first: while the substituted PPPs of the later base year are more appropriate for assessing present and recent poverty, they will be less appropriate for assessing poverty experiences long past. Thus, using 1993 PPPs rather than 1985 PPPs does not provide any obvious gain for assessing the 1980–2001 global poverty trend.

One might think that that this uncomfortable choice may be avoided by using PPPs from different base years in a single time–space comparison. This is not possible, however, because international dollars of different years cannot be meaningfully compared. Moreover, it can be shown that in the case of both EKS and GK PPPs, the use of different base years may lead to downward bias in estimates of changes in poverty headcounts over time (see Reddy and Pogge, 2005, pp. 15–23). In the case of EKS PPPs, the rising proportion of consumption (in both poor and rich countries) accounted for by commodities, such as services, that are relatively cheaper in poor than in rich countries, will lead to declining PPPs and therefore artificially declining poverty lines and poverty headcounts for poor countries over time. In the case of GK PPPs, it can be shown that any shift in consumption—in either rich or poor countries—from tradables to nontradables reduces the PPPs of poor countries and hence, again, their national poverty lines and poverty headcounts. Given that consumption expenditure tends to shift from tradables to nontradables over time, this implies that poverty headcounts based on GK PPPs in different years may show an illusory decline in poverty.

The problem of inter-temporal comparison would not arise if an explicit achievement concept were adopted, since in that case there would be no need to specify a base year to arrive at a set of index numbers. This procedure provides a consistent and robust basis for inter-temporal as well as inter-spatial comparisons.

False precision and mistaken inferences

In addition to errors resulting from the conceptual problems described above, the Bank's estimates of global poverty involve errors due to measurement problems associated with the data used. Some of these errors can be significantly diminished. Others cannot be, but can, at the least, be more explicitly identified. We describe below some of these issues.

Probable error

Despite obvious possibilities of error, the Bank's estimates of the total number of poor in specific countries, regions and the world are reported with six-digit "precision."[15] Kakwani (1993) noted, "No... tests [of the statistical significance of estimates] have been devised for poverty measures because of their complex nature." But since then, it has become possible to construct estimates of standard errors associated with sampling through various procedures (both through assessing the theoretical properties of survey designs and poverty measures and through concrete procedures such as "bootstrapping"). This can be a difficult exercise when sampling designs are complex. In addition, sampling error is only one source of the errors likely to be present in global poverty estimates. However, these are not reasons to avoid providing at least a gross indication of the possible errors involved and their sources. Suggestions of false precision can be avoided even in the absence of well-developed statistical tests.

Above we showed that large fluctuations in the level of headcount poverty in particular countries and regions were caused simply by the choice of PPP conversion factors associated with one base year rather than another. Further uncertainty emerges as a result of the fact that PPPs for a very large number of countries are based on judgments or fitted values rather than on actual observations of prices and quantities of goods consumed in that country. For example, sixty-three countries participated in the International Comparison Program Phase V Benchmark Study in 1985.[16] Relative price levels for the remaining countries were determined through regression estimates, which predicted real per capita income (and thereby PPPs) on the basis of exchange rate incomes, secondary school enrollment ratios, and "post adjustments," which are derived from data about the costs of living of expatriates living in capital cities collected by the International Civil Service Commission and by private sector consultants (Ahmad, 1992). There are, of course, errors associated with a procedure of this kind.

The errors associated with the PPP estimates for countries containing potentially large numbers of poor persons may have especially important implications. India participated in the 1985 ICP benchmark survey but not in the 1993 ICP benchmark survey or subsequent ones. China participated in neither. Thus,

PPPs for these two vast and heterogeneous countries with significant shares of world poverty have been largely based on "educated" guesses. The consumption PPP reported by the World Bank for India in 1993 is based on the updating of its assumed international price level in 1985 by domestic inflation, with some adjustment made for changes in post adjustments and other data. The consumption PPP reported by the World Bank for China is based primarily on an estimate of China's PPP in 1986 produced by academic authors (Ruoen and Kai, 1995) through a bilateral comparison of prices in China and the United States. China's PPP was thus derived in an entirely different way than were PPPs assigned to other countries, and is now quite dated. Since the State Statistical Bureau did not report national average prices for many items, the authors undertook price surveys in a mere ten cities with no coverage of rural areas.

PPPs proposed for China vary by a factor of more than two, reflected in per capita GDP estimates for 1990 spanning the range from $1,300 (IMF), $1,600 (Ruoen), and $1,950 (World Bank) to $2,695 (Penn World Tables).[17] Ruoen and Kai (1995) report that, even when they confine themselves to their favored methodology, reasonable estimates for China's PPP per capita income in 1991 still vary from $1,227 to $1,663. Reddy and Minoiu (2006) present alternative poverty estimates for China associated with the World Bank's IPL and distinct specifications of China's PPP and other parameters. They show that estimates of the extent of poverty in China in 1990 and subsequently are greatly influenced by these choices. Reddy and Minoiu (2006) show that estimates of the extent and trend of East Asian and world poverty are in turn greatly influenced by the assumptions used in assessing poverty in China. This extraordinarily important issue is never once mentioned in the Bank's presentation of its global poverty estimates. More recently, new estimates of PPPs for China have raised altogether new controversies (see, for instance, Keidel, 2007).

Countries that participate in ICP price surveys also differ greatly in the quality of the price observations they collect. There is reason to believe that price and quantity observations in specific regions (for example sub-Saharan Africa) are of poor quality. Quantity observations are typically inferred by dividing estimates of total expenditure on specific commodities (taken from the national income and product accounts) with price data from surveys. Uncertainties about the quality of the national income and product accounts therefore also infect the ultimate results. Missing observations are often replaced through regression methods (using the so-called country-product-dummy method) with associated uncertainties.

Finally, the Bank's global poverty assessments use data on individual consumption from household surveys. It is well known, however, that there are very large discrepancies between consumption reported in household surveys and consumption reported in the national income accounts. Which of these sources is more accurate? There is considerable reason to believe that household surveys are a much more accurate source of private consumption data.

Nevertheless, as noted by Karshenas (2002), "the discrepancy in average consumption between the household survey and national accounts data, apart from definitional discrepancies between the two concepts, is due to possible errors in both sources of data."

The poor may face different prices than the non-poor

The benchmark surveys of the International Comparison Program collect data on prices paid by consumers for specified items at specified points of sale in countries throughout the world. These are typically formal sector enterprises in urban centers.

An important issue is that the poor may face different prices than the non-poor for the goods they consume, because of where they buy (for example in semi-peripheral and rural areas with potentially less-competitive retail market structures), because of the quantities in which they buy (typically smaller than for the non-poor, because of cash-in-hand, credit, and storage limitations), or because of who they are (social marginalization, which may permit adverse retail market discrimination against the poor, or monopolistic price discrimination which may segment the retail market according to consumer income). There is some evidence that the poor pay more for the goods they purchase. For example, Biru (1999) finds that lower income groups pay more for the same commodities in Zambia, and that the differences in the prices paid by the different income groups are greatest in the poorest regions. Similar results are reported by Rao (2000) for rural South India. The use of PPPs based on prices observed to be paid by the non-poor may then be misleading insofar as the poor tend to pay different prices for these same commodities than their non-poor compatriots do.

Automatic poverty "reduction"?

Chen and Ravallion (2004) note that their global poverty estimates are based on data from only ninety-seven countries. Of these, twelve have only a single survey in the 1981–2001 period and twenty more have only two surveys (pp. 163–6). In the absence of up-to-date survey based data on the distribution of consumption, the procedure adopted by the Bank is to "estimate measures for each reference year by applying the growth rate in real private consumption per person from the national accounts to the survey mean—assuming in other words that the Lorenz curve for that country does not change" (Chen and Ravallion, 2001, p. 289). With the distribution of income assumed to be constant, estimated poverty rises and falls with average consumption. The procedure yields merely apparent poverty reductions in countries in which both real private consumption per capita and the inequality in its distribution have increased. This double increase case seems to be quite common in the 1990s.

How much of the vaunted reduction in global poverty is due to the assumption that national Lorenz curves have not changed since the last survey? This is difficult to tell without additional information. But it is quite possible that the 7 per cent reduction in global $1 per day poverty that the Bank has calculated for the 1987–2001 period (Chen and Ravallion, 2004, p. 153) is entirely due to that empirical assumption built into its measurement approach. According to Table A.1 in Chen and Ravallion (2004, pp. 163–6), for many of the countries involved, especially in Africa, the latest survey date lies quite a few years back.

Erroneous estimates: some empirical evidence

In this section, we offer some empirical evidence that the use of an inappropriate PPP concept has led to error (and specifically understatement, *ceteris paribus*) in estimates of the level of global poverty. First, we consider the lower IPL used by the World Bank and show that it makes an enormous difference which PPP concept is used to generate this IPL. We show that the Bank's reliance on general consumption PPPs leads to lower poverty lines (and therefore lower poverty headcounts) than would result from employing an appropriately narrower PPP concept in most countries.

Second, we estimate the increased headcount that would arise in specific countries as a result of employing less inappropriate PPPs. Third, we show that the supposedly close fit between the IPL and official domestic poverty lines for the poorest countries—used by the Bank to motivate the choice of its IPL—breaks down when less inappropriate PPPs are used. We conclude that the use of general consumption PPPs distorts global poverty assessments. Replacing these with PPPs that are related as closely and explicitly as possible to the consumption needs of the poor would constitute an improvement of the money-metric approach. However, we shall argue below that this is an inadequate solution and that a more comprehensive reform of methodology is required.

Inappropriate PPPs and the understatement of local "equivalents" (with an endogenous IPL)

The World Bank generates its IPL on the basis of PPPs for general consumption. But for a limited but still substantial range of countries, PPPs for narrower categories relevant to poverty assessment (in particular "all food" and "bread and cereals" sub-aggregates) are available. These PPPs are calculated from price and quantity data for various items collected in specific "benchmark" years by the International Comparison Program (ICP) under its "basic headings" (comprising internationally comparable product categories). The PPPs for "all foods" and for "bread and cereals"—henceforth "food-based" PPPs—derive from applying the EKS aggregation procedure to the price and quantity data for commodities at the even more detailed "basic heading" level belonging to these sub-aggregate classifications.

Food expenditure plays a significant role in the overall cost of avoiding absolute poverty. "Bread and cereals" PPPs are likely to be especially relevant for poverty assessment, as bread and cereals are likely to play an important role in meeting basic food needs. Other sub-categories making up the ICP "foods" category as a whole in 1985 were "meat," "fish," "milk, cheese and eggs," "oils and fats," "fruits, vegetables and potatoes," and "other food." Although these other categories of foods are also likely to play a role in a balanced diet, they may figure minimally in the most absolutist conception of basic requirements. Using ICP data, Regmi et al. (2001) report that the income elasticities of demand for staple foods (including cereals) are lower than those for non-staple foods in all countries. They also note that this phenomenon is especially marked for the poorest countries. The poor cannot substitute away from staple foods to anything else. Expenditures on these foods play an important role in the actual consumption of the poor, and are also likely to play an important role in the cost of avoiding poverty.

We now examine the effect of adopting food-based PPPs in the construction of an IPL and in its subsequent translation into national currency equivalents. We first followed the Bank's procedure of defining the IPL as the median of the ten lowest official domestic poverty lines (as ranked when the chosen PPP concept is used to convert from national currencies to international dollars), using all of the countries for which we have comprehensive data (i.e. both food-based PPPs and general consumption PPPs) from the same list of official domestic poverty lines (for thirty-three countries) used by the Bank. We call this method A. The IPL constructed by the method is endogenous in the sense that it varies according to the PPP concept used. We then converted the resulting IPL into national currencies, using the same PPP concept as was used in its construction. Table 3.3a lists the IPL and its national currency equivalents constructed in this fashion for each of three distinct PPP concepts ("all consumption," "all food", and "bread and cereals") for which data is available for 1993. In the final column we examine whether the resulting national poverty lines are higher when food-based PPPs are used than when general consumption PPPs are used for both construction and conversion of the IPL. As shown by the summary statistics in Table 3.3b, this is overwhelmingly the case in low income countries—and more so when "bread and cereals" PPPs, likely to be most closely related to the requirements of poverty avoidance, are used. For these poorest countries, the use of "bread and cereals" PPPs rather than general consumption PPPs for both the construction and conversion of the IPL raises "equivalent" national poverty lines by 36 per cent on average (by 26 per cent when weighted by population). Once again, these magnitudes are quite substantial, suggesting that the choice of an alternative PPP concept more reflective

Table 3.3a. 1993 food-based PLs versus general consumption based PL using "endogenous" food-based IPLs calculated by method A

Country	All food PL in national currency ($1.08* PPP food)	Bread and cereals PL in national currency ($1.10* PPP B&C)	All consumption PL in national currency ($1.22* PPP Consume)	Ratio: all food PL / all consumption PL	Ratio: bread and cereals PL / all consumption PL	Country	All food PL in national currency ($1.08* PPP food)	Bread and cereals PL in national currency ($1.10* PPP B&C)	All consumption PL in national currency ($1.22* PPP Consume)	Ratio: all food PL / all consumption PL	Ratio: bread and cereals PL / all consumption PL
Antigua & Barbuda	2.97	3.34	2.83	1.05	1.18	Malawi	1.81	2.21	1.84	0.98	1.20
Australia	1.25	1.74	1.62	0.77	1.07	Mali	139.47	218.23	151.00	0.92	1.45
Austria	17.10	17.95	16.76	1.02	1.07	Mauritius	6.79	6.04	8.37	0.81	0.72
Bahamas	1.26	1.43	1.40	0.90	1.03	Moldova	0.29	0.32	0.22	1.31	1.40
Bangladesh	23.69	25.88	15.36	1.54	1.69	Morocco	3.09	3.17	3.73	0.83	0.85
Belarus	26.08	28.99	17.43	1.50	1.66	Nepal	14.46	15.86	11.17	1.29	1.42
Belgium	42.13	43.71	44.51	0.95	0.98	Netherlands	2.28	2.17	2.48	0.92	0.87
Belize	1.27	1.24	1.42	0.90	0.88	New Zealand	1.66	1.86	1.82	0.91	1.02
Botswana	1.74	2.08	1.68	1.04	1.24	Nigeria	20.93	26.28	13.92	1.50	1.89
Bulgaria	11.73	13.71	9.17	1.28	1.49	Norway	13.05	13.98	11.11	1.17	1.26
Cameroon	149.54	186.78	172.18	0.87	1.08	Pakistan	11.51	11.31	10.00	1.15	1.13
Canada	1.49	1.59	1.55	0.96	1.02	Philippines	7.94	10.34	7.55	1.05	1.37
Congo, Rep.	284.43	287.10	247.51	1.15	1.16	Poland	9.10	9.33	10.07	0.90	0.93
Côte d'Ivoire	194.76	238.64	192.37	1.01	1.24	Portugal	176.39	159.03	141.18	1.25	1.13
Croatia	2.84	2.86	2.44	1.16	1.17	Romania	315.01	193.10	237.76	1.32	0.81
Czech Rep.	11.84	7.74	11.17	1.06	0.69	Russian Fed.	275.95	151.05	225.33	1.22	0.67
Denmark	12.03	13.15	11.16	1.08	1.18	Senegal	134.23	202.53	154.35	0.87	1.31

Country					
Dominica	2.64	3.24	2.35	1.12	1.38
Egypt	1.25	1.50	1.41	0.88	1.06
Fiji	1.01	1.26	1.02	1.00	1.24
Finland	9.49	11.90	7.83	1.21	1.52
France	8.11	8.32	7.97	1.02	1.04
Gabon	543.36	385.40	368.69	1.47	1.05
Germany	2.22	2.46	2.46	0.90	1.00
Greece	228.39	305.17	219.50	1.04	1.39
Grenada	2.41	2.45	2.01	1.20	1.22
Guinea	436.01	534.42	410.29	1.06	1.30
Hong Kong	6.61	7.55	8.74	0.76	0.86
Hungary	42.81	49.42	57.67	0.74	0.86
Iceland	123.85	124.10	103.20	1.20	1.20
Indonesia	715.77	691.24	768.58	0.93	0.90
Iran	326.78	395.18	310.66	1.05	1.27
Ireland	0.81	0.79	0.80	1.01	0.99
Italy	1897.65	1998.46	1808.45	1.05	1.11
Jamaica	16.96	15.77	14.28	1.19	1.10
Japan	295.19	337.21	226.48	1.30	1.49
Kenya	12.97	19.24	14.23	0.91	1.35
Korea, Rep.	1149.98	1600.21	839.85	1.37	1.91
Luxembourg	41.97	41.54	44.86	0.94	0.93
Sierra Leone	398.58	598.12	282.94	1.41	2.11
Singapore	1.29	1.53	1.93	0.67	0.79
Slovak Rep.	10.66	7.35	12.22	0.87	0.60
Slovenia	97.31	102.94	90.15	1.08	1.14
Spain	141.77	175.37	142.02	1.00	1.23
Sri Lanka	19.15	18.74	15.54	1.23	1.21
St. Kitts & Nevis	2.42	3.01	2.31	1.05	1.30
St. Lucia	2.50	3.46	2.24	1.11	1.55
St. Vincent & the Grenadines	2.41	2.52	1.83	1.32	1.38
Swaziland	1.23	1.61	1.46	0.84	1.10
Sweden	12.54	13.82	12.20	1.03	1.13
Switzerland	2.89	2.82	2.67	1.08	1.06
Thailand	17.25	14.13	16.27	1.06	0.87
Trinidad & Tobago	3.52	4.26	3.95	0.89	1.08
Tunisia	0.34	0.29	0.42	0.81	0.68
Turkey	8806.73	7932.93	7174.62	1.23	1.11
Ukraine	0.01	0.01	0.01	1.45	0.72
UK	0.66	0.61	0.76	0.86	0.80
US	1.08	1.10	1.22	0.89	0.90
Vietnam	2413.95	2464.23	1930.36	1.25	1.28
Zambia	341.31	551.61	270.14	1.26	2.04
Zimbabwe	2.25	2.95	2.76	0.82	1.07

Table 3.3b. Summary and analysis of Table 3.3a

	Full sample (all available countries)	No high income countries	No high or middle income countries	Low income countries only
Number of countries	78	54	41	15
Number of countries with ratio > 1 for food PL	47	36	26	9
Number of countries with ratio > 1 for bread & cereals PL	57	41	30	14
Number of countries with ratio < 1 for food PL	31	18	15	6
Number of countries with ratio < 1 for bread & cereals PL	21	13	11	1
Arithmetic mean ratio: food PL / all consumption PL (unweighted)	1.07	1.10	1.10	1.14
Geometric mean ratio: food PL / all consumption PL (unweighted)	1.05	1.09	1.09	1.12
Arithmetic mean ratio: bread & cereals PL / all consumption PL (unweighted)	1.16	1.20	1.19	1.41
Geometric mean ratio: bread & cereals PL / all consumption PL (unweighted)	1.12	1.16	1.14	1.36
Percentage of sample population for whom ratio of food PL / all consumption PL > 1 (1993 population)	59.07%	72.14%	71.20%	61.30%
Percentage of sample population for whom ratio of bread & cereals PL / all consumption PL > 1 (1993 population)	59.45%	61.41%	59.66%	75.62%
Arithmetic mean ratio: food PL / all consumption PL (weighted by 1993 population)	1.10	1.17	1.16	1.18
Geometric mean ratio: food PL / all consumption PL (weighted by 1993 population)	1.08	1.15	1.14	1.16
Arithmetic mean ratio: bread & cereals PL / all consumption PL (weighted by 1993 population)	1.13	1.18	1.15	1.31
Geometric mean ratio: bread & cereals PL / all consumption PL (weighted by 1993 population)	1.09	1.12	1.09	1.26

Notes: For method, see text. Country income level classifications are taken from the World Bank's *World Development Report*, 1994.

of the consumption requirements of avoiding poverty would greatly increase the estimated extent of severe income poverty worldwide.

A possible objection to this procedure is that by choosing the IPL as the median of the bottom ten poverty lines of that set of countries for which all three PPPs were available, we have introduced a systematic selection bias. In particular, our endogenous poverty line for all consumption of $1.22 per day differs from the $1.08 of the Bank due to the loss of eleven countries in the sample for which data on food-based PPPs was not available. To deal with this concern to the extent possible, we construct a second set of endogenous IPLs interpreting the Bank's methodology as involving choosing the median of the bottom 30.3 per cent of countries' domestic poverty lines when the chosen PPP concept is employed to convert these into international dollars. Here we use the median of the bottom seven out of twenty-two usable domestic poverty lines to mirror the Bank's use of the bottom ten out of thirty-three usable domestic poverty lines.[18] This second method (which we call method B) is also endogenous, as the IPL depends on the PPP concept employed. When general consumption PPPs are used, this method results in an IPL of $1.10 in 1993 international dollars (very close to the Bank's $1.08).

The IPLs constructed both through method A and method B along with the values of the official domestic poverty lines for which all three PPPs are available (converted into international dollars using the respective PPP concepts) are exhibited in Table 3.5. In Table 3.4 we report the national poverty lines "equivalent" to the endogenous IPL arising from the alternative PPP concepts (calculated through method B). Once again, it is evident that the use of food-based PPP concepts leads to higher national poverty lines than when general consumption PPPs are used both to calculate the IPL and its national currency equivalents. For the low income countries, the use of bread and cereals PPPs leads to national poverty lines that are on average 42 per cent higher (31 per cent when weighted by population). Once again, these magnitudes are quite substantial, suggesting that the choice of an alternative PPP concept less inappropriate for poverty assessment would increase the estimated extent of severe income poverty worldwide.

The distortion arising from the use of general-consumption PPPs instead of all food or bread and cereals PPPs is greater for the poorer countries, even when the IPL varies endogenously. This is shown in the summary statistics grouped by income class in Tables 3.3b and 3.4b and by the regressions in Tables 3.6a and 3.6b. The regressions show that whatever measure of disadvantage is used (per capita GDP measured at exchange rates or at PPP, infant mortality rate or under 5 mortality rate) the extent to which poverty lines based on food-based PPPs are higher than poverty lines based on general consumption PPPs increases as disadvantage increases. The results involving the PPP measure most closely related to the requirements of poverty avoidance (bread and cereals PPPs) show coefficients of the highest magnitude and at a very high level of

Table 3.4a. 1993 food-based PLs versus general consumption based PL using "endogenous" food-based IPLs calculated by method B

Country	All food PL in national currency ($0.92*PPP food)	Bread & cereals PL in national currency ($1.03* PPP B&C)	All consumption PL in national currency ($1.10*PPP Consume)	Ratio: all food PL / all consumption PL	Ratio: bread & cereals PL / all consumption PL	Country	All food PL in national currency ($0.92*PPP food)	Bread & cereals PL in national currency ($1.03* PPP B&C)	All consumption PL in national currency ($1.10*PPP Consume)	Ratio: all food PL / all consumption PL	Ratio: bread & cereals PL / all consumption PL
Antigua & Barbuda	2.53	3.13	2.56	0.99	1.22	Malawi	1.54	2.07	1.66	0.93	1.25
Australia	1.07	1.63	1.46	0.73	1.12	Mali	118.81	204.34	136.15	0.87	1.50
Austria	14.57	16.81	15.12	0.96	1.11	Mauritius	5.78	5.66	7.55	0.77	0.75
Bahamas	1.08	1.34	1.26	0.85	1.07	Moldova	0.25	0.30	0.20	1.24	1.46
Bangladesh	20.18	24.24	13.85	1.46	1.75	Morocco	2.63	2.97	3.36	0.78	0.88
Belarus	22.22	27.15	15.72	1.41	1.73	Nepal	12.32	14.85	10.07	1.22	1.48
Belgium	35.89	40.93	40.13	0.89	1.02	Netherlands	1.94	2.03	2.24	0.87	0.91
Belize	1.08	1.16	1.28	0.85	0.91	New Zealand	1.41	1.74	1.64	0.86	1.06
Botswana	1.48	1.95	1.51	0.98	1.29	Nigeria	17.83	24.60	12.55	1.42	1.96
Bulgaria	9.99	12.84	8.27	1.21	1.55	Norway	11.12	13.09	10.02	1.11	1.31
Cameroon	127.39	174.90	155.24	0.82	1.13	Pakistan	9.81	10.59	9.02	1.09	1.17
Canada	1.27	1.48	1.40	0.91	1.06	Philippines	6.77	9.68	6.80	0.99	1.42
Congo, Rep.	242.29	268.83	223.16	1.09	1.20	Poland	7.75	8.73	9.08	0.85	0.96
Côte d'Ivoire	165.91	223.45	173.45	0.96	1.29	Portugal	150.26	148.91	127.29	1.18	1.17
Croatia	2.42	2.68	2.20	1.10	1.21	Romania	268.34	180.81	214.38	1.25	0.84
Czech Rep.	10.09	7.24	10.07	1.00	0.72	Russian Fed.	235.06	141.44	203.17	1.16	0.70
Denmark	10.25	12.31	10.07	1.02	1.22	Senegal	114.35	189.65	139.17	0.82	1.36
Dominica	2.25	3.04	2.12	1.06	1.43	Sierra Leone	339.53	560.06	255.11	1.33	2.20
Egypt	1.06	1.40	1.27	0.84	1.11	Singapore	1.10	1.43	1.74	0.63	0.82
Fiji	0.86	1.18	0.92	0.94	1.29	Slovak Rep.	9.08	6.88	11.02	0.82	0.62

Country					
Finland	8.08	11.14	7.06	1.15	1.58
France	6.91	7.79	7.18	0.96	1.08
Gabon	462.86	360.88	332.42	1.39	1.09
Germany	1.89	2.31	2.21	0.85	1.04
Greece	194.56	285.75	197.91	0.98	1.44
Grenada	2.05	2.30	1.82	1.13	1.26
Guinea	371.42	500.41	369.93	1.00	1.35
Hong Kong	5.63	7.07	7.88	0.71	0.90
Hungary	36.47	46.27	52.00	0.70	0.89
Iceland	105.50	116.20	93.05	1.13	1.25
Indonesia	609.73	647.25	692.98	0.88	0.93
Iran	278.36	370.04	280.10	0.99	1.32
Ireland	0.69	0.74	0.72	0.96	1.03
Italy	1616.51	1871.28	1630.57	0.99	1.15
Jamaica	14.45	14.77	12.87	1.12	1.15
Japan	251.46	315.75	204.20	1.23	1.55
Kenya	11.05	18.02	12.83	0.86	1.40
Korea, Rep.	979.62	1498.38	757.24	1.29	1.98
Luxembourg	35.76	38.90	40.45	0.88	0.96
Slovenia	82.89	96.39	81.28	1.02	1.19
Spain	120.77	164.21	128.05	0.94	1.28
Sri Lanka	16.31	17.55	14.01	1.16	1.25
St. Kitts & Nevis	2.06	2.82	2.08	0.99	1.35
St. Lucia	2.13	3.24	2.02	1.05	1.61
St. Vincent & the Grenadines	2.05	2.36	1.65	1.24	1.43
Swaziland	1.04	1.51	1.32	0.79	1.14
Sweden	10.68	12.94	11.00	0.97	1.18
Switzerland	2.46	2.64	2.41	1.02	1.10
Thailand	14.69	13.23	14.67	1.00	0.90
Trinidad & Tobago	3.00	3.99	3.56	0.84	1.12
Tunisia	0.29	0.27	0.38	0.76	0.70
Turkey	7502.03	7428.11	6468.92	1.16	1.15
Ukraine	0.01	0.01	0.01	1.37	0.75
UK	0.56	0.57	0.69	0.82	0.83
US	0.92	1.03	1.10	0.84	0.94
Vietnam	2056.33	2307.42	1740.49	1.18	1.33
Zambia	290.74	516.50	243.57	1.19	2.12
Zimbabwe	1.92	2.76	2.49	0.77	1.11

Table 3.4b. Summary and analysis of Table 3.4a

	Full sample (all available countries)	No high income countries	No high or middle income countries	Low income countries only
Number of countries	78	54	41	15
Number of countries with ratio > 1 for food PL	35	29	23	9
Number of countries with ratio > 1 for bread & cereals PL	59	41	30	14
Number of countries with ratio < 1 for food PL	43	25	18	6
Number of countries with ratio < 1 for bread & cereals PL	19	13	11	1
Arithmetic mean ratio: food PL / all consumption PL (unweighted)	1.01	1.04	1.04	1.08
Geometric mean ratio: food PL / all consumption PL (unweighted)	0.99	1.03	1.03	1.06
Arithmetic mean ratio: bread & cereals PL / all consumption PL (unweighted)	1.21	1.25	1.24	1.46
Geometric mean ratio: bread & cereals PL / all consumption PL (unweighted)	1.17	1.20	1.19	1.42
Percentage of sample population for whom ratio of food PL / all consumption PL > 1 (1993 population)	46.54%	61.96%	61.19%	61.30%
Percentage of sample population for whom ratio of B&C PL / all consumption PL > 1 (1993 population)	60.05%	61.41%	59.66%	75.62%
Arithmetic mean ratio: food PL / all consumption PL (weighted by 1993 population)	1.04	1.10	1.10	1.12
Geometric mean ratio: food PL / all consumption PL (weighted by 1993 population)	1.02	1.08	1.08	1.09
Arithmetic mean ratio: bread & cereals PL / all consumption PL (weighted by 1993 population)	1.18	1.22	1.19	1.36
Geometric mean ratio: bread & cereals PL / all consumption PL (weighted by 1993 population)	1.13	1.16	1.14	1.31

Notes: For method, see text. Country income level classifications from the World Bank's *World Development Report*, 1994.

Table 3.5. Calculation of "endogenous" food-based IPLs for 1993 (following the World Bank procedure)

	Using PPPs for all consumption		Using PPPs for all food		Using PPPs for breads & cereals	
	Countries ordered lowest to highest by converted PL	Domestic PL converted to $/ day using 1993 PPPs for all consumption	Countries ordered lowest to highest by converted PL	Domestic PL converted to $/ day using 1993 PPPs for all consumption	Countries ordered lowest to highest by converted PL	Domestic PL converted to $/ day using 1993 PPPs for all consumption
1	Zambia	0.88	Zambia	0.62	Zambia	0.39
2	Indonesia	1.05	Bangladesh	0.68	Bangladesh	0.64
3	Thailand	1.10	Nepal	0.76	Nepal	0.70
4	Nepal	1.10	Thailand	0.92	Kenya	1.03
5	Bangladesh	1.19	Indonesia	1.00	Indonesia	1.06
6	Tunisia	1.26	Pakistan	1.15	Thailand	1.14
7	Pakistan	1.50	Sri Lanka	1.19	Pakistan	1.20
8	Kenya	1.55	Tunisia	1.38	Sri Lanka	1.24
9	Sri Lanka	1.65	Kenya	1.50	Egypt	1.45
10	Egypt	1.71	Turkey	1.51	Philippines	1.56
11	Morocco	1.78	Egypt	1.71	Tunisia	1.67
12	Turkey	2.10	Morocco	1.90	Turkey	1.71
13	Philippines	2.37	Philippines	1.99	Morocco	1.88
14	Jamaica	2.85	Jamaica	2.13	Jamaica	2.33
15	Poland	4.49	Japan	4.30	Japan	3.83
16	Japan	6.33	Poland	4.40	Poland	4.37
17	UK	7.34	Belgium	7.48	Belgium	7.34
18	Belgium	7.99	UK	7.52	UK	8.24
19	US	10.79	Canada	10.72	Canada	10.23
20	Germany	11.50	US	10.79	Germany	10.34
21	Canada	11.61	Germany	11.27	US	10.79
22	Australia	13.92	Australia	15.92	Australia	11.68

Method A: Median of bottom ten countries in sample

IPL using PPPs for all consumption	1.22
IPL using PPPs for all food	1.08
IPL using PPPs for bread & cereals	1.10

Method B: Median of bottom 30.3% of countries in sample

IPL using PPPs for all consumption	1.10
IPL using PPPs for all food	0.92
IPL using PPPs for bread & cereals	1.03

statistical significance. By using general consumption PPPs, the Bank grossly underestimates the costs in national currency of purchasing a quantity of food equivalent to that which can be purchased in the United States. If the Bank maintains its money-metric methodology of global poverty assessment but substitutes less inappropriate PPPs this can be expected to raise national poverty lines and associated poverty headcounts. We shall ultimately argue, however, that there is a still better alternative.

Table 3.6a. 1993 ratio of food, and bread and cereals PLs to consumption PL using "endogenous" food-based IPLs calculated by method A

	Dependent variable: ratio of 1993 food PL to 1993 all consumption PL				Dependent variable: ratio of 1993 bread & cereals PL to 1993 all consumption PL			
Log per capita GDP in constant 1995 US dollars at exchange rates	-0.032** (0.014) [-2.33]				-0.064*** (0.021) [-3.11]			
Log GDP in US dollars at PPP		-0.044** (0.020) [-2.15]				-0.116*** (0.029) [-3.95]		
Log infant mortality rate			0.026 (0.022) [1.20]				0.088*** (0.033) [2.70]	
Log under 5 mortality rate				0.025 (0.020) [1.24]				0.085*** (0.029) [2.93]
Number of observations	78	78	73	73	78	78	73	73
R-squared	0.07	0.06	0.02	0.02	0.11	0.17	0.09	0.11

Table 3.6b. 1993 ratio of food, and bread and cereals PLs to consumption PL using "endogenous" food-based IPLs calculated by method B

	Dependent variable: ratio of 1993 food PL to 1993 all consumption PL				Dependent variable: ratio of 1993 bread & cereals PL to 1993 all consumption PL			
Log per capita GDP in constant 1995 US dollars at exchange rates	−0.031** (0.013) [−2.36]				−0.067*** (0.021) [−3.10]			
Log GDP in US dollars at PPP		−0.042** (0.019) [−2.18]				−0.120*** (0.030) [−3.93]		
Log infant mortality rate			0.025 (0.021) [1.22]				0.091*** (0.034) [2.69]	
Log under 5 mortality rate				0.024 (0.019) [1.26]				0.088*** (0.030) [2.91]
Number of observations	78	78	73	73	78	78	73	73
R-squared	0.07	0.06	0.02	0.02	0.11	0.17	0.09	0.11

Notes: We obtain our data on per capita GDP at market exchange rates in constant 1995 US dollars and our data on per capita GDP converted at PPP from the Bank's 2000 World Development Indicators. Our data on infant mortality rates and under 5 mortality rates were provided by UNICEF.

The effect of PPP-influenced variation in national poverty lines on poverty headcounts

What is the effect of employing inappropriate PPPs on the apparent incidence of poverty? We answer this question for the set of poor countries for which we have both broad gauge general consumption PPPs and food-based PPPs as well as household survey based data about the size and distribution of income. For these countries, we estimate the headcount poverty associated with different PPP concepts using the POVCAL software program designed and distributed by the Bank. We report all cases for which the necessary data was available and for which the program generated theoretically consistent results.

We find that using food-based PPPs rather than general consumption PPPs both to construct and to convert an IPL into local currency units raises poverty headcount ratios substantially. For the set of countries for which we have a complete set of data, on average, as shown in Tables 3.7a and 3.7b, a 1 per cent increase in the poverty line due to the use of all-food PPPs rather than general consumption PPPs is associated with a 0.96 per cent increase (method A) and a 0.95 per cent increase (method B) in the poverty headcount ratio. Similarly, on average, as shown in the tables, a 1 per cent increase in the poverty line due to the use of bread and cereals PPPs rather than general consumption PPPs is associated with a 0.96 per cent increase (method A) and a 1.02 per cent increase (method B) in the poverty headcount ratio. Roughly, then, a 1 per cent increase in the poverty line is associated with a 1 per cent increase in the poverty headcount ratio. The effect of using all food rather than general consumption PPPs is to raise the average headcount ratio from 39.85 to 44.66 per cent (method A) and from 33.88 to 35.59 per cent (method B). The effect of using bread and cereals PPPs rather than general consumption PPPs is much more dramatic. It raises the average headcount ratio from 39.85 to 60.31 per cent (method A) and from 33.88 to 56.81 per cent (method B).

How "representative" are the World Bank's International Poverty Lines?

A justification offered by the authors of the Bank's poverty measurement methodology for the IPLs they employ is that the domestic poverty lines of several poor countries are close to its lower ($1 per day) IPL when the former are converted into international dollars using general consumption PPPs. Chen and Ravallion (2001) and Ravallion (1998) report regressions attempting to establish this and state, "The poverty rate on this basis must thus be deemed a conservative estimate, whereby aggregate poverty in the developing world is defined by perceptions of poverty found in the poorest countries" (Chen and Ravallion, 2001, p. 288). We show in Figure 3.1, which represents the relation between domestic poverty lines as converted to international dollars using various PPP concepts and consumption per capita, that this statement is not

Table 3.7a. Comparisons of PLs and estimated poverty headcounts, 1993: selected countries' PLs and headcounts using method A

Country	Year	Estimate of headcount ratio for consumption PL (PL = CPI*1.22*PPP Consumption)	Estimate of headcount ratio for all food PL (PL = CPI*1.08*PPP All Food)	Estimate of headcount ratio for bread & cereals PL (PL = CPI*i.10*PPP B&C)	Ratio of headcount for all food PL to headcount for consumption PL	Ratio of headcount for breads & cereals PL to headcount for consumption PL	Ratio of (HC for food PL / HC for consumption PL) to (Food PL / consumption PL)	Ratio of (HC for B&C PL / HC for consumption PL) to (B&C PL / consumption PL)
Bangladesh	1995–6	30.68	63.66	69.56	2.08	2.27	1.35	1.35
Côte d'Ivoire	1995	15.24	15.78	25.66	1.04	1.68	1.02	1.36
Kenya	1994	49.71	44.58	66.12	0.90	1.33	0.98	0.98
Mali	1994	63.39	59.85	77.65	0.94	1.22	1.02	0.85
Nepal	1995–6	33.25	51.29	57.69	1.54	1.73	1.19	1.22
Nigeria	1996–7	79.51	90.36	93.89	1.14	1.18	0.76	0.63
Senegal	1995	16.33	10.94	30.00	0.67	1.84	0.77	1.40
Sierra Leone	1989	60.09	68.53	79.23	1.14	1.32	0.81	0.62
Zambia	1996	66.38	75.99	89.47	1.14	1.35	0.91	0.66
Geometric mean		39.85	44.66	60.31	1.12	1.51	0.96	0.96

Table 3.7b. Comparisons of PLs and estimated poverty headcounts, 1993: selected countries' PLs and headcounts using method B

Country	Year	Estimate of headcount ratio for consumption PL (PL = CPI*1.22*PPP Consumption)	Estimate of headcount ratio for all food PL (PL = CPI*1.08*PPP All Food)	Estimate of headcount ratio for bread & cereals PL (PL = CPI*1.10*PPP B&C)	Ratio of headcount for all food PL to headcount for consumption PL	Ratio of headcount for breads & cereals PL to headcount for consumption PL	Ratio of (HC for food PL / HC for consumption PL) to (Food PL / consumption PL)	Ratio of (HC for B&C PL / HC for consumption PL) to (B&C PL / consumption PL)
Bangladesh	1995–6	23.44	51.72	65.23	2.21	2.78	1.51	1.59
Côte d'Ivoire	1995	11.12	9.55	22.25	0.86	2.00	0.90	1.55
Kenya	1994	44.01	36.09	62.67	0.82	1.42	0.95	1.01
Mali	1994	58.76	52.42	75.4	0.89	1.28	1.02	0.85
Nepal	1995–6	26.47	39.96	53.18	1.51	2.01	1.23	1.36
Nigeria	1996–7	75.8	86.91	93.02	1.15	1.23	0.81	0.63
Senegal	1995	12.21	6.3	26.6	0.52	2.18	0.63	1.60
Sierra Leone	1989	57.73	64.47	77.5	1.12	1.34	0.84	0.61
Zambia	1996	61.71	69.56	88.11	1.13	1.43	0.94	0.67
Geometric mean		33.88	35.59	56.81	1.05	1.68	0.95	1.02

Notes: We construct headcount estimates using the World Bank's Povcal Program (see <http://www.worldbank.org/html/prdph/lsms/tools/povcal/> [accessed on June 15, 2009]). Shaohua Chen of the World Bank has provided data on total national final household consumption expenditure in national currency units. We use population data from the World Bank's 2000 *World Development Indicators*.

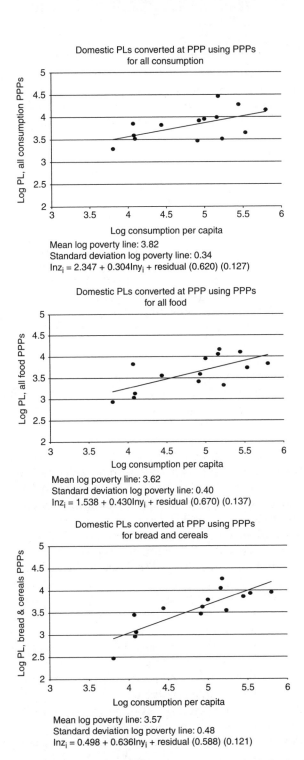

Figure 3.1 Domestic poverty lines converted into dollars using PPPs for food versus PPPs for general consumption, poorest fourteen countries.

necessarily robust to the choice of PPP concept. In that figure, we replicate their core result that there is a (visually) relatively "flat" cluster of poor countries whose official domestic poverty lines are close to one another if they are converted into international dollars using general consumption PPPs. (Our result is not numerically identical to the Chen and Ravallion 2001 result since we use data on consumption per capita from national income accounts rather than the household survey data they use, due to our lack of access to the latter for all countries.) It should be clarified that the purportedly "flat" relationship is not especially flat, since the poverty lines in question vary for the poorest fourteen countries between around 26 to around 87 international dollars (1993) per month.

When these same official domestic poverty lines are converted into international dollars using food-based PPPs, the relationship between consumption and the domestic poverty line is similar, with the highest poverty line for the poorest fourteen countries being around 67 international dollars and the lowest poverty line being around 18 international dollars (1993) per month. When bread and cereals PPPs rather than general consumption PPPs are used, a still steeper relationship between consumption and the domestic poverty line becomes evident, with the poverty lines for the poorest fourteen countries varying between around 12 and around 67 international dollars (1993) per month. The elasticity of domestic poverty lines with respect to per capita income *doubles* for the poorest countries composing the cluster when bread and cereals PPPs rather than all consumption PPPs are used.

It is not obvious that the IPL chosen by the Bank is innocuous because it matches closely the official domestic poverty lines of a wide range of poor countries. The validity of this claim appears to depend on the use of the very PPP concept that is being challenged, and indeed it is not obvious that it is true even when general consumption PPPs are employed: the domestic poverty lines employed by the Bank in its "inductive" procedure for constructing an IPL are fixed by officials of governmental and intergovernmental agencies (in many cases by authors of the Bank's own country documents). Influenced by political and other considerations, such domestic poverty lines may be a poor reflection of "perceptions of poverty found in the poorest countries" (Chen and Ravallion, 2001, p. 288). It has also already been noted that both the lower and the upper IPL are substantially lower than the cost of meeting basic human requirements in the base country (the United States) in relation to whose currency the IPL is defined, which should not be the case if PPPs used are appropriate and the IPL employed corresponds to the cost of attaining basic human requirements.

Comparison of domestic poverty lines in poor countries and the $1 and $2 per day IPLs is possible, by inferring the relative values of these poverty lines from the national headcount estimates associated with these different lines for the same survey years and countries. We have undertaken a detailed study of this kind, using headcount estimates from online databases and World

Development Reports in the 1990s. The conclusion that can be drawn is that for the majority of country years, the $1 per day PPP 1993 line is notably lower, and the $2 per day PPP 1993 line higher than the domestic poverty line. This conclusion suggests that, even to the extent that domestic poverty lines are accepted as indicating "perceptions of poverty" in poor countries, neither IPL really captures these perceptions, although the upper and lower IPL together may offer a better picture of poverty than does either independently.

It is interesting to note that for a large number of "spells" in which poverty estimates are available for the same country and two distinct years, the trends of poverty identified according to the Bank's higher or lower IPL are different in direction than those identified according to national poverty lines. This discrepancy is deeply concerning, and points to the poor state of poverty monitoring worldwide.

For countries in Latin America, the influential poverty estimation methodology of the Economic Commission for Latin America (ECLA), developed by Oscar Altimir in 1979, provides another comparator to the poverty estimates of the Bank. The ECLA methodology makes an attempt to set poverty lines that account for nutritional and non-nutritional requirements. Although there are some reasons to doubt the adequacy of this methodology (in particular its implicit assumption that all households have the structure of a nationally representative household) it seems likely that its poverty estimates are more appropriate for Latin America than those produced by the Bank. It is interesting to note that ECLA estimates of the poverty headcount ratio for its lower poverty line are substantially higher than those of the Bank for its lower ($1.08 per day PPP 1993) IPL.[19] ECLA estimates of the poverty headcount ratio for its higher poverty line are also substantially higher than those of the Bank for its higher ($2.15 per day PPP 1993) IPL. These discrepancies suggest the need for caution in accepting the claim that the IPL captures "perceptions of poverty" in poor countries.

Can the money-metric approach be saved?

In response to the criticisms of the Bank's approach offered by us in early versions of this paper as well as by other authors, a number of proposals have emerged as to how to save the "money-metric" approach to poverty assessment from the difficulties it faces. We discuss three of these proposals here.

The first proposal, initiated by the World Bank in the aftermath of initial circulations of the criticisms in this paper, is the so-called PPPP (or poverty-related PPP) project of the World Bank (in its capacity as host of the International Comparison Program). The proposal is to maintain the Bank's present approach but to introduce new "poverty-related" PPPs focused more directly on the commodities likely to be required to avoid poverty.

In our view, although this proposal constitutes an improvement over the current approach, it is inadequate for a number of reasons. First, it does not address the difficulty of the meaninglessness of the present IPLs, but merely seeks to reduce problems associated with their translation into local currency units. Second, it is impossible to define poverty-related PPPs without having a clear conception of the commodities required to avoid poverty, which in turn requires an achievement-based poverty concept. However, if such a concept exists, then PPPs are not needed at all. Rather, as discussed further in the next section, poverty lines corresponding to this concept can be directly constructed in each country. Existing proposals for the construction of poverty-related PPPs propose that quantity and price data be collected for specific commodities, reflecting the pattern of consumption of lower quantiles of the income distribution in different countries. This proposal is highly unsatisfactory, since the same quantiles of the income distribution have very different real incomes in different countries. In addition, the empirical pattern of their actual consumption, reflecting adaptive preferences and endogenous adjustments to duress, offers an inadequate guide to the costs of poverty avoidance. Third, although PPPPs can diminish the problem of commodity irrelevance in the calculation of PPPs, they do nothing to address the problem of country irrelevance.

The second proposal, presented by Deaton (2000, 2003) recommends the following five step formula:

1. start from the $ PPP 1993 poverty lines in Chen and Ravallion (2001); 2. ask UNDP and World Bank country offices to check these lines; 3. modify the lines to correct serious errors revealed at the country level; 4. update the lines over time using domestic price indexes, without further reference to PPP exchange rates; 5. if step 4 is carried out on an annual basis, as is warranted by the importance of the counts, then major improvements to PPP exchange rates could be incorporated infrequently, no more than once a decade.

It is not clear what Deaton means by checking for "serious errors." Presumably, he has in mind that the poverty lines employed should not reflect a money-metric approach at all but rather reflect an achievement-based conception of some kind. If so, would it not be better to begin with such a conception? As it stands, it is unclear what Deaton's proposed approach achieves other than to arrive at a set of more acceptable poverty lines (one for each country) reflecting potentially very different levels of real income (since there is no requirement to coordinate the process of "checking" the poverty lines in relation to a common achievement-based conception) and misleadingly bearing the common label of "$1 per day" or "$2 per day." This proposal solves the underlying problems of the money-metric approach only by substituting a set of national poverty lines, which possess no common interpretation but bear a common flag, apparently for public relations purposes.

The third approach, recently presented by Kakwani and Son (2006), recommends, as best we understand it, the following six step procedure. First, a reference group deemed appropriate in one or more reference countries deemed appropriate (for example, the bottom quintile of the consumption distribution in Bangladesh) should be identified. For the average food consumption pattern of that reference group the average cost of calories (i.e. the number of calories in the average food consumption basket of the reference group divided by the cost of that basket) in international dollars should be identified. The PPPs used should preferably be ones based on relative international prices of commodities figuring significantly in the consumption pattern of those deemed poor. Call the resulting international dollar amount the international dollar reference cost of calories. Second, translate this international dollar reference cost of calories into local currency amounts in each country by employing PPPs. The resulting "equivalent" local currency value in each country may be called the local currency reference cost of calories. This amount may also be translated into the local currency value of a given survey year through the use of an appropriate and available CPI. Third, a per capita calorie norm should be identified. This calorie norm can if thought appropriate be permitted to vary with type of household (as defined by age and gender composition) and country.

Fourth, the per capita cost to each household of achieving this calorie norm, given the average cost of calories identified earlier in each country (i.e. this cost of calories times the per capita calorie norm) should be identified. This amount may be referred to as the food poverty line for each household.

Fifth, the cost of achieving the non-food requirement for each household in each country should be identified. This should be done as follows. Identify the households in each country whose value of per capita food consumption is the same as the food poverty line for the household. These are households whose local currency average cost of calories is the same as the local currency reference cost of calories. Interpret these households in all countries as consisting of individuals possessing the same level of subjective preference satisfaction. Identify the average per capita local currency value of the total consumption of these households in each country. Subtract the food poverty line from this average per capita local currency value. Identify the resulting remainder as the non-food poverty line for households of each type in each country, making further ad hoc adjustments as thought appropriate in order to capture non-food requirements in each country.

Sixth, identify a household as poor if its per capita consumption falls beneath the total poverty line defined by summing the food poverty line calculated in step four and the non-food poverty line calculated in step five.

There are at least three central problems with this approach. The first problem is that the choice of a reference group and an associated reference consumption basket involves circularity: it cannot be determined what the appropriate choice of reference group is without first resolving the problem that we are attempting to solve—the identification of the poor and the requirements of poverty avoidance. The second problem is that the approach relies on the existence of appropriate PPPs which may be used to determine the international dollar reference cost of calories and its local currency "equivalent." As such, it is subject to all of the problems of country and commodity irrelevance identified above. There is circularity here too: it cannot be known what the appropriate PPPs to employ are without having first identified an invariance concept (in relation to which "equivalent" purchasing power is to be understood) and no such concept is identified here. The third problem is that the interpretation attached to households possessing the same average cost of calories—that they possess a common level of subjective preference satisfaction—can neither be readily justified, nor serve as the basis for constructing a non-food poverty line. It cannot be readily justified because it relies on strong assumptions regarding the uniformity of the preferences of individuals and of the manner in which they transform commodities into final subjective preference satisfaction regardless of the diverse contexts in which they live. It also assumes that subjective preference satisfaction is what we are ultimately concerned with, and that such satisfaction can be inferred and treated as interpersonally comparable. The level of expenditure undertaken by households possessing the same average cost of calories may in fact be insufficient to achieve either the nutritional or the non-nutritional requirements of members of such households.

Conclusion and an alternative

Income poverty is, as we have noted, only one aspect of poverty, and other poverty estimates, based on under-nutrition, infant mortality, access to health services, and other indicators can continue to inform us even in the absence of usable figures concerning global income poverty. International development targets should appropriately continue to focus on these measures of deprivation in the world, which are not to the same extent subject to the concerns we have outlined above, while a new procedure for the global assessment of income poverty is developed and implemented.

A new procedure is urgently needed. There are strong reasons to doubt the validity and meaningfulness of the estimates of the level, distribution and trend of global income poverty provided by the Bank in recent years. These reasons for doubt revolve around the lack of a well-defined IPL that permits meaningful and reliable inter-temporal and inter-spatial comparisons, the use of an inappropriate measure of purchasing power equivalence, the reporting of falsely precise results, and inadequately justified inferences.

All of these flaws are likely to systematically distort estimates of the level and trend of global income poverty. There is some reason to think that the distortion is in the direction of understating the extent of income poverty. Whether this is so cannot be known with confidence in the absence of better founded estimates. Statements that global income poverty is decreasing have no evidential justification in light of the uncertainties associated with present and past estimates of its extent. The problems are avoidable, although their avoidance would require a fundamental change in the methodology of global poverty assessment. The "$1-per-day" poverty estimates regularly calculated and published by the World Bank cannot adequately serve the purposes they are intended to serve. In particular, the monitoring of world poverty, necessary to assess whether the Millennium Development Goals are being achieved, cannot reliably be undertaken at present.

Our rejection of the Bank's procedure does not support the skeptical conclusion that the attempt to provide a standard of income poverty comparable across time and space is doomed to fail. There exists a much better procedure which can be easily implemented. This alternative procedure would construct poverty lines in each country that possess a *common* achievement interpretation. Each poverty line would refer to the local cost of achieving a specific set of ends. These ends should be specified at the global level and can include elementary human requirements such as the ability to be adequately nourished. Each poverty line should reflect the cost of purchasing commodities containing relevant characteristics (for example, calorie content) that enable individuals to achieve the desired ends (such as specified elementary human requirements, however conceived).[20] Poverty lines defined in this way would have a common meaning across space and time, offering a consistent framework for identifying the poor. As a result, they would permit meaningful and consistent inter-country comparison and aggregation. The proposed procedure focuses not on whether the incomes of poor people are sufficient in relation to an abstract IPL but rather on whether they are sufficient to achieve a set of elementary requirements. In effect, it does away with the need for an IPL, by focusing instead on a common poverty concept to be applied in all countries. As such, the proposed procedure altogether eliminates the need for PPPs (which are central to the existing money-metric approach) and avoids the many problems associated with these.

To be sure, income poverty statistics based on the procedure we suggest cannot be objective and precise in the way of measurements of physical distance. There are differences of opinion about the relative significance of various elementary human requirements, about the relevance of interpersonal variations in such requirements, about the quantity and quality of commodities needed to achieve these basic requirements, and about the appropriate degree of deference to local circumstances. Such disagreements can often be narrowed through reasonable collective reflection and debate to a sufficient degree to create a framework for action. If that is not possible, multiple conceptions (concerning, for instance, the relevant elementary requirements and how they are to be empirically interpreted) can be retained. In the context of assessing severe poverty (rather than living standards more generally) such differences will in any case be relatively narrow.

Although approximations will necessarily be involved in an alternative exercise of global poverty measurement (as in any empirical estimation exercise), it will at least be possible to interpret the resulting errors in estimation in a transparent, consistent, and meaningful way. Until and unless the task of counting the global poor is better conducted, we will simply not know very much about the extent of income poverty and its evolution over time. Such ignorance also makes it challenging to determine whether and to what extent the current world order is benefiting or harming the global poor.

The heart of an alternative (and more credible) approach to measuring global poverty is to carry out on a world scale an equivalent of the poverty measurement exercises conducted regularly by national governments, in which poverty lines that possess an explicit achievement interpretation are developed. In many large federal countries in which there are significant internal variations in tastes and in prices, workable means for accommodating internal differences within a consistent aggregate poverty assessment exercise have been implemented. Today a similar approach is needed at the global level. It should begin with a transparent and consultative process of identifying at the global level a core conception of poverty defined in terms of an achievement interpretation. This achievement interpretation can focus on a set of elementary requirements (e.g. the ability to be adequately nourished) and the characteristics of commodities (e.g. nutritional content) necessary to achieve them. This core conception should be used to define poverty lines. These poverty lines can then be applied to available survey data so as to identify the poor. Such a procedure, and such a procedure alone, can produce consistent estimates of poverty that are comparable across space and time.[21] A national poverty commission, supported by international funds, should be empowered in each country to construct and update poverty lines over time, drawing on national and international expertise, undertaking periodic and meaningful public consultations, and presenting its reasoning and conclusions to public scrutiny. Such a commission should strive to maintain an invariant relation between the poverty lines established and the fixed achievement interpretation required to be given to these poverty lines worldwide.

Reddy, Visaria, and Asali (2008) show that inter-country comparisons of poverty based on the construction of poverty lines related to a common achievement concept is possible, even employing existing surveys that were not designed to support such comparison. They adopt a nutritional norm and construct poverty estimates for three countries in three continents (Nicaragua, Tanzania, and Vietnam). They show that both ordinal and cardinal comparisons of poverty can be influenced by whether the money-metric approach or a requirement-based approach of this admittedly limited type is used.

Improvement and coordination in survey protocols, so as to create an improved basis for such analysis, are also required. A new international effort to create common protocols for survey design and analysis, and for poverty line construction, is necessary. Such an effort is complementary to, and can substantially strengthen, national poverty assessment exercises. The UN's historic achievement in promoting a common statistical protocol in the form of the System of National Accounts—an achievement which could not have been dreamed of before the Second World War—testifies to the important role of international coordination in such a process. It is necessary today to launch the equivalent of this effort in the area of poverty estimation.

We are surprised that the Bank has been publishing regular income poverty statistics for twenty years now—which are reported with six-digit precision and widely used in academic research, policy analyses, and popular media all over the world—without even a hint of public recognition of the deep flaws in their construction. It is hard not to see this fact as indicative of the low priority that has hitherto been attached to the global problem of persistent severe poverty.

Notes

* An unabridged version of this paper is available at www.socialanalysis.org. We are grateful to Yonas Biru, Shaohua Chen, Branko Milanovic, Martin Ravallion, and other World Bank staff for their assistance with our queries and also thank for helpful suggestions Sudhir Anand, Christian Barry, Andre Burgstaller, Don Davis, David Ellerman, Greg Garratt, Julia Harrington, Richard Jolly, Stephan Klasen, Howard Nye, Benjamin Plener, D. S. Prasada Rao, Lisa C. Smith, S. Subramanian, Ling Tong, Robert Wade, Michael Ward, and many individual correspondents.

1. The New School for Social Research, Department of Economics.
2. Yale University, MacMillan Center and Department of Philosophy.
3. See Ahluwalia, Carter, and Chenery (1979).
4. Remarks to the G-20 Finance Ministers and Central Governors, Ottawa, November 17, 2001. Wolfensohn relied on how the number of persons living below $1 per day was said to have evolved in World Bank (2001, p. 8). Not long after his speech, the World Bank revised this estimate, affirming that the number of those living below $1 per day had declined by "almost 400 million" between 1981 and 2001 (Chen and Ravallion, 2004, p. 141).
5. See WDR 1999/2000, p. 25. This is the very period for which the Bank later showed the steepest decline in the global poverty headcount (World Bank, 2001, p. 8).
6. In two recent papers, Sala-i-Martín (2002, 2006) has produced a set of estimates of global income poverty. His methodology, however, involves applying the World Bank's $1 (and $2) a day poverty lines to a world income distribution profile generated using country GDP data converted at PPPs, and is therefore subject to all of the objections we make to the World Bank's estimates of global poverty, as well as to others that we do not state here. The alternative estimates provided in Bhalla (2002) and in Deaton and Dupriez (2009) are subject to similar concerns.
7. <http://iresearch.worldbank.org/PovcalNet/jsp/index.jsp> accessed on June 15, 2009.
8. "A ... representative, absolute poverty line for low income countries is $31, which (to the nearest dollar) is shared by six of the countries in our sample, namely Indonesia, Bangladesh, Nepal, Kenya, Tanzania, and Morocco, and two other countries are close to this figure (Philippines and Pakistan)" (Ravallion, Datt, and van de Walle, 1991).
9. The following statement is illustrative: "PPPs measure the relative purchasing power of different currencies over equivalent goods and services. They are international

price indexes that allow comparisons of the real value of consumption expenditures between countries in the same way that consumer price indexes allow comparisons of real values over time within countries...The resulting PPP indexes measure the purchasing power of national currencies in 'international dollars' that have the same purchasing power over GDP as the US dollar has in the United States" (Notes to Table 4.10, World Bank World Development Indicators 1998).

10. Two short, thoughtful research notes by Michael Lipton (1996) and Shahin Yaqub (1996) contain a few of the insights we have developed further here regarding the importance of PPPs in global poverty assessment. The issue is also noted although not fully explored by Deaton (2000).

11. For a fuller discussion of the conceptual relation between index numbers expressing money "equivalence" and concepts of achievement invariance, see Reddy and Plener, 2006.

12. An example is the *Economist*'s "Big Mac" PPP index, which assesses the purchasing power of all national currencies in relation to a single commodity by valuing each currency in inverse proportion to the retail price of a Big Mac.

13. This refers to the property that rank orderings of countries are maintained when the procedure for PPP estimation is applied only to a proper subset of the countries.

14. The underlying problem is that the vector of PPPs for 1993 is not a scalar multiple of the vector of PPPs for 1985.

15. Chen and Ravallion (2001, pp. 290). There is more modest five-digit precision in WDR 2000/1, p. 23, and Chen and Ravallion (2004).

16. We have not been able to find any public enumeration of the countries that participated in the 1993 benchmark survey.

17. These different estimates and their differences are discussed in Heston (undated).

18. The Bank used the median of the converted poverty lines of the following countries to construct its $1.08 1993 PPP poverty line: Bangladesh, China, India, Indonesia, Nepal, Pakistan, Tanzania, Thailand, Tunisia, and Zambia. We lack data on PPP conversions for food and bread and cereals for 1993 for China, India, and Tanzania.

19. See, for example, Appendix E in Reddy and Minoiu (2006).

20. We do not believe that it is necessary finally to resolve here the issue of whether these needs should be conceptualized in terms of elementary capabilities or in some other manner. An adequately operational approach to global poverty assessment need not require final agreement on this issue.

21. See Reddy and Plener (2006).

Bibliography

Ahluwalia, M.S., Carter, N.G., and Chenery, H.B. (1979) 'Growth and Poverty in Developing Countries'. *Journal of Development Economics*, 6, pp. 299–341.

Ahmad, S. (1992) 'Regression Estimates of Per Capita GDP Based on Purchasing Power Parities'. World Bank Policy Research Working Paper 956, Washington DC.

—— (1994) 'Improving Inter-spatial and Inter-temporal Comparability of National Accounts'. *Journal of Development Economics*, 44, pp. 53–75.

Anand, S. and Kanbur, R. (1991) 'International Poverty Projections'. World Bank Policy, Research, and External Affairs Working Paper No. 617, Washington DC.

Bhagwati, J. (1983) 'Why Are Services Cheaper in the Poor Countries?' *Economic Journal*, 94, pp. 279–86.

Bhalla, Surjit S. (2002) *Imagine There is No Country*. Washington, DC: Institute for International Economics.

Biru, Y. (1999) 'The Purchasing Power of the Poor: A Case Study of Zambia'. In F. G. Pyatt and M. Ward (eds.) *Identifying the Poor*, Amsterdam: IOS Press.

Boskin, M. J. et al. (1998) 'Consumer Prices, the Consumer Price Index, and the Cost of Living'. *Journal of Economic Perspectives*, 12, pp. 3–26.

Chen, S. and Ravallion, M. (2001) 'How Did the World's Poorest Fare in the 1990s?' *Review of Income and Wealth*, 47(3), pp. 283–300.

—— —— (2004) 'How Have the World's Poorest Fared since the Early 1980s?' *World Bank Research Observer*, 19, pp. 141–69. <http://wbro.oupjournals.org/cgi/content/abstract/19/2/141> accessed on May 6, 2008.

—— —— and Datt, G. (1994) 'Is Poverty Increasing In the Developing World?' *Review of Income and Wealth*, 40(4), pp. 359–76.

Deaton, A. (2000) 'Counting the World's Poor: Problem and Possible Solutions'. Mimeo, Princeton University.

—— (2003) 'How to Monitor Poverty for the Millennium Development Goals'. Mimeo, Research Program in Development Studies, Princeton University.

—— and Dupriez, O. (2009) 'Global Poverty and Global Price Indexes', Working paper, Princeton University. http://www.princeton.edu/indeaton/downloads/Global_Poverty_and_Global_Price_Indexes.pdf>, accessed September 30, 2009.

Diewert, E. (1990) 'Axiomatic and Economic Approaches to International Comparisons'. In A. Heston and R. Lipsey (eds.) *International and Interarea Comparisons of Prices, Income and Output*, NBER, Chicago: University of Chicago Press.

Geary, R. C. (1958) 'A Note on the Comparison of Exchange Rates and Purchasing Power Between Countries'. *Journal of the Royal Statistical Society*, 121, pp. 97–9.

Heston, A. (undated) 'Treatment of China in PWT 6'. Mimeo.

—— (2000) 'PPP Comparisons in the ESCAP Region: What Have We Learned?' Mimeo.

—— and Lipsey, R. E. (1999) *International and Interarea Comparisons of Income, Output, and Prices*. Chicago: University of Chicago Press.

—— and Summers, R. (1995) 'Price Parities of Components of Gross Domestic Product in 35 Developing Countries: 1985'. Center for International Comparisons at the University of Pennsylvania (CICUP).

—— —— (1997) 'PPPs and Price Parities in Benchmark Studies and the Penn World Table: Uses'. CICUP.

—— —— Aten, B., and Nuxoll, D. A. (1995) 'New Kinds of Comparisons of the Prices of Tradables and Nontradables'. CICUP.

Hildebrand, F. B. (1992) *Methods of Applied Mathematics*. New York: Dover.

Jorgenson, D. and Slesnick, D. (1999) 'Indexing Government Programs for Changes in the Cost of Living'. *Journal of Business and Economic Statistics*, 17(2).

Kakwani, N. (1993) 'Statistical Inference in the Measurement of Poverty'. *Review of Economics and Statistics*, 75(4).

—— and Son, H. H. (2006) 'New Global Poverty Counts'. United Nations Development Programme, International Poverty Center (Brasilia, Brazil), Working Paper No. 29. <http://www.ipc-undp.org/pub/IPCWorkingPaper29.pdf>, accessed July 28, 2009.

Karshenas, M. (2002) 'Measurement and Nature of Absolute Poverty in Least Developed Countries'. Mimeo, School of Oriental and African Studies, University of London.

Keidel A. (2007) 'The Limits of a Smaller, Poorer China'. *Financial Times*, November 13.

Khamis, S. H. (1970) 'Properties and Conditions for the Existence of a New Type of Index Numbers'. *Sankhya*, 32(B).

—— (1972) 'A New System of Index Numbers for National and International Purposes'. *Journal of the Royal Statistical Society*, 135, pp. 96–121.

Kravis, I. B. (1986) 'The Three Faces of the International Comparison Program'. *World Bank Research Observer*, 1(1), pp. 3–26.

Kurabayashi, Y. and Sakuma, I. (1990) *Studies in International Comparisons of Real Product and Prices*. Tokyo: Kinokuniya Company Ltd.

Lipton, M. (1996) 'Emerging Asia, the Penn Tables, and Poverty Measurement'. Poverty Research Unit Newsletter No. 4, School of African and Asian Studies, University of Sussex.

—— (2001) 'The 2015 Poverty Targets: What Do 1990–98 Trends Tell Us?' Mimeo.

Milanovic, B. (2002) 'True World Income Distribution, 1988 and 1993: First Calculation Based on Household Surveys Alone'. *The Economic Journal*, 112, pp. 51–92.

Pogge, T. and Reddy, S. (2006) 'Unknown: Extent, Distribution and Trend of Global Income Poverty'. *Economic and Political Weekly*, 41(22), pp. 2241–7. <http://www.socialanalysis.org> accessed on May 6, 2008.

Rao, V. (2000) 'Price Heterogeneity and Real Inequality: A Case-Study of Prices and Poverty in Rural South India'. *Review of Income and Wealth*, 46(2).

Ravallion, M. (1998) 'Poverty Lines in Theory and Practice'. World Bank Living Standards Measurement Survey Working Paper No. 133, Washington DC.

—— Datt, G., and van de Walle, D. (1991) 'Quantifying Absolute Poverty in the Developing World'. *Review of Income and Wealth*, 37, pp. 345–61.

—— et al. (1991) 'Quantifying the Magnitude and Severity of Absolute Poverty in the Developing World in the Mid-1980s'. World Bank Policy Research Working Paper No. 587, Washington DC.

—— and Chen, S. (1997) 'What Can New Survey Data Tell Us About Recent Changes in Distribution and Poverty?' *The World Bank Economic Review*, 11(2), pp. 357–82.

—— —— and Sangraula, P. (2008) 'Dollar a Day Revisited'. World Bank Policy Research Working Paper No. 4620, Washington DC.

Reddy, S. and Plener, B. (2006) 'The Choice of Index Number: Part I'. Institute for Social and Economic Research and Policy, Columbia University. <http://www.iserp.columbia.edu/research-initiatives/working-paper-series/choice-index-number-part-i-valuation-and-evaluation> accessed on July 28, 2009.

—— and Minoiu, C. (2006), 'Has World Poverty *Really* Fallen?' *Review of Income and Wealth*, 53(3), pp. 484–502.

—— —— (2008) 'Chinese Poverty: Assessing the Impact of Alternative Assumptions'. *Review of Income and Wealth*, 54(4), pp. 572–96.

—— and Pogge, T. (2005) 'How *Not* to Count the Poor,' Version 6.2. <http://www.socialanalysis.org> accessed, July 28, 2009.

—— Visaria, S., and Asali, M. (2008) 'Inter-country Comparisons of Poverty Based on a Capability Approach'. In K. Basu and R. Kanbur (eds.) *Arguments for A Better World: Essays in Honor of Amartya Sen*, Oxford: Oxford University Press.

Regmi, A., et al. (eds.) (2001) 'Cross-Country Analysis of Food Consumption Patterns'. In *Changing Structure of Global Food Consumption and Trade*. Washington DC: Economic Research Service/USDA.

Rogoff, K. (1996) 'The Purchasing Power Parity Puzzle'. *Journal of Economic Literature*, 34, pp. 647–68.

Ruoen, R. and Kai, C. (1994) 'An Expenditure-Based Bilateral Comparison of Gross Domestic Product between China and the United States'. *Review of Income and Wealth*, 40, pp. 377–94.

—— —— (1995) 'China's GDP in U.S. Dollars Based on Purchasing Power Parity'. World Bank Policy Research Working Paper 1415, Washington DC.

Ryten, J. (1998) 'The Evaluation of the International Comparison Program (ICP)'. *International Monetary Fund*. <http://siteresources.worldbank.org/ICPINT/Resources/UNSC30_ICP1_1999.pdf> accessed on July 28, 2009.

Sala-i-Martín, Xavier (2002a) 'The Disturbing "Rise" of Global Income Inequality'. NBER Working Paper No. w8904. <http://www.nber.org/papers/w8904>.

—— (2006) 'The World Distribution of Income: Falling Poverty and...Convergence, Period'. *Quarterly Journal of Economics*, 121, pp. 351–97.

Schiller, B. (2001) *The Economics of Poverty and Discrimination*. Upper Saddle River, NJ: Pearson.

Sen, A. (1984) 'Poor, Relatively Speaking.' In *Resources, Values and Development*, Cambridge, Mass.: Harvard University Press.

Summers, R. and Heston, A. (1988) 'A New Set of International Comparisons of Real Product and Price Levels Estimates for 130 Countries, 1950–1985'. *Review of Income and Wealth*, 34, pp. 1–25.

—— —— (1991) 'The Penn World Table (Mark 5): An Expanded Set of International Comparisons, 1950–1988'. *Quarterly Journal of Economics*, pp. 327–68.

—— —— (1995) 'Standard of Living: SL an Alternative Measure of Nations'. *Current Material Well-Being*, CICUP, 95(5).

United Nations (1992) 'Handbook of the International Comparison Programme'. New York. <http://www. unstats.un.org/unsd/methods/icp/ipco.htm> accessed on July 28, 2009.

United Nations, Department of Economic and Social Information and Policy Analysis (1994) 'World Comparison of Real Gross Domestic Product and Purchasing Power, 1985'. New York. <http://pwt.econ.upenn.edu/papers/World_Comparison_phaseV.pdf> accessed on July 28, 2009.

Vachris, M. A. and Thomas, J. (1999) 'International Price Comparisons Based on Purchasing Power Parity'. *Monthly Labor Review*, 122, pp. 3–12.

Ward, M. (1985) *Purchasing Power Parities and Real Expenditures in the OECD*. Paris: OECD.

World Bank (1990) *World Development Report 1990*. Washington DC: World Bank Press.

—— (1993) *Purchasing Power of Currencies: Comparing National Incomes Using ICP Data*. Washington DC: World Bank.

—— (2000) *World Development Report 1999/2000*. New York: Oxford University Press. <http://www.worldbank.org/wdr/2000/fullreport.html> accessed on May 6, 2008.

—— (2001) *World Development Report 2000/2001*. New York: Oxford University Press. <http://www.worldbank.org/poverty/wdrpoverty/report/index.htm> accessed on May 6, 2008.

—— (2002) *Globalization, Growth, and Poverty*. New York: Oxford University Press. <http://econ.worldbank.org/prr/globalization/text-2857/>.

Yaqub, S. (1996) 'Internationally Comparable Estimates of Poverty'. Poverty Research Unit Newsletter No. 4, School of African and Asian Studies, University of Sussex.

3a

A Reply to Reddy and Pogge

Martin Ravallion[1]

A lay reader of the Reddy and Pogge chapter in this volume might be forgiven for suspecting that the World Bank's data producers and researchers are real scoundrels. Reddy and Pogge (2002, 2008[2]) assert that there are *"deep flaws"* in the Bank's methods of measuring global poverty, and that the Bank has probably understated the extent of poverty in the world and overstated global poverty reduction.[3] Furthermore, they contend that it is no accident that these flaws have gone unchecked for nearly twenty years; this reflects (they claim) the *"low priority that has hitherto been attached to the global problem of persistent severe poverty."* Given that eliminating global poverty is the Bank's self-declared goal, surely only scoundrels could have imparted deep flaws into the institution's measures of progress in attaining that goal? (Yet others claim that we have systematically overstated the extent of poverty in the world to keep ourselves employed fighting poverty.[4] It seems that measuring global poverty is a treacherous business for us scoundrels!)

However, as this chapter argues, the Reddy and Pogge (RP) critique collapses under even moderate scrutiny. They do not provide anything approaching a sound basis for believing that there are "deep flaws" in the Bank's estimates of the extent of global poverty.

The World Bank's poverty measures

Some years ago a consensus emerged in the international development community on the idea of an international poverty line of around $1 a day. This became the basis of the first of the UN's Millennium Development Goals (MDG1), which calls for a halving of the 1990 "$1-a-day" poverty rate by 2015.[5] Reddy and Pogge (2008, p. 2) declare that "$1 a day" is a *"meaningless poverty line,"* which presumably implies that MDG1 is a meaningless goal in their view. RP call for a new approach to measuring global poverty. However, before following their advice, one should take a closer look at how exactly the "$1-a-day" line arose. This should convince anyone that the line has more meaning than RP are willing to acknowledge.

Conceptually, one can think of any poverty line as the monetary cost of a reference level of "welfare" deemed necessary to not be considered poor. As in any true cost of living index (or money-metric utility function), the reference is a matter of choice. When measuring poverty, prior information on the nutritional requirements for good health and normal activity levels is often used to guide that choice.[6] However, it must be acknowledged that there is ample scope for different people to form different judgments on the key parameters in setting a poverty line, including the composition of the food bundle and the allowance made for non-food needs.

The (unsurprising) reality is that people at different levels of living tend to hold different views about what the reference level of economic welfare should be for defining "poverty." The critical level of spending that a poor person would deem to be adequate in order to escape poverty is undoubtedly lower than the level that a rich person would deem adequate. (This has long been recognized in the literature on poverty measurement.)

The same point holds between countries, as well as within a given country. In a background paper produced for the 1990 *World Development Report* (WDR, World Bank, 1990), Ravallion et al. (1991) studied how national poverty lines varied with the mean consumption of a country, when both were converted to a common currency at purchasing power parity (PPP, meaning that the currency conversion rate is intended to assure a common purchasing power over commodities). Among poor countries, they have found that poverty lines tend to be low, and there is also only a modest income gradient across countries in their poverty lines—absolute consumption needs naturally dominate in a poor country. Nutritional requirements for good health and normal activity levels tend to be fairly similar between people in poor countries and rich countries. However, as living standards rise people tend to buy more expensive calories (more meat and higher quality, or more highly processed, food grains) and tend to have more varied diets. And prevailing notions change concerning what non-food needs should be met if one is to not be deemed "poor." Poverty is a socially specific concept. Thus, above a critical level of mean consumption, the national poverty line tends to rise sharply with mean consumption (Ravallion et al., 1991).

This issue has recently been revisited by Ravallion et al. (2008), who have compiled an entirely new database of national poverty lines across seventy-five developing countries. (In Chapter 13 of this volume, Chen and Ravallion summarize the results from this new compilation of national poverty lines.) Their results indicate that the pattern found in the original Ravallion et al. (1991) is quite robust: national poverty lines rise with mean consumption, though with a low elasticity at low consumption. Both the food and non-food components of the national poverty lines rise with mean consumption. As one would expect, the "income" elasticity tends to be higher for the non-food component of the national poverty line, there is still a significantly positive elasticity for the food component (Ravallion et al., 2008).

In this light, the key question is: *By whose definition of "poverty" should we judge its extent in the world as a whole?* One might use the poverty lines that prevail in each country. But then one would not be treating people with the same level of welfare, as measured by real consumption, the same way. By treating absolutely poor people similarly to relatively poor people one would risk diverting the focus away from what is surely the highest priority: to raise the living standards of the poorest in the world. The resulting measures would lose meaning as measures of absolute poverty. Relative poverty lines can still be defended if one believes that relative deprivation matters to a person's welfare.[7] For comparison purposes, the Bank has also produced poverty measures that take this approach (Chen and Ravallion, 2001, 2004). However, in the bulk of its efforts at global poverty monitoring, the Bank has taken the position that to measure absolute poverty on a consistent basis across countries one should use a poverty line with the same real value.

The "$1-a-day" line aims to judge poverty in the world as a whole by the standards of what poverty means in poor countries. The latest available estimates indicate that about 1 billion people live below this line, representing about one-fifth of the population of the developing world (Chen and Ravallion, 2007). This is an explicitly conservative definition; one could hardly argue that the people in the world who are poor by the standards typical of poor countries are not in fact poor. The point is that one cannot reasonably argue that there is less poverty in the world as a whole than is indicated by this calculation. Chen and Ravallion (2001) also argue that the "$1-a-day" line is a defensible lower bound to relative poverty lines.

We do not claim that the "$1-a-day" line is the only line that one would want to use for international comparisons. Indeed, in Chen et al. (1994) we provided estimates spanning a fairly wide range. We regularly publish estimates for a line set at twice the level found in the poorest countries. The "$2-a-day" poverty count is published alongside the "$1-a-day" count in the Bank's *World Development Indicators* for all years in which the numbers have been published. (Pritchett, 2006, has proposed an "upper bound" poverty line of around $10 a day; about 95 per cent of the developing world's population live below this line.)

As one would expect, there are measurement errors and idiosyncratic differences between countries in how poverty lines are constructed, which can be interpreted as noise in the mapping from the underlying welfare space into the income space. So it would not make sense to pick the lowest poverty line in the world; in fact that is well below $1 a day. Some averaging is called for, as is normally the case in economic measurement. The 1990 WDR $1 a day line had been picked by eyeballing the scatter of points in the relationship between national poverty lines and national mean consumption. Since then we have taken an average of the lines for the poorest countries, and provided tests of sensitivity to alternative methods of forming that average.

Having set an international poverty line, we then convert it back to local currency using the same PPPs. The best available consumer price indices (CPIs) are then used to convert the international line in local currency to prices prevailing at the time of the surveys. Next, these poverty lines are applied to distributions of consumption per person (or income if consumption is not available) constructed from nationally representative household surveys—we currently use well over 500 surveys for over 100 countries. Adjustments to the data are often required for consistency, such as assuring that population weights are used to obtain an unbiased estimate of the individual distribution of household consumption per person. Calculations are done from the primary data (either micro data or appropriate tabulations). The latest estimates are found in Chen and Ravallion (2007).[8]

As an aside, the vast bulk of the Bank's analytic and operational work on poverty does not use the "$1-a-day" line, and with good reason. When one works on poverty in a given country, or region, one naturally tries to use a definition of poverty considered appropriate to that setting. Most of the time, the Bank's poverty analysts do not need to know what the local poverty line is worth in international currency at purchasing power parity. In its annual tabulation of the "$1-a-day" poverty numbers, the Bank's *World Development Indicators* (for example, see World Bank, 2007) gives estimates based on national poverty lines side by side with the international lines, and has done so since these data were first published. Behind every one of these country numbers is a body of work as part of the Bank's country *Poverty Assessments* and (more recently for low income countries) the country's own *Poverty Reduction Strategy Paper.*

Purchasing power parity and poverty measurement

PPPs are derived from the country-level price surveys that have been done since 1968 by the International Comparison Program (ICP). Estimating global poverty is only one of many applications of these PPPs in economic research. (For example, they have also been widely used in the vast literature on measuring and explaining differences in real incomes across countries.)

Prior to 2000, the Penn World Tables (PWT) were our main source of the PPP rates derived from the ICP; see, for example, Summers and Heston (1991). In 2000 we switched to the 1993 PPPs estimated by the Bank's Development Data Group. New PPPs have recently become available for 2005, again based on

ICP price surveys (World Bank, 2008). There were numerous data improvements over time and various methodological differences between these sets of PPPs.[9]

RP clearly do not like any of these PPPs. Their main concern seems to be that PPPs (from either PWT or the Bank) do not correspond to the cost of a *well-defined basket of commodities*" which leads them to claim that "... existing PPPs are generally inappropriate for identifying the real incomes of poor households and hence the incidence of absolute poverty" (Reddy and Pogge, 2002, p. 10). They go on to argue in their 2002 paper that "... the only way to avoid this problem is to *start* from a particular reference basket of commodities and to construct PPPs that accurately reflect the relative costs of purchasing *this* basket in different countries." So they appear to be proposing to price a single bundle of goods in each country relative to a reference country.[10] The idea of basing PPPs on a fixed bundle of goods is problematic for well-known reasons. People consume very different things in different countries, reflecting in part the differences they face in relative prices. I would be surprised if any kind of consensus could be reached on what should be included in the single global bundle of goods, comparable to the consensus that has been established around the "$1-a-day" concept.

In fact, the deficiencies of the idea of using a single bundle of goods led to the types of price indices currently in use for constructing PPPs. Ideally the underlying price index would only reflect differences in the cost of a reference level of welfare, fixed across all countries. This means that the reference bundle of goods cannot be the same across countries, given that relative prices vary and hence that consumers can substitute among goods to achieve the same level of welfare—moving along their indifference curves. The PPPs underlying the Bank's global poverty measures are based on the Fisher index, which gives a true cost of living index (reflecting differences in relative prices consistently with consumer preferences) under certain assumptions.[11]

While it would certainly not be progress to follow RP's recommendations, it can be agreed that it would be better to have PPPs designed for poverty measurement, weighted to the consumption bundle of people near the poverty line, using an appropriate iterative estimation method.[12] This was argued by Ravallion et al. (1991) in the first paper estimating the "$1-a-day" global poverty measures, although there was little or no progress toward that goal until the latest round of the ICP. An effort is underway at the Bank to estimate "PPPs for the poor," by re-weighting the 2005 ICP prices to accord more closely with consumption patterns of poor people. Preliminary results reported in Deaton and Dupriez (2007) do not suggest that the re-weighting needed to derive a PPP for the poor will make an appreciable change to the aggregate consumption PPP. However, further work will be needed before we can be confident about the implications for global poverty measurement.

Does the Bank underestimate the extent of global poverty?

The fact that we judge the extent of consumption poverty in the world by the standards typical of low income countries clearly does not mean that we are underestimating the extent of world poverty. Obviously if you use a higher standard you will get a higher poverty count. The "$1-a-day" line does not claim to be anything other than a poverty line typical of poor countries. To say that we are underestimating poverty by this method is like saying that one underestimates length using a ruler calibrated in inches rather than centimeters. If one knows how the ruler is calibrated there should be no confusion.

RP question whether the national poverty lines are reliable as a basis for setting an international poverty line. There appear to be two concerns. First, they claim that the national poverty line may be *"influenced by political and other considerations"*. They appear to be implying that this would lead us to underestimate the extent of global poverty, although this is evidently little more than a casual conjecture on their part, and they give no reason to expect a bias. Our new data set of seventy-five national poverty lines was formed from the World Bank's *Poverty Assessments* and the governments' own *Poverty Reduction Strategy Papers*. In every case, these poverty lines are constructed by professional teams, often comprising staff of the governmental statistics office and economists and/or statisticians working for the Bank. There are (as already noted) idiosyncratic differences in how poverty lines are constructed, which is why we take an average of the poverty lines found among low income countries. Errors certainly cannot be ruled out, but there is no obvious reason to expect systematic bias one way or the other.

Second, RP (2008) claim another fault in our method, stemming from the fact that different low-income countries have different (national) poverty lines. They present results for a truncated sample of the domestic poverty lines for "the poorest fourteen countries," which appears to be the fourteen countries with lowest mean consumption at PPP in the original sample of thirty-three countries used by Ravallion et al. (1991). RP show that there is a variance in poverty lines found among these countries. However, this has never been an issue.[13] Again, some averaging is called for, as we have always argued. RP do not present anything that would lead one to question that the mean poverty line (conditional on consumption) rises with consumption. Note that if RP had not chosen to truncate the Ravallion et al. (1991) sample—and no reason is given for this odd truncation—their readers would no doubt have seen the same strong positive relationship between the poverty line and mean consumption reported in Ravallion et al. (2001), and in Ravallion et al. (2008), for the new sample of seventy-five national poverty lines.

While the aims of the Bank's global poverty measurement effort have not changed over time, there have been many improvements in the underlying data. There has been a huge increase in the country coverage of the Bank's global poverty aggregates; from one national survey for each of twenty-two countries in World Bank (1990) and Ravallion et al. (1991) to well over 500 surveys for 100 countries now. Indeed, the Bank has put substantial effort into expanding the database on household living standards.

The PPPs have changed too, with new and better price data. The 1993 PPPs were an improvement over those for 1985 in terms of country coverage, although there were concerns about data quality. However, the two sets of PPPs are not comparable, so there is no straightforward way to convert the old $1-a-day line at 1985 PPP to a new line with base 1993. Instead, the only defensible approach is to go back to the original poverty lines for the WDR 1990, and recalculate those lines with the new set of PPPs, and re-estimate the relationship between national poverty lines and mean consumption which led to the original $1-a-day lines used in the WDR 1990. The same basic approach has been proposed by Ravallion et al. (2008), based on the updated data set of national poverty lines referred to above, using the PPPs derived from the 2005 ICP price surveys. (Chapter 13 in this volume provides a summary.)

Why not just update the international poverty line for inflation in the US? This would be a valid method if the purchasing power parity principle held (whereby the PPP for a given country evolves over time according to differences in that country's rate of inflation and that for the US) *and* one deemed 1993 PPPs to be beyond question; indeed, under these conditions one would not have needed to do the 2005 ICP. However, neither condition holds. Ravallion et al. (2008) show that the joint implications of the purchasing power parity principle and comparability of the 1993 and 2005 ICP data can be convincingly rejected statistically.

Thus the naive approach of simply adjusting the old line upwards for inflation in the US ignores some key features of how PPPs have evolved over time, including problems of data comparability over time. For example, China's and Indonesia's poverty lines at 1985 PPP are almost identical to their poverty line at 1993 PPP; India's poverty line at 1993 PPP is only 17 per cent higher than its poverty line at 1985 PPP. Yet adjusting the 1985 $1-a-day line for US inflation would entail an upward increase of roughly 50 per cent. In other words, if we had simply adjusted the $1-a-day line for inflation in the US between 1985 and 1993 we would have obtained a poverty line that is well above the median of the ten lowest poverty lines at 1993 PPP, and so we could no longer claim to be using a poverty line that is typical of poor countries. That would certainly entail a re-calibration of the ruler. The same point applies to the switch from the 1993 to 2005 PPPs, as shown in Ravallion et al. (2008).

In the light of these observations, one should not accept the claim by RP, echoed by Wade (2004), that we have devalued the poverty line over time, and hence overestimated the extent of the world's progress against poverty.

We have long recognized these problems in switching PPP base years and data sources. The latest version of RP's critique is more cognizant of the problems than their earlier paper. However, they still do not properly acknowledge that our practice has always been to revise *all* of our estimates back in time (currently back to 1980) when new PPPs become available. The PPP currency conversion is only done at the base data; then the comparisons over time for a given country depend on the best available CPI for that country. The country-level CPIs are not always ideal, but they are the best data we have for making such comparisons over time.

The key point is that, in assessing progress against poverty in the world, we do not need to make comparisons across different (non-comparable) sets of PPPs. So the entire discussion of this issue in RP (2002, 2008) is irrelevant.

As an aside, it was noted in Chen and Ravallion (2001) that the $1.08 line using the 1993 PPP gave a very similar global poverty count to the old $1-a-day line at 1985 PPP for the common reference year in the series, namely 1993. RP assert that it was a *"serious error of reasoning"* on our part to have made this check for whether the poverty counts matched for the same year. This is surely overstated. It is natural to look at how new data and methods affect one's final estimate of (ostensibly) the same thing, and to draw some comfort from their similarity. RP are right that they could have come out at very different poverty counts; that is obvious enough since (as explained above), we did not choose the new poverty line to make the aggregate poverty count similar for any year.

"Methodological revisions," "erroneous estimates," and "false precision"?

As in virtually all aspects of socio-economic data, there is still scope for improving the data underlying the global poverty measures, namely the survey-based distributional data and the price data (both CPIs and PPPs). However, data are improving in the developing world, thanks to the efforts of international agencies such as the Bank, as well as the governmental statistical offices in developing countries. There is no doubt that both data sources have improved enormously in terms of coverage and quality in the time since our estimates of those poverty measures began, around 1990.

As data improve, it is not too surprising that our knowledge gets revised as well. In the light of better data, we have always revised our global poverty estimates accordingly, including back in time (as have other data sources, such as the national accounts).

These revisions to our past estimates provide fuel for many of RP's criticisms, though I expect most people would agree that to *not* revise knowledge in the light of new data would be far worse. In particular, RP criticize the Bank for "*methodological poverty revisions*" (RP, 2002, p. 7). They give a number of examples (Tables 2 and 3 of RP, 2002), drawing on the Bank's published estimates at different dates.

It can hardly be surprising that the numbers change as a result of new data, even for the same country and year. This can arise from changes in the underlying estimate of the PPP exchange rate, revisions to the CPIs at country level and changes in the processing of the underlying survey data (a more consistent consumption or income aggregate may have been formed, for example). For example, quite a few of the "*pure methodological revisions*" they cite (in RP, 2002, Table 2) between the poverty counts using 1985 PPP and 1993 PPP are for the Former Soviet Union (FSU). For 1985 there was only one PPP rate for the FSU, while with the new 1993 price data from the International Comparisons Project it was possible to estimate separate PPP rates for all countries within the FSU. So naturally we revised the estimates for all countries within the FSU. RP chastise us for making such changes. A knowledgeable external consumer of these numbers would surely be far more inclined to criticize us if we had not made these revisions. The fact that RP can see all these changes speaks for itself about our openness in making the necessary revisions in the light of new data.

RP also confuse "*methodological revisions*" with real effects when they also compare our estimates for the same country at different dates (see Table 3 of RP, 2002). They acknowledge the possibility that these changes are real, but assert that this "*seems unlikely*" (p. 7) though they provide no justification for this judgment. Against their interpretation, the substantial increase in the measured poverty rate in Indonesia (for example) between 1996 and 1999, which RP identify as a "methodological revision," is more plausibly attributable to the severe macroeconomic crisis Indonesia faced in 1998, compounded by a poor agricultural year (Ravallion and Lokshin, 2007). While it may "seem unlikely" to RP that such a crisis could have substantially increased poverty, it is very clear from the evidence that it did do so. There are other examples of the same confusion of real effects with revisions in the light of better data.

RP (2002) assert that our methods systematically overstate the rate of poverty reduction for yet another reason, namely the method we use to line surveys up in time. In the latest available estimates at the time of writing, Chen and Ravallion (2008) used almost 700 surveys spanning 115 countries. But these surveys do not (of course) line up neatly in time across different countries, so an interpolation method is needed to obtain an aggregate estimate for any given reference year in the aggregate time series of regional or global estimates. Again, our methods are well documented. The reference years chosen lie comfortably within the range of the data. If there is only one survey for a country, then we estimate measures for each reference year by applying the growth rate in real private consumption per person from the national accounts to the survey mean—assuming that the distribution does not change. However, for almost 100 countries we had two or more surveys. When the reference date is between two surveys, we interpolate from each survey to the reference date and take a weighted mean (Chen and Ravallion, 2001, 2004).

Let us now take a closer look at why RP think we have overestimated the rate of poverty reduction. Though it is not entirely clear from their papers, one reason is that they appear to think that inequality is increasing within countries, thus leading us to overestimate the rate of poverty reduction by the above method. Yet, as we have established in other work and re-established in the latest update to our global poverty numbers, inequality within developing countries is falling about as often as it is increasing (Ravallion and Chen, 1997; Ravallion, 2007). And this is true during spells of growth too; indeed, the sample data for growing economies are almost exactly split between inequality-increasing cases and inequality-decreasing cases. Furthermore, even if RP were right that inequality tends to increase as poor countries grow, note that for all except the countries with only one survey, they would again be wrong since we interpolate in both directions and then take the average. This much could have been readily verified from the documentation they cite (notably Chen and Ravallion, 2001, 2004).

However, it is again important to note that in our published regional and global aggregates we have re-calculated all numbers back in time in the light of improved survey data, revised price indices and new PPPs. RP ignore the fact that in all updates of the Bank's global and regional aggregates, all the numbers have been revised back in time on a consistent basis. So at whatever line one chooses—$1 or $2 per day—the aggregate comparisons are consistent over time.

Another argument they make is that the PPP for food is "... *a more appropriate PPP concept*" for poverty measurement; they also assert that this gives a higher poverty count. However, RP provide no argument, and it is far from obvious, that putting zero weight on non-food goods would give you a better PPP than that based on all consumption, even recognizing that the latter PPP is anchored to the mean consumption bundles. I am not surprised that using a PPP that ignores about half of consumption gives different poverty counts for a fixed poverty line (though they do not present any evidence to suggest that it would give different trends). But this is hardly a convincing basis for saying that the estimates based on consumption PPPs are *"erroneous"* as they claim. RP's calculations are also deceptive given that they ignore the fact that switching to a food PPP would also change the poverty line; Ravallion et al. (2008) show that using the food PPPs implies an appreciably lower poverty line.

RP also accuse us of what they call *"false precision"* in the poverty estimates reported in the various technical papers by Chen and Ravallion, documenting their methods for the Bank's global poverty estimates. "False precision" refers to the fact that the estimates of the global poverty measures (in millions of people and percentages of the population) are given to two decimal places in Chen and Ravallion (2001, 2007; and to one decimal place in Chen and Ravallion, 2004). RP believe that greater rounding off of the estimates would have better revealed their true precision. We choose to give as much accuracy as we could reasonably fit into our published tables, leaving it to the data users to do further rounding off. Maybe RP would be happier to round off the poverty counts to the nearest billion people before publishing them; then the count would have been unchanged (at 1 billion) between 1981 and 2004, even though the number of poor fell by 500.80 million (Chen and Ravallion, 2007). Readers can judge for themselves the merit of RP's claims of "false precision."

How would Reddy and Pogge measure global poverty?

In their conclusions, Reddy and Pogge claim that there is a better way of counting the world's poor. They are rather vague about what this would entail, but refer to a paper by Reddy et al. (2006). This paper measures poverty in three countries (Nicaragua, Tanzania, and Vietnam) using a method that will be recognized by specialists on poverty measurement as a version of what is termed the "cost of basic needs" (CBN) method (Ravallion, 1994, 2008a).[14] By this method one calculates the cost of a bundle of goods deemed to be nutritionally adequate and conforming to local tastes—to give the food poverty line—and one adds to this an allowance for non-food spending consistent with the spending patterns of those near the food poverty line. The Reddy et al. (2006) version of this method is that used by the government of Vietnam (following recommendations from the World Bank). They then repeat the method for the other two countries, using the same caloric cut-off point for all three countries (2,100 calories per person per day) but different (country-specific) food bundles and different allowances for non-food spending (anchored to the spending behavior in each country for the quintile at which 2,100 calories is reached on average).

What is being proposed here is essentially the method most developing countries use to set their own, national, poverty lines; indeed, virtually all of the seventy-five countries in our new compilation of national poverty lines have used some version of the same CBN method (Ravallion et al., 2009). There are of course differences; caloric cut-off points vary somewhat, as do valuation methods and the allowances made for non-food needs. However, to a first order approximation, one expects that the poverty lines generated by Reddy et al. (2006) are more like national poverty lines. In that light, the fact that (as Reddy et al. show) the resulting poverty measures differ from those obtained using an international ($1-or $2-a-day) line is hardly surprising. As noted already, the purchasing power over commodities of the national poverty lines is demonstrably *not* constant, as best that can be measured. So two people with the same absolute standard of living in terms of their command over commodities will be treated differently, depending on where they live. Typically the person living in the poorer country will be less likely to be deemed poor.

RP may object that the Reddy et al. (2006) measures can still be considered "absolute" because they have used the same caloric cut-off point for all three countries. However, this response would ignore an important lesson from the literature on nutrition and poverty (and from common sense), namely that a given food energy intake can be attained in multiple ways, requiring very different levels of income. As already noted, there is a strong income effect on both the food and non-food components of national poverty lines (though stronger for non-food component); for example, one obvious reason why poorer countries tend to have lower poverty lines is that they consume cheaper calories.

So RP have not solved the problem of setting an international poverty line with constant purchasing power over commodities, but rather they have side-stepped that problem. Arguably, RP have not taken the discussion of how best to set an international poverty line any further than its starting point in the 1990 WDR (World Bank, 1990).

Conclusion

Reddy and Pogge begin their chapter in this volume as follows: *"How many poor people are there in the world? This simple question is surprisingly difficult to answer at present"*. I would argue instead that there is nothing simple about the question, and nothing surprising about how difficult it is to answer it. Reddy and Pogge have oversimplified the problem of measuring poverty in the world, have greatly exaggerated the supposed faults in the Bank's methods, and their proposed alternative method does not take us very far in the goal of setting an international poverty line.

Postscript in response to Thomas Pogge's rejoinder

I thought I was just a scoundrel in their eyes, but it seems I am "Nixonesque" to boot. (Although, given that Pogge is "not questioning the integrity of the Bank's researchers," I am left wondering in what sense he sees me as Nixonesque.) Much of what I say above can be repeated in response to Pogge's rejoinder. I will avoid doing so. But there are a couple of points that do require clarification, so readers are not misled by Pogge's rejoinder.

One such issue is Pogge's assertion that the national poverty lines for developing countries (that we use in identifying an international poverty line) are unreliable in that they do not reflect "a level of income or consumption sufficient to meet basic human needs." The national poverty lines we use are all founded on reasonably well-specified "basic needs," and in this respect they are no more "questionable" than (say) the official poverty line of the US. Indeed, they are typically set essentially the same way that Reddy and Pogge advocate that an international line should be set!

Of course, as I pointed out in my reply to Reddy and Pogge, what constitutes a "basic human need" is socially specific—it depends on the standards of living in a specific setting. And national poverty lines in poor countries are clearly not "survival points" below which nobody can live (for if they were there would not be so many people living below them!). Rather they reflect the prevailing notions of what "poverty" means in those societies. I have no objection when Pogge pleads for a higher line, reflecting what he thinks constitutes "basic human needs." The "$1-a-day" line has not claimed to be anything more than a defensible lower bound, by which poverty in the world as a whole is judged by what are seen to be basic human needs in the poorest countries in the world.

Pogge goes on to repeat some textbook-ish points about the properties of PPPs. The original "$1-a-day" paper in 1990 fully acknowledged that standard PPPs (designed for comparing national accounts across countries) were not strictly appropriate for measuring poverty. It took twelve years to get to a new round of the ICP that could do a better job in this respect. The analysis is still underway, but the preliminary results suggest that the "PPPs for the poor" are quite similar to the standard PPPs, and that the global poverty estimates are reasonably robust to this change. I have no disagreement in principle with Pogge on the importance of weighting PPPs and CPIs appropriately to the task of measuring poverty.

However, near the end of his rejoinder, Pogge comes to what he sees as "the most compelling evidence one can have that the method (used by the Bank) is no good," namely that one gets different poverty counts if one changes the base year for the PPPs. Yes, new rounds of the ICP have generated new PPPs that imply changes to our poverty estimates. New ICP rounds bring new and better data on the cost of living in developing countries. Consider the latest ICP round for 2005—almost certainly the biggest global statistical exercise in history, involving numerous international agencies and the government statistics offices of almost 150 countries. This is clearly far superior to past rounds in terms of country participation, survey data collection and processing methods, and the quality and comparability of the price data collected. Nobody who bothers to look into the history of the ICP—from 1970 (crude price surveys for ten countries) to 2005 (state of the art price surveys for 150 countries)—could contend otherwise. It cannot be too surprising that the 2005 ICP has changed our estimates of real volumes for all international economic comparisons, including poverty measures. (My chapter with Shaohua Chen in this volume shows the impacts for China.) There has also been considerable progress in improving the coverage and quality of the household survey data required for measuring poverty. This too has entailed some significant changes to our poverty measures.

The key point here is that the data have improved and that this has led to new *and* better estimates. That hardly means that "the method is no good."

Notes

1. These are the views of the author, and need not reflect those of the World Bank or any affiliated organization. The author is grateful to Shaohua Chen for her comments on this chapter.
2. See <http://www.socialanalysis.org> (accessed on June 16, 2009).
3. In this reply to Reddy and Pogge I will refer to both their chapter in this volume and their (unpublished but widely seen) paper of 2002, under the same title, which goes into more detail on some points.
4. See Bhalla (2002). This raises different issues—see (for example) Bourguignon et al. (2008).
5. See <http://www.un.org/millenniumgoals/>.
6. For an overview of the main approaches to setting poverty lines, see Ravallion (2008a).
7. For further discussion of the theory and evidence on this point, see Ravallion (2008b).
8. We have also created a website, *PovcalNet*, which allows users to replicate our calculations and try alternative assumptions; see <http://econ.worldbank.org/povcalnet>.
9. The PWT used the Geary-Khamis (GK) method, while the Bank used the EKS method, which is the multilateral extension of the bilateral Fisher index. On the differences between the GK and EKS methods and implications for global poverty measures, see Ackland et al. (2006).
10. I say "appear" here because they seem to back away from this position in their 2008 paper, possibly in recognition of the problems readers of their 2002 paper pointed out to them.
11. Notably that the utility function is quadratic. For a recent discussion, see Ackland et al. (2006).
12. Given that one needs to set a poverty line to determine the relevant consumption bundle, but only then can one determine the poverty line; an iterative method for this problem is proposed by Ravallion (1998), in the context of setting national poverty lines.
13. They also show that the variance is higher, and the relationship with mean consumption is steeper, if one uses food PPPs. Given that the underlying national poverty lines were based on both food and non-food needs, it would seem more appropriate to use the full consumption PPP.
14. Reddy et al. (2006) call their method a "capability-based approach." However, the relationship to Sen's (1985) "capability approach" is unclear. The fact of being able to afford a diet that yields (say) 2,100 calories per day does not assure that the functions that come with being adequately nourished will actually be met, even on average, let alone for each individual. A true "capability approach" would presumably look rather different to what Reddy et al. (2006) propose. For further discussion see Ravallion (2008a).

References

Ackland, R., Dowrick, S., and Freyens, B. (2006) 'Measuring Global Poverty: Why PPP Methods Matter'. Mimeo, Research School of Social Sciences, Australian National University.

Bhalla, S. (2002) *Imagine There's No Country: Poverty, Inequality and Growth in the Era of Globalization*. Washington DC: Institute for International Economics.

Bourguignon, F., Ferreira, F., Milanovic, B., and Ravallion, M. (2008) 'Global Inequality'. In K. Reinert and R. Rajan (eds.) *Princeton Encyclopedia of the World Economy*, Princeton, NJ: Princeton University Press (forthcoming).

Chen, S., Datt, G., and Ravallion, M. (1994) 'Is Poverty Increasing in the Developing World?' *Review of Income and Wealth*, 40(4), pp. 359–76.

—— and Ravallion, M. (2001) 'How Did the World's Poor fare in the 1990s?' *Review of Income and Wealth*, 47(3), pp. 283–300.

—— —— (2004) 'How Have the World's Poorest Fared Since the Early 1980s?' *World Bank Research Observer*, 19/2, pp. 141–70.

—— —— (2007) 'Absolute Poverty Measures for the Developing World, 1981–2004'. *Proceedings of the National Academy of Sciences of the United States of America*, 104/43, pp. 16757–62.

—— —— (2008) 'The Developing World is Poorer than we Thought, but no less Successful in the Fight against Poverty'. Policy Research Working Paper 4703, Washington DC: World Bank.

Deaton, A. and Dupriez, O. (2007) 'Poverty PPPs for Latin America and Asia'. Mimeo, Development Data Group, World Bank.

Pritchett, L. (2006) 'Who is *Not* Poor? Dreaming of a World Truly Free of Poverty'. *World Bank Research Observer*, 21(1), pp. 1–23.

Ravallion, M. (1994) *Poverty Comparisons*. Chur, Switzerland: Harwood Academic Press.

—— (1998) *Poverty Lines in Theory and Practice*. Living Standards Measurement Study Paper 133. Washington DC: World Bank.

—— (2007) 'Inequality *is* Bad for the Poor'. In J. Micklewright and S. Jenkins (eds.) *Inequality and Poverty Re-Examined*, Oxford: Oxford University Press.

—— (2008a) 'Poverty Lines'. In Larry Blume and Steven Durlauf (eds.) *The New Palgrave Dictionary of Economics* (2nd edn), London: Palgrave Macmillan.

—— (2008b) 'On the Welfarist Rationale for Relative Poverty Lines'. In Kaushik Basu and Ravi Kanbur (eds.) *Arguments for a Better World: Essays in Honor of Amartya Sen.* Volume II: *Society, Institutions and Development*, Oxford: Oxford University Press.

—— and Chen, S. (1997) 'What Can New Survey Data Tell Us about Recent Changes in Distribution and Poverty?' *World Bank Economic Review*, 11(2), pp. 357–82.

—— —— and Sangraula, P. (2008) 'Dollar a Day Revisited'. *World Bank Economic Review*, 23(2), pp. 1–22.

—— Datt, G., and van de Walle, D. (1991) 'Quantifying Absolute Poverty in the Developing World'. *Review of Income and Wealth*, 37, pp. 345–61.

—— and Lokshin, M. (2006) 'On the Consistency of Poverty Lines'. In Alain de Janvry and Ravi Kanbur (eds.) *Poverty, Inequality and Development: Essays in Honor of Erik Thorbecke*, Springer.

—— —— (2007) 'Lasting Impacts of Indonesia's Financial Crisis'. *Economic Development and Cultural Change*, 56(1), pp. 27–56.

Reddy, S. G. and Pogge, T. W. (2002) 'How *Not* to Count the Poor'. (Version 3.0) Mimeo, Barnard College, New York.

—— Visaria, S., and Asali, M. (2006) 'Inter-Country Comparisons of Income Poverty Based on a Capability Approach'. Department of Economics, Barnard College <http://ssrn. com/abstract=915406>.

Sen, A. (1985) *Commodities and Capabilities*. Amsterdam: North-Holland.

Summers, R. and Heston, A. (1991) 'The Penn World Tables (Mark 5): An Extended Set of International Comparisons, 1950–1988'. *Quarterly Journal of Economics*, 106, pp. 327–68.

Wade, R. (2004) 'Is Globalization Reducing Poverty and Inequality?' *World Development*, 32(4), pp. 567–89.

World Bank (1990) *World Development Report: Poverty*. Oxford University Press for the World Bank.

—— (2000) *World Development Report: Attacking Poverty*. Oxford University Press for the World Bank.

—— (2007) *World Development Indicators*. Washington DC: World Bank.

—— (2008) *2005 International Comparison Program: Tables of Final Results*. Washington DC: World Bank.

3b

How Many Poor People Should There Be? A Rejoinder to Ravallion

*Thomas Pogge**

How many poor people should there be? To this apparently simple question, the world's governments have given two unanimous answers. One is enshrined in the 1948 *Universal Declaration of Human Rights*:

Everyone has the right to a standard of living adequate for the health and well-being of himself and of his family, including food, clothing, housing and medical care (Article 25).

Everyone is entitled to a social and international order in which the rights and freedoms set forth in this Declaration can be fully realized (Article 28).

There is to be no poverty at all, then—at least no severe poverty that would jeopardize the ability of human beings to meet their basic needs.

The other answer, also adopted unanimously, is rather different. It sets an acceptable extreme poverty level for 2015, which is presented as a halving of such poverty by that date. The interpretation of this goal keeps changing. At the 1996 World Food Summit in Rome, 186 governments agreed on "reducing the *number* of undernourished people to half their *present* level no later than 2015."[1] Greatly boosting the political importance of the extreme poverty statistics the World Bank had been supplying since 1990, the first Millennium Development Goal (MDG) then promised "to halve, by the year 2015, the *proportion of the world's people* whose income is less than one dollar a day and the proportion of people who suffer from hunger."[2] The UN and its MDG administrators have since decided that this proportion is to be calculated as a percentage not of world population, but of the faster-growing population of the less developed countries, and that the benchmark year for this and all MDGs should be not the year of their adoption (2000), but 1990.[3] The fate of billions is gravely affected by these as well as by additional decisions about how the evolution of extreme poverty is assessed by the UN and the World Bank. It is in this context that Sanjay Reddy and I have joined the poverty measurement debate.

Let me provide one more piece of background. With some 18 million (30 per cent of) human deaths each year attributed to poverty-related causes (WHO, 2008), the scale of the world poverty problem is staggering in human terms. But in economic terms, the problem is paltry. The Bank now acknowledges that 1.4 billion human beings are living in extreme poverty: below its new international poverty line (IPL) of $1.25 per day (at 2005 purchasing power parities or PPPs) and 30 per cent below this level on average (Chen and Ravallion, 2008, pp. 32, 36). Yet this entire shortfall is said to amount to only 0.33 per cent of global GDP (ibid., p. 23). Using a less extreme definition of poverty, some 2.6 billion people are reportedly living below $2.00 per day (at 2005 PPPs) and nearly 40 per cent below this line on average (ibid., pp. 33, 36). Even their entire shortfall still amounts to only 1.3 per cent of global GDP (ibid., p. 23).[4] This shows that, for the sake of comparatively trivial gains, the world's governments—and we all—are keeping billions trapped in life-threatening poverty by imposing on them the heavy burdens facilitated by the global institutional architecture, such as debt obligations incurred by their illegitimate rulers, public spending restrictions to ensure national debt repayment, monopoly prices for medicines, and protectionist barriers to trade (Pogge, 2008).

Coming to Ravallion's reply, let me emphasize strongly that our concern has always been with the soundness of the Bank's measurement methodology. We are not questioning the integrity of the Bank's researchers. Our main contact at the Bank has been Ravallion's colleague, Shaohua Chen. Without her prompt, full, patient, and cheerful collaboration, we could not have analyzed and reconstructed the Bank's calculations to anything like the extent we have done. Ravallion is entitled to his Nixonesque protestation, of course. But it is not responsive to anything we have written. Nor does his being no "real scoundrel" (p. 86) help show that his method is sound.

Responding to us, Ravallion writes:

> The fact that we judge the extent of consumption poverty in the world by the standards typical of low-income countries clearly does not mean that we are underestimating the extent of world poverty. Obviously if you use a higher standard you will get a higher poverty count. The "$1 a day" line does not claim to be anything other than a poverty line typical of poor countries. To say that we are underestimating poverty by this method is like saying that one underestimates length using a ruler calibrated in inches rather than centimeters. If one knows how the ruler is calibrated there should be no confusion. (p. 91)

This statement repeats many of the mistakes and confusions we have been criticizing. Let me go through them.

A silly objection we do not make

Ravallion is right that one is not underestimating the length of a table when, measuring in inches, one assigns it the number 50—even if, measured in centimeters, its length is 127. He is right to suggest that it would be silly to object to one method and the results it delivers, that another method would deliver different results. But we are not raising this silly objection. Our objection is that the Bank is using a method that is seriously flawed in the following ways.

Arbitrarily set too low, the Bank's IPL sugarcoats the poverty trend

The Bank has defended the *level* of its latest IPL as "anchored to the [domestic poverty] lines found in the poorest countries" (Chen and Ravallion, 2008, p. 9). The "anchoring" is a bit loose. In its first exercise, the Bank chose $1.02 (1985 PPP) as the IPL on the grounds that the domestic poverty lines of *eight* countries were *close to* this amount. Later, it chose $1.075 (1993 PPP) as the IPL because it is *the median* of *the ten lowest* domestic poverty lines. And for its most recent exercise the Bank is choosing $1.25 (2005 PPP) as the IPL because it is *the mean* of the domestic poverty lines *of the fifteen poorest countries*—thirteen of which are small states in Africa (ibid., p. 10).

To make matters worse, the domestic poverty lines relied upon are not exactly "found" by the Bank, but in many cases set by or in collaboration with the Bank itself (ibid., p. 9). There was no examination of whether these lines reflect a level of income or consumption sufficient to meet basic human requirements.

Ravallion responds that it does not matter how high or low the IPL is fixed. Once it is understood how this line is calibrated, there should be no confusion: poverty is whatever the Bank's method measures.[5]

Indeed, there is no confusion. But it does matter how high or low the IPL is set. This matters to the reported headcount trend, which looks ever prettier the lower the IPL is set.[6] It also matters insofar as millions go hungry above the Bank's IPL and are consequently ignored in the MDG1 exercise and by the affluent.

Is the Bank's IPL set at a reasonable level? We have already seen that the goal of eradicating poverty would still be quite feasible if the IPL were set at $2 a day rather than at $1.25 (2005 PPP): relative to the $2 a day standard, there would be 2.6 billion poor people—40 per cent of humanity—collectively living on 2 per cent and collectively lacking 1.3 per cent of global GDP. Assessed at market exchange rates, the eradication of poverty so defined would require a shift of well under 1 per cent of global GDP.

But isn't $2.00 a day rather too sumptuous as a poverty line, and doesn't the Bank's $1.25 (2005 PPP) standard better capture what it means to escape poverty? One can approach this question by converting the Bank's IPL into the currency of one's own country and year, using the conversion methods the Bank uses while claiming that they preserve equivalence of purchasing power. Following this approach, we find that, in the US in 2009, income or consumption of $1.37 per day would get a person counted as non-poor.[7] People living in the US strictly on what can be bought with this amount—$500 per year—would clearly be unable to meet their basic needs.[8] Insofar as the Bank's conversions indeed preserve purchasing power equivalence, we can conclude that its IPL is equally inadequate when converted into local currency unit (LCU) amounts for other country/year settings. Insofar as the Bank fails to register as poor many people who cannot meet their most basic needs, its criterion of poverty is at odds with how its readers understand this word. More importantly, by systematically ignoring very large numbers of people in life-threatening poverty, the Bank is providing misleading information to policy-makers about the distribution and trend (see note 6) of severe poverty, and grossly misleading information to all of us about the magnitude and seriousness of our responsibility to structure the world economy so that severe poverty is reliably avoided.

The Bank's method relies on questionable PPPs

How does the Bank derive its IPLs from domestic poverty lines which, after all, are denominated in many different currencies? And how, more generally, does it compare individual incomes and consumption expenditures denominated in diverse currencies?

Such *cardinal* comparisons—presupposed in averaging—are not as straightforward as Ravallion's analogy to lengths makes them seem. The income of a poor Indian may be higher than that of a poor Mexican in terms of the amount of rice each can buy and yet lower in terms of the amount of meat or gasoline. The comparison of incomes—or expenditures or domestic poverty lines—denominated in different currencies must somehow aggregate over such price data to arrive at an overall judgment of the form: the Indian's rupee income is worth *n* times as much as the Mexican's peso income.

The Bank's comparisons have been relying on general consumption PPPs of some specific base year for converting domestic poverty lines from this base year into US dollars of the same year. The Bank's successive IPLs were defined in different PPP base years: 1985, 1993, and 2005. Once it has defined an IPL in US dollars of a specific base year, the Bank then uses the same PPPs to convert this IPL into all local currencies of the same year. The resulting LCU amounts are then converted further via national consumer price indices (CPIs) to extend the IPL to other years.

Reddy and I have long been pointing out that the quality of the PPPs so heavily relied upon by the Bank's method is highly questionable, especially for the most important countries, China and India. Startled by the Asian Development Bank's recent re-evaluation of PPPs, the World Bank now accepts this point, claiming that it had previously assigned about twice as much purchasing power to the Chinese and Indian currencies as they are really worth (Chen and Ravallion, 2008, p. 8). The Bank offers this overestimate in explanation of the dramatic 50 per cent hike in its reported 2005 global extreme poverty figure. It gives the number of extremely poor as 931.3 million relative to its $1.075 (1993 PPP) IPL and as 1,399.6 million relative to its new $1.25 (2005 PPP) IPL (ibid., Table 5). Below, I will argue that the Bank's dramatic revision reflects not merely bad inputs, and unnecessary ones at that, but a bad method as well.

Let me reiterate that the PPPs employed even in the Bank's latest poverty measurement exercise are highly questionable. Noting that the latest "price survey for China was confined to 11 cities [and] some surrounding areas," the Bank chose to "use existing differentials in urban-rural poverty lines...to correct the national PPP for the purpose of measuring poverty" (ibid., p. 11). Such a "correction" of China's PPP based on existing poverty lines is evidently highly conjectural and moreover ignores that prices in China vary more by province than by rural versus urban (Heston, 2008, p. 68). The employment of a single averaged PPP for all of India is similarly distorting, although greater efforts were undertaken in India than in China to collect rural prices.[9]

Ppps and Cpis are greatly affected by poverty-irrelevant commodities

Even if all prices were perfectly uniform in each country and general consumption PPPs were then calculated for all currencies to everyone's satisfaction, reliance on such PPPs in the context of the Bank's poverty measurement exercise would still be highly problematic. We make two objections in particular. One objection is *commodity irrelevance*. Generally, the more spending some commodity attracts, the more its price will influence calculated PPPs. This is problematic because many commodities are irrelevant to poverty avoidance. Used for purposes of poverty assessment, PPPs are influenced far too much by the prices of luxury goods and services, which the poor cannot afford and do not really need, and influenced far too little by the necessities that are most needed by the poor and on which they concentrate their spending.[10] The fact that an income suffices to meet basic human needs is no assurance, then, that a PPP equivalent income in another country is similarly sufficient. In poor countries, prices of necessities are often higher, and prices of services lower, than what the PPP to the US dollar would suggest.

A numerical example may illuminate the point. Imagine a simple world with three commodities: *necessities*, *discretionaries*, and *services* (always in this order). Suppose the prices of these three commodities are LCU 5, 6, and 1 in some poor country and $3, $4, and $9 in the US. What is the PPP? The answer depends on the spending pattern in both countries. Suppose this pattern, in per cent, is 30, 50, and 20 in the poor country and 10, 50, and 40 in the US. This yields a PPP (calculated by the Bank's method) of 1.55—each LCU is deemed equivalent to

$1.55. But in reference only to necessities, priced at LCU 5 and $3, each LCU is worth only 60 cents. The Bank's reliance on general consumption PPPs ensures that, wherever the actual price of necessities is higher than what such PPPs suggest, many who are very poor, relative to what they really need to buy, do not show up in the Bank's extreme poverty statistics.

There are indications that the Bank will try to address this problem by elaborating PPPs for the poor (PPPPs) based on the actual consumption pattern of the poor. This is an extremely complex undertaking because of the interdependence of three identifications. To ascertain what the poor are actually consuming, the Bank must be able to identify who the poor are. To do this, the Bank must identify the level of the IPL and the PPPPs for converting this line into all currencies. To identify the level of the IPL, which the Bank does by averaging the domestic poverty lines of the poorest countries, the Bank needs PPPPs to make those domestic lines comparable. Each of the required identifications—of PPPPs, of the poor, and of the IPL—thus presupposes the other two. This circularity problem will apparently be attacked through a complex iteration procedure.[11]

This revision may be a step forward insofar as it cuts down the influence of price data about commodities that are irrelevant to the avoidance of poverty. Still, the revision is not fully satisfactory because the observed spending pattern of the poor sometimes fails to disclose what they need most. Unmet needs, ignorance, and advertising often lead poor people to spend some of their income on alcohol, tobacco, or quackery. Yet, unlike higher food prices, a higher price of cigarettes does not make them poorer in an intuitive sense: it does not reduce their ability to meet their basic needs. Conversely, millions of poor people worldwide do not spend any money on buying patented medicines they urgently need. This fact does not show that the price of such medicines is for them irrelevant. In fact, this price is killing many of them. The observed spending pattern of the poor—itself heavily influenced by existing prices and other extraneous factors (tobacco advertising)—is not then a good indicator of what they require to meet their basic needs.

PPPs are greatly affected by poverty-irrelevant data from other countries

Both PPPs and PPPPs are subject to another objection we have made: *country irrelevance*. Considering two countries in isolation, the PPP rate is calculated on the basis of the prices and consumed quantities of all commodities. For example, the more that is spent on services in the US, the more of an influence the prices of services in India and the US will have on the PPP of the Indian rupee to the US dollar. Given that services are (relative to other commodities) especially cheap in India versus the US, high service consumption in the US raises the assessed purchasing power of the Indian rupee and hence the assessed spending power of the Indian poor. Clearly, what Americans are spending their money on is wholly irrelevant to whether persons in India are poor or not. But the Bank's method makes the US spending pattern relevant to identifying the poor in India.

The problem is compounded once third countries enter the picture. Bilateral PPPs calculated without regard to other countries would not satisfy transitivity.[12] But it is, for various reasons, highly desirable that PPPs be transitive[13]—so that, for countries A, B, C:

$$PPP(A, B) \times PPP(B, C) = PPP(A, C)$$

To achieve such transitivity, the calculation of PPPs involves a final step that adjusts all preliminary bilateral PPPs to one another in a way that guarantees transitivity. This adjustment has the consequence that the PPP assigned to any local currency is affected by the prices and spending patterns not only of its home country and the US (base country), but also of every other country. In the Bank's method, then, the classification of any person as poor or non-poor is influenced not merely by the money she has and the prices she faces, but also by the prices and spending patterns of all countries included in the PPP exercise.

A move toward PPPPs would mitigate this problem. If the poor spend little on services, then the price of services in other countries will have little influence on the calculation of their currencies' PPPPs. But such calculations will still be excessively affected by the prices of commodities that are important only elsewhere. For example, if potatoes figure prominently in the spending of the poor in some countries, then India's PPPP will be significantly influenced by what potatoes cost in India and elsewhere. And the classification of Indians as poor or non-poor can then be significantly affected by potato prices even if potatoes are not, and cannot plausibly become, part of the diet of the Indian poor.

CPIs do not track the prices of necessities

Once the Bank has, through the use of PPPs, converted its chosen IPL into corresponding base-year amounts in all other currencies, it uses national CPIs to convert the results into LCUs for other years.

We object to this step as well. Tracking price changes in nationally consumed commodities, a country's CPI is influenced most by the commodities on which most is spent. Reliance on CPIs thus courts, once more, the risk of losing track of the prices of basic necessities. Falling prices of necessities may raise the real standard of living of poor people, even while their incomes are flat and the CPI is rising. Conversely, falling prices of electronics or services may cause the CPI to fall, even while biofuel demand is raising food prices. When this happens, poor people on constant incomes become even poorer in real life, but richer in the Bank's statistics. This is not a mere theoretical possibility. While the Bank is delivering a steady stream of good news from the poverty front, the Food and Agricultural Organization reports steady increases in the number of chronically malnourished people—a number that now exceeds 1 billion for the first time in human history.[14]

This problem could be mitigated by constructing—in analogy to PPPPs—CPIs for the poor (CPIP). Such CPIPs would cut down the influence of the prices of non-necessities. But they would also, implausibly, cut down the influence of the prices of necessities that, because of their high price, are barely consumed by the poor. As far as I know, no revision toward CPIPs is currently being contemplated.

The Bank's method delivers massively inconsistent results

Perhaps the most compelling evidence one can have that a method is no good is that its applications deliver mutually inconsistent results. We have presented such evidence (both analytic and empirical), showing that the Bank's method is not robust with respect to the PPP base year chosen. Unfortunately, this objection was not understood. We were certainly not saying that new data should be ignored—a proposition Ravallion rightly refutes at length.

What then were we saying? The Bank's method requires comparing currency amounts from different countries and years. The Bank makes these comparisons in two steps. It converts each LCU amount into its base year equivalent, using the national CPI. It then converts the result into its base year US dollar equivalent, using base year PPPs. In this way, any income, consumption expenditure, and domestic poverty line—regardless of year, country, or amount—can be mapped onto a common cardinal scale calibrated in US dollars of some chosen base year.

Our objection is that this method is highly sensitive to the choice of PPP base years. A comparison of two monthly incomes—say 280 Canadian dollars (CAD) in 1980 with 831 Australian dollars (AUD) in 1999—yields different results depending on the year whose PPP is used in the conversion. Here is one way the Bank has used to compare such amounts:

$$CAD280(1980) = CAD544(1993) = 426(1993)$$

$$AUD831(1999) = AUD743(1993) = 558(1993)$$

But if the same two local currency amounts are compared via 1985 PPPs, then they turn out to be exactly equivalent. (We know this because the Bank used 1985 as its PPP base year until 1999.) The choice of 1993 rather than 1985 as PPP base year raises the assessed purchasing power of *all* AUD amounts—prices, incomes, consumption expenditures—in all years by 31 per cent relative to that of all CAD amounts. And the choice of 1985 rather than 1993 as PPP base year raises the assessed purchasing power of *all* CAD amounts in all years by 31 per cent relative to all AUD amounts. The outcome of such income comparisons thus is heavily influenced by a factor that is obviously irrelevant to these comparisons: namely by the Bank's arbitrary choice of PPP base year.[15]

As Table 3.1 (pp. 46–8) demonstrates, such base year sensitivity—some of even much larger magnitude—is common across rich and poor countries alike. It is bound to occur, because conversions using CPIs and PPPs are based on very different consumption patterns: the Canadian CPI is based on the Canadian consumption pattern, the Australian CPI on the Australian, and the PPPs of 1985 and 1993 are based on the differing international consumption patterns of those years. No wonder, then, that different conversion paths yield diverse results.

The Bank's choice of PPP base year obviously also affects profoundly who is classified as poor. Let me illustrate this by considering China and Bangladesh which, as it happens, are related like Australia and Canada: the choice of 1993 rather than 1985 as PPP base year raises the assessed purchasing power of all Chinese amounts in all years by 31 per cent relative to all Bangladeshi amounts—and *vice versa*. Now take any pair consisting of a Bangladeshi person in some year living below $1.075 1993 PPP and a Chinese person in some other year living above this IPL and no more than 31 per cent above the Bangladeshi. For each such pair, if 1985 is chosen as PPP base year, then the Chinese person is deemed poorer than the Bangladeshi. If 1993 is chosen, then the Bangladeshi is deemed poorer than the Chinese. The choice of base year affects then the classification of at least one of the two persons. The Bank's method makes the poverty classification of millions of people—today and in past and future years—dependent on the arbitrary choice of PPP base year. This is bad, because the Bank's choice of PPP base year is no more significant to the real situation of human beings than the weather on Jupiter.

The Bank now states that all its extreme poverty headcount figures based on its IPL of $1.075 (1993 PPP) were far too low because it had overestimated the purchasing power of the currencies of many poor countries: "We find that the incidence of poverty in the world is higher than past estimates have suggested. The main reason is that the 2005 ICP price data suggest than past PPPs had implicitly underestimated the cost of living in most developing countries" (Chen and Ravallion, 2008, p. 6). The idea here expressed is that one can use the PPPs of one base year (2005) to correct the PPPs of another (1993). To do this, one would have to rely on the national CPIs covering the intervening period: by adjusting the 2005 PPPs by the national rates of consumer price inflation between 1993 and 2005. Such reliance assumes that a circular journey—from 1993 USD to 2005 USD to 2005 LCU to 1993 LCU to 1993 USD—must lead back to the original amount. If this assumption were sound, then any three of these conversion rates would determine the fourth. But the assumption is false, because the four conversions in the circle are based on national and international consumption patterns that differ greatly from one another.[16]

What can replace the Bank's method of poverty measurement?

If we want to assess income poverty through a headcount measure, then we should find a more direct method than the Bank's: a method that focuses on the prices a person faces in order to determine whether her income suffices to meet her basic human requirements.

Ravallion misunderstands this proposal of ours in two respects. He writes that "they appear to be proposing to price a single bundle of goods in each country relative to a reference country" (p. 90). What we have in fact proposed is to assess each person's income against "the cost of purchasing commodities containing relevant characteristics (for example, calorie content)" (p. 79) that are needed to achieve the basic requirements of human beings.

Ravallion also writes that we "ignore an important lesson from the literature on nutrition and poverty (and from common sense), namely that a given food energy intake can be attained in multiple ways, requiring very different levels of income" (p. 97). We are not quite so ignorant. Our proposal was to define the poor as those whose income affords them *no* acceptable way of meeting their basic human requirements, given the cultural and environmental conditions they face. What these nutritional and other basic requirements are, and what counts as an acceptable way of meeting them, are matters for debate. There is certainly some need for judgment in specifying a poverty criterion of this kind, as there is in any poverty assessment exercise. But making such contestable judgments in the specification phase is certainly much better than choosing a criterion that—even after it has been fully specified—makes its results depend on arbitrary contingencies such as the Bank's choice of PPP base year and the prices and consumption patterns in all countries on earth. Moreover, we have argued that making such judgments should involve transparent participatory processes. This would be in contrast to the approach of the Bank which eschews public consultation behind a false facade of science-like objectivity.

Ravallion asserts that "the Reddy and Pogge critique collapses under even moderate scrutiny" (p. 86). For the sake of the poor, one can only hope that the scrutiny of some readers will not be quite so moderate.

Notes

* Many thanks to Branko Milanovic, Matt Peterson, and Sanjay Reddy for their insightful comments and suggestions.
1. Rome Declaration on World Food Security, 1996, <http://www.fao.org/wfs>, author's emphasis.
2. *UN Millennium Declaration*, General Assembly Resolution 55/2, 2000, <http://www.un.org/millennium/declaration/ares552e.htm>, author's emphasis.

A Rejoinder

3. In terms of the Bank's international poverty line (IPL) at the time, these two reinterpretations of the goals stated in the Millennium Declaration have increased, by roughly 250 million, the number of those whose confinement below the Bank's IPL in 2015 will be deemed acceptable and have thereby cut the envisaged reduction in the number of extremely poor people to less than 20 per cent (Pogge, 2004, pp. 378–80; 2008, pp. 11–13). In terms of the Bank's new IPL, and the much higher extreme poverty count associated with it, the two reinterpretations are raising the acceptable 2015 extreme poverty count by 323 million, from 1,004 million to 1,327 million (calculated on the basis of Chen and Ravallion, 2008, Tables 4 and 5, and UN Population Division, 2009).

4. The average shortfall of those living below some poverty line is the ratio of the relevant poverty gap and headcount indices provided in Chen and Ravallion (2008), Tables 9 and 6 respectively. These calculations are performed in terms of PPPs. Valued at market exchange rates, the global poverty problem is substantially smaller still.

5. Analogous to Edwin Boring's (1923) famous definition of intelligence as whatever these tests measure—or indeed Jacob Viner's crack that economics is what economists do.

6. The Bank's new poverty figures readily confirm this point. Between 1981 and 2005, the reported change in the number of people deemed poor by the Bank's $1.00, $1.25, $2.00, and $2.50 per day (2005 PPP) standards was minus 43 per cent, minus 27 per cent, plus 2 per cent, and plus 15 per cent, respectively. And similarly for the shorter 1990–2005 period, where the change relative to the same four lines is given as minus 33 per cent, minus 23 per cent, minus 6 per cent, and plus 2 per cent, respectively (Chen and Ravallion, 2008, Table 8). With the Bank's choice of IPL, in 2005 we were 34 per cent ahead of schedule toward achieving MDG1. Had $2.00 or $2.50 per day (2005 PPP) been chosen instead, we would in 2005 have been behind schedule by 67 or 112 per cent, respectively (Pogge, 2009, Section 3.2).

7. Following the Bank's method, I have here converted its latest IPL—defined as $1.25 per day in 2005 US dollars (USD)—via the US consumer price index, <http://www.bls.gov/data/inflation_calculator.htm> (accessed June 20, 2009). The Bank's earlier IPLs—$1.02 (1985 PPP), $1.00 (1985 PPP), 1.075 (1993 PPP)—have higher equivalents in 2009 USD, namely $2.03, $1.99, and $1.59, respectively (ibid.).

8. The unabridged version of our paper (<http://www.socialanalysis.org>) cites evidence that such an amount is not nearly sufficient to meet even just the food needs of a human being. The elaborately designed thrifty food plan (USDA, 1999) is an equal-cost revision of the Economy Food Plan first presented in 1961 "as a nutritionally adequate diet for short-term or emergency use." The lowest cost stated for this minimal diet was $80.40 per person per month in 1999. The Bank counts as non-poor anyone who lived in the US in 1999 on $32.42 per person per month (<http://www.bls.gov/data/inflation_calculator.htm>, accessed June 20, 2009). Such a person could have bought about 40 per cent of the USDA's emergency diet—but only by spending *nothing* on clothing, shelter, health care, utilities, and everything else.

9. See <http://siteresources.worldbank.org/ICPINT/Resources/Indian_country_report.pdf>, accessed June 20, 2009.

10. For example, rice accounts for a fraction of 1 per cent of household spending in the US and other affluent countries, and its price therefore plays a minuscule role in determining the PPP of the Indian rupee. But the price of rice is of very great significance for the real value of the rupees that very poor people in India have available to them.

11. Many thanks to Shaohua Chen for conveying information used in this paragraph, which I hope to have summarized accurately. See also Ravallion, Chen, and Sangraula (2008, pp. 19–21).

12. Intuitively speaking, transitivity fails because the left side of the equation in the text is substantially influenced by the spending pattern in country B, while the right side is not so influenced at all.

13. One pertinent reason is this. If PPPs were not transitive, then the Bank's poverty measurement exercise would not be robust with respect to the choice of base country. Then the relation between the domestic poverty lines of any two countries would change depending on which currency they are converted into and compared in.

14. See <http://www.fao.org>, accessed June 20, 2009.

15. Another way of bringing out the problem involves a circular journey of conversions. Using the Bank's method, we can convert our CAD280 (1980) via 1985 PPPs into AUD831 (1999) and then convert this amount back via 1993 PPPs into CAD367 (1980). The blatant failure of transitivity—CAD280 (1980) is surely not equivalent to CAD367 (1980)—shows that the Bank's conversions do not preserve equivalence. Note that I am using in this section two earlier IPLs in my examples because I do not yet have access to country breakdowns for the new $1.25 (2005 PPP) IPL.

16. Another reason mentioned earlier is that bilateral PPPs are adjusted on the basis of data from all other countries so as to achieve transitivity. We see here *en passant* why it makes no sense to insist that the latest available PPP base year is always best. This may be so when one seeks a snapshot of poverty in or near that year. But there is no such advantage with regard to the all-important trend figures delivered by the Bank. The choice of a later base year may give a more accurate picture of the end of the period, but only at the cost of a less accurate picture of its beginning.

Bibliography

Chen, S. and Ravallion, M. (2008) 'The Developing World is Poorer than We Thought, but no Less Successful in the Fight against Poverty'. World Bank Policy Research Working Paper WPS 4703. Available at <http://econ.worldbank.org>, accessed June 20, 2009.

Heston, A. (2008) 'The 2005 Global Report on Purchasing Power Parity Estimates: A Preliminary Review'. *Economic and Political Weekly*, March 15, pp. 65–9.

Pogge, T. (2004) 'The First UN Millennium Development Goal: a Cause for Celebration?' *Journal of Human Development*, 5, pp. 377–97.

—— (2008) *World Poverty and Human Rights: Cosmopolitan Responsibilities and Reforms* (2nd edn). Cambridge: Polity Press.

—— (2009) *Politics as Usual: What Lies behind the Pro-Poor Rhetoric*. Cambridge: Polity Press.

Ravallion, M., Chen, S., and Sangraula, P. (2008) 'A Dollar a Day Revisited'. World Bank Policy Research Working Paper WPS 4620. Available at <http://econ.worldbank.org>, accessed June 20, 2009.

UN Population Division (2009), *World Population Prospects: The 2008 Revision.* Available at <http://esa.un.org/unpp>, accessed June 20, 2009.

USDA (1999). *Thrifty Food Plan, 1999.* Washington DC: USDA. The relevant cost table is available at <http://www.cnpp.usda.gov/Publications/FoodPlans/1999/CostofFood-Nov99.pdf>, accessed June 20, 2009.

WHO (World Health Organization) 2008. *The Global Burden of Disease: 2004 Update.* Geneva: WHO Publications. Available at <http://www.who.int/healthinfo/global_burden_disease/2004_report_update/en/index.html>, accessed June 20, 2008.

4

Raising the Standard: The War on Global Poverty[1]

Surjit S. Bhalla[2]

Introduction

It would be an understatement to say that poverty reduction is one of the most important goals of our time. Much has been written on this topic, and the fight against world poverty is now almost forty years old. In 1973, Robert McNamara, President of the World Bank, made a speech about the need to fight global poverty, a speech that launched concentrated work, effort, and aid towards poverty reduction by the developed and developing world.

The World Bank estimate for world poverty for 2004 was 970 million.[3] That is, close to a billion people have consumption expenditures of less than $1.08 a day at 1993 PPP prices.[4] This number is not that much different from the one that prevailed a decade earlier—1.13 billion in 1990. In 1981, global poverty was estimated as 1.5 billion. What has changed over the last two decades is the composition of the poor—in 1981, both India and China contributed two-thirds (1 billion) to the total. Poverty then was essentially an India–China story. More than two decades of growth later, the importance of India–China is substantially reduced, but for some methods, the share in world poverty for these two Asian economies is around 30 per cent.

Both Bhalla (2002b) and Sala-i-Martín (2006) have contended that world poverty is significantly below the World Bank estimates. Depending on assumptions, our estimates for global poverty for 2005 range from about 200 to 500 million, an order of magnitude lower than the official estimates. Which set of estimates are "correct" has enormous implications for aid and development policy, and for evaluations of how the globalization growth process in the past twenty years has affected the lives of the poorest.

These "new" estimates have been partly based on the old method of estimating poverty, and the one followed universally until the early 1990s (see Ahluwalia et al., 1979 for the first such estimate—the ACC method). The ACC method relies on national account means of per capita consumption, and household survey distributions of consumption (or income).[5] Critics have rejected such estimates of poverty for two reasons: first, survey based estimates of per capita consumption, and not national accounts based estimates, are a more reliable estimate for the "true" mean; and second, if the distribution of the survey distribution is trusted, then the mean must also be trusted. This chapter is *not* about poverty estimates as revealed by household survey data "matched" with national accounts data.[6] Rather, this chapter is about the authenticity and reliability of survey based measures of poverty. If the survey estimates are accurate or "correct," what can we say about poverty, inequality, and growth in the developing economies for the period 1980 to present? If they are not correct, then can alternative more accurate estimates of poverty be presented, based on all the available data, surveys and national accounts?

This chapter is also properly viewed as an extension of the poverty estimates reported in (Bhalla, 2003c, 2004a). Bhalla (2003c) documented how World Bank data and poverty measurement methods (i.e. using survey, not national account means) indicated that the Millennium Development Goals of reducing poverty to 15 per cent of the developing country population by 2015 had already been reached—and reached at about the same time as the goals were being formulated in 2000. Bhalla (2004a) then documented how some of the important parameters of World Bank poverty calculations (e.g. growth in per capita consumption between 1987 and 1998) could *not be reproduced* by the country specific data on survey means made available by the World Bank on its website.[7]

Given this inaccuracy, there is a need to develop alternative estimates of world poverty according to survey means not suffering from World Bank "adjustments." Several agencies now publish estimates of both survey means and distributions, two essential ingredients in the calculation of poverty. WIDER, in particular, provides detailed estimates of distributions.[8] This paper uses data from all available sources to construct three estimates of poverty: (i) the World Bank method with only World Bank data; (ii) the World Bank method with all available data; and (iii) an alternative method also using all available data.[9]

This new method incorporates *all* the characteristics of survey data except one, the noisy and declining character of survey capture: the ratio of household survey means to national account means (S/NA). This method forces the ratio of the survey mean to national accounts mean to be *constant* and reflect the value obtained in an arbitrary year, chosen to be 1987 for all the countries. The reason this year was chosen was because generally, for most countries, the survey capture ratio started to decline somewhat sharply after the mid-1980s. A declining survey to national accounts ratio means that the growth rate in survey consumption is most likely understated, and understated by the percentage decline in the survey to national accounts ratio. If the S/NA is understated, then absolute poverty is overstated.

This new method allows the S/NA to be different across countries, but to stay constant within a country, and constant at its 1987 value or if a survey was not conducted in that year to be constant at the value of the latest survey prior to 1987. The *distribution* of consumption, used here, by the World Bank, Sala-i-Martín, etc. are all similar, if not identical, and are so because they originate from the same source, household surveys; unlike for survey means, researchers have generally refrained from "adjusting" data on distributions.

The three methods yield differing estimates of poverty, but strikingly, the strong results that emerge are that, regardless of the method chosen: developing country poverty in 2005 was already close to the MDG goal of 15 per cent for 2015; world poverty today is essentially about poverty in Africa; and the World Bank estimates of poverty in India seem to be gross overestimates, and estimates not corroborated by other researchers or institutions (for example, the official Indian government estimate for poverty in India, *for the same poverty line* as that used by the World Bank, is about *7 percentage points lower* in 1993/4).

Given this overwhelming evidence in favor of significant poverty reduction in the formerly poorest part of the world, Asia, and especially given the magnitude of poverty reduction in two large countries, India and China, this paper argues that the time has come to raise the decades-old poverty line from $1 a day (1985 PPP prices) to a poverty line significantly higher, around $2.16 per capita per day in 2005 prices.

The plan of the chapter is as follows. The second section provides an overview of the data used in generating poverty estimates. This section also documents that the World Bank poverty line of PPP$1.08 in 1993 prices is exactly equal to the government of India poverty line developed in 1973–4. This equivalence is an important input in documenting the exaggeration present in World Bank poverty estimates. The same poverty line should yield the same level of poverty; but for India, as just noted, the World Bank, inexplicably, has a poverty level that is 7 percentage points higher. The following section analyzes other reasons for different poverty estimates; in particular, the overestimation in poverty caused by the rather slow rate of consumption growth revealed by means based on household surveys, a decline not corroborated by trends in an alternative estimate of consumption, namely the national accounts. The systematic nature of the decline in S/NA should prohibit a blind acceptance of survey means; hence, the need to develop an estimate of growth in survey means.

The fourth section emphasizes the role played by the clustering or congestion of people close to the poverty line; different degrees of this congestion affect interpretation of poverty trends, and interpretation of how good (or bad) economic growth, or initial inequality, has been in reducing poverty. The magnitude of the poverty decline is shown to be independent of initial inequality.

The next section presents estimates of poverty for different time periods and different regions of the world. This section shows that using official, namely government, data and a constant S/NA ratio, and all other parameters the same as the World Bank, world poverty in 2005 is reduced from the World Bank estimate of 970 million to less than 500 million.

The sixth section examines the data on national poverty lines in the world, and concludes that the world poverty line of $1.08 a day is too low. With development, poverty is reduced, and the world's perception of poverty has moved away from absolute poverty to a notion of relative poverty. Most of the developing world, except sub-Saharan Africa, is in that transition mode; hence, time for the aid community to adjust and raise the standard for being poor—and raise it to PPP$1.70 per capita per day in 1993 prices, or $2.16 per capita per day in 2005 prices. The final section provides a conclusion.

Data, methods, and results: an overview

The study of poverty, and its determinants, requires that definitions of three important variables be explicit, and clear. The three variables are poverty, the distribution of consumption (inequality), and growth in per capita consumption. There are several definitions of *poverty*, but the one used here is the head-count ratio: the fraction of the population whose per capita expenditures (or income) are less than, or equal to, a pre-defined level of expenditures given by a "poverty line."

Inequality can be measured by several indices (share of expenditures of the bottom 20 per cent, the ratio of mean expenditures of the bottom 20 relative to the top 20 per cent, the Gini index, etc). All of these are aggregate indices—the point of departure of our analysis is that what matters for the analysis of poverty is not aggregate inequality but inequality *at (or close to) the poverty line*.

Differences in definitions of *growth* and differences in sources of data for growth (and levels) cause very large differences in estimates of levels and trends in poverty. There are, before modifications, *two* sources for consumption means—that obtained from national accounts (NA) data and that obtained from household surveys (S). There are natural differences between the two sources because of differences in definition, coverage (e.g. institutions are part of NA but not of surveys[10]), measurement (survey consumption is measured directly while NA consumption is often a residual), and prices. These differences fail to account for more than a small fraction of the two means, about 5 per cent or so. The differences in *growth* of survey or NA consumption are even smaller (since the differences in levels are likely to persist).

However, there are other problems with World Bank world poverty estimates, in addition to differences between NA adjusted (for definitions and comparability) and survey means. These problems arise because the World Bank adjusts *survey* means for some countries, particularly for the two largest poverty countries, India and China. The same source for distribution and the mean (for example, National Sample Survey, NSS, data for India) should ordinarily yield the same estimate for absolute poverty. For 1993/4, the World Bank estimate of all India poverty is 42 per cent;[11] the government of India estimate for the *same* year, using the *same* NSS data, is a considerably lower 36 per cent; on a population of 900 million, that is an *extra 54 million* people deemed poor in India by the World Bank. The divergence increases for the survey year 1999/2000. Again, for the same poverty line, the World Bank estimates 36 per cent poor, in comparison, the government of India estimate is 26 per cent—that is an extra 100 million poor in India, and the world.

It can be argued that the difference arises because the World Bank uses the international poverty line of PPP$1.08 a day, 1993 PPP prices, while the government of India uses its own national poverty line with a 1973 base year. *But for the 1993/4 NSS survey year, and hence for all years, the $1.08 and the Indian poverty line are identical.* This identity holds for all other years since the two organizations update the poverty lines by inflation, and will hold until either the Indian government, or the World Bank, changes its definition of the absolute poverty line. Bhalla (2002b) argues that a large country, namely India (and a country with the most research on absolute poverty), might have been the basis for the world poverty line; the identity in Indian and World Bank poverty lines may not be a coincidence.

Equivalence between Indian national poverty line and $1.08 per capita per day

The Indian poverty line is defined in terms of thirty days of consumption and in 1993/4 was equal to 206 rupees (INR) in the rural areas and INR286 in the urban areas, or an all India average of INR227 per capita for thirty days. This yields a per day average of INR7.57. The World Bank consumption PPP exchange rate for 1993 is given as INR7.02 yielding the national Indian poverty line, in PPP 1993 terms, of INR7.57/7.02 or $1.08.[12] *This number is exactly the same as the international poverty line.*

Different methods of estimating survey means

The non-reproduction of the poverty estimates for India by the World Bank is one source of difference between our and World Bank poverty figures. A larger difference is caused by the trend in the survey to national accounts ratio. Survey based means (and the implied growth) do not account for the possibility that the survey to national accounts ratio might diverge significantly for different years *for the same country*. The emphasis on the same country is important because differences in methods of data gathering, etc., can and do cause significant differences in S/NA across countries. But for the same country, the S/NA ratio is expected to move in a narrow range across time, as it was for most of the countries of the world until the mid-1980s.

A declining S/NA trend means that the mean survey consumption level declines (relative to a constant S/NA) by 1 per cent for each 1 per cent decline in the S/NA ratio. The headcount ratio of poverty, *ceteris paribus*, increases by approximately 0.5 percentage point with each 1 percentage point decline in the S/NA ratio. To correct for this tendency, our method is to "impute" a survey mean. Recall that the traditional method of estimating survey means was to make them equal to national account means. Our procedure is to adjust the survey mean to a survey mean adjusted for unusual declines (or increases) in the S/NA ratio. This adjusted mean is likely to be closer to the underlying reality than the measured survey mean.

Divergence between survey mean and national accounts mean: an example from India

The trend in S/NA is on the basis of surveyed households. Divergence between this and the "true" mean can arise due to two factors: underreporting of consumption, and non-survey of a large consumption set of households. What might such magnitudes be? In Bhalla (2002b) the issue of greater under-reporting by the rich was examined in detail for one large poor country, India, using its household (NSS) survey for 1993/4 and national accounts data for the same year. The method was to "blow up" the survey based estimates to the NA means for eighteen major consumption items. This means that if a person consumed x per cent of the survey mean, she would consume the same x per cent of the NA mean. If she does not consume potatoes in the surveys, no potatoes are allocated to her in the (adjusted) estimate. If a person does not consume TVs, or cars, none of the "missing" TVs is allocated to this person. This method estimates an adjusted consumption estimate for each household and therefore allows for percentile distributions of the adjusted consumption estimate to be derived. The mean of the survey estimate for each item is "forced" to equal the mean NA estimate for the same item; hence, by construction, the survey mean is made equal to the national accounts mean.

The results were revealing—the bottom 40 per cent of the population understated their expenditures by 29 per cent while the average household understated its expenditure by 34 per cent. The top 20 per cent (the rich) understated their expenditures by 41 per cent. Two conclusions are relevant—first, even the poor understate their true consumption, an occurrence documented by the fact that even for food items, expenditures are increasingly being understated in the surveys. Second, there is a large 12 percentage point gap between the understatement of the rich and the poor. However, since the adjustments are made with reference to *average* expenditures, the "error" between the rich and the poor has only a small magnitude—only 5 per cent. In other words, if India is a typical poor country, the "error" made by using NA per capita expenditures rather than survey expenditures is only around 5 per cent at a particular *point in time*,[13] and almost 0 per cent for changes over time. To reiterate: the matching of survey consumption with national accounts consumption, often involving a large adjustment in the former, fails to reveal any large differences in the magnitude of underestimation between the rich and the poor, at least for five survey years for India (1983, 1987/8, 1993/4, 1999/2000, and 2004/5).

The survey mean does not incorporate the possibility that some rich people are *missed* by the surveys (due to high walls, security guards, etc.). By how much would the survey mean be lower than the NA mean in this instance? One plausible, though not likely, estimate is that the survey fails to sample anyone in the top 2 per cent of the population. Since most of the top 2 per cent reside in the four major cities of India, this assumption means that *no* top 2 per cent household was sampled in the four major cities of Delhi, Mumbai, Calcutta, and Chennai. The expenditure of this top 2 per cent in developing countries is not likely to be more than 10 per cent of total consumption. If the extreme assumption is made that *all* of these 20 million top individuals (2 per cent of the population) were missed by the household surveys in India, it would mean that the S/NA ratio for developing countries should still be close to 90 per cent. In 2004/5, the survey to NA ratio in India was less than 50 per cent.

The consumption share of the top 1 and 2 per cent of the population in India in 1999/2000 (NSS survey) was 7.5 and 3.5 per cent, respectively. This yields 11 per cent as the total share of the top 2 per cent and fits in with the conjecture above. But the argument can be made (and is made!) that the surveyed households are not the "true" top 2 per cent, or at least a large number are not. Banerjee and Piketty (2005) use Indian tax return data to estimate the shares of the top 1 per cent of the population for various years between1952 and 2000. They find the *income* share of the top 1 per cent was 8.5 per cent in 1993/4 and 9 per cent in 1999/2000, for a mean level of INR230,000 for the top 1 per cent in the latter year. But these shares seem to be underestimates. One indication of this possibility is that the consumption share is in the same ballpark. The second indication is provided by estimates of GDP and private income (personal disposable income plus income taxes). For the same year, the two levels are INR19,520 billion and INR14,800 billion, respectively. The population in 1999/2000 was 1 billion, which yields the share of the top 1 per cent at 11.8 per cent of GDP and 15.5 per cent of private income. Simple calculations suggest that such large shares for the top 1 per cent are inconsistent with shares of income observed for the fourth and fifth quintile in India (about 22 and 50 per cent, respectively).

Taking *all* the factors responsible for differences in survey and NA means, including non-coverage of the super rich and larger understatement by the surveyed rich, a very conservative assumption is that household surveys (in a poor country like India) can be expected to miss out on no more than 10–15 per cent of total expenditures in any given year. In contrast, the measured survey to consumption ratio in India was 49 per cent in 2004/5, down from 55 per cent in 1999/2000 and 62 per cent in 1993/4. These are large gaps, gaps that cannot be explained by assumptions of missing out the rich living in gated communities etc. Further, the underestimation is across all commodities, including and especially food. The rich, even with their wealthy incomes, cannot consume all of this unmeasured food, or even most of it, or even more than a small fraction.

A rough break-up of this 15 per cent understatement is that two-thirds of this difference is likely due to definitional and other reasons, and one-third (or 5 percentage points) may be due to extra understatement by the rich, extra with reference to the understatement of the average consumer. This implies that around 85 to 90 per cent is a reasonable estimate of the survey to national accounts ratio; i.e. to make a conversion from national account estimate to the "correct" survey estimate, one should discount or reduce the NA estimate by around 10 to 15 per cent. Survey to NA ratios of 70, 60, or 50 per cent cannot therefore be accurate, given all that we know of the limits to human consumption, especially with regard to food consumption. A lower bound of S/NA is likely to be about 80 per cent; anything below this number is likely to mean that expenditures of the poor are actually being underreported—i.e. household surveys are likely to be overstating poverty for such countries.

Declining S/NA observed for most countries

The breakdown in S/NA in the late 1980s can be illustrated with data for the ratio for a few countries. In India, the S/NA was 78.2 per cent in 1977/8, 71.2 per cent in 1987/8, 55.5 per cent in 1999/2000, and 48.7 per cent in 2004/5. For China, the ratio declined from 91 per cent in 1981 to 82.2 per cent in 2001. For Korea, the ratio was 84.8 per cent in 1971 and 60.3 per cent in 1992. Out of seventy-four non-industrialized countries with more than one expenditure (or income) household survey in the post-1980 period, more than two-thirds (fifty) witnessed a decline between the first and last survey post-1980; only twenty-four witnessed an increase.[14]

Figure 4.1a plots the pattern of the S/NAs for India and China. It is plotted on a dual scale and suggests both that declines have been steep for the two countries (India is larger) and that the *timing* of the decline has been very similar. On average, the S/NA for developing countries declined by about 10 percentage points in the decade 1991–2001 (Figure 4.1b). Given that for the average developing country the S/NA was 82 per cent in 1991, a 10 percentage point decline in subsequent years translates into a decline of 12 per cent in estimated survey consumption, i.e. on average, 12 per cent of the gain in mean

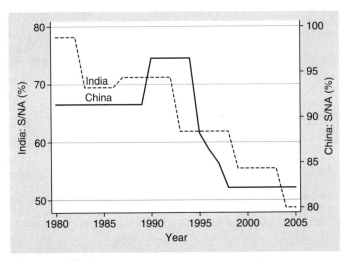

Figure 4.1a Survey to national accounts ratio, India and China, 1980–2005 (%)

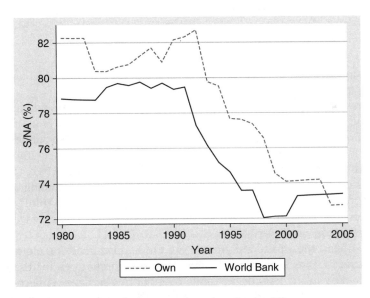

Figure 4.1b Survey to national accounts ratio: two estimates (%)

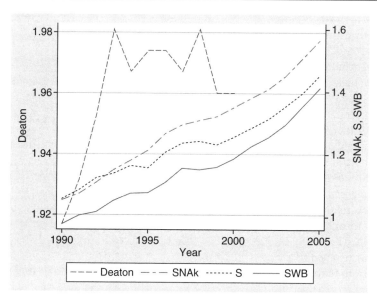

Figure 4.2 Mean consumption in the developing world (per capita per day), 1990–2005

Note: SWB refers to World Bank method and data; S refers to data from all available surveys; SNAk represents the method where the survey to national accounts ratio is kept constant at the observed 1987 level for each country; Deaton represents the data included in Deaton's chapter in this volume.

consumption of the average (or poor person) is "missing" or *unaccounted for in survey expenditures*.

Figure 4.2 documents the evolution of mean expenditures for non-OECD countries (the survey to national accounts ratios reported above are derived from these means) as calculated by Deaton (Chapter 7 in this volume, figure 7.3),[15] by the World Bank (Chen and Ravallion), and by us. The numbers are reported in logs so percentage changes can be read easily from the charts. Data are presented for developing economies, namely economies excluding those of the Western developed countries and those of Eastern European and FSU.

Deaton (Ch. 7) reports survey based growth for non-OECD countries to be 2.8 per cent a year for the ten-year period 1990–2000 (Table 7.3); from his Figure 7.3, we obtain the annualized growth rate to be approximately 0.4 per cent a year (survey means, consumption where possible). Deaton's estimates suggest that the peak in the level of per capita consumption in developing countries was reached in 1993; his three-year growth, 1990–3, is a high 4.4 per cent; his data shows the same peak being reached twice—1993 and 1998; and in his data, over the three-year period, 1998–2000, the average consumption level in 2000 (a recovery year) was more than 20 per cent *lower* than in 1998 (an East Asian crisis year). Thus, all the decadal growth (and more) in Deaton's calculations seems to have occurred in just three years, 1990–3. Both the World Bank and our estimates reveal a slow and gradual increase with some acceleration post-1999.

What these data suggest is that some method needs to be found to adjust the survey means for different countries since levels of S/NA at 40, 50, and 60 per cent, etc. are not helpful in assessing the nature and magnitude of poverty decline in developing countries. Concern is rightly centered on the relative roles of inequality change and consumption growth in affecting poverty; unfortunately, large changes in S/NA introduce a considerable amount of measurement error in poverty calculations. This measurement is larger than all estimates of inequality change or consumption growth.

A suggested method of deriving consumption growth estimates unaffected by *changes* in S/NA is as follows. If growth in survey means is equalized to growth in NA means, then the data can be left uncorrupted by declines (or increases) in S/NA. This is the estimate of survey means reported in this paper. By keeping S/NA constant to its observed 1987 value, one obtains a growth rate in consumption that is a mixture of survey and national accounts data; i.e. the original *level* of consumption from the surveys is adjusted by the *growth* rate in consumption obtained from NA data. The growth rate in per capita consumption is thus made equal to the NA per capita consumption growth rate.

None of the objections to the use of NA consumption data (it is not representative, it is a derived estimate, etc.) apply to the use of *growth* rate in NA consumption. The year 1987 was chosen as the "constant S/NA" year, partly because the trend decline in S/NA seems to have accelerated, in many countries around the world, around the late 1980s. Selection of a different year than 1987 would not change any of the results on growth in means, but would change the results on the level of poverty in any given year. The choice of 1987 is appropriate because it is near the end of the constancy of S/NA and the beginning of the breakdown as indicated by Figures 4.1 and 4.2.

The irrelevance of initial inequality for poverty reduction

Before proceeding to the estimation of poverty findings in the next section, a few comments on what we should expect with respect to poverty decline over the last two decades or so. There has been a lot of discussion about how inequality has hampered the decline in poverty. Indeed, one of the most consistent "findings" in the recent development literature is that poverty reduction is greater, *ceteris paribus*, in more initially equal economies. The reasoning is assumed to be straightforward: lower inequality means a higher share of consumption at a point in time for any given group, say the bottom 20 per cent; this implies that a higher share of the same growth will accrue to the poor in the more equal country; this "higher" growth means a higher magnitude of poverty reduction; hence, the simple conclusion that a more equal distribution of consumption is desirable for poverty reduction. Several documents have offered this logic to advocate a more equal distribution of consumption as a *desirable* starting point in discussions of poverty reduction, including WDR 1990, WDR 2000/1, Ravallion (2001), Klasen (2001), and Datt and Ravallion (2002). Some excerpts from the first and last study illustrate this belief:

> A 10 per cent increase in the incomes of the poor in Bangladesh and India would reduce the incidence of poverty by about 7 percentage points. *Where the distribution of income is more unequal*, as in Venezuela and Brazil, the corresponding figure would be only 3 percentage points (WDR 1990, p. 47, my emphasis).

> Household survey data for developing countries suggest that initial distribution does matter to how much the poor share in rising average incomes; higher initial inequality tends to reduce the impact of growth on absolute poverty. By the same token, higher inequality diminishes the adverse impact on the poor of overall contraction (Datt and Ravallion, 2002).

It turns out that this reasoning is false, and this was demonstrated as early as 1964 by US economist Locke Anderson. He showed that initial inequality was *irrelevant* for poverty reduction. Using data on US poverty, he made the (graphical) point that the rather small decline observed in US poverty in the early 1960s, despite rapid growth in per capita incomes and not much change in the distribution of incomes, was not at all surprising and had a lot to do with "congestion" of the poor near the poverty line.[16]

> For any of these groups, an increase in median income of about 2.5 per cent would reduce the incidence of poverty by 1 percentage point, judging from the slope of the central portion of Figure IV...This analysis suggests that *movements along the poverty curve* corresponding to the existing income distribution will imply a declining rate of reduction of poverty (Anderson, 1964, my emphasis).

Bhalla (2002) summarizes this movement along the poverty curve as the shape of the distribution elasticity or SDE—"a quasi-elasticity that yields the total arithmetic change in the headcount ratio of poverty that can be expected with a 1 per cent change in mean expenditures of individuals clustered around the poverty line." Though Anderson does not offer any empirical values for this congestion, our estimated value for SDE for the US in the early 1960s is around 0.15; a 10 per cent change in average incomes of the poor in the US would affect the headcount ratio by only 1.5 percentage points.

Anderson's important work was ignored by development practitioners (perhaps because it was on a developed economy, US). Thus, discussion of the impact of the congestion at the poverty line on future poverty reductions remained absent until 1990 when the World Bank report on Malaysia was published (see Bhalla and Kharas, 1991; the 1990 *World Development Report* also highlighted its importance—neither study was aware of Anderson's work). These two reports, however, did not offer any theoretical or empirical estimates of SDE.

What the SDE–growth relationship suggests (as per the US example) is that there can be robust growth in incomes of the poor and yet very little poverty reduction. The following admittedly unrealistic but heuristic example is illustrative. Assume the poverty line is 100 and that most of the poor (the center of gravity) are clustered around a mean income of 50, and that the standard deviation of the incomes of the poor is 20. An increase in mean consumption of 10 per cent will have a near-zero impact on the headcount ratio. Now assume that the mean shifts to 95 and the standard deviation is only 10. Now a 10 per cent increase in mean consumption will lead to a very large decline in the headcount ratio. If the poor are now congested at a level close to the poverty line, say 99, the elasticity will be close to infinity. So with the same growth in mean consumption of the poor, one obtains varying elasticities.

Yet another example, this time perhaps more realistic, explains the workings of the SDE on poverty. Growth in expenditures of the poor is the sum of growth from two sources: the mean growth in expenditures of the entire population (this is the popular "headline" growth variable); and the growth in the *share* of expenditures of the poor (change in inequality but only for those close to the poverty line). Thus, if mean expenditures increase by (log) 10 per cent and inequality, measured as the share in total expenditures of the population close to the *poverty line*, worsens by (log) 10 per cent, then there will be no change in net consumption of the poor, and therefore little change in the headcount ratio of poverty.

What these examples substantiate is that initial inequality is *irrelevant* for future poverty reduction. This is because the *change in poverty* is a function of the *change in consumption at the poverty line*. If inequality does not change, then growth cannot have a differential impact. When inequality stays constant, the same amount of growth *will result in the same increase in the consumption of the bottom 20 or bottom 40 per cent or the top 1 per cent*. So if a person was poor in 1987 in unequal Brazil or equal India and consuming $1 a day, and if both societies experienced a 10 per cent change in average consumption, and in both societies inequality did not change, then in both societies the poor person would be consuming $1.10 in 1998, and in both societies the person would be non-poor in 1998; so initial inequality is irrelevant for poverty reduction, as far as a direct (independent of the effect on growth) impact is concerned.

What happened to poverty and growth in 1950–2005?

The theoretical and empirical background provided in the previous sections (the importance of declines in S/NA, the irrelevance of initial inequality, etc.) can yield an informed perspective on the ongoing fierce debate on what *actually*

Table 4.1. World poverty, 1950–2005 (% of population)

Year	Population (million)	$1.08 Poverty Line			$2.16 Poverty Line		
		SWB	S	SNAk	SWB	S	SNAk
1950	1,742	69.7	63.3	66.2	89.1	86.8	87.8
1960	2,120	65.9	59.3	62.5	86.6	84.3	85.2
1970	2,691	57.4	49.7	53.4	82.5	79.6	80.8
1981	3,419	48.2	43.0	44.1	76.1	73.1	73.4
1985	3,716	38.5	35.6	35.0	70.9	68.8	68.4
1990	4,113	33.6	28.6	29.7	67.7	64.0	64.0
1993	4,342	28.9	26.1	23.1	63.8	60.9	58.7
1995	4,492	28.2	24.2	20.6	62.4	59.5	56.1
2000	4,862	25.0	21.6	16.0	57.5	54.1	47.3
2004	5,151	18.6	17.9	9.9	50.4	48.6	40.1
2005	5,225	15.2	14.7	8.4	47.9	45.9	37.2

happened to poverty over the past three decades. There is the authoritative voice of the World Bank, the official referee on poverty, which says that the decline has been painfully, and surprisingly, slow. There is the voice of dissent, the voice of those who argue that the World Bank figures are erroneous because it has mismeasured the growth in consumption and therefore underestimated the decline in poverty. Determining who is right in this debate can be treacherous to one's view of economists, and statisticians. Given this minefield of a background, a useful path for analysis is to first isolate the facts. Statistics presented here for growth and poverty decline cover three different measures of consumption growth (the differences in inequality, or distribution, is of minor importance)—World Bank data (Survey World Bank, SWB), all available data (Survey data, S), and survey to national accounts ratio kept constant at 1987 levels (SNAk).

There should theoretically be little difference in the poverty estimates yielded by the two straightforward unadjusted means and common distribution estimates provided by SWB and S—as shown in Table 4.1, the difference was as much as 6 percentage points in 1990 though in recent years this has lowered. In 1990 we believe the World Bank versus the alternate all data series would have led to an overstatement of global absolute poverty of 350 million; in 2004, the overstatement is a 100 million. Our S/NA constant series shows poverty to be sharply lower than these two series—1,171 million in 1990 (SWB estimate 1,409) and 464 million in 2004 (SWB estimate 760 million).

Substantial poverty decline since 1981

Figures 4.3 and 4.4 document the enormous decline that has taken place in world poverty since 1981. The World Bank acknowledges that world poverty

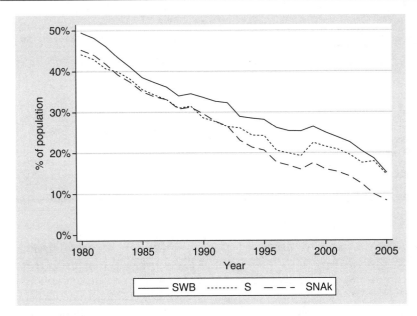

Figure 4.3a Size of poor population, developing world, 1980–2005 (% of population, $1.08 PL)

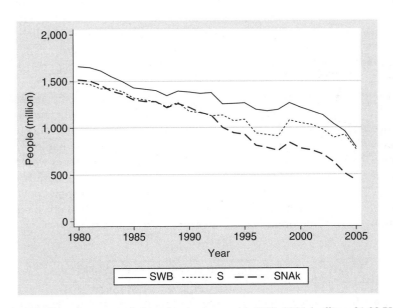

Figure 4.3b Size of poor population, developing world, 1980–2005 (million, $1.08 PL)

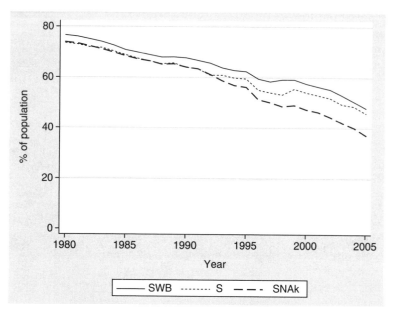

Figure 4.4a Size of poor population, developing world, 1980–2005 (% of population, $2.16 PL)

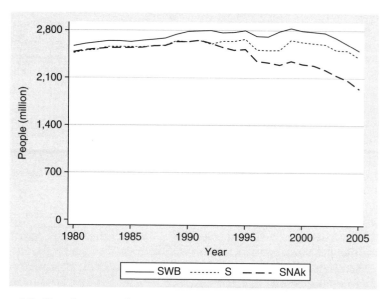

Figure 4.4b Size of poor population, developing world, 1980–2005 (million, $2.16 PL)

Note: S refers to collection of poverty non-World Bank website data (e.g. WIDER); SWB refers to World Bank data obtained from its website; SNAk is the survey to national accounts ratio kept constant at its 1987 value for each country.

has declined from 40 to 21 per cent from 1981 to 2001; our reproduction yields estimates of 48 per cent and 24 per cent in those two years. The more accurate SNAk measure of per capita consumption has poverty declining from 44 to 15 per cent at the $1.08 poverty line, and from 73 to 46 per cent at the $2.16 poverty line. The percentage point decline, regardless of source or poverty line, is a reduction of some 20 to 30 percentage points. The fast pace of developing economy growth since 2001 (including sub-Saharan Africa), has meant a further decline in poverty to 8.4 per cent and 37.2 per cent (at the $1.08 and $2.16 poverty lines respectively) in 2005. These statistics suggest that the time has come to raise the world poverty line from its $1.08 level—a subject explored in the next section.

Mean growth from national accounts, poverty from surveys

Until the early 1990s, the conventional method for estimating poverty was to obtain the distribution from household surveys and impose the mean of per capita consumption obtained from national accounts data. In the 1990s, starting with the World Bank World Development Report 1990 (WDR 1990), the method changed to obtaining poverty from survey means and survey distributions. But in discussions about the impact of growth on poverty, the conventional procedure still remains to use *survey* based poverty measures of poverty and *national account* (NA) based measures of growth (e.g. WDR, 1990; Dollar and Kraay, 2001; Datt and Ravallion, 2002; Besley and Burgess, 2003).

This questionable procedure of inferring survey based poverty trends from NA estimates of consumption growth was dubbed the "Peter-Paul" problem in Bhalla (2002b)—using survey based poverty and growth from national accounts was akin to using Peter's income to determine Paul's poverty. There is only one consistent method of deriving or estimating the impact of growth on poverty—average growth should be calculated from the same source as the growth in individual incomes.

When the growth rate of survey means is close to the growth rate of national account means, S/NA stays constant. This is what was observed in most of the world prior to the 1980s. The fact that S/NA is less than unity is not disturbing, and nor is that it has declined. But the magnitude of the level significantly below unity and the pace of this decline pose serious problems for analysis of trends in poverty.

Assuming that the NA *growth* rate is correct, declining S/NA means that poverty is overstated—the more the decline, the greater the overstatement. To reiterate, the SNAk measure uses the same growth rate for each country as the national accounts, at least since 1987. In the case of India, the decline of S/NA from 71 to 49 per cent (1987 to 2004/5) is a decline of 35 per cent, or an overstatement of poverty of about 20 percentage points.

Regardless of the method of poverty calculation, the estimated figures for 2005 are revealing. They show the following levels of $1.08 poverty for the three different means and methods of poverty estimation, SWB, S, and SNAk measures— 15.2 per cent, 14.7 per cent, and 8.4 per cent respectively. This means that about the time the World Bank and associated international organizations like the UN were getting serious about the Millennium Development Goal of 15 per cent by 2015, the world had already reached that level a decade earlier. This highlights one of the major points of this chapter—it is time to raise the poverty line.

Existing poverty lines: too low

According to our estimates of world poverty, "only" 20 per cent of the world population was poor in 2001 (survey means) and only 15 per cent was poor in the same year if the declining survey to national accounts ratio is frozen for each country at its 1987 value. Even the "high" World Bank estimate of poverty in 2001 is "only" 23.6 per cent poor in 2001, and 19 per cent in 2004. The previous sections have documented that a large part of the difference in our reproduction of World Bank data and World Bank data arises from the unusually high World Bank poverty numbers for India—almost 2 percentage points of global poverty. Little difference was obtained between ours and World Bank estimates for sub-Saharan Africa.

These low poverty estimates are based on a very low level of living, hence the term absolute poverty. What these low levels of numbers signify is that the world poverty problem is different today—it is more of a relative poverty problem than a problem of absolute poverty. Of course, almost half of sub-Saharan Africa is absolutely poor, but this continent contains only about 300 million absolute poor; and most of the rest of the developing world is not absolutely poor.

Latin America and the MENA region (Middle East and North Africa) have for more than a decade now recorded absolute $-a-day poverty levels in single digits. For both these regions, the domestic local poverty lines are above $2 a day. The former Soviet Union and Eastern Europe economies do not have much $1-a-day poverty, which leads one to the conclusion that international agencies should start developing a *relative* measure of poverty.

Despite rapid per capita growth, the world poverty line has not shifted since the original $1-a-day poverty line based on 1985 PPP prices. Indeed, the 1993 PPP poverty line of $1.08 a day, deemed to be the "equivalent" of $1 a day, 1985 prices, entailed a reduction in the poverty line of almost 22 per cent (see Bhalla, 2002, for details). US inflation was close to 30 per cent between 1985 and 1993; since US is the numéraire in PPP calculations, it follows that international price inflation was close to 30 per cent. Hence, $1 a day in 1985 prices is approximately equal to $1.30 a day in 1993 PPP prices.

It is necessary to re-evaluate what it means to be poor; this, by implication, means that it is necessary to raise the international poverty line. What should

Table 4.2a. Poverty headcount ratio, 1981–2005 (%, $1.08 PL)

	Year				
Region	1981	1990	1993	2001	2005
World Bank data and varying S/NA					
Sub-Saharan Africa	43	45	46	40	37
South Asia	60	45	40	36	24
East Asia	58	34	25	18	6
Central Asia	4	4	13	9	6
Latin America	13	15	14	11	10
MENA	6	4	2	4	3
World	48	34	29	24	15
All available data and varying S/NA					
Sub-Saharan Africa	38	45	41	39	36
South Asia	45	27	37	26	22
East Asia	56	32	21	16	4
Central Asia	5	5	9	8	5
Latin America	14	20	19	17	15
MENA	6	4	1	4	3
World	43	29	26	21	15
All available data and constant S/NA					
Sub-Saharan Africa	38	45	42	41	37
South Asia	49	26	25	12	5
East Asia	56	35	22	12	1
Central Asia	5	5	8	7	5
Latin America	14	20	19	16	15
MENA	6	4	2	2	2
World	44	30	23	15	8

Sources: World Bank; WIDER; author's own calculations.

the new international poverty line be? A common, and correct, presumption is that poverty lines should rise with economic development. Ahluwalia et al. (1979) present the first set of world poverty estimates, calculated for 1975. Since then, per capita consumption in the developing world has more than doubled. The elasticity of the poverty line with respect to average consumption is 0.63 as illustrated by the following regression for ninety-two traditional developing countries in 1993:

$$\log(\text{poverty line}) = -0.15 + 0.63 * \log(\text{per capita consumption})$$

Data for 92 countries; $R^2 = 0.65$; t–statistic(log consumption) $= 12.04$

If the $1 a day in 1985 prices is deemed as the appropriate poverty line, then the new poverty line twenty years later in 2005 prices should be higher in real terms, and higher by the amount indicated by the above regression. Mean per capita consumption in the developing world in 2005 was 52 per cent (or log 42 percent) higher than in 1993. Given a log elasticity of 0.63, the new (log) increase in the poverty line should be 0.63*42 or log 26 per cent higher. Thus, the $1.30 per capita per day in 1993 prices needs to be raised by 30 per cent

Table 4.2b. Number of poor, 1981–2005 (million, $1.08 PL)

	Year				
Region	1981	1990	1993	2001	2005
World Bank data and varying S/NA					
Sub-Saharan Africa	170	227	255	271	275
South Asia	551	499	473	490	348
East Asia	841	567	447	336	112
Central Asia	2	2	7	5	3
Latin America	47	64	64	59	58
MENA	15	14	6	14	11
World	1,626	1,373	1,252	1,176	807
All available data and varying S/NA					
Sub-Saharan Africa	150	226	227	262	267
South Asia	419	302	438	361	324
East Asia	816	544	365	299	82
Central Asia	2	3	5	4	3
Latin America	52	87	87	87	86
MENA	14	13	5	16	12
World	1,453	1,174	1,126	1,029	774
All available data and constant S/NA					
Sub-Saharan Africa	150	225	232	274	275
South Asia	454	293	289	165	79
East Asia	816	595	383	234	10
Central Asia	2	3	4	4	3
Latin America	52	87	89	86	84
MENA	14	13	5	7	6
World	1,489	1,216	1,002	770	456

Sources: World Bank; WIDER; author's own calculations

(equivalent of log 26 per cent). Given an initial poverty line of $1 in 1985 PPP or $1.30 in 1993 PPP, this yields $1.69 as the new poverty line in 1993 prices. Between 1993 and 2005, the US GDP price deflator has increased by 28 per cent, which yields an equivalent line in 2005 PPP$ of 2.16 (1.69*1.28). The international community has been using $1.08 and $2.16 as the poverty lines in constant 1993 international prices. It is suggested that $2.16 be the new poverty line in PPP 2005 prices.

Latin America has been using a > $2-a-day poverty line for some time; the average country specific poverty line in Latin America is a high PPP$5.6 a day; in sub-Saharan Africa, the average country specific line is about $1.6. The region with poverty lines needing revision is the region with the fastest growth, Asia. Figure 4.5—which is based on the regression presented above—poignantly illustrates the large existing gap between mean consumption levels and poverty lines in Asia, as well as the rest of the developing world. It is apparent that a majority of countries—and especially China, Indonesia, and India—had in 1993 poverty lines that were far below their *predicted* poverty lines.

Poverty also is relative. Who the Malaysians (or Argentineans) consider poor will be considered middle class in most parts of Asia. It does not make the poor

Table 4.3a. Poverty headcount ratio, 1981–2005 (%, $2.16 PL)

	Year				
Region	1981	1990	1993	2001	2005
World Bank data and varying S/NA					
Sub-Saharan Africa	72	74	74	69	65
South Asia	92	88	85	82	73
East Asia	87	70	62	48	35
Central Asia	20	21	36	23	16
Latin America	31	34	33	30	28
MENA	28	19	18	22	18
World	76	68	64	56	48
All available data and varying S/NA					
Sub-Saharan Africa	67	72	69	66	62
South Asia	86	77	84	74	70
East Asia	84	67	56	43	31
Central Asia	16	18	27	27	17
Latin America	34	42	41	37	36
MENA	26	19	16	23	18
World	73	64	61	53	46
All available data and constant S/NA ratio					
Sub-Saharan Africa	67	72	70	70	66
South Asia	88	76	74	59	47
East Asia	84	68	57	38	26
Central Asia	16	18	25	20	14
Latin America	34	42	41	36	35
MENA	26	19	17	18	14
World	73	64	59	46	37

Sources: World Bank; WIDER; author's own calculations.

Korean any happier to know that several hundred million people are poorer in the rest of the world. Each country has its own poverty line to reflect these different country averages of standard of living. We have seen above that own poverty lines, especially in Asia, are falling behind the poverty lines which *should* be present. Asian and world poverty has declined significantly, and the concept of absolute poverty has receded. Today, absolute poverty in most parts of the developing world is relative; hence the need for a new, and higher, poverty line.

Conclusion

World poverty today (circa 2005) is primarily a sub-Saharan Africa problem. In that region, about half of the population exists on less than the very low absolute poverty line of $1 a day. The number of absolute poor in Africa is around 275 million. The major challenge for the world community is to bring this level of poverty down to Asian, Latin American, and Middle Eastern levels, i.e. less than 10 per cent poor.

Table 4.3b. Number of poor, 1981–2005 (million, $2.16 PL)

	Year				
Region	1981	1990	1993	2001	2005
World Bank data and varying S/NA					
Sub-Saharan Africa	281	376	408	463	477
South Asia	849	980	1,005	1,122	1,078
East Asia	1,259	1,179	1,096	912	689
Central Asia	9	10	19	13	10
Latin America	113	151	156	156	156
MENA	66	60	59	85	73
World	2,576	2,755	2,743	2,752	2,482
All available data and varying S/NA					
Sub-Saharan Africa	261	366	381	443	455
South Asia	798	861	990	1,023	1,037
East Asia	1,222	1,128	988	828	604
Central Asia	7	9	14	15	10
Latin America	125	185	190	196	198
MENA	62	59	52	88	76
World	2,475	2,609	2,615	2,593	2,379
All available data and constant S/NA					
Sub-Saharan Africa	261	365	387	467	483
South Asia	808	850	878	814	698
East Asia	1,222	1,141	1,003	722	504
Central Asia	7	9	13	11	8
Latin America	125	186	191	192	194
MENA	62	60	56	68	56
World	2,485	2,611	2,528	2,275	1,943

Sources: World Bank; WIDER; author's own calculations.

The rapid rates of growth experienced in most of the developing world over the last twenty-five years, and especially over the past ten, has brought about large declines in absolute poverty, for both the $1-and $2-a-day poverty lines. A striking feature of this development has been the improvement of inequality in the developing world, and this improvement has occurred for all the estimates of per capita consumption and distribution that exist. This is an intuitive result, and has occurred because the poorest and the most populous region in the world in 1980, Asia, has witnessed rapid progress. Such progress has been observed in the two giant economies, China and India; it has also occurred in Bangladesh, Indonesia, Laos, Pakistan, Thailand, and Vietnam. It is hard to find one nation in Asia that has fallen behind, though data are not available for the war-torn economy of Afghanistan or the closed economy of Myanmar.

The rapid decline in poverty, to levels unimaginable even a decade ago, means the time has come to revise upwards the absolute poverty line. This line has stayed constant for almost twenty-five years, and indeed was *lowered* when the World Bank changed this line from $1 a day, PPP 1985 prices to $1.08 a day, PPP 1993 prices. As happens in all countries, our notion of absolute poverty changes (increases) with the average level of development. These

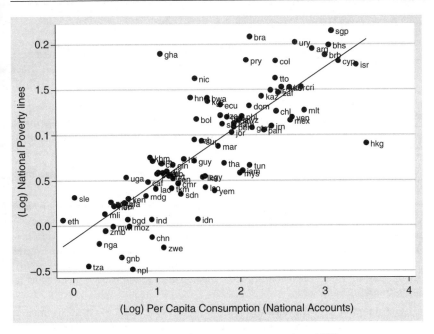

Figure 4.5 National poverty lines and per capita consumption, 1993

perceptions are changing, and a sign of success is that we are moving towards a notion of relative poverty. As a first approximation, it is suggested that we increase the international poverty line to $1.69 in 1993 PPP prices (or about $2.16 in 2005 PPP prices), a level some 45 per cent higher, in real terms, than the old $1.08 poverty line. Coincidentally, the world poor according to this new poverty line would be close to 35 per cent, a level that the world was dealing with at the much lower $1-a-day line in 1985.

On its way to recommending this new poverty line, this chapter also examined some old assumptions about the determinants of poverty. In particular, the question of whether and how initial inequality affects poverty decline was explicitly taken up. The answer to this is negative: there is no theoretical, or empirical, basis to think that initial inequality affects future poverty change. Since poverty depends on the congestion near the poverty line, the response of poverty decline is different for different poverty lines and different income levels. For example, in 1981, for the $1.08 poverty line, a 10 per cent increase in per capita expenditure would be expected to result in a 5.5 percentage point decline in absolute poverty; in 2005, the same growth would result in only a 3.5 percentage point decline. For the $2.16 poverty line, the corresponding responses are the reverse: 10 per cent growth in 1981 would have led to a poverty decline of 3.5 percentage points; today, that same growth would mean a larger, 5.1 percentage point decline.

137

Appendix

For calculation of poverty one needs three items of data—the distribution of consumption, the mean, and the poverty line. Countries undertake surveys only on a periodic basis, yet figures for individual country, and world poverty, are computed on an annual basis. How this is possible is explained below.

Poverty line: This is defined on the basis of 1993 PPP consumption exchange rates published by the World Bank.

Distribution of consumption: There are several sources of data on distribution, and prominent in this collection is the Deininger-Squire effort of compiling inequality data. This exercise has now been undertaken by WIDER and is the primary source of information on distribution. Poverty is defined on the basis of per capita consumption. Several countries around the world, and primarily in Latin America, have not undertaken any consumption survey. For such countries, the income distribution is taken to be equal to the consumption distribution.

Mean consumption: This is available from the survey in local currency. All local currency means are converted to means and therefore distribution in 1993 PPP consumption prices. If a consumption survey was undertaken then the mean is used. If no consumption survey was undertaken, then the income survey to national accounts ratio is assumed to be the same for consumption. Multiplying this S/NA by the national accounts consumption mean (in 1993 prices) yields an estimate of a distribution and mean for the year in question. If a country has both a consumption and income survey, then only the survey to national accounts ratio for the consumption surveys is used.

For years for which there is no survey: The lagging survey to national accounts ratio is assumed for the years going forward and for years going back, in reverse. Assume that a survey was undertaken for two years 1985 and 1995. The national accounts estimate is available for all the years. This estimate is multiplied by the S/NA for all years before and including 1994, and for all years subsequent, the 1995 S/NA is used. With this method, data are available for all the years for a country if even it had only one income or consumption survey.

A country with no survey data is not used in the analysis. It enters the global poverty figures based on the average poverty ratio in the region and year in question.

Notes

1. This chapter is a revised version of a paper presented at the Initiative for Policy Dialogue and Rockefeller Foundation Global Poverty Workshop, March 31–April 1, 2003. I am extremely thankful to Tirthanomoy Das for excellent research assistance and an anonymous referee for helpful comments.
2. Chairman, Oxus Research and Investments, New Delhi, India.

3. Recently, the World Bank has come out with new estimates of PPP data with 2005 as the base year. These estimates are controversial because they show, somewhat inexplicably, that per capita incomes in China, India, and most parts of Asia are about 40 per cent lower than what was believed only a little while previously.

4. There are two World Bank estimates of poverty reported in this chapter: the actual World Bank estimates as reported in Chen and Ravallion (2004) and our estimates of the same, based only on the World Bank method and World Bank data. It is expected that the two will differ, but it is also expected that the two estimates will not differ by much. As it happens, the figures are very close for 2001 and 2004 but somewhat apart in the earlier years.

5. Sala-i-Martín essentially follows the ACC method while this chapter offers a method which uses national account *growth* rates and survey *means*.

6. See Bhalla (2002b) for an extensive discussion of the issues related to poverty measurement.

7. <http://www.worldbank.org>, accessed March 1, 2009.

8. Inequality data (distributions) have been gathered from three major sources, namely, Deininger and Squire (1996), WIDER (2008), and data collected from various projects undertaken at Oxus Research: Bhalla et al. (2003), a report prepared for the Asian Development Bank; Bhalla (2003b), a report prepared for the Planning Commission, government of India; and the Institute of International Economics publication, Bhalla (2002b). Survey means for Middle Eastern economies have been obtained from Adams and Page (2003). Survey data for eighteen Asian countries were obtained from Sachs (2005). For other countries the survey means are taken from various sources; if an independent official source of data was not available, then survey means data were obtained from the World Bank website. (Previously <http://www.worldbank.org/povmonitor>, accessed on March 15, 2002; now <http://iresearch.worldbank.org/PovcalNet/jsp/index.jsp>, accessed on March 1, 2009.)

9. The World Bank data allows for computation of poverty for sixty-one countries—fifty-seven traditional developing countries and four countries from central Asia (formerly part of the Soviet Union). Our sample consists of eighty-seven traditional and four from central Asia. The standard practice (and followed by us as well) is to impute the average percentage poor rate to countries with missing data in order to compute world averages.

10. It has been speculated (see Ravallion, 2000) that the non-governmental organizations (NGO) population in India may be causing a significant part of the divergence between survey and NA means, and growth rates. As pointed out in Bhalla (2003c) the contribution of this factor to overall divergence in survey and NA means is very small.

11. <http://iresearch.worldbank.org/PovcalNet/PovcalNet.html>, accessed on March 1, 2002. It reports an urban poverty level of 21.9 per cent and a rural poverty level of 48.88 per cent for the $1.08 poverty line for 1993/4. The urbanization rate in India for that year was 26.2 per cent. The weighted average of the two poverty levels is 41.8 per cent.

12. If the PPP exchange rate for income is taken (6.0 rather than 7.02) the Indian poverty line, in PPP terms, is not 1.08 but PPP$1.26 per capita per day.

13. An identical exercise was carried out for three other survey years—1983, 1987/8, and 1999/2000. While the average multiplier varied, the relative understatement of the different sectors of the population stayed constant.
14. Why this is happening is a major research undertaking; a likely cause is the wider choice of consumption items (which do not make it to the interview list of questions) and the increasing opportunity cost of time (people do not have time for the typical 5 to 6 hour interview).
15. Deaton's graph contains annual values of per capita expenditure; the chart reading has been transformed by us into a per capita per day reading rather than a per capita per year reading.
16. I am thankful to Angus Deaton for pointing me towards Anderson's work.

Bibliography

Adams, R. H. J. R. and Page, J. (2003) 'Poverty, Inequality and Growth in Selected Middle East and North Africa Countries, 1980–2000'. *World Development*, 31(12), pp. 2027–48.
Ahluwalia, M. S., Carter, N. G., and Chenery, H. B. (1979) 'Growth and Poverty in Developing Countries'. *Journal of Development Economics*, 6, pp. 299–341.
Anderson, W. H. Locke (1964) 'Trickling Down: The Relationship between Economic Growth and the Extent of Poverty among American Families'. *Quarterly Journal of Economics*, 78(4), pp. 511–24.
Banerjee, A. and Piketty, T. (2005) 'Top Indian Incomes, 1982–2000'. *World Bank Economic Review*, 19(1), pp. 1–20.
Besley, T. and Burgess, R. (2003) 'Halving Global Poverty'. *Journal of Economic Perspectives*, 17(3), pp. 3–22.
Bhalla, S. S. (1997) 'Economic Freedom and Growth Miracles: India is Next'. World Bank–IMF Annual Meetings, Hong Kong.
—— (2002a) 'Growth and Poverty in India—Myth and Reality'. In G. Rao (ed.) *Development Poverty and Fiscal Policy: Decentralization of Institutions*, Oxford University Press, Oxford.
—— (2002b) *Imagine there's No Country: Poverty, Inequality and Growth in the Era of Globalization*. Institute of International Economics.
—— (2003a) 'Recounting the Poor: 1983–99'. *Economic and Political Weekly*, January 25, pp. 338–49.
—— (2003b) 'Not as Poor, nor as Unequal, as you Think: India, 1950–2000'. Report on research project 'The Myth and Reality of Poverty in India', Planning Commission, Government of India (May).
—— (2003c) 'Crying Wolf on Poverty: Or How the Millennium Development Goals of Poverty Reduction have already been Reached'. *Economic and Political Weekly*, July 5, pp. 2843–56.
—— (2004a) 'Poor Results and Poorer Policy: A Comparative Analysis of Estimates of Global Inequality and Poverty'. *CESifo Economic Studies*, 50(1).
—— (2004b) 'Pro-Poor Growth: Measurement and Results'. In S. Ahmed and S. Bery (eds.), *Annual World Bank Conference on Development Economics 2003*, World Bank and NCAER, New Delhi.

—— et al. (2003) 'End of Asian Poverty?' Report prepared for research project RETA-5917. Asian Development Bank, Manila (May).

—— and Homi Kharas (1991a) 'Growth, Poverty Alleviation and Improved Income Distribution in Malaysia: Changing Focus of Government Policy Intervention'. *World Bank on Malaysia*, no. 8667-MA, chs. 2–4.

—— and Tirthatanmoy Das (2005) 'Pre- and Post-Reform India: A Revised Look at Employment, Wages and Inequality'. *India Policy Forum*, 2, pp. 183–254.

Bourguignon, F. (2004) 'The Poverty-Growth-Inequality Triangle'. Paper prepared for the Indian Council for Research on International Economics Relations, Delhi, February 4.

Burnside, C. and Dollar, D. (2000) 'Aid, Policies and Growth'. *American Economic Review*, 90(4), pp. 847–68.

Chakravarti, A. (2005) *Aid, Institutions and Development*. Oxford: Oxford University Press.

Chen, S. and Ravallion, M. (2001) 'How Did the World's Poorest Fare in the 1990s?' *Review of Income and Wealth*, 47, pp. 283–300.

Collier, P. and Dollar, D. (2000) *Can the World Cut Poverty in Half? How Policy Reform and Effective Aid Can Meet International Development Goals*. Development Research Group, World Bank, Washington DC (July).

Datt, G. and Ravallion, M. (1992) 'Growth and Redistribution Components of Changes in Poverty: A Decomposition with Application to Brazil and India'. *Journal of Development Economics*, 38, pp. 275–95.

—— —— (2002) 'Is India's Economic Growth Leaving the Poor Behind?' *Journal of Economic Perspectives*, 16(3), pp. 89–108.

Deaton, A. (2001) 'Counting the World's Poor: Problems and Possible Solutions'. *World Bank Research Observer*, 16(2).

Deininger, K. and Squire, L. (1996) 'A New Data Set Measuring Income Inequality'. *World Bank Economic Review*, 10(3), pp. 565–92.

Dollar, D. and Kraay, A. (2002) 'Growth Is Good for The Poor'. *Journal of Economic Growth*, 7, pp. 195–225.

Dubey, A. and Gangopadhyay, S. (1998) 'Counting the Poor: Where are the Poor in India?' Sarvekshana Analytical Report 1, New Delhi: Department of Statistics, Government of India.

Easterly, W., Levine, R., and Roodman, D. (2003) 'New Data, New Doubts: Revisiting Aid, Policies, and Growth', Working Paper No. 26, Center for Global Development, Washington DC.

Kakwani, N. (1980) *Income Inequality and Poverty: Methods of Estimation and Policy Applications*. Oxford: Oxford University Press.

—— (1993) 'Poverty and Economics Growth with Application to Côte D' Ivoire'. *Review of Income and Wealth*, 39, pp. 121–39.

Klasen, S. (2001) 'In Search of the Holy Grail: How to Achieve Pro-Poor Growth?' Mimeo.

Kravis, I. B., et al. (1975) A *System of International Comparison of Gross Product and Purchasing Power*. Baltimore: John Hopkins University Press.

Milanovic, B. (2002) 'True World Income Distribution, 1988 and 1993: First Calculations Based on Household Survey Alone'. *Economic Journal*, 112, pp. 51–92.

Ravallion, M. (2000) 'Should Poverty Measures be Anchored to the National Accounts?' *Economic and Political Weekly*, August 26, pp. 3245–52.

Ravallion, M. (2002) 'Have we already met the Millennium Development Goals for Poverty?' *Economic and Political Weekly*, November 16.

—— (2003) 'Measuring Aggregate Welfare in Developing Countries: How Well Do National Accounts and Surveys Agree'. *Review of Economics and Statistics*, 85(3), pp. 645–52.

—— and Datt, G. (1999) 'When Is Growth Pro-Poor? Evidence from the Diverse Experiences of India's States'. Policy Research Working Paper WPS 2263, World Bank.

Sachs, J. D. (2005). *The End of Poverty*. New York: The Penguin Press.

Sala-i-Martín, X. (2002) 'The Disturbing Rise of Global Income Inequality'. NBER Working Paper 8904, Cambridge, Mass.: National Bureau of Economic Research.

—— (2006) 'The World Distribution of Income: Falling Poverty and Convergence, Period'. *Quarterly Journal of Economics*, 121(2), pp. 351–97.

Srinivasan, T. N. (2004) 'Comments'. In S. Ahmed and S. Bery (eds.) *Annual World Bank Conference on Development Economics 2003*, World Bank and NCAER, New Delhi.

WIDER, United Nations University (2008) Inequality Data Set <http://www.wider.unu.edu/>.

World Bank (1990) *World Development Report 1990: Poverty*. Oxford: Oxford University Press.

—— (1991) *Growth, Poverty Alleviation and Improved Income Distribution in Malaysia: Changing Focus of Government Policy Intervention*. Report 8667-MA. Washington DC.

—— (2001) *World Development Report 2000/2001: Attacking Poverty*. Oxford: Oxford University Press.

—— (2003) *World Development Indicators*. Washington DC.

5

Irrelevance of the $1-a-Day Poverty Line[1]

T. N. Srinivasan[2]

Introduction

Whether or not an individual is deemed to be poor depends not merely on that individual's economic and non-economic endowments but also, equally, if not more importantly, the place of that individual in the socio-economic-political processes of the country of which he or she is a citizen. An important implication of this is that any meaningful indicator that distinguishes the poor from non-poor has to be multidimensional. Nonetheless, most widely used indicators, including the $1-a-day poverty line, are one dimensional and are usually defined as a person's expenditure on consumption or, less often, income.

An indicator of poverty, whether multi- or one dimensional, could serve three distinct purposes. The first is a purely descriptive one of depicting the extent of poverty, the socio-economic profile of the poor, at one or more points of a time, within a well defined unit, such as a nation state or sub-national units, or aggregates of nations (e.g. low income countries of South Asia or the world). Such a depiction provides a potential yardstick for monitoring the performance of national governments and international agencies, such as the World Bank, in achieving their professed objective of poverty reduction. More importantly, it could serve as a prelude to a positive analysis of likely determinants of different dimensions of poverty. However, in such an analysis, aggregations of poverty over very disparate spatial units or over a long time involving major systemic changes would likely mask the influence of different determinants of poverty. The reason is that the relationship between determinants and poverty outcomes almost surely would be very different across the units being aggregated.[3] This being the case, global indicators, such as $1-a-day counts of the poor, are unlikely starting points for any useful analysis of determinants of poverty.

The second purpose is normative: poverty indicators are inputs into the process of formulating policies for poverty eradication. Global indicators, and

143

even national indicators in large, diverse countries, such as India, are not very useful for this purpose either. Determinants of poverty, and hence, policies for poverty alleviation, are unlikely to be the same across diverse regions. Further, a policy is likely to be most effective in reaching its target and achieving its objective if its locus is where the target happens to be. Because most policies targeted at the poor are in the jurisdiction of sub-national (or even lower level) units, poverty indicators at higher levels are not helpful in policy formulation. This is not to say that national and international policies are irrelevant but only that their effects on aggregate indicators are best understood through the aggregation of their effects on indicators of poverty at lower levels.

The third purpose is mobilization of support among citizens, media and governments for the objective of poverty alleviation and for policies at all levels (subnational, national, and international) that presumably could alleviate poverty. Even those who would readily concede that global poverty counts are virtually useless for the first two purposes would agree that they might be effective for the third purpose. Certainly, saying that in 2000 so many millions of people in the world went to bed hungry or lived on less than $1-a-day grabs attention. Thus, such global poverty counts have hortatory and rhetorical values.

The adoption of the Millennium Development Goals at the Millennium Summit by the United Nations, including the goal to reduce global poverty (in terms of the estimated number of people living at less than $1-a-day), indicates a certain purposefulness. It is arguable whether such attention and resolve have concrete value in raising resources for poverty alleviation or changing policies. For example, nearly six decades after the adoption in 1948 by the UN of the Charter on Basic Human Rights, abuses are still widespread. Exhortations based on appalling poverty in developing countries led in the 1970s to the target of 0.7 per cent of gross national product for industrial countries to contribute for development assistance. This target was reiterated in the so-called Monterrey Consensus adopted at the International Conference on Financing Development held at Monterrey, Mexico on March 21–2, 2002. Yet some of the richest countries of the world have not reached the target. Even if it were the case that there would have been faster development or greater poverty reduction with larger development assistance, a case for which the evidence is at best ambiguous, exhortations based on global poverty counts are unlikely to generate more resources from the rich now than they have in the past.[4]

Concept of poverty and choice of poverty line

The possible hortatory value of global poverty counts does not mean that the formidable conceptual and measurement problems underlying them can be ignored. There is a certain unavoidable arbitrariness in the choice of the criteria by which the incidence of poverty in any society at any point in time is to be judged. As Adam Smith recognized long ago, poverty is a social construct. He argued that in defining necessities, one must include not just "the commodities which are indispensably necessary for the support of life" but also those which "the custom of the country renders indecent for creditable people, even of the lowest order to be without. A linen shirt, for example, is, strictly speaking, not a necessary of life. The Greeks and Romans lived, I suppose, very comfortably, though they had no linen. But in the present times, through the greater part of Europe, a creditable day laborer would be ashamed to appear in public without a linen shirt, the want of which would be supposed to denote that disgraceful degree of poverty, which, it is presumed, no body can well fall into without extreme bad conduct." (Smith, 1937, pp. 821–2).

To be non-poor, a person must be able to afford at least the necessities. Following Smith, one should presumably include a "decency" component in them. Obviously these are subjective and would vary over time and space.[5] Moreover, important non-income aspects of poverty such as deprivations in health, educational attainments, enjoyment of citizenship rights, though difficult to measure, cannot be meaningfully combined with income or consumption measures to define a comprehensive poverty indicator of relevance.[6] For example, knowledge of the current health status of an individual is not in itself adequate to project that individual's future survival prospects: these depend both on the future evolution of the environment of sanitation, hygiene, health care and disease vectors of the society, and the individual's own access to the society's system of health care. Proxies for survival prospects such as life expectancy at birth (or more generally age–sex specific mortality rates) are averages and not individual specific. Besides, they describe only the current mortality experience of the population as a whole, rather than its likely future evolution.[7] Moreover, life expectancies and literacy rates usually move too slowly to be helpful for monitoring progress in poverty reduction except in the very long run.

The most easily understood approach for deriving the widely used consumption expenditure based poverty line is to start from a socially defined "poverty consumption" bundle of goods and services for a representative (in size and age–gender composition) household. Allowing for the possibility that some components of the bundle would partly or mostly be provided free (or at subsidized prices) by the state, the value of the components of the bundle that are not provided by the state at appropriate prices, yields the consumption poverty line.[8] There is unavoidable arbitrariness in determining which goods and services (and in what amounts) are to be included in a poverty bundle. Nevertheless, given a poverty bundle for a representative household, appropriate adjustments for differences of any other household in its size and age–gender composition could be made to arrive at a household-specific poverty line. A household would be deemed to be poor if it does not have the resources, measured in terms of either income or total consumption expenditure, to buy the private component of *its poverty bundle at the price it faces.* A household that can afford to but does not buy its poverty bundle obviously is not deemed as poor.

Poverty measurement

Clearly, if data on the resources that each household commands and the prices it faces are regularly collected, say through an annual household survey, it is a straightforward matter to estimate the number of the poor each year, as long as the constituents and the public component of the poverty bundle remain the same over time and space, and surveys in different regions and time periods continue to collect household specific data on resources and prices.

Leaving aside the issue of imputing prices for consumption from home production, only the prices actually paid by an individual (or household) in purchase transactions are relevant for arriving at a poverty line specific to that individual (or household). No household survey collects transaction specific prices. At best one can obtain an average unit cost, if the expenditure and quantity bought of each item of consumption are available from a survey. Annual surveys with requisite data are most unlikely to be available for calculating poverty lines through valuation of a *given* poverty bundle at prices that are specific to each household, region, and period of time. This being the case, a common practice is to use some price index to adjust some poverty line (not necessarily one derived from valuing a poverty bundle) at base year (or base region) prices to arrive at a poverty line for a different year (or region). This is in effect how official poverty lines are updated in India. There is no reason to presume that the commodity weights and the price quotations used in constructing these price indices reflect the commodity weights in the consumption bundle of a representative poor household and the price quotations correspond to the prices faced by it. Deaton and Tarozzi (2005, pp. 34–5) recomputed Indian poverty estimates using price indices based on commodity weights and unit values from household surveys, instead of price indices used in updating poverty lines in official data. They found that "between 1987–88 and 1993–94, there was no great difference in the rate of decline of urban and rural poverty," in contrast to the diverging trends in official poverty estimates. Thus, the use of price index matters. But whatever index is used, the basic, standard textbook index number problem remains and cannot be wished away.

A poverty bundle common to all regions within a geographically and culturally diverse country such as India, let alone for all countries of the world, is hard to visualize even conceptually. If such a bundle could be defined, then the national poverty line at any point in time would be the value of that bundle at the relevant prices in *local currency* in that nation at that point in time. There would be no need for the use of any currency exchange rate in such a calculation. Is the use of an arbitrary global poverty line of $1-a-day and deriving local currency poverty lines by converting $1 at purchasing power parity (PPP) exchange rates a sensible response to the obvious non-existence of such an internationally accepted bundle? Before attempting to answer this question, it is useful to recapitulate how the $1-a-day poverty line originated.

Origin of the $1-a-day poverty line

The very interesting paper of Ravallion et al. (1991) is the origin of the $1-a-day poverty line. Their objective was to quantify absolute poverty in the developing world. They begin their paper with five relevant questions:

What poverty line should be used? Should one use the same poverty line across all countries? How should one adjust for differences across countries in the purchasing power of their currencies at official exchange rates? How should one interpolate from the available grouped data on the distribution of income or consumption? How should one extrapolate to countries for which distributional data are unavailable, or are highly imperfect? (p. 345)

They claim to have proposed, "a methodology for addressing these questions, and give aggregate results for 86 developing countries in the mid-1990s. Our aim is to make a necessarily rough but methodologically consistent assessment of the magnitude and severity of absolute poverty, based on recent available data" (p. 345).

What exactly is their methodology? They begin with two possible interpretations of an absolute poverty line, the first is the cost of "a bundle of goods which is *recognized as constituting an absolute minimum by international standards*" (p. 345, my emphasis). As argued in the previous section, such an internationally recognized bundle obviously does not exist.

Their second concept of the real poverty line comprises "of an 'absolute' component, which is consistent across all countries, and a 'relative' component, which is specific to each country" (ibid.). Prima facie, this approach appears sensible and even seems to accommodate Adam Smith's concern. Although they neither define the notion of consistency analytically nor the sense in which the country specific component is relative, their intended meanings are to be inferred from their empirical implementation, which consists of estimating the following regression:

$$log\ z_i = \alpha + \beta\mu_i - \gamma\mu_i^2 + \text{residual} \qquad (1)$$

"where z_i is poverty line in country i and μ_i is the mean monthly private consumption per capita [both] at constant PPP." The residual is assumed to pick up other "factors influencing the local poverty lines, and measurement error in the letter" (ibid., p. 348). The theoretical foundation, if any, that would rationalize (1) is unclear.

The authors start from poverty lines in local currency for thirty-three countries, both developing and developed, and convert them to a common currency (US dollar) using "estimates presented by Summers and Heston (1988) of the adjustments to official exchanges rates needed to give purchasing power parity (PPP)" (ibid., p. 347), to arrive at z_i and μ_i. They recognize that ideally one would like to construct PPP based on prices most relevant for the absolute poor, but this recognition is not acted upon in any way. The regression provided a good fit with an R^2 of 0.90.

Although it would seem natural to interpret e^α as the absolute component of the poverty line, it is not sensible since α is the expected value of $log\ z_i$ for a country with $\mu_i = 0$, i.e. mean consumption per capita of $0 in PPP. A more appropriate value for the absolute component is the expected value of $Log\ z_i$ for the poorest country, i.e. one with the lowest μ_i. It turned out that among the eighty-six countries that the authors considered, Somalia had the lowest μ_i at $22. When $22 is substituted for μ_i in the estimated regression, it led to an estimate of poverty line of $23 per month for consumption per capita. This happened to be very close to the then Indian poverty line (converted to dollars at PPP) of $23.14. Since among the thirty-three countries used in estimating (1), many low income countries had more generous poverty lines, they decided that "a more generous and more representative absolute poverty line for low-income countries is $31, which (to the nearest dollar) is shared by six of the countries in our sample, namely Indonesia, Bangladesh, Nepal, Kenya, Tanzania and Morocco and two other countries are close to this figure (Philippines and Pakistan). We shall use both these poverty lines, interpreting the lower line as defining 'extreme absolute poverty'" (ibid., pp. 348–9). Thus $31 a month or $1-a-day at 1985 PPP exchange rates came to be the *real absolute poverty line across all developing countries*. The authors justify this on the grounds that the estimates of the parameters of (1) show that poverty lines tend to be less responsive to increases in the mean at low levels of consumption. They note that their absolute poverty line does not allow for differences between countries in relevant non-income (or consumption) factors.

It is clear that the role that PPP exchange rates played in the determination of the $1-a-day poverty line is the very limited one of enabling the estimation of (1) by converting poverty lines and monthly per capita consumption in *local currency* into their US dollar values. Given that the authors themselves recognize that the prices and the consumption baskets used in arriving at the PPP rates of Summers and Heston (1985) are not appropriate for the purpose at hand,[9] one would have expected them to check whether the use of any other available set of exchange rates lead to estimates of (1) that were different and gave a better or poorer fit to the data. They do not report on any such experimentation. A priori, one cannot rule out the possibility that the use of other exchange rates could have yielded as good or better a fit to the data and also the estimated parameters of (1) could have greater sensitivity of the poverty line to per capita consumption of low income countries.

The PPP exchange rate is used *only once* in poverty measurement in each country, it is used in converting the $1-a-day poverty line to local currency terms in *the base year*. For estimating poverty in other years, the so-computed poverty line is moved forward or backward in time, using the local price index. Thus, for arriving at the poverty line at a point in time (the base year), prices associated with the implied consumption basket of PPP are used, but for updating the base year poverty line to other points in time, a *local price index* associated with a different consumption basket is used. In any case, the whole exercise is driven by the objective of deriving a real absolute poverty line in terms of consumption or income across *all* developing countries, an objective that is inherently flawed for the various reasons discussed earlier.

As better and more data become available, the base year for PPP exchange rates is changed. In a later work (Chen and Ravallion, 2001), the base year of PPP rates was changed from 1985 to 1993. The 1993 rates were based on new price and consumption basket data collected by the World Bank through its International Comparison Project, which covered 100 countries. The 1985 rates from Summers and Heston (1988) covered only sixty countries. Regression (1) was re-run for thirty-two of the thirty-three countries used in the earlier regression, now with local currency poverty lines and consumption converted at 1993 PPP rates. For the country with the lowest per capita consumption, the estimated poverty line was $31.96 per month and the median of the poverty lines for the bottom ten countries among the thirty-two in terms of per capita consumption was $32.74, again exhibiting the insensitivity of poverty lines to differences in per capita consumption of poor countries. Again, going from the base year of 1993 to other years, local currency price indexes were used. It should be noted that the time series of poverty counts based on 1985 base year for PPP are not comparable to the ones based on 1993 base year. Thus, the estimated poverty counts for a *given year* for the *same* country based on PPPs for *different* base years could be *different*, the difference arising from the fact that the concept of absolute poverty implicit in the $1-a-day poverty line for the different base years is different. This is very disturbing since it implies a varying notion of absolute poverty, which has nothing to do with changes in the conceptualization of poverty but only with the factors that led to the change in PPP exchange rates.

Growth and poverty

There is a large and growing theoretical and empirical literature on the growth–poverty link. In empirical studies, real GDP growth estimates are based on national accounts statistics (NAS) while poverty estimates are derived from household expenditure surveys (HES). It is well known that consumption expenditures estimated from NAS differ from those estimated from HES in developed (for example, the United States) and developing (for example, India) countries and there are many conceptual and statistical reasons for the discrepancy. Nonetheless, the fact that the discrepancy seems to be growing over time, such as in India, is disquieting. However, attempts to deal with it by using (often) higher per capita mean consumption expenditure estimates from the NAS and its household distribution from HES have no analytical foundation and have to be rejected.

Conclusion

There is an urgent need for a serious research program for reconciliation between NAS and HES data. There should be more experimentation in survey practice. In particular, research is needed for a better understanding of how measurement of consumption is affected by the design of surveys, including the length of reference periods, length and detail of questionnaires, length of interviews, repeat visits to the same household, and whether to have more than one respondent from each household.

Most important of all, Deaton's (2001) plea for finding better ways to set the poverty line is right on the mark. As should be evident from my comments, I prefer to start from a well-defined poverty bundle. Clearly, it has to be defined in terms of characteristics for healthy life and functioning, depending on an individual's age, gender, work activity, and other relevant attributes. But this is impractical. As an alternative, one may try to define a few poverty bundles in terms of goods and services. The need for more than one arises from the fact of variation in climates and dietary habits if nothing else. Given the poverty bundle appropriate to a subset of the population and well-designed surveys, it would be simple to define poverty lines that are specific to that subset and time period, based on prices faced by the poor. But this alternative may not be that much more practical than defining a single global poverty bundle. There is no easy way of determining how many bundles would be needed to capture the variations in relevant dimensions. In any case, once there is more than one bundle and an associated poverty line that is appropriate for each region or subset of the population, index number problems reappear if one attempts to construct a global poverty line that is representative of all the regional poverty lines.

Comparability and global representativeness are therefore impossible to achieve. It is clear that the $1-a-day at a constant PPP exchange rate poverty line does not satisfy either. For this reason and the reason that global poverty counts neither have normative significance nor are of value in a positive analysis of determinants of poverty, I would prefer to abandon the search for the impossible and stick to national poverty lines, even though they also have conceptual weaknesses, though less serious. But if the rhetoric and politics of resource mobilization for poverty alleviation demand global poverty counts, the use of $1-a-day global poverty line, converting it using PPP exchange rate of some base year for deriving poverty lines in local currency terms for each country, and updating them for other years using *local price indices* has some value. However, any claim that such counts are based on poverty lines that are comparable in a conceptually meaningful sense across nations and subnational units, just because the same $1-a-day at PPP exchange rates of some base year is being used in computing local currency poverty lines, cannot be sustained and ought to be dismissed out of hand.

Notes

1. This paper draws extensively from Srinivasan (2001) and references cited therein. I thank Martin Ravallion for his brief comment on an earlier version. His graciously commenting on it should not be taken to mean that he endorses anything I have said in either version.
2. Yale University.
3. There are serious problems with poverty estimates and analysis that take the *household* as the relevant unit. First, they assume, in effect, a unitary model of household decision-making. This precludes a meaningful analysis of poverty of women and children, particularly female children, that arises from their relative weakness in bargaining over intra-household allocations of resources. Second, household surveys define a household as consisting of those who eat from the same kitchen. This definition is constraining when it comes to the analysis of poverty over time since for savings and investment (in human and physical capital) decisions, the relevant unit is a family (nuclear or extended).
4. There is considerable evidence suggesting that political economy constraints at national and international levels, rather than inadequacy of domestic and external resources, are at the root of poor development performance and persistence of poverty.
5. In Srinivasan (2000), I argue that the claim of objectivity often made for a particular poverty line (that is, value of consumption expenditure or income per person) by linking it to the required habitual or long-term intake of food (or, more precisely, its energy content) for an individual to be adequately nourished is untenable. Briefly stated, there are *intra-individual* variations in energy requirements so that, even for a given individual, an unvarying poverty line based on energy requirements is inappropriate. Besides, even if an energy based poverty line could be defined at prices prevailing at a point in time, its updating using *price indices* severs its connection to energy requirements over time. See also Srinivasan (2007).
6. Indicators such as the UNDP's Human Development Index are also subject to the same criticism: they combine indicators that are not commensurable into an index. Attempts to provide a conceptual foundation for this index have not been convincing.

This is true also of UNDP's "capability based poverty measure" and the "human poverty index" that draw on Amartya Sen's concepts of "capabilities and functioning." Apart from lack of a sound conceptual foundation, these indices avoidably lose some of the valuable information contained in individual indicators.

7. It is a little known fact that life expectancy estimates for a number of countries are based on scanty data and on the use of model life tables rather than country specific ones. The reason is that data from reliable population censuses for more than one year are unavailable for such countries.

8. This valuation of the private component is in effect what an expert group did for India's Planning Commission in 1962, in defining poverty lines for rural and urban households in India.

9. This fact is explicitly stated in the report on the preliminary results of 2005 International Comparison Program "PPP provide a measure of the overall price level of an economy, but they may not reflect the expenditure patterns of the poor. Nor do they capture differences in price levels within a country. Additional data and analysis will be necessary before an international poverty rate can be estimated, therefore direct application of these PPPs to the estimation of poverty [lines] levels and rates may yield misleading results" (World Bank, 2007, p. 11).

Bibliography

Bhagwati, J. N. and Hansen, N. (1973) 'Should Growth Rates be Evaluated at International Prices?' In J. Bhagwati and R. Eckhaus (eds.) *Development and Planning*, Cambridge, Mass.: MIT Press.

Deaton, A. (2001) 'Counting the World's Poor: Problems and Possible Solutions'. *The World Bank Research Observer*, 16(2), pp. 125–47.

—— and Tarozzi, A. (2005) 'Prices and Poverty in India'. In A. Deaton and V. Kozel (eds.) *Data and Dogma: The Great Poverty Debate in India*, New Delhi: MacMillan.

Ravallion, M. and Chen, S. (2001) 'How did the World's Poorest Fare in the 1990s'. *Review of Income and Wealth*, 47(3), pp. 283–300.

—— Datt, G., and van de Walle, D. (1991) 'Quantifying Absolute Poverty in the Developing World'. *Review of Income and Wealth*, 37(4), pp. 345–61.

Smith, A. (1937) *An Inquiry into the Nature and Causes of the Wealth of Nations*. Edited by E. Cannan. New York: Modern Library.

Srinivasan, T. N. (2000) 'Poverty and Undernutrition in South Asia'. *Journal of Food Policy*, 25, pp. 269–82.

—— (2001) 'Comment on "Counting the World's Poor"'. *The World Bank Research Observer*, 16(2), pp. 157–68.

—— (2004) 'The Unsatisfactory State of Global Poverty Estimation'. *In Focus*, 4, United Nations Development Program (September).

—— (2007) 'Poverty Lines in India: Reflections after the Patna Conference'. *Economic and Political Weekly*, 42(40), pp. 4155–65.

Summers, R. and Heston, A. (1988) 'A New Set of International Comparisons of Real Product and Price Levels: Estimates for 130 Countries, 1950–1985'. *Review of Income and Wealth*, 34(1), pp. 1–26.

Triplett, J. E. (1997) 'Measuring Consumption: The Post-1973 Slowdown and the Research Issues'. *Federal Reserve Bank of St. Louis Review*, May/June, pp. 9–42.

World Bank (2007) *2005 International Comparison Program: Preliminary Results*. Washington DC: International Bank for Reconstruction and Development, and World Bank.

6

Use of Country Purchasing Power Parities for International Comparisons of Poverty Levels: Potential and Limitations

Bettina Aten[1] and Alan Heston[2]

Introduction

Individual scholars and expert groups have considered both physical and monetary measures to define a poverty line. Physical measures might be based upon caloric intake, or as considered in India, the number of square meals (thoughtfully defined) in a sample period and the purchase of clothing, with some experts also arguing for an inventory of physical household assets. The attraction of choosing physical measures is that they appear to avoid the necessity of converting currencies across countries to a common measure. However, the survey problems of identifying those below such thresholds, or of choosing equivalent food baskets across space to obtain the same caloric intake, involve problems as knotty as those using monetary measures. In any event, the focus of this chapter is on monetary measures of poverty and takes up two interrelated issues of comparing poverty levels: what prices and what expenditure weights should be used when comparing the purchasing power parity (PPP) of currencies, either across or within countries, such as across rural and metropolitan areas.

The first section outlines the usual method of counting those in poverty across different geographic areas, including the limitations of past practice and the potential of modifying current practice using the aggregate PPPs from the International Comparison Program (ICP) and the Penn World Table (PWT). An appendix describes the estimation of PPPs and compares the PWT approach to that of the World Bank. In the second section, the nature of the prices that may be specific to sections of the population (such as the very poor, or the rural versus the urban residents) is discussed, including the work of Deaton, Friedman, and Alata (2004). The final section describes the results of an exercise designed to create more appropriate "poverty PPPs" than currently published.

Generating poverty counts across space

There is a voluminous literature on this subject at the national level where this exercise began in the 1960s. Typically, monetary measures of poverty lines have been based on a particular consumption bundle, or as a per cent of median consumption in the country. In either case, the poverty count provides a snapshot of the number of persons below the line. This type of poverty count has the great policy advantage that it can change, hopefully going down over time.

Within large countries such as India, which first introduced poverty reduction as a national planning goal, there may be lower poverty lines for rural areas, because some prices in the consumption bundle will be lower than in urban areas. If one wants to create an international poverty line, the problem of converting monetary measures becomes critical.

The factor used to make currencies comparable across countries, whether it is an exchange rate or purchasing power parity, does not change the underlying economic inequalities around the world. However, it does significantly affect the perception of the extent of poverty and the economic size of countries. At PPPs, the economies of China and India are ranked among the world's top seven, but not so at exchange rates. Similarly, if one took a simple poverty line such as one-quarter of the world per capita income average, the proportion in poverty was near 80 per cent in Asia at 1980 exchange rates, while at PPPs this proportion is closer to 50 per cent.[3] Since writing this chapter the World Bank has released a benchmark purchasing power parity study for 146 countries for 2005. It provides a much larger spread in country incomes than in previous ICP studies, or in the PWT. In 2005 the report shows that 84 per cent of the population was under half the world per capita income average, while at PPPs the proportion drops to 66 per cent, or two-thirds of the population under the world per capita income average.[4]

Which PPPs should be used?

The ICP was designed to produce detailed data on prices and expenditures of goods and services that entered into the calculation of countries' gross domestic product (GDP). These so-called benchmark comparison surveys have been undertaken for various years beginning in 1970. The surveys enable the calculation of PPPs at various levels of aggregation, from basic heading expenditures such as Food, Transport, Housing, and so forth, to aggregate expenditures such

155

as Consumption, Investment, and Government. The OECD countries now undertake their own surveys producing annual PPP comparisons for a number of European countries, while the PWT group includes other countries and estimates a time series going back to 1950. The World Bank has also produced an aggregate PPP for GDP, and is now leading the efforts for a new global ICP benchmark survey with a reference year of 2011.

The ICP concept of consumption differed slightly from the 1964 SNA (System of National Accounts) framework, because it included private consumption expenditures plus those parts of government expenditures on health and education directly consumed by households. In 1993 the SNA adopted this convention and called it Household Actual Final Consumption, distinguishing it from the old SNA concept of Household Final Consumption Expenditures. The OECD countries have all followed suit, and consumption in PWT 6.1 (2002) is equal to Household Actual Final Consumption when possible, although most developing countries still use the old SNA concept. There is a significant political and economic debate in some countries as to whether publicly provided goods and services should be included in the poverty line, and this is also an important research question. In practice, the question of publicly provided services is beyond the scope of this chapter. If it were possible to add these services to survey data to obtain actual household final consumption by income or expenditure decile, it would clearly be valuable to calculate both SNA concepts.

In the 2005 World Bank Report, the concepts of actual consumption and household consumption are both presented. It is important to note that some of the differences between the 2005 ICP and earlier rounds are due to comparisons for non-priced government services in administration, health, and education.[5] In Africa, Asia and West Asia an adjustment was made that reduced the GDP of these countries by 10 per cent or more compared to the treatment in earlier benchmarks or PWT. However, this adjustment does not affect household consumption, which is the focus of this chapter. For a fuller discussion of the differences between the 2005 and earlier studies see Heston (2008). The likely impact of the new ICP numbers on the World Bank poverty lines and counts is discussed in this volume by Martin Ravillion (Ch. 2).

Use of the PPP for consumption is clearly more appropriate than the PPP for GDP for converting any common international poverty line into local currencies. Both are available from the benchmark ICP surveys (1970, 1975, 1980, 1985, and 1993), and for a larger number of countries in the World Bank, as well as for intermediate years up to 2002 in PWT. Are there other PPP concepts that should be considered? One alternative would be to use consumption weights specific to the poorer income groups. This is a fairly natural extension of what is done in temporal price indices where one might estimate a consumer price index for subgroups of the population like the elderly.

In the second section, we further discuss the sensitivity of PPPs to consumption weights. Since poverty studies have conversion factors for currencies estimated in different ways, we have included in an appendix the PWT methodology and a comparison with the World Bank estimates of consumption PPPs.

What prices should be used?

Estimation of consumption PPPs or some other aggregate PPP, such as Food PPPs, or Housing PPPs, is not easy, even if there is agreement on all the methods to be employed. This is partly because there are multiple layers of items within each basic heading, such as Flour, Meat, Rice, and Vegetables within Food, or Household Appliances and Furniture within Housing. One of the key issues involves the common practice of obtaining a national average item price from each country. For example, the price of one pound of a bag of white flour[6] within the Food basic heading can be averaged across a number of outlets and several time periods. But when we are focused on a particular population group, namely those in poverty, do national average prices make sense? They probably do in small countries, because most of the evidence suggests that the poor are affected by the lack of capital that constrains them to buy in small quantities, not necessarily that they pay higher prices for the same items. However, in larger countries, there may be significant regional price differences that require more than one poverty line in order to not over-count the poor in some areas and under-count them in others.

Items consumed by the poor

Consider an item about which millions of us are experts: haircuts. On a summer day in Beijing circa 2000 one could get a haircut at shops with varying amounts of amenities. Excluding hotels, the charges might range from CNY10 to CNY15 in shops down to CNY1 or CNY2 for a no-overhead service on the street. Most PPP estimates will choose a shop that might be found in a range of other countries. As long as the prices in such shops represent the relative costs of these services in different countries, the comparisons may still be reasonable, even if they do not explicitly price street barbers.

However, the existence of phenomena like street barbers raises some larger questions. If we consider provision of a minimum bundle of necessary goods and services as the basis for determining the cost of a poverty bundle, then what do we do about items like street haircuts that may only be consumed by the poor? Other examples include rice with broken grains that is indifferently sorted and cleaned, inferior grains like *ragi*, in India, secondhand clothing or cloth remnants, and a wide variety of inferior or makeshift housing. The present state of PPP estimation, at best, only represents consumption of goods and services in the relevant expenditure heading that are available in a wide range of countries.

The prices to the poor question

Outlets and items used in the ICP are those thought important in the expenditures of each country, and often the items representing a heading in one country will be different from those in another country. But do the poor pay different prices for the same items than the middle and upper classes? Those in the PPP estimation business are silent on this issue, and if asked, will say we would be glad to have such data if only countries collected them.

In an early study, Kunreuther (1973) set forth a simple model to examine this question, taking into account size of packaging, type of outlet, and inventory costs of large package sizes or bulk purchases. He found that in New Haven the same package size was more expensive in small stores than chain stores, and that price per physical unit declined with increasing package size.[7] The link to poverty occurs in where stores are located, where the poor make purchases and the size of package they purchase. His result was quite clear. The poor purchased in smaller size packages in smaller stores. Why? Chain stores were not in poor neighborhoods and the poor had less access to their own transport to travel to larger stores. The poor interviewed in the Kunreuther study traveled smaller distances than the more affluent, and had less ability to store goods. In addition to the storage constraint, the poor had weekly per capita purchases that were about two-thirds those of the middle class sample interviewed. The poor also made more frequent purchases suggesting that storage and liquidity constraints may have both operated to produce purchases of smaller size packages.

That was New Haven in 1973. A study in north-east Brazil by Musgrove and Galindo (1988) reported a somewhat different result when they looked at small and large stores in large, medium, and small cities. Their study was in 1985 and in an attempt to overcome the effects of the overall rapid inflation in Brazil, they concentrated the survey into two weeks in a month with only (!) a 5.4 per cent price increase. Whereas Kunreuther found that neighborhood stores sold the same size package at a price typically 10 to 15 per cent higher than the chains, Musgrove and Galindo did not find such a consistent pattern, with some items like manioc flour being sold at lower prices by small retailers. Further, they report that for items sold in bulk, like beans or rice, the price per unit was the same whether the size was a cup or a much larger quantity. A limitation of their study was that it relied solely on the response of store-owners. They did not have direct information on where the poor made their purchases or at what prices. However, it does appear that in urban areas of Brazil the poor do not face different prices for the same goods as the rich, in part because many neighborhoods have a wide range of socio-economic groups living in close proximity, which is not to say that lack of capital does not constrain the size of unit that the poor purchase.

Another question is whether we can learn anything from the prices of goods that are thought to be purchased solely by the poor. Examples of such items are day-old bread, inferior grains, used clothing, or street corner haircuts. In the current round of the ICP several items were consistent for pricing across African countries. If the PPPs are similar to other consumption items between countries, then it would suggest that comparisons across countries can be carried out on the basis of typical items of consumption. However, those purchasing day-old bread or used clothing need no proof that they are in poverty to buy these items, so there is only a presumption that they are mainly purchased by the very poor.

V. Rao (2000) dealt with this question in a study of villages in South India and found that, because the poor buy in very small quantities, the price paid per kilogram of basic food items is higher than for the middle classes. For example, a kilo of yellow split peas would cost INR28, and a 100 gram purchase, INR3.50. While poor families in a week may buy grains in sufficient bulk, important commodities like *pulses* may, as in the above example, have a 20 per cent higher unit cost. Similarly cooking oil is often purchased by the poor in 100 gram lots, raising the unit price. In rural areas, there may be little effect of outlets, but Rao found a significant effect of size of purchases on the cost of a given quantity of consumption goods between the very poor and better off villagers.

What of urban areas of India? Anecdotal evidence abounds. Sales of individual cigarettes at small street stalls reveal the same higher costs per unit as a correlate of low income and/or little liquidity.[8] Even when prices per kilogram are similar for larger and smaller size purchases, there is typically in India a valuable gift with the large package.[9] Is there an outlet effect for the same size of purchase such as in New Haven, but which was not systematically evident in north-east Brazil? Certainly the ICP framework has in the past provided no basis for examining this issue.

An exercise carried out by Perling (2003) collated some 2,800 price observations on thirteen commodities and services in rural and urban areas of China, Hong Kong, Thailand, Malaysia, and Singapore. Although the items surveyed comprised more than the Big Mac, they were not statistically rigorous in terms of the sampling framework, and the results are only suggestive of the type of survey that would address some of the issues raised in this section. The table below provides summary results for three items in Perling's study: a durable item, batteries; a perishable, onions; and a service item, haircuts for men. In Table 6.1 the price level of each item is presented. The base for the comparisons comes from prices collected in outlets in a middle class area of Chengdu, China. For Bangkok, the PPP of the Thai bhat to the Chinese yuan is divided by the exchange rate and expressed as a per cent. For example, the entry of 227 for a kilogram of onions in Bangkok means that it costs the Bangkok middle class 2.27 times as much as in Chengdu at exchange rates.

Taken at face value, what would the information in Table 6.1 suggest about the geographical distribution of poverty within a country? As is well known, the poverty count is inversely related to the level of income in states, provinces or

Table 6.1. Price levels, selected Asian markets, Spring 2002 (base = Chengdu, 100)

	Batteries	Onions	Haircuts
Bangkok: Middle	79	227	208
Bangkok: Poor	79	306	102
Singapore: Middle	135	500	582
Singapore: Poor	101	312	406
Shanghai: Middle	110	151	160
Shanghai: Poor	84	135	107
Fuli: Rural	59	85	22
Shenzen: Middle	109	164	126
Hong Kong: Middle	118	477	835
Chengdu: Middle	100	100	100

any other sub-national unit. This fact is often used to justify policies that promote overall economic growth in a country as the most useful way to reduce poverty. However, it is not inconsistent with that position to also try to measure the poverty in different regions better than we do. In some cases better measures of the geographic dispersion of poverty may facilitate targeted policies that can supplement income growth in raising the economic, educational, or health status of specific groups. (See, for example, Bigman and Fofack, 2000). The numbers for China in Table 6.1 suggest that taking account of price differences within China would reduce the poverty count in rural areas and poorer cities and raise them in better off cities.

A study of the poverty line in the US by Aten (1996) illustrates another aspect of the regional problem. The notion of a national poverty line has been under review in the US for a number of years (Ruggles, 1990). The National Academy of Sciences (1995) made a series of recommendations for a new approach to measuring poverty, including an adjustment for geographic differences in the cost of living. The Census Bureau has been leading an extensive research effort on exactly how to make these adjustments and on alternative poverty measures (Short et al., 1998, 1999; Jolliffe, 2006; Garner et al., 1998; Short, 2001). In the meantime, a number of poor in regions like the Dakotas are over-counted and those in large cities undercounted. In her work Aten, based on Kokoski, Cardiff, and Moulton's (1994) study of inter-area price differences in the US, calculated the cost of the national poverty bundle in 1987 which was then $5,778 per person. This bundle cost $4,867 in the north-central region versus just over $6,970 in San Francisco and New York, hence the likely over-count of those in the north-central and south regions compared to most large US cities. While the government may have had political reasons to shy away from sub-national poverty lines, it has certainly not stopped a number of private firms from selling their estimates of how costly it is to live in different parts of the US.

The Bureau of Labor Statistics approach to spatial price comparisons

ICP price research looked for models in terms of known frameworks for price collection for country consumer price indices (CPI). CPI methodology typically either averages prices across outlets in a city and then takes the time-to-time price relative for an item such as flour (standardized to a unit weight), or takes a price relative at each outlet and averages the relatives across outlets in a city. In either case, information that might have been available on outlet type and average quantity purchased is discarded in the aggregation process. However, in general, price collectors know the location of their outlets, and could easily learn about typical sizes of purchase for items where it is relevant.

The Bureau of Labor Statistics (BLS) in the US changed its framework for CPI price collection in a way that at first glance made the problem of using its data to compare prices across space very difficult. There is a sampling frame at which the price collector checks off for each entry level item (ELI) the outlet, the size, the type of package, and other information about the volume seller within the ELI as indicated by an outlet employee. Examples of ELIs within the Food and Beverages expenditure group would be Flour, Bread, Milk, Chicken, Bananas, etc. When this framework was adopted by BLS in the 1970s it seemed not to lend itself to place to place comparisons because collectors were not asked to price the same item in different outlets. There is no way of knowing in this framework whether, for example, the type of soft drink priced in supermarkets in Denver is the same as those priced in Chicago.

Kokoski, Moulton, and Zieschang (1999) demonstrated that the framework of the CPI lends itself clearly to a hedonic approach. The BLS group began experimenting with the hedonic approach that was also part of early ICP work, namely the Country Product Dummy (CPD) method developed by Robert Summers (1973). The version that Summers used was a very straightforward hedonic regression model akin to those used for temporal studies (Griliches, 1990; Triplett, 1990; Berndt et al., 1995).

The prices are regressed against the two sets of dummy variables as given in equation (1) below: one set contains a dummy variable, D_j for each country other than the numéraire country (country 1), and the second set with a dummy for each item specification, z_i.

$$\ln p_{ij} = \sum_{i=1}^{n} \beta_i z_i + \sum_{j=2}^{m} \alpha_j D_j + \varepsilon_{ij} \qquad (1)$$

The country coefficients (α_j) are the logarithms of the estimated country price levels.[10] The item coefficients (β_i) are the logarithms of the estimates of the average item price in the currency of the numéraire country (which could also be a regional currency).[11]

The innovation of the BLS group was to apply these regressions to US metropolitan areas using the ELI characteristics of the CPI data, resulting in the calculation of inter-area price parities at the level of various expenditure classes or groups. The basic idea was similar to the CPD procedure. The exact same type, brand, and size of apple may not be priced in Philadelphia, Los Angeles, Miami, and Alaska, but as long as there is an overlap of apple characteristics across two or more areas, then a price parity for apples can be obtained for all areas. This framework has been elaborated and a different aggregation used for more recent years by Aten (2006).

The application of this hedonic framework that is proposed for a poverty PPP is set out in (2) below. The subscript j may refer to countries as in the CPD method or, as in the BLS formulation, to regions within a country.

$$\ln p_{ikj} = \sum_{i=1}^{n} \beta_i z_i + \sum_{k=1}^{l} \beta_k z_k + \sum_{j=2}^{m} \alpha_j D_j + \varepsilon_{ij} \qquad (2)$$

The subscript i refers to an income related characteristic, such as outlet type or neighborhood: for example, low, average or high income neighborhood, while the k are item specifications. With this information a simple hedonic regression could tell us whether coefficients for dummy variables in poor neighborhoods were significantly higher than in middle class neighborhoods for different types of items. However, neighborhoods are often not so easily defined, and the poor may make purchases in outlets that are located in higher income neighborhoods, but perhaps it would be possible to broadly identify these differences.

One conclusion is that it would be desirable, in countries with dispersion in prices and incomes across regions, to build up price levels by geographical region and population groups like the poor, perhaps by estimation of hedonic regressions for a number of goods and services. These hedonic equations would explain price *by item characteristics* like size of package, national or local brand and *market characteristics such as* type of outlet, region of the country, rural versus urban location, and within urban areas, poor and other neighborhoods. If the relative importance of different size purchases in rich and poor neighborhoods is known, it could be used to sharpen the PPP estimates for the poor. This would permit regional estimates of price levels, real incomes, and hence numbers in poverty.

Estimation of an international poverty PPP

How is the World Bank poverty line of "$1 a day" a day estimated? Initially, the poverty line for India in rupees was used as a base, and later poverty lines from other low income countries were included. Based on the benchmark ICP studies, these poverty lines could be converted to the US dollar and to other currencies based on their PPPs. As long as a country has expenditure or income distribution data, it is then possible to develop poverty counts based on this international standard. The $1-a-day number proved popular with many users. However, it does not explicitly allow for inflation. In actual applications, the $1 a day line is well over $2.[12]

As discussed briefly in the first section of this chapter, the PPP used for an international poverty line should refer to consumption goods and services, which is clearly more appropriate than the PPP for GDP. However, the PPPs from the ICP involve the budget shares of rich and poor countries as weights so the market basket is quite different from that of the poor. Further, in the case of several aggregation methods, the PPP for consumption is affected by the relative prices of investment goods and government services. The purpose of this section is to make a first pass at examining how sensitive the consumption PPPs are to different methods, to different country groups, and to different reference expenditure distributions. The final section will provide actual estimates of various PPPs for 115 countries, followed by a discussion of their strengths and limitations with respect to using them as the basis for converting an international poverty line.

Sensitivity of PPPs to aggregation methods

The difference between aggregation methods in international comparisons has been extensively researched (for example, in Balk, 2004). We will highlight two of them. The first is the GK (Geary-Khamis) method used in PWT, and the other is the CPD method described earlier with respect to work done by the BLS. The latter is gaining favor in both national and international practice because of its operational flexibility and transparency, as well as some desirable theoretical properties.

Sensitivity of PPPs to country groupings

Should all countries be included in the calculation of a world poverty line? That is, should the prices and quantities of consumption goods in high income countries enter into the aggregation methods at all, and if so, how sensitive are the results to them? In this chapter the world refers to the countries for which we have detailed benchmark data, and they are divided into groups based on their 1996 GDP per capita.

Sensitivity of PPPs to expenditure weights

The question of what prices should be used if we want to estimate anything other than a national average PPP has been discussed briefly in the first section under two headings: "What prices should be used?" and "Items consumed by

Table 6.2. Ratio of poor to average PPPs, 1980

Region	Number of countries	Ratio (poor/average PPP)
Africa	14	0.876
Asia	5	1.205
South America	17	1.310
High income countries	19	1.064

the poor." However, we do not have published national average prices paid by the poor versus the wealthy, nor are there any systematic efforts under way to obtain such differentials, assuming they exist. An example of a survey and a framework for the future was outlined under "The prices to the poor question" and "The Bureau of Labor Statistics approach...". On the other hand, it is possible to obtain expenditure distributions by income groups within countries, and also differential expenditure groupings by countries across the world, and one can look at the sensitivity of the PPPs to these expenditure weighting choices.

Heston (1986) experimented with the first approach using the expenditure weights of the lowest quintile groups in Malawi, India, Brazil, and the US to represent the expenditure distribution in African, Asian, South American, and high income countries respectively. The major surprise was that the weights made as much difference as indicated in Table 6.2.

What drives the results in the low income countries is the relative price of food, which is typically high compared to other headings of consumption. This means that for Asia and South America, using a consumption PPP based upon an expenditure distribution closer to the poverty level would increase the number in poverty.

If we believed the African figures they would suggest the number in poverty in 1980 was substantially overstated, especially compared to Asia and Latin America. Prices of many food items were controlled in Africa in 1980, and while efforts were made to obtain prices of food as a weighted average of ration and free market prices, it is doubtful that this was actually done in many countries. The average ratios in Table 6.2 cover up a fair amount of country variance, but there were only two of the fourteen countries in Africa where the PPP of the poor was higher than of the national average. However, it seems probable that the African PPP for the poor is low because ration prices entered into the estimation with more weight than justified by their quantitative importance. A study carried out by Biru and Ahmad (1994) at the World Bank, based on prices collected in a number of African countries for 1985, produced a result similar to that reported above for Asia and South America.[13]

An iterative approach

An expenditure distribution for those in poverty, either within countries or across countries, departs from the average in obvious ways, such as higher proportion of expenditure on food and other basic necessities. The practical problem of data availability can be resolved by using the two approaches suggested above—within country surveys and across country groupings. But there remains a conceptual issue of simultaneity. We are ultimately seeking a conversion factor appropriate to count those in poverty, but using an existing expenditure survey to group observations means that we are assuming a pre-defined poverty threshold across the observations.

In order to cut through this simultaneity, we develop an iterative procedure as follows: assume an initial distribution of expenditure weights and country groupings, and using the average national prices from the benchmark ICP, estimate a set of initial consumption PPPs. Then adjust the per capita consumption of each country by the latter, and find a new grouping and distribution of expenditures based on this initial PPP for consumption. Repeat the process, using the same average national prices, until the groupings are stable and/or the PPPs converge.

Results

The consumption PPPs reported here refer to 1996 input prices and expenditures, and are derived from benchmark comparisons in different parts of the world between 1993 and 1996 involving 115 countries, rich and poor.[14] For presentation purposes, the PPPs have been converted to price levels, with a price level of 1.00 for the world in the sample. The price level is simply the PPP divided by the exchange rate relative to the US dollar, although any other numéraire country could be used. For example, a price level of 1.66 for the US means that US$1.66 is equivalent to one international dollar. A price level of 0.66 for Tanzania translates into a PPP of TZS381 at an exchange rate of TZS580 US$1. This reduces the number of decimal places and the need to specify the different currency names for all 115 countries. The list of countries and their 1996 exchange rates used in this chapter are in the appendix.

To examine the sensitivity of consumption price levels, seven different alternative combinations of aggregation and weighting methods are discussed and they are presented schematically in Table 6.3. The Geary-Khamis (GK) method has been used in PWT, and the other, the weighted CPD method, is similar to the EKS method used in the European Union (Balk, 2004; Sergeev, 2004; Rao, 2005).

In order to estimate methods (5)–(7), using poverty weights, countries are ordered by their per capita GDP and expressed as a percentage of the US in 1996

165

Table 6.3. Alternative price levels for consumption

	GK method		CPD method		Iterative CPD method
	Consumption within GDP	Consumption	Consumption (only low income countries)		
Super-country weights	(1)	(2)			
Share weights	(3)	(4)			
Poverty weights		(5)	(6)		(7)

Consumption price level directly from PWT
- GK method.
- Super-country weights, a plutocratic weighting scheme.[1]
- All 115 countries are included.
- Aggregation is over GDP although the consumption price level refers only to consumption within GDP.

Consumption PWT (super-country weights)
- As (1) except: Aggregation is only over consumption.

Consumption PWT (percentage share weights)
- As (2) except: Weights are percentage shares, totaling 100 for every country, a democratic scheme.[2]

CPD method (percentage share weights)
- As (3) except: CPD method instead of GK method.

CPD method (poverty weights)
- As (4) except: Countries are grouped by income and their weights are the percentage shares of expenditures of a low income country within a group.

CPD method (poverty weights, no high income countries included)
- Same as (5) except for: Aggregation is only over low income countries (totaling 52).

CPD iterative approach (poverty weights)
- As (5) except: Groupings change to reflect the new ordering after the consumption price levels are calculated, and the process is repeated until there is convergence and the groups remain stable.

1. In practice, PWT uses the nominal GDP modified by a "super-country weight" factor to adjust for the fact that the number of countries that participate in PWT changes every benchmark year. Details are in the appendix.
2. The EKS system, which is commonly used in EU and OECD comparisons, is usually an unweighted version so that Luxembourg is given the same weight as Germany. When the GK system is run with percentage weights, the results are very close to EKS. For comparisons, see Heston et al. (2001).

from PWT (y). For example, in this initial ordering, Tanzania is the poorest, with a y equal to only 1.6. The US is ranked 114 out of 115 countries, with a y equal to 100. Initial poverty thresholds are set at y values less than 5, 10, 20, and 40 respectively for income Groups 1–4, while Group 5 countries had y values greater than 40. Some of the borderline countries were assigned a group depending on their national poverty counts.[15]

The poverty weights used in alternatives (5)–(7) are a set of reference distributions for each group, based on the quintile expenditures of two poor countries: Ethiopia and Guatemala, neither of which participated in the 1996 comparisons.[16] It would clearly be better to have quintile distributions for each country, but using the average expenditures of the poor in a country with a similar

Table 6.4. Poverty weights: reference distributions

Expenditure heading	Country income group				
	1	2	3	4	5
Cereals	48.50	34.00	19.60	18.70	15.00
Meat	2.50	5.20	8.00	7.80	7.10
Fish	0.30	0.40	0.50	0.50	0.40
Eggs, milk	5.50	6.60	7.70	10.00	10.30
Oils	5.60	3.30	1.00	0.80	0.80
Fruit, vegetables	1.90	8.20	14.50	12.30	9.70
Other foods	5.50	6.80	8.20	6.50	8.30
Non-alcoholic beverages	3.80	2.60	1.40	1.30	1.50
Alcoholic beverages	0.40	0.40	0.40	0.30	0.40
Tobacco	0.20	0.20	0.10	0.10	0.20
Clothing	2.90	3.10	3.40	2.80	2.50
Footwear	1.60	1.70	1.70	1.50	1.40
Rent	6.30	8.70	11.10	10.80	10.60
Fuel	1.00	0.60	0.20	0.30	0.70
Furniture	0.50	0.30	0.10	0.20	0.30
Household operation	1.40	2.50	3.70	3.80	3.70
Appliances	0.50	0.30	0.20	0.20	0.30
Health	1.80	3.40	4.90	5.70	6.40
Transport equipment	0.20	0.20	0.20	0.20	0.30
Transport operation	0.20	0.20	0.20	0.70	1.40
Transport services	0.50	1.70	2.90	2.80	3.10
Communication	0.20	0.20	0.20	0.50	0.60
Recreation	0.70	0.80	0.80	1.10	1.60
Education	3.60	3.50	3.50	4.20	5.10
Restaurants	1.30	1.40	1.50	1.50	2.50
Other expenditures	3.90	3.80	3.70	5.40	5.70
Total	100.00	100.00	100.00	100.00	100.00

income at least provides a starting point with which to contrast the national average distributions. These weights are given in Table 6.4.

Figure 6.1 shows a summary of the price level calculations for all countries, with this normalization. That is, the price levels on the Y axis are the averages by income group, and countries in Groups 1–3 average 1. There are seven lines corresponding to the seven alternative price levels, although three of them are highlighted and the remaining four are squeezed between alternatives (1) and (7).

Table 6.5 summarizes the data in Figure 6.1, showing the average price levels by income group for each of the seven alternative calculations. Alternative (0) is the price level of GDP, used in the initial conversion of currencies to international dollars (see also Table 6.2).

Alternative (1) is the price level of consumption from PWT computed with, but not including other expenditures in GDP, while the others are computed only with consumption expenditures. The consumption only alternatives (2)–(7) tend to be flatter than alternative (1), with slightly higher price levels for Group 1 and lower levels for Group 5. Group 2 countries tend to have the

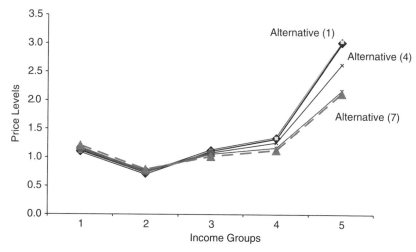

Figure 6.1 Alternative price levels by income group (average of Groups 1–3 = 1.00)

lowest price levels in all alternatives, lower than those in Group 1, giving the lines their U-shape in Figure 6.1 and suggesting that the very poorest countries have proportionally higher price levels for consumption than the low to middle income countries, and sometimes even lower than middle income countries in Group 3.

Tables 6.A1 and 6.A2 show the detailed results for all countries and are included in the appendix. Table 6.A1 has all the price levels, with the average of the countries equal to one. The average of Group 1–3 countries is also given in order to allow comparisons with alternative (6). That is, the price level of any of the other alternatives must be divided by that factor to normalize on the same average as alternative (6).

Do the methods make a difference?

The difference between using GDP price levels and consumption price levels as shown in Table 6.A2 are significant, as many low income countries have lower consumption price levels, and the share of consumption is also relatively high. However, the differences between using the consumption component of GDP—alternative (1)—and only consumption in the GK aggregation method—alternative (2)—are almost negligible. Alternative (2) increases the range slightly, as the differences occur mostly in the extreme low and high income countries.

The differences between the GK method used in alternative (3) and the CPD method in alternative (4) are larger, as expected. They both use the same own

Table 6.5. Summary price levels

Average by income group[1]	(0)[2] GDP	GK (1)[3] Wts	GK (2)[4] Wts	GK (3) %	Alternatives (4) %	Alternatives (5) % POV	CPD (6) % POV (1–3)	CPD (7) % POV Iter
1	1.09	1.10	1.10	1.13	1.12	1.17	1.15	1.21
2	0.76	0.72	0.72	0.78	0.76	0.76	0.75	0.79
3	1.10	1.12	1.12	1.07	1.08	1.06	1.07	1.02
4	1.32	1.34	1.34	1.18	1.26	1.17		1.13
5	2.92	3.02	3.04	2.14	2.63	2.17		2.12

[1]Average of all countries in Groups 1–3 = 1.00.
[2]Alternative (0) is the GDP price level; all others are consumption price levels.
[3]Alternative (1) is consumption as a component of GDP.
[4]Alternative (2) is consumption only, not a component of GDP.

country expenditure share weights but for the majority of the low income countries, the CPD method results in lower price levels, while for the higher income countries, the CPD leads to higher price levels. The largest of these differences are for Nigeria (drops from 2.8 to 2.4) and Bahrain (from 1.8 to 1.4) and Switzerland (increases from 2.2 to 2.7), where the average of all countries is 1.0. At higher incomes, the CPD method is closer to alternative (1)—GK with own country weights—while the GK method with percentage share weights is closer to the CPD method when representative poverty weights are used in the iterative procedure of alternative (7).

Do country groupings make a difference?

There is a small difference, to the second decimal place, between using all 115 countries in alternative (5) and just the Groups 1–3 countries in alternative (6), other things being equal. The difference is positive for lower price levels and negative for higher price levels, that is, the range of price levels is greater when using just the Groups 1–3 countries. However, we only have twenty-six consumption headings, and if there were more detailed price and expenditure data for a greater number of headings, the differences might be more pronounced.

Do expenditure weights make a difference?

There are two sets of comparisons: one between alternatives (2) and (3): super-country versus percentage share weights using the GK method; and the other between alternatives (4) and (5), percentage share weights versus poverty weights using the CPD method. The difference between using plutocratic (super-country) weights and democratic (percentage share) weights is very large. The spread across countries is much wider with lower price levels for lower income countries and higher price levels for high income countries when using plutocratic weights. The pattern is similar for the second comparison: the spread is wider when using democratic weights versus the representative weights, although smaller than when using plutocratic versus democratic weights.

This difference in spread can be seen clearly in Table 6.5, if we focus on differences between income Groups 1 and 3. The average price levels for Group 1 are higher than for Group 3 when percentage share weights or poverty share weights are used—alternatives (3)–(7)—regardless of method. When using plutocratic weights, the Group 3 price levels are slightly higher than the Group 1 levels.

Does simultaneity make a difference?

If the alternative price levels change the relative ranking of countries, then their income groups may change, and hence their representative poverty weight should change as well. In order to verify that these relative changes do not affect the final price level results, we developed an iterative procedure that regroups the countries and recalculates the price levels based on the new income groupings and new poverty weights until the price levels are stable. This occurred after the third iteration, and the difference between the original price levels—alternative (5)—and these iterated price levels—alternative (7)—are similar to the differences when the expenditure weights are changed. That is, for Groups 1 and 2, the iterated price levels are on average higher, but for the remaining groups they are lower, so that the spread is wider in alternative (7).

Do alternative price levels affect poverty counts?

To highlight the difference that the alternative price levels might make to poverty thresholds and counts, we compare the original ordering of countries by per capita GDP relative to the US converted at GDP price levels, with the ordering that would result using alternative (1). The consumption expenditures are given in international dollars (available from PWT), and are labeled "CEX$" in Table 6.A2.

We normalize on the total consumption expenditures of the US for 1996 of just under $20,000 and apply the same 5, 10, 20, and 40 per cent thresholds as in the initial grouping. These are labeled "cy" in Table 6.A2 and correspond to expenditure groupings of $1,000, $2,000, $4,000, and $8,000 respectively, or approximately $3, $5, $11, and $22 international dollars a day.

The general pattern is that lower income countries have a lower consumption price level and this leads to a higher cy (with US=100), although not necessarily a higher CEX$ since the latter depends on whether consumption expenditures are a relatively large proportion of GDP. For example, Guinea's price level of GDP is 0.36 but that of consumption is 0.30, and although its total CEX$ drops to $2,514 from $2,715, its cy jumps to 12.7 from 9.3, and it would be classified as a Group 3 country instead of a Group 2 country.

Table 6.6 shows only the countries that switch income groups, between the original and either alternative (1) or alternative (7). For example, Zimbabwe, which at GDP price levels is only 9.8 per cent of the US, at consumption price levels is over 10 per cent, and moves up into Group 3 using either alternative measure. Korea has a high consumption price level and drops from nearly 50 per cent of the US GDP to just under 40 per cent when we use the iterative method, alternative (7), and to 40.8 per cent using alternative (1). Out of the twenty-five countries that switch groups, sixteen fall into a lower income group using alternative (7) and ten using alternative (1), most of them with ys in the 20 per cent to 25 per cent range. Six countries would

Table 6.6. Countries that switch income groups

				Alternative	
		Initial y	(0)	(1)	(7)
1	Armenia	8.2	2	3 higher	2
2	Bolivia	9.0	2	3 higher	2
3	Guinea	9.3	2	3 higher	3 higher
4	Zimbabwe	9.8	2	3 higher	3 higher
5	Sri Lanka	11.0	3	3	2 lower
6	Ecuador	13.2	3	3	2 lower
7	Turkmenistan	15.5	3	2 lower	2 lower
8	Lebanon	16.9	3	4 higher	4 higher
9	Romania	17.1	3	4 higher	4 higher
10	Bulgaria	20.2	3	4 higher	4 higher
11	Kazakhstan	20.1	4	4	3 lower
12	Botswana	20.8	4	3 lower	3 lower
13	Belize	21.2	4	3 lower	3 lower
14	Latvia	21.2	4	3 lower	3 lower
15	St Lucia	21.5	4	4	3 lower
16	St Vincent	22.0	4	3 lower	3 lower
17	Dominica	23.6	4	3 lower	3 lower
18	Venezuela	23.7	4	4	3 lower
19	Russia	24.3	4	4	3 lower
20	Thailand	24.3	4	3 lower	3 lower
21	Mauritius	40.4	4	5 higher	5 higher
22	Antigua	44.3	5	4 lower	4 lower
23	Slovenia	45.0	5	4 lower	5
24	Bahrain	45.4	5	4 lower	4 lower
25	Korea	49.1	5	5	4 lower

move to a higher income group using alternative (7) and eight using alternative (1).

If we look at Table 6.A2, which has the GDP per capita and the consumption expenditures per capita using alternative (1), we can see that for some countries the differences underlying Table 6.5 are significant. For example, Turkmenistan has a y equal to 15.5 per cent of the US and a per capita GDP of \$4,525, but its consumption per capita drops to \$1,770 and its corresponding cy to only 8.9 per cent of the US. Similarly, Botswana goes from a GDP per capita of \$6,072 and a y of 20.8 down to a per capita consumption of \$2,410 and a cy of 12.1 per cent.

Concluding remarks

This chapter has reviewed some of the strengths and limitations of PWT for providing suitable price levels and PPPs for international poverty comparisons. It compared alternative aggregations and weighting methods and suggested several ways in which estimation of PPPs for the poor might be improved in benchmark ICP comparisons.

It seems clear that a consumption-based PPP is preferable to any GDP-based PPP. Both are available from PWT, and the former, labeled alternative (1) in the chapter, will already significantly affect the ordering of countries. However, the weighting used in PWT is more suitable for national income accounting as it tends to assign greater weight to larger economies, which—in the 1996 benchmark on which these calculations are based—tend to be the wealthier countries. Both China and India were included in the 2005 benchmark and as a consequence, the difference due to weighting between alternative methods was less. But it appears that use of country shares or poverty shares as the weight is a more appropriate way to answer the question about the relative purchasing power of the poor in each country.

Only two aggregation methods were used here and others should be examined. However, previous work has shown that variations of both the GK and CPD are known to be similar to EKS (Sergeev, 2003). An attempt was made here to represent the expenditure distributions of the poor based on household surveys in Guatemala and Ethiopia. Ideally one would like the distribution of expenditures for each country around the likely international poverty line, and then to carry out an iterative procedure such as Deaton et al. (2004) have used for India and Indonesia. However, even the iterations computed here, using only a rough expenditure distribution for the five low income groups, suggest a promising line of research.

Improvements to current methods of using average prices and expenditures to estimate country price levels for poverty comparisons can be summarized as:

• Taking into account the prices paid by the poor into the initial price comparisons when there are geographical concentrations of people, such as in large urban centers of developing countries.

• Using percentage share weights rather than actual weights for each country (democratic versus plutocratic weights).

• Adjusting these share weights to reflect expenditures distributions of the very poor, either by using low income surveys for each country, or an iterative approach that combines representative shares and own country average-income shares. As noted earlier, this will be made easier in the future because of the World Bank effort to classify a large number of household expenditure surveys into the ICP framework.

If direct price surveys are not available, an indirect approach is to use existing surveys to identify the location, outlet and type of neighborhood where prices are collected, and the typical size of purchase. This would improve the underlying price data entering into PPP and subsequently PWT calculations of private consumption that are more appropriate for the poor, both within and between countries. Similarly, expenditure surveys for the poor that are comparable across countries would improve the iterative procedure in that the initial distributions represent individual countries, rather than representative groups of countries.

Since the release of the Final Report of the 2005 ICP in June 2008 (World Bank, 2008), researchers have been provided access to detailed parities for 146 countries. In addition household expenditure surveys for over sixty countries have been put into the same framework of basic headings as the ICP. These surveys provide expenditure distributions for each 20th of the distribution. These data developments permit use of much more sophisticated approaches to generating world poverty lines and poverty PPPs. The work of Deaton and Dupriez (2009) is especially interesting because of the development of new methods including providing errors for their estimates of poverty PPPs. Further, their work using the same basic information from ICP 2005 provides alternative estimates to those of the World Bank Poverty Group, which are used by other international organizations.

Appendix

PWT and other conversion factors for poverty studies

This section sets out the main differences between PWT and other data sets that might be used for studies of international poverty. We first distinguish between the treatment of benchmark and non-benchmark countries. The method of producing current and constant international price estimates is treated next along with the principal differences between the PPP estimates of the World Bank and PWT. A more detailed version of the materials described here is provided in the documentation of PWT 6.1[17] so this discussion will be brief.

Benchmark and non-benchmark countries

Benchmark ICP comparisons have been carried out for over 100 countries, some for just one year, and some for as many as eight years since 1970, originally at five-year intervals, and now every three years for the OECD countries.[18] Benchmark comparisons typically involve detailed price comparisons representing 150 or more basic headings of expenditure on consumption, capital formation, and government. Beginning in 1980 these benchmark comparisons have been organized regionally with various procedures built into the process so that links could be established between countries in different world areas. Some links were provided by countries in both OECD and other groupings, as for example Austria with countries of Eastern Europe, and Japan with the Economic and Social Commission for Asia and the Pacific (ESCAP).

Unfortunately, the last ICP benchmark that represented most of the world regions for a particular date was 1985; it was incorporated in PWT 5.6, with later regional benchmark data. For PWT 6.1, a world comparison was cobbled by using 1996 OECD estimates for member countries plus an equal number of formerly planned economies. Several Latin American countries also made estimates for 1996, and it was possible to update 1993 estimates for the ESCAP countries, Africa, the Middle East, and the Caribbean to 1996, for a total of 115 countries, albeit at the level of only thirty-six headings of expenditure.[19]

Figure 6.A1 illustrates the inputs and procedures used in PWT to obtain the initial 1996 base year price levels (or PPPs) for the three components of GDP: consumption, investment, and government.

First, the ICP benchmark data for the 115 countries are aggregated to the level of Consumption (C), Investment (I), and Government (G) using the Geary-Khamis (GK) method and weights, termed super-country weights, that assign proportional representation of the benchmark countries relative to the world. The World Bank has used a different aggregation method and a different weighting scheme, one that assigns equal weight to each country over all of GDP, so that small countries such as Belize and Luxembourg will have the same importance over all headings as larger countries such as Mexico and Germany. The use of super-country weights in the GK system provides continuity with previous versions of PWT.

The second step is to estimate the PPP of C, I, and G for the non-benchmark countries.[20] In recent versions of PWT these estimates have been made in two stages. First, an estimate of the PPP for Domestic Absorption is made based upon the relationship between various cost of living measures and the PPP for GDP for benchmark countries. The values of these post adjustment indices for the non-benchmark countries are then

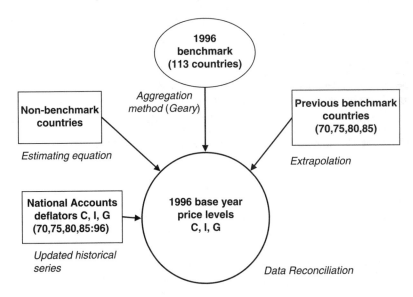

Figure 6.A1 Base year PPPs

175

used in the estimating equation to obtain their Domestic Absorption. This may be contrasted with the method used by the World Bank, also a short cut approach, but one that uses an equation involving education and nominal income but no direct information on prices in non-benchmark countries. In addition, the World Bank does not make estimates for C, I, and G, only for GDP, whereas in PWT the component PPPs are estimated again using a relationship derived from the benchmark countries.

The third and final step is to collate the 1996 benchmark PPPs, the non-benchmark PPPs, and the PPPs from previous benchmark countries that may or may not be part of the 1996 ICP. When countries have multiple benchmarks, the relative PPPs of two countries in two benchmarks usually differs from what would be predicted from relative price movements in the two countries. For example, if the GDP deflator in country A rises by 20 per cent between two benchmarks and that in country B by 30 per cent, then one would expect the $PPP_{B/A}$ to rise between two benchmarks by about 8.3 per cent $[(1 - 1.3/1.2)*100]$. In fact, the two estimates will differ, often by 5 to 15 per cent or more in either direction.

To deal with this empirical finding we use a reconciliation process.[21] The basic idea is to bring previous benchmark estimates of PPPs to a common year by use of the national accounts deflators. For countries with several benchmarks it is necessary to average the different PPP estimates and this is done by giving more recent estimates somewhat greater weight. The reconciled past and present benchmark PPPs, together with the non-benchmark short cut PPP estimates, and the national accounts expenditure data, become the inputs to another multilateral aggregation procedure (GK method, super-country weighting) that will generate the GDP PPPs and international dollar estimates for C, I, and G for the 168 countries in 1996.

It should be noted that these estimates will not necessarily correspond to the initial benchmark comparison for 1996 because both non-benchmark and previous benchmark countries are now included. The World Bank does not attempt this reconciliation process.

PWT estimates in other years

Frequently, international comparisons of poverty, and of wealth, are made at different points in time. One advantage of PWT as a data source for the PPP for such estimates is that it provides a continuous series from which erratic movements that may occur using benchmark estimates in two different years have been removed.[22] Figure 6.A2 illustrates the procedure to obtain the current and constant price series in PWT over time.

For 1996, we have the set of 168 benchmark, non-benchmark, and previous benchmark countries and their component PPPs. For other years, we move the 1996 PPPs backwards and forwards by the changes in the national accounts deflators for each component of each country relative to changes in the US. These become the input PPPs that, combined with the current price national accounts of each country, permit a new multilateral aggregation (GK method, super-country weights) for each year. The result is a set of GDP PPPs and international price estimates of C, I, and G for the 168 countries for 1950–2000.

Several different constant price measures are provided in PWT. It is not clear that researchers would want to use these in poverty comparisons, so the following discussion is highly condensed. A Laspeyres-type measure is given that takes the real value of the components in each year and moves them backward and forward by the national accounts growth rates of the components. The resulting estimates are summed with the

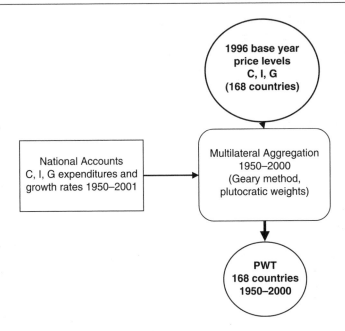

Figure 6.A2 PPP and GDP estimates, other years

net foreign balance in 1996 prices to obtain the GDP in each year. Because the weights of C, I, and G in international prices will not necessarily be the same as those in national prices, the growth rate of GDP in PWT will not be identical to that in national prices. In this PWT differs from most other series and this should be understood in research making use of the growth rates implicit in PWT. The same is true of the chain index in PWT. The chain index applies the national accounts growth rates to the component shares in international prices, derived from the current year multilateral aggregation, obtaining a growth rate for Domestic Absorption (DA) for each pair of consecutive years.

The main differences between PWT and World Bank PPPs can be summarized as follows:

1. The initial *aggregation method* or price index number formula that is applied to the benchmark countries is not the same: PWT uses the GK aggregation with plutocratic weights. Estimates for *non-benchmark* countries are made using short cut methods, but the equations and variables differ: the World Bank uses education and nominal incomes whereas PWT uses information on prices and no education variable.

2. Information on *previous benchmarks* is not used in the World Bank, but is collated and reconciled in PWT.

3. The *current price series*: PWT estimates PPPs and international prices for each component in each year, whereas the World Bank obtains the 1996 GDP PPPs and applies national accounts growth rates to obtain other years.

4. The *constant price series*: PWT's Laspeyres series is based on the growth rate of C, I, and G from the national accounts plus the net foreign balance, the World Bank uses GDP growth rates.

5. *Chain series*: PWT provides a chained constant price series using component shares in international prices for each year.

6. *Consumption PPPs*: PWT provides the PPP and the constant and current international prices for consumption as well as for GDP for all countries and for as many years as there are national accounts series available.

Table 6A.1. Detailed price levels

		GK (1)	GK (2)	GK (3)	CPD (4)	CPD (5)	CPD (6)	CPD (7)
		Consumption in GDP			Consumption			
	y	Wts	Wts	%	%	% POV	% POV (1–3)	% POV Iter
Tanzania	1.6	0.66	0.65	0.69	0.63	0.66	*0.91*	0.74
Malawi	2.5	0.44	0.44	0.58	0.52	0.61	*0.84*	0.64
Madagascar	2.7	0.58	0.57	0.67	0.61	0.66	*0.92*	0.72
Yemen	2.7	1.27	1.27	1.37	1.24	1.56	*2.15*	1.48
Mali	2.8	0.45	0.45	0.60	0.52	0.73	*1.00*	0.72
Zambia	2.9	0.70	0.69	0.79	0.73	0.85	*1.17*	0.86
Nigeria	3.2	1.96	1.94	2.77	2.36	2.72	*3.75*	3.02
Sierra Leone	3.2	0.30	0.30	0.61	0.52	0.62	*0.86*	0.67
Tajikistan	3.4	0.26	0.26	0.42	0.35	0.34	*0.47*	0.42
Benin	3.8	0.57	0.57	0.66	0.62	0.75	*1.03*	0.74
Kenya	4.3	0.37	0.37	0.51	0.44	0.55	*0.76*	0.56
Mongolia	4.3	0.54	0.53	0.51	0.48	0.49	*0.67*	0.50
Nepal	4.4	0.27	0.27	0.29	0.26	0.30	*0.42*	0.26
Senegal	5.1	0.54	0.53	0.68	0.61	0.76	*1.05*	0.75
Bangladesh	5.2	0.38	0.37	0.40	0.36	0.39	*0.54*	0.40
Vietnam	5.7	0.31	0.31	0.31	0.28	0.28	*0.39*	0.27
Congo	5.9	0.74	0.74	1.26	1.00	1.33	*1.87*	1.34
Cameroon	6.5	0.45	0.45	0.72	0.61	0.73	*1.03*	0.74
Côte d'Ivoire	6.7	0.50	0.50	0.75	0.67	0.79	*1.10*	0.77
Pakistan	6.7	0.45	0.45	0.43	0.41	0.39	*0.55*	0.43
Azerbaijan	7.0	0.36	0.36	0.52	0.43	0.34	*0.48*	0.49
Moldova	7.8	0.30	0.30	0.44	0.35	0.33	*0.46*	0.42
Armenia	8.2	0.33	0.33	0.51	0.44	0.35	*0.49*	0.50
Kyrgyzstan	8.9	0.32	0.32	0.42	0.36	0.36	*0.50*	0.42
Bolivia	9.0	0.62	0.62	0.56	0.57	0.57	*0.80*	0.59
Guinea	9.3	0.30	0.30	0.47	0.40	0.51	*0.72*	0.50
Uzbekistan	9.6	0.35	0.35	0.49	0.40	0.45	*0.63*	0.51
Zimbabwe	9.8	0.33	0.33	0.42	0.41	0.48	*0.68*	0.45
Albania	10.5	0.48	0.47	0.56	0.49	0.42	*0.60*	0.51
Philippines	10.7	0.51	0.51	0.48	0.48	0.46	*0.66*	0.46
Sri Lanka	11.0	0.41	0.41	0.45	0.39	0.36	*0.51*	0.41
Egypt	12.7	0.41	0.41	0.48	0.45	0.52	*0.74*	0.52
Jordan	12.8	0.80	0.80	1.01	0.91	1.01	*1.44*	0.97

Morocco	13.0	0.45	0.45	0.68	0.59	0.66	*0.94*	0.69
Jamaica	13.0	0.99	0.99	1.13	1.03	1.17	*1.66*	1.12
Ecuador	13.2	0.87	0.87	0.76	0.79	0.79	*1.12*	0.78
Indonesia	13.3	0.49	0.48	0.50	0.45	0.52	*0.74*	0.42
Syria	13.6	1.92	1.92	2.40	2.13	2.74	*3.92*	2.60
Ukraine	15.1	0.34	0.34	0.45	0.37	0.39	*0.56*	0.42
Peru	15.2	0.89	0.89	0.80	0.82	0.84	*1.21*	0.80
Georgia	15.3	0.39	0.39	0.58	0.50	0.38	*0.55*	0.54
Turkmenistan	15.5	0.16	0.16	0.32	0.22	0.21	*0.30*	0.27
Macedonia	15.7	0.81	0.81	0.78	0.77	0.78	*1.12*	0.75
Lebanon	16.9	1.04	1.03	1.65	1.27	1.73	*2.47*	1.37
Romania	17.1	0.40	0.40	0.47	0.41	0.36	*0.52*	0.41
Grenada	17.2	0.89	0.89	1.03	0.90	1.04	*1.49*	1.01
Swaziland	17.7	0.35	0.35	0.53	0.49	0.60	*0.85*	0.55
Fiji	18.1	0.93	0.93	0.90	0.88	0.82	*1.17*	0.83
Iran	18.3	0.59	0.59	0.66	0.61	0.68	*0.97*	0.71
Panama	19.4	0.82	0.81	0.74	0.75	0.76	*1.08*	0.73
Belarus	19.4	0.38	0.38	0.52	0.43	0.44	*0.62*	0.48
Bulgaria	20.2	0.37	0.37	0.37	0.36	0.37	*0.52*	0.35
Tunisia	20.0	0.38	0.38	0.63	0.53	0.66		0.62
Kazakhstan	20.1	0.40	0.40	0.54	0.45	0.45		0.50
Botswana	20.8	0.49	0.49	0.63	0.64	0.68		0.68
Belize	21.2	0.86	0.86	0.94	0.85	0.93		0.82
Latvia	21.2	0.60	0.60	0.75	0.66	0.61		0.66
St Lucia	21.5	1.04	1.03	1.10	1.01	1.21		1.19
St Vincent	22.0	0.89	0.89	1.06	0.91	1.08		1.05
Turkey	22.0	0.75	0.75	0.71	0.70	0.66		0.62
Lithuania	22.2	0.55	0.55	0.61	0.55	0.54		0.53
Dominica	23.6	0.98	0.98	1.14	0.99	1.10		1.10
Brazil	23.6	1.18	1.18	1.03	1.11	1.06		1.00
Venezuela	23.7	0.88	0.87	0.79	0.80	0.80		0.71
Thailand	24.3	0.84	0.83	0.81	0.79	0.73		0.74
Russia	24.3	0.64	0.64	0.74	0.67	0.66		0.67
Mexico	25.2	0.80	0.80	0.69	0.76	0.71		0.69
Croatia	25.4	1.01	1.01	1.06	1.06	1.03		1.05
Estonia	25.7	0.66	0.66	0.68	0.64	0.66		0.63
Poland	26.4	0.76	0.76	0.83	0.79	0.70		0.70
Hungary	29.8	0.69	0.69	0.65	0.66	0.63		0.60
Gabon	30.4	0.65	0.65	1.33	1.02	1.34		1.51
Chile	30.7	0.94	0.94	0.83	0.87	0.88		0.85
Uruguay	31.8	1.13	1.13	1.05	1.10	1.03		1.00
Trinidad	32.5	0.85	0.85	0.89	0.89	0.96		0.90
Slovakia	34.2	0.56	0.56	0.60	0.58	0.51		0.54
Argentina	36.6	1.22	1.21	1.05	1.12	1.10		1.03
St Kitts and Nevis	39.9	1.00	0.99	1.02	0.97	1.10		1.10
Mauritius	40.4	0.39	0.39	0.63	0.53	0.65		0.60
Greece	43.7	1.58	1.58	1.34	1.43	1.29		1.24
Antigua	44.3	1.38	1.37	1.52	1.45	1.52		1.51
Slovenia	45.0	1.27	1.27	1.03	1.12	1.09		1.05
Bahrain	45.4	1.12	1.11	1.83	1.36	1.27		1.19
Czech Republic	46.1	0.65	0.65	0.62	0.62	0.60		0.57
Portugal	46.3	1.39	1.39	1.17	1.27	1.14		1.11
Korea	49.1	1.40	1.40	1.34	1.34	1.51		1.45
Barbados	50.0	0.48	0.49	1.02	0.72	1.04		0.73
Spain	53.2	1.69	1.70	1.34	1.52	1.36		1.34
Israel	56.4	1.80	1.81	1.38	1.64	1.54		1.50
Bahamas	56.6	1.30	1.30	1.26	1.26	1.38		1.30

(*Continued*)

Table 6A.1. (Continued)

		GK (1)	GK (2)	GK (3)	CPD (4)	CPD (5)	CPD (6)	CPD (7)
		Consumption in GDP			Consumption			
	y	Wts	Wts	%	%	% POV	% POV (1–3)	% POV Iter
Oman	57.1	0.66	0.66	1.36	0.98	1.11		1.03
New Zealand	60.7	1.75	1.76	1.32	1.59	1.43		1.46
Ireland	63.4	1.88	1.89	1.50	1.70	1.44		1.46
Bermuda	64.4	2.44	2.44	2.65	2.67	2.27		2.45
Finland	66.8	2.31	2.31	1.77	2.09	1.84		1.85
Qatar	68.0	0.79	0.79	1.05	0.92	1.21		0.98
UK	68.7	1.74	1.75	1.33	1.56	1.38		1.41
France	69.3	2.26	2.27	1.73	2.07	1.81		1.82
Italy	70.1	1.72	1.72	1.39	1.57	1.45		1.41
Sweden	71.5	2.52	2.53	1.93	2.33	2.02		2.06
Belgium	72.3	2.09	2.10	1.58	1.89	1.64		1.66
Germany	72.3	2.25	2.26	1.70	2.07	1.79		1.88
Austria	73.3	2.22	2.23	1.70	2.02	1.72		1.76
Netherlands	73.4	2.04	2.05	1.56	1.87	1.58		1.61
Iceland	73.6	2.01	2.02	1.62	1.81	1.76		1.71
Australia	78.2	1.70	1.71	1.29	1.54	1.33		1.35
Canada	79.1	1.47	1.48	1.09	1.34	1.20		1.24
Japan	82.4	2.61	2.63	2.09	2.41	2.59		2.53
Denmark	82.5	2.44	2.45	1.91	2.21	2.05		2.01
Switzerland	83.8	2.86	2.87	2.23	2.70	2.31		2.39
Singapore	85.4	1.92	1.92	2.19	1.99	1.42		1.51
Norway	85.4	2.52	2.53	1.95	2.30	2.13		2.10
Hong Kong	89.0	1.45	1.46	1.47	1.46	1.38		1.43
US	100.0	1.66	1.67	1.25	1.57	1.32		1.48
Luxembourg	120.4	2.11	2.12	1.59	1.89	1.70		1.75
Average all		1.00	1.00	1.00	1.00	1.00	1.00	1.00
Average Groups 1–3		0.58	0.58	0.71	0.64	0.71	1.00	0.72

Table 6A.2. GDP versus consumption alternative (1)

	GDP (original)				Consumption alternative (1)			
	PLGDP	GDP$	Y (US = 100)	Income Group	PLC	CEX$	cy (US = 100)	Income Group
Tanzania	0.68	467	1.6	1	0.66	403	2.0	1
Malawi	0.52	730	2.5	1	0.44	689	3.5	1
Madagascar	0.60	788	2.7	1	0.58	720	3.6	1
Yemen	0.92	788	2.7	1	1.27	535	2.7	1
Mali	0.55	817	2.8	1	0.45	703	3.5	1
Zambia	0.71	847	2.9	1	0.70	660	3.3	1
Nigeria	2.02	934	3.2	1	1.96	567	2.9	1
Sierra Leone	0.37	934	3.2	1	0.30	911	4.6	1
Tajikistan	0.26	993	3.4	1	0.26	664	3.3	1
Benin	0.59	1,109	3.8	1	0.57	995	5.0	1

Kenya	0.43	1,255	4.3	1	0.37	998	5.0	1
Mongolia	0.56	1,255	4.3	1	0.54	799	4.0	1
Nepal	0.26	1,285	4.4	1	0.27	895	4.5	1
Senegal	0.61	1,489	5.1	2	0.54	1,236	6.2	2
Bangladesh	0.36	1,518	5.2	2	0.38	1,310	6.6	2
Vietnam	0.32	1,664	5.7	2	0.31	1,306	6.6	2
Congo	0.93	1,722	5.9	2	0.74	1,014	5.1	2
Cameroon	0.58	1,898	6.5	2	0.45	1,581	8.0	2
Côte d'Ivoire	0.65	1,956	6.7	2	0.50	1,454	7.3	2
Pakistan	0.41	1,956	6.7	2	0.45	1,445	7.3	2
Azerbaijan	0.33	2,044	7	2	0.36	1,685	8.5	2
Moldova	0.29	2,277	7.8	2	0.30	1,599	8.0	2
Armenia	0.29	2,394	8.2	2	0.33	2,152	10.8	3
Kyrgyzstan	0.26	2,598	8.9	2	0.32	1,719	8.7	2
Bolivia	0.61	2,627	9	2	0.62	2,029	10.2	3
Guinea	0.36	2,715	9.3	2	0.30	2,514	12.7	3
Uzbekistan	0.35	2,803	9.6	2	0.35	1,557	7.8	2
Zimbabwe	0.44	2,861	9.8	2	0.33	2,061	10.4	3
Albania	0.45	3,065	10.5	3	0.48	2,858	14.4	3
Philippines	0.61	3,124	10.7	3	0.51	2,349	11.8	3
Sri Lanka	0.39	3,211	11	3	0.41	2,392	12.0	3
Egypt	0.51	3,708	12.7	3	0.41	3,371	17.0	3
Jordan	0.68	3,737	12.8	3	0.80	2,212	11.1	3
Morocco	0.59	3,795	13	3	0.45	3,134	15.8	3
Jamaica	0.94	3,795	13	3	0.99	2,492	12.5	3
Ecuador	0.70	3,854	13.2	3	0.87	2,231	11.2	3
Indonesia	0.49	3,883	13.3	3	0.49	2,393	12.0	3
Syria	1.68	3,970	13.6	3	1.92	2,817	14.2	3
Ukraine	0.33	4,408	15.1	3	0.34	2,487	12.5	3
Peru	0.95	4,437	15.2	3	0.89	3,143	15.8	3
Georgia	0.31	4,467	15.3	3	0.39	3,320	16.7	3
Turkmenistan	0.19	4,525	15.5	3	0.16	1,770	8.9	2
Macedonia	0.81	4,583	15.7	3	0.81	3,320	16.7	3
Lebanon	1.07	4,934	16.9	3	1.04	5,232	26.3	4
Romania	0.52	4,992	17.1	3	0.40	4,140	20.8	4
Grenada	1.03	5,021	17.2	3	0.89	3,536	17.8	3
Swaziland	0.42	5,167	17.7	3	0.35	3,686	18.6	3
Fiji	0.86	5,284	18.1	3	0.93	3,543	17.8	3
Iran	0.68	5,342	18.3	3	0.59	3,471	17.5	3
Panama	0.89	5,664	19.4	3	0.82	3,285	16.5	3
Belarus	0.34	5,664	19.4	3	0.38	3,033	15.3	3
Bulgaria	0.33	5,897	20.2	3	0.37	4,040	20.3	4
Tunisia	0.61	5,839	20	4	0.38	4,517	22.7	4
Kazakhstan	0.37	5,868	20.1	4	0.40	4,110	20.7	4
Botswana	0.90	6,072	20.8	4	0.49	2,410	12.1	3
Belize	0.76	6,189	21.2	4	0.86	3,735	18.8	3
Latvia	0.55	6,189	21.2	4	0.60	3,886	19.6	3
St Lucia	1.02	6,277	21.5	4	1.04	4,614	23.2	4
St Vincent	0.64	6,423	22	4	0.89	2,964	14.9	3
Turkey	0.75	6,423	22	4	0.75	4,551	22.9	4
Lithuania	0.54	6,481	22.2	4	0.55	4,309	21.7	4
Dominica	0.78	6,890	23.6	4	0.98	3,470	17.5	3
Brazil	1.16	6,890	23.6	4	1.18	4,377	22.0	4
Venezuela	0.76	6,919	23.7	4	0.88	4,074	20.5	4
Thailand	0.71	7,094	24.3	4	0.84	3,590	18.1	3
Russia	0.66	7,094	24.3	4	0.64	4,538	22.8	4
Mexico	0.81	7,357	25.2	4	0.80	5,451	27.4	4
Croatia	0.99	7,415	25.4	4	1.01	4,448	22.4	4

(*Continued*)

Table 6A.2. (Continued)

		GDP (original)					Consumption alternative (1)		
	PLGDP	GDP$	Y (US = 100)	Income Group		PLC	CEX$	cy (US = 100)	Income Group
Estonia	0.66	7,503	25.7	4		0.66	4,476	22.5	4
Poland	0.80	7,707	26.4	4		0.76	5,791	29.1	4
Hungary	0.84	8,700	29.8	4		0.69	5,651	28.4	4
Gabon	0.96	8,875	30.4	4		0.65	5,352	26.9	4
Chile	0.89	8,963	30.7	4		0.94	5,517	27.8	4
Uruguay	1.06	9,284	31.8	4		1.13	6,462	32.5	4
Trinidad	0.78	9,488	32.5	4		0.85	6,019	30.3	4
Slovakia	0.61	9,984	34.2	4		0.56	7,011	35.3	4
Argentina	1.20	10,685	36.6	4		1.22	7,280	36.6	4
St Kitts and Nevis	0.86	11,648	39.9	4		1.00	5,923	29.8	4
Mauritius	0.53	11,794	40.4	5		0.39	9,458	47.6	5
Greece	1.55	12,758	43.7	5		1.58	10,144	51.1	5
Antigua	1.05	12,933	44.3	5		1.38	5,700	28.7	4
Slovenia	1.19	13,137	45	5		1.27	7,144	36.0	4
Bahrain	1.21	13,254	45.4	5		1.12	5,607	28.2	4
Czech Republic	0.69	13,458	46.1	5		0.65	9,325	46.9	5
Portugal	1.39	13,517	46.3	5		1.39	9,801	49.3	5
Korea	1.32	14,334	49.1	5		1.40	8,096	40.8	5
Barbados	0.86	14,597	50	5		0.48	12,084	60.8	5
Spain	1.66	15,531	53.2	5		1.69	10,721	54.0	5
Israel	1.69	16,465	56.4	5		1.80	9,656	48.6	5
Bahamas	1.24	16,524	56.6	5		1.30	12,234	61.6	5
Oman	0.86	16,670	57.1	5		0.66	9,713	48.9	5
New Zealand	1.68	17,721	60.7	5		1.75	12,075	60.8	5
Ireland	1.81	18,509	63.4	5		1.88	11,760	59.2	5
Bermuda	2.36	18,801	64.4	5		2.44	16,677	83.9	5
Finland	2.12	19,502	66.8	5		2.31	12,611	63.5	5
Qatar	1.13	19,852	68	5		0.79	9,942	50.0	5
UK	1.67	20,056	68.7	5		1.74	15,089	75.9	5
France	2.14	20,231	69.3	5		2.26	13,707	69.0	5
Italy	1.74	20,465	70.1	5		1.72	14,159	71.3	5
Sweden	2.36	20,874	71.5	5		2.52	14,084	70.9	5
Belgium	2.09	21,107	72.3	5		2.09	11,591	58.3	5
Germany	2.29	21,107	72.3	5		2.25	14,625	73.6	5
Austria	2.23	21,399	73.3	5		2.22	14,925	75.1	5
Netherlands	2.05	21,428	73.4	5		2.04	13,405	67.5	5
Iceland	2.09	21,487	73.6	5		2.01	14,728	74.1	5
Australia	1.65	22,830	78.2	5		1.70	15,784	79.4	5
Canada	1.47	23,092	79.1	5		1.47	13,488	67.9	5
Japan	2.58	24,056	82.4	5		2.61	14,637	73.7	5
Denmark	2.40	24,085	82.5	5		2.44	15,965	80.4	5
Switzerland	2.84	24,464	83.8	5		2.86	14,456	72.8	5
Singapore	1.66	24,932	85.4	5		1.92	8,663	43.6	5
Norway	2.39	24,932	85.4	5		2.52	14,701	74.0	5
Hong Kong	1.55	25,983	89	5		1.45	17,482	88.0	5
US	1.66	29,194	100	5		1.66	19,867	100.0	5
Luxembourg	2.05	35,149	120.4	5		2.11	21,047	105.9	5
Average	1.00	9,354	32.0			1.00	6,071	30.6	

Notes

1. US Department of Commerce, Bureau of Economic Analysis.
2. University of Pennsylvania.
3. These comments and parts of this section are based on Heston (1986).
4. See <http://www.worldbank.org/icp>.
5. Typically for non-priced output of government and non-profit organizations, the PPP has been derived from wage comparisons for closely specified occupations. This assumes that productivity of these workers is equal across countries, an assumption that was clearly a gross simplification since the opportunity cost of labor and the capital per worker are higher in more affluent countries. In the 2005 comparison a very rough adjustment was made based on actual or assigned capital per worker in the whole economy for lower income countries. This adjustment has the effect of reducing the output of educational, health, and administrative services by 50 to 100 per cent compared with previous benchmarks.
6. The size and packaging can be standardized to any other specification, and to other characteristics, depending on the richness of the price collection survey.
7. In Kunreuther's sample the price per unit over the range of package sizes was from 50 per cent to 75 per cent going from largest to smallest size. The sample of poor and middle class respondents were well aware of the range of sizes available and the differences in price per physical unit even though this was before mandatory displays of this information in chain stores. In the sample of neighborhood stores, about 20 to 40 per cent stocked the largest package size for each of the eight items sampled by Kunreuther.
8. In fact the pricing of an individual cigarette at INR2 can be fairly close to a package of ten, that may cost something over INR15. And panwallas may use a low price of a single cigarette as a loss leader. But informants in Brazil and Egypt suggest that the mark-up or the single cigarette is typically 10–20 per cent above buying a package.
9. For example a 1 kilogram package of cooking oil may sell for INR55 and a 5 kilogram package at INR225, but the latter will include a plastic bucket valued at INR90 by the seller, but at cost perhaps INR50. A significant percentage of larger size consumer items in India are discounted in this tied manner.
10. The price level is commonly used in the international literature instead of a PPP and often refers to prices expressed relative to a numéraire country currency, such as the US dollar. The analogue in inter-area comparisons is a price expressed relative to one area, or to the average of the areas (as is done in the Euro-area).
11. Chapter 10 of the draft ICP handbook deals extensively with the estimation of basic heading parities using both a weighted (roughly) and unweighted CPD and EKS. In this chapter simulations are developed indicating that the weighted CPD approximates more closely what would be obtained if all prices were available for all products in all countries than other methods.
12. Some users do not regard $1 or so a day as helpful because they believe no one could live on $1 or $2 in the US. Of course, the $1 buys three or four times the amount of goods in a rural area of a poor country than it would in the US. It might be of interest to note that about the time that the $1-a-day poverty line was being discussed, the homeless in Chicago on average had $5 of spending money a day.

13. The exercise reported below was based on fifty-five of the sixty countries in the 1980 ICP benchmark (Eastern Europe was excluded). Two limitations of this exercise should be mentioned. First, the exercise was not on input prices at the basic heading level of 100 or so categories of consumption, but at the level of major expenditure components, about 10–20 summary categories. The summary categories for 1980 had been estimated by the Geary-Khamis (GK) aggregation method. It is possible that the overall quantitative effect of alternative weights would differ from those using more detailed headings, but it is not likely that the use of GK parities would change the qualitative findings. The second limitation of this exercise is that it used representative expenditure weights of a very diverse character: for Africa, the expenditure distribution was of estate workers in Malawi; in Asia, the third decile of rural workers in India; for South America, the lowest quintile in Brazil; and in high income countries, the 1960 expenditure distribution for those in poverty in the US was used.

14. Details of how the price and expenditure data are transformed into PPPs at the various levels of aggregation, such as Consumption, Investment, Government, and GDP are beyond the scope of this paper, but a brief summary of the procedures used in PWT are given in the appendix.

15. Bulgaria was assigned to Group 3 and Tunisia and Kazakhstan to Group 4 although their ys are all around 20.

16. If Guatemala and Ethiopia had participated in the 1996 ICP comparisons, they would be in Groups 3 and 1 respectively. For Group 1, Ethiopia's second quintile was used; for Group 2, the average of Ethiopia's and Guatemala's second quintiles was used. For Groups 3–5, Guatemala's distributions, from second to fourth quintile were used.

17. Technical Documentation, About PWT <http://pwt.econ.upenn.edu>.

18. Actually the EU countries have been carrying out annual estimates since 1993 where about one-third of the underlying items are priced each year, and the remainder updated from the previous years by appropriate time-to-time indices.

19. In 1985 there were only sixty-four countries but a total of 139 basic expenditure headings.

20. There are also countries for which benchmark results are not available but some studies have been made, notably China and Taiwan. For details, see PWT6.1.

21. This reconciliation process was called "consistentization" in previous versions of PWT, but Robert Summers has reluctantly given up the term.

22. The reconciliation process does not remove erratic movements that originate in the national accounts series.

Bibliography

Aten, B. (1996) 'Some Poverty Lines are More Equal Than Others'. Paper presented to the Western Regional Science Association (February). Discussion Paper of the Center for International Comparisons at the University of Pennsylvania, CICUP 95–5.

—— (2006) 'Interarea Price Levels: an Experimental Methodology'. *Monthly Labor Review*, Bureau of Labor Statistics, 129(9).

Balk, B. (2004) 'Aggregation Methods in International Comparisons: What Have We Learned?' Report Series Research in Management ERS-2001–41-MKT (Erasmus Research

Institute of Management, Erasmus University Rotterdam). First version presented at the Joint World Bank–OECD Seminar on Purchasing Power Parities, January30–February2, 2001, Washington DC.

Berndt, E., Griliches, Z., and Rappaport, N. (1995) 'Econometric Estimates of Price Indices for Personal Computers in the 1990s'. *Journal of Econometrics*, 68, pp. 243–68.

Bigman, D. and Fofack, H. (eds.) (2000) *Geographical Targeting for Poverty Alleviation: Methodology and Applications*. Washington DC: International Bank for Reconstruction and Development, World Bank.

Biru, Y. and Ahmad, S. (1994) 'Sensitivity of Poverty Lines to Choices of PPPs'. World Bank Working Paper, November.

Deaton, A. and Dupriez, O. (2009) 'Global Poverty and Global Price Indexes'. Working paper, <http://www.princeton.edu/~deaton/papers.html>.

—— Friedman, J., and Alatas, V. (2004) 'Purchasing Power Parity Exchange Rates from Household Survey Data: India and Indonesia'. Research Program in Development Studies, Princeton University.

Diewert, E. (2002) 'Weighted Country Product Dummy Variable Regressions and Index Number Formulae'. University of British Columbia Department of Economics Discussion Paper 02–15, Vancouver, BC, Canada.

Garner, T. I., Paulin, G., Shipp, S., Short, K., and Nelson, C. (1998) 'Experimental Poverty Measurement for the 1990s'. *Monthly Labor Review*, 121(3).

Griliches, Z. (1990) 'Hedonic Price Indices and the Measurement of Capital and Productivity: Some Historical Reflections'. In E. R. Berndt and J. E. Triplett (eds.) *Fifty Years of Economic Measurement: The Jubilee Conference of Research in Income and Wealth, Studies in Income and Wealth, Vol. 54*, Chicago: University of Chicago Press, pp. 185–206.

Heston, A. (1986) 'Some Problems of Comparing Poverty Levels Across Countries'. Paper presented at Seminar on "Use of Purchasing Power Parities", Luxembourg, Eurostat (November).

—— (2008) 'What Can Be Learned About the Economies of China and India from the Results of Purchasing Power Comparisons'. Revision of paper presented at Indian Council for Research on International Economic Relations (ICRIER), New Delhi, December 6–7, 2007. <http://pwt.econ.upenn.edu/papers/paperev.html>.

—— Summers, R., and Aten, B. (2001) 'Stability of Country Price Structures: Implications for Spatial-Temporal Comparisons'. *UN Economic Commission for Europe Statistical Reporter*, May.

—— —— —— (2002) 'Penn World Table Version 6.1'. Center for International Comparisons at the University of Pennsylvania (CICUP). <http://pwt.econ.upenn.edu/>.

—— —— —— (2006) 'Penn World Table Version 6.2'. Center for International Comparisons at the University of Pennsylvania (CICUP). <http://pwt.econ.upenn.edu/>.

Jolliffe, D. (2006) 'Poverty, Prices and Place: How Sensitive is the Spatial Distribution of Poverty to Cost of Living Adjustments?' *Economic Inquiry*, 44(2).

Kokosky, M., Cardiff, P., and Moulton, B. (1994) 'Interarea Price Indices for Consumer Goods and Services: An Hedonic Approach Using CPI Data'. BLS Working Paper 256.

—— Moulton, B., and Zieschang, D. (1999) 'Interarea Price Comparisons for Heterogeneous Goods and Several Levels of Aggregation'. In A. Heston and R. Lipsey (eds.) *International and Interarea Comparisons of Income, Output and Prices*, Studies in Income and Wealth, Volume 61. Chicago: University of Chicago Press.

Kravis, I., Heston, A., and Summers, R. (1982) *World Product and Income*. Baltimore: World Bank and Johns Hopkins University Press.

Kunreuther, H. (1973) 'Why the Poor May Pay More for Food: Theoretical and Empirical Evidence'. *Journal of Business*, 46(3), pp. 368–83.

Musgrove, P. and Galindo, O. (1988) 'Do the Poor Pay More? Retail Food Prizes in Northeast Brazil'. *Economic Development and Cultural Change*, 37, pp. 91–109.

National Academy of Sciences (1995) *Measuring Poverty: A New Approach*. Washington DC: National Academy Press.

Perling, M. (2003) 'The Effect of Brand and Outlet Variation on Price in Malaysia, China, Singapore and Thailand'. Available from author.

Rao, D. S. P. (2005) 'On the Equivalence of Weighted Country-Product-Dummy (CPD) Method and the Rao-System for Multilateral Price Comparisons'. *Review of Income and Wealth*, 51(4).

Rao, V. (2000) 'Price Heterogeneity and "Real" Inequality: A Case-Study of Prices and Poverty in Rural South India'. *Review of Income and Wealth*, 46(2), pp. 201–11.

Ruggles, P. (1990) *Drawing the Line—Alternative Poverty Measures and Their Implications for Public Policy*. Washington DC: The Urban Institute Press.

Selvanathan, E. A. and Rao, D. S. P. (1994) *Index Numbers: A Stochastic Approach*. Ann Arbor: University of Michigan Press.

Sergeev, S. (2003) 'Equi-representativity and some Modifications of the EKS Method at the Basic Heading Level'. Working Paper No. 8, UN ECE, Geneva, March 31–April 2. <http://www.unece.org/stats/documents/2003/03/ecp/wp.8.e.pdf>.

—— (2004) 'The Use of Weights within the CPD and EKS Methods at the Basic Heading Level'. Mimeo, Statistics Austria.

Short, K. (2001) *Experimental Poverty Measures: 1999*. Current Population Reports, P60–216, US Census Bureau, Washington DC.

—— Shea, M., Johnson, D., and Garner, T. I. (1998) 'Poverty Measurement Research Using the Consumer Expenditure Survey and the Survey of Income and Program Participation'. *American Economic Review*, 88(2), pp. 352–6.

——Garner, T. I., Johnson, D., and Doyle, P. (1999) *Experimental Poverty Measures: 1990 to 1997*. Current Population Reports, Consumer Income, P60–205, US Census Bureau, Washington DC.

Summers, R. (1973) 'International Comparisons with Incomplete Data'. *Review of Income and Wealth*, March.

—— and Heston, A. (1991) 'The Penn World Table (Mark 5): An Expanded Set of International Comparisons, 1950–1988'. *Quarterly Journal of Economics*, 106(2), pp. 327–68.

Triplett, J. E. (1990) 'Hedonic Methods in a Statistical Agency Environments: An Intellectual Biopsy'. In R. Berndt and J. E. Triplett (eds.) *Fifty Years of Economic Measurement: The Jubilee Conference of Research in Income and Wealth, Studies in Income and Wealth, Vol. 54*, Chicago: University of Chicago Press, pp. 207–38

World Bank (2008) *Global Purchasing Power Parities and Real Expenditures: 2005 International Comparison Program*. Washington DC.

7

Measuring Poverty in a Growing World (or Measuring Growth in a Poor World)[1]

Angus Deaton[2]

Introduction

A central issue in the debate about globalization is the extent to which economic growth reduces poverty. When economic growth benefits everyone in equal proportion, the incomes of the poor grow at the same rate as does mean income. The fraction of the population whose incomes are below a fixed poverty line must then decline with growth, although the rate at which it does so depends on the position of the poverty line in the income distribution, with growth in the mean generating more rapid poverty reduction the greater the fraction of the population who are near the poverty line. If economic growth is unequally distributed, the effects of growth on poverty reduction will be less (or more) depending on whether the incomes of the poor grow by less (more) than average. So much, but perhaps not much more, is common ground.

Early debates on growth and poverty, much influenced by Simon Kuznets' (1955) dictum that inequality would increase in the early stages of development, tended to argue that growth did little to reduce poverty. Writing in the 1970s, Hollis Chenery, Montek Ahluwalia et al. (1974), Irma Adelman and Cynthia Morris (1973), Albert Fishlow (1972), and Pranab Bardhan (1973) all argued that economic development either left the poor behind or actually made them worse off, see William Cline (1975) for a contemporary survey. Lance Taylor and Edmar Bacha (1976) constructed a growth model of "Belindia," a tiny rich Belgium in a huge poor India, as an example of "the unequalizing spiral" that they saw as fitting the stylized facts of development. Montek S. Ahluwalia, Nicholas G. Carter et al. (1979), who were among the first to measure global poverty using now-standard methods, argued that the effect of growth was limited both by the relatively low growth of the poorest countries, and by expanding inequality within them. When Gary Fields (1977) argued that in the Brazilian economic miracle of the 1960s, the poor had actually done better than average, he was robustly challenged by Ahluwalia, John Duloy et al. (1980), who showed that Fields' conclusions were not warranted by his data, which were consistent with an uninformatively wide range of differential growth rates of incomes of the poor and non-poor. This was surely the truth of the matter; in 1980, the data were not available to provide a clear answer to the question of whether or not the poor did better, the same, or worse than average during the unprecedentedly high rates of growth in many poor countries in the immediate post-war period. Researchers were forced to rely on a scattering of published distributional measures, whose provenance and reliability were often unclear; and indeed Kuznets' famous article used distributional data for only three rich countries, with a smaller amount of information for three poor ones.

The paper by Ahluwalia et al. (1980) was an important impetus to the establishment of the Living Standards Measurement Study (LSMS) at the World Bank. The original purpose of the LSMS was to measure the living standards of the poor in a standardized way, to remedy the paucity of distributional data in the Third World, and to set up a system of household surveys that would both support and cross-check the national accounts, as well as replicating for living standards measurement what the UN's System of National Accounts (SNA) had done for National Income Accounts around the world, see for example Graham Pyatt (2003).

Thirty years later, the data situation has been transformed. There are two key innovations. First, internationally comparable national accounts, based on purchasing power parity exchange rates, allow comparisons of average living standards across countries in a way that is not vitiated by the gross inadequacies of conversions at market exchange rates. Making comparisons in purchasing power parity units corrects, or at least diminishes, the gross understatement of living standards in poor countries relative to rich, and removes the spurious component of growth among poor countries that comes from the elimination of those differences with economic development. PPP exchange rates were first used for global poverty estimates by Montek S. Ahluwalia et al. (1979) and their use is by now almost universal. Second, there has been an extraordinary growth in the number of household surveys available to the research community, including several dozen LSMS surveys. For example, the World Bank's most recent set of poverty calculations use data from 297 surveys from eighty-eight developing countries, Shaohua Chen and Martin Ravallion (2001). Klaus Deininger and Lyn Squire (1996) have collected and tabulated data on more than 2,600 Gini coefficients as well as many measures of quintile shares; the WIDER extension includes more than 5,000 Gini coefficients. The unit record data from many household surveys are now routinely available to researchers, including such previously inaccessible troves as nearly twenty years of data from the Indian National Sample Surveys back to the early 1980s. Notable by its exclusion is any similar access to Chinese official surveys.

Yet the controversies are no more settled than they were thirty years ago, although there is certainly more common ground among economists than there is in the world at large. The professional consensus, based on the Deininger–Squire data, and on work by them and many others, is that, contrary to the Kuznets hypothesis, and contrary to beliefs in the 1970s, there is no *general* relationship between inequality and growth, and certainly not one in which growth systematically widens inequality, as would be the case of growth left that the poor behind. From this, two important propositions follow. First, *at least on average*, (and much depends on whether we are averaging over countries or people) growth is good for the poor, David Dollar and Aart Kraay (2002), Ravallion (2001), as is the growth that is arguably generated by greater openness Andrew Berg and Anne Krueger (2003). Second, and again *on average*, the fraction of people in poverty should decline as if growth were neutrally distributed. In particular, the relatively rapid growth in the developing world from 1980 to 2000 must have brought about a rapid reduction in the fraction of the world's population that is poor. And indeed, calculations using the Penn World Tables combined with inequality measures, the technique first used by Montek S. Ahluwalia et al. (1979), show rapid poverty reduction in the 1980s and 1990s, see Surjit Bhalla (2002), Xavier Sala-i-Martín (2002), and Francois Bourguignon and Christian Morrisson (2002). According to these calculations, not only has the proportion of poor in the world declined, but the decline has been rapid enough to offset population growth, so that the actual numbers of poor people in the world has fallen. According to Bhalla, the first of the United Nations' Millennium Development Goals, halving the number of people living on less than $1 a day between 1990 and 2015, had already been met when the goal was announced.

These optimistic calculations are starkly at odds with the World Bank's numbers on global poverty. The World Bank, which is endorsed by the UN as official score-keeper for the poverty Millennium Development Goal, uses household survey data to measure the living standards of the poor, ignoring national accounts estimates, and their calculations show relatively little poverty reduction in the 1990s. Chen and Ravallion (2001), which provides the details of the Bank's calculations, shows a reduction in the proportion of the poor living on less than $1 a day from 1987 to 1998 from 28.3 to 23.5 per cent; they argue that this modest reduction comes, not from any expansion in inequality within countries, but from relatively slow growth in mean consumption. Across their eighty-eight countries, the population weighted rate of growth in mean consumption was only 0.90 per cent from 1987 to 1998, compared with 3.3 per cent growth in real per capita consumption in the Penn World Tables over the same period. These estimates exclude the latest (1999–2000) Indian data whose inclusion will increase the growth of the survey means over the 1990s, there remains a large gap between, on the one hand, the direct assessment of the growth of consumption of the poor through surveys, and on the other hand, the growth that is implied by the growth in average accompanied by no general increase in inequality.

The plethora of new data has not resolved the controversy because the new sources are mutually contradictory. According to direct measurement in household surveys, growth among the poor of the world has been sluggish compared with average growth rates of the countries in which they live. Yet there is no documented increase in inequality that would resolve the discrepancy. If we are to accept the surveys, growth in the world is a good deal slower than we are used to thinking from the national accounts data, and what growth there has been in the latest two decades has made only a modest dent in the level of world poverty. If we accept the national accounts, and do not challenge the conclusion that there is no general increase in inequality nor any correlation between growth and changes in inequality, then official poverty numbers are overstated, and we have already made rapid progress towards reducing poverty in the world. This chapter explores these contradictions empirically with an aim to providing a sharper characterization and to advancing some first hypotheses about causes and possible remedies.

A note of caution at the outset. Because countries have vastly different populations, statements about averages are often sharply different depending on whether or not they are population weighted. A third of the world's poor live in two countries, India and China, and the global poverty counts are much affected by what happens there. When we are interested in the well-being of the people of the world, and in the effects of statistical practice and statistical discrepancies on global poverty measurements, we must weight by population. There is no reason to down-weight the well-being of a Chinese peasant relative to a Ghanaian cocoa-farmer, nor to believe that the world is a better place when an African moves out of poverty and an Indian moves in. However, many of my concerns are about the relationship between measurement and the level of development, in which case the appropriate procedure is to take each statistical system as the unit, and to ignore population sizes. Beyond that, many of the political negotiations about poverty, and about measurement, for example those in the councils of the United Nations and the World Bank, are carried on at a nation by nation level. In consequence, I shall typically present both weighted and unweighted results.

Surveys versus national accounts: all countries

In this section, I consider the cross-country and intertemporal relationships between survey and national accounts estimates of consumption expenditure per capita. Many commentators have noted the (sometimes substantial) discrepancies between survey estimates and their national accounts counterparts. As we shall see below, there are also long-standing literatures in India and the United States, not only on level differences, but also on the fact that survey means grow less rapidly than means in the national accounts. My analysis and data overlaps with Martin Ravallion (2003) whose main concern is with regional and global analyses of the statistical significance of discrepancies in the levels and growth rates of the ratios of survey to national accounts consumption. For consumption surveys, Ravallion comes to the optimistic conclusion that the significant discrepancies can be traced back to the disarray in the statistical systems of the transition economies. The lack of significant differences elsewhere reflects the large cross-country variance in the ratios, as well as the fact that when surveys are not weighted by population, the low and falling ratio in India, where about a third of the world's poor live, is lost in the variation of the ratios elsewhere. In consequence, it is possible for the survey to national accounts ratios to be insignificantly different from one another even though the surveys and national accounts data have radically different implications for trends in global poverty.

National accounts estimates of consumption are available for most countries in most recent years, so the countries and dates of the comparison are set by the availability of the surveys. The surveys used here come from a convenience sample assembled from various sources. In most cases, I have survey estimates of mean income or mean consumption from the estimates assembled by Chen and Ravallion, and which appear on the World Bank's poverty monitoring website. To these I have added my own estimates for India, most of which appear in Deaton and Jean Drèze (2002), a number of OECD surveys, particularly from the Consumers Expenditure Survey and Current Population Surveys in the US, and the Family Expenditure Survey (now the Expenditure and Food Survey) in the UK, as well as a number of additional survey estimates supplied by the Bank, but not used in their poverty counts, for example estimates of mean consumption per head from the official Chinese surveys. In all, I have 557 survey-based estimates of mean consumption per head or mean income per head (occasionally both). Table 7.1 shows that these come from 127 countries; that the earliest year is 1979 and the latest 2000. The number of surveys in the data set grows steadily larger overtime; I have only three in 1979 and seven in 1980, but 57 in 1998 (the peak year). There are twenty-two surveys for 1999 and twenty-six in 2000, but this diminution in numbers after 1998 reflects merely the delay in processing and obtaining survey data, rather than any slackening in the growth of usable surveys around the world. For a single country, consumption and income estimates may come from the same survey, for example, China, or from different surveys, for example the US. The fraction of the world's population covered by the surveys shows a strong upward trend, more than doubling from 1980 to 1998, but there is fluctuation in the fraction from year to

Table 7.1. Description of surveys used in the analysis

Year	No of surveys	No of countries	Population covered (bn)	Fraction of world population (%)
1979	3	3	0.35	9.0
1980	7	6	1.33	34.1
1981	5	5	0.27	6.7
1982	3	3	0.33	8.1
1983	2	2	0.97	23.6
1984	7	5	0.48	11.4
1985	13	11	1.59	37.4
1986	21	18	1.75	40.3
1987	23	21	1.82	41.2
1988	26	24	2.92	64.9
1989	31	28	2.14	45.7
1990	23	20	1.69	35.1
1991	29	26	1.95	38.6
1992	37	34	2.16	42.1
1993	45	41	2.61	49.9
1994	35	30	3.22	60.2
1995	51	45	3.67	67.7
1996	48	44	3.82	68.3
1997	43	38	3.38	61.1
1998	57	53	3.86	70.3
1999	22	19	2.16	39.1
2000	26	23	3.54	63.6
All	557	127	..	..

Notes: Surveys are a convenience sample where survey means were readily available. When the number of surveys exceeds the number of countries, some countries have estimates of both mean income and mean consumption per capita. China is included in 1980, 1985, and every year thereafter; India in 1983, 1988, 1994, 1995, 1996, 1997, 1998, and 2000, but not in 1999. (Indian surveys that run from mid-year to mid-year have been arbitrarily allocated to the second year.) There are 278 estimates of mean consumption, and 281 estimates of mean income.

year as individual countries move in and out of the counts. Much depends on whether or not there is an Indian survey in a specific year. China is included in 1980, and from 1985 onwards.

Table 7.2 shows information on the ratios of survey estimates of consumption or income per head to consumption or income per head from the national accounts. The ratios are calculated using nominal values in local currency units (LCU) for both the numerator and denominator. National accounts estimates of household final consumption are the obvious counterparts to survey consumption. For income, most countries do not publish data on disposable household income, so possible counterparts are GDP or, once again, household consumption. The argument for the latter is that much of saving may not be done by households, but by corporations, government, or foreigners, so that household income may be closer to household consumption than to national income. The top panel in Table 7.2 shows summary statistics for ratios of survey to national accounts' consumption per head, the second panel is for the ratios of survey

Table 7.2. Ratios of survey means to means from national income accounts

	No of surveys	Unweighted			Population weighted		
		Mean ratio	Standard error	Standard deviation	Mean ratio	Standard error	Standard deviation
Consumption to cons.							
All	277	0.860	(0.029)	0.306	0.779	(0.072)	0.191
EAP	42	0.819	(0.069)	0.224	0.863	(0.031)	0.110
EECA	59	0.847	(0.038)	0.230	0.796	(0.040)	0.184
LAC	26	0.767	(0.094)	0.329	0.585	(0.078)	0.193
MENA	20	0.955	(0.104)	0.300	0.867	(0.111)	0.270
OECD	33	0.781	(0.052)	0.097	0.726	(0.032)	0.076
SA	23	0.649	(0.063)	0.122	0.569	(0.036)	0.103
SSA	74	1.000	(0.061)	0.415	1.089	(0.089)	0.459
Income to consumption							
All	266	0.904	(0.034)	0.290	1.008	(0.044)	0.174
EAP	32	1.036	(0.065)	0.244	1.057	(0.019)	0.105
EECA	47	0.852	(0.038)	0.231	0.811	(0.030)	0.196
LAC	100	0.893	(0.084)	0.392	1.004	(0.143)	0.416
OECD	75	0.891	(0.020)	0.137	0.910	(0.011)	0.084
SA	8	0.892	(0.028)	0.118	0.874	(0.009)	0.101
SSA	4	1.000	(0.136)	0.420	1.023	(0.204)	0.359
Income to GDP							
All	272	0.569	(0.023)	0.203	0.542	(0.023)	0.113
EAP	32	0.515	(0.031)	0.124	0.512	(0.007)	0.051
EECA	49	0.530	(0.029)	0.157	0.481	(0.016)	0.119
LAC	103	0.616	(0.055)	0.264	0.661	(0.104)	0.288
OECD	76	0.527	(0.027)	0.092	0.586	(0.018)	0.059
SA	8	0.685	(0.009)	0.100	0.659	(0.010)	0.071
SSA	4	0.837	(0.138)	0.512	0.672	(0.098)	0.228

Notes: EAP is East Asia and Pacific; EECA is Eastern Europe and Central Asia; LAC is Latin America and the Caribbean; SA is South Asia; and SSA is sub-Saharan Africa. There are no income surveys for MENA in the sample. Numbers differ slightly from Table 7.1 because the relevant national income magnitudes are not always available. Panel 1 shows the ratio of consumption from the survey to consumption from the national accounts; Panel 2 the ratio of income from the surveys to consumption from the national accounts; and Panel 3 the ratio of income from the surveys to GDP from the national accounts. Standard errors are calculated so as to allow for correlations within countries.

income to national accounts' consumption, and the third panel is for survey income to GDP.

Consumption estimated from the surveys is typically lower than consumption from the national accounts; the average ratio is 0.860 with a standard error of 0.029, or 0.779 (0.072) when weighted by population. (India has particularly low ratios.) The exception is sub-Saharan Africa, where the average ratio of survey to national accounts consumption is unity in the unweighted and greater than unity in the weighted calculations. For the OECD, where survey and national accounts quality is presumably the highest, the surveys pick up only a little more than three-quarters of consumption in the national accounts. These differences come in part from differences in definition—for example, national accounts consumption includes such items as the imputed value of owner-occupied housing, which is nearly always excluded from the surveys—but they also reflect errors and omissions in both surveys and national accounts. In consequence, that the ratios for Middle East and North Africa (MENA) and sub-Saharan Africa (SSA) are close to unity says nothing about the quality of the surveys in those two regions. Indeed, it is possible that the perfectly measured ratio is less than unity, but is actually measured as greater than unity because there is understatement in the national accounts. And it is entirely possible that the high ratios for SSA come from large scale underestimation in the national accounts.

Income measured in the survey is on average larger than consumption measured in the surveys, but is in most cases less than national accounts consumption, and much less than GDP. Survey income is less than 60 per cent of GDP on average.

The standard deviations of the ratios provide one crude indicator of combined survey and national accounts accuracy, including both sampling and non-sampling errors. Without prejudging the relative accuracy of national accounts and the surveys, the latter are more likely to vary from year to year, for example because of sampling and changes in survey design, and from country to country, because survey protocols are less internationally standardized than are national accounts. By this measure, surveys in sub-Saharan Africa are the most problematic, though surveys in Latin America and the Caribbean (LAC) also show great variance, particularly the income surveys. OECD surveys have the lowest variance, followed by South Asia, where high quality household surveys have been in existence for many years. In spite of the difficulties of collecting data in transition economies, the Eastern Europe and Central Asian (EECA) region does not show particularly high variance. In several countries in both EECA and LAC, high inflation poses great problems for both survey and national accounts data.

Figures 7.1 (weighted by population) and 7.2 (unweighted) show how the same three ratios are related to the level of GDP, here GDP per head at 1995 purchasing power parity dollars. (This is the World Bank's current PPP series, divided by the implicit price deflator of GDP in the United States.) Cross-country and time-series data are pooled in these graphs.

There are two points to take away from this figure. First, the top panels in both figures show a negative relationship between the ratio of survey to national accounts consumption on the one hand, and the level of GDP per capita on the other. This relationship is steepest among the poorest countries, is flatter in middle income countries, but resumes its downward slope among the rich countries. The continuous lines in the two top graphs are locally weighted non-parametric regression of the relationship using a bandwidth of 1.5 (units of real log GDP in PPP.) Second, there is no similar relationship among the income surveys, either for the ratio of survey income to national accounts consumption, or for the ratio of survey income to GDP. At least some of the pattern in Figure 7.1 must comes from the fact that consumption is typically much easier to measure in surveys than is income in poor countries, where many people are self-employed in agriculture, while the opposite is true in rich countries, where most people are wage earners and are more reluctant to cooperate with time-consuming consumption surveys.

For assessing trends in global poverty and growth, the most important feature of these data is the behavior of the ratios over time. This issue is explored in Figure 7.3 and Table 7.3. Because the subset of countries for which we have survey means differs from year to year, it is not useful to calculate rates of growth of the survey means on a country by country basis, and then weight by population to obtain estimates of global growth from the surveys. Instead, I have computed population-weighted averages for each year, over whatever subsets of countries have survey data. First, the local currency consumption and income means are converted to PPP dollars by deflation by the consumption PPP exchange rate from the Penn World Tables, Version 6.1, (PWT6.1) and then into real terms by deflation by the US CPI. They are then weighted by population and averaged, excluding the wealthy countries of the OECD. The resulting series are plotted as the bottom two lines in Figure 7.3. They differ in their treatment of country/years where there is both a consumption and an income mean. For the broken, lower line, I have chosen the consumption survey whenever both are available, and for the solid, upper, line, I have chosen the income survey. (The results of choosing income means are almost identical if we take income means for China, and consumption means elsewhere.)

For comparison with these survey based estimates, I have used real consumption from PWT6.1 calculated by applying the consumption share to the chain-weighted GDP series. The top solid line in the figure shows the population weighted average of PWT6.1 consumption for all of the countries that ever appear in the survey data set, excluding only the OECD. The broken line is also a population weighted average of PWT6.1 consumption, but for each year is averaged only over the countries for which there is survey data. This calculation allows a comparison with the survey calculations in which both series are

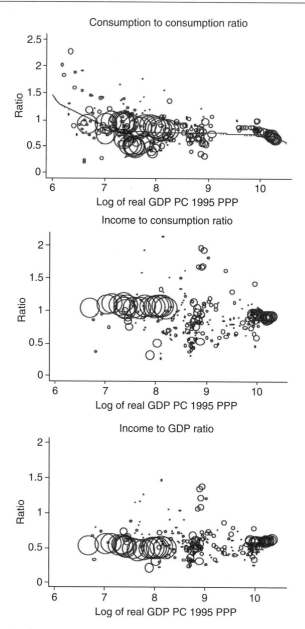

Figure 7.1 Ratio of survey estimates of mean income or consumption per capita to comparable national accounts estimates, weighted, 1979–2000[1,2]

[1] The charts cover 498 surveys across 124 countries.
[2] The diameter of the circles is proportional to national population in the year of the survey.

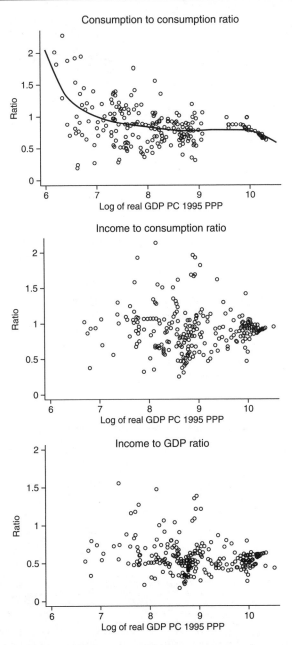

Figure 7.2 Ratio of survey estimates of mean income or consumption per capita to comparable national accounts estimates, unweighted, 1979–2000[1]

[1] The charts cover 498 surveys across 124 countries.

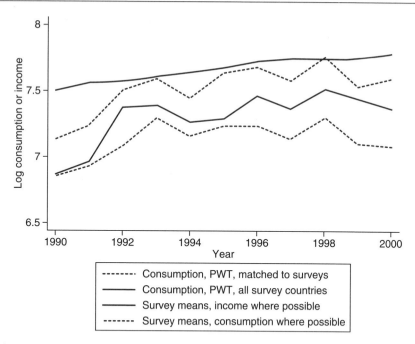

Figure 7.3 Logarithms of population weighted averages of consumption or income

Source: Household surveys and Penn World Tables, v. 6.1.

Table 7.3. Population weighted growth rates, 1990–2000, real consumption or real income, various measures, non-OECD countries (% per annum)

	Surveys with consumption preference	Surveys with income preference	PWT6.1 matching surveys by year & country	PWT6.1 All survey countries
Regression of log on time	1.9	4.0	3.8	2.8
Average rate of growth	2.3	5.0	4.5	2.8

Notes: Columns 1 and 2 show the growth rates of population weighted survey means. In column 1, whenever there is both an income and a consumption mean for a country/year pair, consumption is used. In column 2, whenever there are two surveys, preference is given to income. In both cases, survey means are converted to a constant price PPP basis by dividing by the product of the US CPI and the consumption PPP exchange rate from PWT6.1. For each year from 1990 to 2000, a population weighted average of the survey means is calculated; note that these averages involve different countries in different years—see Table 7.1. The growth rates are then calculated in two ways, by regression of the logarithm on a time trend (first row) or by calculating the average change in the logarithm over the period. These can be quite different when the series is noisy, as is the case here, because countries come in and out of the average. Columns 3 and 4 show comparable population weighted growth rates for real PPP (chain weighted) consumption from PWT6.1. In Column 3, consumption from PWT6.1 is used only for country/year pairs for which a survey mean exists; this column therefore shares the variability in columns 2 and 3 that comes from the varying selection of countries. Column 4 shows the population weighted growth rates for consumption from PWT 6.1 using *all* countries for which there is a survey.

affected similarly by the variation that comes from the fact that survey countries (and thus the composition of the sum across the world income distribution) changes from year to year. And indeed, the year to year variation in the broken line version of the PWT6.1 consumption series is highly correlated with both survey measures. Of course, the year to year (or cyclical) fluctuations in all the series in Figure 7.3 (except for the top line) comes as much from the changing selection of countries with different living standards as it does from any genuine fluctuations in the unobservable survey mean over *all* countries, so that we can use these series only to examine long-run growth, not differences in growth rates over subperiods.

Figure 7.3 shows that national accounts consumption in non-OECD countries, here taken from the PWT6.1 and shown in the top two lines, grew more rapidly over the 1990s than did consumption from poor countries measured from the surveys, shown in the bottom line. Table 7.3 shows that growth of survey consumption is 2.3 per cent a year if we simply take average growth over the decade, or 1.9 per cent a year if we regress its logarithm on a time trend, the difference in the two estimates coming from the variability in the series. This difference is induced by countries with different income levels, particularly India, moving in and out of the survey averages, and is also seen in the comparison growth rates from national accounts consumption, which are 3.8 and 4.5 per cent a year. Whether we take the two low or two high estimates, the growth rate of survey consumption is about a half of the growth rate of national accounts consumption. If instead of using consumption estimates from the surveys, we take income estimates when they are available, the situation is reversed, and we get a rate of growth from the surveys that is *larger* than the corresponding growth rates in national accounts consumption. The higher growth rate when we give preference to income surveys comes almost entirely from the Chinese data. The World Bank's global poverty estimates use income surveys for China, because there are no distributional data for the Chinese consumption figures. However, in the Bank's calculation the Chinese income distribution is scaled down by the ratio of consumption to income in the Chinese national accounts, a ratio that has been rising over time, so that the first column in Table 7.3 and the bottom graph in Figure 7.3 are the relevant ones for thinking about trends in global poverty as measured by the dollar a day counts.

Surveys versus national accounts: India and China

Figure 7.4 shows the ratios of survey to national accounts estimates for China and for India. The Chinese data, which have a discontinuity in 1990, for which there are two estimates, are from the same survey data-base discussed above, while the national accounts data are taken from the 2002 Edition of the World Development Indicators. In China the ratio of survey to national accounts consumption has been declining since around 1990, from a peak of

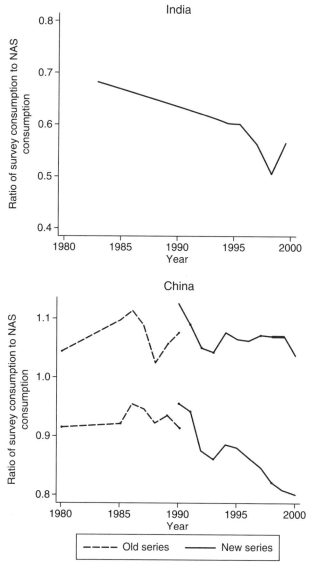

Figure 7.4 Ratios of survey means to national accounts means of consumption and/or income per head, India and China

95 per cent in 1990 to 80 per cent in 2000; the growth rates of the two series thus differ by about 1.7 per cent a year in the 1990s. The ratio of survey income (from the same surveys as consumption) to national consumption did not decline over the same period. However, there is a great deal of household saving in China (which shows up in the surveys in that the top line is much higher than the bottom line), national consumption is not the relevant comparison. Ideally, income should be compared with GDP or, better still, some national accounts estimate of household income. Although I do not have the data to calculate that ratio, there is little doubt that it would also be declining over time. Given the population of China, its increasing discrepancies between survey and national accounts is a major contributor to the global differences. However, it should be noted that many commentators have argued that the growth rates in the Chinese national accounts are too high. The discussions in Angus Maddison (1998), Harry Wu (2000), and Albert Keidel (2001) are all consistent with an overestimation in the rate of GDP growth by between 2 and 4 percentage points a year, and Thomas Rawski (2001) argues for much larger overestimation in the last few years. Removing 2 percentage points a year from NAS consumption growth would eliminate the difference in the growth rates between the NAS and the surveys.

Figure 7.4 also shows the data from India, in this case taken, for national consumption, directly from the latest available edition of the National Accounts, Government of India (2003) and for the survey estimates, from my own calculations from the unit record data. The Indian National Sample Survey (NSS) conducted its latest full scale household expenditure survey in 1999/2000 but, because the questionnaire design was changed from earlier similar surveys, there has been controversy about the interpretation of the results. The estimate of average consumption used here was calculated according to the methods laid out in Deaton (2003) but differs relatively little from the official calculations, much less than is the case for the poverty estimates. In India, survey consumption is much lower relative to national accounts consumption than in China. However, as in China, the ratio of the two estimates of consumption has been declining over time. In 1983, the ratio was 0.68, which declined in 1999/2000 to 0.56, so that national accounts consumption has been growing at 1.1 per cent a year more rapidly than survey consumption. India, like China, accounts for a large share of the world's population, and an even larger share of those who live on less than $1 a day.

The Indian consumption ratio in Figure 7.4 calls for some additional comment, particularly the erratic behavior from 1995 through 1998. The Indian NSS carries out large household expenditure surveys only once every six years or so, with the two most recent being in 1993/94 and 1999/2000. The estimates between those dates come from four smaller NSS surveys that also collect expenditure data. Although the sample sizes of those surveys are sufficient to obtain reliable estimates of the national headcount ratio, there have been questions about their design. The 1998 survey, in particular, lasted only for a half year, and it is arguable that the penultimate observation in the graph should be ignored. Unfortunately, circumstances have conspired to give this and the immediately preceding observation a great deal of weight. Because the 1999/2000 survey was arguably contaminated by changes in the questionnaire, the 1997 and 1998 surveys did not fade into history as quickly as they otherwise would have done. In addition, these were the latest observations for India available to the World Bank for the most recent set of global poverty counts, constructed for the 2000/1 *World Development Report* on poverty. The use of the new data in the next round of global poverty counts will give a more optimistic picture of the rate of global poverty decline, though not as optimistic as would be the case if survey growth had been as rapid as growth in national accounts.

The internal Indian debate on discrepancies between surveys and national accounts has flared up sporadically for at least thirty years, see in particular the papers in T. N. Srinivasan and Bardhan (1974) as well as B. Minhas (1988) and Minhas and S. Kansal (1989). The recent spate of interest has generated a great deal of important detailed work, including collaborative efforts between the NSS and the National Accounts Division of the Central Statistical Office. Much can be learned from that work, not only for India, but also for other countries; discussion on this features in the section "Why do surveys and national accounts diverge?"

Surveys versus national accounts: the UK and the US

Although my primary concern is with the measurement of global poverty, and thus with measurement in poor countries, the issue of statistical discrepancies between surveys and national accounts is a general one, and there is a great deal to be learned by looking at the issue at the other end of the global income distribution. Rich countries tend to have fuller data, so that it is sometimes possible to test general hypotheses about surveys that cannot readily be tested in, for example, India or China.

Figure 7.5 presents the results of survey and national accounts comparisons for the US and the UK. The right-hand chart, which looks at the UK, shows results for the Family Expenditure Survey (FES), since 1995 subsumed into the Expenditure and Food Survey (EFS). Data on real consumption per head were taken from the EFS reports, and were scaled up using population and retail price data from the *Annual Abstract of Statistics*, Office for National Statistics (2003). The figure shows the ratios of these numbers to final consumers' expenditure from the national accounts. The redesign of the survey and the switch from the FES to the EFS results in a discontinuity before and after 1995, for which year there are two estimates. The left-hand chart shows corresponding data from the United States using two different surveys, the Current Population Survey

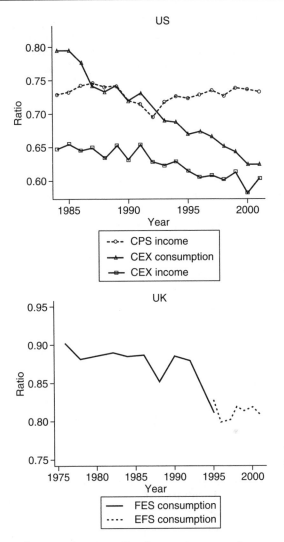

Figure 7.5 Ratios of survey means to national accounts means of consumption and/or income per head

(CPS) and the Consumer Expenditure Survey (CEX). The CEX is the main consumption survey in the US, although it also collects income data, and the two solid lines in the chart show (a) the ratio of consumption from the CES to consumption in the national accounts, the upper solid line, and (b) the ratio of pre-tax income from the CEX to personal income from the national accounts, the lower solid line. The CEX income and consumption estimates are calculated by the Bureau of Labor Statistics from the CEX, and include estimates from both the diary and interview components of the survey, as well as an estimate of the rental equivalence of owner-occupied homes. The CPS, which is the main income survey in the US, and which is used by the Bureau of the Census to calculate the official estimates of poverty, does not collect data on consumption. The broken line in the figure is the ratio of income from the CPS to personal income in the national accounts.

Both sets of consumption figures show the now familiar pattern of declining ratios of survey to national accounts consumption. In the UK, the decline is far from uniform over time, and if the break in the survey in 1995 had been in 1994, it could perhaps have been attributed to the change in design. As it is, the ratio declines by about 10 percentage points over the twenty-five years from 1976 to 2001, so that survey consumption is growing about 0.5 per cent a year less rapidly than consumption in the national accounts. The decline in the corresponding ratio in the US is a good deal more dramatic, from 0.80 to 0.64 from 1984 to 2001, so that the difference in the two growth rates is 1.3 per cent a year, a little more than in India, and a little less than in China. Income from the CEX is also a declining ratio of personal income in the national accounts, although the rate of decline is much slower, less than 5 percentage points over seventeen years. And income in the CPS shows no trend relative to personal income in the national accounts. More careful comparisons between the CEX and national accounts consumption data have been made by Jack Triplett (1997) and by Thesia Garner, George Janini et al. (2003). After making a number of corrections to try to put the two series on a comparable basis, Triplett estimates that from 1984 to 1994, personal consumption expenditures grew at 1.0 per cent a year more rapidly than consumers' expenditure from the CEX. Garner et al., comparing only comparable items, calculate that the CEX to national accounts ratio was 89 per cent in 1992. In 1997 and 2000, the comparable ratio was only 80 per cent, so that the differential growth rate was 2.4 per cent a year until 1997 and 1.5 per cent a year to 2000. The differential behavior of income and consumption ratios may have something to do with the fact that in the US, consumption is much harder to collect than is income. The CEX costs a great deal more per interview as does the CPS and while for most people (those who are not self-employed) income can be collected with only a few questions, consumption requires a long interview or extensive record keeping in diaries. The non-response rate in the CEX has been rising over time, Robert Groves and Mick Couper (1998), while that for the CPS has been constant. It is possible that people are less and less willing to cooperate with the CEX over time, but those who do so are prepared to answer the income questions more fully and more accurately than the consumption questions. The CPS, which does not ask consumption questions, may suffer from fewer problems. Its sample size is also much larger, 60,000 households versus only 5,000 up to 1999, and 7,500 thereafter.

Why do surveys and national accounts diverge?

The previous sections have documented the fact that consumption, measured from surveys, frequently grows less rapidly than consumption, measured from the national accounts. Consistent with this general relationship, the ratio of the two magnitudes is highest in the poorest countries, and lowest in the richest. Within countries as diverse as China, India, the UK, and the US, the ratio falls over time as real income increases. Taking non-OECD countries as a whole, population weighted survey consumption at PPP constant dollars grew at only half the rate of population weighted consumption in the Penn World Tables. The conceptual differences between the two concepts of consumption are broadly the same, but these do not account for the differences in growth rates, so that one or both of the two growth rates are incorrect. If the surveys are wrong, and the national accounts right, either inequality has been widening in ways that our data do not appear to show, or poverty has been falling more rapidly than shown by the $1-a-day counts. If the surveys are right, there has been less growth in the world in the 1990s than usually supposed. Extreme positions apart, we have some combination of underestimation of poverty decline, underestimation of a widening in the distribution of consumption, and overestimation of growth. Quantifying the contribution of each is an urgent task for anyone interested in growth, poverty, and inequality. In this section, I lay out some of the possible explanations.

It is important to note that there can be no general presumption in favor of one or other of the surveys and the national accounts. In particular, that national accounts are familiar, widely used, and in principle comparable (they typically conform to the UN's System of National Accounts) does not imply that the divergences between them and the surveys must be attributed to the latter. While it is certainly the case that there exist "failed" surveys, whose execution is known to have been faulty, where fieldwork was disrupted or inadequately supervised, where sampling procedures were flawed, or where changes in survey design made it impossible to compare the results with earlier surveys, national accounts estimates are also subject to many errors, some of which will be discussed below.

Unit non-response

Not everyone who is asked to participate in a survey agrees to do so, and failure to respond (unit non-response) is known to be different for households with different household characteristics, Groves and Couper (1998). Of particular interest is the case where better-off households are less likely to respond; Groves and Couper report that, in rich countries, the probability of response is negatively related to almost all measures of socioeconomic status, and while survey organizations in poor countries can usually collect data in very poor areas, albeit under difficult conditions, it is often impossible to penetrate the gated communities in which many rich people live. Suppose then that the probability that consumption y is recorded in the survey is $\pi(y)$, and that $\pi(y)$ is monotone declining in x. This situation has been discussed in a recent paper by Johan Mistiaen and Ravallion (2003), who also show how to use aggregate measures of non-response (for example, by region) to correct estimates of poverty and inequality.

If the true (untruncated) density of consumption (or income) is $f(y)$, the density for observed (truncated) consumption is

$$\hat{f}(y) = \frac{\pi(y)f(y)}{\int\limits_{y_0}^{y_1} f(y)\pi(y)dy} = \frac{\pi(y)f(y)}{\bar{\pi}} \tag{1}$$

where y_0 and y_1 are the bottom and top levels of consumption, and $\bar{\pi}$ is mean response in the population. From (1), the difference in the true and actual densities is

$$\hat{f}(y) - f(y) = \frac{\pi(y) - \bar{\pi}}{\bar{\pi}} f(y) \tag{2}$$

so that the observed density is higher or lower according to whether the household's response rate is below or above the mean. Because $\pi(y)$ is monotone decreasing, the truncated density is higher at low levels of x, and lower at high values, so that the distribution function is shifted to the left, i.e.

$$\hat{F} \geq F(y). \tag{3}$$

This inequality says that the truncated distribution is first-order stochastic dominated by the untruncated distribution, which implies that the estimated poverty rate from the actual data will be no less than the estimated poverty rate in the population, no matter what the poverty line, and that estimated mean consumption will be no larger than the population mean.

Mistiaen and Ravallion also consider the effects of the truncation on the Lorenz curve, $L(p)$. In general, the derivative of the Lorenz curve satisfies (see, for example, Kakwani 1987):

$$L'(p) = \frac{F^{-1}(p)}{\mu} = \frac{y}{\mu} \tag{4}$$

where x is the pth quantile of consumption and μ is its mean. Provided that $y_0 > 0$ and $y_1 < \infty$, and provided $\pi(y) > 0$, for all y in the support, so that the support of the truncated distribution is identical to that of the original, the reduction in the mean by the non-response implies that the truncated Lorenz curve is at least as steep as the true Lorenz curve both at the origin and at $(1,1)$, so that either the Lorenz curves are identical, or they must cross at least once. This result, although obtained under special assumptions (for example, if

$x_0 = 0$, it is possible to construct cases where the curves need not cross), tells us that with greater non- response by the rich, there can be no general supposition that estimated inequality will be biased either up or down by the selective under-sampling of richer households. (The intuition that selective removal of the rich should *reduce* measured inequality, which is sometimes stated as obvious in the literature, is false, perhaps because it takes no account of reduction in the mean from the selection.)

If we are prepared to place restrictions on the compliance function $\pi(y)$, we can analyze the effect of inequality on compliance. In particular, suppose (a) that $\pi(y)$, in addition to be monotone decreasing, is convex, and (b) that $y\pi(y)$ is monotone increasing and concave. Then if F_1 and F_2 are two distributions of income with the same mean, such that F_1 second-order stochastically dominates F_2, we have

$$\int \pi(y)dF_1(y) \leq \int \pi(y)dF_2(y) \tag{5}$$

so that average compliance is lower for the more equal distribution. In addition,

$$\int \pi(y)ydF_1(y) \leq \int \pi(y)ydF_2(y) \tag{6}$$

so that, dividing (5) by (6), we have

$$\mu_1 \geq \mu_2. \tag{7}$$

Provided the two monotonicity and convexity/concavity assumptions are satisfied, a mean preserving increase in spread in the true distribution will decrease the truncated mean. The monotonicity assumption in (b) guarantees that, in spite of the non-compliance, reported income increases with actual income. The concavity/convexity assumptions guarantee the result, but do not appear to be required by the logic of the problem.

To sharpen intuition further, consider the following illustrative but not unrealistic case in which a lognormal distribution of income is combined with a probability of compliance that is non-increasing in income. Suppose that x is the *logarithm* of income or consumption, and that the distribution prior to truncation is lognormal with mean (of logs) v and variance (of logs) σ^2. Suppose too that the probability of responding to the survey is unity up to some income level $\exp(v - \theta\sigma)$, for some number θ, but that above $\exp(v - \theta\sigma)$, the logarithm of the compliance probability declines linearly with the logarithm of income; the "kink" in the response function is needed to prevent the probability being greater than unity. Hence if $\pi(x)$ is the probability that a household with (log) income x agrees to cooperate, we have

$$\begin{aligned} \pi(x) &= 1, & x &\leq v - \theta\sigma \\ \pi(x) &= \exp[-a(x - v + \theta\sigma)], & x &\geq v - \theta\sigma \end{aligned} \tag{8}$$

so that the probability of response is unity at the bottom of the distribution. The parameter α is non-negative, and is (minus) the elasticity of compliance with respect to income.

In the Appendix, I show that, provided θ is large enough, so that non-compliance begins far enough below the mean, the observed (truncated) distribution of incomes is approximately lognormal, that the variance of log income is *unchanged*, but the mean of logs is shifted downward from v to $v - \alpha\sigma^2$. Although this result is entirely driven by assumption, it illustrates a number of important points. First, we have a case where non-response drives the difference between the national accounts and the surveys, and where the mean is biased down, but the Lorenz curve is correct. Second, the ratio of survey consumption to true consumption depends on the variance of the true (and truncated) distribution. In particular, If $\hat{\mu}$ and μ are the truncated and true means of income, the ratio satisfies

$$\ln\left(\frac{\hat{\mu}}{\mu}\right) = -\alpha\sigma^2 \tag{9}$$

so that the understatement of income will be greater in places and at times where inequality is higher. In particular, increasing inequality of incomes will drive down the survey estimates in relation to the truth, even though the ratio of survey to the true mean is independent of the *level* of mean income. Third, in this case, the ratio of the truncated to the true mean is independent of mean income, so that, although compliance is declining in income, and although average compliance is declining as the economy expands (at least if the compliance probability in (8) is scaled to respond to actual income, rather than the deviation of income from the mean), the fraction of total income captured by the survey does not decrease with growth.

The compliance probability in (8) can be generalized, for example by introducing a quadratic term in the second branch of (8), which would then be written

$$\pi(x) = 1, \qquad\qquad\qquad\qquad\qquad\qquad x \le v - \theta\sigma$$
$$\pi(x) = \exp[-a(x - v + \theta\sigma) - \frac{\gamma}{2}(x - v + \theta\sigma)2], \quad x \ge v - \theta\sigma \tag{10}$$

The parameter γ can be positive or negative, in the latter case, (10) needs to be modified at high levels of x to stop the probability exceeding 1. Although I do not deal with the complication here, high values of x can be handled in the same way as low values of x in (8). Under the same conditions as before, that θ is large enough, (8) also implies that the truncated distribution will be lognormal, but now both mean and variance of logs are changed. Similar algebra to the linear case gives

$$\hat{\sigma}^2 = \frac{\sigma^2}{1 + \gamma\sigma^2} \tag{11}$$

for the variance of logs in the observed distribution, which can be greater than or less than σ^2 depending on the sign of γ. For the mean of logs, we have

$$\hat{v} = v - \frac{\sigma^2(a + \theta\sigma\gamma)}{1 + \gamma\sigma^2} \tag{12}$$

Once again, the inequality of income affects the ratio of the observed to true mean. However, it is no longer appropriate to replace the mean by its true value, leaving the variance unchanged, because if γ is nonzero the variance is now also affected by the non-compliance, something that we would generally expect to be the case. Note that as in the original case, the ratio of true to measured income does *not* vary with the true mean, so that non-compliance can increase with income, without the ratio of measured to true income falling with increases in mean income.

There are no ideal aggregate data for testing the extent to which mean income and income inequality affect survey means through non-compliance. Although there is a great deal of distributional information in the Deininger–Squire data set, the information for developing countries is neither reliable in itself, nor well-matched to the surveys in the sample discussed above. For the smaller subset of 111 consumption and 77 income surveys for which Gini coefficients are provided on the World Bank's poverty monitoring web-site, there is no significant (unweighted, as is appropriate here) relationship between the log of the ratio of survey to NAS mean and the Gini coefficient, whether or not real GDP per capita is controlled for. (Region by region, there is a marginally significant effect in South Asia where data quality is probably highest; note that the OECD countries are not represented in the poverty monitor countries.) This is also true when the Gini is replaced by the log variance, calculated from the formula for the log standard deviation $\sigma = \sqrt{2}\Phi^{-1}[(g + 1)/2]$ which holds when the distribution is lognormal, J. Aitchison and Alan Brown (1969).

Another place to look is across the states of India, where there exist state net domestic product data which can be compared with the state means from the household surveys. Again, this comparison is far from ideal; the state domestic product accounts are widely believed to be measured with considerable error, and even without error, the ideal comparison would not be with net domestic product, but with consumption. An offsetting advantage, compared with the international data, is that the state survey means and inequality measures are derived from the same surveys using identical questionnaires and procedures in each state. It should also be noted that the Indian NSS Organization consistently maintains that non-compliance is rare, and that numerators make repeated visits until people are available or it is convenient for them. The data from the surveys also carry a notation for whether the household actually surveyed was the one originally intended, or whether it is a substitute for the household targeted for sampling. In the 1999/2000 survey, only 1,200 out of more than 70,000 rural households are listed as substitutes, with 1,900 out of 48,900 urban households. About two-thirds of the substitutions are attributed to the informant being away, and less than a quarter to informants being busy or uncooperative.

The state survey means are well correlated with the state estimates; across the 43rd (1987/8), 50th (1993/4), and 55th (1999/2000) rounds of the NSS, and using means for only the seventeen largest states, the correlations are 0.88 or higher if Delhi is included, and 0.70 or higher if is excluded. If we use the log of the ratio of survey consumption per head to state net domestic product per head as the left-hand side of (6), and the variance of logs from the surveys as the right-hand side, the regression coefficient on the variance of logs is -1.39 ($t = -3.3$) in a pooled regression of the three rounds (fifty-four observations from eighteen states in each of the rounds), including round dummies. Taking each round separately, the corresponding coefficients (and t-values) are -0.69 (-0.8), -0.78 (-2.6), and -1.44 (-2.2) for the 43rd, 50th, and 55th rounds respectively. Figure 7.6 shows the corresponding plots, with each state identified. Taken literally, these estimates suggest that the elasticity of non-compliance has almost doubled in the twelve years between 1987/8 and 1999/2000, which is certainly consistent with a fall in fraction of aggregate consumption captured by the surveys. Inequality, within urban areas, and between urban and rural areas, has also been rising in India, Deaton and Drèze (2002) which would again depress the ratio of survey to NAS means. Of course, these results are consistent with a wide range of other possibilities; for example, as suggested by a referee, states with more inequality could have higher savings rates, and in the absence of good capital markets, a higher share of investment and a lower share of consumption in state GDP, or higher inequality could generate more government expenditure, with similar consequences. So the empirical evidence is weak at best.

These data are not suitable for investigating the important question of whether the ratios are lower when mean consumption is higher. This is because the state net domestic product is used in the calculation of the log ratio, so that to include it in the regression is to guarantee a negative correlation, whether or not one actually exists. Another variable that is plausibly important is the degree of urbanization, if enumerators have greater difficulty contacting or obtaining compliance from urban households. In fact, with the Indian state data, it is difficult to tell the urbanization and inequality explanations apart. Urbanization (the fraction of population in the urban sector) can be used to replace the variance of logs in the regression, with similar t-values, and when both urbanization and the variance are entered together, neither is significantly different from zero. Urbanization and inequality are highly correlated in these data, and we cannot tell whether it is high income that poses the problem for

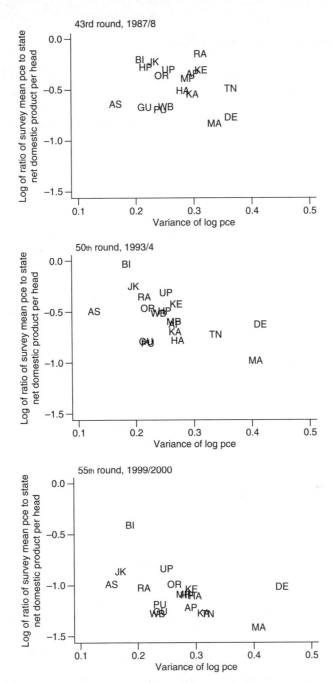

Figure 7.6 Ratio of survey mean of consumption to state net domestic product and variance of log pce, India, three NSS Survey rounds

Note: AP, Andhra Pradesh; AS, Assam; BI, Bihar; DE, Delhi; GU, Gujarat; HA, Haryana; JK, Jammu & Kashmir; KA, Kamataka; KE, Kerala; MP, Madhya Pradesh; MA, Maharashtra; OR, Orissa; PU, Punjab; RA, Rajasthan; TN, Tamil Nadu; UP, Uttar Pradesh; WB, West Bengal.

the surveys. With only eighteen states, I am almost certainly pushing these data too far. Nevertheless, the question of compliance is central to the analysis of survey versus national accounts, and the Indian experience provides some support for the idea that income-related non-compliance explains some part of the shortfall between the surveys and the national accounts, and perhaps even a part of why the shortfall is increasing.

Issues involving national accounts

Although non-compliance almost certainly explains at least some of the discrepancies between surveys and national accounts, and although there are other problems with the surveys beyond non-compliance, there are serious quality issues with the national accounts estimates of consumption and GDP. I discuss some of the most important in this subsection.

Discrepancies between survey and national accounts estimates of consumption can arise both through differences in definition, and through differences in the relative success of meeting those definitions. National accounts statistics are compiled according to protocols laid down in the 1993 version of the Systems of National Accounts, SNA93. The SNA93 establishes what is known as the "production boundary," which defines what is and is not part of consumption and GDP. The production boundary includes all goods and services that are exchanged, as well as *goods* that are non-exchanged, such as food produced for home consumption, but excludes *services* that are not exchanged, such as food preparation, home education of children, or minor home repairs, with the important exception of housing services consumed by owner-occupiers. Because the excluded services tend to be replaced by exchanged services as people become better-off, and substitute market for home-production, the measured growth rate of consumption and GDP will be too high, at least when the true rate of growth is positive. Yet this bias cannot explain any of the growing discrepancy between surveys and national accounts, because the non-exchanged services are not included in the surveys either.

Yet the degree of effective coverage of the non-exchanged items will almost always differ between the surveys and national accounts. Surveys almost never directly collect data on implicit rents for owner-occupiers, (other than the maintenance component) though it is sometimes possible to use data from the surveys on housing characteristics to estimate hedonic rental regressions, provided there is a local rental market. But few of the surveys used for poverty analysis contain such estimates, which undoubtedly contributes to the finding that survey to NAS consumption ratios are typically less than one, and if the share of the NAS consumption attributable to rents to owner-occupiers is increasing over time, it will also help explain the increasing divergence. I have not made any general study of the latter, but in India, the share appears to be more or less constant over time. In the US, the comparison of the CES and the NAS in Figure 7.5 includes imputed rents in both numbers, so that this cannot be the source of the increasing discrepancy between them. There are also likely to be differences in coverage of non-exchanged goods. Consumption of own-production, gifts, and wages in kind, are an important part of the total in poor countries, and many good survey offices devote a great deal of attention to collecting such information. For example, the Indian NSS distinguishes purchases, own production, and gifts for several hundred items. The coverage of non-exchanged goods in the NAS will depend on the methodology employed. Some countries use the survey estimates, but in many and perhaps most cases, consumption is calculated as a residual in a process that begins from production. In principle, this is not a problem, but in many countries, it would be extremely optimistic to suppose that the measurement of production accurately captures home production.

Consumption surveys, as opposed to income surveys, are likely to capture a good deal of illegal or legal, but concealed (for example, to avoid taxes or regulation), activities. *Purchasers* of such goods and services, unlike their *producers*, often have no incentives to conceal their transactions, and individuals who have substantial income from sources that they are unlikely to report, may nevertheless report the consumption that is financed by that income, see Derek Blades and David Roberts (2002), OECD (2002). Because of this, and because many surveys collect comprehensive data on non-exchanged production, it is not surprising that, in some of the poorest countries, consumption measured in the surveys would sometimes be much larger than consumption estimated in the national accounts. As non-exchanged production becomes less important with economic development, the effect will wear off, and could thus account for at least some of the decline in the ratio of the two measures. However, as Blades and Roberts emphasize, claims that the existence of various non-observed activities means that a large share of GDP, as much as a quarter or a third, is missed in the national accounts are almost certainly exaggerated. National income accountants understand the nature of the problems, and although their estimates for the non-observed economy may not be very accurate, they do not omit it.

In addition to imputed rents of homeowners, there are two other important items of consumption that are included in the NAS, but not in the surveys. One is "financial services indirectly imputed," or FISIM, which is an estimate of the consumption value of financial intermediation. FISIM is measured as the difference between interest paid to banks and other intermediaries, less interest paid by them. The idea is that interest charged to borrowers contains, in addition to the market rate of interest, a charge for intermediation services to lenders, in addition to the market rate of interest, while interest paid to lenders is lower than market, with the difference attributed to financial intermediation services to depositors. The difference between interest paid and interest received is therefore a measure of the value of financial intermediation, and since the

1993 revision of the SNA, has been added to national accounts estimates of household consumption. A similar item is included for risk-bearing services, measured from the profits of insurance companies. In India, the value of FISIM increased from close to zero in 1983/4 to 2.5 per cent of consumption in 1993/ 4, A. Kulshreshtha and A. Kar (2002), so that this item alone accounts for 0.25 percentage points per year of the difference in annual growth rates between NAS and survey consumption in India. Note also that, to the extent we are interested in measuring the living standards of the poor, it can reasonably be doubted whether the value of such financial intermediation accrues is relevant. In consequence, even if we accept the argument for the inclusion of FISIM in NAS consumption, neither it nor its rate of growth contribute to the living standards of the poor.

The second potentially important item of consumption included in NAS but not in the surveys is consumption by non-profit institutions serving households (NPISH) which, in most countries, cannot be separated from household consumption. It is unclear how large these items are, or whether such expenditures are growing relative to total consumption. In the UK, NPISH in 2001 was 3.9 per cent of total consumption, almost double the 1970 share of 2.1 per cent. It is possible that NPISH are much more widespread in poorer countries (in India, it is sometimes claimed that there is an NGO in every village), but I know of no data on the subject.

National accounts consumption is typically estimated as a residual using the "commodity flow" method. Starting from an estimate of domestic production of each commodity, net exports and government consumption are deducted, as are the amounts used in investment and intermediate consumption, with the residual attributed to household (and NPISH) consumption. Many of these calculations are done in physical volumes, so that estimation of consumption in currency units, which is what can be compared with the surveys, requires the use of prices and price indexes. There are many opportunities for error along this chain of calculation and, in general, there is no means (other than surveys) of cross-checking the final answer. The measurement of prices is a survey-based activity with its own sampling and non-sampling errors, and it is sometimes difficult to be sure that prices are those actually paid by consumers. Not surprisingly, the monetary value of NAS estimates of consumption are subject to errors and to occasional large revision. K. Sundaram and Suresh Tendulkar (2003) report that the Indian NAS estimate of consumption of fruits and vegetables in 1993/4 in nominal rupees more than doubled between the 1998 and 1999 versions of the national accounts. The estimate for clothing fell by about a half, and that for rent, fuel, and power rose by more than 40 per cent. Even with some canceling out of pluses and minuses, total consumption was revised upwards by 14 per cent, an amount which, if used to calculate poverty rates, would cut the Indian poverty rate by a little less than a half.

For food, which is a large share of consumption in poor countries, domestic production is typically estimated by multiplying the acreage of land under cultivation by an estimate of yields per acre. The former comes from a land census or survey, which in many countries is done quite infrequently, while the latter comes from crop-cutting surveys, themselves of mixed quality. Data on government consumption are usually relatively accurate, as are imports and exports, which typically are subject to direct monitoring by the government. The same cannot be said for intermediate (business) consumption, which is often assessed by applying various ratios to measured production. These ratios come from enterprise surveys, or from input output tables. Once again, these measures are often outdated. For India, Kulshreshtha and Kar (2002) write that their NAS consumption estimated "depend on an assortment of direct and indirect estimates along with various rates and ratios, some of which are based on the results of studies carried out in the distant past."

The use of outdated ratios and correction factors is particularly problematic when the economy is growing and its structure changing. Kulshreshtha and Kar, in their detailed commodity by commodity comparison of food consumption in the NAS and the NSS in India, find that one of the largest discrepancies is for *vanaspati*, a vegetable cooking oil, that is widely used in restaurants. This intermediate use of cooking oil should be deducted in the commodity flow calculations but, in fact, there is no such correction in the Indian national accounts. In consequence, and because consumers' expenditure in restaurants is already included in NAS consumption, restaurant use of *vanaspati* is double-counted in the national accounts. And because consumers switch from domestic cooking to purchased meals as they get better-off, the more rapid is the growth of the economy, the larger will the overstatement of consumption become. The *vanaspati* example is an extreme case, in that there is no correction for intermediate business consumption, but the same exaggeration of growth will be generated by the use of outdated "rates and ratios" to assess intermediate consumption in an economy where growth is reallocating economic activity from own-production to the market.

Overstatement of consumption and consumption growth through a failure to capture intermediate consumption will also lead to an overstatement of the level and growth rate of expenditure-based measures of GDP. This exaggeration is in addition to the exaggeration associated with the general movement of activity, such as services, from a non-exchanged to an exchanged basis, for example as a greater share of food preparation is done by food vendors, which is counted in GDP, rather than by family members, which is not. Both come from the same fundamental trend, which is the increasing marketization, complexity, and "roundaboutness" of production with economic development. Note that not all of these errors in constructing consumption necessarily find their way into GDP. For example, how a commodity flow is allocated between consumption and capital formation will affect the estimation of both, but not of their sum.

Other survey issues

The two previous sections have documented what are perhaps the most likely candidates for explaining the divergence between national accounts and survey-based estimates of consumption. However, it should also be emphasized that there are many other problems some of which are on the survey side. It is clear that details of survey design matter for the results, and that protocols are not the same across countries, or sometimes within countries over time. Many of these are discussed in more detail in Deaton and Margaret Grosh (2000).

Surveys often have less than complete *coverage*, excluding for example students, the military, and institutionalized persons, expenditures by whom are included in NAS estimates of consumption. In some cases, survey coverage excluded rural households, or parts of the country that are expensive or dangerous to visit.

Survey questionnaires differ in the length of the *recall period* over which respondents are asked to report their consumption. The choice of recall period is often thought to involve a trade-off between accuracy of memory, which calls for a short period, and the match between consumption and purchases, which is more accurate when averaged over a long period. But there is little understanding of the effects of different recall periods, particularly in poor, agricultural societies. In India between 1989 and 1998, the NSS experimented with different recall periods, replacing the traditional 30-day recall period for all goods with a 7-day recall period for food and tobacco, and with a 365 day period for durable goods and some other infrequently purchased items. The sample was randomly divided, and half were given the old questionnaire, and half the new, so that it is possible to make a clean evaluation of the effects of the change. The shorter reporting period increased reported expenditures on food by around 30 per cent, and total consumption by about 17 per cent, very much in the right direction to help resolve the discrepancy with the NAS. Because there are many Indians close to the poverty line, the 17 per cent increase was enough to reduce the measured headcount ratio by a half, removing almost 200 million people from poverty. What might seem to be an obscure technical issue of survey design can have a major effect on the measurement of poverty, not only in India, but in the world. It should be noted, however, that the higher consumption totals associated with the shorter recall period, although closer to the NAS estimates, are not necessarily more accurate. Indeed, the NSS has carried out a series of controlled experiments in which, for many foods, the 30-day reference period appears to be more accurate then the 7-day period, see NSSO Expert Group on Sampling Errors (2003).

Survey questionnaires also vary in the number of items that are separately distinguished, and there is some evidence that the greater the degree of disaggregation, the greater is measured consumption in total. There is also no consistency in the treatment of seasonality, with some surveys visiting each household on several occasions throughout the year, while most simply rely on spreading data collection throughout a calendar year, a procedure that should not bias the mean, though there will be biases in higher-order statistics. In some surveys, respondents keep diaries of their purchases over a period, in others, they make oral responses to interviewers based on recall. Surveys vary on who is chosen as respondent, and whether one or more household members are interviewed. However well-informed the household member who reports purchases, "proxy" reports, on the purchases of other family members, are likely to be less accurate than reports about the respondent's own behavior. Indeed, proxy reporting can plausibly contribute to a progressively large share of consumption being missed over time. In a poor, rural community, where everyone eats from the same pot, and food is nearly all of the budget, the housewife's report will be quite accurate. This is much less so in more diverse and better-off households, with some family members working outside of the home, and maintaining partial budgetary independence.

In addition to the *unit* non-response discussed earlier, there is *item* non-response, where household members fail to report at least some expenditures, or provide deliberately misleading reports, for example on alcohol consumption, or on various illegal items. Finally, and in parallel with the national accounts, there are difficulties in finding adequate prices for consumption items that are not purchased in the market; some surveys use market prices to impute home production, some use farm-gate prices, and some use valuation techniques that are not clearly documented.

It would be desirable if the international statistical community could agree on a common set of best-practice protocols for household income expenditure surveys, as a parallel to the SNA for the national accounts. Unfortunately, most of the issues discussed here are neither sufficiently well-researched nor understood to admit of uncontroversial solutions, and many statistical offices are stout defenders of their own particular practices. Yet, as I shall argue in the next section, only household surveys allow us to measure poverty, so that the task of harmonization must be undertaken if we are to put global poverty measurement on a sound basis.

Conclusions and implications for the measurement of poverty

The standard measures of poverty are based on counting the number of people who live in households whose measured per capita consumption is less than a poverty line. When rich households are less likely to cooperate with the survey than poor people, survey-based estimates of consumption will understate mean consumption, and overstate the fraction of people in poverty. Under some conditions, the amount by which average consumption is understated will be larger the greater is the inequality of the true distribution of consumption. Unless consumption inequality is increasing over time, or the fraction of non-cooperating households is increasing, income-based non-cooperation does not, in and of itself, imply that ratio of measured to true consumption is increasing over time.

National accounts estimates of consumption are typically, although not always, larger than survey-based estimates, and there is a tendency, both across countries and over time within important countries, for the NAS estimate of consumption to grow more rapidly than the survey based estimate. While survey based estimates are subject to numerous errors and inaccuracies, there are also problems with national accounts estimates. These are likely to understate consumption in the poorest countries, and to overstate the rate of growth of average consumption, both over time in poor countries, and in comparisons between poor and rich countries at a moment in time. In part, these systematic problems in measuring the rate of growth of consumption carry through to GDP, whose growth rate is also systematically biased upwards. I know of no plausible estimates of the size of the bias.

Given the conflict between survey and NAS estimates of consumption, it is tempting to allow the NAS estimates to play at least some role in poverty measurement, instead of using only the survey data. Indeed, the combination of means from the surveys and Lorenz curves from the surveys has a long history, including Montek S. Ahluwalia et al. (1979), the Indian government prior to 1993, and most of Latin America until today. In some cases, this procedure was adopted because the survey means were unavailable, and in others, such as the Indian case, the practice was abandoned after searching criticism of the quality of the national accounts, see in particular B. S. Minhas (1988) who memorably describes the earlier practice as "mindless tinkering." In general, there is an argument for averaging of multiple estimates, although only estimates of the same thing, so that extensive prior adjustment of any NAS mean would be required before using it to scale up survey estimates. However, there is need for a good deal of caution, and mechanical use of *unadjusted* NAS means, combined with survey-based estimates of distribution around the mean, will certainly give poor measures of poverty. There are at least three reasons why.

First, and most generally, the national accounts are designed to generate estimates of macro-economic aggregates, not estimates of poverty, and the SNA rules are designed with that in mind. National accounts track money, not people. To take an example, the SNA recognizes that production for own consumption is difficult to measure, and recommends that the effort be made only "when the amount produced is likely to be quantitatively important in relation to the total supply of the good in the country," OECD (2002, p. 179). Such a rule makes little sense when our prime objective is to measure poverty.

At the other end of the spectrum, items like FISIM and the rental value of owner occupier homes are (properly) included, although in most cases they are either not consumed by the poor, or comprise less of their budgets. In general, the NAS is more likely to capture larger transactions than smaller ones, which is close to the opposite of what happens in the surveys, where large *transactors* are the least likely to be included.

Second, the differences in coverage and definition between NAS and surveys mean that, even if everything were perfectly measured, it would be incorrect to apply inequality or distributional measures, which are derived from surveys which measure one thing, to means that are derived from the national accounts, which measure another. When national accounts and surveys are measuring different things, it is perfectly possible for the poor to do less well than the average, without any increase in measured inequality.

To illustrate, suppose that we are interested in measuring consumption growth among the bottom $100p$ per cent of the population. We have data on mean consumption, μ, from the national accounts, and data on the share of the bottom $100p$ per cent of households from surveys, s_p. Mean consumption of the bottom p per cent is then estimated to be

$$\mu_p = s_p \mu / p \tag{13}$$

so that the growth rate of consumption for the bottom group is

$$\frac{\dot{\mu}_p}{\mu_p} = \frac{\dot{s}_p}{s_p} + \frac{\dot{\mu}}{\mu}. \tag{14}$$

In (13), the first term on the right hand side comes entirely from the surveys, and the second entirely from the national accounts. The survey mean, $\hat{\mu}$, and the direct survey measure of $\hat{\mu}p = s_p\hat{\mu}$, the average consumption of the bottom $100p$ per cent, are discarded, even though the poor rarely refuse to respond, and provide accurate estimates of their consumption. Moreover, the validity of (13) and (14) depends on being able to apply the survey shares to the NAS means, which not only assumes that the NAS means are perfectly measured, but that both are measuring the same thing. So even if we were to accept that NAS consumption is the concept that we want, and even if we were to believe that it is accurately measured, the shares from the survey are shares of consumption excluding consumption on rents of owner occupiers, excluding FISIM and the profits of insurance companies, and excluding the expenditures of NPISH. Using the survey shares to allocate NAS consumption to the poor and non-poor assumes that these items are distributed between poor and non-poor in the same way as are the goods measured in the survey, an assumption that is not true.

Third, we must recognize that neither mean consumption nor its distribution are accurately measured either in the surveys or the NAS. A particular difficulty comes from the mechanical use of the distributional shares and Gini coefficients that come from the Deininger–Squire (DS) and WIDER compilations. (Shares can be calculated from Gini coefficients if a particular distribution is assumed, for example the lognormal.) For most poor countries, these measures are of dubious quality, as indeed is recognized by DS. And neither DS nor the WIDER compilation provide the information that would be required to make an informed judgment on the way their numbers were calculated. So that if equation (14) is used to construct $\dot{\mu}_p/\mu_p$, and the measures of s_p are noisy, a regression of $\dot{\mu}_p/\mu_p$ on $\dot{\mu}/\mu$ will have a coefficient that is close to one, essentially by construction, and the worse is the measurement error, the closer the estimate to one. So there is no credibility to the claim that globalization has been good for the poor based on a calculation that applies badly measured distributional shares to (upwardly biased) measures of growth from the national accounts. The globalization debate is serious enough that we must genuinely measure the living standards of the poor, not simply assume them. We cannot prove that growth trickles down by assuming that growth trickles down, nor argue that globalization has reduced poverty without measuring the living standards of the poor.

If the task were the purely statistical one of estimating mean consumption, there would be much to be said for using the average of mean consumption from the surveys and from the adjusted national accounts, Deaton (2001). But if we need to measure poverty in a way that will convince those who are skeptical of the idea that average growth reaches the poor, there is little choice but to use the surveys. This argument is reinforced by the impossibility for many countries, and certainly for all, of making the adjustments to NAS consumption estimates that would make them comparable with the survey totals. None of this says that the surveys are correct, nor that current measures of global poverty are doing a good job of measuring the trends. And because not every country has a survey in every year, they are clearly unsuitable for measuring year to year variations, see Figure 7.3. There is too much incompatibility in survey design across countries. The downward bias in survey measures of consumption almost certainly biases upwards the World Bank's global poverty estimates, and since it is unlikely that all of the growth discrepancy between the surveys and the NAS is due to faults in the latter, the rate of poverty decline is likely downward biased. We need an international initiative to provide a set of consistent international protocols for survey design, as well as deeper study into the effects of non-sampling errors, particularly non-compliance.

Appendix: Lognormally distributed income with selective compliance.

Suppose that x is the logarithm of income, and that x is normally distributed in the population with mean μ and variance σ^2. The compliance probability as a function of income is given by equation (1) in the main text. In general, if the true density if $f(x)$, the density function of the truncated distribution is given by

$$\hat{f}(x) = \frac{p(x)f(x)}{\int\limits_0^\infty p(s)dF(s)} = \phi(x)f(x) \tag{A1}$$

In this normal case with the response function given by equation (1) in the main text the truncated density is

$$\hat{f}(x) = \frac{1}{\bar{p}\sqrt{(2\pi\sigma^2)}} \exp\left[-\frac{1}{2}\left(\frac{x-\mu}{\sigma}\right)^2\right], \qquad\qquad x \leq \mu - \theta\sigma$$

$$\hat{f}(x) = \frac{1}{\bar{p}\sqrt{(2\pi\sigma^2)}} \exp\left[-\frac{1}{2}\left(\frac{x-\mu}{\sigma}\right)^2\right]\exp[-a(x-\mu-\theta\sigma)], \quad x \geq \mu - \theta\sigma \tag{A2}$$

where $\bar{p}$ is the population average compliance probability. The second part of (A2) can be rewritten

$$\hat{f}(x) = \frac{1}{\bar{p}\sqrt{(2\pi\sigma^2)}} \exp\left[-\frac{1}{2}\left(\frac{x-\mu-a\sigma^2}{\sigma}\right)^2\right]\exp\left(-a\theta\sigma + \frac{1}{2}a^2\sigma^2\right), \quad x \geq \mu - \theta\sigma \tag{A3}$$

If we integrate $\hat{f}(x)$ over the full range of x, we can derive an expression for the mean compliance probability

$$\bar{p} = \Phi(-\theta) + \Phi(\theta - a\sigma)\exp\left(-a\theta\sigma + \frac{1}{2}a^2\sigma^2\right) \tag{A4}$$

where the first term comes from integrating the first part of (A2) and the second from integrating (A3). These three equations completely characterize the truncated density $\hat{f}(x)$.

If we substitute (A4) into (A3), we get the density of a normal distribution with mean $\mu - a\sigma^2$ and variance σ^2, scaled by the factor

$$\frac{\exp\left(-a\theta\sigma + \frac{1}{2}a^2\sigma^2\right)}{\Phi(-\theta) + \Phi(\theta - a\sigma)\exp\left(-a\theta\sigma + \frac{1}{2}a^2\sigma^2\right)}$$

$$= \frac{1}{\Phi(-\theta)\exp\left(a\theta\sigma - \frac{1}{2}a^2\sigma^2\right) + \Phi(\theta - a\sigma)} \tag{A5}$$

As θ becomes large, the second term in the denominator on the right goes to unity, while the first term goes to zero. Hence, for large θ, with little of the density is to the left of $\mu - \theta\sigma$, the truncated density is approximately (A3), which is approximately

$$\hat{f}(x) = \frac{1}{\sqrt{(2\pi\sigma^2)}}\exp\left[-\frac{1}{2}\left(\frac{x-\mu-\alpha\sigma^2}{\sigma}\right)^2\right], \quad x \geq \mu - \theta\sigma \qquad (A6)$$

so that the truncated distribution of log income is also normal, with the same variance σ^2 as the true distribution, but with mean $\mu - \alpha\sigma^2$ instead of μ.

Notes

1. The Review of Economics and Statistics Lecture, presented at Harvard University, April 15, 2003 and previously published in the Review of Economics and Statistics, 87:1, 1–19, February 2005. I am grateful to Daron Acemoglu, Bettina Aten, Barry Bosworth, François Bourguignon, Shaohua Chen, Russel Freeman, Paul Glewwe, Carol Graham, Tom Griffin, Ivo Havinga, Alan Heston, Michael Kremer, Martin Ravallion, Dani Rodrik, T. N. Srinivasan, Nick Stern, John Williamson, and Jeronimo Zettelmeyer for help in the preparation of this paper, as well as comments on an earlier draft. Anne Case made many invaluable suggestions and corrected several errors. The views expressed here are those of the author alone.
2. Princeton University.

Bibliography

Adelman, I. and Morris, C. T. (1973) *Economic growth and social equity in developing countries*. Stanford, CA: Stanford University Press.
Ahluwalia, M. S., Carter, N. G., and Chenery, H. B. (1979) 'Growth and poverty in developing countries'. *Journal of Development Economics*, 6, pp. 299–341.
—— Duloy, J. H., Pyatt, F. G., et al. (1980) 'Who benefits from economic development? Comment'. *American Economic Review*, 70(1), pp. 242–5.
Aitchison, J. and Brown, A. (1969) *The lognormal distribution*. Cambridge: Cambridge University Press.
Bardhan, P. K. (1973) 'On the incidence of poverty in rural India in the sixties'. *Economic and Political Weekly*, 8 (February special issue), pp. 245–54.
Berg, A. and Krueger, A. (2003) 'Trade, growth, and poverty: a selective survey'. IMF Working Paper 03/30, Washington DC.
Bhalla, S. S. (2002) *Imagine there is no country: poverty, inequality, and growth in the era of globalization*. Washington DC, Institute for International Economics.
Blades, D. and Roberts, D. (2002) 'Measuring the non-observed economy.' *OECD Statistics Brief*, No. 5 (November), pp. 1–8.
Bourguignon, F. and Morrisson, C. (2002) 'Inequality among world citizens: 1820–1992'. *American Economic Review*, 92(4), pp. 727–44.

Chen, S. and Ravallion, M. (2001) 'How well did the world's poorest fare in the 1990s?' *Review of Income and Wealth*, 47(3), pp. 283–300.

Chenery, H. B., Ahluwalia, M. S., Bell, C. L. G., et al. (1974) *Redistribution with growth*. Oxford, Oxford University Press for the World Bank.

Cline, W. R. (1975) 'Distribution and development: a survey of the literature'. *Journal of Development Economics*, 1(4), pp. 359–400.

Deaton, A. (2001) 'Counting the world's poor: problems and possible solutions'. *World Bank Research Observer*, 16(2, Fall), pp. 125–47.

—— (2003) 'Adjusted Indian poverty estimates for 1999–2000'. *Economic and Political Weekly*, January 25, pp. 322–6.

—— and Grosh, M. (2000) 'Consumption'. In M. Grosh and P. Glewwe (eds.) *Designing household questionnaires for developing countries: lessons from fifteen years of the living standards measurement study*. Washington DC: World Bank, pp. 91–133.

—— and Drèze, J. (2002) 'Poverty and inequality in India, a reexamination'. *Economic and Political Weekly*, September 7, pp. 3729–48.

Deininger, K. and Squire, L. (1996) 'A new data set measuring income inequality'. *World Bank Economic Review*, 10, pp. 565–91.

Dollar, D. and Kraay, A. (2002) 'Growth is good for the poor'. *Journal of Economic Growth*, 7, pp. 195–225.

Fields, G. S. (1977) 'Who benefits from economic development? A reexamination of Brazilian growth in the 1960s'. *American Economic Review*, 67(4), pp. 570–82.

Fishlow, A. (1972) 'Brazilian size distribution of income'. *American Economic Review*, 62(1/2), pp. 391–402.

Garner, T. I., Janini, G., Passero, W., et al. (2003) *The consumer expenditure survey in comparison: focus on personal consumption expenditures*. Washington DC: Bureau of Labor Statistics.

Government of India (2003) *National Accounts Statistics*. Ministry of Statistics and Programme Implementation <http://mospi.nic.in/national_account_main.htm> accessed March 1, 2003.

Groves, R. M. and Couper, M. P. (1998) *Nonresponse in household interview surveys*. New York: Wiley.

Kakwani, N. (1987) 'Lorenz curve'. In J. Eatwell, M. Milgate, and P. Newman (eds.) *The new Palgrave: A dictionary of economics*, Vol. 3, London and Basingstoke: Macmillan, pp. 242–4.

Keidel, A. (2001) 'China's GDP expenditure accounts'. *China Economic Review*, 12(4), pp. 355–67.

Kulshreshtha, A. C. and Kar, A. (2002) 'Estimates of food consumption expenditure from household surveys and national accounts'. World Bank Working Paper <http://www.worldbank.org/indiapovertyworkshop>.

Kuznets, S. (1955) 'Economic growth and income inequality'. *American Economic Review*, 45(1), pp. 1–28.

Maddison, A. (1998) *Chinese economic performance in the long run*. Paris: OECD.

Minhas, B. S. (1988) 'Validation of large-scale sample survey data: case of NSS household consumption expenditure'. *Sankhya*, Series B, 50(Supplement), pp. 1–63.

—— and Kansal, S. M. (1989) 'Comparison of NSS and CSO estimates of private consumption: some observations based on 1983 data'. *The Journal of Income and Wealth*, 11, pp. 7–24.

Mistiaen, J. A. and Ravallion, M. (2003) *Survey compliance and the distribution of income*. Washington DC: World Bank.

NSSO Expert Group on Sampling Errors (2003) 'Suitability of different reference periods for measuring household consumption: results of a pilot study'. *Economic and Political Weekly*, January 25, pp. 307–21.

Organization for Economic Cooperation and Development (2002) *Measuring the non-observed economy: a handbook*. Paris.

Office for National Statistics (2003) *Annual Abstract of Statistics*. London: HMSO.

Pyatt, G. (2003) 'Development and the distribution of living standards: a critique of the evolving data base'. *Review of Income and Wealth*, 49(3), pp. 333–58.

Ravallion, M. (2001) 'Growth, inequality, and poverty: looking beyond the averages'. *World Development*, 29(11), pp. 1803–15.

——— (2003) 'Measuring aggregate welfare in developing countries: how well do national accounts and surveys agree'. *Review of Economics and Statistics*, 85(3), pp. 645–52.

Rawski, T. G. (2001) 'What is happening to China's GDP statistics?' *China Economic Review*, 12(4), pp. 347–54.

Sala-i-Martín, X. (2002) *The disturbing 'rise' of global income inequality*. NBER Working Paper No. 8904, Cambridge, Mass.

Srinivasan, T. N. and Bardhan, P. (1974) *Poverty and income distribution in India*. Calcutta: Statistical Publishing Society.

Sundaram, K. and Tendulkar, S. (2003) 'NAS-NSS estimates of private consumption for poverty estimation: a further comparative estimation'. *Economic and Political Weekly*, January 25, pp. 376–84.

Taylor, L. and Bacha, E. L. (1976) 'The unequalizing spiral: a first growth model for Belindia'. *Quarterly Journal of Economics*, 90(2), pp. 197–218.

Triplett, J. E. (1997) 'Measuring consumption: the post-1973 slowdown and the research issues'. *Federal Reserve Bank of St Louis Review* (May/June), pp. 9–42.

Wu, H. X. (2000) 'China's GDP level and growth performance: alternative estimates and the implications'. *Review of Income and Wealth*, 46(4), pp. 475–99.

8

Poverty or Income Distribution: Which Do We Want to Measure?[1]

Robert Johnston

The concepts of poverty, poverty line, levels of income and expenditure, low income, and inequality have been in the statistician's vocabulary for more than a century. While statisticians have considerable experience to draw on in trying to understand them, we can also see from this history that there has always been considerable confusion and overlap among them. I propose that we can benefit by studying concepts of poverty on the one hand and income distribution (including inequality) on the other separately, rather than trying to subsume them in a single analysis. This will provide a better basis for deciding what it is we define as "poverty" for measurement purposes, at least from an international development perspective (only one of many perspectives which might be used, of course), and will then help us to consider how to measure it and with what available tools.

My main conclusion is somewhat paradoxical. The "elimination of extreme poverty" target in the United Nations' Millennium Development Goals (MDGs) is basically not about money or income distribution; it is about deprivation and distress at the levels of individuals and households, notably hunger and malnutrition, ill health and death, and lack of shelter. Deprivation and distress can take many forms and we can and do measure a large number of these in many ways. The paradox is that money, as a generalizable measure, is the most convenient general yardstick. Fortunately, with the recent international consensus on the MDGs and targets, we now have a short, workable list of other yardsticks suited to measure directly significant dimensions of human distress and deprivation which are not well captured by the money dimension (United Nations, 2000, 2001).

A short historical note on poverty statistics

The concept and measurement of poverty have had a chequered history in statistical work over the past century. Probably the world's first large-scale poverty survey was undertaken at the end of the nineteenth century by Charles Booth, who wanted some measure of the wretched living conditions of the working class in London. This work has achieved enduring fame at the Museum of the City of London in a fine exhibit on its conduct and results. Booth's work was soon followed up by B. S. Rowntree in York, England, who seems to have invented a precursor of the modern household survey for this purpose, using on-the-spot interviews with family members and a standard set of questions. As Claus Moser and Graham Kalton tell the story (Moser and Kalton, pp. 7–9), Rowntree also seems to have invented the concept of what we are now calling extreme poverty, that is "total earnings insufficient to obtain the minimum necessaries for the maintenance of merely physical efficiency," using a practical household budget-based standard (Moser and Kalton's paraphrases).

These surveyors apparently had no interest in the distribution of income or inequality as such. It seems that the wretched conditions and large but unknown numbers of the poor were the main motivations, not invidious comparisons with the well-off. Such comparisons were certainly a main motivation of Marx (himself a regular user of statistics) but inequality and distribution of income did not enter the practicing statistician's vocabulary until much later. To my mind, as I will try to show in the next part of this story, the later concern with inequality, equity or more generally distribution of income, has been a diversion and ultimately a serious distraction from the overriding issue of meeting fundamental human needs.

The distribution of income approach gained attention in international statistics from the 1960s onwards. This approach has tried to have it both ways; opening the door to considerations of inequality as well as level of impoverishment. Since a poverty line can be set anywhere along an income or expenditure distribution with reference to the correlation of that level of income or consumption with observable non-monetary needs and conditions, it came to be widely assumed that a good place to start studying poverty was with the distribution of income. Even better, the degree of inequality itself can be used as a measure implying a lower stratum in more or less dire straits. However, this change in focus to income distribution had, in my view, the unfortunate effect of muddying the waters. What was needed was a poverty line that had an intuitively understandable referent in everyday life, but instead, the notion that all poverty was purely relative came into prominence. The study of income distribution has achieved some major conceptual and methodological advances but has contributed little, in my view, to the understanding or measurement of extreme poverty, other than providing a lot of non-standardized data to try to work with.

Extensive work on the more traditional notion of inadequacy, however measured, followed on from the early work of Booth and Rowntree. Some new policy implications of this approach crystallized after the Second World War in the notion of "standard of living," which turned on the idea of determining what an "acceptable" working class salary would be in any given country—obviously a relative concept—with a view to also measuring regular "cost of living" increases which could be used to adjust wages. This has given statisticians, policy analysts, politicians, and interest groups plenty of work right up to the present day.

In the United Nations, the official statisticians started talking in the 1950s about a more neutral variant, the idea of "levels of living," that is standard of living without any explicit component of inadequacy (United Nations, 1954, 1961). Perhaps because any notion of inadequacy was left out, thereby draining the concept of relevance to social development policy, this early work did not have much of a discernible impact on development policy planning or analysis. It was taken up and substantially broadened in concept and method at the end of the 1960s by the United Nations Research Institute for Social Development (UNRISD), an autonomous research institute in Geneva, but did not reappear on the agenda of the Statistical Commission of the United Nations Economic and Social Council until some years later.

UNRISD sponsored research had tried another variation by expanding the income and poverty concepts into a more comprehensive index of levels of living (Drewnowski, 1974) but again there was little follow-up until the much later Human Development Index (HDI), established for the annual *Human Development Report* of the United Nations Development Programme. But in this variant, the technique was quite different and led quickly to professional and political controversies official statisticians were at some pains to avoid.

The first official statistical work that seemed to bring poverty and levels of living concepts into a single overall framework was the 1968 Level of Living Survey in Sweden. This work arose from a political debate in the Swedish parliament as to the extent of poverty in Sweden, generally considered a "model" country in terms of living conditions and social equality. This gave rise to a considerable debate between the Swedish Institute for Social Research, which favored a broad and explicit levels of living approach, and Statistics Sweden, which argued that Swedish statistics were already adequate to look at the many component elements of levels of living, and that they already had an internationally agreed income distribution survey. In the event, it ended up that the Institute wrote the survey it wanted and Statistics Sweden implemented it in the field.

Ironically, the Institute protagonist, Sten Johansson, went on some years later to become the Director-General of Statistics Sweden. Johansson succeeded in bringing the focus back to levels of living issues and at the same time making explicit the income and poverty focus by fully incorporating and focusing on the concept of low income. He and Erik Allardt also broadened and formalized the levels of living approach by explicitly reviewing the components of levels of living in terms of social policy concerns, drawing on the much earlier United Nations and UNRISD work. The rationale sounds very similar to that of the later HDI ("command over resources"), but without the index and with systematic attention to non-monetary but poverty related concerns.

At about the same time, Claus Moser developed for the UK a more detailed survey with similar coverage but without the explicit social policy underpinnings, in the General Household Survey. This survey became the mainstay source of many social measures for the UK, including income and poverty, and continues to this day.

Meanwhile, at the United Nations the official international statisticians were proceeding along much more conservative lines, with the appearance of the renowned *A System of National Accounts* (1968), later of *Towards a System of Social and Demographic Statistics* (1975), and then of *Preliminary Guidelines on Statistics of the Distribution of Income, Consumption and Accumulation of Households* (1977). In this work the concept "poverty" or levels of living is nowhere mentioned. Later, in the late 1980s, there was a period of enthusiasm in the Statistical Commission for looking at new issues and ideas and a poverty working group was formed, chaired by the World Bank. However, it soon concluded that there was no technical possibility of designing international standards for poverty measurement and that it was basically a policy issue to which the international statistician had very little to contribute, and the group disbanded in 1990.

Nevertheless, a countertrend in the United Nations had been at work for some time. United Nations publications in the 1970s took poverty and level of living measurement seriously as part of development statistics and indicators (United Nations, 1977, 1978, 1989, 1991), and while these publications had modest impact, they were part of a trend that was slowly ripening in the background.

In summary, I conclude first, that income and poverty are quite different concepts and distribution of income is a poor way to get to a poverty measure, but low income, carefully defined, can give us a good measure of deprivation. I have not talked much about the definition of income for this purpose, but I will say (again, paradoxically) that SNA-based definitions, such as those spelled out in (United Nations, 1977) and (United Nations Economic Commission for Latin America and the Caribbean, 1983) can serve the purpose quite well.[2]

Poverty and the Millennium Development Goals

Moving now to very recent times, the United Nations' Millennium Declaration and its follow-up have adopted the World Bank's $1.08PPP (1993) a day measure of poverty (hereafter referred to as the "$1-a-day" poverty line) in the

MDGs and targets (United Nations, 2000, 2001). This has had the effect, for global policy applications, of ratifying the wide international use of this particular measure, notwithstanding the extensive ongoing debates on its technical and philosophical merits.

Clearly the $1-a-day measure takes us back through several generations of basic needs measurements (in various guises) to the original concept in the UK surveys of dire straits—the complex and elastic question of what is socially justifiable is subordinated to the intuitively simpler question of what should not have to be endured.

If we ignore the many technical questions which have been discussed on this measure and accept the notion that it is not at all concerned with income distribution or various similar variants in terms of more or less relative poverty lines, then where is the $1-a-day measurement taking us?

There are signs of a slow but steady reformulation of the 1970s' Bank dictum, "growth with equity." As equity or lack thereof has been more and more closely scrutinized as a globalization issue, it has emerged from behind the shadow of growth. More precisely, the idea that growth automatically provides benefits to all has been seriously reconsidered, if only because experience on the ground seems to show otherwise. It is now acceptable to suggest that growth and poverty are to some degree independent, and we can now see fairly clearly how various growth and social policies have ended up favoring the middle classes, some have favored the rich, some the poor, and some have disfavored the poor, often to considerable effect. On balance, though, in the least developed countries, where progress in achieving the poverty target has generally been minimal, we are still far from understanding very well how to make growth work for the elimination of extreme poverty.

Meeting the target—how to close the gap?

The discussion to this point leads naturally to two immediate questions: what is the percentage of population in a given country or countries with total consumption or income below the World Bank's extreme poverty line (less than $1.08 a day, in 1993 PPP dollars, to continue with the World Bank's concept), and what is the shortfall between consumption or income and the $1-a-day PPP poverty line? Approaching the analysis in this way keeps the immediate focus for present purposes on need and deprivation, not inequality.

The World Bank publishes estimates of population below the poverty line based on extensive analysis of household surveys in most developing countries. However, its "poverty gap index," described as the mean shortfall from the poverty line as a proportion of the poverty line taken across the whole population, does not readily allow the calculation of the total absolute amount of the gap relative to total income. Neither does it address what might intuitively be of more immediate interest, the shortfall of the poor themselves, since the shortfall is taken as a ratio relative to the whole population. It is difficult to calculate either of these ratios because the current poverty line estimates use PPP 1993 dollars, and estimates of total current income in 1993 PPP dollars are not readily available.

The Bank's regional estimates of the percentage of population in extreme poverty in 2003 are given in Table 8.1. These seem plausible enough, and more or less in line with the United Nations identification among the developing countries of categories of countries with special needs, the least developed and the landlocked. These two special groupings, and their overlaps, are shown in Figure 8.1 and provide a good quick guide to where the most serious problems lie.

In order to see how large the poverty line shortfall might be, I take Bangladesh as an example. Figure 8.2 shows an old, and therefore purely illustrative, income distribution curve from Bangladesh (Jain, 1974) applied to total GDP 2000 in 1993 PPP dollars, so that the 1993 $1-a-day poverty line (actually $1.08, equaling $393.12/year) can also be used. The figure shows that the average income ranges from $199 in the lowest decile to $1,563 in the highest. Actual income below the poverty line is shown in light shading and the actual income differences below and above the poverty line in dark shading. The dark portions of bars in the four deciles with actual incomes below the line represent the poverty gap, while those in the six deciles above the poverty line show the total "surplus."

The Bank's poverty gap ratio, taking the amount of the poverty gap as a percentage of poverty line income for the whole population works out to 10.81 per cent. However, the ratio of the gap to income above the line is 27 per cent. As a percentage of the total national income (GDP), it is 7 per cent. The figure of 27 per cent answers the question of how much of the income

Table 8.1. Population below $1 PPP per day (%)[1]

Region	% of population living below $1/day		
	1990	1999	2001
Northern Africa	2.6	2.0	1.9
Sub-Saharan Africa	46.9	42.7	46.4
Latin America and the Caribbean	10.9	10.6	10.0
Eastern Asia	33.0	17.8	16.6
Southern Asia	39.7	30.5	30.4
South-eastern Asia	18.4	10.8	10.2
Western Asia	1.6	4.2	3.7
Commonwealth of Independent States	0.5	10.3	5.0
Transition countries of south-eastern Europe	0.4	1.7	2.1

[1] High-income economies, as defined by the World Bank, are excluded.

Source: Compiled and estimated by the World Bank for the United Nations Millennium Indicators Database, World and Regional Totals (<http://millenniumindicators.un.org>, accessed May 2004). The latest estimates are at <http://mdgs.un.org/unsd/mdg/Default.aspx> under World and Regional Totals (accessedOctober 2006).

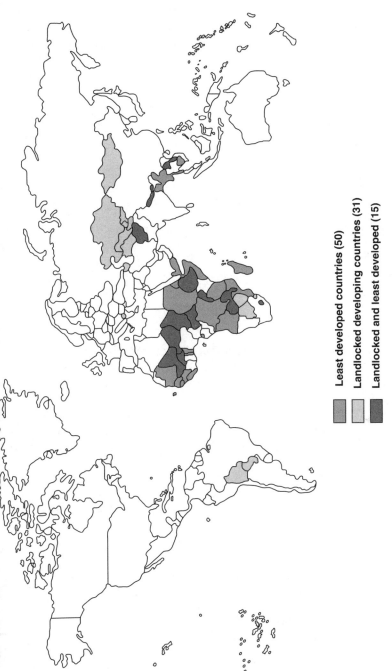

Least developed countries (50)

Landlocked developing countries (31)

Landlocked and least developed (15)

Figure 8.1 Least developed countries and landlocked developing countries (as at June 2004)

Source: United Nations Statistics Division and United Nations Office of the High Representative for Least Developed Countries, Landlocked Developing Countries, and Small Island Developing States, June, 2004.

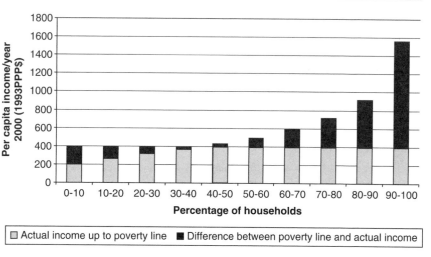

Figure 8.2 Illustrative income distribution, Bangladesh, 2000

Sources: Calculations by the author based on gross national income per capita in 2000 equal to PPP$1,501 (World Bank estimate) and decile shares for the Lorenz Curve from Jain (1974), based on a 1966/7 national survey.

above the line would have to be redistributed below the line to bring everyone at least up to the line. It seems fairly clear that this is well beyond political practicality, even assuming there were some effective control over the distribution process.

Another way to consider it is to take the figure of 7 per cent (the poverty gap as a proportion of total income) and multiply it by the total GDP to obtain a dollar amount for the gap. In this case it is US$3.53 billion using year 2000 prices and exchange rates. This tells us how much money would be needed, if it were perfectly targeted only on the extreme poor, to bring them up to the extreme poverty line but no more. By way of comparison, total official development aid to Bangladesh in 2000 was US$1.1 billion (United Nations, 2006: Table 74).

This is an admittedly highly speculative calculation but provides some background to consider ways the gap could be filled. It is also worth pointing out at this stage that once everyone has reached the poverty line, presumably thereby eliminating extreme deprivation by this standard, there is no basis to choose one or another income distribution as socially preferred. In other words, if there is no extreme poverty by the $1-a-day standard, the MDG target is achieved and the distribution of income is irrelevant.

Further complicating the picture, there is another phenomenon at work here. Some rough calculations seem to show that the total GDP per capita in $PPP for

Bangladesh in 2001 is about twice the per capita household income based on its income and consumption surveys. The $PPP 1993 per capita income from household surveys in 2000 was about $585, while total per capita $PPP GDP was about $1,150. Some of this difference can be accounted for by other sources and destinations of the national product in the form of investment, government expenditure, flows to and from the rest of the world and the like, but basically only a fraction. As other chapters in this volume show in some detail, large discrepancies such as this have been found in many countries and seem to be growing, and despite some considerable research in a few countries, they cannot at present be satisfactorily explained. It is very much to be hoped that when the phenomenon is better understood, it will be possible to design more effective policies for tapping resources to improve the income and consumption of the very poor.

There are three ways of addressing the gap that come to mind: redistribution from above the line to below it; redistribution into a country from abroad; and growing the economy as a whole, with some unspecified portion of the growth occurring among those below the line until they are above it. All poverty strategies rely on one or a combination of these approaches but of course there are considerable debates, not always well grounded in quantitative analysis, at least for most developing regions, on which are, or might be, more effective.

A notable exception to this lack of rigor is provided by the work of the United Nations Economic Commission for Latin America in its *Social Panorama 2003*. As discussed further below, it clearly demonstrates the near impossibility of "growing the poor" out of poverty without a higher rate of growth of poor compared to non-poor incomes, at least in that region.

This is where ethical judgments on inequality are frequently brought in, which, it can be argued, crowd out the further analysis of income generation and distribution of free and subsidized services which is needed. The first approach, straight redistribution from above the line to below it, apparently violates the constraint of Pareto optimality—that is there are obviously losers above the line who will be worse off in a simplistic approach. A simplistic approach, however, usually based on the concept of progressive taxation, belies a more realistic and careful analysis of the distribution of public services, subsidies and other important components of consumption which are part and parcel of any government's real workings.

The second approach, redistribution from abroad, is of course already a major factor in many developing countries in such forms as aid, income and workers' remittances from abroad. Here data and analysis are relatively scarce. Likewise, there are some data and considerable discussion of foreign direct investment, but relatively little macro-analysis or time series on the household income and consumption it generates in a country or its distribution.

Finally, there is the growth strategy, or the notion that a rising tide floats all boats. Unfortunately, literally speaking, a rising tide floats all boats equally in absolute terms, whereas in an economic calculus, equality is sought in the percentages. An equal percentage growth rate starting from $1 per day is profoundly different from a starting point of $10 or $100 per day (United Nations ECLAC, 2002). The poverty analyses already cited from United Nations ECLAC demonstrate conclusively, based on a large and well-structured collection of survey micro data from that region, that where there is a significant proportion of the population poor or extremely poor, long-term growth rates in the absence of major changes in the distribution patterns imply absurdly long timetables for the poor to change their poverty status. It should be possible to do some analyses on the distribution of investment by income level needed to change production and productivity curves by income level but that is another line of research which it is impossible to pursue here.

Continuing with the Bangladesh example, we can look at it again in the light of our consideration of exactly what we are trying to achieve with the MDG poverty goal, which aims to eradicate extreme poverty. That is, we want everyone to be at least level with the extreme poverty line. This we take to be the minimal satisfaction of a moral imperative, or arguably of a human right. In the system of international organizations, the entire huge apparatus of relief is built on that imperative and a fairly high degree of social intervention is widely accepted to meet these basic needs. We can now see that the conclusion from the Bangladesh example and its follow-up, that national redistribution of existing resources is not going to help much, except for the caveat that we do not have a very good idea where 30–40 per cent of the national income is actually going.

All of this is rather speculative but does lead me to think that we have hardly begun to put the available statistical and analytical tools to work. We have very considerable bodies of statistics on production, consumption, income, and investment in national accounts; we have very detailed trade and financial flow statistics; and we have a tremendous amount of data on employment by class, occupation, and industry, and on living conditions among various classes, defined in various economically important ways. But we do not seem to have made much progress in applying these data to mapping out viable and detailed economic and social development strategies that are able to bring together consistently the macroeconomic data and the household survey income and consumption data to explain better than we can now where and how real dollars need to go to meet the poverty target, and where they might come from.

That is where I see that the real challenge lies. The great ship of economic and social development may have started to change course, but there is still a long way to go.

Conclusions and ways forward

To sum up:

1. The concept of extreme poverty based on observable individual and household distress and degradation is as serviceable now as it was a century ago.

2. There is good correspondence between the World Bank's concept of the $1 a day threshold for extreme poverty and the still-relevant concept of poverty as an umbrella concept for distress and degradation. It is entirely appropriate that this concept should be adopted for the MDGs as there is a good international consensus for the alleviation of basic suffering through humanitarian and development assistance.

3. The related concept of minimum standard of living, based on negotiations over minimum "decent" wages for the working classes, is based on the concept of the "relative poverty line," which is drawn according to national conditions and politics. This concept does not have any clear application or value in the international implementation of the MDGs.

4. Likewise, inequalities in national income distributions, judging from limited evidence, may have an important role in the MDGs relating to the elimination of poverty, but they are highly resistant to change for the better, at least with the policy tools known and tried to date, such as taxes. Thus, targeting redistribution per se seems, on historical evidence, unlikely to have a very significant impact on poverty. There are also considerable problems in consistent and comparable data collection, analysis, and interpretation of income and consumption distribution data which make any kinds of conclusions based on them rather speculative.

5. The concepts and definitions of the international System of National Accounts, as concern household income and consumption, provide a sound conceptual apparatus for measuring income and consumption levels at and below any given poverty threshold, even at so-called subsistence levels. However, there is relatively little systematic guidance available, or incentive, to less experienced national statistical services to apply these appropriately and consistently in national household surveys.

6. There are many physical manifestations of extreme poverty, and many other highly desirable development objectives, that should be separately measured. These are reasonably well covered by the consensus MDGs and targets, and statistically well specified in the indicators and data series agreed for measuring them.

7. Hardworking and hard-pressed national statistical offices, and the World Bank, have collected and compiled a remarkable amount of data on

poverty in the developing regions. Nonetheless, we have very little analysis as yet around the overall dimensions of needed income, expenditure, and investment to alleviate and eliminate poverty, or the relative contributions national economic growth, development assistance, and reallocation of expenditures might make to these. This analysis is complicated by the extremely discrepant aggregate sizes of household income and consumption produced by household surveys and national accounts methods, for which at present there is no explanation.

In a few words, I think our statistical toolbox for the measurement of poverty is in pretty good shape as far as concepts and methods are concerned, and these tools are more helpful in analyzing and targeting poverty than income distribution concepts and methods. However, support for consistent implementation of the available tools and standards in developing regions is at best uneven, and good methods, or "best practices," for reconciling household survey and national accounts data have yet to be fully worked out. As far as empirically grounded policy analysis and prescriptions go, I think it is fair to say that we are still a long way from a technical consensus on what policies can have a significant and measurable impact on the alleviation of extreme poverty.

Notes

1. The author is a retired staff member of the United Nations Statistics Division. The views expressed are not necessarily those of the United Nations Secretariat. I would like to acknowledge the assistance of Statistics Division staff members Virgilio Castillo and Javier Terán in preparing the maps and charts, and the helpful and encouraging comments of colleagues in the Statistics Division and the former Development Policy Analysis Division, United Nations Department of Economic and Social Affairs, on some of these ideas in the "zero" draft of this paper, as well as the very helpful comments and suggestions of the referees, none of which, of course, can be held responsible for any of the conclusions here.
2. These comprise compensation in cash and kind, entrepreneurial income in cash and kind, property income, and current transfers, which add up to total household income. These components are spelled out and defined in detail in the sources cited. The ECLAC source refines them even further for use in the study of rural poverty.

Bibliography

Allardt, E. (1975) 'Dimensions of Welfare in a Comparative Scandinavia Study'. Research Group for Comparative Sociology, University of Helsinki, No. 9.
Drewnowski, J. (1974) *On Measuring and Planning the Quality of Life*. The Hague: Mouton.

Glennerster, H., et al. (2004) *One Hundred Years of Poverty and Policy.* York: Joseph Rowntree Foundation. <http://www.jrf.org.uk/publications/one-hundred-years-poverty-and-policy>, accessed on June 24, 2009.

Jain, S. (1974) *Size Distribution of Income—A Compilation of Data.* Washington DC: World Bank.

Johansson, S. (1973) 'The Level of Living Survey: A Presentation'. *Acta Sociologica, Journal of the Scandinavian Sociological Association,* 16(3), pp. 211–19.

Moser, C. A. and Kalton, G. (1972) *Survey Methods in Social Investigation.* New York: Basic Books.

Ravallion, M., et al. (1991) 'Quantifying Absolute Poverty in the Developing World'. *Review of Income and Wealth,* 37(4), pp. 345–61.

United Nations (1954) Report on "International Definition and Measurement of Standards and Levels of Living", Committee of Experts convened by the Secretary-General of the United Nations jointly with the International Labour Organization and the United Nations Educational, Scientific, and Cultural Organization (E/CN.3/179).

—— (1961) *International Definition and Measurement of Levels of Living, An Interim Guide.*

—— (1968) *A System of National Accounts.* Series F, No. 2, Rev. 3.

—— (1975) *Towards a System of Social and Demographic Statistics.* Series F, No. 18.

—— (1977) *Provisional Guidelines on Statistics of the Distribution of Income, Consumption and Accumulation of Households.* Series M, No. 61.

—— (1978) *The Feasibility of Welfare-Oriented Measures to Supplement the National Accounts and Balances: A Technical Report.* Series F, No. 22.

—— (1979), *Improving Social Statistics in Developing Countries: Conceptual Framework and Methods.* Series F, No. 25.

—— (1984) 'Income, Consumption and Expenditure'. In *Handbook of Household Surveys* (rev. edn.). Series F, No. 31, Ch. X.

—— (1989) *Handbook on Social Indicators.* Series F, No. 49.

—— (1991) *Compendium of Social Statistics and Indicators.* Series K, No. 9, Table 30.

—— (2000) 'Millennium Declaration'. General Assembly resolution A/RES/55/2). <http://mdgs.un.org/unsd/mdg/Host.aspx?Content=/Products/> accessed on June 24, 2009.

—— (2001) 'Road Map towards the Implementation of the United Nations Millennium Declaration'. Report of the Secretary-General (A/56/326). <http://mdgs.un.org/unsd/mdg/Host.aspx?Content=/Products/> accessed on June 24, 2009.

—— (2006) *Statistical Yearbook.* 50th issue.

United Nations Development Programme (annual) *Human Development Report,* New York. <http://hdr.undp.org/en/reports> accessed on June 24, 2009.

United Nations Economic and Social Commission for Latin America and the Caribbean (1983), *Measurement of Employment and Income in Rural Areas.* Estudios e Informes de la CEPAL 19, International Labour Organization Regional Employment Programme for Latin American and the Caribbean, Employment Office of the Secretariat for Labour and Social Welfare of the Government of Mexico, Santiago: United Nations.

—— (2003) *Social Panorama 2003.*

United Nations Research Institute for Social Development (1971) *Contents and Measurement of Socioeconomic Development.* Report by D. V. McGranahan, C. Richard-Proust, N. V. Sovani, and M. Subramanian, New York: Praeger Publishers.

9

A Note on the Mis(Use) of National Accounts for Estimation of Household Final Consumption Expenditures for Poverty Measures

Ivo Havinga, Gisèle Kamanou, and Vu Quang Viet[1]

This chapter addresses whether the national accounts concept of final household consumption (expenditures) can be used to supplement household survey data for the purpose of poverty measures. We reinforce some of the views expressed by many authors—that the national accounts estimate of household final consumption, as used in the current procedures to estimate poverty, is not appropriate. We also try to clarify some misconceptions of the national accounts procedures and methods of estimation of final household consumption, and suggest ways for supplementing household surveys with individual consumption of government and non-profit institutions serving households (NPISH) and other components from national accounts not generally captured through household surveys.[2] Likewise, some suggestions are made to guide future work on the harmonization of household income and expenditure surveys for their use in national accounts compilations and poverty measures.

This chapter should not be considered as a comprehensive response to the recent debate over the use of national accounts in poverty measures. Rather, it should be viewed as a stimulus for further work on a more coherent use of national accounts in poverty measurements.

Is income or consumption more appropriate for measuring poverty?

Since the 1990s there has been a broad agreement that poverty encompasses multiple dimensions, going beyond material deprivation. However, this chapter is concerned only with comparability between the national accounts (NA) and household survey (HS) estimates of household consumption and their implications for poverty measures when consumption is the preferred indicator of well-being.

Conceptual approaches to the measures of well-being are well known. A case is generally made to favor consumption over income when it comes to the measure of living standards. However, there are cases where income is a better measure of well-being than consumption; such as when well-being is viewed as the capability of a household to consume rather than what is actually consumed by the household (Ravallion, 1992).

In addition to conceptual considerations, there is also a general consensus on the practical level that consumption is better captured than income through household surveys and we share that view. Income is often perceived as being less reliable than consumption. People might have difficulty remembering or conceptualizing non-wage income or income might be deliberately underreported for tax evasion.

In national accounts, the income concept used for measuring the capability to consume is disposable income, which requires more complex imputations and adjustments than consumption by individual households included in the surveys. Table 9.1 presents the national accounts concept of disposable income and indicates which components should be surveyed and those to be imputed. Table 9.2 shows for some selected countries, the components of adjusted disposable income of the household sector in national accounts, which also takes into account social transfers in kind from the government and NPISH. In these countries, compensation of employees makes up from 36 to 60 per cent of the total adjusted disposable income. The Philippines and Vietnam have a larger component of unincorporated household enterprises than Malaysia, thus having a higher share of mixed income in disposable income. Social transfers in kind from the government to households are more significant in Vietnam thus resulting in a higher share in "others." The statistics here may help indicate where household income from household surveys deviate from national account household income.

Comparability between national accounts and household survey estimate of final household consumption

Consumption is not an easy flow to measure either. The concerns that poverty estimates are sensitive to the survey design are well justified. Another challenge are the over time and cross-country comparisons of poverty measures, given the variation in survey design over time and across countries. The reliability of survey estimates of household consumption critically depends for example on the choice of the recall period. Other technical aspects such as the training and commitment of field staff and the degree of cooperation of the sampled

National Accounts and Poverty Measures

Table 9.1. Compilation of disposable income by individual households

	Components of disposable income	Contents covered in national accounts	Estimation method
+	Compensation of employees	Includes wages and salaries, payments in kind, and employers' social contributions to pension funds and other insurance schemes.	Should be surveyed.
+	Withdrawals of income from quasi-corporations	Withdrawals of income for own use by owners of unincorporated enterprises but with full set of business accounts, such as partnership.	Should be surveyed.
+	Mixed income	Income left for own use to owners of household enterprises without business accounts after deducting from output intermediate cost of goods and services as well as depreciation and taxes on production.	Should be surveyed in association with survey on household production.
+	Property income receivable	Interest, land rent, dividends received, and property income attributable to insurance policy holders imputed as received from pension funds.	Should be surveyed. Interest received should be adjusted to include financial service charges already deducted from interest received. Property income attributable to insurance holders must be imputed on the basis of insurance held.
+	Social benefits other than social transfer in kind	Social security benefits in cash, private funded social benefits (pension benefits), unfunded social benefits by employers, and social assistance benefits in cash.	Should be surveyed and or use of pension funds data.
+	Other current transfers in cash receivable	Net non-life insurance claims, current transfers from government, current transfers from relatives, and others.	Should be surveyed and adjusted to exclude insurance service charges.
+	Social transfers in kind	Individual final consumption of government and NPISH.[1]	Imputed by analyzing government and NPISH expenditure with regards to types of households that benefit.
−	Social contributions	Contributions to social security fund, pension funds, and other insurance schemes.	Should be surveyed and compared with data from government, pension funds, and insurance companies.
−	Property income payable	Interest and land rent paid.	Should be surveyed and compared with data from financial corporations and adjusted to exclude financial service charges, which are treated in the NA as final consumption.

–	Taxes on income	Regular income, property, and wealth taxes.	Should be surveyed and compared with data from government.
–	Current transfers payable	Net non-life insurance premiums paid and current transfers from relatives and others.	Should be surveyed and compared with data from insurance companies and adjusted to exclude insurance service charges.
=	Disposable income (adjusted)		

[1] Individual final consumption of the government and NPISH is defined as the final consumption expenditure incurred by those respective institutions for the benefit of individual households (SNA, para. 9.80) such as expenditure on health care, education, disposal of household waste, etc.

Table 9.2. Components of adjusted disposable income of households, selected countries

	Malaysia (1996)	Philippines (1993)	Vietnam (1999)
Per capita GDP in in 1999 (US$)	3,613	1,033	373
Total adjusted disposable income (%)	100	100	100
Compensation of employees (%)	60	38	36
Mixed income (%	32	56	49
Net property income (receivable less payable, %)	11	9	3
Others (%)	−2	−2	12

Sources: Distribution and use of income accounts and capital account 1996, Department of Statistics Malaysia, 2000; Vietnam Economy in the Years of Reform, General Statistical Office of Vietnam 2002, 2003; unpublished information from a national account project in the Philippines.

household are also important criteria for good sample estimates. Still, survey estimates of household consumption can be improved with adequate survey instruments and appropriate sampling methods. One serious conceptual problem of the consumption approach, however, is the valuation of consumption of goods provided through social transfers in kind by the government and NPISH. Its inclusion in actual household consumption has to be derived from national accounts and imputed to individual household through allocation indicators principally obtained from household surveys, in addition to crude allocations of government expenditures.

Table 9.3 presents the concept of actual household final consumption (AHFC) based on a harmonized approach to household surveys. It indicates the type of information that should be collected from a household survey and the adjustments to be made to be compatible with the concept of AHFC in national accounts.

Table 9.3. National accounts concept of actual household final consumption within a harmonized approach to household surveys

Components of actual household final consumption	Estimation methods
+ Goods and services purchased for final consumption.	Should be surveyed.
+ Goods and services provided by employers.	Should be surveyed.
+ Own-produced consumption, including imputed rent for own-occupied dwellings.	Should be surveyed along with household production through unincorporated enterprises and household dwelling ownership.
+ Goods and services bartered for consumption.	Should be surveyed.
+ Current transfers in kinds other than social transfers in kind.	Should be surveyed.
= Household Final Consumption Expenditures (from HS).	
+ Financial intermediation services indirectly measured (FISIM).	Adjusted through NA.
+ Insurance service charges.	Adjusted through NA.
= Household Final Consumption Expenditures (in NA).	
+ Social transfers in kind from government and NPISH.	Adjusted through NA from information on government and NPISH data.
= Actual household final consumption.	

It is important to point out that in national accounting there are two concepts of household final consumption. *Household final consumption expenditure* (HFCE), as the wording of the concept indicates, measures the expenditure of households for its own consumption. HFCE includes those items of household final consumption (HFC) that are conventionally available through household surveys (such as goods and services purchased for final consumption, goods produced for own consumption, goods and services bartered, goods consumed and obtained from transfer in kind, and imputed rent for own-occupied dwellings). In addition to the expenditures components covered, adjustments need to be made for financial intermediation services indirectly measured (FISIM) and for insurance service charges. The concept of *actual household final consumption* (AHFC) measures both household final consumption expenditure and the individualized consumption paid for by the government and NPISH, like education, health care, and other community and social services. The estimation methods of the individual consumption provided by government and NPISH rely fully on imputations based on valuation assumptions on cost structures of the services rendered.

The concept of actual household final consumption captures better what is actually consumed by a given household. This might partially explain the empirical findings that household consumption expenditure obtained through household surveys from many countries tends to be lower than the total final consumption expenditures from NA. For example, Ravallion (2003) found that for 77 per cent of the eighty-eight developing countries studied, the ratio of the two consumption estimates ranged between 0.2 and 2.4 and averaged to 0.826.

Precisely, because there could be a sizable difference, it has been suggested by some authors in recent literature that NA estimates of the household final consumption expenditure should be used to adjust household survey estimates of household consumption (Bhalla, 2002). This practice is feasible if the un-measured components of household consumption can be allocated/imputed to individual households. Still, there has been strong opposition to this adjust-ment, the main two reasons being that there are no solid justifications for the accuracy of the NA estimates and that the observed gap between the two is not distributional neutral among the households. In fact there is a misconception about the (lack of) accuracy/reliability of the country estimates of total final household consumption expenditure. The most recent reference on the com-pilation of consumption in the NA cited to support arguments against this adjustment is Ruggles and Ruggles (1986). However, since then, and with the implementation of the 1993 System of National Accounts (SNA), it has been advocated among countries to estimate household final consumption expen-ditures through more direct methods based on surveys using a commodity flow approach within a supply and use table framework.

National accounts aim to measure the final household consumption of the total economy. The aggregate household consumption from national accounts is therefore not an aggregate of income or final consumption by individual households and cannot provide information on the distribution of income or consumption for the purpose of poverty measures.

Advocators of the use of NA over household surveys have used distribution of consumption over households from previous years, assuming it remained un-changed. While this assumption might hold in some macroeconomic contexts, it remains to be proven in its generality.

Concluding notes and recommendations

The fact that household surveys might underestimate true consumption does not necessarily mean that household survey is not an appropriate tool for measuring household consumption. Neither does it imply that NA esti-mate of household final consumption is incorrect because adjustments are made to the survey estimates, mainly through the commodity flow ap-proach. The recent debate has been centered around whether poverty mea-sures should be based on national accounts and not on household surveys. We believe that is the wrong question to debate, since there are clear con-ceptual and empirical justifications of the gap between the two figures. A more useful and important question is how the two methods can be improved and reconciled. Below we summarize our views and make some suggestions for further work.

1. Household surveys are more adequate than national accounts for income/consumption distributional information.

2. The practice of household surveys need to be improved. In particular, it is necessary to establish global standards for household surveys. This can be accomplished fairly easily, given an abundance of experiences accumulated over the past two decades. Empirical work has shown that in many cases the samples were not representative, forms and methods of data collection were not consistent over time, and the types of questions asked may not be appropriate; in addition, there was also a lack of proper interviewer training.

3. The clarification of national accounts concept of household final consumption is needed and an appropriate list of imputed consumption should be developed.

4. Finally, methods for imputation at a single household level need to be worked out to assist the harmonization of national accounts and household survey data.

5. International agencies and other organizations should give high priority to developing global standards for harmonized household surveys as a tool that could generate reliable estimates for poverty, consistent across countries and time. This harmonized tool should, in addition, support a direct measure of household consumption in the national accounts.

Notes

1. The views expressed here are those of the authors and do not necessarily reflect those of the United Nations.

2. Individual final consumption of the government and NPISH is defined as the final consumption expenditure incurred by those respective institutions for the benefit of individual households, such as expenditure on health care, education, disposal of household waste, etc. United Nations (1993). In analyzing household consumption, we focus on the concept of *household consumption*, which is more comprehensive than the concept of *household consumption expenditure* since the former includes expenditure by the government and NPISH for the benefit of individual households.

Bibliography

Bhalla, S. S. (2002) *Imagine There's No Country: Poverty, Inequality and Growth in the Era of Globalisation.* Washington DC: Institute for International Economics.

Deaton, A. (2001) 'Counting the World's Poor: Problems and Solutions'. *World Bank Research Observer*, 16(2), pp. 125–47.

—— (2003) 'How to Monitor Poverty for the Millennium Development Goals'. RPDS Working Paper No. 221, Princeton University.

Ravallion M. (1992) *Poverty Comparisons: A Guide to Concepts and Methods*. Washington DC: World Bank.

—— (2000) 'Should Poverty Measures Be Anchored to the National Accounts?' *Economic and Political Weekly*, August 26, pp. 3245–52.

—— (2001) 'Comment on Counting the World Poor by Angus Deaton'. *World Bank Research Observer*, 16(2), pp. 149–56.

—— (2003) 'Measuring Aggregate Welfare in Developing Countries: How Well do National Accounts and Surveys agree?' *Review of Economics and Statistics*, 85(3), pp. 645–52.

Ruggles, R. and Ruggles, N. D. (1986) 'The Integration of Macro and Micro Data for the Household Sector'. *Review of Income and Wealth*, 32(3), pp. 245–76.

Srinivasan T. N. (2001) 'Comment on Counting the World's Poor by Angus Deaton'. *World Bank Research Observer*, 16(2), pp. 157–68.

Sundaram, K. and Tendulkar, S. D. (2003) 'NAS-NSS Estimates of Private Consumption for Poverty Estimates; A Further Comparative Examination'. *Economic and Political Weekly*, January, pp. 376–84.

United Nations (1993) 'System of National Accounts 1993, ST/ESA/STAT/SER.F/Rev.4'. <http://unstats.un.org/unsd/sna1993/toctop.asp>.

10

Unequal Development in the 1990s: Growing Gaps in Human Capabilities[1]

Sakiko Fukuda-Parr and David Stewart

Introduction

Questions about global income inequality inspire some of the most contentious debates among not only academics but politicians and the public at large. People look to data on income inequality as they might a stock market index to gauge how the world is doing. Are things on the right track? Is enough being done? In this age of globalization, the question is inevitably about whether "Globalization"—meaning liberalization of economies and the integration of global trade and capital flows—brings prosperity or not. The controversies raging today over the many studies coming to different conclusions depend on how the questions are asked, and which data series are used. Such debates indicate little more than how economists and statisticians can find many answers to the seemingly same questions. More fundamentally, these debates mask attention on the growing disparities in human lives.

The aim of this chapter is to assess the empirical development trends of the 1990s by focusing on human well-being rather than on incomes alone. It argues that by these measures, the decade was one of unprecedented improvement for some but not for others, and that there is a growing gap among developing countries as well as among all countries of the world.

Measuring disparities in human lives

Despite the wide recognition among scholars and practitioners of development that development and poverty concern the well-being of human lives,[2] and that this has multiple dimensions beyond income, almost all the empirical studies on global inequalities focus on income measures. The data on income and income inequalities are far from satisfactory for reasons of both data availability as well as measurement tools being used. Indeed, several chapters of this volume address this problem in greater detail.

As Amartya Sen has argued, development is about enlarging the capabilities that people have to lead lives they value, or human development. Capabilities such as being able to lead a long and healthy life, being able to read and write, being able to enjoy the respect of others and participate in the life and decision-making of a community are universally valued (see Sen, 1999). Incomes are important means to achieving and expanding such capabilities, and correlate with capability achievements in such areas. But there is no perfect relationship between income and these capabilities. Countries such as Pakistan and Vietnam have similar levels of GDP per capita but have stark differences in life expectancy. Korea and the US have the same levels of life expectancy but Korea has less than half the income of the US (UNDP, 2003b).

To understand how the world is faring we must look beyond economic growth alone to indicators that capture important human capabilities more directly. This is not only conceptually desirable but also feasible. Some would argue that capabilities are too complex and involve too many dimensions. Such arguments dominated the debates that led to the development of the Human Development Index (HDI), as Amartya Sen's own account makes clear.[3] Furthermore, one of the most contentious issues among scholars of capability is about whether important capabilities can be identified. While some—Martha Nussbaum being the foremost author—argue that a 'list' can be constructed, others, notably Amartya Sen, argue that such lists should be made only by democratic debate in society.[4] However, in the context of undertaking a global evaluation of development based on capability expansion as a criterion, it is possible to use the internationally comparable data that exist in dimensions that are universally accepted as priority areas of improving human well-being.[5] It was on this basis that the HDI was constructed by Mahbub ul Haq and the UNDP Human Development Report team, together with Amartya Sen and Sudhir Anand.[6] These include the capabilities in areas such as child mortality, hunger, school enrollment, and the spread of HIV/AIDS that allow a comparison of how different countries of the world are faring.

A human development crisis in the 1990s

By measures of human capabilities as well as incomes, development in the 1990s was the best in years and the worst in years. Some regions and countries saw unprecedented progress, while others stagnated or reversed. What is most striking is the extent of the stagnation and reversals—signaling a human development crisis not seen in previous decades.

This is apparent in the HDI, the summary measure of key dimensions of human development. The index usually moves steadily upwards—though usually slowly because two of its key components—literacy and school enrolment rates—take time to change. So when the HDI falls, it indicates crisis, with nations depleting their basis for development—people, their real wealth. The human development crisis is also evident from other indicators of human development that are not included in the HDI. The HIV/AIDS pandemic continues to spread and its impact deepen throughout the world. Only one country has definitively reversed the epidemic once it reached crisis proportions (UN-AIDS, 2002). Some fifty-four countries are poorer now than in 1990 and income poverty rates increased in thirty-four of the sixty-seven countries that have trend data. In twenty-one countries a larger proportion of people are going hungry. In fourteen countries more children are dying before the age of five. In twelve countries primary school enrolment rates have fallen. And in many countries things are neither worsening nor improving, with stagnation setting in (UNDP, 2003b).

Declines in the HDI

After a steady increase since the mid-1970s, there has been a deceleration in HDI progress. The slowdown, particularly in the late 1980s and first half of the 1990s, was led by countries in Central and Eastern Europe and the Commonwealth of Independent States (CIS). Many of these countries had already started on a downward spiral in the mid-1980s, but between 1990 and 1995 the HDI declined on average in the region. In sub-Saharan Africa overall growth in the HDI merely slowed, but some countries suffered terrible declines.

The HDI declined in twenty-one countries in the 1990s. This is a new phenomenon: only four countries saw their HDIs fall in the 1980s (see Table 10.1). Much of the decline in the 1990s can be traced to the spread of HIV/AIDS, which lowered life expectancies, and to a collapse in incomes, particularly in the CIS (UNDP, 2003b).

Table 10.1. Countries with decreases in HDI, 1980–2001

Period	Number	Countries
1980–90	4	Democratic Republic of Congo; Guyana; Rwanda; Zambia
1990–2001	21	Armenia;[1] Belarus;[1] Botswana; Burundi; Cameroon; Central African Republic; Democratic Republic of Congo; Côte d'Ivoire, Kazakstan;[1] Kenya; Lesotho; Moldova; Russian Federation; South Africa; Swaziland; Tajikistan;[1] Tanzania;[1] Ukraine;[1] Zambia; Zimbabwe.

Note: Based on a sample of 113 countries with complete data.
[1] No data for 1980–90; the fall in HDI may have begun before 1990.
Source: United Nations Development Program, *Human Development Report 2003*.

Increasing spread of HIV/AIDS

In recent decades the greatest shock to development has been HIV/AIDS. The first cases were recognized in the early 1980s, and by 1990 some 10 million people were infected. Since then that number has more than quadrupled, to about 42 million. Moreover, the disease has already killed 22 million people and left 13 million orphans in its wake (UNAIDS, 2002).

HIV/AIDS is crippling parts of Africa—at least 1 in 3 adults is infected in Botswana, Lesotho, Swaziland, and Zimbabwe, 1 in 5 in Namibia, South Africa and Zambia and more than 1 in 20 in 19 other countries. The disease kills rich and poor, including teachers, farmers, factory workers, and civil servants. Zambia lost 1,300 teachers to the disease in 1998—two-thirds of those trained each year (ibid.). By 2020 the hardest-hit African countries could have lost more than one-quarter of their workforces (FAO, 2001).

HIV/AIDS destroys more than lives. By killing and incapacitating adults in the prime of their lives, it can throw development off course. The disease's impact on the HDI occurs through its devastating effect on life expectancy in the worst-affected countries.

The spread continues. Uganda is the only sub-Saharan country to have halted and reversed the epidemic once it reached crisis proportions. In Zambia HIV prevalence among young women fell 4 percentage points between 1996 and 1999, offering hope that it would become the second country in the region to reverse the crisis. Senegal is another success story, having kept HIV/AIDS under control from the beginning through an immediate and concerted response (UNAIDS, 2002).

Though sub-Saharan Africa accounts for three-quarters of HIV/AIDS cases, the epidemic is spreading in other regions. Almost 0.5 million people are infected in the Caribbean, 1.0 million in East Asia, 1.0 million in Eastern Europe and the CIS, 1.5 million in Latin America, and 5.6 million in South Asia (ibid.).

China, India, and the Russian Federation—all with large populations and at risk of seeing their infection rates soar—are of particular concern. About 7 million people are infected in these countries, and in sub-Saharan Africa 7 million cases exploded to 25 million in a decade (Eberstadt, 2002). The course of the epidemic depends on social characteristics and responses to the

Table 10.2. Reductions in life expectancy due to HIV/AIDS (years)

	Life expectancy without HIV/AIDS 2000–5	Years of life expectancy lost due to HIV/AIDS 2000–5
Botswana	68.1	28.4
Zimbabwe	67.6	34.5
Swaziland	62.2	27.8
Lesotho	59.0	23.9

Source: United Nations, *World Population Prospects 1950–2050: The 2000 Revision.*

Table 10.3. The potential effects of HIV/AIDS by 2025, selected countries

Country	Estimated HIV/AIDS cases	Estimated reduction in life expectancy (years)
China	70 million	8
India	110 million	13
Russia	13 million	16

Source: Eberstadt (2002).

threat. But even in a moderate scenario, by 2025 almost 200 million people could be infected in these three countries alone (see Table 10.3).

Failing economic growth

Failed economic growth lies behind the faltering HDI and the inability of many countries and regions to reduce income and human poverty. Seldom if ever is income poverty reduced in a stagnant economy, and the regions growing fastest economically are also the ones that have reduced income poverty most. That provides a clear message: economic growth is essential for income poverty reduction. But the link between economic growth and income poverty reduction is far from automatic (see Tables 10.4 and 10.5). In Indonesia, Poland, and Sri Lanka poverty rose in the 1990s despite economic growth (see World Bank, 2002).

For many countries, economic growth in the 1990s was far from impressive. Of 153 countries with data, only 30 had annual per capita income growth rates above 3 per cent in the 1990s. Among the rest, fifty-four countries saw average incomes fall, and in seventy-one countries annual income growth was less than 3 per cent (UNDP, 2003b).

What are the consequences of this dismal growth performance? At the turn of the millennium more than 1.2 billion people were struggling to survive on less than $1 a day—and more than twice as many, 2.8 billion, on less than $2 a day (World Bank, 2002). Living on $1 a day does not mean being able to afford what $1 would buy when converted into a local currency, but the equivalent of what $1 would buy in the US: a newspaper, a local bus ride, a bag of rice.

Globally the proportion of people living on less than $1 a day dropped from nearly 30 per cent in 1990 to 23 per cent in 1999 (ibid.). But the story is not one of good overall progress. Rather, it is one of some countries forging ahead while others see bad situations get even worse. Much of the impressive reduction in global poverty has been driven by China's incredible economic growth of more than 9 per cent a year in the 1990s, lifting 150 million people out of poverty (ibid.).

Of sixty-seven countries with data, thirty-seven saw poverty rates increase in the 1990s. But others achieved impressive reductions in poverty rates: Brazil,

Table 10.4. Economic growth and income poverty reduction, 1990–9 (% change)

Region	Growth (annual per capita income growth)	Poverty reduction (percentage point reduction)
East Asia and the Pacific	6.4	14.9
South Asia	3.3	8.4
Latin America and the Caribbean	1.6	−0.1
Middle East and North Africa	1.0	−0.1
Sub-Saharan Africa	−0.4	−1.6
Central and Eastern Europe, and the CIS	−1.9	−13.5

Note: Poverty reduction change measured is measured using the $1-a-day poverty line, except for Central and Eastern Europe, and the CIS (for which the $2-a-day poverty line was used, as it is considered a more appropriate extreme poverty line for this region).
Source: World Bank, *Global Economic Prospects 2003*.

Table 10.5. Links between economic growth and income poverty, selected countries

	Increases in poverty (percentage points)	Growth (%)
Poland (1987/8–1993/5)	14.0 (from 6% to 20%)	2.41
Indonesia (1990–9)	3.1 (from 15.1% to 18.2%)	3.23
Sri Lanka (1991–6)	6.3 (from 33.0% to 39.3%)	4.13

Source: Growth rate calculations based on World Bank (2003); poverty rates based on World Bank (2000, 2002).

Chile, India, Uganda, Thailand, and Vietnam. Many of the countries where poverty rates soared were in Eastern Europe—particularly Central Asia—though other notable cases include Algeria, Mongolia, Nigeria, Pakistan, Venezuela, and Zimbabwe.[7]

When populations grow, reductions in the proportion of poor people often have little impact on their total number. Only in East Asia did the number of people in extreme poverty decline significantly in the 1990s. In South Asia, home to almost 0.5 billion poor people, the number hardly changed. In all other regions the number of poor people rose—notably in sub-Saharan Africa, where a further 74 million people, the population of the Philippines, ended the decade in extreme poverty. And in Eastern Europe and the CIS the number of poor people more than tripled, from 31 million to almost 100 million.[8]

Reversals in Hunger

Each day around 800 million people go hungry, among them 170 million children (FAO, 2002); a further 2 billion people suffer from diverse micronutrient deficiencies whose impacts range from illness to severe disability (Millenium Project Task Force, 2003). The consequences when a child goes hungry can be particularly devastating—over 15,000 children die every day as a result and at current rates of progress about 1 billion children will be growing up by 2020 with impaired mental development (ibid.).

The proportion of malnourished people has fallen from 21 per cent in 1991 to 18 per cent in 1999, but again population growth masks the human suffering behind this seeming success: the total estimated reduction since 1991 has been only 39 million people—at this pace if would be close to 150 years until hunger was eradicated (FAO, 2002).

As with income poverty, behind these averages lie vast disparities between countries and regions successfully addressing the problem and others where the situation continues to deteriorate. In East Asia and the Pacific the proportion of those hungry has fallen dramatically, from 16 per cent to 10 per cent. But in the world's hunger hot spots there has been little overall change, in South Asia 1 in 4 people are still malnourished and in sub-Saharan Africa as many as 1 in 3 still go hungry (FAO, 2002).

There are twenty-one countries where the number of undernourished people actually increased (UNDP, 2003b). And while data on child malnutrition is limited, of only of the thirty-three countries with data, ten have experienced reversals in the 1990s (World Bank, 2003). It is important to note, however, that these reversals are not all happening in the world's poorest countries, some dramatic success in reducing hunger have been achieved in sub-Saharan Africa: in the weakest regions some countries are finding ways to succeed and in the strongest, some are continuing to fail.

Child mortality

On an average day more than 30,000 children in the world die of preventable causes—from dehydration to hunger (UNICEF, 2003). The challenge is enormous: in Sierra Leone, 18 per cent of children born alive will not live to see their first birthday—a greater proportion than in England at the beginning of the seventeenth century (Maddison, 2001). Progress has been made in large parts of the developing world in reducing deaths in children under five, but it has been uneven, with some regions progressing much faster than others. Again the hot spots are South Asia and sub-Saharan Africa, and again South Asia is progressing, from 12.5 per cent to around 10 per cent, while sub-Saharan Africa is being left behind: 17 per cent of children will not live to see their fifth birthday.

Inequalities in child mortality between rich and poor countries have become unambiguously worse. In the early 1990s children under five were nineteen times more likely to die in sub-Saharan Africa than in rich countries—and today, twenty-six times more likely. Among all developing regions only Latin America and the Caribbean saw no worsening in the past decade relative to rich

Table 10.6. Likelihood of a child dying before its fifth birthday, relative to a high income OECD country

	1990	2001
Arab States	9.4	11.0
East Asia and the Pacific	6.0	6.5
Latin America and the Caribbean	5.5	5.2
South Asia	13.1	14.7
Sub-Saharan Africa	18.8	26.3
Central and Eastern Europe and the CIS	3.9	5.5

Source: Calculations based on World Bank (2003).

countries, with children still about five times more likely to die before their fifth birthdays (see Table 10.6).

There are fourteen countries where a greater proportion of children were dying at the end of the decade than at the beginning, and a further fourteen where a child's chances of survival have not improved. Eleven of these hot spots are in sub-Saharan Africa, but the problem is not in Africa alone. These countries include Algeria, Cambodia, and Iraq as well as three countries from Central Europe and the CIS (UNDP, 2003b).

Much is known about reducing child mortality, and a key factor in countries that have succeeded has been successful immunization programs. However, after impressive increases in the 1970s and 1980s there have also been reductions since in the 1990s in some developing regions, most noticeably sub-Saharan Africa and East Asia (UNICEF, 2003). Immunization, however, is far from enough. Of the countries performing best and worst in reducing under five deaths the immunization rates are similar—it is inaction against the ravages of HIV/AIDS that is currently proving a child's worst enemy. In three of the five countries with the greatest increases in child mortality, HIV/AIDS prevalence among children mirrors the increases in child deaths (World Bank, 2003).[9]

Achieving universal primary education

Currently 115 million school age children do not attend primary school—94 per cent from developing countries—but encouragingly all of the world's regions experienced improvements in primary enrolment in the 1990s. East Asia and the Pacific, Eastern Europe and the CIS, and Latin America and the Caribbean are converging on universal primary education. South Asia is further behind but progressed in the 1990s, increasing the number of children enrolled to 75 per cent. While enrolments in sub-Saharan Africa increased by 6 per cent over 1991–2001, still only 60 per cent of children are enrolled.

While there has been progress overall, there are twelve countries where primary enrolments have actually fallen. In Botswana, Madagascar, and Zambia primary enrolment fell by over 10 percentage points in the 1990s. While the biggest declines were in sub-Saharan Africa, countries from other regions that were performing well as a whole were also having setbacks—Hungary and Iran saw falls of 9 percentage points (World Bank, 2003).

Enrolling in primary school, however, is only the first step. To receive a meaningful education families must resist the temptation of forgone income and work in the home to ensure primary education is completed. Data are sparse on school completion and so a general picture is hard to paint. In South Asia completion rates are around 70 per cent and in Africa little over one-half of children who start primary school will be there at the end (Millennium Project Task Force, 2003). Combined with low enrolments this means that little over one in three children in sub-Saharan Africa are currently completing primary education in the region.

While enrolling and completing primary school is a means to education, being able to read and write is one of its most fundamental ends. Among 862 million adults, 1 in 4 in the developing world is illiterate. Encouragingly youth literacy is far above adult literacy in all regions suggesting future improvements in educational levels (UNDP, 2003b).

Inequalities within countries: groups being left behind

This chapter focuses on national averages and the countries which are being left behind as development fails. However, it is important not to lose sight of what national averages can hide in terms of growing internal inequalities and groups that are not sharing in human development progress. For example, while China as a whole has forged ahead, it is the coastal provinces that have driven its success. Shanghai has a life expectancy and income similar to Portugal, and Beijing is comparable to Costa Rica, but many inland provinces have fared much worse: Guizhou has an income per capita little over $1,000 (US PPP), more comparable to Tajikistan (UNDP, 2003b).

The problem is much more widespread than this single example. Between 1980 and the mid-1990s income inequalities increased in forty-three of seventy-three countries with complete and comparable data; in only six of the thirty-three developing countries with data was there a significant reduction in income inequality (Cornia and Kiiski, 2001). Where data are available, these changes in inequalities within countries can be traced in dimensions of human development beyond income: of fourteen countries with data where child mortality is improving at the national level, in eight the gaps between rich and poor are increasing, in five inequality remains stable, and in only one are child mortality rates between rich and poor narrowing (Minujin and Delamonica, 2003).

Data on gaps between groups within countries are severely lacking and form one of the crucial challenges of data collection for human development. However, one area where data is available that reveals consistent gaps from the

Table 10.7. Child mortality rates: inequalities within countries versus changes in national averages, 1980s and 1990s, selected countries

Child mortality rates		Relative gap (between rich and poor)		
		Narrowing	Constant	Widening
Average level	Improving	Guatemala	Egypt Mali Morocco Peru Senegal	Bangladesh Bolivia Brazil Colombia Dominican Republic Ghana Indonesia Uganda
	Constant	Togo Zambia	Burkina Faso Cameroon Niger	Philippines Tanzania
	Worsening		Kenya	Kazakhstan Zimbabwe

Source: Minujin and Delamonica (2003).

richest to poorest countries is gender. Women throughout the world play critical roles in development, their contributions impacting on households; communities, and national economies (Millennium Project Task Force, 2003). Yet gender equality remains a long way off: some two-thirds of the worlds 876 million illiterates are women (UNESCO, 2002), women still earn only 75 per cent as much as men on average (UNDP, 2003b), and around the world at least one woman in every three has been beaten, coerced into sex, or otherwise abused (Millennium Project Task Force, 2003). It is estimated that there are as many as 100 million "missing" women, missing due to infanticide, neglect, and sex-selective abortions (UNDP, 2002). Until women hold political power some of these injustices may be slow to change: currently only 14 per cent of the world's parliamentarians are women and this number is changing only slowly (UN, 2003).

The countries being left behind

In each area of development there are countries with intense human poverty struggling to move forward, or where the situation is even deteriorating. In many countries these development failures are happening in not just one area of development, but many. These countries are being left behind and comprise the most urgent priority for reducing global poverty and global inequalities.

The *Human Development Report 2003* (UNDP, 2003b) identifies fifty-nine countries (out of 147 with data) that are in this greatest of crises where entrenched human poverty is combining with failed progress across multiple dimensions of human development. These fifty-nine countries are classified as priority countries, and are further sub-divided into "top" and "high priority" countries.

Though they come from all the world's regions, the most by far are from sub-Saharan Africa: thirty-eight out of fifty-nine. There are also four from East Asia and the Pacific, six from the Arab States, five from Central and Eastern Europe and the CIS, four from Latin America and the Caribbean, and two from South Asia.

Though no single factor can explain the predicament of these countries, many of the top-priority and high-priority countries share common features which deserve consideration in diagnosing their situation. For example, many are landlocked or have a large portion of their populations living far from a coast. In addition, most (fifty-five) are small—only five contain more than 40 million people. Being locked far from world markets and having a small economy could be important factors, complicating diversification away from primary commodities to less volatile exports with more value added. Indeed, in twenty-one of twenty-six countries with data primary commodities make up more than two-thirds of their exports. Small size and geographic location as well as dependence on primary commodities are major factors behind poor economic performance. Analysis of eighty-four countries over 1980–98 found that countries with inland populations (over 75 per cent of the population living at least 100 kilometers from the coast) fared consistently worse in economic growth than coastal countries. Small countries (with populations below 40 million) that also had inland populations did particularly badly; of fifty-three countries with these characteristics, only twenty-four had positive growth rates and the average per capita growth rates for the group as whole was −0.2 per cent; countries in other categories all registered positive growth rates (see Table 10.8).

On export patterns, transition economies and fuel exporters experienced highly negative growth rates in the 1980–98 period (−1.7 per cent and −1.5 per cent respectively) as did non-fuel commodity exporters (−0.1 per cent). Of the sixty-one countries in this last category, only twenty-nine countries had a

Table 10.8. Economic growth by population size and location, 1980–98

Geographic location	Small countries			Large countries		
	Countries with growing GDP per capita	Average annual growth, GDP per capita (%)	Population living in countries that grew, 2001 (million)	Countries with growing GDP per capita	Average annual growth, GDP per capita (%)	Population living in countries that grew, 2001 (million)
Inland populations	24 of 53	−0.2	379 of 799	10 of 10	2.5	3,087 of 3,087
Coastal populations	15 of 17	1.9	118 of 130	3 of 4	3.2	341 of 418

Source: United Nations Development Program (2003).

Table 10.9. Economic growth by country group, 1980–98

Group	Countries with growing GDP per capita	Average annual growth, GDP per capita
Technology innovators	18 out of 18	1.7
Transition countries	4 out of 12	−1.7
Fuel exporters	2 out of 13	−1.5
Manufacturing exporters	23 out of 24	2.7
Commodity (non-fuel) exporters	29 out of 61	−0.1

Source: United Nations Development Program (2003b).

positive growth performance. This contrasts starkly with manufacturing exporters, where twenty-three out of twenty-four countries experienced positive average annual growth rates with an overall average of 2.7 per cent per capita (see Table 10.9).

But poor performance in improving human well-being can be attributed to factors other than economic growth. These could include government social policy that influences public income rather than private income, such as expenditures on education, immunization, and so on. Another factor is the spread of HIV/AIDS. Yet another is violent conflict. More research is needed on the factors that lie behind the reversals in important human well-being indicators such as education, nutrition, and survival (Marshall, 2000).

Conclusions

The 1990s were a decade of prosperity during which most rich countries enjoyed an economic boom, where much of south-east Asia and south Asia registered major gains in poverty reduction, including the historically unprecedented achievement of lifting 150 million people out of income poverty in China.

Yet another trend of the 1990s in human development, focusing on both income and capability measures, was stagnation and unprecedented reversals, which signaled a decade of development crisis.

Proponents of globalization would argue that world market forces propelled poverty reduction in China and elsewhere—if so, why did they so systematically bypass the fifty-nine priority countries? They would argue that weak economic policies and governance are to blame, often combined with civil conflict. This chapter points to other factors which deserve consideration, such as the structural constraints. The fifty-nine countries are almost all low human development countries, which in itself is a disadvantage. They also face constraints over which they have little control such as global disease, falling commodity prices, and trade rules. More attention needs to be given to these longer-term structural constraints that need to be unblocked before the priority countries can take advantage of global market forces for human development.

Notes

1. This paper was based on work for the Human Development Report 2003. It reflects the views of the authors and is not a policy statement of UNDP.
2. For example, the World Bank's *World Development Reports* on poverty (2000) and equity (2004) focus on factors such as access to health care, education, jobs, capital, and secure land rights, as well as political power, as key elements of redressing poverty and inequality. These analyses go far beyond income as the central element of poverty and inequality.
3. Sen (2000).
4. Sen (2005). Also see the discussion of this point in Robeyns (2005).
5. It is on this basis that the Human Development Index was constructed. See United Nations, *Human Development Report* (1990) and successive *Human Development Reports*.
6. Haq (1994).
7. Covers different periods between 1990 and the mid- to late 1990s for countries with data on national poverty trends (World Bank, 2002; ECLAC, 2002; UNCTAD, 2002; World Bank, 2000a; Milanovic, 1998).
8. Measured using the $2 a day poverty line, which is considered a more appropriate extreme poverty line for Central and Eastern Europe and the CIS (UNDP, 2003a).
9. The three countries are: Swaziland, Botswana, and Zimbabwe. The other two are Equatorial Guinea and Kenya.

Bibliography

Cornia, G. A. and Kiiski, S. (2001) 'Trends in Income Distribution in the Post-World War II Period: Evidence and Interpretation'. Discussion paper 2001/89, United Nations University, World Institute for Development Economics Research, Helsinki.

Eberstadt, N. (2002) 'The Future of AIDS'. *Foreign Affairs*, 81(6).

Economic Commission for Latin America and the Caribbean (2002) *Social Panorama for Latin America and the Caribbean*. Santiago: United Nations. <http://www.eclac.org/cgi–bin/getProd.asp?xml=/publicaciones/xml/5/11245/P11245.xml&xsl=/dds/tpl–i/p9f.xsl&base=\tpl–i\top–bottom.xsl> accessed March 2003.

Food and Agricultural Organization (2001) 'The Impact of HIV/AIDS on Food Security'. Paper presented at the 27th Session of the Committee on World Food Security, Rome.

—— (2002) *The State of Food Insecurity in the World 2002*. Rome.

Haq, Mahbub ul (1994) *Reflections on Human Development*. New York: Oxford University Press.

Maddison, A. (2001) *The World Economy: A Millennial Perspective*. OECD.

Marshall, M. G. (2000) *Major Episodes of Political Violence, 1946–1999*. University of Maryland Center for Systematic Peace, College Park.

Milanovic, B. (1998) 'Income, Inequality, and Poverty during the Transition from Planned to Market Economy'. Washington DC: World Bank.

Millennium Project Task Force (2003) 'Halving Global Hunger'. Task Force Paper 2.

—— (2003) 'Achieving Universal Primary Education by 2015'. Task Force Paper 3.

Minujin, A. and Delamonica, E. (2003) 'Equality Matters for a World Fit for Children. Lessons from the 90s'. UNICEF Staff Working Papers, Division of Policy and Planning Series No. 3.

Sen, A. (1999) *Development as Freedom*. Oxford: Oxford University Press.

—— (2000) 'A Decade of Human Development'. *Journal of Human Development*, 1(1), pp. 17–23.

—— (2005) 'Amartya Sen talks with Bina Agarwal, Jane Humphries, and Ingrid Robeyns; Capabilities, Lists, and Public Reason: Continuing the Conversation'. In B. Agarwal, J. Humphries, and I. Robeyns (eds.) *Amartya Sen's Work and Ideas: A Gender Perspective*, London: Routledge.

Joint United Nations Program on HIV/AIDS. (2002) 'Report on the Global HIV/AIDS Epidemic'. Geneva.

United Nations (2000) *World Population Prospects 1950–2050: The 2000 Revision*. New York: Department of Economic and Social Affairs, Population Division.

—— (2003) *Millennium Indicators Database*. New York: Department of Economic and Social Affairs, Statistics Division.

United Nations Conference on Trade and Development (2002) 'The Least Developed Countries Report 2002. Escaping the Poverty Trap'. Geneva.

United Nations Development Program (1990) *Human Development Report 1990*. New York: Oxford University Press.

—— (2002) *Human Development Report 2002*. New York: Oxford University Press.

—— (2003a) *Correspondence on the use of $2 a day as Extreme Poverty Line*. New York: Regional Bureau for Europe and the CIS.

—— (2003b) *Human Development Report 2003*. New York: Oxford University Press.

United Nations Educational, Scientific and Cultural Organization (2002) *EFA Global Monitoring Report 2002: Is the World on track?* Paris.

United Nations Children's Fund (2003) *The State of the World's Children 2003*. New York: Oxford University Press.

World Bank (2000a) *Making Transition Work for Everyone: Poverty and Inequality in Europe and Central Asia*. Washington DC.

—— (2000b) *World Development Report 2000/2001: Attacking Poverty—Opportunity, Empowerment, Security*. Washington DC.

—— (2002) *Global Economic Prospects 2003*. Washington DC.

—— (2003) *World Development Indicators 2003*. Washington DC.

—— (2004) *World Development Report 2004: Equity and Development*. Washington DC.

Part II

Regional and Country Studies

11

Improving Measurement of Latin American Inequality and Poverty with an Eye to Equitable Growth Policy[1]

Albert Berry

Introduction

In Latin America, the past thirty years have seen enormous strides in the measurement of inequality and poverty at the national (and subnational) level and in the feasibility of making meaningful comparisons across countries and over time in the same country. Latin America is around the norm for developing countries as a whole in this regard; the availability and accuracy of its data is better than in some other regions but weaker than in others. It now permits reasonable guesses as to the true level of inequality in most countries of the region, makes it clear that inequality is higher in some than in others and, usually with less confidence, allows some judgments on trends. The regional distinctions are basically more feasible than the over time judgments, because the observed variance is several times higher; thus the reported Gini coefficient in Brazil is usually around 0.60 and that in Uruguay is around 0.40,[2] so the likelihood that non-comparability of estimates would negate the conclusion that inequality is much greater in Brazil than in Uruguay is extremely remote. Over time it is rare to see the reported Gini coefficient for a given country vary by more than 0.04–0.05, so if the error of estimate changed considerably over the period of that change, it is less assured that a true change did occur. Reported changes of up to about 0.05 in the Gini coefficient make it necessary to attach a probability statement to any surmise as to whether a change really occurred. Such caveats notwithstanding, our knowledge has increased greatly, both about the level of inequality per se, its components (e.g. how much is associated with inequality of labor income) and several of its correlates, and with respect to the nature of the remaining measurement errors. The fact that reported inequality tends to be very stable in most countries, in the absence of identifiable changes in measurement (e.g. in the nature of the questions asked in the surveys), suggests that true inequality is also stable. The main possible exception to this generalization is that overall measurement error could change over time in a way closely related to changes in true capital income distribution and/or true capital share; thus reported capital income and its impact on reported inequality might not change while true capital income and true overall distribution did. Such a change might result from financial liberalization, frequently argued to have contributed to rising inequality in developing countries (Cornia, 2004; Behrman et al., 2000).

What are the remaining weaknesses in the measurement of inequality and what do we lose as a result? Inequality data are used in part for broad descriptive purposes like those just alluded to. To this end they are now reasonably satisfactory for most countries of the region. They are also used to assess overall economic performance (e.g. did inequality rise or fall in the last decade?) and as evidence on the impact of specific policies (e.g. did inequality fall when a new pension system was implemented?). For this purpose, the quality is not nearly so adequate since much greater precision is required if one is to be in a position to identify relatively small changes in overall inequality or more specific changes (e.g. related to certain subgroups within the population). Few changes either in policy or in the mechanisms of the development process are likely to affect the Gini coefficient by more than a couple of percentage points, which is clearly well within the normal error of estimate of reported to real Gini. To have a chance to detect impacts on inequality one must therefore have a good idea of the likely serial correlation of the errors of observation. Fortunately, there is good reason to believe that such correlation will tend to be high, so this provides a reasonable chance to identify impacts. Chances of such identification are also raised by the fact that many policies are expected to influence only certain groups within the overall population and with adequate detail the income of these groups can be traced.

The extent of poverty, as it is traditionally conceived in economics, may be thought of as implicit in the evidence on average income and its distribution or average consumption and its distribution, depending on whether poverty is defined in income or in consumption terms. Thus all of the measurement issues that affect that part of the distribution not too far above the poverty line are relevant to the discussion of poverty as well as to that of inequality. The one additional issue relating to poverty is where to draw the line or lines. We do not address that complicated question here, beyond noting that one reason that it is important to have a clear picture of most of the income or consumption profile in a country is precisely that there is always a degree of arbitrariness in where poverty lines are drawn. Poverty conclusions are most persuasive when they are not very sensitive to where the poverty line(s) are drawn.

In the remainder of this chapter we first review the state of information on inequality/poverty in Latin America, then consider the main gaps that it would be desirable to fill in light of the major policy issues most urgently needing to be addressed. Since this latter list of priorities is a matter of personal judgment, any conclusions drawn with respect to priority improvements in the database are naturally by implication a matter of judgment as well. A few brief conclusions on priorities are presented in the final section.

Measurement weaknesses, their relative importance and the feasibility of addressing them

Distribution of private income and private consumption

In most developing countries, estimates of inequality of private income and private consumption can now be based on periodic household surveys taken annually or more frequently. So frequency of data points is much less a problem than it was a few decades ago. In some parts of the world the main focus is on measuring consumption, in others (including Latin America) on measuring income. It is desirable to have both these distributions; which is more important to know with precision depends on, among other things, which policy issues it is most important to analyze. If one knows one of them with reasonable precision it is possible to guess at the other one with a certain degree of success. It is accepted that the distribution of consumption (or of total expenditure) can be more accurately measured than the distribution of income; this can be a factor in the choice of which distribution to focus on. It may even be that the best way to get a good feel for the distribution of income is to begin with a good measure of the distribution of consumption, then use a variety of other information to map this distribution onto that of income. The best approach, of course is to strive for accurate measurement of both, and to use non-survey information to cross-check the relationship between the two. The greater potential accuracy of measurement of consumption and its distribution comes with a higher minimum cost of data collection, since it is necessary to have a quite detailed questionnaire.[3] As a result many countries perform these surveys with less frequency than the income surveys.

Household surveys allow the analyst to focus on the distribution of income among earners, among families ranked by per capita or total income, or among persons ranked by per capita family income. Per capita measures may be improved a little by using per adult-equivalent variables. If data on both consumption and on income are collected, it is possible to identify the functional relationship between savings and income. Typically household surveys fail to incorporate publicly provided goods and services (public consumption) and may or may not take account of most taxes and transfers, and thus must be considered to provide only part of the whole distributional story.

Apart from their failure to capture the impact of the public sector on distribution, household surveys suffer from a set of common and predictable measurement problems, the resolution, or not, of which determines the accuracy of the information collected. These include:

1. imprecision of the income data for most self-employed groups, especially those in activities where gross income varies considerably over time, where the calculation of net income requires subtracting out various inputs, and where the informant does not keep books. Most small agriculture fits into this category, but the problems are accentuated there by the long-run seasonal fluctuations and the usually higher cost of data collection due to distance.

2. weak data on high income recipients, especially those whose earnings come mainly from capital. Many such people have complicated earnings structures; this is compounded by a reluctance to report income fully through fear of taxes or other negative consequences.

3. weak data on income in kind, especially prevalent in small-farm agriculture, which raises special difficulties since the earner often does not think of it as income at all, and even after being pressed to provide the relevant information, may be hampered by the fact that no market price is attached to the outputs involved. Imputed rent on owner-occupied housing is an important form of income in kind, especially for urban dwellers. Not all surveys include estimates of it, but it is less difficult to approximate reasonable numbers than for some other forms of income in kind, since the characteristics of a dwelling are observable and the owner may know roughly how much it would cost to rent such a dwelling. This element of income is increasingly, but by no means always, included in surveys.

4. weak data on illegal income, which may reach significant levels in some countries. People who have to pay protection probably seldom report it as an expenditure nor do those who receive it report it as income. In this respect crime-related and other illegal forms of income are like some components of capital income.

The above weaknesses have been expressed as the result of inaccurate or incomplete responses by households who are captured in the survey. A different problem arises when households refuse to participate in the survey or are not at home/not easily locatable. This "unit non-response" problem is also very unlikely to be uncorrelated with income and other relevant variables, and hence adds another type of bias to reported figures. Mistiaen and Ravallion's (2003) analysis of US data leads them to conclude that correction for this bias appreciably increases mean income and inequality, as a result of decreasing compliance as income rises.[4] Though they see no presumption that their results, even in qualitative terms, will hold elsewhere, the finding of a significant impact for the US makes it highly probable that differential compliance has some sort of impact in many developing countries. It thus increases the likely magnitude of error in reported figures on inequality.

As a result of the various weaknesses and challenges noted, the most reliable information in household surveys comes from those individuals on fixed salaries, a datum easy both to remember and to verify. The main contours of many reported income distributions are dominated by the incomes of these mainly middle class people. Altimir (1998, pp. 48, 76) sums up the distribution data for Latin America noting that the income data usually refer to household disposable cash income, after direct tax payments. "Income in kind and imputed income . . . is either explicitly excluded or so poorly measured as to be considered excluded in most of the surveys, . . . which are labor or income surveys." In light of the severity of reporting problems for major groups, it is not surprising that it may be necessary to resort to consumption data to get a better feel for distribution. Individuals are less reluctant to report such data, and it is conceptually simpler than income data, even if it is necessary to collect data on a long list of items, some of which are purchased only infrequently. It is implicit in the above observations that consumption data are especially important in learning about the incomes of agricultural earners, informal sector workers and higher income people, given the difficulty of approaching income measurement directly.

How serious are the above weaknesses, relative to each other and to absolute accuracy? This depends most directly on the policy issue for which the data are needed, but also on the economy, its structure and its level of development, as well on the quality of the data collection process. In still very agricultural economies, the problems of measuring home consumption are great and failure to get a reasonable reading on this component means missing a significant share of income, especially in the case of poor subsistence farmers. Even if only a few per cent of GDP were involved, it would be easy to understate the incomes of the bottom decile or so by 20–40 per cent in this way. This could make a great difference to estimates of poverty and the poverty gap in rural areas. With agriculture and rural populations declining in Latin America, and with subsistence agriculture also less and less common, this problem has also been declining in relative importance. But since, according to existing figures, one-third of the poor and nearly half of the very poor (indigent) are still found in rural areas (CEPAL, 2004, p. 50) it remains important. The measurement problems among workers in the informal sector, where errors of 25–50 per cent for many individuals are quite possible, are of increasing relative importance given the trend towards informalization of the urban economy that has accompanied the slow growth in most countries over the last quarter century. As with low income agriculture, the measurement problem here takes on special importance because many people in the sector are poor. The largest chunk of national income typically missed in surveys is the capital and business income of high income earners. In a survey whose quality was such that 70–90 per cent of paid labor income was reported, the figure for capital income might be as low as 20–30 per cent; the reporting ratio for this income seldom appears to reach 50 per cent, when the benchmark or point of reference for the estimate is the national accounts figure. Imputed income from owner-occupied housing is the easiest large component of capital income to measure; most other components are difficult.

Estimates of income and consumption underreporting in household surveys[5] are themselves subject to much uncertainty in most Latin American countries because the accuracy of the national accounts figures, the only overall source of a feasible cross-check for the household survey data, appears to vary widely also. There is typically little independent evidence to go on to judge how seriously the figures may be in error. Most observers assume the bias is typically downward, which means that estimated measurement error in household surveys, when based on a comparison with the national accounts, will also tend to be downward biased. Ideally, one should compare each of consumption, savings, and income from the household surveys with the corresponding figures from the national accounts, bearing in mind that in some cases the national accounts figures make use of the household survey data in their construction.

One may therefore have a true cross-check between independent estimates of the same economic variable only for some components of each of these three variables. Completeness of reporting for some household surveys can be partially assessed by comparing them to others taken at nearly the same time and having higher quality standards. Average underreporting of income in household surveys can sometimes be deduced up to a point by comparison with consumption figures from the same survey; if the comparison implies an implausibly low savings rate or high dissavings rate, this suggests income underreporting. Aggregate savings and some of its components may be approximated in other ways also, in particular with financial system data; these can provide a useful cross-check for both the household survey and the national accounts estimates, though the latter are sometimes based in part on such data. In short, the accuracy with which income and consumption distribution can be ascertained depends on the total body of information available, some of which provides direct evidence and some of which provides cross-checks of various sorts. In some countries very little data is available to permit useful cross-checks (e.g. where the national accounts are not very reliable, financial information is scarce, etc.) whereas in others (most notably India) much good work has been done to compare survey data with other sources and thus narrow down the range of uncertainty. Though in principle the whole body of data useful to undertake such cross-checks should be thought of as the information base for analysis of inequality, very few studies have taken full advantage of it.

Capital incomes constitute in many ways the biggest challenge in the measurement of inequality, though not of poverty since poor people usually have little income of this sort; they are especially hard to measure with reasonable accuracy either as part of the national accounts exercise or in household surveys. In the former context they are typically derived as a residual between national income accruing to the private sector and labor income. Two major problems are involved in that estimation. First, as a residual between two bigger numbers, the per cent error which the estimate of capital income may suffer due to a modest error of estimate in one or both of the larger variables is great. Second, one is mainly interested in net capital income (i.e. after depreciation), but gross capital income is better measured in the national accounts since depreciation is a tricky concept, even in theory, and the simple accounting-type rules usually used to define it could be well off the target in some situations. Thus in trying to assess total net capital incomes, or net capital incomes accruing to individuals (total minus those remaining in the hands of corporations), one has to work with substantially inaccurate estimates from both sources. This is a major problem in analysis of distribution since capital shares do appear to be high in many developing countries, and they clearly constitute much of the income of the top few percentiles of the distribution.

Cross-country comparisons, especially of the top part of the distribution, could be seriously in error if, as must be expected, the completeness of reporting of this income component varies substantially from country to country. The reliability of over time analyses is also seriously prejudiced. This problem is of special relevance in Latin America, both because of the high observed levels of inequality and because the major factor contributing to the recent increase in reported inequality has taken place at the top of the distribution. Whether the increases in the share of the top few per cent have been exaggerated or understated is an important issue from a welfare point of view and in terms of the social efficiency of growth.

One relatively simple and frequent adjustment to correct for the relative underreporting of capital income involves adjusting reported capital income up by the same per cent for each person (or family) reporting such income, that per cent being based on the overall degree of relative underreporting of capital income based on comparison with the national accounts figures for each of labor and capital income. Altimir's adjustments to estimated inequality in a number of Latin American countries take account of this factor (see Table 11.1) are a variant of this approach. Broadly speaking, his procedure involved adjusting upward each type of income where the average amount reported in the surveys was less than that implicit in the national accounts, except for monetary property incomes where underreporting was assumed to be concentrated totally in the upper quintile (Altimir, 1987, pp. 151–2). This adjustment increased the Gini coefficient by up to 6 percentage points in a number of cases but in others by very little.

Altimir (1987, p. 146) notes that items like property income received in cash by households are likely to be grossly underestimated in the national accounts of some countries, and although there have been some improvements since he

Table 11.1. Impact of upward adjustment to capital incomes on measures of inequality, selected countries

Country	Year	Original distribution			Adjusted distribution		
		Lower 40%	Upper 10%	Gini	Lower 40%	Upper 10%	Gini
(a) National level							
Brazil	1972	7.0	50.6	0.605	5.6	58.7	0.662
Colombia	1972	5.9	50.8	0.618	6.5	50.1	0.607
Mexico	1963	10.2	42.2	0.530	7.5	50.2	0.606
	1968	10.6	42.1	0.521	8.1	48.3	0.586
	1977	11.5	36.3	0.482	10.4	40.1	0.518
Peru	1971/2	7.0	42.9	0.568	5.7	46.2	0.603
Venezuela	1971	10.3	35.7	0.494	9.8	36.3	0.505
(b) Urban areas							
Argentina	1970	16.0	28.8	0.385	13.6	35.8	0.448
Brazil	1972	8.6	47.0	0.569	6.3	54.8	0.633
Colombia	1975	8.0	43.6	0.565	8.1	45.2	0.572
Mexico	1968	11.7	40.1	0.498	9.3	45.4	0.553
Peru	1971/2	12.2	36.3	0.471	11.6	38.8	0.489
Uruguay	1967	14.3	30.5	0.419	13.3	35.7	0.454

Source: Altimir (1987)

wrote, the broad picture is probably similar. Such weaknesses in the national accounts mean that the adjustment reported here probably still leaves most or all of the Gini coefficients below their true values.[6] Only with the detailed study of capital incomes, and more generally the incomes of the top few percentiles of populations, will it be possible to achieve reasonably reliable estimates of overall inequality. Better household surveys will be part of that effort but need to be complemented by a battery of other types of information. Analysis of the economic conditions of the rich in developing countries requires special effort, something along the lines of Kuznets' (1953) path-breaking study for the US half a century ago. Although Latin America has a number of studies of rich families and how they got that way, for example Majul (1997) for Argentina and Miranda (2000) for Paraguay, they do not take the sort of approach which would contribute to the quantitative measurement of inequality.

One form of income based on ownership of capital but not included in the national accounts (since it does not correspond to current production) is the appreciation or depreciation of assets. Since it does constitute part of people's disposable income, for purposes of analysis of distribution it should be taken into account. In principle, therefore, it should be included in household surveys designed to measure inequality; in practice, high reporting errors might produce results of little value. It would be more plausible to pursue information on this component of income together with data on wealth distribution. I am unaware of studies in Latin America that have tried to incorporate this form of family income, either on the basis of evidence at the family level or based on some more indirect approach. The study of wealth distribution is in and of itself interesting (e.g. to link it to political power), but has additional merit as a way to improve the accuracy of all capital-related components of income distribution, especially capital gains. Wealth studies have been few in developing countries outside Asia, including those of Latin America (Davies and Shorrocks, 2005).

Bhatia's pioneering study for the US found that over the period 1948–64 accrued capital gains on corporate stock, real estate, and livestock were as much as 12 per cent of reported personal income (Bhatia, 1972, p. 869). Realized capital gains were a much smaller 2.6 per cent, but this is the less relevant figure. Of accrued gains, the bulk (60.6 per cent) was from corporate stocks, 28.7 per cent from non-farm residential real estate, and 12.6 per cent from farm real estate. As expected, accrued gains were erratic, exceeding a quarter of regular personal income in a couple of years but turning substantially negative in others. Pending comparable studies in Latin American countries, it seems plausible that the ratio of capital gains to production-related income may reach the 5–10 per cent range or even higher in some of them. Including this element of income inevitably makes inequality more severe, since it is likely to be more or less proportional to wealth (or to other components of capital income), which is distributed in a way substantially more unequal than is income itself. Urbanization and stock market booms tend to increase the appreciation component of income. It is also substantially more volatile than other components, so in periods of general economic crisis, when the value of real estate, stocks, etc., tends to fall, overall income distribution including this factor will be less unequal than income excluding it. But in the long run it is an inequality-increasing factor.

While income from sources like rent on capital, capital appreciation, or criminal activities is particularly unlikely to show up in survey figures on income, the consumption which it facilitates is much more likely to, hence data on consumption inequality may provide a valuable cross-check on that for income inequality. It is recognized that consumption inequality is less than that of income by several Gini percentage points.[7] Unfortunately consumption surveys have not been sufficiently frequent in Latin America to permit enough analysis of the determinants of how income and consumption distributions differ to permit a sort of calibration which would allow fairly precise estimation of levels and trends in one of the two if one had only the other.

The distribution of secondary income: handling taxes and transfers

It is important, especially as the level of development advances, to distinguish income levels before and after taxes and (monetary) transfers. In-kind transfers have to be dealt with separately because of the special valuation problem they create. The *primary distribution* of income is that which emerges from the functioning of the economy before any subsequent redistribution through taxes and transfers: the *secondary distribution* includes their effects. Most income surveys focus just on current disposable income after any withholding of taxes, this being the easiest figure for the respondent to understand and provide. If income taxes must be paid on an annual basis they are no doubt often missed. In many countries such taxes are only paid by a minority of individuals. Monetary transfers received from private or public sources tend to be caught, especially if they are regular. The impact of sales taxes is already taken account of since the prices used to deflate incomes include these taxes. The implication of these patterns is that the typical reported distribution is a combination of the before and the after tax and transfer monetary distributions, usually closer to the latter.

Proper assessment of the overall impact of the tax and transfer system on income (or consumption) distribution requires a general equilibrium analysis. Such analyses are rare and difficult, especially with respect to the impact of the system on distribution through its effects on savings, investment, and growth. The indirect effects of some transfers (e.g. pensions to low income people) may be relatively small, although even in such cases there may be a substitution effect for inter-family transfers and multiplier effects on local incomes where the money is spent. The broader question of how all public sector interactions with families affect distribution includes the impact of the provision of public services in kind to families, which requires a special analysis as noted below, and the impact of monetary subsidies and provision of public services in kind to businesses; since the first-round effects of these benefits from government show up in family incomes, they need no further consideration unless and until one attempts to estimate the general equilibrium effects of the public sector's activities.[8]

Publicly provided goods and services

Judging by the few careful and relatively complete studies available, education, health care, and other public services, together with subsidies, often have significant impacts on the distribution of both income and consumption (publicly provided services are part of both income and consumption). Measurement of these benefits is less straightforward, or at least less reliable, than of benefits from transfers and losses through payment of taxes, because the decision on quantity and quality of the service available to a given person or family is made by the government rather than by the individual or family.[9] The standard assumption is that benefits are distributed proportionately to cost of provision among those receiving "the same" service, with total benefits equaling total costs. That each recipient benefits equally will never be precisely true and may not be close to accurate; that total benefits equal total costs of provision may also be well off the mark in either direction. If one took literally some of the very high rate of return figures estimated for primary education, total benefits could be two or three times total costs. But benefits could also fall short of costs where quality is very defective. The degree of mismeasurement of the benefits from some services can be lowered through surveys including respondent judgments on relative or absolute value of those services. In the absence of anything to go on but total cost of provision, it is desirable to undertake some analysis to check for the sensitivity of overall inequality to the assumptions used.

Selowksy's (1979) study for Colombia was the first of the few thorough studies in Latin America to probe the impact of public spending on income distribution. Others have followed (e.g. Velez, 1996; Bravo et al., 2000) and an increasing number of countries (including Argentina, Colombia, Costa Rica, and Ecuador) have used special modules in their household surveys to identify the destination of some public expenditures.[10] The magnitude of the effort required for full-scale attacks on this problem makes them infrequent, which in turn complicates attempts to judge how distribution, duly including these goods and services, is changing. Hopefully the increasing use, widening scope, and improved interpretation of household survey modules recording some important types of public spending will gradually fill in much of this gap in our understanding. Efforts are needed to find fairly reliable proxies for the distribution of public expenditure benefits, calibrated on the basis of the infrequent detailed studies undertaken.

What to do about market misinformation?

As just noted, publicly provided goods and services complicate the measurement of income/consumption since the fact of consumption does not reflect the client's judgment on benefits relative to costs. A somewhat similar issue arises when, although the consumer does choose to buy, he does so on the basis of misinformation about the product. For frequently purchased items it is legitimately assumed that the associated losses will be small and learning will be quick. This is less so in the case of infrequent purchases, especially of goods where advertising is misleading or good information is simply hard to obtain. The most extreme case of loss through misinformation is probably that of addictive substances, in which case after making the wrong decision the buyer is unable to reverse course and correct the error. Under such circumstances, high expenditures on an item (e.g. drugs) may be reflective of low levels of benefit rather than high. The issue here is related to but not identical to some raised by the happiness literature (see below).

The inclusion of natural "goods" and "bads"

All goods and services that are purchased are in principle included in national income, together with some of those home produced and consumed items for which a market exists. But it is clear that human welfare is also affected by numerous other factors, many of which are free. Serious attempts to measure levels of welfare and the distribution of that welfare should thus take these other determinants into account when possible—things like weather, beauty of surroundings, effects of surroundings on health, and degree of economic insecurity. The inevitable (because of inherent difficulties) failure to do so means that our measures of income, consumption, and their distribution may not correspond very closely to true levels of satisfaction and its distribution.

Accordingly, comparison of income levels and distributions across countries or over time may not reflect with any precision how satisfaction levels and distribution differ across populations, and must therefore be treated with the appropriate level of caution. Although the general response to this problem is to simply ignore it and accept that we can only get at some of the presumed determinants of satisfaction, it is worth asking whether and when it may be partially corrected. This is the case when a "good" which is naturally available in one country or region or time period is absent in another, leading to the production and purchase of partial substitutes. An example is the use of insurance to buy economic stability. In an over time analysis of income and its distribution in a country in which insecurity rises, for example because of the way the economy is structured and functions, one may often legitimately conclude that after purchase of insurance that provides a partial protection against an insecurity which was not there before, people are still worse off than before on this specific account. In such a case it would be legitimate to subtract all expenditures for purchase of insurance from disposable income and from consumption as one compares current income and consumption with the levels before the threat of insecurity arose.[11] Another important example is crime; even after the cost of protection from it (which enters the national accounts as a "good"), a society may be deemed to be worse off than it was before the crime arose. Such a case produces the irony, in comparisons across countries or over time, that a country or period with a proclivity to crime both suffers the direct loss from that crime and also pays the costs of curbing it, yet that cost enters the national accounts as a positive service (which it is vis-à-vis the benchmark situation of a still worse situation without the protection). With a few important phenomena of this sort, estimated incomes could be rising while the standard of living as perceived by people was falling.

Most non-marketed "goods" or "bads" do not accrue equally to everyone and thus constitute another component of a more broadly defined inequality. The effects of crime tend to fall disproportionately on the poor, partly because they are naturally more vulnerable and sometimes because government-provided protection against crime is not distributed fairly. Most poor people cannot buy safety, since some public goods are differentially available by socio-economic class. Sickness is another typical feature of poverty, since it is closely associated with socio-economic context—lack of clean water, lack of sanitation facilities, vulnerability to disease through malnutrition, etc. AIDS, while afflicting all social classes, is a special scourge to the poor since they have less options for earning a living and protecting their children than the better off. Certain types of mental illness have been noted to be prevalent in urban shantytowns where families live in overcrowded quarters, income is inadequate to the needs of the family, and insecurity and stress contribute to such illness (Rogler and Hollingshead, 1965; Rogler et al. 1989). Children living in such settings are especially vulnerable to abuse from family members or others.

Looking at income volatility, long-run average income, and wealth

Almost everyone's income changes over time, so point of time snapshots of inequality and poverty can be misleading. Income fluctuations are of particular importance to people and families who are poor at least some of the time, i.e. the fluctuations can pull them out of poverty or push them into it. Unfortunately, short- and medium-run income fluctuations are notorious for some groups with high average poverty, most notably small farmers and lower income people in the informal sector. Thus, both to understand the nature of poverty as it afflicts these groups and to design policy to alleviate it requires an understanding of the short- and medium-run income dynamics of these groups. Such analysis, increasingly common in industrial countries over the past few decades, usually requires panel data to follow families over periods of a year to a few years. It allows a useful distinction between the chronically poor and the transitorily poor and a corresponding distinction, where appropriate, between policies to deal with their respective problems (Hulme and Shephard, 2003; McKay and Lawson, 2003). Although panel features in household surveys in some Latin American countries date back several decades, their use has not been widely institutionalized, with the result that we know much less about poverty dynamics than we should.[12] Such knowledge would be helpful in the framing of a number of policies, including most obviously some targeting programs designed to alleviate poverty (see below). In fact, the informational needs of targeting programs have enriched the body of information on income distribution through the surveys and analyses undertaken, beginning with Chile's CASEN program (MIDEPLAN, 1990) and replicated in several other countries within the region.

Apart from income fluctuations that can quickly change a family's relative position in the income hierarchy and/or its poverty status, there are longer-run trends that also change relative positions in the hierarchy and imply that inequality measured over longer periods differs from point of time inequality. Most people agree that one should be more interested in inequality of long-run average income or consumption across people or families than in short-run inequality. Both logic and empirical evidence suggest that longer-run inequality tends to be moderately less than short-run inequality.[13] This finding seems to be of only modest policy importance per se, however, since it seems unlikely that large cross-country differences or over time changes in short-term inequality would not be fairly faithfully reproduced in the corresponding longer-term figures. Too little analysis has been done in this area to allow any guesses for the developing countries, including those in Latin America. The kinds of panel data which are necessary to do this sort of analysis properly are virtually never available for representative samples of populations over more than a year. In their absence, however, there is often considerable advantage to be gained by using the social security registers, which allow the tracking of a person's earnings over long periods of time. These are most likely to be useful in those countries where the labor force is relatively formalized, such as Argentina, Uruguay, Chile, and Costa Rica, but are valuable in many others as well. In keeping with the general need to use different sources in a complementary way, this body of information deserves more attention than it has received.

Wealth is an important determinant both of current and of future income, so knowing a family's wealth level adds to one's picture of its welfare, both because wealth affects future income and (related) because it serves as a source of economic security (Schneider, 2004, p. 5). Wealth inequality, regardless of the definition employed,[14] tends to be far greater than income inequality. Wolff

(1996) reports 1980s Gini coefficients of 0.69–0.79 for Canada, France, and the US and data for several other countries suggesting Ginis in that same range while the estimates for Italy, Japan, and Korea are lower, at around 0.60 (Schneider, 2004, pp. 51–2). Wealth inequality seems to have declined significantly over the longer run (a century or more) in each of the industrial countries (US and a few European nations) for which estimates are available. Wealth distribution in Latin America has received very little quantitative analysis. This is in rather striking contrast to the situation of the larger Asian countries—India, China, and Indonesia—all of which have useful data (Davies and Shorrocks, 2005).

Allowing for differences in/changes of the price vector

Levels of and changes in inequality are easiest to measure when all families at all of the points of time compared face the same relative prices for the items they purchase. Since this condition is rather far from being met, especially in the case of comparisons between quite unlike countries or over longer periods of time, considerable misinterpretation can result from failure to confront the problem. For point of time estimates of inequality in a given country the issue is partly one of inter-regional or inter socio-economic group price differences, and an increasing number of studies do address it, most often by using regional price data or a broad urban versus rural distinction, or a combination of these.[15] The use of differing price vectors may improve accuracy of estimates a great deal in situations where higher incomes (e.g. in certain urban areas) are mainly or wholly a response to/reflection of higher prices. Unfortunately where decisions on spatial location are heavily influenced by intangibles (or, more specifically, things which are not purchased), such deflation may actually diminish the accuracy of inequality estimates, since higher prices may often be correlated with the presence of such intangibles. While it is possible to use earnings differentials together with price differentials to make estimates of the relative value of such intangibles in different regions, it would be unrealistic to expect such refinement in any but the most in depth analyses of inequality.

Because the composition of consumption is substantially different between poorer people and richer people, it is possible that differences across countries in the distribution of income or consumption, or changes over time in the same country, will not correspond to differences in (changes in) real income or consumption. This factor is too seldom taken into account either in inter-group or region cross-country or over time comparisons although in principle it is relatively easy to do. It is probable that differences (or trends) in real income inequality would differ measurably from differences in (changes in) current price income inequality whenever there are significant changes in relative prices. Poor families spend up to 70–80 per cent of their total consumption on food, most of that on a few staples. The rich have a very different consumption bundle, including cars, tourism, and other luxury goods and services. Distribution in real terms worsens relative to distribution in nominal terms when a famine sharply raises the price of staples (Ravallion, 1987; Drèze, 1999). Less extreme but still substantial changes in relative prices have occurred in some countries during the process of liberalization. In cases where staple food prices were previously controlled and subsidized while luxury imports (and the components for them) paid hefty tariffs, liberalization would be expected to lower the relative price of the rich family consumption basket vis-à-vis that of the poor family. Use of current price data would thus lead to an underestimate of the increase (overestimate of the decrease) in inequality associated with the liberalization.

Some countries officially produce more than one consumer price index, e.g. one for white collar workers and one for blue collar workers (a lengthy Colombian tradition). Even when this is not done, the consumption basket of various income groups is available from consumption surveys and can be used to develop separate price indices for as many groups as deemed appropriate. Meanwhile, cross-country studies in real terms can be facilitated through use of the purchasing power parity database on prices for a large number of countries around the world. In short, it is somewhat surprising that so little attention has been addressed to this possibly significant aspect of inequality differences and changes.

Getting closer to the measurement of satisfaction or welfare

An unjust or unfair society could legitimately be defined as one in which either welfare or the potential for (access to) welfare is quite unevenly distributed. In recognition of the fact that the study of inequality should in principle not be restricted to the more clearly economic elements of welfare, a number of authors have addressed the question of just how strong or weak the links between income and welfare are. A major body of data has been collected on people's reported level of satisfaction or happiness and its correlates. The responses of people in the industrial countries (where such surveys have been carried out with some frequency and over long periods) about their happiness and its correlates indicate a much smaller role for income than standard economic theory would suggest. It is moderately significant when the comparison is between people at different levels of the income hierarchy at a point of time but less so—some authors say virtually insignificant, as a factor in how average societal welfare changes over time, even when average incomes have risen considerably (Easterlin, 1974, 2002; Scitovsky, 1976; Oswald, 1997). Most such studies reveal that the strongest influence among economic variables comes from employment; people with jobs are much happier than those without them.[16] Low inflation also makes people feel happier. The educated are on average happier than the uneducated, the self-employed than employees, and the retired than the economically active. The precise meaning of most of this evidence remains to be drawn out; in particular a deeper understanding of the small apparent role of income cries out for analysis[17]—so do the differences in results across countries whose economies and societies contrast in interesting ways.

One might plausibly guess that income would be a more significant determinant of self-reported happiness in lower income (developing) countries, and most of the available data does tend to confirm this.[18] Frank (1997, p. 1834) notes that "most careful studies find a clear time-series relationship between subjective well-being and absolute income at low levels of absolute income." Where most people lack minimally adequate shelter and nutrition, additional income yields significant and lasting improvements in subjective well-being (Diener and Diener, 1995). Reported satisfaction levels are markedly lower in extremely poor countries than in rich ones, and within countries the positive link between income and satisfaction is significant primarily at the lowest levels of relative income. "For individuals in the middle and upper portions of the income distribution, variations in income explain less than 2 per cent of variation in reported satisfaction levels" (Frank, 1997, pp. 1834–5, citing Diener and Diener, 1995). Having concluded that average satisfaction levels within a country are not significantly correlated with income over time, Frank puts great emphasis on relative status as a source of respect and a determinant of well-being.

The surprising findings (to many economists at least) on the relative unimportance of income as a determinant of societal welfare is only one of several reasons for a reconsideration of the conceptual basis for poverty policy. The role of a sense of belonging to a community in human welfare is obvious at one level, but it remains to be factored into discussions of economic policy. The same may be said of "social capital" (the ability to work effectively with others). Participatory poverty assessments uncover some of the correlates of welfare and deprivation as experienced by the respondents. In his study in the Republic of Guinea, Shaffer (1998) found that, although consumption data revealed no relative deprivation of women vis-à-vis men, two other dimensions which disproportionately affect women surfaced clearly—excessive workload and lack of decision-making authority/respect. Graham and Felton (2005, p. 12) report that, in contrast to the US and Europe where women are on average happier than men, the opposite is true in Latin America, perhaps due to unequal gender rights.

In what is, to my knowledge, the most detailed analysis of the happiness evidence for Latin American countries, Graham and Felton (2005, p. 17) find that many of the patterns observed elsewhere hold up and that inequality in Latin America seems to make the poor (here the bottom two quintiles of people ranked by wealth) much less happy and the rich (the top quintile) moderately happier. Though the qualitative nature of the questions used to rank happiness makes any quantification of such effects problematic, the authors consider those effects to be large.

The combination of evidence to the effect that more income does make the individual better off than his counterparts with less income but that when everyone's income rises over time there is a smaller effect on average reported happiness is consistent with the general notion that people's welfare depends on relative status, which in modern societies is affected by relative income and consuming power. Given such attitudes, deprivation—the reason one is interested in poverty as a problem—can be alleviated mainly by reducing the degree of income inequality. But, as many authors have emphasized, a more basic implication of such a situation is that society is dysfunctional since, with satisfaction defined mainly in relative terms, there is no way to make everyone much better off. The gain of the low income person who is now closer in status to those above him is a loss to the latter, who can no longer enjoy the feeling of superiority which gave them satisfaction before. A society with attitudes less individualistic and competitive and more positively community or society oriented has the chance to benefit much more from economic advance. In short, the empirical evidence, especially that from the industrial countries, suggests that attitudinal change may be more important than economic growth, and that without the former the latter may remain largely irrelevant. Although this is less true of the developing countries, to the extent that they replicate the attitudinal patterns of the rich countries it will become their problem too. A key objective of any society should be to reduce the "zero-sum" component of what gives people satisfaction.

However important one considered economic inequality to be before taking account of the findings of the happiness literature, that importance is accentuated when it is taken into account. Inequality now matters not just because it implies low purchasing power for those towards the bottom of the income hierarchy, but also because the gap between them and those above them imposes an added psychological cost. From a measurement point of view this not only enhances the importance of having and using good quality data on income and consumption distribution, but also suggests the value of collecting information on other likely correlates of welfare[19] and on attitudes to inequality and poverty, studying their correlates, etc. Sociologists have advanced a good way in this direction but their work needs to be drawn on more extensively by economists and applied more directly to choices of economic policy. In Latin America the existence for about a decade of the Latinobarometro happiness surveys (used by Graham and Felton, 2005) and their considerable richness of information should continue to generate useful insights and lead to expansion of the database in new directions.

Key policy uses of distribution data: implications for what is needed

Judgments as to the most important gaps to be filled or refinements to be made to the battery of statistics available on inequality and poverty should be made with reference to the policy issues on which such improvements might bear. Where policy changes are expected or argued to influence the degree of poverty at an aggregate level, then overall poverty figures of adequate quality and without undue delay will be important. And where the mechanisms of the expected impact imply differing effects on different groups, it is important to have data that corresponds to and can throw light on those mechanisms.

Hypotheses relating to inequality and poverty tend to originate in one of two distinct ways. One type begins with the desire to understand the impacts of certain policies or phenomena on inequality. Another begins with the observation that inequality has changed significantly in either direction, thus offering an especially useful laboratory from which to learn about the factors influencing it. Whereas the first type of analysis focuses on a given policy and tries to trace its impacts, the second by nature considers all policies that might have played a role in the observed change in inequality. The data needs tend to be somewhat different depending on which type of analyses is being undertaken.

Where the hypothesis under consideration is a broad one (e.g. globalization has significantly worsened income distribution) good aggregate distribution data are a natural tool to help test it, but they are never sufficient by themselves since, given the inevitable presence of competing hypotheses, the overall data base is unlikely to be sufficient to sorting out their relative validity without complementary information. That complementary information can help to validate the hypothesis by tracing the phenomenon's presumed impact on different groups of people, as a complement to the analysis of its overall impact on distribution. Sometimes the types of data needed to assess whether the hypothesized mechanisms were in play are included as standard components of income distribution data sets. If the hypothesis relates to the impact of increasing educational levels, we have the advantage that the educational level of the individual is almost always reported together with income. If the hypothesis relates to size of the firms in which people work, such information is sometimes available but more often not. Accordingly, some uses of distribution data call for special modules to be added to questionnaires in order to permit a tracing of the mechanisms under discussion. At a third level, most causal analyses involving distribution data need to be complemented by other, independent information, for purposes of cross-checking, adding essential items, and so on, as per the examples below.

Some policies would not be expected to affect overall income or distribution levels enough to have a detectable effect in the aggregate data. In such cases data on the incomes of specific groups, together with their place in the bigger distributional picture will be the key ingredient to the analysis. Sometimes what is needed is a good picture of income structure such that it is possible to deduce *ex ante* the likely impact of a policy change. Thus, to predict the impact of an improvement in the quality of primary education on distribution, one needs to know where in the distribution the persons whose quality of education will be affected are, and have some idea of what will happen as a result of their getting better education.

Among approaches to identifying the impacts of policies on inequality and poverty, a broad trade-off exists between those which rely more heavily on the use of broad distribution data to test hypotheses and those which rely more heavily on subgroup income data plus complementary information. Consider, for example, the hypothesis that microcredit brings benefits to the poor by raising the productivity and incomes of the loan recipients. A first step in the validation of this hypothesis is to verify that the borrowers do see more income due to higher productivity in their enterprises. But such evidence would not by itself prove that the project helped the poor since there could be negative side effects of the loans on the businesses of the competitors of the loan recipients. It is more difficult to detect such side effects through direct investigation than to identify the positive effects on the presumed beneficiaries and hence it is difficult to estimate the net overall impact on the population. Here the avail-ability of more general income distribution data is important. Where the policy or phenomenon under analysis is of a magnitude such that it might be expected to influence, say, the average incomes of several deciles towards the bottom of the distribution, such effects may be best tested for with data on the incomes of those deciles. Approaching validation this way, however, gets one into the "competing explanations" problem; if one cannot take account of other possi-ble factors at work in determining trends in average income and its distribution, one falls victim to the "omitted variables" problem. The essential trade-off is thus between (i) the capacity to specify all major determinants of changes in income and its distribution well enough so that one does not have to trace the effects of the specific policy of interest at the microeconomic level to be reason-ably sure they are taking place and producing the final observed effect on income and its distribution; and (ii) the generation of enough detail about the income structure of the population to be able to verify more directly the mechanisms of policy impact. Where, for whatever reason, it is not feasible to model the impacts either of the policy under analysis or of other causal factors well enough to be able to study them effectively through their final impacts on income and its distribution (e.g. where too little is known about the lags with which they appear after the policy goes into play) then extra distributional detail and complementary information on the mechanisms linking the policy to the final outcomes will have a higher payoff. The two approaches are by definition complementary to each other, since it is preferable to be able to use both, as well as substitutes, since neither can ever be perfect. But with a given level of resources available for the two together, there is always the question of what combination is most effective.

Another complicated issue is the impact of market reforms on growth and inequality. As discussed in more detail below, the cross-country time series approach to identifying the impact of the various reforms, individually and as a group, is unlikely to provide reliable results given the many ambiguities about the mechanisms connecting these changes to the outcomes, and especially about the time lags involved between policy change and outcome change. These complexities, together with the great difficulty in specifying in an econometrically manageable way the other elements in the puzzle, like ongoing technical change, make such exercises very challenging, and unlikely to yield relatable results in the near future. It will therefore be important to have the needed combination of information on income structure and on other relevant variables so that the mechanisms hypothesized to connect liberalization and distributional outcomes can be traced in some detail. Exactly what data are needed on distribution is a matter for analysts to specify, but things like the distinction between earners connected to tradables production versus those connected to non-tradables production would be one obvious need. So, probably, would data on who is connected to firms of differing sizes and technologies.

Major issues in recent times whose distributional implications are important include:

- the impact of the recent market-friendly economic reforms, with special attention to trade reforms;
- agricultural development, especially in Africa;
- the impact of changes in technology;
- education and health policy;
- financial development and regulations on the financial system, including microfinance;
- small and medium enterprise (SME) policy;
- targeting of assistance to specific poor or vulnerable groups such as women, orphans, single parent families, families afflicted by HIV/AIDS, or the elderly through food aid, pensions, or subsidies for school attendance; and
- privatization [part of the first issue above but often discussed separately].

Several of these phenomena are included both because it is important to know what their distributional impact may be and because they are already hypothesized as candidates in explaining the marked increases in inequality which have plagued a number of the countries of the region at various points of time over the past quarter century. Attempts to unravel the *role of the market-friendly reforms* in that worsening serve as a useful example of what sort of information is needed, in the context of a probably complicated set of mechanisms. Of the several multicountry studies that have addressed this issue, the Inter-American Development Bank (IDB, 1997) and Morley (2001) employed similar data and econometric analysis but reached somewhat different results. The former concluded that the main worsening of income distribution was in the 1980s, with no further significant increases in the 1990s, and that the reforms—including the trade reforms—actually improved distribution in comparison with what it would otherwise have been as well as contributing to growth. Morley, working from the reform indices developed by the IDB authors but extending and improving them and applying a more thorough econometric analysis, concluded that the reforms had a modestly negative effect on distribution and a small positive impact on growth. Berry and associates' (Berry, 1998) series of country case studies judged that the frequent timing coincidence between the reforms (mainly trade reform) and the associated opening up and worsening inequality suggested a causal relationship.[20] Without much more detailed probing and comparison, it is not possible to sort out which of the existing studies, if indeed any of them, gets close to the facts of the matter. A prudent judgment might be that the truth probably lies between the Morley results (small negative impact on inequality) and a pessimistic reading of the Berry results in which all or nearly all of the distributional worsening that coincided with the reforms was caused by them. In the latter case, the reforms could have accounted for increases in the Gini coefficient of up to 5 percentage points in a number of the countries—but not in all, so that the average impact would be perhaps half that much.

Successful analysis of this issue would require both better distribution data, better complementary data on other variables (like the reform indices used[21]), better capacity to link income status of individuals and families to the hypothesized mechanisms (e.g. employment in production of tradables or nontradables, size and technology of employing firm), and more total effort to probe competing hypotheses, allow for differences across countries in the mechanisms involved, etc. Among the weaknesses in the distribution data per se have been ambiguity in several countries (including Colombia and Chile) as to which time series on inequality to use, as well as the twin weaknesses of serious underreporting of capital income and the very limited analysis of the impact of changing relative prices on real inequality. Both of these flaws create a serious possibility that the impact of the reforms was more negative than any of the studies has concluded, especially in the light of the findings reported by Cornia and Court (2001) on the role of interest income in observed increases in inequality in several developing countries.

Support for small agriculture

It has been widely argued that productive small scale agriculture is a key to equitable growth and development (Johnston and Clark, 1982). Most calculations show land productivity to be a more or less monotonically decreasing function of farm size (Binswanger, Deininger, and Feder, 1995; Lipton, 1993). Several authors note, however, that in many settings farms below a certain size are not sustainable so their operators eventually have to sell and go out of the business (Zimmerman and Carter, 2003). So is a land reform that breaks large farms into smaller units good for distribution and for poverty reduction or not? When can good support programs for small farms make the difference? Is their success related closely to the system of property rights and if so which systems are the best?[22] The ideal battery of information with which to address this set of issues would include: unusually good income and consumption surveys—they must be of above average quality to hope to get reliable information on the people in a sector where income is erratic and the economics of the business often complicated; and good data on the agricultural activities of families, of the sort usually collected in agricultural censuses, with the potential to link this data to the income and consumption data usually provided by household surveys, and which includes the income from non-agricultural activities. The data base should also include information on property rights, access to support services, and quality of relevant infrastructure. Data on land distribution and how it is changing are also important, together with income and production data over a period of time sufficient to permit identification of trends, and (very important) data on the non-agricultural incomes of families engaged in agriculture. Some data sets are satisfactory for part of this list of needs, but it is rare to be able to merge agricultural census type information with the other variables.

Technological change

It is arguable that the most negative factor in the increasing inequality witnessed in many developing countries over the past few decades has been the nature of the technological change impinging on them, with the arrival of the new information and communication technologies (ICT) and the dramatic spread of supermarkets being two of the most obvious components of the process. Broadly speaking, the premature arrival of inappropriately capital-intensive technologies is an important aspect of the process, perhaps even more so than when the concept became popular in development thinking in the 1970s (Stewart, 1977; Singer, 1982). The mechanisms and pace of technological change are associated in various ways with international economic integration—for example foreign direct investment plays a role, but the details are not well enough understood to permit reliable predictions as to when this process will be severely damaging to inequality and poverty and when it will not. Though there has been considerable research around ICT (Perez, 1994; Lall, 2004), very little has focused adequately on following the links whereby the new technology interfaces with inequality and poverty, except perhaps through the work on formal sector–informal sector and firm size relationships. Within Latin America it is a strong hypothesis that the widening productivity gaps by firm size (Stallings and Peres, 2000) have had a significant impact on income distribution through their impacts on different segments of the labor force, but little research has attempted to trace the chain of effects from newer technology through the productivity changes by groups of firms (e.g. categorized by size or type of technology) to the earnings of individual workers and their families. The modeling exercise carried out by Adelman and Robinson (1978) for Korea exemplifies one useful approach. Sometimes the technology choice will be the result of or co-caused with other patterns, such as the distribution of land rights. In such cases it is likely that the only way to identify the major sources of changes in inequality and poverty is very detailed country studies which use as a main source of information household surveys with inequality data, alongside a wide range of complementary information (here on technologies employed, among other things), collected around a series of competing hypotheses.

Health and education

Analysis of the distributional impact of health policy requires crossing data on health status, access to, and cost and quality of health services with data on income levels. Relevant over time data on groups presumably affected by health interventions (e.g. HIV/AIDS sufferers) can in a fairly straightforward way relate the resulting benefits to income levels. In cases where specific diseases are attacked (e.g. control of malaria) declining incidence can also be easily related to socio-economic status, as long as the health information is collected with appropriate frequency. The impact of more general health services is harder to identify with comparable precision. Since health status is a major component of welfare, and varies greatly by socio-economic status in many countries, such analysis is an important element of thinking about policy on welfare distribution. Recent promising efforts in this area include Knaul et al.'s (2005) look at the extent to which large (relative to income) health expenditures push families into poverty in Mexico and the potential for health insurance to prevent that outcome; studies of the determinants of the rich–poor gap in child health status (e.g. Wagstaff, 2002); and the overall impact of disease on the poor (Gwatkin and Guillet, 2000).

The effect of educational policies on inequality is an important but difficult research question, difficult in part because the effects on economic and more general well-being are delayed and more general than those of many health interventions. Economists and others have at times held out serious hopes that a better distribution of educational attainment could provide a feasible route, perhaps the only feasible route, to a significantly better distribution of income in many countries.[23] For Latin America, this hope has not been borne out, for reasons that need to be analyzed in more detail. Earnings gaps by level of skill have risen worldwide over the last couple of decades,[24] a pattern more often interpreted as reflecting the character of technical change during this period than what has happened or not happened on the educational front, though Londoño (1996) and IDB (1997), for example, do blame inadequate educational development. It would be surprising if the low and sometimes declining quality of primary and sometimes secondary education had not played a role. Although Latin America has achieved considerable increases in the coverage of education at these two levels, quality has not come along with quantity. Coverage usually comes last to the more marginal and hard to reach populations. With poorer students, less educational background in the home, and greater resistance on the part of teachers to working in these zones, it is almost a foregone conclusion that quality of education (as defined by the usual objective measures—performance in languages, maths, etc.) will be low. Only concerted and professional efforts, with the expenditures of relatively large amounts of resources, would be likely to reverse this pattern. Such is the background within which data on income distribution are used to try to sort out the distributional impacts of various patterns of educational advance and reform. The challenge of using the now widely available household survey data on income distribution to assess the impacts of educational change include, together with the universal need to worry about other factors which may be determinants of absolute and relative earnings of different people, several special ones:

1. the need for data on the quality (as well as the quantity) of education of people in the sample—data on test scores is now much more widely available than a couple of decades ago, but researchers are still sorting out how quality so measured relates to the subsequent payoff in economic and other terms;

2. the desirability of over time data for individuals, to allow analysis of the age profiles of earnings for quality-specific groups;

3. the need to deal with the impacts of labor market segmentation in the statistical analysis (Rosenzwieg, 2002);

4. the continuing challenge of measuring ability and motivation and their interactions with educational attainment;[25]

5. the lack of any very clear idea of how education pays off, in ways that help to understand the earnings gaps by level of education. This is relatively easier when the focus is on specific skills and groups like computer operators, but much less so when the group is people with primary school education engaged in a very wide range of activities.

In the cases both of health and education, it is desirable to understand the reasons for non-access to some services or to a better version of them.

Progress is being made in this challenging area, with a number of recent studies using micro-simulation based analysis to investigate the impact of educational changes on income distribution (e.g. the case studies presented in Bourguignon et al., 2005). This approach is probably the most promising at this time, although it will take some time for it to be effectively merged with the analysis of how economic structure and macroeconomic events and institutional patterns mediate the relationship in question. The increasing availability of test scores has given researchers new insights into important policy issues, such as the use of vouchers to give parents a greater say in their children's education and to increase competition among suppliers.[26]

Finance and financial reform

Financial development has been hailed in recent years as an important factor contributing to economic growth (Levine, 1997, 2003). The financial reforms which have been undertaken as part of the market-friendly reforms are also seen by some as contributing to economic equality; analysts have argued, on either theoretical (Balassa et al., 1986, p. 94) or empirical grounds (Jaramillo et al., 1993) or both, that ending financial repression would improve income distribution by tending to equalize access as between larger, better placed firms and smaller ones. It has been difficult to assess this hypothesis empirically, and the evidence is, at this point, inconclusive (Berry, 2004). International financial opening is more often seen as contributing to inequality by improving the credit access of large (international or national) firms relative to that of smaller and more labor-intensive competitors (Hawkins, 2000). Burgess and Pande (2003) provide what appears to be the most convincing evidence thus far that what one might call the "downward expansion" of the banking system to previously underserved regions can reduce inequality, though it must be noted that the expansion in question was not the result of market forces alone but rather what they term the "Indian social banking experiment."[27]

Much more attention has been given to microfinance as a poverty-reducing instrument. Though it is clear that much of the credit gets to at least fairly low income people, the empirical evidence on the magnitude of net social benefits remains scanty. Khandker's (1998) study seems to provide the most solid evidence that the benefit/cost ratio is good for the institutions in Bangladesh that he studied. The further step of linking those benefits to changes in income distribution has not thus far been taken, to my knowledge. In a few countries where the magnitude of microfinance is large enough, including Bangladesh, it would be worthwhile to undertake econometric tests of the overall microfinance–income distribution links. Otherwise, and this would be the general case in Latin America,[28] one must fall back on (and in any case should carry out) attempts to trace microcredit benefits and costs to those groups most likely affected by them, including non-borrowers. Our understanding of the impact on inequality of financial developments along the various paths mentioned above will need to rely on a microdata base which allows the analyst to connect income levels (both of individuals and of the firms where they work) with the financial system. To this end, special modules attached to household surveys can be quite productive.

Small and medium enterprise policy

Proponents of a flourishing SME sector argue that it uses generally appropriate technology, can achieve good levels of efficiency while at the same time being relatively labor intensive and thereby contributing to a relatively equitable distribution of income. Though comparisons suggest that countries with strong SME sectors suffer lower inequality than those with highly dualistic economies (where most of the capital is in the large scale sector and most of the workers in the informal or small scale sector), the required confirmation that size distribution is amenable to policy and that the distributional impact of an increased SME share is significantly positive has been hard to marshal, in part because of the few examples of a significant shift in size composition towards SMEs. Korea is the most cited case, with the SME share, at least in manufacturing, rising dramatically since the mid-1970s. Nugent and Yhee (2002, p. 113) noted the timing coincidence for Korea between the rapid rise of the SME sector after the mid-1970s and the decrease in inequality. Adelman and Robinson (1978) incorporated the size distribution of industry in their modeling exercise to study the trends in distribution in the same country. The SME sector has generally played a smaller role in Latin America than in many countries of East Asia, and it is urgent to understand what its potential is. To this end we need far more empirical analyses of the links between size, technology, and income distribution, based at least in part on more information about the size, technology, and labor productivity of the firms in which individuals work and their position in the distribution of income.

Targeting

Data on income distribution are important, almost by definition, in programs targeted either at the poor as a whole or at specific subgroups thereof. Targeting by income level requires either data on income itself or, more practically, data on good but simple proxies for income. As targeting programs evolve, the nature of the appropriate information base does as well, calling for a response from those in charge of such information. As is true of several of the other policy areas discussed, the need is not so much for more detail on incomes and their distribution per se as for more surrounding information, needed in this case to provide the useful proxies (characteristics of housing and other assets, health conditions, etc.).

The experience with targeting in Latin America and elsewhere has, in return, enriched our understanding of certain aspects and correlates of poverty, among them the dynamics and fluctuations related to the malady. Perhaps more important, the special problems of vulnerable groups: single parent families, orphans, and elderly people without family support deserve more attention, partly through their identification and study using household income and consumption surveys and partly through complementary data, including special modules attached to the household surveys. The analysis of poverty must be pushed increasingly towards distinctions among the poor according to their characteristics and the sources of their poverty. This general need is perhaps especially patent in Latin America, where poverty is no longer the norm.

Brazil's rural social security system, instituted in the 1990s, provides a safety net for the bulk of former workers in agriculture and other primary sector activities and has had a large effect on rural poverty levels through a cost of about 1 per cent of GDP (Schwarzer and Querino, 2002; Morley, 2003). It exemplifies the importance of group specific poverty policies. Gender inequalities can be relatively well described using normal household survey data but getting deeper into both the nature of the problem and the mechanisms at work requires a combination of additional information (especially on aspects of intrafamily inequality) and panel data to trace processes at work.

Privatization

Privatization has generated much controversy within developing countries; one contentious issue is its impact on income distribution and poverty. Outcomes appear to vary widely by country, industry involved, and the process (corruption has often worsened the distributional impact). Birdsall and Nellis (2002) conclude that most privatization programs appear to have worsened the distribution of assets and income, at least in the short run. Jones (2004, p. 5) concludes that "popular opinions on the negative distributional impact of privatization are not broadly supported by the available empirical evidence."[29] The difference between these two views may reflect that fact that Birdsall and Nellis included in their sample transition economies, where negative effects have in some cases been dramatic. Those economies aside, the outcome may depend a good deal on the efficiency of the public enterprise versus the private one, and the extent to which the latter will be subject to adequate competition or regulation. Good distribution data, linked to evidence on use of services (say electricity, water or telephones), can clarify many of the possible impacts on consumers and workers in these enterprises. Sometimes the distributional impact turns on whether privatization leads to an expansion of the service into lower income areas previously without it (Jones, 2004). Loss of jobs is usually unlikely to contribute to poverty since few people in families close to the poverty line are employed by public enterprise.

Summary and conclusions

Major improvements in the quality and frequency of income and consumption distribution data in Latin America have provided a useful base for assessing trends and analysing the factors (including policies) that have an impact on inequality. It seems likely that accuracy is now good enough in most countries to pick up significant changes in true inequality (however measured) as long as those changes are not concentrated in the components of income or consumption which are particularly badly measured—capital income accruing to upper income groups (including that from appreciation of assets), or infrequently measured—consumption of public goods. Ability to deal with changes in these components of income and consumption would require better data and/or a better understanding of when lower quality data sets are likely to be decent proxies for higher quality ones. Changes in the real distribution due to relative price changes between the consumption baskets of groups at different socio-economic levels can be analysed with existing data, though they seldom are, creating another possibly significant source of erroneous conclusions on inequality trends.

Arguably the highest potential pay-off among the easily feasible improvements to the standard data collection procedures is in the panel area. Deaton (1995, p. 1802) notes the benefits reaped from those of the World Bank's Living Standards Surveys which incorporated that feature.[30] But this is the sort of innovation to the traditional collection procedure that may not last unless there is expertise around, inside or outside the data collection agency, to keep it going.

Since the main source for checking on the degree of coverage of income and consumption surveys are the national accounts and their component parts, the accuracy of that source may constrain improvements in our understanding of distribution as much as do the household survey data themselves. Until household surveys are greatly improved from their present levels, other types of information will remain the main source on capital income.

The third major source of potential improvement is in the information that allows better testing of hypotheses about the determination of distribution and its changes. Some of that information is quite independent of the distribution data per se (e.g. indicators of market reforms) but much needs to be collected together with the distribution data so that it can be used jointly with the latter in statistical analysis. Some of what is needed is already collected in most surveys (e.g. data on educational level) but most is not (data on educational quality, data on type of firm in which the person works). The full range of information that would be useful cannot be collected frequently due to cost and limitations on length of interviews. For some analyses, just having the data once might answer most of the interesting questions. But often it is important to track changes. To that end some sort of rotating special module system is desirable. Some countries have something of this sort, but even in the best of cases the total provision of information is far below what it would be useful to have. At this point it appears likely that extension of the distribution-relevant data base in this direction is the highest priority in many countries. Aspiring to decent quality data on capital incomes is optimistic, whereas much reliable data helpful in the analysis of important issues can be collected with household surveys. Decisions on what to collect and how to do it need to involve the analysts who will be the ultimate users.

Notes

1. I have benefited from the comments of two referees of the chapter and from workshop participants.
2. Thus the 2002 Human Development Report (UNDP, 2002, pp. 194–5) gives a figure of 0.607 for Brazil (1998) and 0.423 for Uruguay (1989).
3. The potentially greater accuracy of consumption surveys has led to some cost-cutting attempts to measure expenditure through relatively simple questionnaires, but this also produces data of generally low quality.
4. In their baseline estimate, the Gini coefficient rises from the observed 0.450 to 0.508 as a result of the correction (Mistiaen and Ravaillon, 2003, p. 16).
5. ECLAC has undertaken over the years to present available data in an orderly way and IBD has invested in improving the data systems. At an earlier stage ECLAC systematically compared the expanded household survey income data with the national accounts, and in so doing provided much useful feel for the relative completeness of the household survey data (e.g. CEPAL, 1987). It did not, nor has anyone else to my knowledge, undertaken systematic reviews of the quality of the national accounts (and any other sources used for such checks) in Latin America.
6. At the high end of the spectrum, Rodriguez (2004, p. 330) suggests that the true Gini coefficient in Venezuela during the 1990s was above 0.60, even though that for labor incomes was around 0.4. (For this period most of the reported Gini coefficients for household income were in the mid to high 40s, according to the WIDER database on inequality.) His contention is that due inclusion of capital income would increase the Gini coefficient by much more than the 6 percentage points constituting the upper end of the range reported by Altimir. In allocating his estimate of capital income to individuals he uses the same procedure cited above—assuming the same degree of underreporting of such income for all those who reported any.

7. Berry (1987, p. 424) used the few cases for which two comparable figures were available to conclude that the ratio of Gini coefficients of consumption inequality tended to fall in the range 0.85–0.90 as high as the corresponding ones for income. Thus if the coefficient for income was about 0.5, a reasonable estimate of that for consumption would be 0.43–0.45. Some cross-country regressions to explain inequality have included a dummy variable to distinguish income from consumption data, reaching the same conclusion. De Ferranti et al. (2003, pp. 48–9) refer to the analysis by Elbers et al. (2003) in which a small 1996 pilot survey in parts of Brazil was used to estimate the national Gini for consumption, giving the conclusion that, at something under 0.5, it was far below the Gini for household per capita income of 0.6.

8. If, for example, a group of farmers had not received subsidized credit, the price of their product might have been higher, hence their nominal income higher, and so on. In the absence of implausibly sophisticated general equilibrium models, such analyses are seldom carried out.

9. A comparable problem arises when someone in a family makes choices on the consumption basket on behalf of the whole family. Where the chooser suffers inadequate information, as to the tastes of some family members, this constitutes misinformation. Some intrafamily decisions, though against the preference of the consumer, are good ones since the selector knows what is the right choice for the consumer better than the consumer. The same issue arises in government selection of levels and contents of public goods; the government may know either less well or better than the consumers what is good for them.

10. I am indebted to Luis Beccaria for this observation.

11. Canada's Centre for the Study of Living Standards has supported a number of studies on the implications of economic insecurity, e.g. the rising impermanence of jobs (see Osberg, 1998; Sharpe, 2002).

12. In an interesting study Neri and Thomas (2000) use Brazil's rotating panel design to analyze vulnerability to shocks and worker response. Studies of employment and poverty mobility have used the panels in Argentina, Costa Rica, Peru, and Mexico.

13. Paglin (1975) did the first major empirical study of this for the US.

14. Defining wealth inequality is as complicated, or more so, than defining income inequality. The broadest definitions might include not only all obvious forms of private wealth (land, real estate, financial assets, consumer durables) but also occupational pension rights, state pension rights (old age pension, etc.), and even human capital. Sometimes consumer durables are excluded, as are state pension rights, and human capital is to my knowledge never actually included. For a useful discussion see Davies and Shorrocks (2000).

15. See, for example, Ferreira et al. (2003) for Brazil. Gino et al. (2005) present a good review of price deflation across social groups.

16. This is presumably due in part to unhappy people having trouble finding jobs but longitudinal studies by psychologists have demonstrated that this is not the only cause (Oswald, 1997, p. 1822).

17. Rising average income does not appear to lead to anything like commensurate increases in average happiness. There is a significant cross-section relationship between happiness and income, but it is far from overwhelming. In the European data for 1975–86, 18.8 per cent of the bottom quintile report being "very happy"

compared with 28.4 per cent for the top one, while 26.7 per cent report being "not too happy" compared with 13.1 per cent for the top quintile (Di Tella et al., 1996). Part of this correlation would be due to the higher unemployment rates of the lower income groups. Over time the happiness of the unemployed shows much more fluctuation than that of the employed, for reasons as yet unexplained.

18. Though the results of Graham and Felton (2005), discussed below, do not point in this direction for Latin America, possibly because most of the countries are in the middle income range.

19. The use of more than one measure simultaneously calls for a multi-dimensional approach, discussed by Bourguignon and Chakravarty (2003).

20. The set of studies reported by Bulmer-Thomas (1996) points in this direction as well.

21. A serious flaw in many analyses in this area has been lack of attention to which index of trade reform to use, and to the relatively low correlation among some of the candidates (Pritchett, 1996).

22. Property rights reform may increase the concentration of land if liquidity-constrained farms are induced to sell to those already wealthier agents with access to credit (Carter and Olinto, 2003).

23. This hope was probably borne in part of desperation, as the belief solidified that income and consumption distribution are largely determined by the distribution of income producing assets (broadly defined), that land distribution could not be tampered with much due to the political resistance that attempts at land reform would face and have faced in Latin America, and that it is unrealistic to expect the distribution of non-agricultural capital to be anything but quite concentrated (as it tends to be in all capitalist countries). This left only human capital as a factor of production whose distribution could presumably be affected by public policy (that distribution is not highly concentrated in countries with relatively equitable income distribution, like Taiwan, but is highly concentrated in countries at the other end of the inequality spectrum, like Brazil) and which affects a substantial share of total income (since the labor share, including imputed labor income of the self-employed appears to be above 60 per cent in nearly all countries).

24. In Chile, for example, whereas private returns to primary and secondary education were at 12 per cent in 1970 and to higher education 18 per cent, by 1997 the former rates were unchanged but the higher had risen to 25 per cent (Contreras et al., 1998, cited by Mizala and Romaguera, 2000).

25. Early studies on the role of ability include Boissiere, Knight, and Sabot (1985), and Psacharopoulos and Vélez (1992)

26. In an interesting test of the effects of Chile's pioneering voucher system, whereby private subsidized schools have been allowed to compete with municipal (public) schools since the early 1980s, Mizala and Romaguera (2000, p. 409) report that, though the former outperform the latter in terms of average student scores when no other determinants of scores are taken into account, when such variables are added to the regressions the gap between subsidized private and municipal schools is small or nonexistent. Private fee-paying institutions continue to outperform the other two groups of schools, explicable by the higher level of inputs to the educational process.

27. In 1977 the central bank of India, with a view to reducing regional differences in financial development and in income, instituted a rule whereby in order to open a branch in an already banked location a public commercial bank had to open four branches in locations without banks. The authors conclude that the bulk of the very considerable rural bank expansion which followed was the result of this policy. They also report (Burgess and Pande, 2003, p. 12) that rural poverty reduction was more rapid in financially more developed states both before 1977 and after 1990 (when the program was ended) but that pattern was reversed between those two years.
28. Westley (2001) discusses the impact of financial market policies, microcredit, and credit unions on inequality in Latin America.
29. An interesting recent study by Galiani et al. (2005) finds that in districts where water was privatized in Argentina in the 1990s child mortality fell overall by 8 per cent (relative to districts where it was not) and the impact was largest (26 per cent) in the poorest areas. This impact came through the reduction of water-related diseases.
30. See also Rosenzweig (2003).

Bibliography

Adelman, I. and Robinson, R. (1978) *Income Distribution Policy in Developing Countries: A Case Study of Korea*. Stanford University Press for the World Bank.

Altimir, O. (1987) 'Income Distribution Statistics in Latin America and their Reliability'. *Review of Income and Wealth*, 33(2), pp. 111–55.

—— (1998) 'Income Distribution and Poverty through Crisis and Adjustment'. In A. Berry (ed.) *Poverty, Economic Reform and Income Distribution in Latin America*, Boulder, Colo.: Lynne Rienner Publishers.

Balassa, B., Bueno, G. M., Kuczynski, P-P., and Simonsen, M. H. (1986) *Toward Renewed Economic Growth in Latin America*. Colegio de Mexico, Mexico City, Institute for International Economics, Washington DC, and Fundação Getulio Vargas, Rio de Janeiro.

Behrman, J., Birdsall, N., and Szekely, M. (2000) 'Economic Reform and Wage Differentials in Latin America'. Working Paper 435, Inter-American Development Bank, Washington DC.

Berry, A. (1987) 'Evidence on Relationships among Alternative Measures of Concentration: A Tool for Analysis of LDC Inequality'. *Review of Income and Wealth*, 33(4), pp. 417–29.

—— (1998) *Poverty, Economic Reform, and Income Distribution in Latin America*. Boulder, Colo.: Lynne Rienner Publishers.

—— (2003) 'Methodological and Data Challenges to Identifying the Impacts of Globalization and Liberalization (GL) on Inequality'. Paper prepared for United Nations Research Institute on Social Development.

—— (2004) 'Finance and Pro-Poor Growth'. Paper prepared as part of Pro-poor Economic Growth Research Studies, Development Alternative Incorporated and Boston Institute of Development Economics for USAID.

Bhatia, K. (1972) 'Capital Gains and the Aggregate Consumption Function?' *American Economic Review*, 62(5), pp. 866–79.

Binswanger, H. P., Deininger, K., and Feder, G. (1995) 'Power, Distortions, Revolt and Reform in Agricultural Land Relations'. In J. Behrman and T. N. Srinivasan (eds.) *Handbook of Development Economics, Volume 3B*, Amsterdam: Elsevier.

Birdsall, N. and Nellis, J. (2002) 'Winners and Losers: Assessing the Distributional Impact of Privatization'. Working Paper No. 6, Center for Global Development, Washington DC.

Boissiere, M., Knight, J., and Sabot, R. (1985) 'Earnings, Schooling, Ability and Cognitive Skills'. *American Economic Review*, 75, pp. 1016–30.

Bourguignon, F. and Chakravarty, S. (2003) 'The Measurement of Multi-Dimensional Poverty'. *Journal of Economic Inequality*, 1(1), pp. 25–49.

—— Ferreira, F., and Lustig, N. (2005) *The Microeconomics of Income Distribution Dynamics in East Asia and Latin America*. Washington DC: The World Bank and Oxford University Press.

Bravo, D., Contreras, D., and Millan, I. (2000) 'The Distributional Impact of Social Expenditure in Chile'. In *Poverty and Income Distribution in a High-Growth Economy: The Case of Chile 1987–1998*, Washington DC: The World Bank.

Bulmer-Thomas, V. (ed.) (1996) *The New Economic Model in Latin America and its Impact on Income Distribution and Poverty*. New York and London: St Martin's Press in association with the Institute of Latin American Studies.

Burgess, R. and Pande, R. (2003) 'Do Rural Banks Matter? Evidence from the Indian Social Banking Experiment'. STICERD Suntory Centre, London School of Economics and Political Science, Discussion Paper No. 40.

Carter, M. C. and Olinto, P. (2003) 'Getting Institutions "Right" for Whom? Credit Constraints and the Impact of Property Rights on the Quantity and Composition of Investment'. *American Journal of Agricultural Economics*, 85(1).

Comisión Económica para América Latina y el Caribe (1987) *Antecedentes de la distribución del ingreso: Argentina, 1953–1982*. Santiago: CEPAL.

—— (2004), *Panorama Social de América Latina, 2002–2003*. Santiago: CEPAL.

Contreras, D., Bravo, D., and Medranao, P. (1998) 'Measurement Error and Skill Bias in Estimating the Returns to Schooling in Chile'. Mimeo, Department of Economics, University of Chile.

Cornia, G. A. (ed.) (2004) 'Inequality, Growth and Poverty: An Overview of Changes over the Last Two Decades'. In Cornia, G. A. (ed.) *Inequality, Growth, and Poverty in an Era of Liberalization and Globalization*. Oxford and New York: Oxford University Press.

—— and Court, J. (2001) *Inequality, Growth and Poverty in the Era of Liberalization and Globalization*. Helsinki: UNU-WIDER.

Davies, J. B. and Shorrocks, A. (2000) 'The Distribution of Wealth'. In A. B. Atkinson and F. Bourguignon (eds.) *Handbook of Income Distribution*, North-Holland.

—— —— (2005) 'Wealth Holdings in Developing and Transition Countries'. Paper prepared for the Luxembourg Wealth Study conference on Construction and usage of Comparable Microdata on Wealth, Perugia, January 27–9.

Deaton, A. (1995) 'Data and Econometric Tools for Development Analysis'. In J. Behrman and T. N. Srinivasan (eds.) *Handbook of Development Economics, Volume 3A*, Elsevier.

De Ferranti, D., Perry, G., Ferreira, F., and Walton, M. (2004) *Inequality in Latin America: Breaking with History*. Washington DC: World Bank.

Diener, E. and Diener, C. (1995) 'The Wealth of Nations Revisited: Income and the Quality of Life'. *Social Indicators Research*, 36(3), pp. 275–86.

Di Tella, R., MacCulloch, R., and Oswald, A. J. (1996) 'The Macroeconomics of Happiness'. Mimeo, Oxford and Warwick.

Drèze, J. (1999) *The Economics of Famine*. Edward Elgar.

Elbers, C., Lanjouw, L., Lanjouw, P., and Leite, P. G. (2003) 'Poverty and Inequality in Brazil: New Evidence from Combining PPV-PNAD Data'. Washington DC: World Bank.

Easterlin, R. A. (1974) 'Does Economic Growth Improve the Human Lot? Some Empirical Evidence'. In P. A. David and M. W. Reder (eds.) *Nations and Households in Economic Growth: Essays in Honor of Moses Abramovitz*, New York and London: Academic Press.

—— (ed.) (2002) *Happiness in Economics*. Cheltenham, UK: Edward Elgar.

Ferreira, F., Lanjouw, P., and Neri, M. (2003) 'A Robust Poverty Profile for Brazil Using Multiple Data Sources'. *Revista Brasileira de Economia*, 57(1), pp. 59–92.

Frank, R. (1997) 'The Frame of Reference as a Public Good'. *Economic Journal*, 107(445), pp. 1832–47.

Galiani, S., Gertler, P., and Schargrodsky, E. (2005) 'Water for Life: The Impact of the Privatization of Water Services on Child Mortality'. *Journal of Political Economy*, 113(1), pp. 83–120.

Gino, E., Lopez, H., and Server, L. (2005) 'Getting Real About Inequality: Evidence from Brazil, Colombia, Mexico and Peru'. Mimeo, World Bank.

Graham, C. and Felton, A. (2005) 'Does Inequality Matter to Individual Welfare: An Initial Exploration Based on Happiness Surveys From Latin America'. CSED Working Paper No. 38, Brookings Institution, Washington DC.

Gwatkin, D. R. and Guillet, M. (2000) 'The Burden of Disease Among the Global Poor'. Washington DC: World Bank, Human Development Network.

Hawkins, P. (2000) *Financial Constraints and the Small Open Economy*. PhD dissertation, Stirling University.

Hulme, D. and Shepherd, A. (2003) 'Conceptualizing Chronic Poverty'. *World Development*, 31, pp. 403–23.

Jaramillo, F., Schiantarelli, F., and Weiss, A. (1993) *The Effect of Financial Liberalization on the Allocation of Credit: Panel Evidence for Ecuador*. Washington DC: World Bank.

Inter-American Development Bank (1997) *Economic and Social Progress in Latin America: Latin America After a Decade of Reforms*. Washington, DC: IDB.

Johnston, B. F. and Clark, W. C. (1982) *Redesigning Rural Development: A Strategic Perspective*. Baltimore: Johns Hopkins University Press.

Jones, L. P. (2004) 'Privatization and the Poor: Issues and Evidence'. Paper prepared as part of Pro-poor Economic Growth Research Studies, Development Alternative Incorporated and Boston Institute of Development Economics for USAID.

Khandker, S. (1998) *Fighting Poverty with Microcredit: Experience in Bangladesh*. New York: Oxford University Press.

Knaul, F. M., et al., (2005) *Preventing Impoverishment, Promoting Equity and Protecting Households from Financial Crisis: Universal Health Insurance Through Institutional Reform in Mexico*. Mexico: Fundación Para la Salud (FUNSALUD).

Kuznets, S. (1953) *Shares of Upper Income Groups in Income and Savings*. National Bureau of Economic Research.

Lall, S. (2004) 'The Employment Impact of Globalization in Developing Countries'. In E. Lee and M. Vivarelli (eds.) *Understanding Globalization, Employment and Poverty Reduction*, Houndsmills, UK and New York: Palgrave Macmillan.

Levine, R. (1997) 'Financial Development and Economic Growth: Views and Agenda'. *Journal of Economic Literature*, 35 (June), pp. 688–726.

—— (2003) 'More on Finance and Growth: More Finance More Growth'. *Federal Reserve Bank of St. Louis*, 85(4), pp. 31–46.

Lipton, M. (1993) 'Land Reform as Unfinished Business: The Evidence Against Stopping'. *World Development*, 21(4).

Londoño de la Cuesta, J. L. (1996) *Poverty, Inequality, and Human Capital Development in Latin America, 1950–2025*. Washington: World Bank.

Majul, L. (1997) *Los nuevos ricos de la Argentina: tiburones al acecho: Julio Ramos, Manuel Antelo, Alfredo Coto, Carlos Avila*. Buenos Aries: Editorial sudamericana.

McKay, A. and Lawson, D. (2003) 'Assessing the Extent and Nature of Chronic Poverty in Low Income Countries'. *World Development*, 31(3), pp. 425–39.

Ministerio de Planificación y Cooperación (1990) *Programas sociales: su impacto en los hogares chilenos, casen 1990*. Santiago de Chile: MIDEPLAN.

Miranda, A. (2000) *Dossier Paraguay: los dueños de grandes fortunas*. Asunción: Miranda & Asociados.

Mistiaen, J. A. and Ravaillon, M. (2003) 'Survey Compliance and the Distribution of Incomes'. World Bank Policy Research Working Paper #2956.

Mizala, A. and Romaguera, P. (2000) 'School Performance and Choice: The Chilean Experience'. *Journal of Human Resources*, 35(2), pp. 392–417.

Morley, S. A. (2001) *The Income Distribution Problem in Latin America and the Caribbean*. Santiago: ECLAC.

—— (2003), 'Reducing Poverty in Brazil: Lessons Learned and Challenges for the Future'. Prepared as part of Pro-poor Economic Growth Research Studies, carried out by Development Alternative Incorporated and Boston Institute of Development Economics for USAID.

Neri, M. and Thomas, M. (2000) *Household Response to Labor Market Shocks in Brazil, 1982–99*. Rio de Janeiro: Fundacio Getulio Vargas.

Nugent, J. B. and Yhee, S-J. (2002) 'Small and Medium Enterprises in Korea: Achievements, Constraints and Policy Issues'. *Small Business Economics*, 18(1–3).

Osberg, L. (1998) *An Index of Economic Well-being for Canada*. Ottawa: Human Resources Development Canada, Applied Research Branch.

Oswald, A. (1997) 'Happiness and Economic Performance'. *Economic Journal*, 107(464), pp. 334–49.

Paglin, M. (1975) 'The Measurement and Trend of Inequality: A Basic Revision'. *American Economic Review*, 65(4), pp. 598–609.

Perez, C. (1994) 'Technical Change and the New Context of Development'. In L. Mytelka (ed.) *South-South Cooperation in Global Perspective*, Paris: OECD.

Pritchett, L. (1996a) 'Measuring Outward Orientation in Developing Countries: Can It Be done?' *Journal of Development Economics*, 49(2), pp. 307–35.

Psacharopoulos, G. and Vélez, E. (1992), 'Schooling, Ability and Earnings in Colombia, 1988'. *Economic Development and Cultural Change*, 40(3), pp. 629–43.

Ravallion, M. (1987) *Markets and Famines*. Oxford: Clarendon Press.

Rodriguez, F. (2004) 'Factor Shares and Resource Booms: Accounting for the Evolution of Venezuelan Inequality'. In G. A. Cornia (ed.) *Inequality, Growth, and Poverty in an Era of Liberalization and Globalization*, Oxford and New York: Oxford University Press.

Rogler, L. H. Malgady, R. G., and Rodriguez, O. (1989) *Hispanics and Mental Health: A Framework for Research*. Robert E. Krieger Publishing Company.

—— and Hollingshead, A. B. (1965) *Trapped: Families and Schizophrenia*. Wiley.

Rosenzwieg, M. R. (2002) 'Schooling, Economic Grwoth and Aggregate Data'. In G. Saxonhouse and T. N. Srinivasan (eds.) *Development, Duality, and the International Economic Regime: Essays in Honor of Gustav Ranis*, Ann Arbor: University of Michigan Press.

—— (2003) 'Payoffs from Panels in Low-Income Countries: Economic Development and Economic Mobility'. *American Economic Review*, 93(2), pp. 112–17.

Schneider, M. (2004) *The Distribution of Wealth*. Cheltenham, UK and Northampton, Mass.: Edward Elgar.

Schwarzer, H. and Querino, A. C. (2002) 'Benefiions sociais e Pobrreza: Programas Nao Contribuvios de Seguridade Social Brasileira'.' Sao Paulo Instituto de Pesquisas Economicas e Administrativas (IPEA), Working Paper 929.

Scitovsky, T. (1976) *The Joyless Economy*. Oxford: Oxford University Press.

Selowsky, M. (1979) *Who Benefits from Public Expenditure? A Case Study of Colombia*. Oxford: Oxford University Press for the World Bank.

Shaffer, P. (1998) 'Gender, Poverty and Deprivation: Evidence from the Republic of Guinea'. *World Development*, 26(12).

Sharpe, A. (2002) *The Review of Economic Performance and Social Progress 2002; Towards a Social Understanding of Productivity*. Ottawa: Institute for Research on Public Policy.

Singer, H. (1982) *Technologies for Basic Needs*. Geneva: International Labour Office.

Siregar, M. G. (1995) *Indonesia's Financial Liberalization; An Empirical Analysis of 1981–1988 Panel Data*. Singapore: Institute of Southeast Asian Studies.

Stallings, B. and Peres, W. (2000) *Growth, Employment and Equity: The Impact of the Economic Reforms in Latin America and the Caribbean*. UNECLAC and the Brookings Institution.

Stewart, F. (1977) *Technology and Underdevelopment*. Macmillan.

United Nations Development Programme (2002) *Human Development Report 2002: Deepening Democracy in a Fragmented World*. New York: Oxford University Press.

Vélez, Carlos Eduardo (1996) *Gasto social y desigualdad: logros y extravíos*. Bogota: Departamento Nación de Planeación, Misión Social.

Wagstaff, A. (2002) *Inequalities in Health in Developing Countries: Swimming Against the Tide?* Washington DC: World Bank.

Westley, G. D. (2001) 'Can Financial Market Policies Reduce Income Inequality?' Sustainable Development Technical Series. Washington DC: Inter-American Development Bank.

Wolff, E. N. (1996) 'International Comparisons of Wealth Inequality'. *Review of Income and Wealth*, 42(4), pp. 433–51.

Zimmerman, F. J. and Carter, M. R. (2003) 'Asset Smoothing, Consumption Smoothing and the Reproduction of Inequality under Risk and Subsistence Constraints'. *Journal of Development Economics*, 71(2), pp. 233–60.

12

The Changing Nature of Urban Poverty in China[1]

Carl Riskin[2] and Qin Gao[3]

Introduction

Poverty in China has famously declined since the beginning of the reform period in the late 1970s. Most of the decline occurred in rural areas, where the great bulk of poverty was located in the past. In this chapter, we explore some of the unknown or poorly understood dimensions of *urban* poverty in China and its evolution over time, from the early state of the reform and transition period until the beginning of the present century. Urban absolute poverty was, by most accounts, insignificant in size before the reform period began in the late 1970s, and generally ignored both then and afterwards, when it started to increase. Only recently has research in China and abroad begun to focus on the urban poor.

In the pre-reform era, urban residence was restricted, food rationed, and rural–urban migration thus difficult or impossible to undertake. Employment at state-set wages was guaranteed in urban areas. Under these conditions, while urban living standards were meager and spartan, there was little absolute poverty, with the exception of those unable to work. As Hussain (2005) puts it, "There were poor people in urban areas and the living standard was generally low. However, poverty relief was confined to the small section of the urban population characterized by 'three no's': no ability to work, no savings or other income source, and no relatives to depend on." In the 1990s, however, urban poverty was increasingly perceived to be a problem. Hussain points to several changes that gave rise to this perception: the number of urban poor was growing; income inequality increased, making the urban poor stand out more clearly; and the new urban poor, unlike in the past, were often able to work but were no longer guaranteed a job.

Even when urban poverty began to attract attention, it was treated separately from rural poverty. A different poverty line was used, reflecting not only rural–urban differences in cost of living but also different expectations of living standards. The issues raised by the idea of a single poverty line for all of China are similar to those raised by a single global poverty line, such as the World Bank's PPP$1-a-day line. One such issue is the necessarily "relative" character of even "absolute" poverty lines. While these are usually based on physiological requirements, such as minimum caloric intake, they also encompass the idea that the individual should be able to participate fully in society. What is required to meet this standard varies among countries and cultures and increases as living standards improve with economic development. Thus, national poverty lines are correlated with per capita GDP. If a global poverty line is tightly defined by minimum physiological standards, it risks neglecting entirely the social aspects of poverty that can isolate and oppress people, even when they are fed and sheltered at physiologically adequate levels. While it would be a signal accomplishment if everyone in the world had adequate nourishment, shelter, and health care, this would not by itself mean the end of absolute poverty.[4]

This problem is particularly relevant to China because of the long-time administered separation of urban from rural society. While income levels and expectations might have been quite different in the two sectors even without this wall separating them, the existence of the wall essentially eliminated the equalizing force of migration and enabled the state to create a monotonic urban environment without serious poverty and with a living standard far above the rural. Urban residents enjoyed full employment, job security, and a full array of social benefits, none of which were available to their rural cousins.[5] What was regarded as "poor" in urban society would have amounted to doing quite well in much of the countryside, whereas real rural poverty was unimaginable in the cities. Thus the estimates of Chinese poverty in terms of the World Bank's PPP$1-a-day line excluded significant urban poverty until recently because virtually nobody in urban China had less income than that.[6]

What has happened to urban poverty in China? There are different and conflicting "stylized facts" about China's urban poverty. One belief is that it emerged only in the 1990s as a result of state-owned enterprise (SOE) restructuring, inflation, and the disappearance of guaranteed full employment. This implies that urban poverty increased from the 1970s until the early years of the new century. A contrary view is that urban poverty was quite high in the 1970s and fell, like rural poverty, as a result of rapid economic growth and/or recent changes in government policy emphasizing the establishment of new social benefit programs and a more effective safety net. In this chapter, we review some literature on this question, and then use national household survey data to throw further light on China's urban poverty.

Our analysis is based upon the three-round China Household Income Project (CHIP) surveys of household income carried out by an international team under the aegis of the Institute of Economics, Chinese Academy of Social Science.[7] The CHIP studies defined household disposable income to include direct subsidies, income in kind, and the rental value of owned housing, in keeping with standard international practice. Income thus defined has exceeded income as officially defined and has changed differently, as well, especially in urban areas where formerly large subsidies faded away while rental value of owned housing burgeoned with the housing reform (Khan and Riskin, 2001, 2005). After summarizing available estimates of the size and trends of urban poverty, we use an urban poverty line fashioned by Khan (Khan and Riskin, 2001; Khan, 2004) to examine the changing characteristics of China's urban poor, and then explore whether recent declines in urban poverty are the fruits of the direct benefits and safety net programs that China has been establishing.

Poverty measures and trends

Urban poverty trends depend upon chosen urban poverty lines, and of these there is some variety in China, which lacks an official urban poverty line. As layoffs from state enterprises and unemployment increased in the 1990s, however, many towns and cities constructed diagnostic poverty lines as aids to policy-making.[8] These have been aggregated to provide a national urban poverty line or, in one case, two separate lines for inland and coastal provinces respectively. A single national urban line, calculated by the National Bureau of Statistics (NBS) for the years 1991 to 2000, is shown in Table 12.1. This line is two to three times as high as the rural poverty line.

There is also, of course, the World Bank's PPP$1-a-day and $2-a-day lines, the purpose of which is really to facilitate international comparisons but which

Table 12.1. "Diagnostic" urban poverty lines of the NBS (CNY)

Year	A	B
1991	752	
1992	837	
1993	993	
1994	1,300	
1995	1,547	
1996	1,671	1,850
1997		1,890
1998		1,880
1999		1,860
2000		1,875

Note: The two columns differ in the prices used for costing basic necessities.
Source: Asian Development Bank (2004).

302

Table 12.2. Headcount poverty rates, China (%)

Poverty line	1981	1990	2004	2007
New World Bank PPP$1 poverty line	71–77		13–17	
World Bank "cost of basic needs" poverty line (= old PPP$1 line)[1]	64	33	10	7

[1] The World Bank "cost of basic needs" poverty line coincides with its old $1/day PPP line (by chance, not construction) and remains the basis for the Bank's poverty assessments in China (from personal communication with David Dollar).
Source: World Bank, 2008: Appendix

have been applied to urban China. The poverty rates generated by these lines are shown in Table 12.4 for most years between 1990 and 1999. The $1-a-day line is so low as to essentially eliminate urban poverty, but the $2-a-day line results in poverty rates significantly above zero. However, the World Bank has abandoned its use of GDP PPP conversion rates for measuring poverty on the grounds that the market basket consumed by the poor is a much narrower one, heavily dominated by food and other basic necessities.[9] The Bank has issued some preliminary results of its project to construct and apply special poverty conversion rates. Table 12.2 shows *national* headcount poverty rates (i.e. including both urban and rural populations) for selected years using the new PPP$1 line, as adjusted for poverty measurement purposes, as well as the old PPP line:

The new PPP$1 a day poverty line raises the headcount poverty rate over that generated by the old one in both early and late years. Because the rise is higher for 1981 than for 2004, the *decline* in poverty generated by the new line is actually greater: some 59 per cent of the population was lifted above the new PPP poverty line, compared with 54 per cent using the old one. However, the application of a recently derived PPP exchange rate to the China of twenty-five years ago, when prices were quite different, is a questionable procedure.

Ravallion and Chen (2007) calculated an urban equivalent of the very low official rural poverty line which also eliminates urban poverty, but this line has not been seriously entertained for application to urban China. However, they also developed a new urban poverty line in collaboration with the NBS. The new line is based upon province-specific food bundles valued at median province prices. The food bundles, in turn, are taken from the actual food consumption of the urban population lying between the lowest 15th and 25th percentiles nationally. They are scaled up or down to reach 2,100 calories per person per day with a further constraint imposed that food grains provide 75 per cent of calories. Non-food consumption is then added, based on actual non-food spending of households whose *total* expenditures equaled the food poverty line. This yielded an urban poverty line of CNY1,200 (2002 prices), some 41 per cent higher than the rural poverty line (a differential equal to the estimated difference in cost of living between town and country), worked out in a similar manner. Quite austere, this line exceeds the average food expenditure of the poorest urban decile by only 6.4 per cent in 2002.[10] It is more than a third lower than the diagnostic urban poverty line used by the NBS and reported in Table 12.1 which, like "most studies on poverty in the PRC", put the urban poverty line at two to three times the rural one (GHK and International Institute for Environment and Development, 2004).[11]

A study of poverty based on data from the CHIP surveys in 1995 and 2002 (Khan, 2004) found sharp reductions in urban poverty between those two dates. Khan's urban poverty threshold is also based upon a food consumption level of 2,100 calories per day, but it is much higher than the Ravallion and Chen line.[12] Hussain (2002; see also Hussain, 2005) in a study carried out for the Asian Development Bank, used methods similar to Khan in estimating urban poverty and found similar results. Hussain had access to the 1998 urban household survey of the NBS, with a sample of 17,000 households from all thirty-one provinces of China. His poverty line is also based on a 2,100 calorie daily diet. The relevant food bundle is chosen from the actual consumption pattern of the lowest quintile of the population, ranked by expenditure per capita (excluding expenditure on consumer durables) and then scaled up or down to meet the 2,100 calories requirement. The non-food component of the poverty line is then estimated by regression as predicted non-food expenditure of those whose expenditure on food just equals the food poverty line. The provincial urban poverty lines in 1998 generated by this method range from CNY1,616 in Shanxi Province to CNY3,118 in Beijing Municipality and the national mean is CNY2,310, quite close to the one derived by Khan (CNY2,291 in 1995, CNY2,534 in 2002), and similar in the ratio of poverty threshold to mean per capita income (Table 12.3).

A similar method was also used by Meng et al. (2005, 2007), and applied to a portion of the government's urban household income and expenditure survey samples for 1986–2000 for twenty-nine of China's thirty-one provinces.[13] Their poverty lines are calculated for individual provinces to reflect differences in prices and tastes, and are estimated in a manner that allows for changes in the poverty food bundle and substitutions between food and non-food items, as relative prices and tastes change. They do not provide an average national poverty line, but their provincial lines in 2000 range from CNY1,730 (Anhui Province) to CNY3,771 (Shanghai).

There are thus various differences in the way different poverty lines have been constructed. A striking element of these differences is the variation in ratio of urban to rural poverty threshold. This ranges from a 41 per cent differential in the case of the Ravallion and Chen line, based upon estimated urban–rural cost of living differences, to a multiple of two or three (as in the case of the government's diagnostic poverty lines), much higher than can be explained by such differences. The well-known justification for such a wide gap is that so-called absolute poverty lines, although anchored to a biological standard (such as 2,100 kilocalories per day), generally include a relative component: they express a minimum standard of living judged necessary in a given social setting not only to survive physically and reproduce, but also to participate in society. This norm changes as standards of living advance, just as it differs among countries of different levels of development. It is not unreasonable, in a country with a rural population that for many years was walled off from the urban allowing large differences in real income to develop, for the absolute poverty lines greatly to diverge (Khan and Riskin, 2001).

One useful way of comparing poverty lines is to examine their respective ratios to average urban per capita income. This is done in Table 12.3, which illustrates the considerable range of austerity embodied by the various thresholds. The Ravallion and Chen line is at the austere end of the spectrum, at only 15.6 per cent of mean urban per capita income in 2002, compared to 30 per cent for the government's diagnostic line in 2000.[14] It generates poverty rates that hover at or below 1 per cent of the urban population over the entire period from 1981–2002, with the exception of a few years in the early and late 1980s and 1990–1 (Table 12.4). This includes the period from the mid-1990s on when layoffs from re-structuring state enterprises created a widespread perception that urban poverty was becoming a serious problem. At the top of the spectrum are the Khan (1995) and Hussain (1998) lines, which come to 40 per cent and 38 per cent, respectively, of mean per capita income.

According to the Ravallion and Chen headcount rates, there were a total of only 2.5 million urban poor among the 400 odd million urban residents in 2000, a poverty rate of 0.63 per cent. In contrast, China's Ministry of Civil Affairs, which is responsible for urban poverty relief, stated that in September 2000 there were approximately 14 million urban residents with incomes below

Table 12.3. Alternative urban poverty lines and their relation to average income

	Year	Ratio of PL to national mean urban income (%)
NBS Diagnostic Line	2000	30
World Bank original PPP$1	1995	17
World Bank original PPP$2	1995	34
Khan 1995	1995	40
Khan 2002 (excluding migrants)	2002	26
Khan 2002 (including migrants)	2002	28
Hussain 1998 (income-based)	1998	38
Meng et al. 2005[1]	2000	22–28
Ravallion and Chen 2007 (new PL)	2002	16

Note: "Mean urban income" is urban per capita disposable income as reported in the Statistical Yearbook of China, except in the case of the Khan estimates, where it is the China Household Income Project estimate of urban per capita disposable income as defined in Khan and Riskin (2001).

[1] Meng et al.'s poverty lines are province-specific, to take into account differences in cost of living and taste. The percentages given are ratios of the lowest and highest provincial lines to the national mean urban disposable income.

the local poverty lines, which would have amounted to a poverty rate of 3.1 per cent. In 2007, some 22 million people were said to be eligible for minimum livelihood supplements, or about 3.9 per cent of the urban population (Xinhua, 2007). An earlier Xinhua report quoted unnamed economists as claiming that urban poverty was between 6 and 8 per cent (Xinhua, 2004). While still modest, these rates do not suggest that urban poverty was nonexistent in China.

The minimum livelihood line, from which several of these rates derive and which governs benefits eligibility, varies from place to place in accordance with local budget constraints. Hussain (2002, 2005) provides some examples of the poverty lines established by individual cities and towns as the basis for their minimum livelihood subsidy allocations as of late 2000. These range from CNY2,400–3,828 in annual amount in the biggest cities and municipalities, to CNY1,320–1,680 in provincial capital cities and CNY935–1,320 in small, county level towns. Note that Chinese cities and towns, whose benefits programs were dependent on their budget resources and which were not inclined to be overly generous, had substantially higher minimum livelihood lines than the Raval-lion and Chen CNY1,200 line except for the smallest group, the county towns. They range from 14.9 per cent to 60.8 per cent of the national average urban per capita income for 2000.[15]

The poverty headcount rate for 1998 generated by Hussain's line ranges from 4.73 per cent of the urban population (14.7 million people) to 11.87 per cent (37.1 million), depending on whether the poverty line is interpreted as an income line or an expenditure line respectively. Similarly, Khan's line generates urban poverty rates of 8.0 per cent in 1995 and 2.2 per cent in 2002. Meng et al.'s poverty rates range from 5.5 to 1.9 per cent. Shown in Table 12.4, these three sets of numbers are more consistent with other information about devel-opments in urban China than the very low urban poverty headcount rates generated by the more austere urban lines. A striking finding of Hussain's study is that the urban poverty rate is highly sensitive to the poverty line, meaning that a large share of the urban population has incomes located close to the poverty line. For instance, raising it by 25 per cent more than doubles the income poverty rate, from 4.73 per cent to 11.07 per cent.

These headcount rates and others based upon official surveys of urban house-hold income exclude migrants living in cities but lacking an urban *hukou* (household registration). Mostly from rural areas, such migrants have com-prised an increasingly large proportion of China's urban population since the 1980s. Estimates based on China's 2000 population census put the total num-ber of migrants living in Chinese cities at 79 million in that year (Liang and Ma, 2004). Standard household income surveys exclude these migrants from their sample frames, but some special surveys of migrants are available and are used by Hussain (2002, 2005) and Khan (2004). The latter study finds that, while the income of rural–urban migrants is on average double that of their native villages, it remains more than one-third less than that of full status urban

Table 12.4. Alternative headcount rate estimates of urban income poverty, 1981–2003 (%)

	(1) Old $1/ day	(2) Old $2/ day	(3) RC "New" PL	(4) Khan	(5) CPDR	(6) Hussain	(7) Meng et al.
1981			6.01				
1982			2.16				
1983			1.56				
1984			1.27				
1985			1.08				
1986			3.23				2.6
1987			1.62				1.9
1988			2.07	6.7			2.8
1989			7.05				3.2
1990	1.0	20.7	2.58				2.1
1991			1.66				2.5
1992	0.8	13.2	1.13				3.4
1993	0.7	13.8	1.01				5.0
1994	0.9	13.5	1.19				5.2
1995	0.6	9.7	0.85	8.0			5.5
1996	0.5	9.3	0.61				4.7
1997	0.5	9.1	0.70				5.3
1998	1.0	9.0	1.16			4.7	4.4
1999	0.5	6.8	0.57				3.5
2000			0.63				3.7
2001			0.50				
2002			0.54	2.2			
2003					4.5		

Note: The World Bank's original "PPP$1 a day" line is equal to $1.08 in 1993 prices, and the $2 line is accordingly $2.16. No estimates of urban poverty using the Banks' new poverty-adjusted PPP line were available when this paper was completed.

Sources: (1) and (2) Chen and Wang, 2001; (3) Ravallion and Chen, 2007, Table 3; (4) Khan and Riskin (2001), Khan (2004); (5) China Population and Development Country Report; (6) Hussain (2005); (7) Communication from Xin Meng containing data from which Figure 2 in Meng et al. 2007 was calculated. This series is for one of the two methods used to calculate poverty rates in that paper.

residents. Moreover, it is distributed much more unevenly (Khan and Riskin, 2005). These two facts alone imply a higher poverty rate among the migrants than among full status residents. Khan (2004) estimated that the poverty rate for migrants in 2002 was 14.4 per cent, and the poverty rate for the combined urban population of full status residents and migrants was 4.4 per cent—twice that of the full status residents alone.

Khan's findings have migrant poverty rates seven times as high as that of permanent residents, a startling but not implausible result. Using both a different methodology and different data, Hussain (2002, 2005) found that the poverty rate among migrants in 1999 was 50 per cent higher than among permanent residents. For migrants it was 15.2 per cent and for permanent residents 10.3 per cent. This result is not necessarily inconsistent with Khan's, given especially the difference in data sources.[16] The difference in ratios of migrant to local permanent resident poverty rate is due more to the difference in estimates of the poverty rate among full status residents (10.3 per cent compared to 2.2 per cent) than to the difference in rate for migrants (15.2 per cent versus 14.4 per cent).[17]

The variety of extant estimates of urban poverty, summarized in Table 12.3, indicates that there continues to be more than a modicum of uncertainty about the basic dimensions of Chinese poverty, and even about trends. Are the "stylized facts," described above, about urban poverty trends supported by the available data? The only relatively long series of estimates is that of Ravallion and Chen (2007), which covers the years 1981–2002, albeit from the vantage point of a very austere poverty definition. This series starts relatively high, at 6 per cent in 1981 and then falls sharply, rising again in 1989. Thereafter it subsides to 1 per cent or below for most remaining years. This pattern is consistent with the view that urban poverty was slight in pre-reform years, and it accords with a fairly draconian government austerity in 1981, engineered to reduce inflationary pressures and enable the state to regain control of investment (Riskin, 1987, p. 345), which could explain the spike in 1981. It is also consistent with the extraordinary stagflation in 1989 that was one of the precipitating factors of the student demonstrations at Tiananmen. But it is inconsistent with the many indications, sampled above, of growing urban poverty associated especially with SOE reform beginning in the 1990s. And, of course, being based on full status urban residents only, it cannot incorporate evidence of much higher poverty rates among rural–urban migrants.

The series of poverty estimates generated by the World Bank PPP$2 a day poverty line appears to tell a different story, one of urban poverty steadily declining from about 21 per cent of the urban population in 1990 to less than 7 per cent at the end of the decade. The only inference that can be drawn for pre-reform urban poverty from this series is that it must have been very high: real per capita GDP in 1978 was only 42 per cent as high as in 1990, so even with greater inequality of distribution in 1990, a poverty rate over 20 per cent suggests even higher rates in 1978 and before. But this is a faulty inference from misleading numbers. The PPP$2 line is being applied to a concept of per capita income that omits a substantial portion of that income, namely, the various subsidies and elements of income in kind that provided as much as 42 per cent of urban residents' incomes in pre-reform days and made the difference between destitution and a low but secure and adequate standard of living. Thus, the CHIP studies, which attempted to estimate income comprehensively to include all of its components, generated a mean per capita urban income in 1988 that was 55 per cent higher than the official estimate. Partly for the same reason that the early poverty rates are overstated by the PPP$2 line, the decline in urban poverty is similarly overstated. But an additional reason is that the subsidy component of urban income declined over time, so that actual income (including subsidies) rose more slowly than officially reported income (which excludes them).

Meng et al.'s series runs from 1986–2002 and shows urban poverty rising from the 1980s to the 1990s, despite rapid urban income growth, peaking around 1997 and then falling again. The three Khan estimates for 1988, 1995, and 2002, respectively, are consistent with the pattern of Meng et al.'s longer series, albeit with wider fluctuations. Such a pattern of rising and then falling urban poverty rates, we believe, fits well with other information about urban China during the period in question. The earlier rising trend is ascribable to growing urban income inequality, rising unemployment, and rising prices of food and other necessities in a context of disappearing state subsidies and a largely non-existent safety net. The sharply falling poverty rate after 1997 came about as economic growth took on a far less disequalizing character (Khan, 2004), raising the question whether the emergence of redistributive public policies, including a new safety net (the minimum livelihood guarantee program), commensurate with government rhetoric about making growth more equitable, might have contributed to the decline in urban poverty beginning in the late 1990s. We return to this question at the end of this chapter.[18]

To put China's urban poverty in international perspective, even the poverty rates generated by the less austere poverty lines are low in comparison with those of other developing countries. For instance, India's urban poverty rate is said by the Planning Commission to have fallen from 33 per cent in 1993/4 to 24 per cent in 1999/2000.[19] The average urban poverty rate for the World Bank's $1.08 a day (1993 PPP) poverty line among eighty-seven low and middle income countries in 2002 was 24.55 per cent (Ravallion et al., 2007), many times higher than the highest estimate for China.

Determinants and characteristics of the urban poor

We now use the CHIP data—the same data sets as Khan (2004) and Khan and Riskin (2001, 2005)[20]—as well as the poverty line developed by Khan (2004), to examine the characteristics of the urban poor over the three surveyed years, as one way of ascertaining whether the nature of urban poverty has changed. We do this by estimating a simple probit model for each of the three survey years:

$$P_i = X\beta + \varepsilon_i$$

where P_i is the probability that the per capita income of household i falls below the poverty line in the survey year, X is a vector of demographic and socioeconomic characteristics, some of the household head and others of the household as a whole, and ε_i is a standard error term. The income measure used is household per capita disposable income according to the CHIP definition. The objective is to examine how the likelihood of a household's members falling below the poverty line is influenced by these various characteristics.

Table 12.5 presents the results. The coefficients are marginal effects, namely the change in probability of being poor (based on the Khan definition) due to a

Table 12.5. Probit regression results on poverty status

Household head characteristics	1988	1995	2002
Age (50–59 yrs omitted)			
21–29	0.032**	0.064**	0.016
	(0.012)	(0.024)	(0.017)
30–39	0.006	0.006	−0.004
	(0.005)	(0.011)	(0.005)
40–49	−0.001	−0.018*	−0.003
	(0.004)	(0.009)	(0.005)
60+	−0.012**	−0.027**	0.013
	(0.003)	(0.009)	(0.012)
Education (2-year college or higher omitted)			
Primary school or less	0.042**	0.096**	0.117**
	(0.012)	(0.023)	(0.039)
Junior high school	0.020**	0.043**	0.059**
	(0.006)	(0.011)	(0.015)
Senior high school	0.010	0.023*	0.033*
	(0.006)	(0.011)	(0.014)
Secondary technology school	0.015+	0.011	0.030
	(0.008)	(0.011)	(0.019)
Employment status (employed omitted)			
Retired	0.006	0.045*	−0.000
	(0.025)	(0.018)	(0.014)
Unemployed	—	0.179**	0.178*
		(0.064)	(0.089)
Employment sector (employed in central/provincial SOEs or public institutions omitted)			
Employed in local SOEs or public institutions	−0.007**	0.044**	0.016
	(0.003)	(0.008)	(0.011)
Employed in collective enterprises	0.021**	0.075**	0.019
	(0.006)	(0.018)	(0.016)
Employed in private sector	0.037	0.077	0.017+
	(0.034)	(0.051)	(0.011)
Employment tenure nature (permanent worker omitted)			
Long- or short-term contract worker	0.027	0.007	0.009
	(0.026)	(0.007)	(0.006)
Proprietor or self-employed	−0.001	0.099	0.011
	(0.014)	(0.070)	(0.012)
Other	—	0.024	0.025
		(0.033)	(0.024)
Ethnic minority	−0.003	0.014	−0.007
	(0.005)	(0.014)	(0.006)
CCP member	−0.011**	−0.013*	−0.010*
	(0.003)	(0.006)	(0.004)
Household characteristics	1988	1995	2002
Household size	0.007**	0.017**	0.007**
	(0.002)	(0.004)	(0.002)
Number of children <18 years old (zero omitted)			
1	0.010*	0.032**	0.011*
	(0.004)	(0.007)	(0.005)
2	0.069**	0.208**	0.066*
	(0.015)	(0.035)	(0.029)
3+	0.261**	0.451**	0.256
	(0.055)	(0.141)	(0.232)

Number of elders > 60 years old (zero omitted)			
1	0.002	0.014	−0.001
	(0.004)	(0.010)	(0.006)
2+	0.013	0.023	−0.003
	(0.010)	(0.019)	(0.007)
Region (eastern omitted)			
Central	0.074**	0.107**	0.020**
	(0.006)	(0.010)	(0.005)
Western	0.037**	0.078**	0.029**
	(0.010)	(0.012)	(0.007)
Observations	30,602	21,417	20,604
Pseudo R^2	0.30	0.21	0.20

Notes: Dependent variable is 1 if family is poor, 0 otherwise; marginal effects presented with robust standard errors in parentheses; + significant at 10%; * significant at 5%; ** significant at 1%. "—" denotes that the category is dropped because there are no observations in that category.

one-unit change in an observable characteristic, or, for categorical variables, the change in probability of being poor relative to that probability in the omitted category. For instance, in 1988 households whose heads were aged 21–29 had a 3.2 per cent higher probability of falling into poverty than those with heads aged 50–59 (the omitted group) and this disadvantage was higher at 6.4 per cent in 1995 but disappeared in 2002. The standard errors in parentheses are corrected for the fact that per capita incomes within households are assumed equal.

Most of the regression results are as expected and consistent with findings from a recent study using large samples (Meng et al., 2007). With regard to household head characteristics, age is a significant predictor of poverty in 1988 and 1995, with relative youthfulness (aged 21–29) increasing it and old age (60 years or above, relative to the reference group of 50–59) decreasing it. The latter finding is perhaps surprising. With male retirement at 60 and wages in the old state enterprises highly correlated with seniority, men (most household heads are men) of 50–59 years are in their prime earning years. Why should post-60 year olds have an even lower probability of being poor? Probably because the old pension system, still fully operative in 1988 and largely so in 1995, provided a very generous income by international standards (replacing some 70 per cent of maximum wage earned), and most retired people able to do so also held post-retirement jobs. Interestingly, in 2002 age of household head was no longer a significant predictor of poverty status.

In pre-reform days, the returns to education in China were extremely low. This has changed dramatically. Recent studies, including those coming out of the CHIP survey for 2002, confirm that nowadays, education and especially higher education is an important path to higher income (Hannum and Park, 2007). It is also, evidently, an increasingly potent protector against poverty. In 1988 and 1995, those living in a household headed by someone with a primary school education

311

or less had 4.2 per cent and 9.6 per cent higher probability, respectively, of being poor than those whose head had two or more years of higher education. By 2002 this greater likelihood of being poor had increased to 11.7 per cent and these results are significant at the 1 per cent level. Households headed by someone with a junior high school education had the next highest probability of being poor, and the effect is stronger in 2002 than in previous years.

As for employment status of household head, unemployment has the biggest impact on the likelihood of being poor, increasing it (relative to being employed) by 18 per cent in both 1995 and 2002.[21] In 1988 the category of unemployed did not exist, as China had not yet abandoned the fiction that unemployment was non-existent under socialism. Those who were de facto unemployed were mostly workers laid off from state enterprises who still considered themselves employees of their *danwei* (work unit). Even in 1995, when open unemployment had become more serious and was more widely acknowledged, many laid off workers still received a subsistence stipend from their work unit and would not consider themselves formally unemployed. Nor did the government treat them as such in its statistics. Thus, the fact that only 4 per cent of the poor had household heads who said they were unemployed in 1995 (as shown in Table 12.6, which describes demographic characteristics of the poor) may well reflect the persistent psychology of dependence in the urban work force rather than constituting an accurate measure of the unemployment-poverty nexus. And the fact that that number had risen to 23 per cent in 2002 might conversely reflect the change that had occurred in that psychology.

Nevertheless, despite the growth of urban unemployment in the 1990s and its strong association with the simultaneous increase in poverty, the working poor remained the dominant category of poor. Of those falling below the poverty line in 1988, 1995, and 2002, respectively, 93 per cent, 81 per cent, and 61 per cent had household heads who were employed, as shown in Table 12.6.

Retirement status has a significant positive effect on probability of being poor only in 1995. By 2002, the sign on the coefficient, although no longer significant, had become negative, indicating that retirement status might have become protective against poverty as government funding of the new social security system increased.

The impact of sector of employment changes over time. In 1988, being employed in a local state enterprise actually reduced the probability of being poor relative to employment in a central or provincial SOE. In that year, the proportions of poor employed in central/provincial units and in local units were 52 and 21 per cent, respectively (see Table 12.6). By 1995, these had reversed to 15 per cent central/provincial and 61 per cent local. This explains why employment in a local enterprise was now associated with 4.4 per cent higher probability of being poor than in a central enterprise. But by 2002 it appears to have made no difference. Indeed, in the CHIP sample for that year, the proportions of the poor with household heads in these two sectors were

Table 12.6. Demographic characteristics of poor families

	1988	1995	2002
Household head characteristics			
Age (mean)	42.85	43.30	47.14
21–29	7%	9%	3%
30–39	30%	34%	24%
40–49	40%	29%	39%
50–59	19%	16%	19%
60+	4%	11%	15%
Ethnic minority	3%	7%	5%
CCP member	22%	23%	12%
Education (mean years of schooling)	n/a	8.99	8.28
primary school or less	29%	18%	20%
junior high school	42%	37%	50%
senior high school	14%	20%	22%
secondary technology school	9%	12%	5%
2-year college	5%	9%	3%
4-year college+	2%	3%	0%
Employment status			
employed	93%	81%	61%
retired	7%	15%	16%
unemployed	0%	4%	23%
Among the employed sector			
state-owned, central/provincial	52%	15%	33%
state-owned, local	21%	61%	32%
urban collective	24%	19%	12%
private sector	3%	5%	22%
Employment tenure nature			
permanent	96%	76%	25%
contract (short- or long-term)	1%	19%	50%
proprietor or self-employed	2%	4%	19%
other	0%	1%	5%
Household characteristics			
Household size (mean)	4.71	3.87	3.73
Number of children 018 (mean)	1.86	1.17	0.93
0	7%	14%	24%
1	26%	57%	60%
2	45%	27%	15%
3+	22%	2%	1%
Number of children 06 (mean)	0.32	0.30	0.16
Number of elders > 60 (mean)	0.27	0.36	0.40
0	80%	73%	71%
1	14%	17%	18%
2+	6%	9%	10%
Number of elders > 65 (mean)	0.20	0.25	0.27
Region			
eastern	6%	11%	19%
central	80%	62%	47%
western	13%	27%	34%

Source: Authors' calculations using the CHIP data.

about the same (33 and 32 per cent, respectively). Collective enterprise employment conduced to higher likelihood of being poor in 1988 and 1995, but no longer in 2002. The share of poor heads of households employed in collective enterprises fell from 24 per cent in 1988 and 19 per cent in 1995 to only 12 per cent in 2002. By contrast, poor household heads employed in the private sector increased significantly to 22 per cent by 2002 from less than 5 per cent in the previous years. Consequently, employment in the private sector is associated with an increased 1.7 per cent probability of being poor in 2002.

Regarding employment tenure, contract or temporary status increases the likelihood of being poor in all years, but these results are not statistically significant. Contingent work has always carried pay and benefits inferior to those of full status state employees in China, and this was a well-known source of conflict during the Cultural Revolution years. The only unexpected aspect to the finding, therefore, is its lack of statistical significance.

Belonging to an ethnic minority had no significant impact on probability of poverty in the CHIP sample, but having a household head who belonged to the Communist Party was significantly protective against poverty in all three years.

With respect to characteristics of the household as a whole, both size of household and number of children were highly significant in predicting poverty. An additional household member raised the probability of being poor by 0.7 per cent in 1988, 1.7 per cent in 1995, and 0.7 per cent again in 2002.[22] Having one child increased the probability by between 1 and 3 per cent for all three years, relative to having no children. And that increase grew substantially in all three years for additional children: a second child raised it by 7 per cent in 1988 and 2002 and by 21 per cent in 1995; a third child raised it by 26 per cent in 1988 and 2002 and by 45 per cent in 1995. Of course we must be careful about assuming causation. It is possible that poor urban residents were likely to have more children, rather than that people with more children became poor or that both kinds of interaction were involved. Interestingly, we found no significant effect for number of household members older than 60.[23]

Table 12.7 shows the macro-regional distribution of poverty rates in the CHIP samples.[24] Hussain (2005) argued that such a broad definition of region hides much variation within each region, and he adopted instead a six-region breakdown that contains more homogeneous regions. However, with only eleven

Table 12.7. Overall and regional poverty rates (%)

Region	1988	1995	2002
Eastern	1	2	2
Central	11	14	4
Western	4	8	4
All	6	8	3

Source: Authors' calculations using CHIP data.

provinces included in the CHIP urban sample, so fine a definition is not possible, so we use the common east–central–west breakdown. This indicates that the highest poverty rates are found in the central region, except in 2002, when western rates equal central ones.

The probit results for region are consistent with this regional distribution. Residing in the central region is highly conducive to being poor, relative to the eastern region, but such a negative impact decreased between 1995 and 2002. Western location is also a cause of increased probability of poverty, although this also declines in 2002. The implication of these trends is that, while overall urban poverty was falling over time, the share of it in the eastern region was increasing, and such indeed was the case, with the east's share rising from 6 per cent in 1988 to 19 per cent in 2002 as shown in Table 12.6.

In sum, urban poverty in China was highly regional in nature, but has become less so over time. It is perhaps less associated with age than in the 1980s, but more associated with educational deprivation, contingent labor, and unemployment. More or less unchanging factors associated with urban poverty are non-SOE employment,[25] family size, number of children below 18 years, and being a non-Party member.

Urban poverty and changing state policies

The findings of Khan (2004) and Meng et al. (2007), that urban poverty fell sharply after the mid-1990s, raise the question of whether this result was connected to an evolution in state policies toward a more "pro-poor" policy stance.

The rhetoric of Chinese government pronouncements suggests just such a policy evolution, at least since the sixteenth National Party Conference in 2003, which introduced the new leadership of Hu Jintao and Wen Jiabao. Premier Wen's Report to the National People's Congress in early 2004 heralded a shift from "blind pursuit of GDP growth" to a more balanced set of objectives that would be more people-centered, sustainable, and equitable in pursuit of the longer-term goal of a "modestly well-off" (xiaokang) society. Subsequent rhetoric continued and enhanced this theme. Even before 2003 there was evidence of concern among the national leadership about the implications for social stability of growing inequality, increasing insecurity, and unchecked corruption. At the time of the "Asian crisis" in 1997–8, for instance, the government decided to counter the negative effects of the crisis on aggregate demand in China with a large domestic investment program of CNY100 billion that would focus on infrastructure development. Moreover, it was decided specifically to concentrate this spending in the more backward regions of western and central China. This grew into the Western Development Initiative that was formally introduced in 1999. Various subsidies to poorer regions and people also began to increase during this period (Wong, 2007). Meng et al. (2007) suggest that the decline in poverty after 1998 may have been due to the minimum livelihood guarantee (*dibao*) program, which was fully implemented after 1999.

There is other evidence of policy changes consistent with official rhetoric, as well. Khan (2004) found that urban growth was less disequalizing than before 1995, in the sense that (a) more GDP growth was reaching households as personal income, and (b) the Gini ratio of urban household per capita income fell for the 1995–2002 period. For those reasons, and unlike the period from 1988 to 1995, when China's poverty fell relatively slowly in comparison with its rapid rate of economic growth, the post-1995 period has been characterized by a much higher gross income elasticity of poverty reduction with respect to per capita income.[26] For urban China, this elasticity rose from 0.1 to 2.6. In other words, a given amount of income growth was accompanied by far greater reductions in poverty between 1995 and 2002 than was the case earlier. Riskin (2007) attributed the fall in income inequality to improved distribution of housing income (both rental subsidies and imputed rental value of owned housing), a reduction in the regressive nature of net taxes, and better targeting of welfare payments to low income residents. Gao (2008) showed that social benefits provided over 80 per cent of total income for the lowest decile of the urban population, ranked by pre-tax pre-transfer income, in 2002. Wong (2007) reported that state subsidies to local social security schemes, local minimum livelihood stipend programs and living stipends to workers laid off from SOEs had all burgeoned to significant amounts of money by the early 2000s. All of this suggests that the recent rhetoric of China's leaders promising the adoption of a more equitable growth strategy might have been effectively translated into more equitable policies. It is therefore of interest to examine the composition of income of the urban poor and of those near the poverty line, to see whether direct subsidies and other benefits have been flowing to them in more significant amounts than before.

Figure 12.1 presents the composition of the income of the urban poor, as well as the near-poor (defined as those with incomes between the poverty line and 150 per cent of the poverty line) and from this an interesting change can be seen: over time, for both groups the share of earnings in total income first rises very sharply (1988–95) and then falls again (1995–2002), though not to its original level.

The share of earnings in income rose from 1988 to 2002 mainly because of the decline in subsidies as transition to a market economy gathered force. Total subsidies fell from 39 per cent of income in 1988 to 6 per cent and 4 per cent for the poor and near-poor respectively in 2002. For the urban population as a whole, they fell from 39 per cent of income to about 2 per cent. But there was an important difference between the situation of the lowest income groups and that of the urban population as a whole: a large component of total subsidies had been the implicit rental subsidies comprised by very low rents on housing

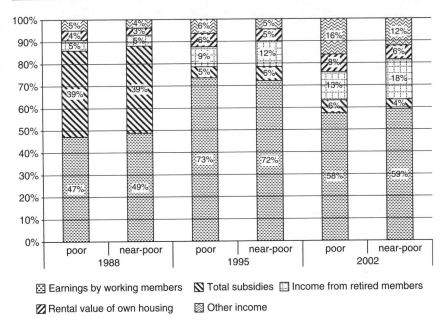

Figure 12.1 Share of income sources among the poor and near-poor (total per capita disposable income, %)

rented from one's work unit or from the state. As these subsidies disappeared over time, housing reform enabled higher income groups to purchase their housing (usually at big discounts from market prices) and receive the imputed rental value of their now privately owned housing. The fall in rent subsidies was matched by the rise in imputed rents. But for the poor, this did not happen. Rent subsidies declined far more than imputed rents rose. This is shown in Table 12.8. Note that the sum of housing subsidy and rental value of owned housing remains stable at around 20 per cent of total income for the urban population as a whole. However, for the poor, this share is cut in half, falling from 20 per cent in 1988 to 10 per cent in 2002, and for the near-poor the decline is even sharper.

There were two reasons for this growing relative deficit in "housing income" among the poor: first, their owned housing had less value than that of the non-poor; and second, fewer of the poor ended up with housing ownership in 2002. Of these two reasons, however, the first must have been considerably more important, since the relative deficit of the poor in home ownership was not large. Table 12.9 shows that home ownership increased from about 14 per cent among all urban population in 1988 to over 79 per cent in 2002, whereas for the poor it increased from 21 per cent to 74 per cent. Therefore, the lag in rental

Table 12.8. Shares of housing subsidy and rental value of owned housing in total income (%)

	1988	1995	2002
Poor			
Housing subsidy	16	4	2
Rental value of owned housing	4	6	8
Near-poor			
Housing subsidy	16	5	2
Rental value of owned housing	3	5	6
Urban population as a whole			
Housing subsidy	18	10	2
Rental value of owned housing	4	11	18

Table 12.9. Change in home ownership (% of families who own their homes)

	1988	1995	2002
Poor	21	49	74
Near-poor	14	42	77
Non-poor	14	42	80
All	14	43	79

value of owned housing among the poor must be due mostly to low house values of the poor relative to those of the non-poor.

The other striking change shown in Figure 12.1 is a rise in the shares of income of retired persons and income from "other" sources over the period concerned, especially between 1995 and 2002. By 2002 these two components together comprised nearly 30 per cent of the income of both the poor and the near-poor, up from about 10 per cent in 1988. For the poor, retirement income increased from 5 per cent of total income in 1988 to 13 per cent in 2002, and for the near-poor it rose from 5 per cent to 18 per cent. This income was mainly from pensions, rather than post-retirement earnings (Table 12.10). The greater increase for the near-poor suggests that one source of poverty may have been the inability of insolvent SOEs to fulfill their pension obligations to retired employees, a problem that may be in process of resolution as state infusions of funding into the new pension system have increased. On the other hand, the rise in retirement income of the poor/near-poor mirrors its rise in the urban population as a whole from 6.8 per cent of total income in 1988 to 14.8 per cent in 2002, due to an aging workforce (Khan and Riskin, 2005).

Table 12.10. Post-retirement income of poor and near-poor (%)

	1988	1995	2002
Poor retirees			
Pensions	4	9	12
Earnings	0	0	1
Near-poor retirees			
Pensions	4	11	16
Earnings	1	1	2

Table 12.11. Share of private/individual enterprise income in total income (%)

	1988	1995	2002
Poor	1	3	11
Near-poor	1	1	8

"Other" income of the poor rises from 5 per cent in 1988 to 16 per cent in 2002, and that of the near-poor grows from 4 per cent to 12 per cent. What is "other income"? It includes income from private enterprises, from property, and miscellaneous income that is mainly private transfers. Of these, the component that changed most notably was the first: income from private or individual enterprises, as shown in Table 12.11.[27] By 2002 private/individual sector income comprised 11 per cent of the income of the poor and 8 per cent of that of the near-poor, both far higher than the 2.7 per cent that it comprised for the urban population as a whole (Khan and Riskin, 2005). There are two possible interpretations of the sharp rise in private sector income of the poor/near-poor: one is that the spread of market-oriented activity presented an opportunity for low income residents frozen out of the formal economy by SOE reform to earn some income in the informal sector. The opposite side of this coin is that, with the disappearance of guaranteed employment and other welfare benefits, poor urbanites had nowhere else to turn for a living than to the informal sector. These are merely different ways of viewing the same facts. No doubt both are true, as the informal sector provided a resource to the poor but also represented for many a last resort.

While this look at the composition of income of low income urban residents reveals some interesting changes, it does not in general support the view that greater welfare spending in the form of direct subsidies to the poor—except perhaps for pensions—played an important role in the decline in urban poverty rate between 1995 and 2002.[28] Table 12.12 examines direct subsidy payments to the poor and near-poor other than housing subsidies and pension income. The table reveals that after the huge decline in such subsidies between 1988 and 1995—they fell as a share of the income of the poor from 23 per cent to 1 per cent—there was a small recovery in 2002 to 4 per cent. For the near-poor

Table 12.12. Share of total income from subsidies other than housing or pensions (%)

Year	Poor	Near-poor
1988	23	23
1995	1	1
2002	4	2

the recovery was even smaller, making it difficult to argue that such direct aid was responsible for their avoidance of poverty.[29]

In view of the abundant evidence, cited above, that state policy has begun to shift noticeably toward the promotion of a more egalitarian approach to development, our inability to find much evidence of that in the household micro-data on urban poverty is striking. There are several possible explanations. The amounts of funding concerned, while growing rapidly, still amount to very modest sums on a per capita basis. Much state spending, e.g. investment in infrastructure in economically undeveloped regions, or to raise salaries of local government cadres, would not be targeted at the urban poor. There might be little overlap between those people our method identifies as poor and those who officially qualify for aid such as *dibao* (minimum livelihood program) payments. Much of the spending that has gone to fund new social insurance programs, such as the social security and unemployment insurance systems, goes to non-poor urban residents. Leakage inherent in China's decentralized fiscal system tends to cause money earmarked for poor people to be siphoned off at various intermediate levels before it reaches the intended beneficiaries. These and doubtless other reasons may explain the evidently limited penetration of urban poverty relief.[30]

Summary and conclusion

Urban poverty has only recently been put on the research and policy agenda in China and among scholars of Chinese poverty. In this chapter we examine several different standards that have been used for defining and measuring it and the resulting estimates of poverty rate and trend. Estimates by Hussain (2002, 2005), Khan (2004), and Meng et al. (2007) seem most consistent with the recent economic history of urban China. These indicate an urban poverty rate between 2 and 8 per cent for the period between the mid-1980s and 2002, depending on the exact year and the particular method used. These are very low rates in comparison with other large developing countries, but still well above the almost zero rates generated by the most austere poverty lines. Moreover, urban poverty followed a pattern of rising from the 1980s into the 1990s and then falling after about 1997. Rural–urban migrants are excluded from these analyses. Although their inclusion would raise the urban poverty rate, it is unclear what impact this would have on the trend of urban poverty.

An examination of the characteristics of the urban poor in 1988, 1995, and 2002 reached a number of conclusions. Regional location has been an important predictor of urban poverty, with higher poverty rates in central and western China than in the eastern coastal provinces. However, poverty rates have fallen in the central and western regions while remaining low and stable in the east, thus reducing the regional disparity. Employment in other than a state operated enterprise, living in a larger household, and having more children below 18 years of age all increase the probability of a household falling below the poverty line in all three years examined. A head of household who was very young (21–29 years) or relatively old (over 60) inclined a household toward poverty in 1988 and 1995 but not in 2002. Higher educational level was strongly protective against poverty and increasingly so through the three years. An unemployed head strongly inclined a household toward poverty in 1995 and 2002, but the majority of the poor nevertheless lived in households whose heads worked. Having a head who was a member of the Communist Party slightly but significantly decreased the likelihood of a household being poor.

The decline in urban poverty from the late 1990s raises the question whether a change in government development strategy toward a more equitable one featuring increased income redistribution and strengthened social benefits programs for low income urbanites might have been an important cause of the decline. To test such a hypothesis, we examine the changing composition of the income of poor and near-poor urban residents. Like other urban Chinese, these have experienced a steep fall in most subsidies and benefits between 1988 and 2002. Only pensions increased substantially as a fraction of their total income, and this at least partly reflects an aging population as well as the shoring up of the financial status of the new pension system by the government toward the end of the period. Otherwise, there is no evidence of a significant impact of direct benefit payments on the incomes of the poor and near-poor. What distinguishes the composition of their income from that of the urban population as a whole is a much larger share of private (informal) sector income (8 per cent for the poor compared with 2.7 per cent for the entire urban population) and a much lower share of imputed rental income of owned housing (8 per cent versus almost 18 per cent). Both of these differences are indications of disadvantage on the part of the poor.

China's social safety net and other benefits programs are still works in progress. While they have been injected with growing amounts of funding by the government in recent years, by 2002, with the possible and important exception of the new social security system, they were still not making a measurable impact on urban poverty or near poverty. This does not imply that government policy bears no responsibility for the reduction in urban poverty after 1997, only that direct benefits programs other than pensions evidently were not the cause.

Notes

1. We would like to acknowledge the gracious and useful help of Shaohua Chen, Athar Hussain, and Xin Meng in answering queries about various issues dealt with in this chapter. Thanks are also due to anonymous readers who provided useful comments.
2. Department of Economics, Queens College, CUNY; Weatherhead East Asian Institute, Columbia University.
3. Graduate School of Social Service, Fordham University.
4. Amartya Sen (1983) puts this point particularly clearly, arguing that "absolute deprivation in terms of capabilities relates to relative deprivation in terms of commodities, incomes and resources". On the other hand, Ravallion et al. (2007) argue that absolute poverty should be defined to rule out change in the aggregate measure of poverty from simply moving individuals between urban and rural areas (or countries) without change in their real consumption, and that, therefore, absolute poverty measures must have "a constant real value both between countries and between urban and rural areas within countries" (p. 7).
5. It is true, however, that periodically during the pre-reform period these expectations fell short of full realization. Thus, when the pace of economic growth, using Soviet-derived capital-intensive technology, could not absorb all available urban labor, a form of de facto unemployment developed known as "waiting for work", in which school graduates entering the workforce might wait many months to be assigned to a job. However, once assigned, their continued employment was guaranteed.
6. In addition to the basic general problem of using existing PPP estimates to examine poverty (Pogge and Reddy, chapter 3 in this volume), the problem in China is made more acute by the fact that China had not until very recently participated in a comprehensive price survey, which is what provides the empirical basis for a country's PPP exchange rate. Thus, the empirical foundation for the use of the PPP$1-a-day poverty line for China has been very weak. The results of a new price survey for China were finally announced by the Asian Development Bank in 2007, and had the effect of greatly reducing the PPP estimate of China's GDP and increasing the headcount of PPP$1-a-day poor. See World Bank, 2008. See also Asian Development Bank, 2007 and Keidel 2007. This information became available too late to be incorporated in the present chapter, which therefore uses the World Bank's old PPP estimates.
7. For a description of the surveys, see Khan and Riskin (2001).
8. Diagnostic poverty rates are constructed to identify the poor, and are to be distinguished from what might be called "benefit lines", meaning cut-off thresholds for benefit eligibility. The latter are constrained by budget limitations and other policy considerations. See Hussain (2005), p. 7 ff.
9. The use of the PPP$1-a-day poverty line had been sharply criticized. See Pogge and Reddy in chapter 3 of this volume.

10. See National Bureau of Statistics (2003) Table 10.7, p. 348.
11. There is an enormous literature on poverty and its measurement, beginning perhaps with Sen (1976). For some accessible discussions of the issues, see Maxwell (1999) and Khan (2004).
12. It comes to CNY2,291 in 1995 and CNY2,534 in 2002. This amounted to 40 per cent and 26 per cent of average urban per capita income in the two respective years. However, income as defined in Khan's study is quite a bit higher than the official estimate, and Khan's poverty line is also based on this definition of income. Khan also generated a "low" urban poverty line equal to 70 per cent of the original line. We discuss here only the original one and its results.
13. They exclude Tibet because of its small sample size. The number of provinces grew from twenty-nine to thirty with the elevation of Hainan to province status in 1990, and to thirty-one in 1997 with the elevation of Chongqing, previously part of Sichuan Province, to separate provincial status. Meng et al. (2007) kept Chongqing in Sichuan for the duration of their series (source: communication from Xin Meng).
14. Relative austerity also depends on time, which correlates with level of income. The higher the mean income, the smaller the ratio of any given poverty line to it, *ceteris paribus*.
15. The high figure of 60 per cent is unlikely to apply to any actual locality, because the localities with the most generous minimum livelihood lines (e.g. Shanghai) also have the highest average incomes, so their percentage would be lower than 60 per cent. Conversely, localities with the lowest lines are likely to have lower incomes, thus raising their percentages above 14 per cent.
16. Hussain used a 1999 one-time survey of urban residents, including migrants, which collected information for only the single month of August in which the survey was carried out rather than for a full year, as in the case of the regular household incomes surveys. This has obvious disadvantages, among them the inability to distinguish between "temporary" and "permanent" income. Many more households were found to report zero income, for instance, than typically do in the normal household surveys.
17. Hussain's estimate of 10.3 per cent for permanent residents does not contradict his finding of a 4.7 per cent rate reported in Table 12.2. The former rate derives from a different and more limited sample, corresponding to the one for migrants (see previous note), and a different methodology.
18. The decline in urban poverty is also consistent with the finding of Ravallion et al. (2007) that China has experienced a "ruralization of poverty" since the late 1990s, in the sense that the urban share of PPP$2-a-day total poverty has fallen.
19. See Deaton and Kozel (2005). The reported decline in poverty is controversial and the 1999/2000 figure represents a lower bound.
20. The samples are described in Khan and Riskin (2001, 2005).
21. Meng et al. (2007) do not directly examine unemployment as a contributor to poverty. It is implicitly present in the characteristic, "per cent of members working," the reciprocal of the dependency rate.
22. Meng et al. (2007) also showed household size to be highly significant, and also found this effect to rise from 1986 until 1997 and then to fall again.

23. Meng et al. (2007) showed mixed results with respect to seniors, whom they identify as those over 65 and break down by sex. For some years in their series they got significant coefficients and for others they did not. For the two years that overlap with our surveys, 1988 and 1995, they got significant results only for older women in 1988.
24. For a discussion of the geographic distribution of the population, and other demographic characteristics as derived from the 2000 census, see Fan (2002).
25. The distribution of income from employment in the private sector is bipolar, including many poor self-employed in the informal sector, as well as some well-off employees of large private or foreign invested enterprises (see Khan and Riskin, 2005). On balance, the coefficients on private sector employment in the probit exercise are positive and significant. If the sample could be broken into its two parts and only the first examined, we conjecture that the coefficients would be much higher and the significance level greater.
26. The gross elasticity of poverty reduction is defined as the percentage decline (rise) in poverty rate divided by the percentage rise (decline) in per capita income. Thus, it includes poverty changes caused by other factors than income.
27. "Individual enterprises" are private enterprises with a small number of employees. The term was a means by which the state permitted the spread of private economic activity while using an ambiguous nomenclature that avoided the ideologically loaded term, "private" and thus reduced the risk of going into business.
28. Of course, other progressive changes in policy could have played a role in reducing poverty, such as providing job retraining or early retirement to laid off workers, pumping funds into the new social security program, or simply investing in labor-intensive activities that would provide employment.
29. For those below Khan's lower poverty line, equal to 70 per cent of the one we are using in this chapter, the shares of subsidy income in total income of the poor and near-poor are slightly higher, 6 per cent and 4 per cent, respectively.
30. A new study of the effectiveness of China's Minimum Living Standard program finds that, while the program slightly reduced the observed poverty rate of program participants in 2002, using the same poverty line as in this chapter, it had virtually no impact on the poverty rate among all eligible people (including non-participants). See Gao et al. (2009).

Bibliography

Asian Development Bank (2004) *Poverty Profile of the People's Republic of China.* Manila.
—— (2007) *Purchasing Power Parities and Real Expenditures.* Manila.
Chen, S. and Wang, Y. (2001) 'China's Growth and Poverty Reduction: Trends Between 1990 and 1999'. World Bank Working Paper.
Deaton, A. and Kozel, V. (2005) *The Great Indian Poverty Debate.* Delhi: Macmillan India.

Dollar, D. (2008) 'New PPPs Reveal China has had More Poverty Reduction than we thought,' March 4. East Asia and Pacific on Rise (World Band blog) <http://eapblog.worldbank.org/content/new-ppps-reveal-china-has-had-more-poverty-reduction-than-we-thought>, accessed March 15, 2008.

Fan, C. (2002) 'Population Change and Regional Development in China: Insights Based on the 2000 Census'. *Eurasian Geography and Economics*, 43(6), pp. 425–42.

Gao. Q. (2008) 'Social Benefits in Urban China: Determinants and Impacts on Income Inequality in 1988 and 2002'. In Wan, G. (ed.) *Understanding Inequality and Poverty in China: Methods and Applications*. Palgrave Macmillan.

—— Garfinkel, I., and Zhai, F. (2009) 'Anti-Poverty Effectiveness of the Minimum Living Standard Assistance Policy in Urban China'. *Review of Income and Wealth*, 55(s1), pp. 630–55.

GHK and International Institute for Environment and Development (2004) *China Urban Poverty Study*. DFID.

Hannum, E. and Park, A. (2007) *Education and Reform in China*. London: Routledge.

Hussain, A. (2002) *Urban Poverty in PRC*. Asian Development Bank.

—— (2005) *Urban poverty in China: Measurement, Patterns and Policies*. Geneva: International Labour Office.

Keidel, A. (2007) 'The Limits of a Smaller, Poorer China'. *Financial Times*, November 14.

Khan, A. R. (2004) 'Growth, Inequality and Poverty in China: A Comparative Study of the Experience in the Periods Before and After the Asian Crisis'. ILO, Issues in Employment and Poverty, Discussion Paper 15.

—— and Riskin, C. (2001) *Inequality and Poverty in China in the Age of Globalization*. Oxford and New York: Oxford University Press.

—— —— (2005) 'China's Household Income and its Distribution, 1995 and 2002'. *China Quarterly*, June (182), pp. 356–84.

Khan, H. (2004) 'The Measurement of Poverty: Some Fundamental Issues'. ADB Institute, Discussion Paper 12.

Liang, Z. and Ma, Z. (2004) 'China's Floating Population: New Evidence from the 2000 Census'. *Population and Development Review*, 30(3).

Maxwell, S. (1999) 'The Meaning and Measurement of Poverty'. ODI Poverty Briefing 4.

Meng, X., Gregory, R., and Wan, G. (2007) 'Urban Poverty in China and Its Contributing Factors, 1986–2000'. *Review of Income and Wealth*, 53(1), pp. 167–89.

—— —— and Wang, Y. (2005) 'Poverty, Inequality, and Growth in Urban China, 1986–2000'. *Journal of Comparative Economics*, 33(4), pp. 710–29.

National Bureau of Statistics (2003) *Statistical Yearbook of China 2003*. Beijing: Statistical Publishing House of China.

Ravallion, M. and Chen, S. (2007) 'China's (Uneven) Progress Against Poverty'. *Journal of Development Economics*, 82, pp. 1–42.

—— —— and Sangraula, P. (2007) 'New Evidence on the Urbanization of Global Poverty'. World Bank Policy Research Working Paper 4199.

Reddy, S. and Minoiu, C. (2006) 'Has World Poverty Really Fallen in the 1990s?' SSRN Working Papers, Barnard College, New York.

Riskin, C. (1987) *China's Political Economy: The Quest for Development since 1949*. Oxford and New York: Oxford University Press.

—— (2006) 'The Fall in Chinese Poverty: Issues of Measurement, Incidence and cause'. In J. K. Boyce, S. Cullenberg, P. K. Pattanaik, and R. Rollin (eds.), *Human Development in the Era of Globalization*. Edward Elgar.

—— (2007) 'Has China Reached the Top of the Kuznets Curve?' In V. Shue and C. Wong (eds.) *Paying for Progress in China*, London and New York: Routledge.

Sen, A. (1976) 'Poverty: An Ordinal Approach to Measurement'. *Econometrica*, 44(2), pp. 219–31.

—— (1983) 'Poor, Relatively Speaking'. Oxford Economic Papers, 35, pp. 153–69.

Wong, C. (ed.) (2007) 'Can the Retreat from Equality be Reversed? An Assessment of Redistributive Fiscal Policies from Deng Xiaoping to Wen Jiabao'. In *Paying for Progress in China*, London and New York: Routledge.

World Bank (2008) *China Quarterly Update, January 2008*. <http://web.worldbank.org/wbsite/external/countries/eastasiapacificext/chinaextn/0,contentmdk:21639655~menuPK:3968048~pagePK:64027988~piPK:64027986~theSitePK:318950,00.html>, accessed on March 15, 2008.

Xinhua (2004) '800,000 More Chinese Live in Poverty in 2003'. Xinhua News Agency, reported in *China Daily* <http://www.chinadaily.com.cn/english/doc/2004–07/20/content_350069.htm> accessed on July 20, 2004.

—— (2007) 'China Increases Urban Minimum Living Subsidy in Wake of Inflation.' <http://www.chinadaily.com.cn/bizchina/2007-08/08/content_6017675.htm>.

13

China is Poorer than We Thought, but No Less Successful in the Fight against Poverty[1]

Shaohua Chen and Martin Ravallion[2]

Our previous estimates of global poverty measures revealed a substantial contraction in the incidence of poverty in China over the period 1981–2004; the latest update in Chen and Ravallion (2007) indicates that the proportion of China's population living below an international poverty line of $1.08 a day at 1993 prices fell from 64 per cent in 1981 to 10 per cent in 2004; the number of poor by this measure fell by about 500 million.

This international poverty line was converted to local currency using the 1993 Purchasing Power Parity (PPP) rate for China produced from the country-level price surveys done by the International Comparison Program (ICP). The PPP gives the conversion rate for a given currency into a reference currency (the US$) designed to assure parity in terms of purchasing power over commodities. However, these calculations for China rested on an estimate of the country's PPP for 1993 that was not based on a 1993 price survey, but rather was an updated version of an older (1986) PPP for China.[3] China's estimated level of poverty in 2004 was thus rooted in a PPP rate that was almost 20 years old, and even then was not drawn from the ICP.[4]

In this light, the new estimates in World Bank (2008) of China's PPP rate for 2005, based on the ICP price survey for that year, are undeniably important new data. The results for China's first participation in the ICP have already attracted considerable attention, as they suggest that China's economy in 2005 is 40 per cent smaller than we thought. For example, Keidel (2007) claims that the new PPP for China adds 300 million to the count of the country's poor. Some observers have gone further to claim that the new PPP casts doubt on the extent of China's, and (hence) the world's, progress over time against poverty.[5]

All this begs for a more careful scrutiny of China's new PPP and its implications for the extent of poverty in the country and how much progress it has made against poverty. This chapter focuses solely on the implications of the new consumption PPP released by World Bank (2008).[6] Our analysis combines the results of the 2005 ICP with a new compilation of national poverty lines for developing countries and tabulations of the distribution of consumption and income in China provided by the National Bureau of Statistics (NBS), based on their household surveys, and our interviews with NBS staff.

The 2005 PPP rate for China

The 2005 ICP is clearly the most complete assessment to date of how the cost of living varies across the countries of the world. The ICP collected primary data on the prices of a list of internationally comparable goods and services from each of a large number of outlets within 146 countries. The 2005 ICP is a clear improvement over the ICP effort for 1993, which was the last base-year used for our global poverty measures. The number of countries participating in the price survey is larger (146, compared with 117 in 1993) and the surveys have been implemented on a more scientific basis. New methods were used for measuring government compensation and housing. Ring comparisons (linking regional PPP estimates) were also done for a much larger set of countries (eighteen in all), which priced global goods. The 2005 data were also subjected to more rigorous validation methods. Otherwise, the PPPs calculated from the ICP data (and presented in World Bank, 2008) follow standard methods; as in the past, the Bank uses a multilateral extension of the bilateral Fisher price index.[7]

Given that this is the first time that China has participated in the ICP, one can hardly be very surprised to find that the new PPP differs from the old one. But the difference is large indeed. The new estimate of the consumption PPP for China is CNY3.46 to US$1 (CNY4.09 if one excludes government consumption), as compared to a PPP rate of 1.42 for 1993. The corresponding "price level indices" (PPP divided by market exchange rate) are 0.52 in 2005 versus 0.25 in 1993.

This chapter focuses on the implications of this major data revision for our knowledge about the extent of poverty in China by international standards. China merits close attention because it is not only the world's most populous country, but also the country that has made the greatest progress against poverty since about 1980s. (In due course we will also produce new estimates for the rest of the developing world.)

However, while China's participation in the 2005 ICP is clearly an important step, that participation was *partial* in that the government only agreed to implement the ICP price survey in eleven metropolitan areas, namely Beijing, Chongqing, Dalian, Guangzhou, Harbin, Ningbo, Qingdao, Shanghai, Wuhan,

Xiamen, and Xi'an. The price survey was implemented by China's NBS. Using the data from these eleven cities, the ICP has estimated national average prices and the PPP rate. To properly assess the implications of China's new PPP we need to look carefully for possible sample bias associated with the fact that the ICP price survey only included these eleven cities.

Sources of bias in the 2005 PPP for China

Our discussions with NBS staff responsible for implementing the ICP price survey revealed that the choice of these eleven cities was influenced by expectations about the likely availability of the types of goods referred to in the ICP survey, notably the more "international" goods, not readily available throughout China. One would not expect to find that all the commodities identified in the ICP price survey schedule are readily available in most rural areas of China, or even in many urban areas.

Here we try to assess what bias this might entail in the PPP for China. The estimation of "national prices" from the data for eleven cities by the ICP did attempt to re-weight the data to make them nationally representative. Each of the eleven cities was assigned to one of four regional clusters (Capitals, Coastal, Northern, Inner China) and weights were then applied based on urban and rural expenditures shares across eight commodity groups, derived from NBS household surveys.[8] The issue at hand is whether there is sufficient common support between the data for eleven cities and the national distribution to believe that the bias could be eliminated by such a re-weighting of the data.[9]

The data for the eleven cities included surrounding "rural" areas, but only about one-fifth (22 per cent) of the 1,700 outlets from which prices were obtained were in these non-urban areas (World Bank, 2008). We discussed the survey design with the senior statistician of NBS managing the unit implementing the ICP for China and other staff of NBS in Beijing. We were assured that the "rural" coverage was little more than the suburban areas at the urban fringe, and could not be considered representative of prices in rural areas.[10] This will be a source of bias if price levels differ between urban and rural areas. Evidence from China and other developing countries suggests that such differentials do exist and can be sizable (Ravallion et al., 2007). These urban–rural price differentials can be particularly large for items of consumption that are important for the poor, notably food.

When the aim is to measure poverty in China, the best available way of comparing the cost of living facing the poor between urban and rural areas is the new set of poverty lines constructed for China as part of a research project by NBS, in collaboration with the present authors.[11] These have entailed estimating the cost of food bundles (deemed adequate for basic nutritional attainment given Chinese food tastes) in both urban and rural areas of all China's provinces, and then adding an allowance for non-food goods. Region-specific food bundles were used, with separate food bundles for urban and rural areas, valued at median unit values by province. The food bundles were based on the actual consumption of those between the poorest 15th per centile and the 25th per centile nationally. These bundles were then scaled to reach 2,100 calories per person per day, with a maximum of 75 per cent of the calories from food grains.[12] Median unit values (expenditure divided by quantity at the commodity level) in urban and rural areas of each province were used for valuation. Allowances for non-food consumption were based on the non-food spending of households in a neighborhood of the point at which total spending equals the food poverty line in each province (and separately for urban and rural areas). These estimates indicate that the urban cost of living for the poor is 37 per cent higher than in urban areas in 2005; the cost of food alone is 42 per cent higher in urban areas.

Figure 13.1 plots the poverty lines for 2002 by province, split urban–rural, and identifies the provinces containing the eleven cities. There are two key observations to be made. First, the eleven cities roughly span the range of the poverty lines for *urban* areas. So it appears to be plausible that the re-weighting done by the ICP team could deliver a credible estimate for urban China. Indeed, assigning the eleven cities to their respective provinces, we see that the range is identical (Figure 13.1). The urban poverty line varies from a minimum of CNY1,061 (per person per year) to a maximum of CNY1,358 across China's

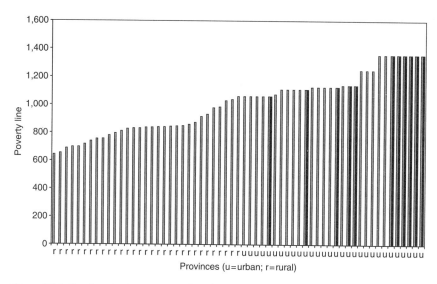

Figure 13.1 Rural and urban poverty lines by province (CNY/year)

Note: The dark bars correspond to the urban areas of the provinces that include the 11 cities used in the ICP price survey for 2005.

provinces. The food component of the poverty line varies across provinces from CNY784 to CNY1,229 while among the eleven cities it varies from CNY800 to CNY1,229. The cost of living facing the poor in the eleven cities comes reasonably close to matching that found in urban China as a whole.

The second observation from Figure 13.1 is that the eleven cities have a far higher implied cost of living for the poor than found in rural areas. The (population-weighted) mean of the urban poverty lines for the provinces containing the eleven cities is CNY1,243, as compared to CNY1,195 for all urban areas; by contrast the mean for the rural lines is CNY849.[13]

These tests cannot be considered conclusive, given that the eleven cities may well have higher prices than other urban areas, in the same province. Non-negligible price differentials between large and small cities are known to exist elsewhere.

However, from these observations, it is reasonably clear that the prices obtained in the 2005 ICP survey are un-representative of China's *rural* areas, where prices are appreciably lower for many goods, especially food for which the poor tend to have the highest budget share. And it is plain that there is no way one could credibly correct this problem by re-weighting the data, given the narrow region of common support evident in Figure 13.1. The direction of bias is clear: the new consumption PPP overstates the cost of living in China, and this bias is likely to be larger for the poor, who naturally have a high budget share for food. As we will see in the next set of calculations, it remains true that China is poorer than we all thought, but not as much so as the uncorrected 2005 consumption PPP suggests.

International poverty lines

Chen and Ravallion (2004, 2007) used a line of $32.74/month at 1993 PPP, or $1.08 per day. This was chosen as a deliberately conservative line, whereby the amount of absolute poverty in the world was judged by the standards of what "poverty" means in the poorest countries of the world; naturally, better off countries tend to have higher poverty lines, as shown in Ravallion et al. (1991). The precise line used was set at the median of the lowest ten lines in a sample of thirty-three national poverty lines, though this was shown to be virtually the same poverty line if instead one estimated the expected value of the poverty line in the poorest country, which gave a line of $31.96 per month ($1.05 per day). (This was estimated by Chen and Ravallion, 2001, using a regression of the log of the poverty line on a quadratic function of the level of mean consumption per person at PPP.)

The simplest way one might imagine updating the old "$1-a-day" line for 1993 to 2005 prices would be to apply the US rate of inflation over that period. Updating the $32.74/month 1993 PPP for inflation over 1993–2005 (using the

CPI for the US) gives $44.25 ($1.45 a day). However, this calculation makes two strong assumptions: (1) that the 1993 PPPs on which the old "$1-a-day" line was based are correct; and (2) that the principle of purchasing power parity holds, whereby the PPP for a given country evolves over time according to differences in that country's rate of inflation and that for the US. We have already noted the problems with the 1993 ICP and that there are a number of comparability problems between the 1993 and 2005 ICP data. Ravallion, Chen, and Sangraula (2008) provide an econometric test using a new set of national poverty lines (which we return to below). Their test firmly rejects the joint implications of the PPP principle and comparability of the 1993 and 2005 PPPs. They also show that if one compares fixed national poverty lines (fixed in local currency at a given date) valued at the 1993 versus 2005, the estimated poverty line at the 2005 PPP corresponding to the 1993 line of $32.74 is $36.06 (with a standard error of $4.07). This is significantly lower than the figure of $44.25 for 2005 obtained by only adjusting for inflation in the US.

These observations echo those made in Chen and Ravallion (2001, 2004) concerning the 1993 round of the ICP. Then it was also noted that there was a serious comparability problem, in that case between the 1985 PPPs based on Penn World Tables (PWT) and the Bank's PPPs at base 1993; the comparability problems related to both the primary data and the methods used. So Chen and Ravallion (2001) also argued that it is wrong to simply adjust for inflation in the US between 1985 and 1993 to update the poverty line.[14]

Given these concerns, a better approach is to return to the basic idea behind the "$1-a-day" poverty line. From the outset, this was designed to be a representative poverty line for low income countries. The original $1 a day poverty line was chosen as being representative of the poverty lines found among low income countries (Ravallion et al., 1991). The same principle was applied by Chen and Ravallion (2001) in updating the poverty line using the new PPPs for 1993. As we showed in that paper, simply adjusting for inflation in the US between 1985 and 1993 to update the international poverty line gives a line that is well above those found in low income countries.

However, the set of national poverty lines used in all our previous papers are now rather old, being essentially the same set of poverty lines used by Ravallion et al. (1991).[15] Ravallion, Chen, and Sangraula (2008) have compiled an entirely new set of seventy-five national poverty lines from the Bank's country-specific poverty assessments. In each case the national poverty line was converted to 2005 international dollars using the individual consumption PPP.

Figure 13.2 plots the Ravallion et al. (2009) poverty lines against mean consumption per person (from national accounts data) also using the same 2005 PPPs. The same pattern found by Ravallion et al. (1991) and Ravallion (1998) using the older compilations of national poverty lines is evident in Figure 13.2, with the poverty line rising with mean consumption, but with a low elasticity initially. Thus absolute poverty appears to be the dominant

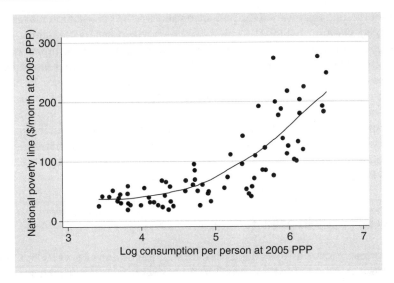

Figure 13.2 National poverty lines plotted against mean consumption, 74 developing countries, 2005 consumption PPP

Note: Fitted values use a LOWESS smoother with bandwidth=0.8.

concern in poor countries, with relative poverty emerging at higher consumption levels; for further discussion of why this happens see Ravallion (2009).

There are a number of ways one might set a new international poverty line consistent with the original idea of using a line that is typical of the poverty lines found in the poorest countries. Although the relationship in Figure 13.2 is quite flat at low consumption levels, there is still a sizable variance. The lowest poverty line in the data set is $19.05, though this is found at well above the lowest consumption level; the corresponding consumption level is slightly under $80 per month. The poverty line corresponding to the country with lowest mean consumption (Malawi) is $26.11.

However, these estimates are undoubtedly sensitive to measurement errors. Idiosyncratic differences in the data and methods used for setting national poverty lines are also likely to be playing a role. Some averaging is clearly needed. Chen and Ravallion (2001) used a semi-log parametric model for this purpose, in which the log of the national poverty line is regressed on a quadratic function of the level of consumption per capita at PPP. Using the same method on the new data set of national poverty lines gives an estimate of the log poverty line of 3.52 ($33.75 per month) for the expected poverty line in the poorest country in the sample, with a White standard error of 0.105. Figure 13.2 also gives a more flexible non-parametric regression of the national poverty lines against log mean consumption; the predicted values give the estimated mean poverty line at any given level of mean consumption.[16] The lowest predicted value is $37.14

per month and the mean of the predicted values in the poorest fifteen countries is $37.98 per month. Since this method does not impose any parametric functional form on the data, it can be considered a more robust estimate of the expected value of the poverty line in the poorest country. Based on these observations, Ravallion et al. (2009) propose an international poverty line of $1.25 a day for 2005 ($38 per month).[17]

It should be noted that the poverty line of $44.25 for 2005 that one obtains if one updates the old (1993) international line of $32.74 for inflation in the US is clearly well above the lines found in the poorest countries in Figure 13.2 (echoing the finding of Chen and Ravallion, 2001, comparing the 1993 and 1985 PPPs).

New poverty estimates for China

Our primary focus in this chapter is assessing the extent of poverty in China based on an international poverty line. Of course, this need not agree with the national poverty line in any one country. Naturally, the PPP for China has no bearing on the poverty counts using national poverty lines (such as reported for China in Ravallion and Chen, 2007). Both the official poverty line for China and the (higher) line used by Ravallion and Chen (2007) are lower than the international line used here. China's official poverty line for rural areas is about $20 per month, making it one of the lowest lines in the developing world. The line used by Ravallion and Chen is closer to the international line, though still lower (at about $30 per month). (China's official poverty line has not been updated in real terms since the mid-1980s, even though mean household consumption has increased by a factor of about four. At the time of writing, proposals to raise the official poverty line were being seriously considered within the government of China.)

In estimating China's poverty rate using the international poverty lines our estimation methods follow Chen and Ravallion (2004, 2007). We focus initially on household consumption expenditure as the welfare indicator for measuring poverty. This follows our past practice in measuring global poverty. However, we also report results for income poverty measures, which are more common in poverty analysis for China.

We readily acknowledge that the sense in which the old and new poverty lines can be meaningfully compared is rather limited, given that so much has changed (as we have emphasized above). However, it is natural to ask what the combined effect of all our changes has been. (The underlying distributional data are the only thing that has not changed, beyond updating the series to 2005.)

Table 13.1 gives estimates using both the old (1993) PPP and two new poverty lines. One of these lines simply updates the 1993 line for inflation in the US

Table 13.1. Consumption poverty rates, China, 1981–2005

	1993 PPP				2005 PPP		
		Without adjustment for lower rural prices			With adjustment for lower rural prices (PL in urban prices)		
	$Z=\$1.08$	$Z=\$1.25$	$Z=\$1.45$	$Z=\$2.00$	$Z=\$1.25$	$Z=\$1.45$	$Z=\$2.00$
				% living below poverty line			
1981	63.8	87.4	92.0	98.2	83.8	89.8	97.8
1984	41.0	78.1	84.4	95.0	69.1	78.6	92.8
1987	28.7	67.7	74.6	87.8	53.8	64.6	83.5
1990	33.0	71.8	77.4	87.9	60.7	69.9	84.9
1993	28.4	67.3	72.9	82.7	54.7	64.4	79.4
1996	17.4	52.3	59.9	73.4	37.1	46.8	65.9
1999	17.8	49.1	55.9	68.4	35.7	44.3	61.5
2002	13.8	40.1	46.3	58.4	27.8	34.9	50.5
2004	9.9	33.9	40.0	52.2	22.1	28.4	43.3
2005	5.5	26.4	32.9	46.7	15.6	20.9	35.7

Note: Poverty line is in dollars per person per day.

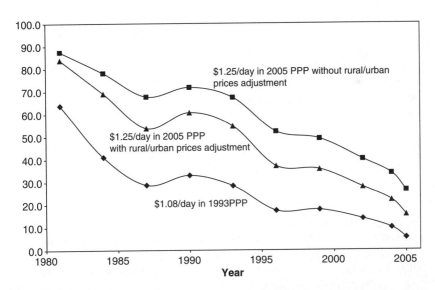

Figure 13.3 China's poverty rate over time, 1993 and 2005 PPPs (with and without correction for ICP sampling bias, %)

Table 13.2. Income poverty rates, China, 1981–2005

| | | 1993 PPP | | | 2005 PPP | | | |
| | National poverty lines* | | Without adjustment for lower rural prices | | | With adjustment for lower rural prices (poverty line in urban prices) | | |
		$Z=\$1.08$	$Z=\$1.25$	$Z=\$1.45$	$Z=\$2.00$	$Z=\$1.25$	$Z=\$1.45$	$Z=\$2.00$
				% living below poverty line				
1981	52.8	62.3	85.3	89.8	97.1	81.6	87.5	96.7
1984	24.1	25.6	70.5	78.5	91.8	54.6	67.4	87.5
1987	16.8	21.5	63.0	70.2	83.5	45.7	57.2	78.0
1990	22.2	23.0	61.8	68.6	81.2	46.0	56.3	75.3
1993	20.0	21.0	55.0	62.2	74.9	39.9	49.0	67.4
1996	9.8	10.4	38.4	46.6	63.7	23.9	31.7	50.9
1999	7.6	8.0	30.2	37.6	54.0	17.8	24.2	41.0
2002	7.3	7.6	25.1	31.4	45.8	15.3	20.0	33.5
2004	5.3	5.8	20.0	25.5	39.0	11.8	15.6	27.0
2005	5.2	5.4	17.3	22.0	34.9	10.4	13.5	23.4

Note: Poverty line is in dollars per person per day.
Sources: Ravallion and Chen (2007); *China Statistical Yearbook*, National Bureau of Statistics (1982–2006)

Table 13.3. Size of poor population, China (million)

| | Consumption poverty | | Income poverty | |
	1993 PPP $Z=\$1.08$	2005 PPP $Z=\$1.25$ (adjusted for lower rural prices)	1993 PPP $Z=\$1.08$	2005 PPP $Z=\$1.25$ (adjusted for lower rural prices)
1981	638.0	838.9	623.4	816.2
1984	428.0	720.9	267.2	569.9
1987	314.0	587.9	235.0	499.1
1990	377.5	693.7	263.0	526.2
1993	336.1	648.3	248.9	472.9
1996	212.5	454.2	127.3	292.4
1999	223.5	448.9	100.6	224.0
2002	177.2	357.3	97.6	196.6
2004	128.6	286.8	75.4	153.7
2005	71.6	204.3	70.6	135.4

Note: Population figures are end-year from *China Statistical Yearbook* (1982–2006). Poverty line is in dollars per person per day.

($44.25 per month). However, as noted above, this gives a poverty line that is well above that found in the poorest countries (due to some combination of a failure of the PPP principle to hold and non-comparabilities of the two sets of PPPs). So we also give results for a 2005 poverty line of $38 per month, as proposed by Ravallion et al. (2009), which is the mean poverty line for the poorest fifteen countries (based on Figure 13.2), and $60.83 per month ($2 a day) which is about the median ($60.81) of seventy-five countries' national poverty lines used by Ravallion et al. (2009). The "adjusted" estimates assume that the urban price level facing the poor is 37 per cent higher than in rural areas. Figure 13.3 plots the estimated poverty rates over time using both the $32.74 per month ($1.08 a day) line based on the 1993 PPP and the $38 per month ($1.25 a day) line, with and without our correction for the sampling bias in the 2005 ICP price data.

As expected, there is a marked upward revision to the estimated poverty count for China, though the marked decline over time in the poverty rate remains evident. Indeed, the new PPP suggests an even larger absolute reduction in the poverty rate since 1981. Using our corrections for sampling bias in the ICP data for China, and our new international poverty line of $1.25 a day in 2005 prices, the poverty rate fell by 68 percentage points over 1981–2005, as compared to 58 points using our previous "$1-a-day" line based on the 1993 PPP.

So far we have focused on consumption poverty, which has been our preferred approach to global poverty measurement in past work. However, given that discussions of poverty in China have typically focused on income poverty, we also present results for this measure in Table 13.2. The first column includes an update of the income poverty series we estimated in Ravallion and Chen (2007). The rest of the table corresponds to Table 13.1.

Table 13.3 gives our estimates of the number of poor, comparing the old 1993 international poverty line with the new one. We give results for both consumption and income. Comparing 2005 with 1981, there were 635 million fewer people with household consumption per person below our new 2005 poverty line, as compared to 566 million fewer poor using the old 1993 line. Comparing the old and new "$1-a-day" international poverty lines, we find that an extra 133 million people in China live in poverty in 2005. Using income instead, the difference drops to 64 million.

Conclusions

A careful scrutiny of the new PPP for China does not suggest that its implications for the extent of poverty in that country (by international standards) are anywhere near as dramatic as some casual observers have suggested. On a priori grounds, it was plain that the 300 million count for the increase in the number of China's poor was a gross exaggeration because it ignored the (documented) fact that the 2005 ICP price survey is not representative of the cost of living in rural China, where prices (particularly for the goods such as food for which the poor have a high budget share) are appreciably lower than in urban areas. Instead of an extra 300 million people deemed to be poor by the standards of what "poverty" means in low income countries, our calculations suggest the figure is closer to 130 million for consumption poverty and about half that figure for income poverty.

Of course, there can be no denying that this is a large upward adjustment in our assessment of China's poverty. Given that China had never agreed to participate in the ICP prior to 2005, it is possibly not too surprising that the prior estimates of China's PPP rate from non-ICP sources were so far off the mark. This reaffirms the importance of global participation in the ICP.

However, even if we had not done any of the calculations reported in this chapter, it should have been obvious enough that the new PPP rate alone cannot entail the sort of downward revision to China's rate of progress against poverty over time that some observers have claimed. That is because the real growth rates are unaffected by the change in the PPP, and it is China's high growth rates that have driven poverty reduction. Given that the same growth rate can have different implications for the change in the poverty count depending on the initial level of poverty, one may well find even greater progress. That is indeed what we find when we re-estimate China's poverty measures over time by our new international poverty line.

Notes

1. For useful discussions and other forms of help the authors are grateful to Angus Deaton, Yuri Dikhanov, Olivier Dupriez, Prem Sangraula, Changqing Sun, Eric Swanson, and Fred Vogel. These are the views of the authors and should not be attributed to the World Bank or any affiliated organization.
2. Development Research Group, World Bank.
3. More precisely, the previous PPPs were derived using a bilateral comparison of 1986 prices between the United States and China as documented in Ruoen and Kai (1995).
4. Blades (2007) speculates on the reasons why China has been reticent to participate in the ICP.
5. For example, the Bretton Woods Project (a NGO) claims that the new PPPs " ... undermine the much-trumpeted claims that globalization has reduced the number of people living in extreme poverty" (<http://www.brettonwoodsproject.org/art-560008>. Also see the similar comments in Pogge (2008).
6. For the 2005 round the ICP global office has been housed in the World Bank; the Asian Development Bank was the Asia regional office.
7. As was argued in Ravallion et al. (1991) and reiterated in subsequent papers, the weights attached to different commodities in the conventional PPP rate may not be appropriate for the poor. An effort is underway to address these concerns in the future. Preliminary results reported in Deaton and Dupriez (2007) do not suggest that the re-weighting needed to derive a "PPP for the poor" will make an appreciable change to the aggregate consumption PPP.
8. The method is described in World Bank (2007, p. 68) and in greater detail in Dikhanov (2005).
9. Re-weighting the data can only be used to correct for sampling bias as long as the sample spans the range of values found in the population; in other words, there must be adequate common support to believe that re-weighting is feasible.

10. NBS had never claimed that the data for the eleven cities was representative of China as a whole, and had made that clear to the ICP authorities. The preliminary report of the 2005 ICP notes the possibility of bias due to incomplete coverage of rural areas (World Bank, 2007, pp. 12, 68).

11. For further discussion, see Ravallion and Chen (2007). The methods closely follow those in Chen and Ravallion (1996). Note that these are not the current official poverty lines for China.

12. Without the latter condition, the rural food bundles were deemed to be nutritionally inadequate (in terms of protein and other nutrients) while the urban bundles were considered to be preferable. The condition was binding on both urban and rural bundles.

13. Note that these numbers imply a 41 per cent urban–rural differential in 2002; allowing for the different inflation rates in urban and rural areas gives a differential of 37 per cent in 2005.

14. In the light of these observations, we clearly do not accept the claim by Reddy and Pogge (2002) and Wade (2004) that we lowered the real value of the poverty line in Chen and Ravallion (2001) (as compared to Ravallion et al., 1991) because its real value in the US had fallen. This would only be correct if the principle of purchasing power parity holds and the PPP methods are comparable over time. Neither condition holds, either in the switch from 1985 to 1993 PPPs or the switch from 1993 to 2005. For further discussion see Chapter 3a in this volume.

15. The only prior update was done by Ravallion (1998), who included a number of new observations for Africa (which was clearly under-represented in the Ravallion et al., 1991, data set). The results were reasonably similar to the earlier study.

16. We use a Locally Weighted Scatter Plot Smoothing, also known as LOWESS. Figure 13.2 gives the default bandwidth in the STATA program for LOWESS. Ravallion et al. (2009) discuss sensitivity to the choice of smoothing parameter.

17. Note that Ravallion et al. (2009) also argue in favor of a slightly higher line, $1.25 a day, which is the mean of a reference group of the poorest fifteen countries. This raises the level of poverty in China slightly, but does not change our main conclusions.

Bibliography

Blades, Derek (2007) 'China in ICP 2005'. Consultant report to the OECD, Paris.

Chen, S. and Ravallion, M. (1996) 'Data in Transition: Assessing Rural Living Standards in Southern China'. *China Economic Review*, 7, pp. 23–56.

—— —— (2001) 'How Did the World's Poor fare in the 1990s?' *Review of Income and Wealth*, 47(3), pp. 283–300.

—— —— (2004) 'How Have the World's Poorest Fared Since the Early 1980s?' *World Bank Research Observer*, 19(2), pp. 141–70.

—— —— (2007) 'Absolute Poverty Measures for the Developing World, 1981–2004'. *Proceedings of the National Academy of Sciences of the United States of America*, 104(43), pp. 16757–62.

Deaton, A. and Dupriez, O. (2007) 'Poverty PPPs for Latin America and Asia'. Mimeo, Development Data Group, World Bank.

Dikhanov, Y. (2005) 'China: Estimating National Average Prices'. Mimeo, ICP Global Office, World Bank, Washington DC.

Keidel, A. (2007) 'The Limits of a Smaller, Poorer China'. *Financial Times*, November 13.

National Bureau of Statistics (1981–2006) *China Statistical Yearbook*. Beijing: NBS.

Pogge, T. (2008) 'Growth and inequality: Understanding recent trends and political choices'. *Dissent*, Winter, pp. 66–76.

Ravallion, M. (1998) 'Poverty Lines in Theory and Practice'. Living Standards Measurement Study Paper 133, World Bank.

—— (2009) 'On the Welfarist Rationale for Relative Poverty Lines'. In K. Basu and R. Kanbur (eds.) *Arguments for a Better World: Essays in Honor of Amartya Sen*, Oxford: Oxford University Press.

—— and Chen, S. (2007) 'China's (Uneven) Progress Against Poverty'. *Journal of Development Economics*, 82(1), pp. 1–42.

—— —— and Sangraula, P. (2007) 'New Evidence on the Urbanization of Global Poverty'. *Population and Development Review*, 33(4), pp. 667–702.

—— —— —— (2009) 'Dollar a Day Revisited'. *World Bank Economic Review*, 23(2), pp. 1–22.

—— Datt, G. and van de Walle, D. (1991) 'Quantifying Absolute Poverty in the Developing World'. *Review of Income and Wealth*, 37, pp. 345–61.

Reddy, S. G. and Pogge, T. W. (2002) 'How *Not* to Count the Poor'. (Version 3.0) Mimeo, Barnard College, New York.

Ruoen, R. and Chen, K. (1995) 'China's GDP in US Dollars based on Purchasing Power Parity'. World Bank Policy Research Working Paper 1415.

Wade, R. (2004) 'Is Globalization Reducing Poverty and Inequality?' *World Development*, 32(4), pp. 567–89.

World Bank (2007) 'A Briefing Note on Outstanding Issues with China's Consumption PPP and Poverty Estimates'. Mimeo, Data Group, Development Economics Senior Vice-Presidency, World Bank.

—— (2008) *2005 International Comparison Program: Tables of Final Results*. Washington DC: World Bank.

14

Poverty Decline in India in the 1990s: A Reality and Not an Artifact

K. Sundaram and Suresh D. Tendulkar[1]

Doubts have been raised about the comparability of the size distributions and the poverty measures based on them from the 50th (1993–4) and the 55th (1999–2000) rounds of Consumer Expenditure Surveys (CES) carried out by the National Sample Survey Organization (NSSO). We resolve the comparability problems by using the unit level records of the 50th round of CES and those relating to consumer expenditure from the employment–unemployment survey (EUS) of the 55th round. In particular, we show that the estimated monthly per capita consumer expenditure (MPCE) from the 55th round of CES based on the 30-day recall period have not been biased upwards (as maintained by the critics) by an alleged extrapolation by the respondents of their prior responses to questions on the 7-day recall (if the latter were canvassed first) and that therefore they are comparable to the (recalculated) ones from the 50th round estimates.

Using comparable estimates of four measures of poverty and the Sen index at the all-India level, it is shown that poverty in India declined in the 1990s in terms of all the five measures of poverty in rural India and in the country as a whole, and in urban India on all the measures of poverty except the number of urban poor. Also, normalized for the length of the time interval and the base year levels of poverty measures, the average annual rate of reduction in poverty was higher in the last six years of the 1990s than that recorded during the 10.5 year period preceding 1993–4. This is so on all the five poverty measures and this difference is particularly significant in respect of the number of poor.

CES comparability problems, solutions, and implications

The two problems of comparability

The primary and most widely debated problem is that information in the 55th round CES concerning household spending on a group of frequently purchased food items—comprising "food, beverages, paan, tobacco and intoxicants" (henceforth referred to as the "the food groups"[2])—was canvassed on two alternative reference or recall periods of thirty days and seven days, among the *same set of households,* and recorded on the schedule of enquiry in blocks located side-by-side. While only 30-day reporting was published in the 55th round CES, critics maintained that this reporting might have been biased upwards if households were first canvassed on the 7-day reference period and they subsequently extrapolated their response on the 7-day reporting to the 30-day entry by rough multiplicative adjustments. If this were indeed true, then there would be strong grounds to believe that the 55th round overstated consumer expenditures on these items in comparison with all the earlier quin-quennial ("thick") rounds. For, one of the key results to emerge from the four "thin" rounds preceding the 55th round survey (51st–54th) which canvassed the items in "food group" on alternative reference periods on independent sets of sample households, was that the estimates based on the 7-day recall were considerably higher than the corresponding estimates based on 30-day recall.

Lending credence to the perception that the responses from one reference period had influenced the response from the other reference period is the fact that respective monthly per capita expenditures (MPCE) on the food group from the 7- and 30-day reference periods converge to an unexpectedly high degree in comparison to the results from the set of four experimental annual, "thin" rounds of CES conducted prior to the 55th round.

To illustrate, in the 55th round, the difference between the two estimates (on the 7-day relative to the 30-day recalls) of overall mean per capita expenditure on "total food" was 6.5 per cent and 5.7 per cent for the all-India rural and urban population respectively (NSSO, 2000b). Over the four rounds of annual surveys, however, the corresponding differences averaged 30 per cent and 33 per cent.

Since the food group dominates the consumption basket of poor households, in the annual surveys, headcount ratios based on the size distribution of per capita total expenditure (PCTE) from the 7-day recall were also about half the magnitude of those based on the 30-day recall (Visaria, 2000). In the 55th round, the comparable differential considerably narrowed to 10–12 per cent.

The divergence between the 7- and 30-day results in the annual surveys was an expected consequence of two types of possible errors—recall error and telescoping error—which operate on the frequent and less salient expenditures in the food group respectively. Whereas recall error increases with a longer recall period, telescoping error increases with a shorter recall period. For this reason both phenomena skew results for the 7- and 30-day recalls in opposite directions (Deaton and Grosh, 2000).

The narrowing differential in the 55th round may have arisen as follows: when confronted with having to report consumption for the same list of items, involving frequently consumed items which are non salient events in respondent's memory on two alternative recall periods, the respondents would try to economize on their effort by adjusting their reporting for the second reference period on the basis of a rough extrapolation from the first one.

Accordingly, there are two possibilities that could result in narrowing the difference between the 7- and 30-day recalls observed in the 55th round of CES. Possibility 1 (P1) is that the 7-day recall was the first to be canvassed, and that respondents subsequently reported the 30-day equivalent by making a rough multiplicative adjustment. P1 would clearly impart a downward bias in the estimated headcount ratio for 1999–2000 in comparison with earlier rounds. Hence it would overstate the comparable extent of decline in poverty, as asserted by critics of officially released poverty estimates. If P1 is true for a sizeable proportion of households, the results of the 55th round with respect to the specified items would therefore be non-comparable with respect to all previous NSS rounds.

The other possibility (P2) is that respondents may have been asked first to recall consumption for the past thirty days, and subsequently reported their consumption during the previous seven days by use of crude division.[3] It can easily be seen that either P1 or P2 would produce the narrowed 7- versus 30-day differential observed in the 55th round CES. P1 would bias upwards the reporting for the 30-day recall, whereas P2 would bias downward results for the higher 7-day recall. However, if P2 were true, the results of the 55th round would indeed turn out to be comparable to the 50th round—provided one adjusts the latter for the mixed reference period used in the 55th round.

The second and less widely recognized problem is that, in the 55th round, consumer expenditure on certain infrequently purchased items, namely "clothing," "footwear," "durables," "education," and "health care" (institutional), was collected only on a 365-day reference period. The published results for all remaining items were based on a 30-day reference period. Accordingly, in the published results, the size distribution of monthly PCTE as per the NSS 55th round CES for 1999–2000 are based on a mixed reference period (MRP). In contrast, the published size distribution of PCTE from the NSS 50th and all earlier rounds is based on data collected with a uniform reference period (URP) of thirty days for all items of expenditure. In particular this was also true for the published results of all the quinquennial surveys carried out earlier in 1972–3, 1977–8, 1983, and 1987–8.

These comparability problems are, however, not intractable.

A resolution of the 7-day/30-day problem

We resolve the 7-day/30-day problem by showing that the reported consumer expenditure on the food group collected in the 55th round of CES indeed reflected 30-day recall. To establish this we compare the CES results with consumer expenditure data from the 55th round's employment–unemployment survey (EUS) which was canvassed on an *independent sample of households* distinct from those in CES but from the same universe of population and only used *the 30-day recall period* for items in the food group and a 365-day recall period for the above-listed infrequently purchased items. So that, on this score, a size distribution based on the EUS would be comparable to the published 55th round CES results with a 30-day reference period for the food group. It is then ascertained whether the observed difference between the CES and EUS estimates could be attributed to the possible biases introduced in the CES estimates by the canvassing of the household expenditures on these items on two alternative recall periods. This is done by comparing the CES–EUS differential with the corresponding average differential in the estimates of consumer expenditure of these items emerging from independent schedules with 7- and 30-day recall periods canvassed on independent samples during the experimental annual CES surveys conducted from the 51st to the 54th rounds of NSS.

However, this comparison needs to take account of the fact that the EUS is likely to understate consumer expenditures compared with the CES. In the EUS, per capita consumer expenditure was merely a classificatory variable for tabulation of employment characteristics and not the main subject of enquiry. Therefore, consumer expenditure details were canvassed with a considerably abridged schedule. International experience and a priori reasoning suggest that for a given recall period, a detailed listing of items helps reduce recall error. Conversely, an abridged listing leads to a greater recall lapse and hence to an understatement of consumer expenditure in comparison to reporting based on a more detailed listing (Deaton and Grosh, 2000).

Whereas the CES enquiry canvassed a detailed schedule of 330-odd items spread over some fifteen pages, the EUS enquiry canvassed a one-page schedule comprising thirty-three items. According to the explanation provided on the relevant enquiry block, this part of the survey was deemed to serve as a "worksheet" for recording household consumer expenditure. However, not all the items would have been affected by this abridgment to the same degree. For a given recall period, *understatement from recall lapse is expected to be the greater the more heterogeneous the basket* contained in the abridged description. The recall lapse is affected by the diversity in consumer purchases and fluctuations in their consumption during the recall period, as well as the concomitant frequency and salience of the respective consumption events in the respondent's memory.

So, given the impact of the abridgment effect, we can expect the 30-day CES estimates based on a detailed schedule to be higher than the corresponding EUS estimates using an abridged schedule. If, in addition, P1 had indeed eventuated as has been maintained by the critics, then the reported 30-day recall-based estimates from CES would also have been pulled up by the 7-day reporting, compared with what they would have been had the 30-day recall been canvassed independently. This would accentuate the EUS–CES difference beyond that arising from the use in the EUS of an abridged schedule. In order to test the possibility P1, relative differences in Tables 14.1a and 14.1b provide the excess of CES estimates over those from the EUS as a percentage of the latter. Accordingly, the CES–EUS relative differences indicate *the excess of allegedly overstated CES estimates in relation to expectedly understated EUS-based estimates.*

Now, the central question is how large should this excess be in order to validate P1? As noted earlier, the annual 51st to 54th "thin sample" rounds of the NSS provide unbiased estimates of the order of magnitude of this excess (NSSO, 2000a). Accordingly, given the expected understatement in the EUS, if P1 holds, we expect the excess of CES over EUS to be unequivocally greater than the excess of the 7-day estimates over the corresponding estimates, averaged over the four "thin" rounds (or average 7-day/30-day difference). If this does not hold, P1 is not proven. This leaves us with possibility P2 as having eventuated. If this is so, then, the 55th round would indeed have captured the 30-day recall rendering it comparable to all the earlier rounds of NSS as far as food group is concerned.

It needs to be stressed that the empirical support for P2 does not rest solely on the absence of validation of P1. Specifically, as we shall see presently, in the case of many significant item groups, the size of the CES–EUS differential is quite small and thus consistent with P2 being true, after allowing for abridgment effect and sample variability.

Comparing CES and EUS by commodity groups

In the light of the foregoing a priori considerations, we now undertake an empirical implementation of the suggested test procedure to resolve the 7-day/30-day recall controversy. It is organized in two parts. The first compares the CES and the EUS at the aggregate level of the total rural/urban population but separately across all the comparable commodity groups identified in the abridged EUS schedule. This information is collected in Table 14.1a for the rural population, and Table 14.1b for the urban population. The second part performs a similar comparison, but only for the contested commodity groups, and at a disaggregated level, dividing the population into twenty fractile groups of 5 per cent each. A CES–EUS comparison is given for each fractile group. The commodity group details in this part are confined only to those item groups that are affected by the 7-day/30-day controversy. The information is presented for rural and urban populations in Tables 14.2a and 14.2b.

Table 14.1a. A comparison of estimates of monthly per capita expenditures by item group: all India, rural population (NSS 55th round, July 1999–June 2000)

	Item	CES	EUS	Difference	Difference (%)	Average difference (7 days versus 30 days)
1	All goods and services	486.16	443.11	43.05	9.71	
2	Cereals and substitutes	108.11	106.24	1.87	1.76	12.92
3	Pulses and products	19.14	18.19	0.95	5.22	48.18
4	Milk and milk Products	42.56	37.47	5.09	13.58	19.62
5	Edible oil	18.16	18.05	0.11	0.61	22.83
6	Vegetables	29.98	29.75	0.23	0.77	55.25
7	Fruits (fresh and dry)	8.36	6.65	1.72	25.71	60.27
8	Eggs, fish, and meat	16.14	15.72	0.42	2.67	54.16
9	Other food (sugar, salt, spices, and beverages)	46.36	30.04	16.32	54.32	54.57
10	Total food	288.81	262.11	26.7	10.19	30.01
11	Paan, tobacco, and intoxicants	13.96	12.11	1.85	15.28	43.13
12	Fuel and light	36.56	32.03	4.53	14.14	
13	Entertainment	2.02	1.02	1.00	98.03	
14	Non-institutional medical services	22.94	22.43	0.51	2.27	
15	Toilet articles	11.62	14.66	−3.04	−20.74	
16	Travel/conveyance	14.28	10.70	3.58	33.46	
17	Rent	1.89	1.95	−0.06	−3.08	
18	Other misc. goods and services	26.65	12.69	13.96	110.01	
19	Education (tuition, newspapers, books, stationery, etc.)	9.38	13.91	−4.53	−32.57	
20	Institutional medical services	6.66	6.32	0.34	5.38	
21	Cloth and clothing	33.28	32.68	0.60	1.84	
22	Footwear	5.37	5.39	−0.02	−0.37	
23	Durable goods	12.76	15.62	−2.86	−18.31	

Notes: CES and EUS figures are for mean MPCE in rupees. Average difference (7 days versus 30 days): excess of estimated MPCE as per Sch. Type 2 (with 7-day reference period for food, paan, tobacco, and intoxicants) over that based on Sch. Type 1 (with uniform reference period of 30 days) as a percentage of the estimates on the 30-day reference period, averaged over the four "Annual" Rounds (1994–5, 1995–6, 1996–7, and Jan.–June 1998).
Source: NSS (2001a, 2001b); authors' own calculations.

Table 14.1b. A comparison of estimates of monthly per capita expenditures by item group: all India, urban population (NSS 55th round, July 1999–June 2000)

	Item	CES	EUS	Difference	Difference (%)	Average difference (7 days versus 30 days)
1	All goods and services	854.92	762.93	91.99	12.06	
2	Cereals and substitutes	106.02	102.34	3.68	3.60	15.94
3	Pulses and products	25.20	24.22	0.98	4.05	42.08
4	Milk and milk Products	74.17	66.91	7.26	10.85	12.24
5	Edible oil	26.81	27.02	−0.24	−0.78	22.30
6	Vegetables	43.90	47.86	−3.96	−8.27	52.48
7	Fruits (fresh and dry)	20.68	17.26	3.42	19.81	69.28
8	Eggs, fish, and meat	26.78	25.90	0.91	3.40	50.44
9	Other food (sugar, salt, spices, and beverages)	87.39	52.26	35.13	67.22	53.42
10	Total food	410.95	363.77	47.18	12.96	32.91
11	Paan, tobacco, and intoxicants	16.22	13.79	2.43	17.62	41.50
12	Fuel and light	66.26	58.79	7.47	12.71	
13	Entertainment	9.88	4.87	5.01	102.87	
14	Non-institutional medical services	30.95	29.57	1.38	4.67	
15	Toilet articles	26.34	25.41	0.93	3.66	
16	Travel/conveyance	47.19	30.14	17.05	56.57	
17	Rent	38.16	38.58	−0.42	−1.09	
18	Other misc. goods and services	67.02	33.06	33.96	102.72	
19	Education (tuition, newspapers, books, stationery, etc.)	37.06	55.83	−18.77	−33.62	
20	Institutional medical services	12.33	11.60	0.68	6.29	
21	Cloth and clothing	51.76	50.33	1.43	2.84	
22	Footwear	10.05	10.22	−0.17	−1.66	
23	Durable goods	30.85	36.98	−6.13	−16.58	

Notes: CES and EUS figures are for mean MPCE in rupees. Average difference (7 days versus 30 days): excess of estimated MPCE as per Schd. Type 2 (with 7-day reference period for food, paan, tobacco, and intoxicants) over that based on Sch. Type 1 (with uniform reference period of 30 days) as a percentage of the estimates on the 30-day reference period, averaged over the four "Annual" Rounds (1994–5, 1995–6, 1996–7, and Jan.–June 1998).

Source: NSS (2001a, 2001b); authors' own calculations.

Let us turn to an examination of Tables 14.1a and 14.1b. For as many as eight out of the nine items in the food group in both tables, the differences between CES and EUS estimates are well short of the benchmark average 7-day/30-day difference emerging from the 51st to 54th annual rounds. In fact, the estimates are amazingly close to each other, given the impact of the use of an abridged schedule in the EUS.[4]

The only exception to the above result is the omnibus category of "Other food", comprising sugar, salt, spices, beverages, and processed foods including cooked meals. This shows the highest percentage excess within the food group. An excess of 54 per cent almost touches the 7-day/30-day norm for the rural population, whereas for the urban population the CES–EUS difference for this item group at 67 per cent overshoots the 53 per cent norm emerging from the "thin" rounds. This item group by itself accounts for nearly two-thirds (61 per cent in rural India and 64 per cent in urban India) of the total difference between the CES and the EUS in the total food category.

Before proceeding to discuss further the CES–EUS difference in respect of the items in the food group it is useful to review the relative difference between CES and EUS estimates for items outside the food group. Identical reference periods are used for these items in both the 55th round CES and EUS.[5] Therefore, if CES estimates are higher, it is due entirely to the abridgment effect in the EUS. This would provide some benchmarks for the pure abridgment effect.

Only for three item groups—"Entertainment," "Travel/conveyance," and the catch-all category of "Other miscellaneous goods and services"—do CES estimates exceed EUS estimates by more than 30 per cent. This does not account for items for which the EUS estimates actually exceed the CES estimates namely "Education," "footwear," and "Durable goods". In both rural and urban India, the difference is more than 100 per cent in the case of both "Entertainment" and "Other miscellaneous goods and services." Each of these constitutes a heterogeneous basket where the abridgment effect is expected to be significant, as has been observed in similar cases all over the world.

Notably, the category of "Other miscellaneous goods and services" accounts for a major part of the cumulated difference between CES and EUS estimates outside the food group: 40 per cent of the sum of absolute differences in rural India, and 36 per cent in urban India. To reiterate, any observed excess of CES estimates over the EUS estimates in respect of all the items outside the food group are due to the impact of abridgment in the EUS and of sampling variability and *not* the result of any interference due to recall on any alternative recall period.

With this assessment of abridgment effect outside the food group that is free from recall-period effect, let us now revert to a consideration of the CES–EUS differences for items in the food group where both the effects are present.

In eight out of the nine item groups, as noted previously, the excess of CES estimates over the corresponding EUS estimates (as a percentage of the latter) are well below the average 7-day/30-day difference observed in the four "thin" rounds preceding the 55th round NSS, with only the heterogeneous group of "Other food" as the exception. The exception is on expected lines as it is consistent with a priori reasoning and attributable to the abridgment effect based on the evidence from international surveys.

Further, in rural India, for four item groups ("Cereals and substitutes," "Edible oils," "Vegetables," and "Egg, fish, and meat"), the CES–EUS difference is less than 3 per cent, with this difference slightly exceeding 5 per cent for "Pulses and products". In urban India, the CES–EUS difference is below 5 per cent for the same five item groups (including two cases, "Edible oils" and "Vegetables," where the EUS estimates exceed the CES estimates). In both segments, these five item groups accounted for close to two-thirds of the average expenditure on all food in CES.

In respect of all these item groups, a CES–EUS difference of the order of 5 per cent or less, (and way below the 7-day/30-day difference in the "thin" rounds) is quite consistent with the absence of an effect on the 30-day response of a *prior response* on the 7-day reference—if the latter was canvassed first—allowing for the presence of abridgment effects and sampling variability.

This leaves us with three item groups—"Milk and milk products" (CES–EUS difference of above 5 per cent and below, but close to the 7-day/30-day difference); "Paan, tobacco, and intoxicants" (CES–EUS difference above 10 per cent but well below the 7-day/30-day difference); and the heterogeneous group of "Other food"—with the CES–EUS difference being large and close to or above the 7-day/30-day difference.

In respect of "Milk and milk products" (where the CES–EUS difference is 14 per cent in rural India and 11 per cent in urban India), a plausible benchmark for the "order of magnitude" of CES–EUS difference that is unaffected by the 7-day/30-day controversy and that reflects only the effects of abridgment and sampling variability is provided by the case of another compositionally diverse group of "Fuel and light" which also has a sizable share in overall PCTE. In the case of "Fuel and light," the CES–EUS difference is 14 per cent in rural India and 13 per cent in urban India. Further, given that there are five major item categories where the size of the CES–EUS difference is small enough (5 per cent or less) to be consistent with the hypothesis of no upward bias in CES on account of the presence of 7-day questions, it does not appear plausible to argue that the responses of the households on the 7-day recall influenced their reporting on the 30-day recall for "Milk and milk products" but not for, say, "Vegetables" when these item categories are not very dissimilar in terms of salience and frequency of purchase.

In respect of "Other food" and "Paan, tobacco, and intoxicants", a rough indication of the size of the CES–EUS differential that can be expected for a very heterogeneous group, even in the complete absence of any influence of an alternative reference period on the 30-day recall, and reflecting only the effects of abridgment and sampling variability, is provided by the differential for the group "Miscellaneous goods and services" in the non-food category: 100 per cent for rural India and 103 per cent for urban India. As can be readily seen, in respect of both "Other Food" and "Paan, tobacco, and intoxicants", the observed CES–EUS differences are well below these bench-mark levels. If this is accepted, even in respect of the two heterogeneous item-groups in the food category which show a large CES–EUS difference, the 55th round CES estimates can be taken to reflect the responses on the 30-day recall.

In all these cases, therefore, the size of the CES–EUS differential, allowing for the abridgment effect and sampling variability, is consistent with the possibility P2 rather than the 55th round CES estimates on items in the food group indeed reflect responses on the 30-day recall and hence are *comparable to those in the earlier NSS rounds.*

Critics of the 55th round might argue that the test for resolving the 7-day/ 30-day controversy, when implemented at the aggregate level for the entire population, may conceal uneven incidence of the recall problem at the disaggregated level, affecting certain population groups. Indeed, if the 7-day recall had biased upward the 30-day estimate in CES at the lower end of the size distribution, this would overstate consumer expenditure for poorer groups, and hence lead to an understatement in corresponding poverty indicators.

In order to evaluate this possibility, the percentage excess of CES estimates over EUS estimates are mapped across twenty fractile groups of 5 per cent size each in Table 14.2a for the rural population and 14.2b for the urban population. As mentioned earlier, we apply this analysis only to those items which have been involved in the 7-day/30-day controversy, namely: food, beverages, paan, tobacco, and intoxicants. The first line in both tables provides the respective norms for the 7-day/30-day difference derived from the average over the "thin" 51st–54th rounds, as used also in Tables 14.1a and 14.1b. These broad yardsticks continue to be used as the common standard of comparison because differentials derived from comparable "thin samples" at the fractile-group level are expected to carry higher relative standard errors.

Remarkably, in both Tables 14.2a and 14.2b, CES–EUS differences for all but one of the item groups lie well below the yardsticks provided by the 51st–54th rounds. The exception is provided by the same group that stood out in Tables 14.1a and 14.1b—namely "Other food." The reason is also the same: this is an aggregate of heterogeneous items for which abridgment effect is expected to be very pronounced. However, it is remarkable that for the bottom 40 per cent of the rural population, even this diverse group of items registers relative CES–EUS differences well below their respective yardsticks. Further, in almost all fractile groups in the bottom 40 per cent, the CES–EUS difference is 5 per cent or less for at least four item categories.

What we have therefore shown is that the observed differences between the 30-day-based CES estimates and EUS estimates overwhelmingly reflect the

Table 14.2a. Excess of CES estimates over EUS estimates of MPCE in food, paan, tobacco, and intoxicants (1990–2000): all India, rural population, 5% fractile groups (%)

Fractile group	Cereals and substitutes	Pulses and products	Milk and milk products	Edible oils	Vegetables	Fruits and nuts	Eggs, fish, and meat	Other food	Total food	Paan, tobacco, and intoxicants
(1)	(2)	(3)	(4)	(5)	(6)	(7)	(8)	(9)	(10)	(11)
A. All India average difference, 7 versus 30 days (%)	12.9	48.2	19.6	22.8	55.3	60.3	54.2	54.6	30.0	43.1
B. Excess of CES over EUS (%): all fractile groups	1.8	5.2	13.6	0.6	0.8	25.7	2.8	54.3	10.2	15.3
B.1: 0–5	5.6	-7.1	-14.1	-2.5	12.7	30.7	-11.8	34.8	6.2	14.3
B.2: 5–10	3.4	-2.3	-2.8	-2.3	13.6	17.2	-17.8	42.7	6.2	15.6
B.3: 10–15	3.8	1.2	-2.3	-0.7	10.6	-1.7	-8.2	45.3	7.0	9.1
B.4: 15–20	3.0	-0.5	7.1	-2.8	6.6	3.4	-4.5	41.0	6.3	13.4
B.5: 20–25	0.7	2.3	15.0	0.0	6.9	13.8	-4.0	46.2	6.9	6.8
B.6: 25–30	1.8	3.6	9.3	-20.9	2.0	19.2	-7.6	46.3	6.4	18.4
B.7: 30–35	0.5	5.3	11.1	1.4	7.0	6.7	-4.0	49.8	7.4	17.4
B.8: 35–40	0.9	2.7	15.9	0.1	8.2	16.5	6.0	49.9	8.8	12.4
B.9: 40–45	2.3	5.8	11.0	-2.3	5.5	12.7	-2.4	53.2	8.7	14.1
B.10: 45–50	0.3	3.9	12.1	1.6	4.0	17.2	3.7	54.4	8.5	17.3
B.11: 50–55	0.5	6.9	14.6	2.7	6.1	29.5	2.7	49.3	9.4	12.7
B.12: 55–60	-0.4	8.3	11.1	2.9	0.6	34.8	16.1	56.2	9.6	9.8
B.13: 60–65	-0.4	5.4	14.1	3.2	1.8	20.9	-2.7	59.3	9.3	6.6
B.14: 65–70	2.2	4.6	16.7	4.0	-0.5	21.5	5.2	55.6	11.1	14.4
B.15: 70–75	1.0	7.5	13.7	1.8	1.5	21.0	4.2	51.6	10.2	9.7
B.16: 75–80	2.4	5.3	12.0	1.4	-1.5	25.1	6.7	54.9	10.8	13.2
B.17: 80–85	1.8	6.9	21.0	-0.7	-3.2	26.9	-4.4	57.7	11.9	5.6
B.18: 85–90	0.1	6.7	16.7	2.1	-4.9	28.8	11.6	51.3	11.5	12.1
B.19: 90–95	5.0	12.4	13.7	1.6	-7.6	32.5	13.4	52.9	13.7	19.7
B.20: 95–100	4.3	8.5	15.5	0.9	-7.0	39.3	8.8	67.9	17.4	38.2

Notes: Average difference, 7 versus 30 days (%): ratio of 7-day recall based estimate to corresponding 30-day recall based estimate expressed as a percentage and averaged over the 51st to 54th rounds of NSS. 0–5 denotes bottom 5%, 5–10, the next 5% of the population, and so on.

Sources: NSS (2000a); authors' own calculations based on the 55th round of NSS.

Table 14.2b. Excess of CES estimates over EUS estimates of MPCE in food, paan, tobacco, and intoxicants (1990–2000): all India, urban population, 5% fractile groups (%)

Fractile group	Cereals and substitutes	Pulses and products	Milk and milk products	Edible oils	Vegetables	Fruits and nuts	Eggs, fish, and meat	Other food	Total food	Paan, tobacco, and intoxicants
(1)	(2)	(3)	(4)	(5)	(6)	(7)	(8)	(9)	(10)	(11)
A. All India average difference, 7 versus 30 days (%)	15.9	42.1	12.2	22.3	52.5	69.3	50.4	53.4	32.9	41.5
B. Excess of CES over EUS (%): all fractile groups	3.6	4.1	10.9	-0.8	-8.3	19.8	3.4	67.22	13.0	17.6
B.1: 0–5	9.9	3.2	5.3	-3.3	1.8	-6.9	-14.1	60.8	10.9	9.3
B.2: 5–10	5.7	1.7	7.9	-0.7	3.2	1.7	2.3	56.9	10.3	8.2
B.3: 10–15	6.9	1.7	3.1	0.1	1.2	20.8	4.3	56.4	10.9	0.7
B.4: 15–20	2.1	4.2	7.2	0.6	-1.6	20.9	-3.3	64.4	9.5	2.5
B.5: 20–25	4.3	2.2	5.8	-0.3	-3.9	15.5	0.6	57.9	9.3	9.1
B.6: 25–30	2.2	9.1	4.5	2.8	-0.7	12.7	1.8	58.7	9.8	13.5
B.7: 30–35	5.0	2.8	2.9	2.4	-3.4	8.8	-0.6	60.1	9.8	28.4
B.8: 35–40	4.6	4.3	3.4	-1.5	-5.7	10.5	1.0	62.7	9.6	24.4
B.9: 40–45	8.1	9.8	4.4	-1.1	-5.0	13.2	3.7	58.6	11.3	3.5
B.10: 45–50	7.0	3.2	7.6	0.1	-4.1	12.3	8.0	58.0	11.6	16.9
B.11: 50–55	4.2	7.0	16.1	0.2	-5.0	17.3	-2.4	67.7	13.0	9.2
B.12: 55–60	6.3	4.3	11.1	0.7	-7.6	24.2	9.0	65.0	13.2	9.8
B.13: 60–65	2.6	6.2	15.2	1.7	-7.1	22.0	3.0	61.6	12.2	4.6
B.14: 65–70	-0.3	4.4	17.3	2.1	-9.5	24.1	-5.8	65.9	11.7	4.4
B.15: 70–75	-0.5	4.6	11.9	1.4	-14.6	25.7	7.4	69.7	11.9	24.3
B.16: 75–80	4.0	5.4	15.5	-1.7	-12.6	18.1	-0.4	55.8	12.0	1.5
B.17: 80–85	3.0	5.9	11.3	0.3	-10.8	19.2	6.1	65.7	13.5	16.9
B.18: 85–90	4.9	0.6	9.7	-2.7	-12.0	16.4	9.7	67.1	13.9	28.6
B.19: 90–95	-0.3	5.2	15.6	Neg	-12.7	30.2	2.0	61.4	14.6	18.1
B.20: 95–100	-2.5	9.7	9.1	-10.1	-18.2	20.4	12.1	65.2	14.3	57.2

Notes: Average difference, 7 versus 30 days (%): ratio of 7-day recall based estimate to corresponding 30-day recall based estimate expressed as a percentage and averaged over the 51st to 54th rounds of NSS. 0–5 denotes bottom 5%, 5–10, the next 5% of the population, and so on.

Sources: NSS (2000a); authors' own calculations based on the 55th round of NSS.

combined impact of the abridged schedule in the EUS and sampling variability. These differences in turn are too small to support the hypothesis that the CES estimates on the 30-day reference period have been artificially inflated because households extrapolated their 30-day reporting from a 7-day recall. Therefore, the narrowed differential between the 7- and 30-day recall-based estimates in the 55th round CES has to be due to possibility P2, which requires that the households predominantly reported expenditures on the 30-day recall and may subsequently have adjusted their 7-day estimates accordingly.

Adjusting the 50th round result for mixed reference periods

As mentioned previously, in the CES for 1993–4 (50th round), information on clothing, footwear, durables, education, and health (institutional) was collected from each sample household for two alternative reference periods of 30 days and 365 days. Notably, for all the remaining items in the 50th round, a uniform 30-day recall was used. It is thus possible to compute two alternative size distributions for the 50th round: one based on a uniform reference period (URP) of 30 days, and another based on a mixed reference period (MRP) of 365 days for the above mentioned items, and 30 days for the remaining items. This is important for establishing recall period comparability between the 50th round and the 55th round, in view of the shift to MRP in the latter.

Before we report the results of our exercise, it is useful to raise the question of whether canvassing two alternative recall periods in the case of the 50th round raises possible problems of the first recall influencing the reporting for the second, of the kind discussed in connection with the food group in the previous sections. In the 50th round CES, the items of concern are: (a) clothing; (b) footwear; (c) durables; (d) education; and (e) institutional health expenditures. As noted above, information on these items was collected in the 50th round on two alternative recall periods of 30 days and 365 days, from the same set of sample households. In the schedules of enquiry, the blocks relating to (a) to (c) were placed one after the other, with the 30-day recall coming first, whereas for (d) and (e), they were side by side. Prima facie, it cannot be completely ruled out that this might pose problems.

In our judgment, however, their incidence is likely to be minimal, for the following reasons. First, expenditures on (a) to (e) relate to events that are relatively less frequent and more salient in the respondent's memory than those in the food group. Accordingly, expenditures over the last 30 days can be more easily distinguished from those in the last 365 days. This is not the case with the items in the food group. Purchases of these food items are likely to have been more frequent and less memorable, providing greater incentive to minimize the additional effort required to accurately recall expenditures. Second, it is deemed significant that there was some previous experience in the use of the two recall periods in the case of clothing, etc. Information on items (a) to

Table 14.3a. Estimates of MPCE for clothing and durables by broad fractile group, 50th–53rd NSS CES rounds: all India, rural population (INR)

Clothing

	50th round		51st round		52nd round		53rd round	
	30-days	365-days	30-days	365-days	30-days	365-days	30-days	365-days
Bottom 40%	2.63	14.09	3.43	10.64	2.84	12.38	2.59	10.79
Middle 40%	10.14	21.29	12.54	16.44	10.44	18.91	8.44	18.07
80–90	27.03	29.23	31.68	23.88	28.44	26.79	21.73	27.28
90–95	47.48	33.21	49.94	28.48	56.39	32.86	36.84	28.60
95–100	98.74	46.92	136.85	44.88	130.48	45.88	105.45	48.80
All	15.12	21.18	21.78	21.21	26.63	26.43	27.60	28.11

Durables

	50th round		51st round		52nd round		53rd round	
	30-days	365-days	30-days	365-days	30-days	365-days	30-days	365-days
Bottom 40%	1.00	2.60	1.18	1.23	1.12	1.33	0.70	1.08
Middle 40%	3.04	5.22	3.40	2.46	3.76	2.85	3.45	2.67
80–90	7.28	10.33	8.84	5.71	8.68	5.81	7.25	6.10
90–95	11.09	14.70	17.49	8.54	16.40	8.79	14.58	8.59
95–100	95.54	33.44	196.91	30.41	113.80	29.96	85.82	26.54
All	7.67	6.57	16.12	6.29	15.36	8.25	17.34	9.28

Source: Authors' own calculations based on NSS (2000a).

Table 14.3b. Estimates of MPCE for clothing and durables by broad fractile group, 50th–53rd NSS CES rounds: all India, urban population (INR)

Clothing

	50th round		51st round		52nd round		53rd round	
	30-days	365-days	30-days	365-days	30-days	365-days	30-days	365-days
Bottom 40%	3.58	18.51	3.75	14.11	3.31	15.71	2.44	14.73
Middle 40%	15.94	32.90	17.68	26.62	16.84	27.97	14.02	25.81
80–90	40.46	48.47	41.97	39.82	49.43	42.56	36.55	41.77
90–95	62.07	62.07	66.62	49.57	73.72	54.57	67.00	54.07
95–100	129.62	84.12	154.25	72.67	213.29	79.00	150.86	95.06
All	21.43	32.72	28.11	34.26	42.65	40.10	37.62	43.61

Durables

	50th round		51st round		52nd round		53rd round	
	30-days	365-days	30-days	365-days	30-days	365-days	30-days	365-days
Bottom 40%	1.20	3.02	1.72	1.71	1.48	1.60	1.30	1.59
Middle 40%	5.14	8.82	5.04	3.89	5.08	4.79	4.43	4.53
80–90	13.77	18.62	14.72	11.81	16.72	13.82	14.37	16.27
90–95	26.53	32.95	21.44	19.75	26.26	15.13	23.22	22.46
95–100	198.64	78.44	226.09	59.00	308.81	74.58	198.94	92.94
All	15.16	12.17	22.89	12.47	38.75	18.31	32.33	23.44

Source: Authors' own calculations based on NSS (2000a).

(c) had been collected from the same set of households, eliciting information on the basis of the same two alternative recall periods, for the three quinquennial rounds preceding the 50th round. In addition, field officials had been explicitly instructed to check the recorded entries against the two recall periods, presumably to keep some check on the investigators.

What light does the evidence from the "thin" rounds throw on this issue of the 50th round estimates of consumer expenditure on the 365-day reference period being influenced by the prior responses on the 30-day recall in respect of items of low frequency purchase? We have tabulated, for all of India, but separately for the rural and the urban populations, the estimates of consumer expenditure on the two recall periods for the 50th round and three full-year "thin" rounds (51st, 52nd, and 53rd) for "Clothing and durables." This has been done for broad fractile groups—the bottom 40 per cent and the middle 40 per cent, with the top 20 per cent being split into three groups: the 80–90th percentile; the 90–95th percentile and the top 5 per cent. For the 50th round these are exact percentiles, but, for the "thin" rounds, they would be approximate—obtained by aggregating the estimates for (fixed) expenditure—classes.[6] The outcome is presented in Tables 14.3a and 14.3b.

For the population as a whole, in the "thin" rounds, the expenditure reported on the two reference periods are fairly close to one another for clothing in the rural population while the urban population reported higher expenditure on the 365-day recall than that for 30 days. However, in respect of durables the 365-day estimates are substantially lower than the estimates on the 30-day recall, for both the segments.

In the 50th round, the overall monthly per capita expenditure (MPCE) on clothing on the 365-day recall was about 40 per cent higher than that on the 30-day recall. In the case of durables, however, the estimated expenditure on the 365-day recall was *lower* by about 14 per cent (rural) and 20 per cent (urban). Tables 14.3a and 14.3b show that there are differences in consumer behavior in respect of these relatively infrequently purchased items across fractile groups.

Now, focusing on the bottom 40 per cent, we find that the estimates of expenditure on clothing on the 365-day recall are substantially higher than those on the 30-day recall in both the 50th round and in the "thin" rounds—but the differential is greater in the 50th round. Broadly, the same is also true in respect of the durables: an excess of estimates on the 365-day recall over those on the 30-day recall of between 4 and 54 per cent in the "thin" rounds and of 160 per cent in the 50th round. (See Tables 14.3a and 14.3b.) In other words, for the poor population these items are much more infrequent in their purchases of the past 30 days as compared to those during the past 365 days.

For purposes of poverty estimates we may focus on the above-stated results for the bottom 40 per cent: that the excess of the estimates of expenditures on clothing and durable on the 365-day recall over those on the 30-day recall are greater in the 50th round relative to the differentials yielded by the "thin" rounds. If the argument is that canvassing the two alternative recall periods on the same set of households has biased the estimates on the 365-day recall because of their *prior* responses on the 30-day recall by minimizing their recall efforts, then such an interference should have brought the comparable *monthly* estimates on the two recall periods *closer* relative to the differences emerging from the "thin" rounds. This has not happened. The estimates on the two recall periods appear to be indeed based on independent recall efforts on the part of the respondents.

Tables 14.4a and 14.4b present, respectively for the rural and the urban populations, the size distributions of total household consumer expenditure in the 50th round with uniform and mixed referenced periods according to 5 per cent fractile groups. The households are ranked according to the size of monthly per capita total consumer expenditure (PCTE).

It may be noted that a shift from 30-day recall to 365-day recall in respect of clothing, footwear, durables, education, and institutional health expenditure leads to a higher mean PCTE for fractile groups in the bottom 85 per cent of the rural population and the bottom 95 per cent of the urban population. In other words, for these sections of the population, mean per capita monthly expenditure on the above-mentioned items was higher on the basis of 365-day recall

Table 14.4a. A comparison of size distribution by 5% fractile groups between uniform and mixed reference periods, 50th NSS round: all India, rural population

Fractile group	Cumulative % of population	Average PCTE URP	Cum % CE, 30-day	Average PCTE MRP	Cum % CE, 365-day
0–5%	5	101.3139	1.80	110.2837	1.93
5–10%	10	131.1899	4.13	141.7052	4.41
10–15%	15	147.2251	6.75	158.7001	7.18
15–20%	20	160.8434	9.61	172.626	10.20
20–25%	25	172.7032	12.67	184.7478	13.43
25–30%	30	183.6508	15.94	196.1252	16.86
30–35%	35	195.0225	19.40	207.5231	20.49
35–40%	40	206.4848	23.07	218.9433	24.32
40–45%	45	218.0165	26.94	231.0298	28.36
45–50%	50	230.531	31.04	243.5303	32.61
50–55%	55	243.749	35.37	256.804	37.10
55–60%	60	257.9355	39.95	270.8079	41.84
60–65%	65	273.5705	44.82	286.229	46.84
65–70%	70	291.2079	49.99	303.3376	52.15
70–75%	75	312.0809	55.53	322.6343	57.79
75–80%	80	337.115	61.52	345.9822	63.84
80–85%	85	371.5535	68.13	376.3839	70.42
85–90%	90	419.6128	75.58	419.0215	77.75
90–95%	95	499.0608	84.45	490.8102	86.33
95–100%	100	875.375	100.00	781.9013	100.00
0–100%		281.4032		285.9563	

Note: Average PCTE URP, cumulative % CE, and average PCTE MRP figures are all revised estimates.
Source: Authors' own calculations based on the 50th NSS round.

Table 14.4b. A comparison of size distribution by 5% fractile groups between uniform and mixed reference periods, 50th NSS round: all India, urban population

Fractile group	Cumulative % of population	Average PCTE URP	Cum % CE, 30-day	Average PCTE MRP	Cum % CE, 365-day
0–5%	5	133.0799	1.45	144.2726	1.56
5–10%	10	175.8905	3.37	188.5886	3.59
10–15%	15	201.9348	5.58	215.6687	5.92
15–20%	20	222.8357	8.01	237.9062	8.49
20–25%	25	242.3559	10.65	258.9554	11.28
25–30%	30	261.9733	13.51	279.101	14.29
30–35%	35	281.1159	16.58	298.7234	17.51
35–40%	40	302.5225	19.88	319.4199	20.96
40–45%	45	323.6575	23.42	341.5709	24.65
45–50%	50	346.5325	27.20	365.0693	28.59
50–55%	55	370.3242	31.24	389.3419	32.79
55–60%	60	397.9061	35.58	416.542	37.28
60–65%	65	430.2546	40.28	447.7376	42.11
65–70%	70	467.1801	45.38	484.4874	47.34
70–75%	75	513.6512	50.99	528.6223	53.04
75–80%	80	569.3199	57.20	583.3929	59.33
80–85%	85	641.3186	64.20	651.9997	66.36
85–90%	90	742.1016	72.30	747.8689	74.43
90–95%	95	911.4375	82.25	911.5722	84.26
95–100%	100	1626.268	100.00	1457.917	100.00
0–100%		458.083		463.4379	

Notes: Average PCTE MRP and cumulative % CE 365-day figures are all revised estimates.
Source: Authors' own calculations based on the 50th NSS round.

than it was for the preceding 30-day recall. In contrast, for the top 10 per cent of the rural population and top 5 per cent of the urban population, the mean monthly per capita household expenditure on these items was lower with a 365-day reference period in this instance. The overall mean PCTE turns out to be marginally higher (by 1.6 per cent in rural India and by 1.2 per cent in urban India) with the mixed reference period.

The corresponding Lorenz curves presented in Figure 14.1 for the rural population and in Figure 14.2 for the urban population, show that the Lorenz curve based on a mixed reference period (MRP) lies uniformly inside the Lorenz curve based on 30-day uniform reference period (URP). Consequently, the summary measure of relative inequality based on the Lorenz curve, namely the Gini coefficient, is distinctly lower when it is based on an MRP than on a URP. The respective Gini coefficients for rural and urban population are 0.2581 and 0.3184 for the MRP, and 0.2859 and 0.3438 for the URP.

Since the reported PCTE for the bottom fractile groups is higher under MRP than that under URP, for 1993–4, the headcount ratios based on MRP are expected to be lower than those based on URP.

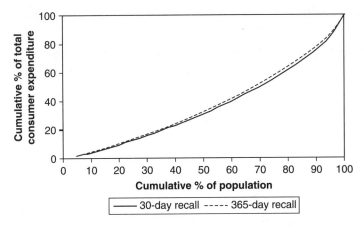

Figure 14.1 Lorenz curve, India: rural population (NSS 50th round, cumulative % PCTE)

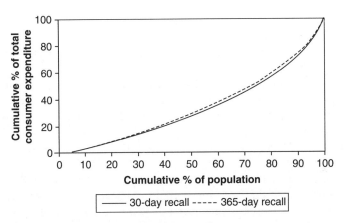

Figure 14.2 Lorenz curve, India: urban population (NSS 50th round, cumulative % PCTE)

Poverty outcomes in the 1980s: the all-India picture

Comparable headcount ratios and related measures of poverty

In the previous section we discussed the problems of comparability pertaining to consumer expenditure surveys from the 50th and 55th rounds of the NSS, which have been highlighted during recent debates about poverty trends in the 1990s in India. Our empirical analysis, based partly on the published results, and partly on unit-level records of the 50th and the 55th rounds of NSS, have established the following:

1. The published size distribution of the first five quinquennial rounds, including the 50th round in 1993–4, is based on a uniform, 30-day reference period (URP) and headcount ratios calculated from them are comparable.

2. The published size distributions of the 50th round for 1993–4, and the 55th round for 1999–2000 are not directly comparable because of the differences in the recall period, namely, URP in the 50th round and a mixed reference period (MRP) in the 55th round.

3. As regards the 7-day/30-day controversy besetting the CES in the 55th round, evidence presented in this chapter suggests that the size distribution of the CES in the 55th round based on 30-day recall for the food group is comparable to the MRP-based size distribution of the 50th round.

4. The size distribution of the 50th round can be recast for MRP, and we have recalculated it with MRP to make it directly comparable to the 55th round.

These points enable us to calculate comparable poverty indicators in order to assess India's much-debated aggregate poverty outcomes over the 1980s and 1990s. To this end we use five summary indicators that capture different dimensions of absolute deprivation.

The first and generally the most widely used indicator is the headcount ratio (HCR), which specifies the proportion of the population that is estimated to be at or below an exogenously defined poverty line. However, it ignores size of the poverty gap, that is, how far below poverty line different poor households are in terms of their PCTE relative to the poverty line. It also does not take account of relative inequality among the poor.

The second indicator is a poverty gap index (PGI), which sums up the poverty gaps of poor households and normalizes the resulting aggregate (weighted) poverty gap. This is done by reference to the maximum possible poverty gap for the entire poor and non-poor population, derived from the product of the poverty line and the total population. Accordingly, given two populations with the same level of HCR, the one with higher PGI will have a larger concentration of the poor population living further away from the poverty line. Hence it is taken to describe the depth of poverty.

The third and fourth poverty indicators are the squared poverty gap (SPG) and the Sen Index (SI; Sen, 1976). In addition to the headcount ratio and the poverty gap, these indicators take into account the relative inequality among the poor. However, SPG and SI differ from each other in terms of the underlying summary measure of relative inequality. SPG incorporates squared coefficient of variation, whereas the SI uses the Gini coefficient among the poor population. Because of their sensitivity to relative inequality, SPG and SI are taken to measure the severity of poverty. Indeed, because they incorporate as component measures the HCR and the poverty gap, as well as the measure of relative inequality among the poor, these indicators are by far the most comprehensive measures of absolute deprivation. Accordingly, given the same HCR and PGI for two populations, the one with higher SPG and SI reflects a greater severity of poverty.[7]

We may add that HCR, PGI, and SPG are special cases of general class of decomposable poverty indicators suggested by Foster et al. (1984).

The fifth and final indicator of poverty used in this chapter is the size of the poor population—variously described also as the "absolute headcount," "the numerical magnitude," or simply "the number of poor people." It is given by a multiplication of the sample survey-based *estimated* headcount ratio (HCR) and the *estimated* total population at the midpoint of the survey period. Both components of the product are *estimated* independently of each other and are not based on direct observations: HCR is based on the estimated size distribution of PCTE among the universe of all households, which, in turn, is based on an appropriately selected sample of households. Similarly, "total population at the midpoint of the survey period" is an interpolated, or projected, figure. Consequently, the size of the poor population is to be regarded as a probabilistic point estimate of the aggregate macro-level order of magnitude of the poor population.

Three comments are warranted on the interpretation of the final indicator. First, it does not permit physical identification of poor persons or households at the micro-level. This would require a complete census. Second, a change in the size of the poor population during the time interval between the two surveys merely indicates the net change in the estimated number of poor people between the midpoints of the two survey periods from all sources. Third, this change in size has two components: (a) change due to changes in the HCR between two time points, which is then applied to the base year population; and (b) change in the total population between two time points, which is applied to the HCR in the terminal year. Notice that (b) is always positive while (a) will be negative in cases where the headcount ratio declines. Either component may dominate the other.

The five summary indicators of poverty are presented in Table 14.5. They are shown for the rural, urban, and total population at the all-India level, mapped across three time points: 1983, 1993–4, and 1999–2000. The choice of years is governed by a specific set of considerations. The idea is to monitor descriptively the progress in poverty reduction over the past two decades and in the process also bring out differences in the level comparability of HCR, arising from uniform and mixed reference periods. To represent the decade of the 1980s, we could have chosen to compare the 43rd round for 1987–8 with the 38th round for 1983. However, poverty—in particular rural poverty—is known to be affected by abnormal harvests and 1987–8 was a meteorological drought year. Hence that year was excluded from consideration. So that, in our subsequent

Table 14.5. Alternative measures of poverty: all India, 1983, 1993–4, 1999–2000

Segment/Measure	Measures on URP		Measures on MRP	
(1)	1983 (2)	1993–4 (3)	1993–4 (4)	1999–2000 (5)
All India: rural				
1. Headcount ratio (%)	49.02	39.66	34.19	28.93
2. Poverty-gap index	0.1386	0.0928	0.0728	0.0579
3. SGP	0.0545	0.0315	0.0232	0.0173
4. Sen Index	0.1882	0.1278	0.1014	0.0806
5. Number of poor ('000)	268,593	261,380	225,330	210,673
All India: urban				
1. Headcount ratio (%)	38.33	30.89	26.41	23.09
2. Poverty-gap index	0.0995	0.0749	0.0600	0.0504
3. SGP	0.0366	0.0265	0.0202	0.0160
4. Sen Index	0.1362	0.1034	0.0833	0.0695
5. Number of poor ('000)	65,798	72,633	62,099	63,987
All India: all areas				
1. Headcount ratio (%)	46.47	37.35	32.14	27.32
2. Poverty-gap index	0.1293	0.0881	0.0694	0.0558
3. SGP	0.0502	0.0302	0.0224	0.0170
4. Sen Index	0.1758	0.1214	0.0966	0.0775
5. Number of poor ('000)	334,391	334,013	287,429	274,660
Memorandum item				
Total population ('000)	719,587	894,188	894,188	1,005,339
Urban population (% of total)	23.86	26.30	26.30	27.57

Notes: All figures in column (4) are revised estimates. Official poverty lines in terms of MPCE of INR49.09 (rural) and INR56.64 (urban) at 1973–4 prices have been used in these calculations. They have been adjusted for changes in prices using the price indices specifically compiled for the poor population. The numerical values of the price adjusted PLs in terms of MPCE at current prices are given below for the years used in this study:

	1983	1993–4	1999–2000
Rural	93.16	211.30	335.46
Urban	111.25	274.88	451.19

Sources: Tendulkar, Sundaram and Jain (1993); authors' own calculations based on the 50th NSS rounds.

discussion, we refer to the 10.5-year period between the 1983 and 1993–4 surveys as the decade of the 1980s and the 6-year period between 1993–4 and 1999–2000 as representing the decade of the 1990s. Other analysts, notably Sen and Himanshu (2004) take the 6-year period between the 1987–8 and the 1993–4 surveys to represent the decade of the 1980s.

Table 14.5 provides two estimates for 1993–4, one based on uniform reference periods (URP) and another based on mixed reference periods (MRP). The estimates based on URP are comparable to the 1983 estimates while the MRP-based estimates for 1993–4 are comparable to the estimates for 1999–2000.

Poverty outcomes in India in the 1980s

To contextualize this exercise, and to provide a point of reference for the changes in poverty over the 1990s, let us first consider briefly the changes in poverty over the 10.5 years between July 1, 1983 and January 1, 1994. In both rural and urban India, and hence, also at the all-India level, there is a clear reduction in the HCR, PGI, SPG, and Sen Index. In rural India, the annual average decline in the headcount ratio over the 10.5 year period was a little under 0.9 percentage points. In urban India, the corresponding decline was 0.7 percentage points per year. For rural and urban areas taken together, the average decline in HCR was just below 0.9 percentage points per annum.

In terms of the estimated number of people living below the poverty line, or, the poor population, there is a clear rural–urban contrast. While in rural India the size of the poor population declined by a little under 7.2 million over the 10.5 year period, translating into an annual average decline of 0.69 million, in urban India, the number of poor people increased by 6.8 million between July 1, 1983 and January 1, 1994, despite the reduction in the corresponding HCR. Consequently, for both rural and urban areas taken together, the number of poor people in India increased marginally by 0.38 million.

However, the rise in population of the poor in urban India, which more than offset the decline in the size of the poor population in rural India, has to be seen in the context of a rapid growth in urban population, from 171.7 million to 235.2 million. This corresponds to a growth rate of over 3 per cent per annum.

We may caution also that the entire increase in urban population cannot be attributed to rural–urban migration. A rise in the urban population also takes place: (a) because of natural population growth in areas which remain classified as urban across survey years; (b) because of the addition of population from the areas that in the base year were rural but re-classified as urban in the terminal year; and (c) because of inter-census growth of this population.

Poverty in India in the 1990s

What happened to poverty in India across the 1990s? A shift from URP to MRP for 1993–4 resulted in an HCR for 1993–4 that is nearly *5.5 percentage points lower* than that on the uniform reference period for rural India. For urban India, the difference is much lower (4.5 percentage points). For the country as a whole (that is taking the rural and the urban population together), the HCR for 1993–4 on the mixed reference period is lower by 5.2 percentage points. Accordingly, an uncorrected and hence inappropriate comparison based on the published results (URP for 1993–4 and MRP for 1999–2000) would overstate the decline over the six years by the same magnitude.

Using comparable MRP-based measures for both 1993–4 and 1999–2000, we find that, except in respect of the number of poor in urban India, all measures of poverty showed a clear decline in both rural and urban areas and, therefore, also for the country as a whole.

Consider first the rural population. At the all-India level over the 6-year period from January 1, 1994 to January 1, 2000, the HCR declined by over 5 percentage points translating to an average decline of a slightly under 0.9

percentage points per annum—roughly the same as that realized between 1983 and 1993–4. It is necessary further to normalize by reference to the initial level value of the indicator for appropriate comparability.[8] By taking the annual average decline by reference to the base year level values (of 49 per cent on URP for 1983 and of 34 per cent on MRP for 1994), the rate of annual average decline between 1993–4 and 1999–2000 at 2.6 per cent is higher than that achieved between 1983–1993–4 (1.8 per cent). In terms of the *number of rural poor*, the 1990s witnessed a decline of just under 14.7 million over the 6-year period, i.e. an annual average decline of just under 2.5 million. This may be contrasted with the annual average decline of a little over 0.7 million between 1983 and 1993–4. As noted above, PGI, SPG, and Sen Index also record a decline for the rural population between 1993–4 and 1999–2000.

For urban India too, HCR, PGI, SPG, and the Sen Index record a decline between 1993–4 and 1999–2000. Taken as they are, the annual average decline in all these indices are slightly smaller in the 1990s than that between 1983 and 1994. However, when normalized by reference to the relevant base year values, the rates of annual average decline are slightly higher between 1993–4 and 1999–2000. There was a rise in the number of poor in urban India in both periods. However, aided by a slightly slower growth in urban population, the annual average increase (0.3 million) between 1993–4 and 1999–2000 was less than half the annual average increase in the number of urban poor between 1983 and 1993–4 (0.65 million).

The picture for the country as a whole parallels that for the rural population with declines in all the poverty indicators between 1993–4 and 1999–2000, with the normalized (with reference to base year values) annual average declines being higher for the 1990s than for the 1980s. Particularly noteworthy is the decline in the absolute number of poor; 2.7 million per annum compared to an increase (albeit marginal) between 1983 and 1993–4.

Our assessment of a clear decline in poverty in India in the 1990s is now shared by almost all analysts of the poverty situation in India with differences being limited to the extent of decline. Tied to this question of the *extent* of decline is the issue of whether or not there has been a decline in the number of poor in the country.

The alternative view that the number of poor in India *increased* between 1993–4 and 1999–2000 has been argued in an important paper by Sen and Himanshu (2004). Central to their result of a *rise* in the number of poor, in rural India and in the country as a whole is their estimates of HCR for 1999–2000 derived by altering the 55th round CES size distribution by "adjusting pro-rata its unit level data item-wise and state-wise with corrections for 'contamination'" (ibid. p. 4255).

A few comments are in order. First, based on their "estimates of over estimation due to 'contamination' in 30-day estimates of the 55th Round Consumer Expenditure Survey" (ibid. p. 4254), Sen and Himanshu note that these results "attribute bulk of CES–EUS difference to EUS underestimation and return strikingly small estimates of CES 'contamination'."

It needs to be emphasized that, having arrived at this judgment, we take the size distribution from the NSS 55th round CES on the 30-day recall for items in the food group *as they are* to generate poverty measures for 1999–2000. In particular, *we do not alter the reported 55th round CES size distribution* as Sen and Himanshu do.

We have deliberately refrained from doing any such pro-rata "item-wise and state-wise" adjustment of the 55th round unit-level data. Our reasoning for *not* doing so is detailed below.

First, as can be seen from Tables 14.2a and 14.2b, the CES–EUS differences are uneven across fractile groups and, in respect of "Other food" which accounted for the bulk of the CES–EUS difference for the food group taken as a whole, the CES–EUS differences for the bottom 40 per cent are lower than the average. So that, if at all any adjustment to unit-level data are to be made "item-wise and state-wise," then the extent of "contamination" too needs to be specified *by fractile groups* (preferably 5 per cent fractiles) *for each state and each of the affected items*. Even for a state as a whole, the CES and the EUS estimates of item-wise expenditure may be expected to carry sizable "sampling errors."

The size of these errors will necessarily be larger when these are sought to be estimated for deciles or 5-per cent fractile groups. It needs to be emphasized that, having arrived at this judgment, we find pro-rata adjustment in observed behavior to be inappropriate and consequently we take the size distribution from the NSS 55th round CES on the 30-day recall for items in the food group *as they are* to generate poverty measures for 1999–2000.

Second, it needs to be re-iterated that our derivation of an alternative MRP-based size-distribution for 1993–4 merely involves re-combining at the unit level the households' own responses on the 365-day reference period for clothing, footwear, durables, education, and (institutional) health care and on the 30-day reference period for all other items. Specifically, no pro-rata scalar adjustments have been made to unit level data. On this, Sen and Himanshu (2004, p. 4251) have noted that, "...it must be accepted that S-T (Sundaram & Tendulkar) were correct in treating poverty estimates from the 50th round MRP as a valid objective method of dealing with the 365-day issue."

Finally, if we use the Sen and Himanshu MRP estimates for 1993–4 and their "unadjusted" estimates for 1999–2000 (on a judgment that their adjustment is inappropriate for the reasons indicated above), it can be readily shown that the number of poor in both rural and urban India did decline between 1993–4 and 1999–2000.

Thus, using the population estimate given in Table 14.5 and the Sen and Himanshu HCR estimates for 1993–4 based on MRP (rural, 31.6 per cent; urban, 27.9 per cent; Table 4, p. 4253) and their unadjusted estimates for 1999–2000 (pp. 4255–6) of 27.0 per cent (rural) and 23.4 per cent (urban), the absolute number of rural poor declines from 208.3 million in 1993–4 to 196.6 million in 1999–2000. For the country as a whole—considering both rural and urban areas—the number of poor declined from 273.9 million to 261.5 million (a fall of 12.4 million) between 1993–4 and 1999–2000.

Summary and conclusions

There were two key changes in the design of the NSS 55th round CES: first, the canvassing on two alternative reference periods of thirty days and seven days of household consumer expenditure on food, paan, tobacco, and intoxicants, recorded in adjacent blocks; and second,the use of a single 365-day reference period in respect of expenditure on clothing, footwear, education, and (institutional) health care. These changes had raised serious doubts about the comparability of the size distributions and of the poverty measures based on them from the NSS 50th (1993–4) and the 55th (1999–2000) rounds of CES. Set against these doubts, our effort in this chapter has been to derive a set of comparable estimates of poverty measures, separately for the rural and the urban populations, at the all-India level.

Comparability of the poverty measure for 1993–4 and 1999–2000 has been established in two steps. First, the 30-day CES estimates have *not* been artificially biased upwards by the simultaneous canvassing on the 7-day reference period. This has been done by undertaking a comparison of the CES estimates of consumer expenditure on individual items in the food group with those identified in the 55th round EUS—canvassed with a single reference period of thirty days over an independent sample of households drawn from the same population. This exercise showed that the 30-day estimates from the CES were strikingly close to the independent EUS estimates with divergences overwhelmingly reflecting the use of a highly abridged worksheet in the EUS.

For generating estimates of poverty measures for 1993–4 that are comparable to the estimates for 1999–2000 (with a 365-days recall for clothing, footwear, durables, education, and (institutional) health care, and a 30-days recall for all other items including the food group) we derive, from the responses of the households about their expenditure on clothing, footwear, etc. on a 365-day reference, a new size distribution with a mixed reference period comparable to that used in the NSS 55th round CES. This was possible because the 50th round collected information on the infrequently purchased items on both the 30-days and the 365-days recall periods. Poverty measures for 1993–4 comparable to the estimates for 1999–2000 (labeled MRP estimates) are estimated using the size distribution of consumer expenditure derived as described above.

Using comparable estimates of poverty measures for 1993–4 and 1999–2000 derived as above it has been shown in this chapter that in rural India and in the country as a whole there has been a clear decline in poverty over the 1990s on all the five measures—the headcount ratio, the poverty gap index, the squared poverty gap, the Sen Index, and the absolute number of poor. In urban India declines in poverty were seen on all poverty measures, except the number of poor, which experienced a small rise.

Finally, we provide a word of caution regarding the interpretation of these results. In this chapter, we have deliberately avoided bringing in a discussion of the possible factors explaining the decline in poverty. In this vein, we would also like to caution that the average annual percentage point decline is not expected to be spread evenly over the intervening years. In an earlier paper, one of us had brought out the complexity of causal mechanisms impacting poverty on the basis of poverty calculations from 1970–1 to 1993–4 (Tendulkar, 1998). It was argued that a poverty outcome in a given year is a combined consequence of: (a) the impact of economic reforms and reform-related factors; (b) the impact of other secular factors operating since pre-reform years; and (c) the impact of year-specific abnormal factors, such as a drought.

We also emphasize that the expected favorable effects of economic reforms and reform-related factors on poverty operate through their impact on the long-term growth of the economy. Higher growth rates, in turn, generate sustainable productive employment opportunities which provide the only enduring solution to poverty eradication.

A postscript: some results from the NSS 61st round survey, 2004–5

The release of the results of the NSS 61st round CES 2004–5 has revived the debate on the poverty outcomes in India in the 1990s.

The published results provide the size distribution of consumer expenditure on a uniform 30-day reference period but, with the exception of one table on the size distribution of households, *not* on a mixed reference period. Himanshu (2007) presents the argument about very little progress in poverty reduction between 1993–4 and 1999–2000 in two steps. In the first step, broadly comparable estimates of poverty ratios for 1993–4 and 2004–5 on a URP are presented. At the all-India level, the rural HCR is estimated to have declined from 37.2 per cent in 1993–4 to 28.7 per cent in 2004–5 and in urban India from 32.6 per cent to 25.9 per cent over the same period.

In the absence of CES 2004–5 results on the mixed reference period used in 1999–2000, Himanshu presents estimates of HCR on MRP based on the (abridged) one-page schedule canvassed in the NSS 55th and the 61st round EUS (1999–2000 and 2004–5). These show over a 9 percentage point decline in rural HCR (from 34.0 to 24.9 per cent) and a near 4 percentage point decline in urban HCR (from 28.9 to 25.0 per cent) between 1999–2000 and 2004–5. If one accepts both these results, then, the inference is obvious: that almost all of the decline in poverty between 1993–4 and 2004–5 took place between 2000 and 2005 with little or no decline in poverty between 1993–4 and 1999–2000.

In a recent paper by one of this chapter's authors (Sundaram, 2007) it has been argued that, at least at the all-India level, there is a better alternative to using the EUS for generating comparable poverty estimates for 1999–2000 and 2004–5: namely, the size distribution of *households* on the mixed reference period presented in Tables 6R and 6O in NSSO (2006b). This can be used directly to estimate, in the first instance, the proportion of households below the poverty line in 2004–5 with parallel estimates from the NSS 55th round CES. And, corresponding to the proportion of *households* below the poverty line (from CES, 2004–5) we can derive the proportion of *persons* below the poverty line or HCR from the 61st round EUS.[9]

Using the official all-India poverty lines, Sundaram (2007) has shown that, at the all-India level, the order of decline between 2000 and 2005 in the proportion of below poverty line households (4.5 percentage points in rural India and 1.5 percentage points in urban India) and that in HCR for persons (4.3 and 1.5 percentage points in the two population segments respectively) are roughly the same. It can be readily seen, that, these estimates of decline in HCR (persons) between 2000 and 2005, based on official poverty lines and MRP size distribution of households from the 61st round CES, are much smaller than Himanshu's (2007) estimates based on EUS for 1999–2000 and 2004–5. This suggests that the latter may need to be substantially revised downwards.

Using the methodology outlined above, but using our alternative poverty lines, Table 14.6 presents comparable estimates on URP for 1993–4 and 2004–5 (Panel A) and on MRP for 1993–4, 1999–2000, and 2004–5 (Panel B).

On a comparable basis, the decline in HCR between 1993–4 and 2004–5 is roughly the same on both uniform and mixed reference periods, with the decline under MRP being somewhat larger in rural India and somewhat smaller in urban India, as well as for the total (rural plus urban) population.

On the MRP, our estimates indicate a distinct slowdown in the pace of poverty decline in the first five years of the twenty-first century relative to that between 1993–4 and 1999–2000. Between 1994 and 2000, rural HCR declined by 0.88 percentage points per year on average and urban HCR by 0.55 percentage points per year. Normalized for base year levels, rural HCR declined at the rate of 2.7 per cent per annum and urban HCR at 2.2 per cent per annum.

In the first five years of the 2000s, rural HCR declined by 0.6 percentage points per annum, or at the rate of 2.1 per cent per annum. In urban India, the corresponding numbers would be 0.05 percentage points, and 0.2 per cent, per annum.

As we have argued elsewhere (Sundaram, 2007), this slowdown in the pace of poverty decline between 2000 and 2005 relative to that between 1994 and 2000 is also consistent with the slowdown in real wages of workers in rural India and

Table 14.6. Estimates of poverty in India, 1993–4, 2004–5

Panel A: Uniform reference period

Year	Rural		Urban		All areas	
	Headcount ratio (%)	Number of poor ('000)	Headcount ratio (%)	Number of poor ('000)	Headcount ratio (%)	Number of poor ('000)
1993-4	39.66	261,380	30.89	72,633	37.35	334,013
2004-5	31.80	248,029	26.74	74,102	29.47	322,131
(PL)	(INR371.29)		(INR546.20)			

Panel B: Mixed reference period

Year	Rural		Urban		All areas	
	Headcount ratio (%)	Number of poor ('000)	Headcount ratio (%)	Number of poor ('000)	Headcount ratio (%)	Number of poor ('000)
1993-4	34.19	225,330	26.41	62,099	32.14	287,429
1999-2000	28.93	210,673	23.09	63,987	27.32	274,660
2004-05	25.95	202,401	22.84	71,504	25.06	273,905
(PL)	(INR371.29)		(INR546.20)			

Notes: Total population: 2004–5 ('000s): rural, 779,967; urban, 313,064; total, 1,093,031. Estimates for 1993–4 and 1999–2000 are drawn from Table 14.5.

an absolute decline in urban real wages between 2000 and 2005 (relative to the 1994–2000 period); and also with the almost universal slowdown in labor productivity growth between 2000 and 2005.

As such, our assessment of the poverty outcomes in India over the 1990s, that the poverty decline over this period is a reality rather than an artifact, remains unaltered by the results from the NSS 61st round surveys for 2004–5.

Notes

1. Centre for Development Economics, Delhi School of Economics.
2. We will use "food group" to denote food, beverages, paan, tobacco, and intoxicants, whereas "total food" is used to denote the total for food and beverages only and excludes paan, tobacco, and intoxicants.
3. The initial instructions to NSS field staff did not explicitly mention the sequence in which information was to be elicited from respondents for the two recall periods. However, nearly 1.5 months after the field work was launched for the 55th round, a letter was sent by the sampling design and research division of NSSO, dated August 19, 1999, asking the investigators to elicit information first for the 30-day recall for all items of the food group, and then seek the same (again from the beginning) for the last seven days. Which sequence was in fact followed, however, remains an open question. We bypass this aspect of the issue by directly examining the outcome through a comparison of the CES estimates of monthly per capita expenditure (MPCE) on the specified items with the EUS-based estimates of MPCE canvassed with a single 30-day reference period—albeit with an abridged schedule.
4. The only item group where the percentage difference between the CES and EUS estimates, though less than the difference between the 7- and 30-day estimates, is somewhat close to the latter, is milk and milk products. Like the item group, "Other food", this is also a somewhat heterogeneous item group, which accounted for less than 5 per cent of total consumption for the lowest 30 per cent of the rural population in 1993–4. For urban India, the corresponding proportion was a little over 7 per cent (Sundaram and Tendulkar, 2001).
5. This is strictly not true in respect to two items forming a part of the education category. Unlike in the CES, two components, namely tuition fees and newspapers, magazines, etc. have a 30-day reference period in the EUS, whereas they—along with school books and other educational articles—are all canvassed with a 365-day reference period in the CES. This could be a factor in explaining why the EUS estimates exceed the CES estimates.
6. Ideally, one would have preferred to have set up a similar comparison in respect of fractile groups formed after *excluding* the expenditures on the items on the 365-day recall. Unfortunately, the unit record data for the 51st–54th NSS rounds provide information only on the 30-day reference period.
7. See Sundaram and Tendulkar (1993) for a discussion of these measures.
8. We hold the view that it is important to normalize the average annual decline by reference to the initial level value of the poverty indicator. Alternatively, one may opt for compound annual change which is also normalized in a similar fashion. Both

procedures yield the same conclusion, namely, the pace of poverty decline was higher in the six-year period of 1990s than in the previous 10.5 years.

9. A similar methodology was used previously to analyze the poor in the Indian labor force (Sundaram and Tendulkar, 2003).

Bibliography

Deaton, A. and Grosh, M. (2000) 'Consumption'. In M. Grosh and P. Glewwe (eds.) *Designing Household Survey Questionnaires for Developing Countries, Lessons from 15 Years of the Living Standards Measurement Study*, Washington DC: World Bank.

Foster, J. E., Greer, J., and Thorbecke E. (1984) 'A Class of Decomposable Poverty Measures'. *Econometrica*, 52(3), pp. 561–76.

Himanshu (2007) 'Recent Trends in Poverty and Inequality: Some Preliminary Results'. *Economic and Political Weekly*, February 10.

National Sample Survey Organization (2000a) *Choice of Reference Period for Consumption Data*. Based on NSS 51st to 54th rounds, Report No. 447 (March).

—— (2000b) *Household Consumer Expenditure in India, 1999–2000, Key Results*. NSS 55th round, July 1999–June 2000 (December).

—— (2001a) *Level and Pattern of Consumer Expenditure in India, 1999–2000*. NSS 55th round, July 1999–June 2000, Report No. 457 (May).

—— (2001b) *Employment and Unemployment Situation in India, 1999–2000*. Part I, NSS 55th round, July 1997–June 2000, Report No. 458 (May).

—— (2006a) *Employment and Unemployment Situation in India, 2004–05*. NSS 61st round, July 2004–June 2005, Report No. 515, New Delhi (September).

—— (2006b) *Level and Pattern of Consumer Expenditure in India, 2004–05*. NSS 61st round, July 2004–June 2005, Report No. 508, New Delhi (December).

Sen, Abhijit and Himanshu (2004) 'Poverty and Inequality in India-I'. *Economic and Political Weekly*, 39(38), pp. 4247–63.

Sen, A. (1976), 'Poverty: An Ordinal Approach to Measurement'. *Econometrica*, 44(2), pp. 219–31.

Sundaram, K. (2007) 'Employment and Poverty in India, 2000–2005'. *Economic and Political Weekly*, July 28.

—— and Tendulkar, S. D. (1993) 'Poverty in Asia and the Pacific: Conceptual Issues and National Approaches to Measurement'. *Economic Bulletin for Asia and the Pacific*, 44(2).

—— —— (2001) 'NAS-NSS Estimates of Private Consumption for Poverty Estimation: A Dis-aggregated Comparison for 1993–94'. *Economic and Political Weekly*, 36(2), pp. 119–29.

—— —— (2003) 'The Poor in India's Labour Force, Scenario in the 1990s'. *Economic and Political Weekly*, 39(48), pp. 5123–32.

—— —— and Jain, L. R. (1993) 'Poverty in India, 1970–71 to 1988–89'. ARTEP Working Paper, New Delhi.

Tendulkar, S. D. (1998) 'India's Economic Policy Reforms and Poverty'. In I. J. Ahluwalia and I. M. D. Little (eds.) *India's Economic Reforms and Development, Essays for Manmohan Singh*, Delhi: Oxford University Press.

Visaria, P. (2000) 'Alternative Estimates of Poverty in India'. *Economic Times*, June 29.

15

Living Standards in Africa

David E. Sahn and Stephen D. Younger[1]

Introduction

Sub-Saharan Africa is one of the poorest regions in the world. Whether it is *the* poorest region is difficult to establish, for all of the conceptual and practical problems in inter-country poverty comparisons laid out in other chapters of this volume. We can avoid some of those problems, though certainly not all, when we make inter-temporal poverty comparisons in one country. Here, too, Africa's performance is disappointing. Poverty reduction has been halting and irregular in Africa, in contrast to other regions of the world that have grown more rapidly and made greater progress on poverty reduction. The first task of this chapter is to substantiate these two claims—that Africa is poor compared to the rest of the world and that poverty in Africa is not declining consistently or significantly—while fully recognizing the problems inherent in using income and expenditure data in Africa and elsewhere.

However, given the reservations about income poverty comparisons, a second important feature of this chapter is that we consider not only income (or expenditure) poverty, but also other dimensions of well-being, especially education and health. There are many reasons for this, both theoretical and practical. On the theory side, Amartya Sen has argued convincingly that we should understand that well-being is multidimensional, comprising capabilities such as good health, adequate nutrition, literacy, and political freedoms. More traditional money metrics of poverty, particularly as measured by income (or consumption expenditure) are *instrumentally* important to these capabilities, but it is the capabilities themselves that are *intrinsically* important, and merit recognition and measurement in their own right (Sen, 1985, 1987). Even though Sen's argument is widely accepted in theory, in practice it is usually ignored. Most empirical poverty research still focuses on measuring material living standards.

Beyond the compelling theoretical argument, there are many reasons to measure poverty (and inequality as well) in non-income dimensions of well-being. First, and most importantly in the context of this volume, measurement error is much less a problem for the non-income variables that we use than it is for standard economic measures of deprivation. We discuss measurement problems later in this chapter. Here we simply note that collecting income and expenditure data is a complex process involving dozens, sometimes hundreds, of questions, not all of which respondents want to answer truthfully and not all of which they find easy to answer. Data on non-income measures of well-being, especially anthropometry and years of schooling, are easy to collect and straightforward to answer. Further, respondents cannot misreport anthropometry data, and reasons to misreport educational attainment are less than those for incomes and some expenditures. Of course, measurement error is still possible for these variables, but it is more likely to be random—uncorrelated with other variables of interest in the survey.

A second reason for considering poverty in dimensions such as health and education is that public policy has an important role in providing for the basic needs of the population in these areas. While publicly funded income transfers also have a compelling logic, they remain rare in developing countries, and it is often far easier to mobilize public support for targeted programs to improve non-income living standards, as manifested in outcomes such as improved nutrition and better education. This both reflects a commonly held welfarist conception of the state and, in developing countries, non-governmental organizations as well. But an additional argument for focusing on deprivation in health and education is that improvements in these areas have tangible externalities, including benefits for the non-poor, that are not as manifest for income transfers.

Third, we can measure outcomes such as nutrition, health, and education at the individual rather than household level. Income and expenditures, in contrast, are measured for households, necessitating arbitrary assumptions about how resources are allocated among household members. Assuming that household income is equally shared among members, the most common approach is potentially misleading in ways that the study of intra-household allocation is only beginning to understand (Kanbur and Haddad, 1992; Sahn and Younger, 2009). A related challenge in employing income measures is the need to make arbitrary and unidentifiable assumptions about economies of scale and equivalence units (Deaton and Muellbauer, 1980). Such problems do not arise when measuring individual outcomes.

Finally, we note that many non-income measures of well-being, especially those that concern health, are not highly correlated with incomes, either within a given country or across countries (Haddad et al., 2003; Behrman and Deolalikar, 1988, 1990; Appleton and Song, 1999). This is important because it indicates that these variables contain additional information about well-being not captured by income or expenditures alone.

With these considerations in mind, this chapter analyzes evidence on levels and trends of poverty in Africa during the late 1980s through the early part of the present decade. We augment the available evidence on expenditures with measures of health and education because these are two fundamental dimensions of well-being whose importance almost everyone can agree upon. The particular variables that we use are per capita expenditures for income poverty; children's height-for-age and women's body mass for health poverty; and women's years of school completed for education. Throughout, we are particularly interested in whether and the extent to which there is consistency between poverty changes measured in these four dimensions.

In the remainder of the chapter, we present some aggregate figures on the three dimensions of poverty in Africa, comparing the continent's performance to other regions in the developing world. The following section provides a presentation of changes in poverty. We begin with a discussion of the data used, distinguishing between the reliance on expenditure data, and the health and education indicators employed. As noted above, the most important results of this section are that Africa is generally poorer than other regions of the world, the one exception being in terms of stunting rates of pre-school age children, and that poverty is not declining consistently on the continent for any of our measures, with the possible exception of women's years of schooling.

Given the ongoing debate over the relative importance of growth versus distribution in affecting poverty levels, we decompose the share of the population that falls below the poverty line into two components: one due to changes in the mean of the distribution and another due to changes in its dispersion (Datt and Ravallion, 1992; Kakwani, 1997).

The discussion in the first few sections deals with the poverty indicators distinctly, each examined as an independent outcome. But it is possible to make multivariate poverty comparisons that account for the correlation of deprivations in different dimensions of well-being (Duclos, Sahn, and Younger, 2006a, b). The penultimate section presents an example of a robust multidimensional poverty comparison over time in Uganda. Finally, we summarize and discuss the overall findings with some concluding comments and insights.

Africa in the global context

We begin our discussion with continent-level data that examine progress in alleviating poverty in Africa and elsewhere since 1960 (when the data permit). We use six indicators of well-being that are readily available and frequently used in cross-country research: dollar-a-day income poverty, gross primary enrolment rates, average years of schooling for adults, the share of children under

Table 15.1. Population falling below the poverty line of $1 per day (estimates, % of total population)

Region	1981	1990	1999	2004
Sub-Sahara Africa	42.24	46.77	45.94	41.09
MENA	5.08	2.33	2.08	1.47
Latin America and the Caribbean	10.77	10.19	9.62	8.64
South Asia	49.57	43.05	35.04	30.84
East Asia	57.73	29.84	15.40	9.05
East Europe/Central Asia	0.70	0.47	3.60	0.95

Source: World Bank, PovcalNet. <http://iresearch.worldbank.org/PovcalNet/jsp/index.jsp>, accessed on July 15, 2008.

five who are underweight, infant mortality rates (IMR), and life expectancy at birth. While the limitations of these continental aggregations are manifest, not least because they are often based on extrapolations and interpolations that compensate for missing and poor quality data, as a first order approximation, the results here set the context for our more detailed analysis of household survey data.

Table 15.1 reports the share of people living on less than $1 per day. The data from the most recent year, 2004, indicate that the headcount is markedly higher in Africa than any other region of the world. In South Asia, the next poorest region, less than one-third of the population is living below the $1 per day poverty line. In East Asia, just over 1 in 10 people live under this threshold, and an even smaller share does so in Latin America and the Caribbean. Going back to the beginning of the 1980s, Africa's share of poor people was markedly less than East Asia and South Asia. However, all this changed by 1990, by which time Africa's poverty headcount actually increased, while steep declines were reported in other regions. The pattern of continued improvement in the poverty numbers occurred throughout the rest of the world in the 1990s, while Africa stagnated and the share of the poor remained relatively constant.

For schooling, we examine two indicators of access: primary school gross enrollment rates and average years of schooling. Gross enrollment is defined as the number of children in primary school divided by the number of children in the age groups associated with primary school.[2] The data for the most recent year, 2000, reveal that sub-Saharan Africa lags markedly behind other regions. For example, the average gross enrollment rate in sub-Saharan Africa is 77 per cent, versus the next lowest value of 97 per cent in the Middle East/North Africa (MENA) region (Table 15.2). And in terms of average years of school among adults, the 3.4 years in sub-Saharan Africa is substantially lower than the 4.6 years in South Asia and 6.2 years in East Asia (Table 15.3). But perhaps of greater interest is that in 1960 the average years of school among adults was somewhat higher in sub-Saharan Africa than South Asia and MENA. However, by 1980 this was no longer the case.

Table 15.2. Primary school gross enrollment rates (% primary school age population)

Region	1960	1970	1980	1990	2000	2005
Sub-Saharan Africa	40	51	80	73	114	95
MENA	59	79	89	97	120	104
Latin America and the Caribbean	91	107	105	105	120	118
South Asia	41	71	77	95	95	113
East Asia	87	90	111	119	114	111
East Europe/Former Soviet Union (FSU)	103	104	100	98	100	103

Note: The gross enrollment ratio is calculated by expressing the number of students enrolled in primary (secondary or tertiary level of) education, regardless of age, as a percentage of the population of official school age for that level; therefore percentages can be over 100%.

Sources: Glewwe and Kremer (2006); <http://devdata.worldbank.org/edstats/query/defaultGrp.htm>, accessed on July 15, 2008.

Table 15.3. Average years at school, adults age 15+

Region	1960	1970	1980	1990	2000
Sub-Saharan Africa	1.7	2.0	2.3	3.0	3.4
MENA	1.4	2.2	2.9	4.1	5.4
Latin America and the Caribbean	3.2	3.7	4.4	5.3	6.0
South Asia	1.5	2.0	3.0	3.8	4.6
East Asia	2.5	3.4	4.6	5.6	6.2
East Europe/FSU	6.5	7.6	8.5	9.0	9.7

Source: Barro and Lee (2001).

Underweight is the most widely used indicator for assessing the general health and nutritional status of children. Falling below standardized norms is considered an excellent indicator of deprivation from both inadequate dietary intake relative to needs, and disease and infection that impede normal growth and weight gain (Beaton et al., 1990; WHO, 1983). We observe that in the most recent year, 2005, nearly 30 per cent of children were underweight in sub-Saharan Africa (Table 15.4). However, the share of underweight children is actually higher in South Asia. What is of greater concern, however, is that the share of underweight children in Africa has virtually remained constant over the past three decades, despite a temporary decline in the 1980s. In contrast, the share of underweight children in South Asia, like all other regions, shows a marked and steady decline from more than two in three children being underweight in 1975, to 40 per cent of the children being underweight in 2005.

The results on the evolution of changes in infant mortality paint a similarly sobering picture for sub-Saharan Africa. During the 1960s, Africa's 154 deaths per 1,000 live births was similar to the figures from the Middle East and South Asia. East Asia too had a high IMR of 133 (Table 15.5). Over the next couple of decades the rate of improvement in Africa and South Asia was markedly slower than other regions, especially East Asia where dramatic drops in IMR were noted. While the 1980s witnessed continued and rapid reductions in IMR in

Table 15.4. Prevalence of underweight preschool children (0–60 months), developing countries, 1975–2005 (%)

Region	1975	1980	1985	1990	1995	2000	2005
Sub-Saharan Africa	31.4	26.2	26.7	27.3	27.9	28.5	29.1
MENA	19.8	17.5	16.4	15.6	14.8	14.0	13.2
Latin America and the Caribbean	19.3	14.2	12.2	10.2	8.3	6.3	4.3
South Asia	67.7	58.1	54.5	50.9	47.3	43.6	40.0
East Asia	43.6	43.5	39.9	36.2	32.6	28.9	25.3

Source: The Fourth Nutrition Situation Report. SCN <http://www.unscn.org/layout/modules/resources/files/rwns4.pdf>. The 1975 data is from the First Nutrition Situation Report <http://unscn.org/layout/modules/resources/files/rwns1.pdf>

Table 15.5. Infant mortality rate (deaths before age 1 per 1,000 live births), developing countries, 1960–2005

Region	1960	1970	1980	1990	2001	2005
Sub-Saharan Africa	154	145	120	112	107	101
MENA	154	128	91	59	47	43
Latin America and the Caribbean	105	86	61	43	28	26
South Asia	146	130	115	89	70	63
East Asia	133	84	55	43	33	26
East Europe/FSU	76	68	55	44	30	29

Source: UNICEF (2007) <http://www.childinfo.org/areas/childmortality/infantdata.php>, accessed on July 15, 2008.

the rest of the world, by 1990 sub-Saharan Africa had distinguished itself by the slow level of improvement in infant mortality. This trend of modest gains in Africa continued through 2005.

At the same time, initial low levels of life expectancy (Table 15.6), which were in the 40- to 50-year range in Africa, Asia, and the Middle East, showed steady improvements through the 1960s and 1970s; progress was especially rapid in Asia. Progress in Africa, however, was considerably slower. The creeping improvements in life expectancy in Africa continued through 1990, reaching 50 years, in contrast to 58 years in South Asia, the second worst region. Over the next 15 years, however, life expectancy in Africa has fallen to 46, the recent decline largely due to the rise in AIDS-related deaths. However, with the exception of Eastern Europe, life expectancy has continued to rise in all other regions of the world, reaching 64 in South Asia, the next lowest number compared to 46 in sub-Saharan Africa.

Despite reservations about data quality, these results provide a sobering perspective on the evolution of poverty in Africa since 1960. Of course, the types of aggregates presented do not tell the story of the complexity and variations within Africa (and the other regions). We next turn to a more careful treatment of the changes in poverty in Africa that relies on good quality household survey data to estimate various measures of well-being.

Table 15.6. Life expectancy (years), developing countries, 1960–2005

Region	1960	1965	1970	1975	1980	1985	1990	1995	2001	2005
Sub-Saharan Africa	40	42	44	46	48	49	50	50	48	46
MENA	46	48	52	54	57	57	63	64	67	69
Latin America and the Caribbean	54	57	60	60	62	64	68	70	70	72
South Asia	46	49	48	58	60	60	58	65	62	64
East Asia	46	49	58	58	60	60	66	65	69	71
East Europe/FSU			66				68		69	67

Source: UNICEF; <http://earthtrends.wri.org/text/population-health/variable-379.html>, accessed on July 15, 2008.

Survey-based estimates of changes in poverty

Income/expenditure surveys

We begin by looking at changes in economic measures of deprivation. While the standard approach to measuring deprivation in material living standards in developed countries is to use income or assets, household consumption expenditures have been widely accepted as the more appropriate approach to measuring economic deprivation in developing countries. The conceptual basis for relying on consumption is that it is the goods and services that people consume that capture their economic well-being, and income and assets only serve to enable that consumption. In addition, however, there are practical reasons for using consumption data rather than income to measure economic deprivation that revolve around the relative ease of measuring the former. These include: that income is far more volatile, varying greatly by season and even across years due to weather and other shocks; that there are formidable challenges in calculating net revenues from agriculture and other own-account enterprises in which most people are engaged in developing countries; that income derived from assets is difficult to estimate; and that there is often a reluctance to divulge information on earnings (and assets), especially in Africa where tax avoidance is widespread and tax authorities are viewed with great suspicion.

The primary sources of data used in Africa to assess economic deprivation are Living Standard Measurement Surveys (LSMS) conducted by, or with the support of, the World Bank. In addition, there are several countries where statistical agencies have conducted income/expenditure surveys that can be used to create expenditure aggregates and derive poverty lines. Both sources of data have been cataloged and collated by the World Bank, and subsequently used to derive poverty measures. We rely on the poverty headcount calculations made by the World Bank in order to examine spells of change for countries in sub-Saharan Africa. We do so, first, because of the difficulty in getting access to many of the relevant surveys. Governments and statistical agencies are notoriously reluctant to allow individuals access to data they collect. We therefore could not get access to many surveys which the World Bank has permission to use. Furthermore, the analytical requirements to create consumption aggregates are formidable (Deaton and Zaidi, 2002). Repeating the enormous effort that the World Bank has put into this enterprise would not only be prohibitively time consuming and expensive, but a fool's errand.

Given our interest in making comparisons of poverty changes that are roughly comparable across countries, we also rely on the $1 per day poverty headcount ratios (HCRs) that were calculated by the World Bank.[3] All the figures that we report are based on household surveys that were designed to be nationally representative. There are a total of twenty-three countries in sub-Saharan Africa that have one or more relatively recent spells of money metric poverty changes over time. Of those, only fifteen have a spell that includes the current decade.

While considerable care went into the Bank's attempt to ensuring some degree of comparability across surveys, concerns remain about the appropriateness of using them to measure changes in living standards over time. The first set of concerns revolves around the ability of the surveys themselves to collect comparable consumption data. There are many challenges in this regard. First and foremost is that in developing countries we are almost exclusively reliant on the recall of respondents. The accuracy of the recall is conditioned by the limitations of the memories of respondents. However, the nature of the survey design is also a critical element in determining the quality of recall data; and so, too, is the training and technical competence of enumerators that are charged with overcoming the challenges of memory loss.

To amplify, it is now well understood that the design of the survey instrument is important in eliciting accurate information. Among the major design parameters that are critical to overcoming memory problems are issues of the number of items that consumption data are collected on, the recall period, and the nature of choices available to respondents in terms of units of consumption. In the case of the list of consumption goods, there is solid evidence that a shorter list reduces the overall estimate of the value of consumption (Joliffe and Scott, 1995; Steele, 1998; Pradhan, 2001). Regarding recall period, which is related to the design issues of the number of visits to the household, the trade-offs between accuracy and representativeness have been well documented in the literature. However, there is also evidence that longer recall periods, which may in fact capture the more typical pattern of consumption (e.g. food versus non-food consumption), will also tend to underestimate total consumption (Silberstein and Scott, 1991; Scott and Amenuvegbe, 1990). As for the choice of consumption units, some surveys allow considerable latitude in responses, including bottle caps of oil, gourds of rice, and so forth, while others do not. The direction of bias introduced by these choices is less clear, although there is little doubt that they affect how well consumption is measured.

There are also a number of related issues that will affect the consumption estimates, such as how often the enumerator visits the household, whether and how the respondents are prompted about consumption of specific items, and whether questions are posed in terms of consumption since the last visit, or alternatively, as usual consumption in a similar time period. Another factor that can affect the reliability and comparability of consumption data concerns the issue of who is interviewed in the household and the gender of the enumerators. In some societies there may be cultural taboos against women working as enumerators, and/or women responding to questionnaires. Likewise, in some cases both the head and the spouse respond, while in others it is one or the other. These types of variability in survey protocols will all affect the reliability and accuracy of recall.

A second set of concerns revolves around deflators and purchasing power parity (PPP) conversion factors. Price data that are required to construct a price index are notoriously deficient in developing countries. The lack of capacity of statistical agencies is compounded by the fact that spatial price variability tends to be far greater in poorly integrated markets where transaction costs are high. Thus, even if good price deflators are available for the capital city, they are likely of little relevance in remote rural areas. Another critical challenge is that unlike in developed countries where patterns of consumption tend to be quite similar across regions, in developing countries this is not the case. So, even if it were possible to collect prices at different locations with some degree of accuracy, the lack of a common consumption basket will make creating appropriate deflators difficult (and likewise for the formulation of a consumption-based poverty line). Furthermore, unlike in developed countries where prices are easily determined at the grocery store or at the local market, this is often not the case in developing countries where prices are not posted and are an outcome of a bargaining process.

In response to these types of problems, some (but not all) surveys rely on prices derived from questions administered to the household, rather than community questionnaires or routine government price reconnaissance. This can involve explicitly asking households about the price per standardized unit, or alternatively, from the calculation of unit values from quantity and expenditure data. Of course, unit values are not prices, but only a first approximation. They are affected by a range of household choices, such as quality choices, size of the purchase, choice of market, and so forth. One way of addressing this variability is to use a measure of central tendency of prices within a sampling cluster as the local price. But again, considerable judgment (and skill) is involved in this process.

In creating a comparable data set across countries, the additional challenge of generating PPPs to derive headcounts is extensively discussed in the literature. Various options exist in this regard, most noteworthy being the Penn World Tables (PWT) which generally serves as the standard for such calculations. However, there are a variety of criticisms of using PWT PPP for poverty comparisons, including their reliance on average prices and expenditures. These concerns have contributed to attempts to create alternative (food-based) PPP. While we are not going to engage with the technicality of the arguments for and against various alternatives, again, the subjective nature of this choice will potentially have important effects on inter-temporal and spatial comparisons.

Other issues, unrelated to sample design and price deflators plague the calculation of economic deprivation using consumption data. For example, economic measures of well-being are collected at the household level. Equal sharing relative to need is generally assumed. Clearly this is not correct as there may be individuals who capture a relatively larger share of consumption in the household. Likewise, the use of household size as the divisor for total consumption represents an unidentifiable assumption. Indeed, there are undoubtedly economies of scale, even in poor households, and these certainly differ by location, household composition, household size, household income, and so forth. But as it is difficult, perhaps impossible, to estimate these scale economies (Deaton, 1997) in the absence of an identification strategy for deriving equivalence scales, the use of per capita expenditure seems as defensible as any other assumption, but certainly as arbitrary.

An examination of the details on the surveys used by the World Bank and referenced below indicates a great deal of variability along all the dimensions cited above, both across time in specific countries, and across countries. While some analysts have made heroic efforts to deal with changes in survey design,[4] there is little doubt that these variations in methods contribute in an important way to the poverty headcounts. We therefore admonish considerable caution in interpreting these results.

A casual examination of the results suggests that our skepticism about using these data for making country-specific inter-temporal comparisons is warranted. For example, the extremely high poverty figures from Uganda seem somewhat implausible, at least compared to other countries in the region (Table 15.7). Similarly, the numbers indicate that poverty in Kenya fell by more than half between 1994 and 1997. A decline in poverty of a similar magnitude is reported for Mali between 1994 and 2001 and Gambia between 1992 and 1998. Similarly, Cameroon, Mauritania, Senegal, and South Africa reported poverty reductions in short intervals that seem quite implausible. The reduction of poverty reported for Senegal during the 1990s is extraordinary, 45.4 to 16.8, and seems completely inconsistent with developments in that economy. Despite such questionable findings, we summarize the results from the Bank data as a point of departure for examining alternative metrics of poverty that are based on more comparable and reliable survey data.

Among the forty-nine spells of poverty changes, quite a few are of a small magnitude—often 2 or 3 percentage points. Given that there are no standard errors on the point estimates, and the inevitable measurement errors, for the sake of distinguishing whether poverty increased/decreased/remained the same across spells, we arbitrarily define "no change," as a difference in the headcount

Table 15.7. Headcount ratio of economic poverty

Country	Survey year(s)	1st survey	2nd survey	3rd survey	4th survey	5th survey	6th survey	7th survey
Benin	2003	30.79						
Botswana	1985, 1993	33.30	28.53					
Burkina Faso	1994, 1998, 2003	51.38	44.85	28.65				
Burundi	1992, 1998	44.07	54.56					
Cameroon	1996, 2001	35.77	20.15					
Cape Verde	2001	1.91						
Central African Republic	1993	66.58						
Côte d'Ivoire	1985, 1987, 1988, 1993, 1995, 1998, 2002	4.71	3.28	7.46	9.88	12.29	15.53	15.72
Ethiopia	1981, 1995, 2000	32.73	31.25	21.60				
Gambia	1992, 1998	53.69	27.91					
Ghana	1987, 1988, 1991, 1998	46.51	45.45	47.24	36.17			
Kenya	1992, 1994, 1997	33.51	26.54	12.41				
Lesotho	1986, 1993, 1995	30.34	43.14	36.40				
Madagascar	1980, 1993, 1997, 1999, 2001	49.18	46.31	49.76	66.03	61.04		
Malawi	2004	20.76						
Mali	1994, 2001	72.29	36.35					
Mauritania	1987, 1993, 1995, 2000	46.67	49.37	28.6	25.94			
Mozambique	1996, 2002	39.84	36.18					
Namibia	1993	34.93						
Niger	1992, 1994	41.73	54.76					
Nigeria	1985, 1992, 1996, 2003	65.72	59.19	78.21	71.18			
Rwanda	1994, 2000	35.01	60.29					
Senegal	1991, 1994, 2001	45.38	24.04	16.82				
Sierra Leone	1989	57.03						
South Africa	1993, 1995, 2000	10.02	6.30	12.37				
Swaziland	1994, 2000	68.21	47.58					
Uganda	1989, 1992, 1996, 1999, 2002	87.67	90.26	87.94	84.92	82.28		
United Republic of Tanzania	1991	32.74						
Zambia	1991, 1993, 1996, 1998, 2004	65.65	73.57	72.22	65.65			
Zimbabwe	1990, 1995	54.39	56.12					

Source: World Bank, PovcalNet.

of less than 3 percentage points. Out of the forty-nine spells, twenty-three indicate a decline in poverty, eleven indicate a worsening of poverty, and fifteen indicate no change. A more encouraging result is found when looking at spells with the most recent year being between 2000 and 2004. Among the fifteen spells that end during the present decade, ten indicate a decline in the poverty headcount, two suggest an increase, and three show no change. Again, it should be kept in mind that there are many cases where even a casual examination of reported magnitudes of the declines in the share of the population falling below the $1 a day poverty line look suspect, suggesting a healthy degree of skepticism be accorded to these findings.

Health and education

We next turn to a discussion of changes in non-income dimensions of well-being, focusing on health and nutrition, which in addition to income are the other two pillars of the Human Development Index (HDI). To begin we discuss briefly the data employed, and then turn to the results. But before doing so, we want to emphasize that we believe these metrics of deprivation have far fewer problems than the standard income and expenditure variables. First and foremost, measuring deprivation in terms of health is done at the individual level. We need not concern ourselves with making assumptions about allocations within the household, or issues of unidentifiable economies of scale parameters. Second, price deflators and PPP calculations are not an issue here: centimeters are centimeters and kilos are kilos the world over. Measurement error is also small, and to the extent that it exists, it is random. Putting a child on a scale and recording a correct weight is simpler, less costly, less time consuming, and less subject to personal judgment than collection of consumption data. Nor are any complex calculations required to get from the field data to our measure of well-being.

Demographic and Health Survey (DHS) questionnaires are nearly identical across time and across countries, and the training of enumerators and field staff follow a standard set of procedures. This again, contrasts dramatically with the LSMS and consumption/expenditure surveys discussed above. Likewise, the questions on health do not rely on memory, and to the extent that the education question does, recall of the highest grade completed is likely not as affected by memory lapses and the types of measurement errors that affect consumption recall.

Despite these dramatic advantages in the measurement of deprivation, there is one common concern with the LSMS and DHS type surveys: the potential of changes in sampling frames which can compromise the comparability of results over time. While in principle the analysis of repeated large, nationally representative surveys that follow the same design is the most appropriate way to understand change in the well-being of the population, the potential pitfall of changes in the sampled populations may lead to spurious estimates of poverty changes. This issue has been examined in some detail in two recent papers using DHS surveys where we compare the sample means of individual or household characteristics that should not change over time in the two data sets (Glick, Sahn, and Younger, 2006; Glick and Sahn, 2007).[5] Among the relatively small number of surveys compared, the authors do find several instances where there is evidence that the DHS samples are not identical. While statistical differences in certain characteristics are frequently uncovered, they are generally of a very small magnitude. While this problem undoubtedly plagues most, if not all the surveys that are the basis of the income-determined poverty figures, it does suggest the need for some caution in interpreting changes for individual spells, especially when differences are small in magnitude. Nonetheless, we would argue that the bigger picture we present based on sixty-four surveys is not affected by this potential problem.

DATA

We analyze data from sixty-four DHS conducted in twenty-three African countries that have at least two such surveys. Overall, we have forty proximal spells of change in health and education poverty in our analysis, usually around five years long. A large share of the most recent surveys are from the current decade, making the comparisons current, although for most countries they do not extend back into the 1980s.

The DHSs are nationally representative surveys with large sample sizes and questionnaires that are virtually identical across time and countries. In most surveys, households are selected based on a standard stratified and clustered design, and, within the household, one woman, aged 15–49, is selected at random as the focus of the interview. In addition, all living children up to a given age (usually 60 months, but sometimes 36 months) born to that woman are weighed and measured. The data that we use pertain to these women and children.

There are many potential health and education variables, and related "poverty" lines that can be used to measure deprivation in these dimensions. Since we are interested in *distributions* of well-being, any useful measure must apply to individuals (as opposed to populations), and must also be continuous (which rules out indicators such as the infant mortality rate or HDI). Likewise, we cannot rely on predicted variables, because the prediction equation will compress the distribution.

For a variety of reasons which we discuss elsewhere (Sahn and Younger, 2005, 2006), the first health indicator that we employ is the standardized height of pre-school age children. There is a large body of evidence to argue that a child's growth is an excellent objective indicator of his/her general health status

(Cole and Parkin, 1977; Mata, 1978; Tanner, 1981; Mosley and Chen, 1984; WHO, 1995; Martorell et al., 1975; Beaton et al., 1990; Strauss and Thomas, 1995; Behrman and Deolalikar, 1988, 1990). As summarized by Beaton et al. (1990), growth failure is "...the best general proxy for constraints to human welfare of the poorest, including dietary inadequacy, infectious diseases and other environmental health risks." They go on to point out that the usefulness of stature is that it captures the "...multiple dimensions of individual health and development and their socio-economic and environmental determinants" (p. 2).

Most analyses of children's heights (or weights) measure them in z-scores: the distance the child's height is from the median of a reference population of healthy children, measured in standard deviations and standardized by age and gender (WHO, 1983). But z-scores can be negative (and usually are for poor populations), while most standard distributional statistics require that the underlying measure of well-being be positive. We thus work with "standardized heights," instead of z-scores. This variable is calculated, given a child's z-score (whatever the age and gender), by assigning that child the height corresponding to the same z-score in the 24-month-old girls' distribution. Thus, the height derived is that which the child would have if s/he were a 24-month old girl. The standardization allows us to compare children of different ages and genders while maintaining a positive value for each child. The poverty line that we assign for this variable is the standardized height that is two standard deviations below the median of the distribution of the reference population of healthy children, a practice that is standard in the literature.

A second health indicator we employ to assess the health of the adult population is the Body Mass Index (BMI) for women aged 15–49, calculated as (weight in kilograms)/(height in meters squared). As with children's heights, we use a conventional cut-off point of 18.5 as a poverty line for this variable. It is important to note that, unlike height, education, or income, welfare does not necessarily increase monotonically with body mass, which violates one of the standard axioms of most distributional measures (the monotonicity axiom, or "more is better"). Yet in Africa, the share of women who are obese is sufficiently small that we can interpret our results for this variable as if "more is better" applies over the observed range of weights.

For education, we use the number of years of schooling for women aged 22–30 as our indicator of well-being, defining education poverty as not completing six years of primary schooling. We limit our analysis to women above 22 because we want to avoid censoring for women who have not yet reached the age at which they should have completed post-secondary school. Likewise, since we want to focus our attention on those who have finished their schooling in the not-too-distant past, we use an upper age limit of 30 years of age.[6] A potential weakness of using years of schooling as a measure of well-being is that it does not control for differences in school quality and is thus an imperfect measure of the well-being that comes from education. However, given that our comparisons are within countries and over relatively short time periods (usually five years), the implicit assumption that school quality is constant may not be too restrictive. We define the education poverty line as completing six years of schooling. Since this is somewhat arbitrary, we have tested the sensitivity of our results to this assumption by varying the education poverty line three years in each direction, and find little difference in our results.

Since the DHSs follow the same structure and format, and the indicators are strictly comparable and do not involve challenges such as employing deflators, we are quite confident in making inter-temporal comparisons using these data. Likewise, we expect that most measurement error will be random—unlike measurement error in income. The fact that we estimated the headcounts ourselves also allows us to not only ensure the same analytical procedures were employed in calculating poverty indexes, but we can also make statistical comparisons over time employing the standard errors we estimate.[7]

RESULTS

Headcount indexes

We next examine the headcounts for the three measures of well-being. Table 15.8 presents the changes in the share of stunted children between proximal spells. Among the thirty-nine spells for which we have data, there were thirteen cases where the headcount worsened (e.g. more stunting), thirteen where the headcount declined, and thirteen where it remained the same.[8] Of course, this summary of the changes in spells obscures important inter-country differences, as well as differences within a country where we have more than one spell. For example, there was a substantial decline in the share of children who were in poor health in Namibia between 1992 and 2000, but just the opposite is the case in Niger. But perhaps of greater interest is that in those countries with two or more spells, it is usually the case that the changes over time do not tend to work in the same direction. For example, Zimbabwe witnessed a large decline in stunted children between 1988 and 1994, only to witness a substantial worsening between 1994 and 1999. In a similar vein, the deterioration in the health of Nigeria's children that occurred between 1986 and 1990, and again between 1990 and 1999, reversed itself by 2003 where there was a substantial decline in the stunted share. Thus, whether we look at all the spells across the continent or sequences of spells in individual countries, there is no clear evidence of steady improvement (or deterioration) in children's health.

We have information for fewer spells in the case of the share of underweight women. This is because women's anthropometry was not a standard part of the health module of the DHS in the earlier surveys. The results, however, differ somewhat from the information on child health. In the majority of cases there

Table 15.8. Poverty headcount ratios for children's heights

	Survey	Headcount ratio	Tests for equality[1] versus first	versus second	versus third
Burkina Faso	1992	0.353			
	1999	0.383	1.96		
	2003	0.406	4.09	1.76	
Benin	1996	0.294			
	2001	0.320	1.82		
Côte d'Ivoire	1994	0.289			
	1998	0.245	−2.61		
Cameroon	1991	0.272			
	1998	0.355	4.65		
	2004	0.348	4.42	−0.42	
Chad	1997	0.431			
	2004	0.437	0.41		
Ethiopia	2000	0.511			
	2005	0.475	−2.62		
Ghana	1988	0.320			
	1993	0.307	−0.78		
	1998	0.236	−5.20	−4.33	
	2003	0.304	−1.00	−0.20	4.24
Guinea	1999	0.284			
	2005	0.371	5.00		
Kenya	1993	0.355			
	1998	0.355	0.00		
	2003	0.347	−0.60	−0.59	
Madagascar	1992	0.567			
	1997	0.564	−0.25		
	2003	0.502	−4.32	−4.17	
Mali	1987	0.272			
	1995	0.368	5.45		
	2001	0.408	7.87	3.75	
Malawi	1992	0.496			
	2000	0.506	0.71		
Mozambique	1997	0.440			
	2003	0.425	−1.09		
Nigeria	1986	0.302			
	1990	0.425	8.11		
	1999	0.504	10.80	4.65	
	2003	0.422	7.57	−0.19	−4.63
Niger	1992	0.439			
	1998	0.497	4.18		
Namibia	1992	0.330			
	2000	0.238	−5.60		
Rwanda	1992	0.489			
	2000	0.427	−4.47		
	2005	0.479	−0.66	3.62	
Senegal	1986	0.230			
	1992	0.262	1.66		
	2005	0.164	−3.38	−7.16	
Togo	1988	0.341			
	1998	0.262	−4.86		
Tanzania	1992	0.451			
	1996	0.466	1.19		
	1999	0.442	−0.58	−1.47	
	2004	0.385	−5.75	−6.67	−3.62

(*Continued*)

387

Table 15.8. (Continued)

	Survey	Headcount ratio	Tests for equality[1] versus first	versus second	versus third
Uganda	1988	0.472			
	1995	0.412	−4.25		
	2000	0.407	−4.53	−0.38	
Zambia	1992	0.428			
	1996	0.448	1.58		
	2001	0.512	6.40	4.95	
Zimbabwe	1988	0.321			
	1994	0.254	−4.04		
	1999	0.312	−0.52	3.51	

[1] These are t-test statistics of the equality of the poverty statistic between the two surveys indicated.

Table 15.9. Poverty headcount ratios for women's BMI

	Survey	Headcount ratio	Tests for equality[1] versus first	versus second	versus third
Burkina Faso	1992	0.137			
	1999	0.125	−1.50		
	2003	0.197	9.12	11.07	
Benin	1996	0.140			
	2001	0.101	−5.02		
Côte d'Ivoire	1994	0.079			
	1998	0.082	0.53		
Cameroon	1998	0.070			
	2004	0.064	−0.89		
Chad	1997	0.194			
	2004	0.202	0.93		
Ethiopia	2000	0.281			
	2005	0.246	−5.38		
Ghana	1993	0.113			
	1998	0.107	−0.68		
	2003	0.091	−2.77	−2.15	
Guinea	1999	0.113			
	2005	0.121	1.09		
Kenya	1993	0.094			
	1998	0.109	2.19		
	2003	0.118	4.05	1.43	
Madagascar	1997	0.190			
	2003	0.184	−0.74		
Mali	1995	0.146			
	2001	0.114	−5.43		
Malawi	1992	0.086			
	2000	0.080	−0.97		
Mozambique	1997	0.109			
	2003	0.081	−4.45		
Nigeria	1999	0.156			
	2003	0.141	−1.75		
Niger	1992	0.177			
	1998	0.190	1.49		

Namibia	1992	0.128			
Rwanda	2000	0.082			
	2005	0.092	2.07		
Senegal	1992	0.137			
	2005	0.174	4.48		
Togo	1998	0.105			
Tanzania	1992	0.089			
	1996	0.088	−0.16		
	2004	0.095	1.25	1.35	
Uganda	1995	0.089			
	2000	0.094	0.78		
Zambia	1992	0.097			
	1996	0.083	−2.25		
	2001	0.141	7.08	10.14	
Zimbabwe	1994	0.047			
	1999	0.054	1.45		

[1] These are t-test statistics of the equality of the poverty statistic between the two surveys indicated.

was no change in the share of women who are underweight; only in four of twenty-five spells did the share of underweight women increase, while it declined in six cases. (Table 15.9).

Our final indicator of deprivation is years of schooling for women aged 22–30. We select this group because, first, the women in this cohort are old enough that schooling is likely not censored. In addition, these young women represent a cohort that has recently passed through the years in which they would have been in school and are also recent entrants into the labor market. We use a cut-off point of six years of schooling for our poverty line (Table 15.10).[9]

Overall we observe a more positive story than the health indicators: out of the thirty-nine spells, schooling poverty declined in twenty cases, worsened in two cases, and remained constant in seventeen cases. Kenya and Zimbabwe are notable for their quite dramatic improvements across multiple spells. In contrast, there are a number of countries with extremely high shares of women who have not completed six years of schooling. These are concentrated in Francophone West Africa, and the sobering statistics capture both low starting values, and the fact that there has been little improvement over the years. In fact, the progress reported for Cameroon between 1991 and 1998 is the only case where a substantial and statistically significant improvement in the share of women who have competed six years of schooling is found in Francophone West Africa.

Decompositions of changes in health and education

In considering the changes in poverty headcounts along various dimensions, an interesting question that arises is the extent to which the relatively limited progress observed is attributable to adverse distributional changes. That is, we

Table 15.10. Poverty headcount ratios for women's years of learning

	Survey	Headcount ratio	Tests for equality[1] versus first survey	versus second survey	versus third survey
Burkina Faso	1992	0.940			
	1999	0.947	0.95		
	2003	0.905	−4.64	−5.71	
Benin	1996	0.893			
	2001	0.898	0.54		
Côte d'Ivoire	1994	0.862			
	1998	0.835	−1.80		
Cameroon	1991	0.718			
	1998	0.543	−9.37		
	2004	0.523	−11.83	−1.29	
Chad	1997	0.966			
	2004	0.947	−2.88		
Ethiopia	2000	0.878			
	2005	0.870	−1.17		
Ghana	1988	0.507			
	1993	0.530	1.23		
	1998	0.492	−0.83	−2.04	
	2003	0.494	−0.73	−1.98	0.12
Guinea	1999	0.927			
	2005	0.931	0.52		
Kenya	1988	0.482			
	1993	0.386	−6.41		
	1998	0.276	−14.38	−7.75	
	2003	0.261	−15.76	−9.01	−1.14
Madagascar	1992	0.726			
	1997	0.748	1.51		
	2003	0.741	1.01	−0.56	
Mali	1987	0.943			
	1995	0.933	−1.12		
	2001	0.929	−1.64	−0.65	
Malawi	1992	0.809			
	2000	0.739	−5.52		
Mozambique	1997	0.924			
	2003	0.893	−3.93		
Nigeria	1986	0.661			
	1990	0.809	8.87		
	1999	0.625	−2.04	−15.34	
	2003	0.599	−3.41	−16.49	−1.84
Niger	1992	0.972			
	1998	0.947	−4.08		
Namibia	1992	0.408			
	2000	0.228	−11.13		
Rwanda	1992	0.762			
	2000	0.640	−8.81		
	2005	0.804	3.39	13.72	
Senegal	1986	0.910			
	1992	0.903	−0.68		
	1997	0.871	−3.70	−3.16	
	2005	0.848	−6.32	−5.92	−2.54
Togo	1988	0.836			

	1998	0.881	3.38		
Tanzania	1992	0.433			
	1996	0.320	−8.29		
	1999	0.328	−6.36	0.44	
	2004	0.346	−6.68	1.98	1.14
Uganda	1988	0.795			
	1995	0.758	−2.59		
	2000	0.699	−6.62	−4.41	
Zambia	1992	0.453			
	1996	0.465	0.79		
	2001	0.476	1.44	0.67	
Zimbabwe	1988	0.532			
	1994	0.286	−13.15		
	1999	0.157	−21.61	−8.89	

[1] These are t-test statistics of the equality of the poverty statistic between the two surveys indicated.

ask the question: to what extent are changes in inequality contributing to, or impairing, progress in terms of the overall reduction in poverty? To address that question, we build on the earlier work of Datt and Ravallion (1992) who show that the change in the share of the population that falls below the poverty line can be decomposed into two components: one due to changes in the mean of the distribution and another due to changes in its dispersion. More precisely, any distribution can be characterized by its mean and its Lorenz curve. As a result, the share of a population that is poor can be expressed as a function of its mean, μ, its Lorenz curve, L, and the poverty line, z. We then decompose the change in poverty between period t and $t + n$ into a growth component, defined as the change in poverty due to a change in the mean of the distribution while holding the Lorenz curve constant at that of the reference sample, and the redistribution component, defined as the change in the Lorenz curve while keeping the mean of the distribution constant at that of the reference sample (Datt and Ravallion, 1992).

The Datt and Ravallion decomposition is not robust to the choice of the reference sample. To avoid this problem we rely on Kakwani's (1997) approach to the decomposition problem and average the Datt and Ravallion decompositions calculated with each sample as the reference. We have previously adopted this practice (Sahn and Younger, 2005), as have others (McCulloch, Cherel-Robson, and Baluch, 2000; Dhongde, 2002; Shorrocks and Kolenikov, 2001). Besides having the advantage of being consistent with the axiomatic properties proposed by Kakwani, it eliminates the residual in the methodology developed by Datt and Ravallion, which is difficult to interpret.

Before presenting the results of our decomposition analysis for the two health indicators and education, we note that there are many examples from Africa of similar decomposition exercises for income poverty. The results of such efforts are summarized by Christiaensen, Demery, and Paternostro (2002), who conclude that the mean shifts are far more important in determining changes in

Table 15.11. Datt-Ravallion-Kakwani decompositions for children's heights

Country	Period	First	Second	Difference	t-value	Mean	Dispersion
Burkina Faso	1992–9	0.351	0.380	0.030	−1.940	0.053	−0.023
	1999–2003	0.380	0.402	0.021	−1.584	0.003	0.018
Benin	1996–2001	0.290	0.318	0.028	−1.920	0.024	0.004
Côte d'Ivoire	1994–8	0.286	0.240	−0.046	2.697	−0.052	0.006
Cameroon	1991–8	0.271	0.349	0.078	−4.405	0.035	0.043
	1998–2004	0.349	0.346	−0.003	0.154	−0.011	0.008
Chad	1997–2004	0.426	0.434	0.009	−0.604	0.011	−0.002
Ethiopia	2000–5	0.509	0.471	−0.037	2.705	−0.071	0.034
Ghana	1988–93	0.320	0.303	−0.016	0.984	−0.026	0.009
	1993–8	0.303	0.232	−0.071	4.333	−0.057	−0.014
	1998–2003	0.232	0.301	0.068	−4.268	0.050	0.018
Guinea	1999–2005	0.282	0.368	0.086	−4.952	0.063	0.023
Kenya	1993–8	0.352	0.352	0.000	0.003	−0.031	0.031
	1998–2003	0.345	−0.007	0.004	0.000	−0.011	0.000
Madagascar	1992–7	0.567	0.562	−0.005	0.339	−0.011	0.006
	1997–2003	0.562	0.502	−0.060	4.089	−0.084	0.024
Mali	1987–95	0.271	0.366	0.095	−5.412	0.069	0.025
	1995–2001	0.366	0.406	0.040	−3.771	0.025	0.015
Malawi	1992–2000	0.491	0.505	0.014	−0.963	−0.009	0.022
Mozambique	1997–2003	0.438	0.423	−0.015	1.128	0.017	−0.032
Nigeria	1986–90	0.301	0.421	0.119	−7.902	0.073	0.046
	1990–9	0.421	0.502	0.081	−4.783	0.035	0.047
	1999–2003	0.502	0.420	−0.082	4.639	−0.045	−0.037
Niger	1992–8	0.437	0.495	0.058	−4.177	0.068	−0.010
Namibia	1992–2000	0.329	0.235	−0.094	5.686	−0.080	−0.014

Rwanda	1992–2000	0.486	0.424	-0.062	4.487	-0.093	0.030
	2000–5	0.424	0.474	0.050	-3.512	0.066	-0.016
Senegal	1986–92	0.230	0.258	0.028	-1.434	0.000	0.028
	1986–2005	0.230	0.162	-0.067	3.460	-0.073	0.005
	1992–2005	0.258	0.162	-0.095	6.980	-0.078	-0.017
Togo	1988–98	0.340	0.259	-0.082	4.969	-0.083	0.001
Tanzania	1992–6	0.448	0.463	0.015	-1.178	0.006	0.009
	1996–9	0.463	0.441	-0.022	1.357	0.001	-0.024
	1999–2004	0.441	0.382	-0.059	3.730	-0.059	0.001
Uganda	1988–95	0.470	0.408	-0.062	4.376	-0.052	-0.010
	1988–2000	0.470	0.404	-0.066	4.619	-0.051	-0.015
	1995–2000	0.408	0.404	-0.004	0.341	-0.002	-0.003
Zambia	1992–6	0.426	0.446	0.020	-1.539	0.018	0.002
	1996–2001	0.446	0.508	0.062	-4.790	0.054	0.008
Zimbabwe	1988–94	0.319	0.252	-0.066	4.033	-0.082	0.016
	1994–99	0.252	0.306	0.054	-3.311	0.004	0.050

Table 15.12. Datt-Ravallion-Kakwani decompositions for women's BMI

Country	Period	First	Second	Difference	t-value	Mean	Dispersion
Burkina Faso	1992–9	0.137	0.125	−0.011	1.501	0.011	−0.022
	1999–2003	0.125	0.197	0.071	−11.069	0.006	0.065
Benin	1996–2001	0.140	0.101	−0.039	5.016	−0.090	0.051
Côte d'Ivoire	1994–1998	0.079	0.082	0.004	−0.534	−0.023	0.027
Cameroon	1998–2004	0.070	0.064	−0.006	0.888	−0.038	0.032
Chad	1997–2004	0.194	0.202	0.008	−0.931	−0.023	0.031
Ethiopia	2000–5	0.281	0.246	−0.035	5.379	−0.045	0.011
Ghana	1993–1998	0.113	0.107	−0.007	0.677	−0.029	0.022
	1998–2003	0.107	0.091	−0.016	2.155	−0.066	0.050
Guinea	1999–2005	0.113	0.121	0.008	−1.092	−0.004	0.012
Kenya	1993–8	0.094	0.109	0.015	−2.188	0.001	0.014
	1998–2003	0.109	0.118	0.009	−1.429	−0.044	0.053
Madagascar	1997–2003	0.190	0.184	−0.006	0.736	−0.047	0.041
Mali	1995–2001	0.146	0.114	−0.031	5.429	−0.066	0.035
Malawi	1992–2000	0.086	0.080	−0.006	0.972	−0.016	0.011
Mozambique	1997–2003	0.109	0.081	−0.027	4.445	−0.056	0.028
Nigeria	1999–2003	0.156	0.141	−0.015	1.747	0.030	−0.044
Niger	1992–8	0.177	0.190	0.013	−1.487	0.011	0.002
Rwanda	2000–2005	0.082	0.092	0.010	−2.074	0.009	0.000
Senegal	1992–2005	0.137	0.174	0.036	−4.483	−0.036	0.072
Tanzania	1992–6	0.089	0.088	−0.001	0.163	−0.012	0.011
	1996–2004	0.088	0.095	0.007	−1.355	−0.018	0.025
Uganda	1995–2000	0.089	0.094	0.005	−0.776	−0.030	0.034
Zambia	1992–6	0.097	0.083	−0.014	2.253	−0.010	−0.004
	1996–2001	0.083	0.141	0.058	−10.144	0.035	0.023
Zimbabwe	1994–9	0.047	0.054	0.008	−1.446	−0.014	0.022

Table 15.13. Datt-Ravallion-Kakwani decompositions for women's years of schooling

Country	Period	First	Second	Difference	t-value	Mean	Dispersion
Burkina Faso	1992–1999	0.940	0.947	0.007	-0.950	0.016	-0.009
	1999–2003	0.947	0.905	-0.043	5.710	-0.052	0.009
Benin	1996–2001	0.893	0.898	0.006	-0.536	-0.012	0.018
Côte d'Ivoire	1994–1998	0.862	0.835	-0.026	1.802	-0.095	0.068
Cameroon	1991–1998	0.718	0.543	-0.175	9.367	-0.189	0.014
	1998–2004	0.543	0.523	-0.020	1.288	-0.038	0.018
Chad	1997–2004	0.966	0.947	-0.019	2.880	-0.021	0.002
Ethiopia	2000–2005	0.878	0.870	-0.008	1.175	-0.011	0.002
Ghana	1988–1993	0.507	0.530	0.023	-1.227	-0.026	0.049
	1993–1998	0.530	0.492	-0.039	2.044	-0.029	-0.009
	1998–2003	0.492	0.494	0.002	-0.121	0.032	-0.030
Guinea	1999–2005	0.927	0.931	0.004	-0.520	0.006	-0.001
Kenya	1988–1993	0.482	0.386	-0.095	6.411	-0.039	-0.057
	1993–1998	0.386	0.276	-0.110	7.753	-0.122	0.012
	1998–2003	0.276	0.261	-0.015	1.138	0.036	-0.051
Madagascar	1992–1997	0.726	0.748	0.022	-1.508	0.017	0.005
	1992–2003	0.726	0.741	0.014	-1.014	-0.017	0.031
	1997–2003	0.748	0.741	-0.008	0.559	-0.017	0.010
Mali	1987–1995	0.943	0.933	-0.010	1.117	-0.014	0.004
	1995–2001	0.933	0.929	-0.004	0.647	-0.010	0.006
Malawi	1992–2000	0.809	0.739	-0.070	5.518	-0.136	0.066
Mozambique	1997–2003	0.924	0.893	-0.030	3.930	-0.022	-0.008
Nigeria	1986–1990	0.661	0.809	0.148	-8.869	0.136	0.011
	1990–1999	0.809	0.625	-0.184	15.337	-0.147	-0.038
	1999–2003	0.625	0.599	-0.026	1.837	-0.092	0.066

(Continued)

Table 15.13. (Continued)

Country	Period	First	Second	Difference	t-value	Mean	Dispersion
Niger	1992–1998	0.972	0.947	−0.025	4.076	−0.049	0.024
Namibia	1992–2000	0.408	0.228	−0.180	11.126	−0.127	−0.054
Rwanda	1992–2000	0.762	0.640	−0.121	8.811	−0.126	0.005
	2000–2005	0.640	0.804	0.163	−13.722	0.078	0.085
Senegal	1986–1992	0.910	0.903	−0.007	0.676	0.044	−0.052
	1992–1997	0.903	0.871	−0.032	3.163	−0.059	0.028
	1997–2005	0.871	0.848	−0.023	2.537	−0.072	0.049
Togo	1988–1998	0.836	0.881	0.045	−3.378	0.026	0.019
Tanzania	1992–1996	0.433	0.320	−0.113	8.290	−0.014	−0.099
	1996–1999	0.320	0.328	0.007	−0.441	−0.007	0.014
	1999–2004	0.328	0.346	0.018	−1.144	−0.014	0.033
Uganda	1988–1995	0.795	0.758	−0.036	2.589	−0.036	0.000
	1995–2000	0.758	0.699	−0.059	4.409	−0.145	0.086
Zambia	1992–1996	0.453	0.465	0.012	−0.794	−0.042	0.055
	1996–2001	0.465	0.476	0.010	−0.671	−0.039	0.049
Zimbabwe	1988–1994	0.532	0.286	−0.246	13.151	−0.199	−0.046
	1994–1999	0.286	0.157	−0.129	8.890	−0.027	−0.102

poverty than the contribution of the distribution component. We are therefore interested in whether the same holds true for well-being measured in terms of health and education. The results of such an analysis are found in Tables 15.11, 15.12, and 15.13. For children's heights, in twenty-nine spells the absolute value of the share of the mean component of the decomposition is larger than the dispersion share, while the opposite is true in only nine spells. For one spell they are the same. It is also the case that whenever there are relatively large changes in the share of stunted children, this is driven by changes in the mean component. A good example of this is found in the three spells from Ghana; in each case the share of the overall change contributed to by the mean shift is more than twice the magnitude of the change in the dispersion.

The fact that the predominance of the changes in the mean is driving changes in stunting, however, is not to say that the dispersion component is trivial or unimportant. Take the case of Nigeria between 1986 and 1990. There was a large increase in the share of stunted children, from 30 to 42 per cent. Over one-third of this increase was attributable to the worsening distribution of standardized heights in the population. Similarly, more than half of the increase in stunting over the spell from 1991 to 1998 was accounted for by the worsening inequality in children's health. We similarly note cases where the distribution and mean components move in opposite directions, and occasionally cancel each other out. This was the case in Kenya between 1993 and 1998. There are also interesting cases such as Rwanda between 1992 and 2000 where the decline in the share of stunted children would have been substantially greater if not for worsening inequality in the population. Overall, in fact, the mean and dispersion components for children's heights move in the same direction in only fifteen out of thirty-nine spells. This is somewhat contrary to our expectation that we would find these moving in the same direction, given that there is an obvious upper bound to children's heights and we might expect that any improvements would be concentrated in the left part of the distribution.[10] But it also reinforces the fact that distributions matter, albeit not as much as mean components.

When we examine the BMI decompositions, somewhat in contrast, we find that only in half of the cases are the mean shifts of a greater magnitude than the dispersion effects. Once again, an example of the importance of the dispersion effect is the case of the most recent spell in Burkina Faso. Between 1999 and 2003, the share of severely wasted women increased from 12.5 per cent to 19.7 per cent. Ninety per cent of this increase was due to worsening inequality, with the mean component remaining nearly constant. Another interesting case of the mean shift and dispersion effects working in opposite directions is the case of Mozambique. In the absence of worsening inequality, the decline in the share of women who are severely wasted would have been nearly 50 per cent. However, the worsening distribution of weights contributed to a far smaller decline in the share of wasted women, falling from 14.6 per cent to 11.4 per cent between 1997 and 2003.

One final finding of note with regard to the BMI results is that, unlike the case for the share of stunted children, the overwhelming share of spells involves an increase in inequality. That is consistent with a story of women at the upper end of the standardized weight distribution seeing larger gains in weight than those thinner and wasted women we are primarily concerned about.

Our final indicator of deprivation is years of schooling for women aged 22–30. As noted above, we use a poverty line of six years of schooling. As we observed with the child health indicator, the mean shift is of a greater magnitude than the impact of the changes in dispersion in terms of explaining overall differences in the headcount. This is the case in twenty-eight out of forty spells. Overall, the average dispersion effect is also smaller than the mean shift effect, indicating it is the latter which is driving improvements in the education poverty headcount. Nonetheless, once again the dispersion effects are sometimes quite important in explaining the overall level of improvement, or lack thereof. In a case such as Uganda between 1995 and 2000, the education headcount fell by 6 percentage points from 76 to 70 per cent. However, if it were not for the increased inequality in education, the decline in the share of women not completing primary school would have been much greater, to 61 per cent. Similarly, the improvement in the share of women completing six years of schooling in Nigeria between 1999 and 2003 would have been 10 percentage points, rather than 3, if inequality was not worsening during the period.

We also note that like BMIs, but unlike children's heights, the mean and dispersion effects tend to move in opposite directions. And likewise, the dispersion effect is more often in the direction of increasing education poverty, i.e. increasing inequality in this outcome.

Given these findings, we next present a series of figures that put them all together: they plot the results of survey data across the four dimensions we have examined—household expenditures per capita, children's heights, women's BMI, and women's years of schooling (Figure 15A.1). The graphs are all plotted on the same axes so as to be comparable across countries. The poverty value in the first survey in the series is assigned zero, so that the subsequent data points capture absolute changes, either positive (more poverty) or negative (less poverty), in the headcount measures. So, a change in the share of the poor from 50 per cent to 58 per cent will be plotted exactly the same as a change in the headcount ratio from 4 to 12 per cent.

Among the most important generalizations that emerge from these graphs is that money metric poverty tends to show more volatility and more dramatic changes over time than other indicators, as indicated by the steeper slopes of the lines connecting the spells between surveys. The fact that the changes in headcounts across spells are greater for money metric poverty might in part be attributable to the role of genuine income fluctuations that households cannot smooth, but many of the measurement error issues that we discussed above may also contribute significantly to this volatility.

The second big story is that indicators often move in opposite directions. Indeed, the education poverty headcounts almost always declines, as discussed above. But there is no sense that the size or direction of change is related to changes in money metric poverty. Likewise, there seems to be little correspondence between the direction of changes in money metric poverty and the measures of health poverty.

Multidimensional poverty comparisons

Throughout this chapter, we have found it useful to evaluate changes in non-income dimensions of well-being as we try to understand poverty changes in Africa. But we have done this for each measure of well-being individually, and independently of any evaluation of changes in income poverty. It is possible, however, to evaluate poverty reduction in multiple dimensions jointly. Duclos, Sahn, and Younger (2006a, b) develop multidimensional methods that are consistent with the stochastic dominance approach to poverty comparisons (Atkinson, 1987; Foster and Shorrocks, 1988a, b, c). These methods are useful in cases when one dimension of well-being is improving while another is not. As we have seen, this is a common occurrence in Africa. As Duclos, Sahn, and Younger (2006a) show, it is possible for certain types of multidimensional poverty measures to be declining over time even if one of the elements of well-being is not improving.[11]

In this section, we examine the particular case of Uganda in the 1990s. In that period, economic growth was quite rapid (by African standards) and consumption poverty declined significantly (Appleton, 2001a, b). Yet there is concern in Uganda that living standards are not improving by anything like the quantitative analysis of household expenditures suggests. In particular, policy-makers and public health professionals have noted that that non-income measures of well-being such as infant mortality and children's nutritional status are not improving over time despite the substantial increases in income (Ministry of Finance, Planning, and Economic Development, 2002; Task Force on Infant and Maternal Mortality, 2003; Uganda Bureau of Statistics, 2001).

METHODS

The stochastic dominance approach to *uni*variate poverty comparisons compares the cumulative density function[12] of a measure of well-being like expenditures or income per capita. If one such poverty incidence curve is everywhere below the other, then it must be the case that poverty is lower in the first population for any poverty line and for any poverty measure that has these four properties: they must be additively separable, non-decreasing, anonymous, and continuous at the poverty line. By "additively separable," we mean that the poverty measure can be expressed as a weighted sum of the poverty status of individuals. By "non-decreasing," we mean that if any one person's income increases, then the poverty measure cannot increase as well. By "anonymous," we mean that it does not matter which person occupies which position or rank in the income distribution. "Continuous at the poverty line" means that the poverty measure cannot change dramatically when someone crosses the poverty line. It is helpful to call all the poverty measures that have these characteristics the "class" Π^1. Π^1 includes virtually every standard poverty measure except the headcount, but in the particular comparison in the example that follows, the headcount is also covered because it is the poverty incidence curve's y-coordinate. Clearly, such comparisons are very robust.

Figure 15.1 gives an example for Uganda, comparing expenditures per capita in 1992 and 1999. Because the poverty incidence curve for 1999 is everywhere below that for 1992, we know that for any poverty line and for the very large class of poverty measures Π^1, poverty was lower in 1999 than it was in 1992. For reasons that will become clear shortly, this is called "first-order poverty dominance." The generality of this conclusion makes poverty dominance methods attractive. However, such generality comes at a cost. If the cumulative density functions cross one or more times, then we do not have a clear ordering—we cannot say whether poverty is lower in one year or the other. This is the case in Figure 15.2, which graphs the cumulative density functions (CDF) for children's height-for-age z-score in 1995 and 2000 in Uganda. These curves are quite close

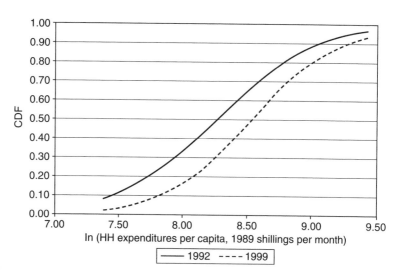

Figure 15.1 Poverty incidence curves, Uganda, 1992 and 1999

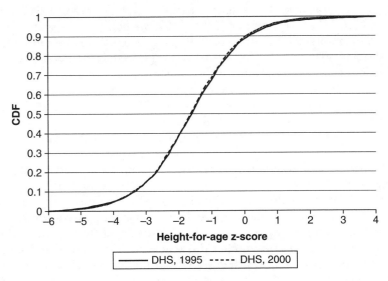

Figure 15.2 Poverty incidence curves for children's heights, Uganda, 1995 and 2000

together, and they cross at several points, including some that are well below a "reasonable" poverty line. In such cases, we cannot conclude that poverty was unambiguously lower in one year or the other.

There are two ways to deal with this problem, both which are still considerably more general than the traditional method of a fixed poverty line and a single poverty measure. First, it is possible to conclude that poverty in one sample is lower than in another for the same large class of poverty measures, but only for poverty lines up to the first point where the CDFs cross (Duclos and Makdissi, 2005). If reasonable people agree that this crossing point is at a level of well-being safely beyond any sensible poverty line, then this conclusion may be sufficient.[13] Second, it is possible to make comparisons for a smaller class of poverty measures. For example, if we add the condition that the poverty measure respects the Dalton transfer principle, then it turns out that we can compare the areas under the CDFs shown in Figure 15.2. If it is the case that the area under one curve is less than the area under another for all reasonable poverty lines, then poverty will be lower for the first sample for all poverty measures that are additively separable, non-decreasing, anonymous, continuous at the poverty line, and that respect the Dalton transfer principle. This is called "second-order poverty dominance," and we can call the associated class of poverty measures Π^2. While not as general as first order dominance, it is still quite a general conclusion. Note that we can make this comparison by integrating the two curves in Figure 15.2, yielding "poverty depth curves," and comparing them to see if one is everywhere above the other.

If the poverty depth curves also cross, then we can proceed to a more restricted set of poverty measures, those that are additively separable, non-decreasing, anonymous, continuous at the poverty line, that respect the Dalton transfer principle, and that respect the principle of transfer sensitivity.[14] To make dominance comparisons for this class of poverty measures, called Π^3, we compare the area under the poverty depth curves by integrating them again and checking to see if one is entirely below the other. If so, then we have "third-order poverty dominance." It is possible to continue integrating the curves in this manner until one dominates the other, but intuition for the class of poverty measures generally ends at third-order comparisons.

Bivariate poverty dominance comparisons extend the univariate methods discussed above. If we have two measures of well-being rather than one, then Figure 15.1 becomes a three-dimensional graph, with one measure of well-being on the x-axis, a second on the y-axis, and the CDF on the z-axis (vertical), as in Figure 15.3. Note that the CDF is now a surface rather than a line, and we compare one CDF surface to another, just as in Figure 15A.1. If one such surface is everywhere below another, then poverty in the first sample is lower than poverty in the second for a broad class of poverty measures, just as in the univariate case.

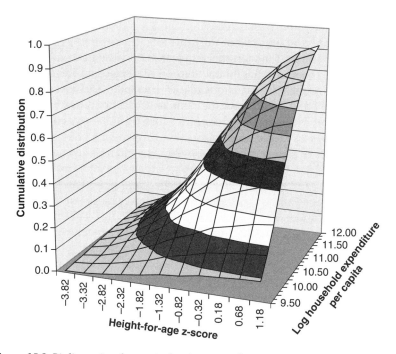

Figure 15.3 Bi-dimensional poverty dominance surface

That class, which we call $\Pi^{1,1}$ to indicate that it is first order in both dimensions of well-being, has the same characteristics as the univariate case—additively separable, non-decreasing in each dimension, anonymous, and continuous at the poverty lines—and one more: that the two dimensions of well-being be substitutes (or more precisely, not be complements) in the poverty measure. This means, roughly, that a transfer of well-being in one dimension from a person who is richer to one who is poorer in that dimension should have a greater effect on poverty if these two people are poorer in the other dimension of well-being.[15]

Practically, it is not easy to plot two surfaces such as the one in Figure 15.3 on the same graph and see the differences between them, but we can plot the differences directly. If this difference is always positive or always negative, then we know that one or the other of the samples has lower poverty for all poverty lines and for a large class of poverty measures $\Pi^{1,1}$.

If the surfaces cross, we can compare higher orders of dominance, just as we did in the univariate case. This can be done in one or both dimensions of well-being, and the restrictions on the applicable class of poverty measures are similar to the univariate case.

In addition to the extra condition on the class of poverty indices, multivariate dominance comparisons require us to distinguish between union, intersection, and intermediate poverty measures. We can do this with the help of Figure 15.4, which shows the domain of dominance surfaces—the (x,y) plane. The function $\lambda_1(x,y)$ defines an "intersection" poverty index: it considers someone to be in poverty only if she is poor in both of the dimensions x and y, and therefore if she lies within the dashed rectangle of Figure 15.4. The function $\lambda_2(x,y)$ (the L-shaped, dotted line) defines a union poverty index: it considers someone to be in poverty if she is poor in *either* of the two dimensions, and therefore if she lies below or to the right of the dotted line. Finally, $\lambda_3(x,y)$ provides an intermediate approach. Someone can be poor even if her y value is greater than the poverty line in the y dimension if her x value is low enough to lie to the left of $\lambda_3(x,y)$.

For one sample to have less intersection poverty than another, its dominance surface must be below the second sample's everywhere within an area like the one defined by $\lambda_2(x,y)$. To have less union poverty, its surface must be below the second sample's everywhere within an area like the one defined by $\lambda_2(x,y)$, and similarly for intermediate definitions and $\lambda_3(x,y)$. These are the sorts of comparisons that we will make in the applications that follow.

RESULTS

Table 15.14 gives descriptive statistics for poverty rates, based on the household asset index, and children's stunting rates for the three DHSs surveys in Uganda. All areas/regions of the country show declines in poverty as determined by household assets, a result that is comparable to the household expenditure results from income/expenditure data in Uganda (Appleton, 2001a, b). In fact,

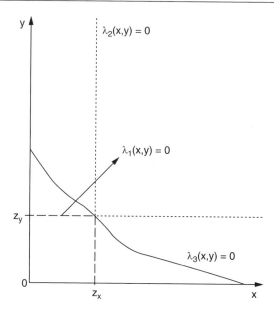

Figure 15.4 Intersection, union, and intermediate dominance test domains

these declines, and even the levels of poverty, are similar to poverty rates as determined by household expenditures per capita. This supports the use of the asset index as a proxy for more standard measures of well-being.

The stunting data, however, are less positive. We find only modest declines in stunting rates over time, mostly between 1988 and 1995. In fact, in urban areas, the stunting rate rises from 1995 to 2000, back to its 1988 level, so the national improvement over the entire period is due only to reductions in rural areas. In addition, the only region with steady improvement in children's heights is the northern region. The western region actually has a significant increase in stunting from 1995 to 2000. Note also that in all cases, assets and children's heights are only modestly positively correlated, a result now common in the literature (Haddad et al., 2003).

Table 15.15 gives the dominance test results for all of Uganda comparing the 1995 and 2000 DHS data. Each cell reports a t-statistic for the difference in the dominance surfaces at the asset index and height-for-age z-scores (HAZ) values shown on the axes. Note that the origin, with the poorest people, is in the lower left-hand corner. To establish dominance, the dominance surfaces should be significantly different in regions similar to those described in Figure 15.4, and of the same sign. Here, there is no dominance for any union poverty measure, and dominance only for a limited range of intersection poverty measures, up to the third decile of the asset distribution. If we examine the top and right edges of the test domain, we see that there is clear univariate dominance for the asset

Table 15.14. Uganda: descriptive statistics for income poverty and stunting, 1988, 1995, and 2000

	Poverty[1]			Stunting[2]			Sample size			corr(asi,haz)[3]		
	1988	1995	2000	1988	1995	2000	1988	1995	2000	1988	1995	2000
National	0.63	0.47	0.35	0.44	0.39	0.39	3,701	4,503	4,939	0.16	0.15	0.18
Rural	0.69	0.52	0.38	0.46	0.41	0.40	3,098	3,249	3,868	0.10	0.07	0.14
Urban[4]	0.08	0.07	0.04	0.26	0.23	0.26	603	1,254	1,071	0.21	0.20	0.24
Central	0.41	0.24	0.19	0.33	0.34	0.35	1,378	1,306	1,377	0.16	0.26	0.22
Eastern	0.65	0.46	0.33	0.45	0.36	0.36	676	1,294	1,350	0.05	0.12	0.12
Western	0.75	0.55	0.39	0.53	0.43	0.48	1,520	1,196	1,437	0.15	0.07	0.17
Northern	0.93	0.65	0.56	0.45	0.42	0.37	127	707	775	0.09	0.12	0.18

[1] Poverty is the headcount ratio, or the share of the sample below the poverty line, based on an index of household assets. We chose the poverty line such that the national headcount is equal to Appleton's (2001a) for the 2000 survey.

[2] Stunting is the share of the sample below −2 z-scores.

[3] The correlation is between the household asset index (ASI) and the height-for-age z-score (HAZ).

[4] The 1988 DHS collected no data in urban areas in the Northern region.

Sources: 1988, 1995, and 2000 DHS.

Table 15.15. $\Pi^{1,1}$ dominance test results, 1995 and 2000 DHS

asset index										
4.89	0.37	0.80	1.71	0.75	1.60	1.44	2.08	2.58	2.47	0.22
0.63	0.27	0.79	1.32	0.39	1.06	1.06	1.35	1.53	0.68	−1.64
0.07	0.31	0.20	0.22	−1.22	−0.61	−0.88	−0.75	−1.05	−2.34	−4.92
−0.12	0.24	−0.27	−0.87	−2.66	−2.40	−3.31	−2.98	−3.33	−4.60	−7.21
−0.22	−0.54	−0.92	−1.46	−3.73	−3.72	−5.12	−4.64	−5.22	−6.60	−8.89
−0.30	−0.96	−2.01	−2.62	−4.80	−4.94	−6.45	−5.77	−6.54	−8.16	−10.47
−0.37	−1.68	−3.09	−3.36	−5.55	−6.25	−7.76	−7.43	−8.31	−9.75	−12.00
−0.43	−2.69	−3.61	−3.84	−5.89	−6.42	−7.94	−7.89	−8.95	−10.24	−12.36
−0.51	−3.80	−5.50	−6.32	−8.02	−8.25	−9.17	−9.03	−9.76	−10.85	−12.51
−0.60	−3.95	−5.50	−6.09	−7.11	−6.82	−6.91	−6.88	−7.45	−8.47	−9.84
0.00	**−3.37**	**−2.69**	**−2.29**	**−1.95**	**−1.61**	**−1.30**	**−0.92**	**−0.51**	**0.10**	**5.71**

haz

Table 15.16. $\Pi^{1,1}$ dominance test results, 1988 and 2000 DHS

asset index						haz					
4.89	−4.43	−6.32	−5.75	−5.08	−5.48	−4.15	−4.07	−2.76	−0.02	1.19
0.58	−4.55	−6.50	−6.24	−5.92	−6.60	−5.44	−5.62	−5.03	−4.24	−6.35
0.03	−4.56	−6.96	−7.31	−7.20	−7.89	−7.20	−7.56	−6.81	−6.84	−8.60
−0.16	−5.47	−8.65	−9.54	−10.76	−12.09	−12.24	−13.45	−13.62	−14.78	−17.33
−0.26	−6.67	−9.96	−11.48	−12.76	−14.49	−15.22	−16.97	−17.67	−19.43	−22.38
−0.34	−7.68	−11.14	−13.07	−14.77	−16.93	−18.14	−20.23	−21.21	−23.35	−26.23
−0.41	−7.96	−12.06	−13.61	−15.22	−17.91	−19.47	−21.54	−22.70	−24.56	−26.91
−0.48	−8.84	−13.25	−15.53	−17.52	−20.30	−21.71	−23.86	−25.39	−27.13	−29.40
−0.55	−9.21	−13.17	−15.07	−16.87	−19.13	−19.89	−21.67	−23.00	−24.12	−26.02
−0.63	−7.81	−10.64	−12.31	−13.73	−14.77	−15.41	−16.77	−17.24	−17.80	−19.20
0.00	**−3.49**	**−2.82**	**−2.41**	**−2.04**	**−1.71**	**−1.38**	**−1.01**	**−0.59**	**0.03**	**5.76**

index (the right edge), i.e. poverty measured by assets declined significantly over the period. However, there is no statistically significant improvement in the dimension of children's heights (the top edge), and, in fact, the 2000 surface is above that for 1995. Results for $\Pi^{2,2}$ (not shown here) are somewhat more positive, yielding dominance for intersection poverty lines up to the sixth decile for the asset index and for all poverty lines in the HAZ dimension. Higher order tests, up to $\Pi^{1,3}$ and $\Pi^{3,3}$, yield results that are qualitatively similar to those in Table 15.15, never showing univariate dominance for heights, and thus never showing any bivariate dominance for union poverty measures. For intersection measures, no comparisons show bivariate dominance for intersection poverty measures at greater than the sixth decile of the asset distribution. Thus, we cannot make a robust conclusion that bivariate poverty declined between these two sample periods unless we are willing to claim that no reasonable poverty line in the asset dimension would be higher than the sixth decile and even then, only for intersection poverty measures.

For a longer time period, Table 15.16 shows that bivariate poverty clearly fell between 1988 and 2000, for any poverty line and for any union or intersection poverty measure.[16] Thus, the overall picture is one of significant declines in bivariate poverty early in the 1990s, but inconclusive results later in the decade. That is inconsistent with Appleton's (2001a, b) results for poverty based on expenditures alone, but it is in line with policy-makers' concerns about lack of progress in the late 1990s, especially on the health front.

Conclusions

We have explored the extent to which countries in sub-Saharan Africa have been successful in alleviating poverty over the past couple of decades. Our analysis suggests that Africa is poor compared with the rest of the world and that poverty is not declining consistently or significantly in most African countries. We arrive at this conclusion by considering not only deprivation in the material standard of living (i.e. income or expenditure poverty), but also other dimensions of well-being, especially education and health. We adopt this strategy for theoretical and practical reasons. In the case of the former, poverty should be understood as more than economic deprivation and includes such capabilities as good health, adequate nutrition, literacy, and political freedoms. Expanding our purview to include deprivation in health and education is particularly important. Many measures of well-being, especially those that concern health, are not highly correlated with incomes, so their analysis adds information on deprivation that is not available in incomes. In addition, garnering public support to improve health and education outcomes is easier than for income transfer programs, especially given the externalities associated with such efforts.

Exploring deprivation in health and education also has a number of practical advantages. These variables are measured at the individual level; they are less prone to measurement error; and they are more easily comparable across time and space. Finally, there is a paucity of survey data on incomes or expenditures in Africa. This is both surprising and disappointing in light of the original promise of the LSMS initiative, as well as subsequent international efforts such as the Millennium Project. Unfortunately, government statistics agencies in Africa have not been able to pick up the ball that was dropped with the decline in World Bank funding for data collection efforts that were initiated with the LSMS program. In contrast, the DHSs continue to provide a solid foundation for measuring the non-material standard of living, especially health.

Our findings paint a relatively sobering picture of economic and social progress in Africa. The broad regional comparisons suggest that Africa continues to fall behind relative to other areas of the developing world, a trend that began in the 1970s and continues basically unabated until the present. Country level results indicate that economic poverty has witnessed large fluctuations. With a few notable exceptions, sustained and significant reductions have not been realized. We are somewhat skeptical about the reliability of the headcount numbers based on money-metric measures, for reasons related to the comparability of surveys and the difficulty of defining poverty in terms of the material standard of living. In addition, there are relatively few recent surveys with reliable income and expenditure data required to make inter-temporal comparisons. We therefore focus on issues of deprivation in terms of health and education. In this regard, the one relatively bright spot seems to be the general increase in primary school enrollments. Substantial progress has been made, although countries in Francophone West Africa continue to lag behind.

Similarly, our measures of child health and the health of the mother show very mixed results, both across survey spells of individual countries, and when comparing progress across countries. When we explore the extent to which the lack of progress can be attributed to increasing inequality, our decomposition analysis suggests that while the distribution component is often important, changes in levels of education and health deprivation in African countries are largely driven by the lack of improvements at the mean. This finding is broadly consistent with what has been reported elsewhere for economic poverty.

In examining changes in health, education, and economic well-being for individual countries, we also note a lack of consistency in the movement of the indicators. During similar periods, we often find them moving in opposite directions. We therefore present and apply to the case of Uganda a method to evaluate poverty reduction in multiple dimensions. This approach is particularly useful when one dimension of well-being is improving while another is not, as is often the case in Africa. The results of the multidimensional poverty comparisons reinforce the importance of considering deprivation beyond the material standard of living and provide insight into how to reconcile differing stories that arise from examining each indicator separately.

Appendix

Figure 15A.1 Changes in poverty headcount ratios by country, 1985–2005 (absolute percentage changes)

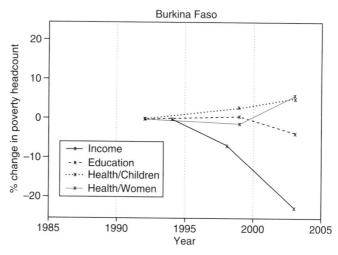

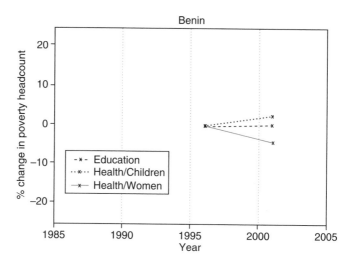

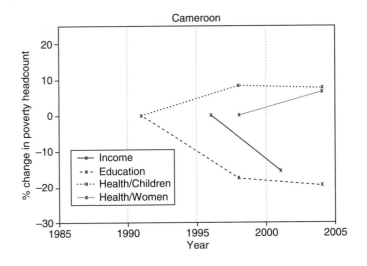

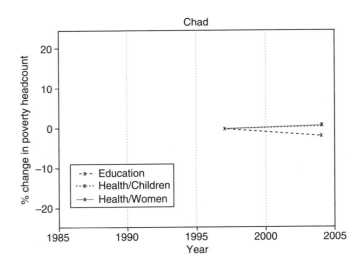

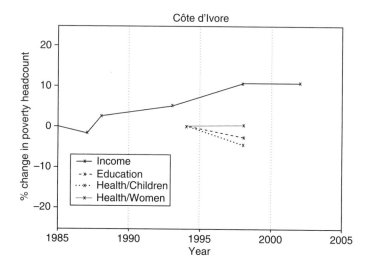

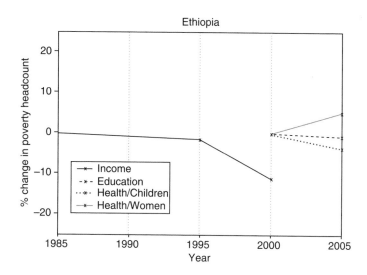

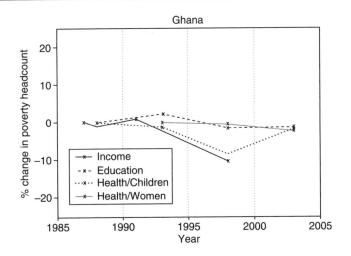

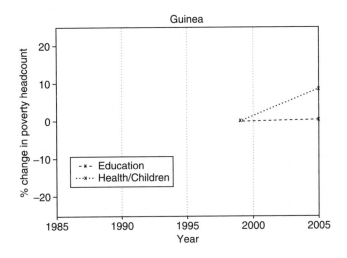

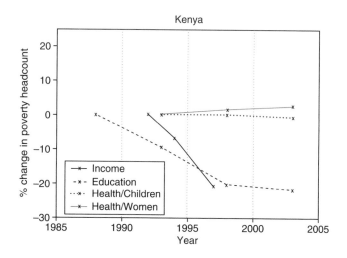

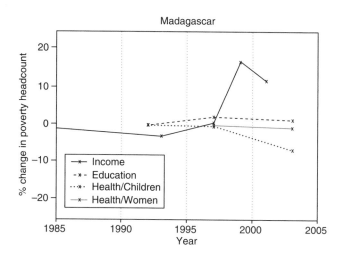

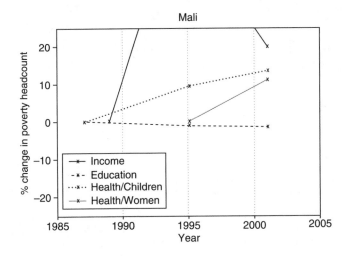

Mali

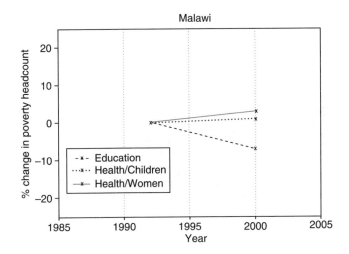

Malawi

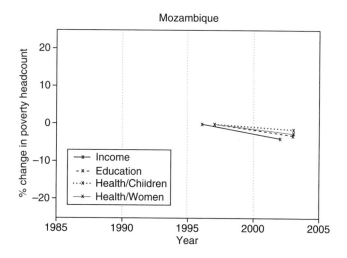

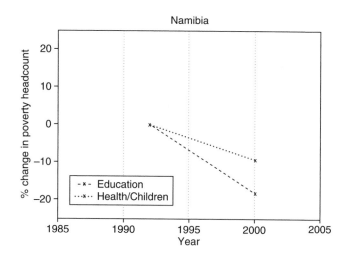

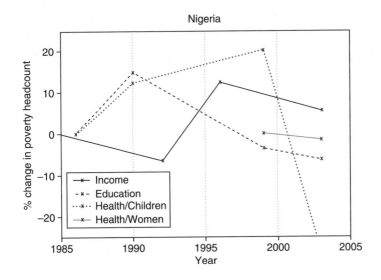

Nigeria

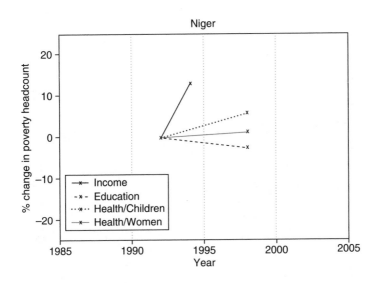

Niger

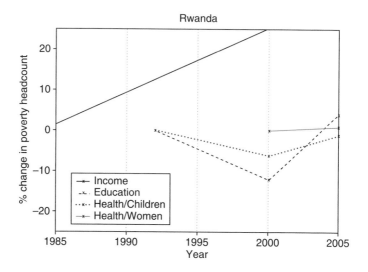

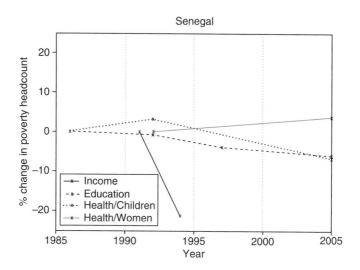

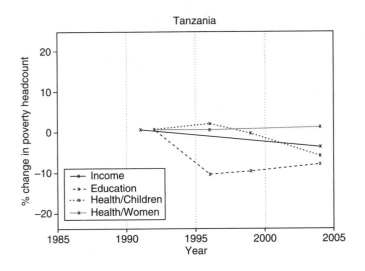

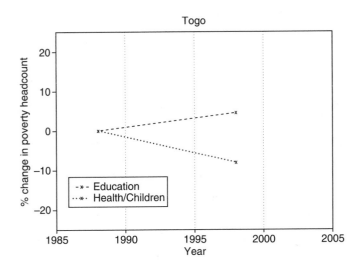

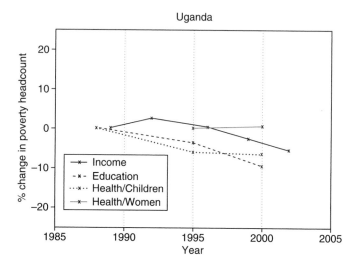

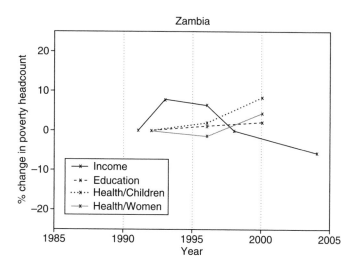

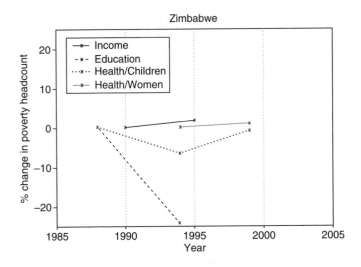

Zimbabwe

Notes

1. Cornell University.
2. This ratio can exceed 100 per cent if, owing to problems such as grade repetition and delayed enrollment, there are many children outside the age normally associated with the grade range of primary school.
3. The details of each survey, and the methods used to calculate the poverty numbers are reported at <http://iresearch.worldbank.org/PovcalNet/jsp/index.jsp>. In addition, several papers and World Bank documents discuss global trends in poverty employing these data. See for example, Chen and Ravallion (2004, 2007).
4. See for example, Appleton (2001a, b) for Uganda; Canagarajah, Ngwafon, and Okunmadewa (2000) for Nigeria; and Coulombe and McKay (2001) for Ghana.
5. Most useful here are characteristics that should not be changing at all over time, such as the mean years of education of a cohort of adults (individuals born in the same year or say, five-year period) that is beyond school age. Mean heights, ethnicity, and religion of individuals in the cohort would be other good measures. If the sampled populations are the same in two surveys, these means should be statistically equivalent.
6. Note that very few women actually attend post-secondary school in these samples, so we could use a younger sample of even more recent graduates using 18 rather than 22 as our lower age limit. The results that we report later for education are almost identical if we do this.
7. Estimated standard errors consider only sampling error, not measurement error. Since the Foster-Greer-Thorbecke (FGT) poverty measures are sums of random variables (the poverty gaps raised to the appropriate power), their variance is the sum of the variance of those poverty gaps. The sample variance of the poverty gaps is a consistent estimate. For comparisons across surveys, we use the sum of the two variances, using the independence of the two samples.

8. A 10 per cent confidence level is used to establish statistically significant differences.
9. Because the choice of six years is arbitrary, we also checked results at three years and nine years. While the headcounts obviously change, the pattern of changes over time is consistent with the results presented here.
10. We do, in fact, find this consistently in Latin America (Sahn and Younger, 2006).
11. It is also possible for multidimensional poverty to increase even though each individual dimension improves, if the correlation of deprivation in the multiple dimensions increases.
12. Ravallion (1994) calls these "poverty incidence curves" because of their relation to the headcount, which is also the FGT (1984) measure with its parameter set to one.
13. In the case of Figure 15.3, that is not likely, since the standard cut-off for stunting is –2 z-scores.
14. The principle of transfer sensitivity says that if we make two equal but offsetting transfers, one from a richer to a poorer person, and the other from a poorer to a richer person, but both of the latter being poorer than the participants in the first transfer, then poverty should decline. The idea is that the benefit of the transfer from a richer to a poorer person, or the cost of a transfer from a poorer to a richer person, is larger the poorer are the two participants.
15. Bourguignon and Chakravarty (2003) discuss this in detail, calling it a "correlation increasing switch," as do Duclos, Sahn, and Younger (2006a).
16. Note that many more districts were not covered in the 1988 DHS for security reasons. We limit this analysis to districts that were covered in both 1988 and 2000, so the 2000 data are not the same as those in the previous section, which included all districts covered in the 2000 DHS. The districts that are excluded are mostly in the north, where bivariate poverty did decline between 1995 and 2000, so it is unlikely that their exclusion explains the difference in the results between Table 15.15 and Table 15.16.

Bibliography

Appleton, S. (2001a) 'Poverty Reduction during Growth: The Case of Uganda, 1992–2000'. Mimeo.
—— (2001b) 'Changes in Poverty and Inequality'. In R. Reinikka and P. Collier (eds.) *Uganda's Recovery: The Role of Farms, Firms, and Government*, Washington DC: World Bank.
—— and Song, L. (1999) 'Income and Human Development at the Household Level: Evidence from Six Countries'. Mimeo, Oxford University, Oxford.
Atkinson, A. B. (1987) 'On the Measurement of Poverty'. *Econometrica*, 55, pp. 749–64.
Barro, R. and Lee, J-W. (2001) 'International Data on Educational Attainment: Updates and Implications'. *Oxford Economic Papers*, 53(3), pp. 541–63.
Beaton, G. H., Kelly, A., Kevany, J., Martorell, R., and Mason, J. (1990) 'Appropriate Uses of Anthropometric Indices in Children: A Report Based on an ACC/SCN Workshop'. United Nations Administrative Committee on Coordination/Subcommittee on Nutrition, ACC/SCN State-of-the-Art Series, Nutrition Policy Discussion Paper No. 7, New York.

Behrman, J. R. and Deolalikar, A. B. (1990) 'The Intrahousehold Demand for Nutrients in Rural South India: Individual Estimates, Fixed Effects, and Permanent Income'. *Journal of Human Resources*, 25(4), pp. 665–96.

—— —— (1988) 'Health and Nutrition'. In H. Chenery and T. N. Srinivasan (eds.) *Handbook of Development Economics*, Vol. 1, North-Holland Press, Amsterdam, pp. 631–711.

Bourguignon, F. and Chakravarty, S. R. (2003) 'The Measurement of Multidimensional Poverty'. *Journal of Economic Inequality*, 1(1), pp. 25–49.

Canagarajah, S., Ngwafon, J., and Okunmadewa, F. (2000) 'Nigeria's Poverty: Past, Present, and Future'. Mimeo, World Bank, Nigeria Country Department, Washington DC.

Chen, S. and Ravallion, M. (2004) 'How Have the World's Poorest Fared Since the Early 1980s?' *World Bank Research Observer*, 19(2), pp. 141–69.

—— —— (2007) 'Absolute Poverty Measures for the Developing World, 1981–2004'. Development Research Group, World Bank, Washington DC. <http://iresearch.worldbank.org/PovcalNet/Publications/poverty%20measures%20for%20the%20developing%20world.pdf>.

Christiaensen, L., Demery, L., and Paternostro, S. (2002) 'Growth, Distribution, and Poverty in Africa: Messages from the 1990s'. Policy Research Working Paper #2810, World Bank, Washington DC.

Cole, T. J. and Parkin, J. M. (1977) 'Infection and Its Effect on Growth of Young Children: A Comparison of the Gambia and Uganda'. *Transactions of the Royal Society of Tropical Medicine and Hygiene*, 71, pp. 196–8.

Coulombe, H. and McKay, A. (2001) 'The Evolution of Poverty and Inequality in Ghana over the 1990s: A Study based on the Ghana Living Standards Surveys'. Mimeo, Office of the Chief Economist, Africa Region, World Bank, Washington DC (May).

Datt, G. and Ravallion, M. (1992) 'Growth and Redistribution Components of Changes in Poverty Measures: A Decomposition with Applications to Brazil and India in the 1980s'. *Journal of Development Economics*, 38(2), pp. 275–95.

Deaton, A. (1997) *The Analysis of Household Surveys: Microeconometric Approach to Development Policy.* Baltimore: Johns Hopkins University Press.

—— and Muellbauer, J. (1980) *Economics and Consumer Behavior.* Cambridge: Cambridge University Press.

—— and Zaidi, S. (2002) 'Guidelines for Constructing Consumption Aggregates for Welfare Analysis'. Living Standards Measurement Study Working Paper # 135, World Bank, Washington DC.

Dhongde, S. (2002) 'Measuring the Impact of Growth and Income Distribution on Poverty in India'. Mimeo, Department of Economics, University of California, Riverside.

Duclos, J-Y. and Makdissi, P. (2005) 'Sequential Stochastic Dominance and the Robustness of Poverty Orderings'. *Review of Income and Wealth*, 51(1), pp. 63–88.

—— Sahn, D. E., and Younger, D. E. (2006a) 'Robust Multidimensional Poverty Comparisons'. *Economic Journal*, 116(514), pp. 943–68.

—— —— —— (2006b) 'Robust Multidimensional Spatial Poverty Comparisons in Ghana, Madagascar, and Uganda'. *World Bank Economic Review*, 20(1), pp. 91–113.

Foster, J. E., Greer, J., and Thorbecke, E. (1984) 'A Class of Decomposable Poverty Measures'. *Econometrica*, 52 (3), pp. 761–76.

—— and Shorrocks, A. F. (1988a) 'Poverty Orderings'. *Econometrica*, 56, pp. 173–7.

———— (1988b) 'Poverty Orderings and Welfare Dominance'. *Social Choice and Welfare*, 5, pp. 179–98.

———— (1988c) 'Inequality and Poverty Orderings'. *European Economic Review*, 32, pp. 654–62.

Glewwe, P. and Kremer, M. (2006) 'Schools, Teachers, and Education Outcomes in Developing Countries'. In E. A. Hanushek and F. Welsh (eds.) *Handbook on the Economics of Education*, Elsevier.

Glick, P. and Sahn, D. E. (2007) 'Changes in HIV/AIDS Knowledge and Testing Behavior in Africa: How Much and for Whom?' *Journal of Population Economics*, 20(2) pp. 383–422.

———— and Younger, S. D. (2006) 'An Assessment of Changes in Infant and under-Five Mortality in Demographic and Health Survey Data for Madagascar'. Cornell Food and Nutrition Policy Program Working Paper #207, Cornell University, Ithaca, NY.

Haddad, L., Alderman, H., Appleton, S., Song, L. and Yohannes, Y. (2003) 'Reducing Child Malnutrition: How Far Does Income Growth Take Us?'. *World Bank Economic Review*, 17 (1), pp. 107–31.

Joliffe, D. and Scott, K. (1995) 'The Sensitivity of Measures of Household Consumption to Survey Design: Results from an Experiment in El Salvador'. Policy Research Department, World Bank, Washington DC.

Kakwani, N. (1997) 'On Measuring Growth and Inequality Components of Changes in Poverty with Application to Thailand'. Mimeo, School of Economics, The University of New South Wales, Sydney.

Kanbur, R. and Haddad, L. (1992) 'Is There an Intrahousehold Kuznets Curve? Some Evidence from the Philippines'. *Public Finance*, 47 (suppl.), pp. 77–93.

Martorell, R., Habicht, J-P., Yarbrough, C., Lechtig, A., Klein, R. E., and Western, K. A. (1975) 'Acute Morbidity and Physical Growth in Rural Guatemalan Children'. *American Journal of Diseases in Childhood*, 129, pp. 1296–301.

Mata, L. (1978) *The Children of Santa Maria Cauque: A Prospective Field Study of Health and Growth*. Cambridge, Mass.: MIT Press.

McCulloch, N., Cherel-Robson, M., and Baluch, B. (2000) 'Growth, Inequality and Poverty in Mauritania 1987–96'. Mimeo, Institute of Development Studies, University of Sussex, Brighton.

Ministry of Finance, Planning, and Economic Development (2002) 'Infant Mortality in Uganda, 1995–2000: Why the Non-Improvement?', Kampala, Uganda.

Mosley, W. H., and Chen, L. C. (1984) 'An Analytical Framework for the Study of Child Survival in Developing Countries'. *Population and Development Review*, Vol. 10 (Supplement), pp. 25–45.

Pradhan, M. (2001) 'Welfare Analysis with a Proxy Consumption Measure: Evidence from a Repeated Experiment in Indonesia'. Cornell Food and Nutrition Policy Program Working Paper #126, Cornell University, Ithaca, NY.

———— Sahn, D. E., and Younger, S. D. (2003) 'Decomposing World Health Inequality'. *Journal of Health Economics*, 22(2), pp. 271–93.

Ravallion, M. (1994) *Poverty Comparisons*. Chur, Switzerland: Harwood Academic.

Sahn, D. E. and Younger, S. D. (2005) 'Improvements in Children's Health: Does Inequality Matter?' *Journal of Economic Inequality*, 3(2), pp. 125–43.

────── (2006) 'Changes in Inequality and Poverty in Latin America: Looking Beyond Income'. *Journal of Applied Economics*, 9(2), pp. 215–34.

────── (2007) 'Measuring Health Inequality: Explorations Using the Body Mass Index'. *Health Economics*, 18(51), pp. 513–36.

Scott, C. and Amenuvegbe, B. (1990) 'Effect of Recall Duration on Reporting of Household Expenditures: An Experimental Study in Ghana'. Social Dimensions of Adjustment in Sub-Saharan Africa Working Paper 6, World Bank, Washington DC.

Sen, A. (1985) *Commodities and Capabilities*, Amsterdam: North Holland.

────── (1987) 'The Standard of Living: Lecture II, Lives and Capabilities'. In G. Hawthorn (ed.) *The Standard of Living*, Cambridge: Cambridge University Press, pp. 20–38.

Shorrocks, A. and Kolenikov, S. (2001) 'Poverty Trends in Russia during the Transition'. Mimeo, World Institute of Development Research, Helsinki, and University of North Carolina.

Silberstein, A. and Scott, S. (1991) 'Expenditure Diary Surveys and their Associated Errors'. In P. Biemer, R. Groves, L. Lyberg, N. Mathiowetz, and S. Sudman (eds.) *Measurement Errors in Surveys*, New York: John Wiley and Sons, pp. 303–26.

Steele, D. (1998) 'Ecuador Consumption Items'. World Bank, Development Research Group, Washington DC.

Strauss, J. and Thomas, D. (1995) 'Empirical Modeling of Household and Family Decisions'. In J. Behrman and T. N. Srinivasan (eds.) *Handbook of Development Economics*, Vol. IIIA, North-Holland, Amsterdam, pp. 1883–2023.

Tanner, J. M. (1981) *A History of the Study of Human Growth*. Cambridge University Press, New York.

Task Force on Infant and Maternal Mortality (2003) 'Report on Infant and Maternal Mortality in Uganda'.

Uganda Bureau of Statistics and ORC Macro (2001) 'Uganda National Household Survey: Report on the Socio-economic Survey'. Calverton, MD.

World Health Organization (1983) *Measuring Change in Nutritional Status: Guidelines for Assessing the Nutritional Impact of Supplementary Feeding Programmes for Vulnerable Groups*. Geneva.

────── (1995) 'An Evaluation of Infant Growth: The Use and Interpretation of Anthropometry in Infants'. *Bulletin of the World Health Organization*, 73, pp. 165–74.

World Bank (ongoing) PovcalNet <http://iresearch.worldbank.org/PovcalNet/jsp/index.jsp>

Index

Note: Page numbers in *italics* indicate *maps, diagrams* and *tables*. There are frequently also textual references on the same pages. Page numbers in **boldface** indicate chapters.